# VISUAL BASIC 2005

## IN A NUTSHELL

# Other Microsoft .NET resources from O'Reilly

**Related titles**

Programming C#
C# in a Nutshell
Programming ASP.NET
ASP.NET in a Nutshell
ADO.NET in a Nutshell
Programming Windows
    Presentation Foundation
C# Cookbook

.NET Gotchas
Programming Visual Basic
    2005
Visual Basic 2005
    Jumpstart
Visual Basic 2005: A
    Developer's Notebook
ASP.NET 2.0 Cookbook

**.NET Books
Resource Center**

*dotnet.oreilly.com* is a complete catalog of O'Reilly's books on .NET and related technologies, including sample chapters and code examples.

*ONDotnet.com* provides independent coverage of fundamental, interoperable, and emerging Microsoft .NET programming and web services technologies.

**Conferences**

O'Reilly brings diverse innovators together to nurture the ideas that spark revolutionary industries. We specialize in documenting the latest tools and systems, translating the innovator's knowledge into useful skills for those in the trenches. Visit *conferences.oreilly.com* for our upcoming events.

Safari Bookshelf (*safari.oreilly.com*) is the premier online reference library for programmers and IT professionals. Conduct searches across more than 1,000 books. Subscribers can zero in on answers to time-critical questions in a matter of seconds. Read the books on your Bookshelf from cover to cover or simply flip to the page you need. Try it today with a free trial.

# VISUAL
# BASIC 2005

## IN A NUTSHELL

**Third Edition**

*Tim Patrick, Steven Roman,
Ron Petrusha, and Paul Lomax*

O'REILLY®

Beijing • Cambridge • Farnham • Köln • Paris • Sebastopol • Taipei • Tokyo

## Visual Basic 2005 in a Nutshell

by Tim Patrick, Steven Roman, Ron Petrusha, and Paul Lomax

Published by O'Reilly Media, Inc., 1005 Gravenstein Highway North, Sebastopol, CA 95472.

O'Reilly books may be purchased for educational, business, or sales promotional use. Online editions are also available for most titles (*safari.oreilly.com*). For more information, contact our corporate/institutional sales department: (800) 998-9938 or *corporate@oreilly.com*.

**Editor:** Jeff Pepper

**Production Editor:** Darren Kelly

**Copyeditor:** Chris Downey

**Proofreader:** Genevieve Rajewski

**Indexer:** Johnna VanHoose Dinse

**Cover Designer:** Pam Spremulli

**Interior Designer:** David Futato

**Illustrators:** Robert Romano, Jessamyn Read, and Lesley Borash

**Printing History:**

| | |
|---|---|
| August 2001: | First Edition. |
| April 2002: | Second Edition. |
| January 2006: | Third Edition. |

 This book uses RepKover™, a durable and flexible lay-flat binding.

ISBN: 0-596-10152-X

[M]  [5/06]

# Table of Contents

# Part II. Reference

# Part III. Appendixes

# Preface

Microsoft Visual Basic began its life back in 1991 as a kind of amalgamation of Microsoft's QBasic programming language and a graphical interface design program developed in part by Alan Cooper. Since then, it has become one of the most popular programming languages in the world.

The 10th anniversary of Visual Basic coincided with the announcement of Microsoft's new .NET platform, and with it a totally revised and revamped version of Visual Basic named "Visual Basic .NET." With the initial release in 2002, the language was streamlined and modernized, and many old "compatibility" elements were dropped from the language. Since that first release, VB.NET has been enhanced and improved through two more general releases (in 2003 and 2005).

Pre-.NET versions of VB included a "good try" implementation of standard object-oriented features, but they often came up short. Teamed with .NET, Visual Basic is now a fully object-oriented programming (OOP) language, with the inclusion of the long sought-after class inheritance feature, as well as other OOP elements. The 2005 release adds operator overloading to the language, something that was absent in the initial .NET version.

Before .NET, Microsoft's Component Object Model (COM) technology played a significant role in application development, especially when it became part of the foundation of Visual Basic 4.0. With the advent of .NET, COM begins to take its exit from the Windows programming stage, as .NET includes a new namespace-based component integration system. This is somewhat unfortunate, since Visual Basic developers have a lot of time and source code invested in COM components. As great as COM was, it was also complex, and there were numerous compatibility issues when sharing components between Visual Basic, Visual C++, and other languages that either produced or consumed these "ActiveX" libraries. All core compatibility issues are banished with .NET, and although you can still take advantage of your substantial investment in COM components through .NET's "interop" features, the enhancements available through .NET will certainly draw all developers eventually to abandon the COM system.

For developers who have made the switch from .NET, the best news of all is that Visual Basic is now an "equal player" with other languages, in terms of programming power and accessibility of Windows features and services. In the past, Visual Basic served as a "wrapper" that simplified and hid much of the complexity of Windows and its Application Programming Interface (API). Now, Visual Basic programmers have full and easy access to all features of the .NET and Windows platforms, just as Visual C++ and C# programmers do.

The extensive changes to the language and the introduction of the .NET platform make a reference guide to the Visual Basic language more essential than ever. At the same time, they make it easy to delineate this book's subject matter. This is a book that focuses on the language elements of .NET-powered Visual Basic—on its statements, functions, procedures, directives, and objects.

This book provides essential information on the Visual Basic language for the .NET platform, but there are some things this book is not:

- It is not a reference guide to Visual Basic for Applications (VBA), the programming language used in all of the major applications in the Microsoft Office suite, as well as in dozens of other third-party applications. VBA served as the core programming language in earlier versions of Visual Basic. However, VBA is not the programming language for the .NET versions of Visual Basic. Microsoft Office Version 12 (not named as of this writing) will include Visual Studio Tools for Applications (VSTA), a new .NET replacement for VBA.

- It is not a reference guide to the .NET Framework Class Library. The Framework Class Library is discussed in these pages, and a number of its classes and their members are documented in this book's reference section. But that documentation just scratches the surface; the Framework Class Library consists of about 200 namespaces (one of which, incidentally, is *Microsoft.VisualBasic*, the namespace that defines many features of the Visual Basic language), several thousand types (including classes, interfaces, delegates, and enumerations), and an enormous number of members. In selecting the .NET Framework classes to document in this book, we've tried to focus on .NET elements that replace commonly used features in pre-.NET versions of Visual Basic, as well as on .NET elements that expand and enhance the productivity of Visual Basic developers.

- It is not a reference guide to the attributes that you can apply to program elements. Chapter 9 introduces attribute-based programming, and there are entries for important language-based attributes in the reference section. But with hundreds of attributes available in the .NET Framework Class Library, only language-related attributes and the general-purpose attributes VB developers are most likely to use are documented in this book.

- It is not a guide to developing full applications or components using Visual Basic or .NET. The text includes simple code fragments that illustrate relevant syntax and code usage, to demonstrate how a language element works. But it doesn't show you the big-picture activities, such as how to use the Windows Forms package to build a Windows application, how to develop a web application using ASP.NET, or how to implement a web service.

# Why Another Visual Basic Book?

Each major release of Visual Basic leaves shelves full of tutorial and training books in its wake. The 2005 release of Visual Basic is no exception, especially since Microsoft expects adoption of Visual Basic on the .NET platform to dramatically increase with this edition. The majority of VB books assume that you're a complete novice and slowly introduce you to basic concepts such as variables, arrays, and looping structures.

This is a different kind of book. It is a detailed, professional reference to the Visual Basic language—a reference that you can use to jog your memory about a particular language element or a particular parameter. It will come in handy when you need to review the rules for a particular language element, or when you want to check that there isn't some "gotcha" you've overlooked with a particular language feature.

In addition, this book serves as a valuable reference for VB 6 programmers who are upgrading to .NET and for existing .NET programmers who need to know about specific differences found in each subsequent release of the Visual Basic language. To this end, we have devoted considerable space to the extensive language differences between VB 6 and VB.NET 2002, and the versions beyond. For each relevant language entry in the large reference chapter (Chapter 12), we have included a "Version Differences" section that details the usage changes for the language element between VB 6 and the 2002, 2003, and 2005 releases of Visual Basic.

# Who This Book Is For

Just like any reference, this book will be useful to many types of readers:

- Developers who have used previous versions of Visual Basic
- Developers who are new to Visual Basic, but who have been developing applications in other programming languages, such as C++
- Those who are learning VB as their first language and would like to have a definitive language reference on their shelf

## Readers New to Visual Basic

If you are new to the Visual Basic language, then you will want to pay particular attention to the first part of the book, which discusses many important areas of programming in .NET with Visual Basic, including variables, data types, the basic principles of object-oriented programming, and error-handling techniques.

## VB and VBScript Developers New to .NET

Some critics have argued that with .NET, Microsoft has introduced an entirely new VB language, separate and distinct from VB 6. While we wouldn't go quite that far, we do recognize that beyond the syntax changes, the new .NET platform brings a paradigm shift that affects the way we think about application development. As a VB 6 or VBScript developer new to .NET, you may find yourself in a position similar to that of a developer who is new to all flavors of Visual Basic.

This book will ease your transition to .NET from earlier versions of Visual Basic. In particular, the first 11 chapters of the book offer a rapid introduction to VB and .NET and to their new features. Appendix D discusses many of the major language changes between VB 6 and VB.NET 2002, while Appendix G lists VB 6 language elements that are no longer supported in .NET editions. The "Version Differences" entries in Chapter 12 also provide support for your migration to .NET.

## Existing .NET Developers

Early adopters of Visual Basic for the .NET platform have been vindicated, as the Windows development world has followed their lead in droves. And while programmers coming fresh into the language with the 2005 release will experience a completely new level of software development, the update introduces changes that keep VB a moving target even for experienced .NET programmers. That's why *Visual Basic 2005 in a Nutshell* includes Appendix E and Appendix F, which document the major changes introduced into the language since the initial 2002 release. You will also find some use for the "Version Differences" entries in Chapter 12.

# How This Book Is Structured

*Visual Basic 2005 in a Nutshell* is divided into three parts. Part I, *The Basics*, is an introduction to the main features and concepts of Visual Basic programming. If you are new to Visual Basic or .NET, this part of the book is essential reading. It is divided into the following chapters:

Chapter 1, *Introduction*
    In this chapter, you will read how Visual Basic has been transformed into its .NET variation and get some sense of how and why the .NET version is different from previous editions of Visual Basic.

Chapter 2, *The .NET Framework: General Concepts*
    This chapter surveys some of the features of the .NET Framework that most impact the VB developer. These include namespaces, the Common Language Runtime (CLR), and assemblies.

Chapter 3, *Introduction to Object-Oriented Programming*
    This chapter discusses the basic concepts of object-oriented programming and shows how to implement VB's object-oriented features in your code.

Chapter 4, *Variables and Data Types*
    This chapter looks at the standard Visual Basic data types and how to use them. Behind the scenes, VB takes advantage of the .NET Framework's Common Type System, so the chapter also examines the .NET data types and the way in which VB wraps these data types.

Chapter 5, *Operators*
    This chapter surveys the operators you use to manipulate data in VB. It also introduces operator overloading, a new feature with the 2005 release.

Chapter 6, *Program Structure*

This chapter discusses the entry points that allow the .NET runtime to execute your code and shows how to structure the code in a Visual Basic program.

Chapter 7, *The .NET Framework Class Library*

The .NET Framework Class Library (FCL) replaces portions of the Win32 API, as well as many of the individual object models familiar to pre-.NET VB programmers. This chapter offers a fast-paced overview of the Framework Class Library and some of its features.

Chapter 8, *Delegates and Events*

While handling events was more or less automatic in previous versions of VB, events in .NET are "wired" through the source code itself. This chapter shows how events work and what they mean to you as a programmer.

Chapter 9, *Attributes*

The .NET Framework supports attributes, an extensible mechanism that lets you "decorate" program elements (such as classes and class members) with tags that describe or alter the use of those elements. Attributes are stored in the assembly's "metadata" and can be used to influence the compiler, the design time environment, or the runtime environment. This chapter explains attributes and shows you how to use and define them.

Chapter 10, *Generics*

Visual Basic 2005 includes a new feature called "generics" that lets you better control the objects managed by other general-use classes. This chapter describes the feature and provides examples for its use.

Chapter 11, *Error Handling in Visual Basic*

Visual Basic now offers two techniques for error handling. The first, which uses the OnError statement, is termed *unstructured error handling* and is a traditional part of VB. The second, which uses the Try...Catch...Finally construct, is termed *structured exception handling* and is new to the .NET implementation. In this chapter, we'll show you how to use both.

Part II of the book thoroughly details all the functions, statements, directives, objects, and object members that make up the Visual Basic language.

Chapter 12, *The Language Reference*

This chapter provides syntax and usage information for all major VB language features, plus information on some of the more useful .NET Framework features that are not officially part of the VB language.

Chapter 13, *The 'My' Reference*

This chapter fully documents the *My* Namespace feature, a convenient new library introduced with Visual Basic 2005.

The third and final section, Part III, consists of the following appendixes:

Appendix A, *Language Elements by Category*

A listing of all VB functions, statements, and major keywords, grouped by category.

Appendix B, *Namespace Hierarchy*
A hierarchical listing of the .NET namespaces from *System* on down, plus the hierarchy of the Visual Basic *My* Namespace feature.

Appendix C, *Constants and Enumerations*
A list of VB intrinsic constants, as well as VB enumerations and their members.

Appendix D, *What's New and Different in Visual Basic .NET 2002*
A discussion of language changes from VB 6 to Visual Basic .NET 2002.

Appendix E, *What's New and Different in Visual Basic .NET 2003*
A discussion of language changes introduced with Visual Basic .NET 2003 and the .NET Framework, Version 1.1.

Appendix F, *What's New and Different in Visual Basic 2005*
A discussion of language changes introduced with Visual Basic 2005 and the .NET Framework, Version 2.0.

Appendix G, *VB 6 Language Elements No Longer Supported*
A list of the language elements that have dropped out of the Visual Basic language as a result of its transition to the .NET Framework.

Appendix H, *The Visual Basic Command-Line Compiler*
Visual Basic includes a command-line compiler—you can actually use Notepad as your primary "development environment" for Visual Basic and use the compiler to compile your code. This appendix documents the operation of the Visual Basic command-line compiler and its options.

## About the Third Edition

The first two editions of *Visual Basic 2005 in a Nutshell* (which were both named *VB.NET Language in a Nutshell*) focused solely on the initial release of Visual Basic .NET (the 2002 release) and related .NET features (the .NET Framework, Version 1.0). This third edition incorporates all new and significant features added in both the 2003 and 2005 releases of Visual Basic. Part I, *The Basics*, has been reorganized to better support the learning process for programmers new to Visual Basic and .NET concepts in general. The largest change is the addition of two new chapters: *Generics* (Chapter 10) and *The 'My' Reference* (Chapter 13). Chapter 5, *Operators*, is also a new chapter, although it existed in the second edition as an appendix. While the third edition focuses on Visual Basic 2005, it is still useful with earlier releases of VB.NET; all feature differences between the various releases of Visual Basic for .NET are clearly marked throughout the book.

When the first release of Visual Basic for .NET appeared in 2002, the official name of the product was "Visual Basic .NET," a naming convention that was retained in the 2003 release. However, beginning with the 2005 release, the language name has officially reverted back to plain "Visual Basic." As this book focuses on the 2005 release of Visual Basic, this name change is reflected throughout the text. In most cases, the meaning of "Visual Basic" or "VB" will be clear through context, but in situations where confusion may exist, the text will specify the version discussed. Because Appendixes D and E specifically discuss the

2002 and 2003 releases of Visual Basic, they still include references to "Visual Basic .NET" and "VB.NET." There are also a few other places in the text where such usage is warranted.

## Using Code Examples

This book is here to help you get your job done. In general, you may use the code in this book in your programs and documentation. You do not need to contact O'Reilly for permission unless you're reproducing a significant portion of the code. For example, writing a program that uses several chunks of code from this book does not require permission. Selling or distributing a CD-ROM of examples from O'Reilly books does require permission. Answering a question by citing this book and quoting example code does not require permission. Incorporating a significant amount of example code from this book into your product's documentation does require permission.

We appreciate, but do not require, attribution. An attribution usually includes the title, author, publisher, and ISBN. For example: "*Visual Basic 2005 in a Nutshell,* by Tim Patrick, Steven Roman, Ron Petrusha, and Paul Lomax. Copyright 2006 O'Reilly Media, Inc., 0-596-10152-X."

If you feel your use of code examples falls outside fair use or the permission given above, feel free to contact the publisher at *permissions@oreilly.com.*

## Conventions Used in This Book

Throughout this book, we've used the following typographic conventions:

Constant Width

> Constant width in body text indicates a language construct, such as a VB keyword (like For or Do While), or a named element from an adjacent block of sample source code. Members of the *Microsoft.VisualBasic* namespace usually appear in constant-width text as well. Code fragments and code examples appear exclusively in constant-width text. In syntax statements and prototypes, text set in constant width indicates such language elements as the function or procedure name and any invariable elements required by the syntax.

Constant Width Italic

> In syntax statements and code prototypes, constant width italic indicates replaceable parameters.

Italic

> Italicized words in the text indicate intrinsic or user-defined namespaces, classes, functions, procedures, and other member names (except for those in the *Microsoft.VisualBasic* namespace). Many system elements, such as paths and filenames, are also italicized. In addition, URLs and email addresses are italicized. Finally, italics are employed the first time a term is used or defined.

Code prototypes use a simplified Backus-Naur notation, presenting all optional elements of the syntax in square brackets ([ and ]). Curly braces ({ and }) surround a set of choices from which one must be chosen. The individual choices, whether required or optional, are delimited by a vertical bar (|).

This icon indicates a note, which is an important aside to its nearby text.

 This icon indicates a warning.

## Safari® Enabled

 When you see a Safari® Enabled icon on the cover of your favorite technology book, it means the book is available online through the O'Reilly Network Safari Bookshelf.

Safari offers a solution that's better than e-books. It's a virtual library that lets you easily search thousands of top tech books, cut and paste code samples, download chapters, and find quick answers when you need the most accurate, current information. Try it for free at *http://safari.oreilly.com*.

## How to Contact Us

We have tested and verified all the information in this book to the best of our ability, but you may find that features have changed (or even that we have made mistakes). Please let us know about any errors you find, as well as your suggestions for future editions, by writing to:

O'Reilly Media, Inc.
1005 Gravenstein Highway North
Sebastopol, California 95472
(800) 998-9938 (in the United States or Canada)
(707) 829-0515 (international/local)
(707) 829-0104 (fax)

You can also send messages electronically. To be put on our mailing list or to request a catalog, send email to:

*info@oreilly.com*

To ask technical questions or comment on the book, send email to:

*bookquestions@oreilly.com*

It's our hope that, as the Visual Basic language continues to grow and evolve, so too will *Visual Basic 2005 in a Nutshell* and that the book will come to be seen by VB developers as the "official unofficial" documentation on the Visual Basic language. To do that, we need your help. If you see errors here, we'd like to hear about them. If you're looking for information on some VB language feature and can't find it in this book, we'd like to hear about that, too. And finally, if you would like to contribute your favorite programming tip or "gotcha," we'll do our best to include it in the next edition of this book. You can request these fixes, additions, and amendments to the book at our web site, *http://www.oreilly.com/catalog/vb2005ian3*.

Steven Roman maintains a web site at *www.romanpress.com* that includes information on his other books published by O'Reilly (and others), articles on VB/VBA and VB.NET, and a variety of software.

Tim Patrick's web site, *www.timaki.com*, includes information on his software development books and links to his technical articles written for Visual Basic and .NET programmers.

## Acknowledgments

Writing a book always requires a substantial commitment of time and effort, and for that we are grateful to our spouses and families for their support in helping to bring this project through to completion. Steve would like to thank Donna; Ron would like to thank Vanessa, Sean, and Ami; Paul would like to thank Deb, Russel, and Victoria; Tim would like to thank Maki and Spencer.

In expectation of the 15th anniversary of Visual Basic, we would also like to acknowledge the contributions of the designers and developers who transformed Visual Basic from an idea into a reality. Truly, it has been a monumental accomplishment that has changed the way in which applications are created.

We'd also like to thank the book's original technical reviewers, Daniel Creeron, Budi Kurniawan, and Matt Childs, for their thoughtful, careful reviews of our work. We'd also like to thank Alan Carter, Chris Dias, Amanda Silver, Sam Spencer, Jay Roxe, and Joe Binder at Microsoft for their help in answering our annoying questions and for reviewing portions of the manuscript. Scott Isaacs, William Murray, and Gerry O'Brien provided great technical reviews for the third edition.

# The Basics

This section serves as a general introduction to Visual Basic for the .NET platform. Taken together, the chapters in this section form an extremely fast-paced introduction to the most critical VB and .NET programming topics. If you're an experienced programmer who is learning VB as a second (or additional) programming language, the material should familiarize you with VB in as short an amount of time as possible.

In addition to its role as a tutorial, Chapter 4 is an essential reference to the data types supported by VB. Chapter 5 also plays the part of a half-tutorial, half-reference chapter.

Part I consists of the following chapters:

# Introduction

Since its introduction in 1991, Microsoft Visual Basic has enjoyed unprecedented success. In fact, in slightly more than a decade, it has become one of the world's most widely used programming languages, with millions of productive developers using various flavors of the language.

The reason for this success is twofold. First, Visual Basic has excelled as a rapid application development (RAD) environment for corporate and commercial applications. Second, Visual Basic offers a programming language and development environment noted for its simplicity and ease of use, making it an extremely attractive choice for those new to programming.

With the introduction of the .NET platform, Microsoft also released a new version of the Visual Basic language, Visual Basic .NET. VB.NET is a from-the-ground-up rewrite of Visual Basic that not only adds a number of new features but also differs significantly from previous versions of Visual Basic. From a high-level view, two of these differences are especially noteworthy:

- Until the release of .NET, Microsoft focused on creating a unified version of Visual Basic for Applications (VBA), the language engine used in Visual Basic, which could serve as a "universal batch language" for Windows and Windows applications. With Version 6 of Visual Basic, this goal was largely successful: VB 6.0 featured VBA 6.0, the same language engine that provided macro language functionality to the Microsoft Office suite, Microsoft Project, Microsoft FrontPage, Microsoft Visio, and a host of popular third-party applications such as AutoDesk's AutoCAD and Corel's WordPerfect Office suite. With the release of .NET, this emphasis on a unified programming language has, for the moment at least, faded into the background; .NET did not become the macro language platform for Microsoft Office or other applications. (That may change over time; SQL Server 2005, for instance, provides significant support for stored procedure scripting using .NET languages.)

- Since Version 4, Visual Basic had increasingly been used with COM and ActiveX. The development of ActiveX components was generally straightforward in VB, and the language could also take advantage of an increasing number of Microsoft-supplied and third-party ActiveX components, including ActiveX Data Objects (ADO), Collaborative Data Objects (CDO), and the Outlook object model. Although .NET supports COM for reasons of backward compatibility, it is designed primarily to work with .NET Framework-generated components rather than with COM.

You may be wondering why Microsoft would totally redesign a programming language and development environment that is so wildly successful. As you shall see, there is some method to this madness.

# Why Visual Basic .NET?

When Visual Basic was introduced in 1991, Windows 3.0 was a fairly new operating system in need of application and utility software. Although Windows 3.0 itself had proven successful, the graphical applications that offered native support for Windows—and upon the release of which the ultimate success or failure of Windows would depend—were slow in coming. The major problem was that C and C++ programmers, who had produced the majority of applications for the MS-DOS operating system, were faced with a substantial learning curve in writing Windows applications and adapting to Windows' event-driven programming model.

The introduction of Visual Basic immediately addressed this problem by offering a programming model that was thoroughly consistent with Windows' graphical nature. Although Windows marked a radical change in the way programs were written, C and C++ programmers continued to produce code as they always had: a text editor was used to write source code, the source code was compiled into an executable, and the executable was finally run under Windows. Visual Basic programmers, on the other hand, worked in a programming environment that its critics derisively labeled a "drawing program." Visual Basic automatically created a form (or window) whenever the developer began a new project. The developer would then "draw" the user interface by dragging and dropping controls from a toolbox onto the form. Finally, the developer would write code snippets that responded to particular events, such as the window being resized or a button control being clicked. Visual Basic's initial success was due to its ease of use, especially the simplicity of its graphical programming environment that was entirely consistent with the graphical character of Windows itself.

To get some sense of the revolutionary character of Visual Basic, it is instructive to compare a simple "Hello World" program for Windows 3.0 written in C (see Example 1-1) with one written in pre-.NET Visual Basic (see Example 1-2). While the former program is over two pages long, its Visual Basic counterpart takes only three lines of code—and two of them are provided automatically by the Visual Basic environment.

*Example 1-1. "Hello World" in C*

```c
// "Hello World" example
//
// The user clicks a command button, and a "Hello World"
// message box appears.
#include <windows.h>

LRESULT CALLBACK WndProc (HWND, UINT, WPARAM, LPARAM);

int WINAPI WinMain (HINSTANCE hInstance, HINSTANCE hPrevInstance,
                    PSTR szCmdLine, int iCmdShow)
    {
    static char szAppName[] = "SayHello" ;
    HWND hwnd ;
    MSG msg ;
    WNDCLASSEX wndclass ;

    wndclass.cbSize        = sizeof (wndclass) ;
    wndclass.style         = CS_HREDRAW | CS_VREDRAW ;
    wndclass.lpfnWndProc   = WndProc ;
    wndclass.cbClsExtra    = 0 ;
    wndclass.cbWndExtra    = 0 ;
    wndclass.hInstance     = hInstance ;
    wndclass.hIcon         = LoadIcon(NULL, IDI_APPLICATION) ;
    wndclass.hCursor       = LoadCursor(NULL, IDC_ARROW) ;
    wndclass.hbrBackground = (HBRUSH) GetStockObject(WHITE_BRUSH) ;
    wndclass.lpszMenuName  = NULL ;
    wndclass.lpszClassName = szAppName ;
    wndclass.hIconSm       = LoadIcon(NULL, IDI_APPLICATION) ;

    RegisterClassEx(&wndclass) ;

    hwnd = CreateWindow(szAppName, "Hello World",
                        WS_OVERLAPPEDWINDOW,
                        CW_USEDEFAULT, CW_USEDEFAULT,
                        CW_USEDEFAULT, CW_USEDEFAULT,
                        NULL, NULL, hInstance, NULL) ;

    ShowWindow(hwnd, iCmdShow) ;
    UpdateWindow(hwnd) ;

    while (GetMessage(&msg, NULL, 0, 0))
        {
        TranslateMessage(&msg) ;
        DispatchMessage(&msg) ;
        }
    return msg.wParam ;
    }

LRESULT CALLBACK WndProc(HWND hwnd, UINT iMsg, WPARAM wParam,
                        LPARAM lParam)
    {
    int wNotifyCode ;
```

*Example 1-1. "Hello World" in C (continued)*

```c
HWND hwndCtl ;
static HWND  hwndButton ;
static RECT  rect ;
static int   cxChar, cyChar ;
HDC          hdc ;
PAINTSTRUCT  ps ;
TEXTMETRIC   tm ;

switch (iMsg)
    {
  case WM_CREATE :
     hdc = GetDC(hwnd) ;
     SelectObject(hdc, GetStockObject(SYSTEM_FIXED_FONT)) ;
     GetTextMetrics(hdc, &tm) ;
     cxChar = tm.tmAveCharWidth ;
     cyChar = tm.tmHeight + tm.tmExternalLeading ;
     ReleaseDC(hwnd, hdc) ;
     GetClientRect(hwnd, &rect) ;

     hwndButton = CreateWindow("BUTTON", "&Say Hello",
                  WS_CHILD | WS_VISIBLE | BS_PUSHBUTTON,
                  (rect.right-rect.left)/20*9,
                  (rect.bottom-rect.top)/10*4,
                  14 * cxChar, 3 * cyChar,
                  (HWND) hwnd, 1,
                  ((LPCREATESTRUCT) lParam) -> hInstance, NULL) ;

     return 0 ;

  case WM_SIZE :
     rect.left   = 24 * cxChar ;
     rect.top    =  2 * cyChar ;
     rect.right  = LOWORD(lParam) ;
     rect.bottom = HIWORD(lParam) ;
     return 0 ;

  case WM_PAINT :
     InvalidateRect(hwnd, &rect, TRUE) ;

     hdc = BeginPaint(hwnd, &ps) ;
     EndPaint(hwnd, &ps) ;
     return 0 ;

  case WM_DRAWITEM :
  case WM_COMMAND :
     wNotifyCode = HIWORD(wParam) ;
     hwndCtl = (HWND) lParam ;

     if ((hwndCtl == hwndButton) && (wNotifyCode == BN_CLICKED))
        MessageBox(hwnd, "Hello, World!", "Greetings", MB_OK) ;

     ValidateRect(hwnd, &rect) ;
```

*Example 1-1. "Hello World" in C (continued)*

```
        break ;

    case WM_DESTROY :
        PostQuitMessage (0) ;
        return 0 ;
    }
    return DefWindowProc (hwnd, iMsg, wParam, lParam) ;
}
```

*Example 1-2. "Hello World" in Visual Basic*

```
Private Sub Command1_Click( )
    MsgBox "Hello, World!", vbOKOnly Or vbExclamation, "Greetings"
End Sub
```

While Version 1.0 of Visual Basic was relatively underpowered, Microsoft displayed a firm commitment to Visual Basic and worked very hard to increase its power and flexibility with each new release. By the time Version 3.0 was released, Visual Basic offered a programming paradigm that was completely intuitive, making it easy for novice programmers to get started and produce simple applications very quickly. At the same time, particularly through its ability to access the Windows Application Programming Interface (API) and through its support for add-on controls, Visual Basic had become a programming tool capable of creating applications of considerable sophistication and complexity. Professional developers now had an additional language selection beyond the usual choices of C and C++.

Visual Basic Version 4.0, which was released in 1995 to support Microsoft's 32-bit family of operating systems, was a complete rewrite of Visual Basic. It featured limited support for object-oriented programming in the form of class modules (CLS files) and the ability to generate not only Windows executables but ActiveX DLLs (also known as COM components) as well.

At about this same time, the character of programming in general changed dramatically. The rise of the Internet as an application platform meant that programmers needed to do more than write single-user, locally installed, standalone Windows applications. The increased prominence of distributed applications that assumed the presence of the Internet marked a huge change in programming focus. Visual Basic continued to be a great tool for implementing Windows desktop applications, and it was a reasonable choice for developing middle-tier components, but those strengths didn't translate easily into situations that required more direct interaction with the Web.

This disparity between Visual Basic's strengths and the new distributed and disconnected programming paradigm created something of a contradiction. On the one hand, Visual Basic excelled at graphically depicting the Windows interface. On the other hand, developers were creating more and more applications that ignored the Windows interface completely. When it came to the Internet, programmers were now using Visual Basic to write source code that would eventually be compiled into middle-tier components. Ironically, a programming environment whose real strength was its graphical character was now being used as a text editor, in very much the same way that the first generation of Windows programmers used text editors to create C source code for graphical Windows applications.

Moreover, as the popularity of the Internet grew, it became clearer that Visual Basic was not a particularly good platform for developing Internet applications. With VB 6, Microsoft introduced Web Classes as the preferred technology for Internet application development in VB. The metaphor presented by Web Classes (which focused on separating a web application's presentation from its programmatic functionality) was confusing to developers, and, as a result, Web Classes never became popular. While VB remained critically important for developing middle-tier components for distributed applications, both it and the Visual Basic community that grew up around it remained strangely isolated from the Internet as an application platform.

Numerous detractors have labeled the .NET-era Visual Basic offering as an entirely new language with little relationship to previous versions of Visual Basic—a dubious innovation foisted on the Visual Basic community by Microsoft in an attempt to sell a new version of its development products. However, that argument ignores one of the main reasons why Visual Basic, or any language, exists: to develop software applications in the most effective and efficient manner possible. The introduction of Visual Basic .NET was a logical and even necessary step forward in the development of Visual Basic as a premier programming language. .NET addresses the limitations of Visual Basic as a development language and brings it into the Internet age so that it can remain a major platform for developing applications of all kinds. Just as Visual Basic 1.0 offered a graphical interface that was suitable for Windows applications, the .NET flavors of Visual Basic and Visual Studio provide a graphical interface that is suitable for developing both desktop and web-based applications. No longer a glorified text editor, Visual Basic (built on the object-oriented foundation of .NET) can now take full advantage of the Internet as an application-development target and will continue to be a tool of choice for developing Windows applications and components.

# What Is Visual Basic .NET?

Visual Basic .NET is a programming language designed to create applications that work with Microsoft's .NET Framework. The .NET platform, in turn, addresses many of the limitations of "classic" COM, Microsoft's Component Object Model, which provided one approach toward application and component interoperability. These limitations included type incompatibilities when calling COM components, versioning difficulties when developing and installing new versions of COM components (known as "DLL hell"), and the need for developers to write a certain amount of code (mostly in C++) to handle the COM "plumbing." In contrast to pre-.NET VB, with its reliance on COM, Visual Basic as a .NET language offers a number of new features and advantages. Let's take a look at some of these.

## Object Orientation

With the release of Version 4, Visual Basic added support for classes and class modules and, in the process, became an object-oriented programming (OOP) language. Yet the debate persists about whether pre-.NET Visual Basic was a "true" object-oriented language, or whether it only supported limited features of object orientation. Detractors point out that Visual Basic did not support *inheritance* of a base class's functionality, only of its interface or signature. While Visual Basic still had a solid base of object-oriented features, purists emphasized the very real limitations in VB's OOP implementation.

While the object-oriented character of previous versions of VB may be in doubt, there is no question that .NET is an object-oriented programming platform. In fact, even if Visual Basic .NET is used to write what appears to be procedural code, it is object-oriented "under the hood." As an example, consider the clearly procedural, non-object-oriented program shown in Example 1-3.

*Example 1-3. A procedural program in .NET*

```
Module Module1
    Public Sub Main( )
        Dim x As Integer
        x = 10
        MsgBox(Increment(x))
    End Sub

    Private Function Increment(ByVal baseValue As Integer) As Integer
        Return baseValue + 1
    End Function
End Module
```

If you use ILDASM (.NET's equivalent of a disassembler) to look at the IL ("Intermediate Language," somewhat similar to assembly language in the non-.NET world) generated for this source code (see Figure 1-1), you see that internally, Module1 is in fact defined as a class that has two methods, Increment and Main.

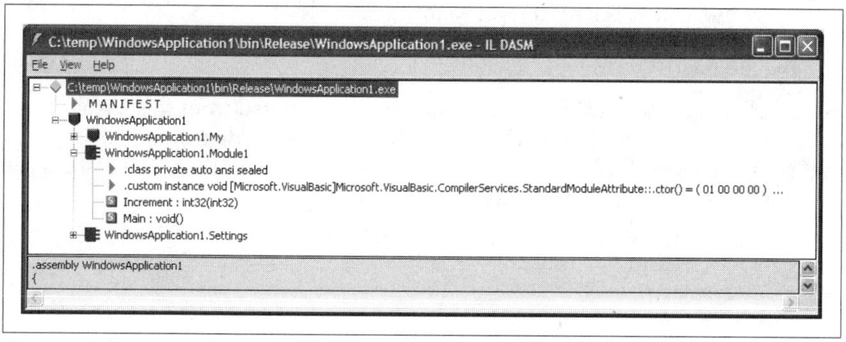

*Figure 1-1. A program viewed through ILDASM*

## A Common Type System

Traditionally, one of the problems of calling routines written in other languages from Visual Basic, or of calling Visual Basic routines from other languages, is that such inter-language calls presuppose a common type system. This is the case when calling Win32 API functions from Visual Basic, but it also applies to attempts to call methods in a VB COM component from other languages, or to call methods in a non-VB COM component from VB.

For instance, until the addition of the AddressOf operator, which obtained the memory address of a procedure, there was no way to indicate a "callback" function, a requirement of many Win32 API enumeration functions. As another example, it is expected that members of structures passed to Win32 API functions be aligned or padded in specific ways, something that VB programmers had great difficulty accomplishing.

Problems of type compatibility tended to occur most often when scripted applications were used to call and pass arguments to COM components. An excellent example is the attempt to pass an array from a script written in JScript to a COM component. COM sees JScript arrays as a string of comma-delimited values rather than as a COM-compatible array (called a SafeArray). This, and similar problems, caused no end of type-related headaches.

The .NET platform removes these difficulties by providing a Common Type System (CTS). Ultimately, all data types are either classes or structures defined by or inherited from the .NET Base Class Library. Having this Common Type System means that .NET components are truly language-independent, and that a .NET component written in one language will be seamlessly interoperable with .NET components written in any other .NET language. The problem of incompatible types simply disappears.

On the surface, VB appears to have retained its old type system. VB still supports the Long data type, for instance, although it is now a 64-bit data type instead of the 32-bit data type of VB 4 through VB 6. Most of the following .NET code is strikingly similar to VB 6 in its use of data types.

```
Public Module GeneralCode
    Public Sub Main( )
        Dim infoText As String = "This is a string."
        Dim bigNumber As Long = 12344
        Dim tinyNumber As Integer = 10
    End Sub
End Module
```

However, if you use ILDASM to examine the IL generated from this Visual Basic code, you see that VB data types are merely wrappers for data types provided by the .NET Framework. Where you expect to see Integer and Long, you instead see int32 and int64, two of the core .NET data types.

```
.method public static void  Main( ) cil managed
{
  .entrypoint
  .custom instance void
      [mscorlib]System.STAThreadAttribute::.ctor( ) = ( 01 00 00 00 )
  // Code size       17 (0x11)
  .maxstack  1
  .locals init ([0] int64 bigNumber,
           [1] string infoText,
           [2] int32 tinyNumber)
  IL_0000:  ldstr      "This is a string."
  IL_0005:  stloc.1
  IL_0006:  ldc.i4     0x3038
  IL_000b:  conv.i8
```

```
IL_000c:  stloc.0
IL_000d:  ldc.i4.s    10
IL_000f:  stloc.2
IL_0010:  ret
} // end of method GeneralCode::Main
```

# Access to System Services: The Framework Class Library

Ever since VB added support for calls to the Windows and Win32 APIs, many Visual Basic programmers have come to regard API programming as a kind of black art. Not only was there a confusing and seemingly limitless array of functions that might be called, but the craft of passing parameters to routines and receiving their return values was equally mysterious. Moreover, with the growing emphasis on object-oriented programming, the Win32 API, with its procedural approach to programming, seemed more and more archaic.

The Declare statement still appears in the .NET Visual Basic language, and programmers can continue to use the Win32 API and routines from other external Windows DLLs. However, many of the common system services provided by the Win32 API and other COM components are now available through the .NET Framework Class Library. The Framework Class Library is a collection of classes, class members, and other OOP-enabled elements, arranged in a convenient hierarchy of logical "namespaces" (read more about these in Chapter 2).

To get some sense of the difference in programming style between the Win32 API and the .NET Framework Class Library, as well as to appreciate the simplicity and ease with which the Framework Class Library can be accessed, compare Examples 1-4 and 1-5. Example 1-4 is a VB 6 routine that adds an entry in the registry that will load a particular program on Windows startup. As is clear in the code, all API constants must be defined, as must the API functions themselves. The API functions must be called correctly, using the ByVal keyword, to avoid passing a BSTR rather than a C null-terminated string to the *RegSetValueEx* function. Neglect this important rule if you like to see applications crash frequently for no apparent reason.

*Example 1-4. Writing to the registry using the Win32 API*

```
Private Const ERROR_SUCCESS = 0&

Private Const HKEY_CLASSES_ROOT = &H80000000
Private Const HKEY_CURRENT_CONFIG = &H80000005
Private Const HKEY_CURRENT_USER = &H80000001
Private Const HKEY_DYN_DATA = &H80000006
Private Const HKEY_LOCAL_MACHINE = &H80000002
Private Const HKEY_PERFORMANCE_DATA = &H80000004
Private Const HKEY_USERS = &H80000003

Private Const REG_SZ = 1

Private Const KEY_SET_VALUE = &H2

Private Declare Function RegCloseKey Lib "advapi32.dll" _
    (ByVal hKey As Long) As Long
```

*Example 1-4. Writing to the registry using the Win32 API  (continued)*

```
Private Declare Function RegOpenKeyEx Lib "advapi32.dll" _
    Alias "RegOpenKeyExA" _
    (ByVal hKey As Long, ByVal lpSubKey As String, _
    ByVal ulOptions As Long, ByVal samDesired As Long, _
    phkResult As Long) As Long
Private Declare Function RegSetValueEx Lib "advapi32.dll" _
    Alias "RegSetValueExA" _
    (ByVal hKey As Long, ByVal lpValueName As String, _
    ByVal Reserved As Long, ByVal dwType As Long, lpData As Any, _
    ByVal cbData As Long) As Long

Private Sub LoadByRegistry()
    Dim hKey As Long
    Dim nResult As Long
    Const cPGM As String = "C:\Test\TestStartup.exe"

    nResult = RegOpenKeyEx(HKEY_CURRENT_USER, _
        "Software\Microsoft\Windows\CurrentVersion\Run", 0, _
        KEY_SET_VALUE, hKey)

    If (nResult = ERROR_SUCCESS) Then
        RegSetValueEx hKey, "MyVBApp", 0, REG_SZ, ByVal cPGM, Len(cPGM)
        RegCloseKey hKey
    End If
End Sub
```

In contrast, Example 1-5 shows the comparable .NET code that uses the *RegistryKey* class in the Framework Class Library's *Microsoft.Win32* namespace. The code is short and simple and, therefore, far less error-prone.

*Example 1-5. Writing to the registry using the Framework Class Library*

```
' ----- "Imports Microsoft.Win32" included at top of file.

Private Const TargetFile As String = "C:\Test\TestStartup.exe"

Private Shared Sub LoadByRegistry()
    Dim hive As RegistryKey = Registry.CurrentUser
    Dim targetKey as RegistryKey = hive.OpenSubKey( _
        "Software\Microsoft\Windows\CurrentVersion\Run", True)
    targetKey.SetValue("MyVBApp", TargetFile)
    targetKey.Close()
End Sub
```

No worries about putting ByVal in the right place. No messy declarations muddying up the code. Just nice, clean, obvious logic. This code could be simplified even more by using the registry management features available in the new Visual Basic *My* Namespace feature. See the *Registry Object* entry in Chapter 13 for additional information.

The .NET Framework Class Libraries (FCL) is a gigantic set of classes, built upon the smaller Base Class Libraries (BCL). FCL adds a lot of the convenience features, such as the Windows Forms namespaces (for Windows desktop development). When you are using the .NET libraries, there is no clear division between BCL and FCL; there are no BCL or FCL prefixes on class names. Somewhere at Microsoft there is probably a document that clearly lists the differences, but for most programmers, it really doesn't matter. Whatever you call it, it's still a big heap of functionality. Many resources use the terms interchangeably, and this book continues that practice.

## A Common Runtime Environment

Although VB had traditionally shielded the developer from many of the intricacies of Windows as an operating system, or of COM as a method for interoperability, some knowledge of how the system worked was still essential to maintain problem-free applications. Programs and components written with one tool did not always work well with code from other tools. Working with the Win32 API often required a more advanced introduction to Windows development concepts than the typical novice Visual Basic programmer was ready to handle. Not all COM components were created equal either. It was quite easy to generate a COM component in C++ that could not be used in VB, and vice versa. Such incompatibilities kept many a programmer from developing and deploying components in their language of choice.

Under .NET, many problems like these are eliminated because of the .NET platform's *Common Language Runtime* (CLR). The CLR, as its name clearly implies, provides a variety of common services to applications and processes running under the .NET platform, regardless of the language in which they were originally written. These services include memory management and garbage collection. They also include a unified system of exception handling and the ability to use the same set of debugging tools on all code, regardless of the original .NET language used. A common set of data types ensures that data and classes interact easily between the various .NET languages. Many of these features are described later in Part I of this book.

## Naming Conventions

Although naming conventions are not strictly part of a programming language, most Visual Basic developers had adopted some form of the prefix-based "Hungarian" naming system developed many years ago by Charles Simonyi. With the release of .NET, Microsoft now recommends a new naming system. This system dispenses with the endless lists of type-specific prefixes and instead assigns names to elements (classes, functions, local variables, global constants, etc.) based solely on what they are. So a variable that holds a customer name is no longer sCustName (with "s" for "string) or even lpszCustName (don't ask); you now simply use customerName.

The new conventions include two types of naming: "Pascal Casing" and "Camel Casing." All names are mixed case, with a capital letter appearing at the start of each new word within the name. Pascal Casing also capitalizes the first letter, and it is used for all public class members and global elements. Camel Casing includes a lowercase initial letter, and it is used for private members, procedure arguments, and local variables. There are some additional details to the rules, and some people differ on when to use Pascal Casing and when to use Camel Casing. The online help included with Visual Studio includes an entry that discusses these conventions in more detail.

In keeping with the spirit of .NET programming, all .NET examples in this book employ the new naming conventions.

## What Can You Do with Visual Basic .NET?

With its language enhancements and its tight integration into the .NET Framework, Visual Basic is a thoroughly modernized language that has become one of the premier development tools for creating a wide range of .NET applications. In the past, Visual Basic was often seen as a "lightweight" language that could be used for particular kinds of tasks but was wholly unsuited for others. (It was often argued, sometimes incorrectly, that you couldn't create such things as Windows dynamic link libraries or shell extensions using Visual Basic.) In the .NET Framework, Visual Basic emerges as an equal player; Microsoft's claim of language independence—that programming language should be a lifestyle choice, rather than something forced on the developer by the character of a project—is realized in the .NET platform.

This means that Visual Basic can be used to create a wide range of applications and components, including the following:

- Standard Windows applications
- Windows console mode applications
- Windows services
- Windows controls and Windows control libraries
- Web (ASP.NET) applications
- XML Web services
- Web controls and web control libraries
- .NET classes and namespaces
- Applications that interact with legacy COM components

Most importantly, with the release of .NET, Visual Basic becomes an all-purpose development environment for building Internet applications, an area in which it has traditionally been weak. Each successive release of Visual Basic should further enhance its position as the tool of choice for developing state-of-the-art software, both now and long into the future.

## Versions of Visual Basic for .NET

.NET brought about a major progression in the Visual Basic language, but it wasn't a once-and-for-all change. Since VB's initial .NET release in 2002, it and the underlying .NET Framework have been updated several times to include new functionality. As of this writing, there have been three major releases of Visual Basic.

- *Visual Basic .NET 2002.* This was the original release of Visual Basic .NET and was packaged with Version 1.0 of the .NET Framework. Internally, this release is known as Visual Basic 7.0. For a list of changes between Visual Basic 6.0 and the 2002 release of VB.NET, see Appendix D.

- *Visual Basic .NET 2003.* The second release of Visual Basic was a "minor" release, with limited functionality changes. It shipped with Version 1.1 of the .NET Framework and was identified internally as Visual Basic 7.1. For a list of changes between the 2002 and 2003 releases of VB.NET, see Appendix E.

- *Visual Basic 2005.* The third and most recent release of Visual Basic is a "major" update to the language. Internally, it is known as Visual Basic 8.0, and it comes with a parallel update to the .NET Framework, Version 2.0. For a list of changes between the 2003 and 2005 releases of VB, see Appendix F.

When .NET first appeared, it significantly raised the learning curve for first-time developers looking to try out Visual Basic. It was designed as a professional tool for professional programmers. The 2005 release of Visual Basic attempts to bring new programmers back into the Visual Basic world by expanding the usability range of the product line. Visual Studio 2005 includes several distinct audience-targeted packages.

- *Visual Studio 2005 Express Edition.* This is the entry-level product, and it is available as a more specific Visual Basic 2005 Express Edition. (Actually, each .NET language is a separate product in the Express Edition line.) This package includes a simplified development environment interface, some restrictions on functionality (at least through the development environment), and features that help first-time developers become more productive in Visual Basic. A companion product (though included in Visual Studio 2005 Express Edition) is Visual Web Developer 2005 Express Edition, a simpler and more lightweight web application development tool. Express Edition users who want to develop web applications must install Visual Web Developer.

- *Visual Studio 2005 Standard Edition.* The standard edition of Visual Basic 2005 uses the same simplified development environment as the Express Edition but adds some extra functionality. It includes the full MSDN documentation set (instead of just *Getting Started* guides), a class designer, full support for building Windows Forms applications, richer XML features, support for source-code-control integration, application-deployment support through the new "ClickOnce" deployment feature, and access to SQL Server's reporting services. You can also target mobile devices with this package.

- *Visual Studio 2005 Professional Edition.* Visual Basic 2005 Professional Edition part of the professional Visual Studio release, includes all the features of the Standard Edition but adds more enhanced features for the full-time developer. The simplified user interface is replaced with the full Integrated Development Environment (IDE). The package also includes Crystal Reports, support for remote debugging, the ability to generate 64-bit applications, full access to system services and databases (including SQL Server), and full deployment support through both ClickOnce and Windows Installer projects. A copy of SQL Server 2005 Developer Edition also appears at this level.

- *Visual Studio 2005 Tools for the Microsoft Office System.* This product is similar to the Professional Edition but includes additional tools that make development with Microsoft Office easier. The package adds tools for specifically working with Microsoft Access databases. However, some Professional Edition-level features are removed. This edition includes no support for mobile devices, and you cannot generate 64-bit applications. Visual J# and Visual C++ are absent as well.

- *Visual Studio 2005 Team System.* This product is actually three distinct packages targeted at (1) software architects, (2) software developers, and (3) software testers. A fourth "suite" package combines all the features of the other three. All of the packages are designed for projects with multiple developers and include tools for testing and profiling .NET applications. Source code control and project management tools also appear. A separate package, *Visual Studio 2005 Team Foundation Server*, is a server-side product that provides additional collaborative and support features for all team members.

- *SQL Server 2005.* Although not officially a Visual Studio development language, Microsoft released the 2005 edition of its premier database platform at the same time that it released Visual Studio 2005. (Some Visual Studio editions include a developer's version of SQL Server 2005.) SQL Server 2005 includes support for .NET application development, especially through its use of stored procedures written in any .NET language.

# 2

# The .NET Framework: General Concepts

This chapter provides a high-level overview of the most important .NET Framework concepts. There are many concepts that are new and different from Visual Basic's pre-.NET days, but some of them are quite technical or esoteric and are beyond the scope of this book. The discussion here is limited to those essential features that you must know to program effectively using .NET. For a more thorough coverage of .NET concepts, see Thuan Thai and Hoang Q. Lam's book, *.NET Framework Essentials* (O'Reilly).

## Common Language Runtime

The *Common Language Runtime* (CLR) is an environment that manages code execution and provides application-development services. It provides all of the common features required by all .NET-enabled languages. Visual Basic and other .NET languages are simply wrappers that expose the CLR's functionality. Because the CLR provides all of the core functionality for all .NET languages, components written in different .NET languages can interact with each other immediately, with no language-specific conflicts. Even data types are shared among .NET languages through the CLR's *Common Type System* (CTS). While data types may have different names in Visual Basic than they do in C#, they will all be based on underlying CLR data types.

The *Common Language Specification* (CLS) defines the minimal set of .NET features that must be implemented by a .NET-compliant compiler. Components developed to be CLS-compliant may be limited in their ability to interact with applications and components that use a wider range of .NET features.

The output of a .NET compiler includes *metadata*, which is information that describes the objects that are part of the generated application or library. The metadata describes the following:

- Data types and their dependencies
- Objects and their members

- References to required components
- Information (including versioning information) about components and resources that were used to build the application or library

Metadata is used by the CLR to support functionality such as:

- Manage memory allocations
- Locate and load class instances
- Manage object references and perform garbage collection
- Resolve method invocations
- Generate native code
- Make sure that the application has the correct versions of necessary components and resources
- Enforce security

By including metadata in a compiled software component, that component becomes "self-describing." This tells the CLR everything it needs to prepare and execute a .NET application, and to allow it to interact with other .NET components.

# Managed Code

Code created within the CLR environment is called *managed code*. Applications and libraries created using non-.NET tools, such as VB 6 applications, and COM and ActiveX components, are *not* managed code. You can still use unmanaged components in your .NET applications, but they must be referenced through special "interop" conduits to prevent the unmanaged code from having any detrimental impact on the managed side of the application.

Having a central manager of all things .NET like the CLR makes possible some nice centralized functionality. One such feature in .NET is the *garbage collection* system, which automatically disposes of all variables and data objects when an application is finished with them, reclaiming every byte and releasing all references to the related memory.

*Managed execution* is the process of running your .NET applications in the context of the CLR, although this process officially starts when writing your first line of .NET source code. There are three simple steps to managed execution.

1. Write code using one or more .NET compilers. Some compilers (like the C++ compiler for .NET) can generate code that is unmanaged or that falls outside the official CLS. Such code cannot easily interact with components from other .NET languages, so avoid it in mixed-language applications.

2. Compile the code. The compiler translates source code to *Intermediate Language* code (IL), also called *Microsoft Intermediate Language* (MSIL) or *Common Intermediate Language* (CIL), and generates the necessary metadata for the application.

3. Run the code. When .NET code is executed, the IL is compiled into CPU-specific native code by a *Just In Time* (JIT) compiler. The resulting application is run within the context of the CLR.

One benefit of running applications within the CLR-managed environment is that data within the application is kept safe. The CLR keeps errant code and malformed data from interfering with the rest of memory, either in your application or elsewhere in the system.

# Namespaces

The notion of a *namespace* plays a fundamental role in the .NET Framework. In general, a namespace is a logical grouping of types (classes and similar constructs) for the purposes of identification and navigation. There are so many classes and features in .NET that there are bound to be name conflicts. And since third-party libraries can be integrated into the class space just like the Microsoft-supplied libraries, namespaces keep everything neat and orderly.

Imagine that, in a certain business, there is an executive named John Smith, a secretary named John Smith, and a custodian named John Smith. In this case, the name John Smith is ambiguous. When the paymaster stands on a table and calls out the names of people to receive their paychecks, the executive John Smith won't be happy if he rushes to the table when custodian John Smith's paycheck is in the paymaster's hand.

To resolve the naming ambiguity, the business can define three namespaces: Executive, Secretarial, and Custodial. Now the three individuals can be unambiguously referred to by their fully qualified names:

- Executive.John Smith
- Secretarial.John Smith
- Custodial.John Smith

Namespaces in .NET look a lot like these references to John Smith. They are simply names used to group and organize all of the .NET classes into a hierarchy. Namespaces can be nested. Consider the following three possible namespaces.

- America Namespace
- America.Washington Namespace
- America.Washington.Seattle Namespace

Each of these namespaces can include classes (and other types) and additional namespaces. And the same class name can appear in multiple namespaces, even in nested namespaces.

- America.Demographics Class
- America.Washington.Demographics Class
- America.Washington.Seattle.Demographics Class
- America.Montana.Demographics Class

The .NET *Framework Class Library* (FCL) consists of several thousand classes and other types (such as interfaces, structures, and enumerations) that are divided into about 200 namespaces. All classes considered to be the "core" language-neutral classes of .NET appear in the *System* namespace, or in one of the nested namespaces within *System*. The namespaces supplied with .NET provide basic system services, such as:

- Basic and advanced data types and exception handling (the *System* namespace)
- Data access (the *System.Data* namespace)
- User-interface elements for standard Windows applications (the *System.Windows.Forms* namespace)
- User-interface elements for web applications (the *System.Web.UI* namespace)

Many Visual Basic language features are implemented within the classes of the *Microsoft.VisualBasic* namespace. (The C# and J# languages have corresponding namespaces.)

All classes (and other types) exist in a namespace, even the classes of your application. By default, your project's namespace is at the top of the hierarchy (next to *System*) and is named after your project's name. You can alter this by using the Namespace statement at the beginning of a code file, or by defining a different project namespace through the Project Properties.

## Types and Objects

Pretty much everything in a .NET application is contained in a *type*. Types include:

- Classes, which are basically collections of data values, and the related code that manages that data. Usually a class has both data and code, but a particular class might just have either data or code. In Visual Basic, a Module is a variation of a class.
- Interfaces, which are class "skeletons." Interfaces define the basic structure of a class but without the actual implementation. They are useful for defining a common layout of features to be shared by many related classes.
- Delegates, which .NET uses to implement its event-driven infrastructure.
- Enumerations, which are collections of named numeric elements.
- Value types and reference types. Normally, when you create an object (an in-memory instance of a class), that object sits in memory somewhere, and your object variable contains the memory location of the object block. (It's like a *pointer*, for those familiar with the C language parlance.) These are *reference types*. The .NET type system also supports *value types*. A value type variable stores the actual data value instead of a memory address to the true location of the data.
- Other similar things. You can subdivide the type system forever, but everything is eventually called a type.

From the Visual Basic point of view, all types are really classes. Of course, all data objects are instances of classes, but even your source code—even your *Sub Main* routine—is part of a class, and it *must* be part of a class to be part of a .NET application.

Classes define a chunk of related data and functionality. When you design a class, you are saying, "I'm planning on creating an object that has these features and that stores this type of data and information." *Objects* are the actual in-memory instances of a class. For a much richer description of objects and other object-oriented concepts, see Chapter 3.

The root of the type hierarchy is the *System.Object* class. All new classes you design eventually tie back to the *System.Object* class. This class provides some basic functionality required of all classes and provides a convenient way to generically identify any object in your application.

## Assemblies

An *assembly* is a single .NET executable (EXE file) or library (DLL file). Since these file types existed before .NET was invented, why bother to give them a special name? Well, it's not just the type of file; it's what is in the file that counts. (By the way, a .NET purist will insist that a single assembly can be split into multiple files. While this is true, it rarely happens, especially since it can't be done from within the Visual Studio development environment.)

An assembly is a *unit of deployment*; that is, it's a file that can be deployed on a user's system. .NET applications are made up of one or more assemblies, all working together for a common goal. Inside of an assembly, you find the following:

- The executable code of your application. Generally you will have a single primary EXE assembly, plus optional DLL assemblies.
- Embedded data, such as resources (graphics, strings, etc.).
- .NET-specific security permissions required for the assembly.
- The types (classes and so on) used in the assembly, including public classes that can be accessed by other assemblies (applications).
- Listings of the external types and references needed by the assembly, including references to other assemblies. These references also indicate the specific or minimum version number expected for those external components.
- Version information for the assembly. Assemblies include a four-part version number (major, minor, revision, and build, as in "2.1.0.25"), and this version number determines how the assembly interacts with other assemblies and components. .NET allows you to install different versions of an assembly on a single machine and have specific versions accessed by other applications. For instance, you may have Versions 1.0 and 2.0 of a spellchecking component installed on a workstation, one for an old word processor (that requires Version 1.0) and one for a newer email system (that uses Version 2.0). Both versions can reside on the same system without conflict. In fact, both versions can be actively running at the same time, a feature known as *side-by-side execution*.

Much of this information is stored in the assembly's metadata, which was discussed earlier. As a unit, this metadata is known as the assembly's *manifest*.

Although this is somewhat repetitive, the manifest contains at least the following information.

- The name of the assembly
- Version information for the assembly
- Security information for the assembly
- A list of all files that are part of the assembly
- Type reference information for the types specified in the assembly
- A list of other assemblies that are referenced by the assembly
- Custom information, such as a user-friendly assembly title, description, company name, copyright information, and product information

If your application is split up into multiple assemblies, each assembly is only loaded into memory as it is needed. One interesting side effect of this as-needed access is that you can update an assembly file *while the application that uses the file is still running*. If you replace a DLL, the application will start using the new DLL the next time it has fully discontinued use of the old DLL. Of course, this generally happens when you exit and restart the application, but in some complex applications, you could perform a live update of an assembly.

# The Framework Class Library

Although .NET itself is very powerful and very cool, it doesn't provide much in the way of specific functionality. The .NET Framework provides a generic system for application development, but it's really all plumbing. It's not that different from the old-style C++ or Pascal compilers. If you want to sort a list of strings in reverse order by length, draw a line on the screen, interact with a database, or send a data packet across the Internet, you still have to write all of that functionality yourself. Or do you?

Fortunately, you don't have to do it all by yourself. The .NET Framework includes a library of prewritten features that provide a lot of the functionality you really wanted, but that you didn't want to write yourself. This library uses a layered approach. At the bottom of the library is the *Base Class Library* (BCL), which defines the central and common features that every .NET language will use, such as:

- Implementation of all core data types
- Data structures, such as stacks, queues, and collections
- Diagnostic and tracking features
- Basic input and output with various sources, such as files and serial ports

On top of this foundation you find the FCL, which is pretty much everything else that Microsoft thought programmers (including programmers designing the .NET system) would find useful. Among the many library classes are:

- XML manipulation tools
- ADO.NET, a collection of generic and platform-specific database interaction components

- GDI+, the core drawing system for on-screen and printed output
- Windows Forms, a package for creating desktop applications
- ASP.NET, a web-based programming system

## Application Deployment

Once you write your VB application, you still have to install it on each user's system. .NET provides two deployment methods. The first method, *Windows Installer deployment*, was actually around for a while before the first release of the .NET Framework. Windows Installer deployments are basic Setup packages that the user installs from a single ".msi" file. All releases of .NET-centric Visual Basic (except for some of the more entry-level 2005 editions) allow you to create a deployment project, the output of which is an ".msi" file packed with all the files needed to install your application. Since the basic installer project features in Visual Studio include limited support for custom installation scenarios, several third-party vendors provide enhanced products for generating more advanced Windows Installer files.

*New in 2005.* The .NET Framework, Version 2.0, part of the 2005 release of Visual Studio, includes a new deployment method called *ClickOnce*. Because Windows Installer deployments often update important system files or registry entries, the user installing the package usually needs to be a local administrator on the workstation to complete the installation. ClickOnce deployments get around this by installing the application in its own protected environment (that is, the rest of the workstation is protected from it!). ClickOnce-installed applications are convenient for users; they are designed for easy single-click installation from a web site, and they can be configured to automatically check for and install updated versions.

## The .NET Framework and Visual Basic

Visual Basic, as a .NET language, uses all of the core features of the Common Language Runtime, the Common Type System, namespaces, assemblies, types, and all other .NET elements, packaging them up in a nice, neat programming system.

To write a Visual Basic application, you create classes that implement your desired functionality and data manipulation features. All application data is stored in memory using the Common Type System data types that Visual Basic uses for its own basic data types. The application manipulates this data using many of the prewritten classes in the Framework Class Library. All of this code gets organized into namespaces of your choosing and is compiled into one or more assemblies. Your application is now ready to deploy and run.

# 3

# Introduction to Object-Oriented Programming

Before you can write quality Visual Basic applications on the .NET platform, you must have a good understanding of objected-oriented programming (OOP) concepts. This chapter presents a brief introduction to these concepts.

Visual Basic has included at least some object-oriented programming features since Version 4. But these features were limited, and some workarounds were required to simulate the missing features, if they could be simulated at all. The advent of .NET infused Visual Basic with a more complete set of OOP features.

You may be saying to yourself: "I prefer not to use object-oriented techniques in my programming." Unfortunately, this is not an option in the .NET flavor of Visual Basic. Every line of code, apart from a few statements that appear in the declarations section of each code file, appears within a class—one of the core building blocks of object-oriented software development. Also, all features contained within the Framework Class Library are built on object-oriented principles.

## Principles of Object-Oriented Programming

Object-oriented programming is a software development architecture that uses the object—a "black box" of data and related functionality—as its focus. These objects are built on four main facets of OOP design: *abstraction*, *encapsulation*, *inheritance*, and *polymorphism*. This section introduces each of these concepts and also the notion of an *interface* as the means of interaction with the contents of an object's black box.

### Objects and Classes

An *object* is a software-based collection of data elements and related procedures that act on those data elements. Obviously, objects are the central theme of "object-oriented" programming. In Visual Basic and other similar OOP languages, a *class* is the source code design of an object. An object is an in-memory instance of a class in a running program. Multiple object instances based on a single class can exist in memory at the same time.

Although the terms "class" and "object" have distinct meanings, the terms are used somewhat interchangeably in this chapter, at least in those cases where the distinction is not necessarily important.

## Abstraction

An *abstraction* is a view of an entity that includes only those aspects that are relevant for a particular situation. It takes something from the real world—an employee, a book, a chart of accounts, a galaxy, a grain of sand—and breaks it down into individual elements that can be managed with software. Consider a software component that provides services for tracking an employee's information. The first step in designing such a component is to identify the items or features that would be managed by the component. Some of these items may be:

- Employee full name
- Employee home address
- Company ID for the employee
- Current salary
- Length of employment
- Features to adjust the salary based on a rule

This list includes not only basic data values, or *properties*, but also common actions to be taken on the data, or *methods*. Properties of the class, such as the employee's full name, are sometimes called fields, and they may have limits on the type or range of data allowed. Methods may require additional information (such as a table of salary adjustment rules for the salary adjustment feature) to work properly. These actions are sometimes referred to as operations or behaviors. Together, the properties and methods are known as *members* of the abstraction.

The properties and methods of a class are relevant to that class. Although the *Employee* class could have included properties for IQ or the number of hairs on the employee's head, these data values have no relevance to the purpose of the class. Even though they are part of each employee, they provide no value to the class and are therefore excluded.

In short, the true employee has been abstracted—the class includes only those properties and methods of employees that are relevant to the needs of the class. Once the abstraction is complete, the properties and methods can be built into a software component.

## Encapsulation

*Encapsulation* is the process of converting an abstraction into a usable software component—the black box—and exposing to the public only those portions of the abstraction that are absolutely necessary. The complete logic needed to manage each public property or method is fully contained ("encapsulated") inside the black box.

Encapsulation serves three useful purposes:

- It permits the protection of these properties and methods from any outside tampering.

- It allows the inclusion of validation code to help catch errors in the use of the public interface. For instance, the encapsulation can be programmed to prevent a negative number from being used for an employee's salary.

- It frees the user from having to know (or worry about) the details of how the properties and methods are implemented.

High-level programming languages already perform some encapsulation to simplify the work required by the programmer. For instance, the SByte data type, introduced in Visual Basic 2005, is an 8-bit integer data type that supports a range of numbers from -128 to 127. But how exactly does it record those 128 negative numbers? If you are familiar with binary representation, you know that each bit of the integer number represents a power of 2: the right-most bit (bit 0) represents $2^0$, the bit just to the left of that (bit 1) represents $2^1$, and so on up to the left-most bit (bit 7), which represents $2^7$. Setting each of these bits results in a different number. For instance, the binary number 00100110 sets bits 1, 2, and 5, and the sum of $2^1$, $2^2$, and $2^5$ is 38 (decimal). In unsigned data, the binary number 11111111 equals 255 decimal. But that's all the bits. How do you get a negative number?

Visual Basic uses a system named *two's-complement representation* to handle negative numbers. Basically, any time the leftmost bit is set to 1, the number is negative. Then there are various rules used to interpret the remaining bits, depending on whether the leftmost bit is set or not.

Do you want to know those rules? Do you really need to know those rule, or how negative values are managed at all? The great answer is: no! In most programming, you don't have to worry about how Visual Basic stores negative numbers at the binary level. Who cares? You only need access to negative numbers, not to the complex rules about how they are processed in the computer. Visual Basic wraps up all of this functionality for you automatically in the SByte data type. This is the essence of encapsulation: just the right amount of visible functionality, all of the messy details hidden from view.

Moreover, encapsulation protects programmers from making errors. For instance, if every programmer had to do the negating by setting each bit manually and following all of the various and sundry rules, some important step would be forgotten. The encapsulated data type takes care of this automatically.

Encapsulation has yet another important feature. Any code written using the exposed interface of the SByte data type remains valid, even if the internal workings of the SByte data type are changed for some reason. If Microsoft decided to have the SByte data type use *one's complement representation* (another method for managing negative numbers), it wouldn't matter to programs that used SByte, as long as the interface to the data type did not change.

# Inheritance

*Inheritance* makes it possible for OOP code to build classes that extend or restrict features in other existing classes, without the need to fully rewrite the original class. For instance, a class of *Pet* may have generic data fields such as *Name*, *Age*, and *Color*. This single class could be extended into other, more specific classes through inheritance. A class named *Dog* that is *derived* from *Pet* would automatically include the *Name*, *Age*, and *Color* members, but it may add additional canine-specific members such as *Breed* and a *ShedsHair* flag. In this situation, the *Dog* class *inherits* from the *Pet* class.

Inheritance used in this manner certainly reduces duplication of code, since the *derived class* does not have to rewrite the code for the existing *base class*'s members. But inheritance also makes interactions between these objects easier, since an object of type *Dog* is also a true object of type *Pet*. Objects of a derived class are also objects of the base class, and they can be used in code as if they were actually members of the base class. (The reverse is not true; objects of type *Pet* are not necessarily objects of type *Dog*).

Some languages allow a class to inherit from multiple base classes at the same time. Visual Basic does not support this feature.

# Interfaces

The public members of an object are known as its *interface* (or *public interface*). Usually, an object has a single public interface, since its class was designed with a single purpose in mind. But sometimes it is useful for a class to have multiple interfaces. For instance, along with the *Pet* class, consider another class called *House*. These two classes have some common aspects and tasks that apply to both, one of which is a cleaning strategy. While you could add distinct *CleanNow*, *CleanserName*, and *CleaningTimeRequired* members to each class, it would be more convenient to have a separate interface, called the *Cleaning interface*, that could then be applied to both *Pet* and *House*. Then your code could call the cleaning-related members on any object that implemented the *Cleaning interface*.

Interfaces are simply templates of desired functionality. To make these templates a functional reality, they must be *implemented* through a class. Implementing is a little different from inheriting. With inheritance, the new class receives the existing functionality of the base class; the new class doesn't have to reinvent this functionality. When implementing an interface, the new class is responsible for providing all of the functionality of the interface.

While Visual Basic classes cannot inherit from multiple base classes, a single class can implement multiple interfaces at the same time.

# Polymorphism

The term *polymorphism* means having or passing through many different forms. The *Dog* class, derived from the *Pet* class, automatically receives the prewritten members of the *Pet* class. However, if one or more of these members needs to be extended in a special way to meet the needs of the new derived class (*Dog*), special

*Dog*-specific versions of those members can be added to the *Dog* class. Any *Dog* object that calls these methods will use the *Dog*-specific versions; any general *Pet* object will use the default *Pet*-specific versions. If your code is currently treating a *Dog* object as a more generic *Pet* object, it will still use the *Dog*-specific versions, since the object is still a *Dog*.

Sound confusing? Welcome to polymorphism. Fortunately, the Visual Basic compiler figures out all of these relationships for you; you just need to write your code to enable the class-specific actions you require.

## Overloading

Sometimes it is useful to have more than one way of performing the same action in a single class. For instance, if your *Dog* class has a *TakeForWalk* action, you might require several ways of taking this action to mimic real-world actions. For instance, you might want to call *TakeForWalk* with a time duration ("30 minutes") for a generic time-based walk, or call it with instructions for a specific path-based exercise plan. You would need one version of this action that takes a number (time-based) and one that takes a path plan (path-based), perhaps sent as a string.

When a class includes multiple versions of the same member that differ by their argument signatures (that is, by the parameters and return values of those members), that is *overloading*. This allows the member to take an action, but with different types of input data. Overloading most often occurs with actions taken on the object's data. The ability to provide differing sets of supporting data to an action can greatly expand the functionality of a class.

*New in 2005.* The original .NET release of Visual Basic did not include *operator overloading*. This form of overloading allows you to provide custom meanings to the standard language operator symbols, such as the + (addition) and <> (not equal to) operators. The 2005 release of Visual Basic adds this form of overloading to the language. See the "Operator Overloading" section of Chapter 5 for information on this enhancement, including examples.

# OOP Development in Visual Basic

The .NET Framework is an OOP-rich development environment. Within that environment, Visual Basic provides access to most OOP features.

The primary OOP entity in Visual Basic is the *class*, but the language also supports two additional variations of this standard entity: (1) the *structure*, a value-type variation (always derived from *System.ValueType*) of the normally reference-type class, and (2) *modules*, a class in which all members are shared and public by default. These three primary development entities, along with a few other entities, such as enumerations, fall under the broad name of *type* in .NET parlance. Unless otherwise noted, all discussions of class features apply also to structures and modules.

# Classes in Visual Basic

Most Visual Basic development establishes a one-to-one relationship between a class and a source code file. However, a single file may include multiple classes. Beginning in 2005, the code for a single class may also be split among multiple source code files by using the new `Partial` keyword. See the entry for that keyword in Chapter 12 for additional information on its usage.

The basic source code needed to define a class is pretty simple.

```
Public Class className

End Class
```

Once a class is defined, it can be used by creating an *instance* of the class, which is what is really known as the *object*. (Some class members can be used without creating an instance; these "shared members" are discussed below.) Instantiating an object requires (1) a variable to hold the object and (2) the creation of the object using the `New` keyword. These two steps are often performed in two separate VB statements.

```
Dim myInstance As SimpleClass  ' Defines the variable
myInstance = New SimpleClass   ' Creates the object
```

These two steps can be combined into a single statement:

```
Dim myInstance As SimpleClass = New SimpleClass
```

A shortcut syntax makes the instantiation even simpler:

```
Dim myInstance As New SimpleClass
```

## Class Members

Visual Basic classes contain the following types of members:

*Field Members*
> This includes member variables and constants. Enumerated data types defined within a class fall into this category.

*Event Members*
> Events are procedures that are called automatically by the Common Language Runtime in response to some action that occurs, such as an object being created, a button being clicked, a piece of data being changed, or an object going out of scope. Events can also be manually fired through code.

*Method Members*
> This refers to both functions and subroutines. A special method subroutine called a *constructor* is used to help create new instances of the class.

*Property Members*
> Properties combine aspects of both function methods and fields. They are often used to provide access to a hidden class field through a pair of property procedures, one for updating the data and one for retrieving the current data value.

*Type Members*
Classes may be *nested*, with one class contained completely within another.

The following Person class sample illustrates all of the various member types except class nesting.

```
Public Class Person
    ' ----- Field Members -----
    Private fullName As String
    Private currentAge As Short
    Public Const MaxAge As Short = 120

    ' ----- Event Member -----
    Public Event Testing( )

    ' ----- Constructor Method Members -----
    Public Sub New( )
        ' ----- Default constructor.
        fullName = "<unnamed>"
    End Sub

    Public Sub New(ByVal newName As String)
        ' ----- Simple constructor to set an initial field.
        fullName = newName
    End Sub

    ' ----- Method Members -----
    Public Sub Test( )
        ' ----- Test the class-defined event.
        RaiseEvent Testing( )
    End Sub

    Public Overrides Function ToString( ) As String
        ' ----- Returns a friendly string related to the instance.
        '       NOTE: The 'Overrides' keyword will be discussed
        '             later in the chapter.
        Return fullName & ", Age " & currentAge
    End Function

    ' ----- Property Members -----
    Public Property Age( ) As Short
        ' ----- This property performs simple error checking.
        Get
            Return currentAge
        End Get
        Set(ByVal value As Short)
            If (value < 0) Or (value > MaxAge) Then
                Throw New System.ArgumentException( _
                    "Age ranges from 0 to " & MAX_AGE & ".", "Age")
            Else
                currentAge = value
            End If
        End Set
    End Property
```

```
Public Property Name( ) As String
    ' ----- This property adds no special logic; it could
    '        have been a public field instead.
    Get
        Return fullName
    End Get
    Set(ByVal value As String)
        fullName = value
    End Set
End Property
End Class
```

## Class Member Accessibility

Generally, the members of a class constitute that class's public interface. But some members may exist only for the internal use of the class instance itself. Each member of a class includes an *access modifier*. These special keywords indicate just how visible a particular member is to code outside of the class. Table 3-1 shows the five available access modifiers.

*Table 3-1. Access Modifiers*

| Access modifier | Description |
| --- | --- |
| Public | Public members are accessible to any code that accesses an instance of the class or structure, or that has access to the module containing the member. If a class has a public member, and an instance of that class is accessed from a separate project, application, or component, the public member is fully accessible to that external code. |
| Protected | Protected members are accessible within the confines of a class and can be used in any code derived from that class, but they cannot be accessed outside of the class. Protected members only apply to classes; they are not available to structures or modules. |
| Friend | Friend members are accessible anywhere within the assembly, but no further. Instances of a class with a friend member consumed outside of the assembly hide the member from that external code. Friend members can be used in classes, structures, and modules. |
| Protected Friend | Using Protected and Friend together grants a member all the benefits of both; such members are accessible within the class and all derived classes, and within the assembly, but not outside of it. Protected Friend members can be used in classes, but not in structures or modules. |
| Private | Private members are accessible anywhere within a class, structure, or module, but not outside. They are also hidden from the custom members of derived classes. |

A class itself also has an access modifier, one of Public, Friend, or Private. Public classes can be accessed by another assembly that uses your class' assembly; Friend classes are accessible throughout your assembly, but not outside of it; and Private classes are only accessible within their "declaration context." Generally, Private is similar to Friend, but nested classes can be limited to use only within their parent class by using the Private keyword.

## Field Members

Variables, constants, and enumerations declared inside of a class, but outside of any class member procedure, are field members. (Enumerations can also be declared outside of classes altogether.) They are simple to declare and use, as done in the Person class earlier.

```
Private fullName As String
Private currentAge As Short
Public Const MaxAge As Short = 120
```

Private field members are often used in tandem with member property procedures to provide logic-controlled access to a data field in the class.

Public field members are available through instances of your class.

```
Dim onePerson As New Person
MsgBox("Maximum allowed age is " & onePerson.MaxAge & ".")
```

## Event Members

Events members provide a way to tap into the event-controlled interfaces of the .NET Framework. The declaration and use of events is fully described in Chapter 8. The 2005 release of Visual Basic adds a new feature called *custom events* that provides more control over the lifetime of an event. This feature is also discussed in Chapter 8.

## Method Members and Constructors

The function and sub procedures contained within your classes will generally make up the bulk of your Visual Basic application. (Procedures that intercept events are also considered method members.) Methods contain two main parts: (1) the declaration and (2) the body.

```
' ---- This is the declaration...
Public Function AgeInDogYears(sourceAge As Decimal) As Decimal
   ' ----- ...and this is the body.
   Return sourceAge * 7@
End Function
```

The declaration of a method is often referred to as its *signature*. The signature includes the specific argument list and the return value; the method name is not part of the signature.

Private methods can only be called within the class itself. Public members can be used within your class or by external users of the class.

```
' ----- This code resides outside of the class that defines
'       the AgeInDogYears function.
Dim meAsFido As Decimal
meAsFido = theDog.AgeInDogYears(38@)
```

When an object of a particular class is created, the compiler calls a special procedure within the class called a *constructor* or *instance constructor*. Constructors initialize an object when necessary. (Constructors take the place of the Class_ Initialize event in pre-.NET versions of VB.)

Constructor procedures always have a name of New; more than one New procedure may appear in your class, provided each one has a different argument signature. (Normally when two procedures with the same name appear in a class, the

Overloads keyword—described later in this chapter—must be added to each declaration. However the New procedure is a special case; it does not require the Overloads keyword.)

For classes that require no special initialization of their public or private members, the constructor can be omitted from the class; Visual Basic will provide a default constructor when no defined constructor exists in a class. But many classes require some basic initialization, and the constructor is the place to do it. The Person class defined earlier includes two constructors.

```
Public Sub New( )
    ' ----- Default constructor.
    fullName = "<unnamed>"
End Sub

Public Sub New(ByVal newName As String)
    ' ----- Simple constructor to set an initial field.
    fullName = newName
End Sub
```

The first constructor is the *default constructor*; since it includes no arguments in its declaration signature, it is used by default when an instance is created that lacks any initialization arguments. The second constructor is a *custom constructor*; it is called when an instance is created that passes a single string argument.

```
' ----- Uses the default constructor.
Dim byDefault As Person = New Person

' ----- Uses the custom constructor.
Dim byCustom As Person = New Person("John Q. Public")
```

The arguments included in the instance declaration must match one of the constructor signatures as declared in the class.

If a class lacks any constructors, a default constructor is added automatically that does nothing beyond instantiating an object. If you want to force the class to be created with a custom constructor only, add at least one custom constructor to the class.

## Property Members

Consider the following simple class.

```
Public Class AnotherPerson
    Public Name As String
    Public Age As Short
End Class
```

This class includes some of the functionality of the Person class defined earlier. However, the Age property has some problems. Because it is a simple public field, any instance of the class can have its Age field set to any Short value, whether 25, 87, 3349, or -23. Some of these ages are certainly invalid. How do you keep the user from setting the Age field to an invalid value?

While you could add specialized function members to set and retrieve the age, .NET includes *properties* that provide a more elegant solution. Within the class, properties look just like specialized functions; to the user of a class, they look like fields. (When a Visual Basic application is compiled, properties actually become method members.) The Person class defined earlier includes a more protected Age property.

```
Private currentAge As Short
```

...and later...

```
Public Property Age( ) As Short
    Get
        Return currentAge
    End Get
    Set(ByVal value As Short)
        If (value < 0) Or (value > MaxAge) Then
            Throw New System.ArgumentException( _
                "Age ranges from 0 to " & MAX_AGE & ".", "Age")
        Else
            currentAge = value
        End If
    End Set
End Property
```

The property procedure includes two distinct *property accessors*, one for setting the hidden tandem value (the Set procedure) and one for retrieving the current value (the Get procedure). You can create a read-only property by supplying only the Get component and adding the ReadOnly keyword to the property definition.

```
Public ReadOnly Property Age( ) As Short
    Get
        Return currentAge
    End Get
End Property
```

The WriteOnly keyword allows you to similarly define a property with only a Set component.

*New in 2005.* The 2005 release of Visual Basic allows you to specify different access levels (such as Public and Friend) to the Get and Set accessors.

## Type Members

Classes may include nested classes as needed.

```
Public Class Level1Class
    Private Class Level2Class
        ' ----- Add level 2 class code here.
    End Class

    ' ----- Add other level 1 class code here.
End Class
```

If the nested class is private, it will only be accessible within the outer class.

## Instance Members Versus Shared Members

Members of a class can either be *instance members* or *shared members*. Instance members are only useful in a specific instance of the class, that is, from an object. Until an instance of the object exists, these members cannot be used or referenced in any way. Instance members belong to specific instances of the class instead of to the class as a whole. The members added to the sample Person class above are all instance members.

```
Public Class SimpleClass
    ' ----- This is an instance member.
    Public Comment As String
End Class
...
' ----- In some other code.
Dim myInstnace = New SimpleClass
myInstance.Comment = "I am not shared!"
```

Shared members (sometimes called *static members*) can be accessed without the presence of any particular instance of the class. They belong to the whole class, but they are also "shared" among all instances of the class. Shared members are accessed by qualifying the name of the member with the name of the class.

```
Public Class SimpleClass
    ' ----- This is an instance member.
    Public Shared Comment As String
End Class
...
' ----- In some other code.
SimpleClass.Comment = "I am shared!"
```

All members of a Module are automatically shared, even though the Shared keyword is not used on each member of the module.

Consider a class that keeps track of how many instances of itself have been created.

```
Public Class Tracker
    ' ----- Shared variables can be private.
    Private Shared totalInstances As Integer

    Public Sub New()
        ' ----- Each constructor call increments the total.
        totalInstances += 1
    End Sub

    Public Shared Function GetInstanceCount() As Integer
        ' ----- Provide read-only access to the count.
        Return totalInstances
    End Function

    Protected Overrides Sub Finalize()
        ' ----- Decrement the count in the destructor.
        totalInstances -= 1
        MyBase.Finalize
    End Sub
End Class
```

Code such as the following accesses the shared member:

```
Dim firstUse As New Tracker
MsgBox(Tracker.GetInstanceCount())    ' --> Displays "1"

Dim secondUse As New Tracker
MsgBox(Tracker.GetInstanceCount())    ' --> Displays "2"
```

This sample code does have a few issues. Although the *Finalize* destructor (called when an instance is destroyed, and described more fully later in this chapter) will eventually be called, there is no guarantee that it will be called in a timely manner. Even if a Tracker object goes out of scope or is specifically destroyed by setting the object variable to Nothing, the *Finalize* method may not be called for quite some time, and the instance count may appear to be inaccurate.

Another problem appears because Visual Basic is a multithreaded programming language. If separate threads of your application each create an instance of Tracker at the same time, their respective calls to the New constructor may overlap and produce invalid results. The .NET Framework includes classes that guard against such overlapping code. *Mutexes*, *semaphores*, and *monitors* can be used to manage conflicts between threads in your application. Visual Basic includes a SyncLock statement that also supports some conflict resolution between threads. This statement is described in the *SyncLock Statement* entry in Chapter 12.

## Finalize, Dispose, and Garbage Collection

An instance of an object can be specifically destroyed by setting the variable that refers to the instance to Nothing.

```
Dim usefulObject As New SimpleClass
...
usefulObject = Nothing
```

An object is also automatically destroyed when all variable references to that object go out of scope or otherwise cease to exist. When an object is destroyed using any of these methods, the *garbage collection* process begins.

The .NET Framework includes a garbage collection system that exists to accurately reclaim memory used by objects within .NET applications. When the garbage collector determines that an object is no longer needed, it automatically runs a special *destructor method* of the class called *Finalize*. However, there is no way to determine exactly when the garbage collector will call the *Finalize* method. It will be called at some time in the future, but it may not happen immediately. The .NET Framework uses a system called *reference-tracing garbage collection*, which periodically releases unused resources according to its schedule, not your program's schedule.

*Finalize* is a Protected method. It can be called from a class and its derived classes, but not from outside the class. (Since the *Finalize* destructor is automatically called by the garbage collector, a class should never call its own *Finalize* method directly.) If a class has a *Finalize* method, that method should in turn explicitly call its base class's Finalize method as well. The general syntax and format of the *Finalize* method is:

```
Protected Overrides Sub Finalize( )
    ' ----- Cleanup code goes here, and then...
    MyBase.Finalize( )
End Sub
```

(The MyBase and Overrides keywords are discussed later in this chapter.) Garbage collection is automatic, and it ensures that unused resources are always released without any specific interaction on the part of the programmer. In most cases, the programmer has no control over the garbage collection schedule; a garbage collection event may occur many minutes after you release an object. This may cause some resources to remain in use longer than necessary.

Since some classes may acquire resources that must be released immediately upon completed use of an object instance, .NET supports a "second destructor" called *Dispose*. Its general syntax and usage is:

```
Class className
    Implements IDisposable

    Public Sub Dispose( ) Implements IDisposable.Dispose
        ' ----- Immediate cleanup code goes here.
    End Sub

    ' ----- Other class code.
End Class
```

(The Implements keyword is discussed later in this chapter.) The *Dispose* method is *not* called automatically by the .NET Framework. Any code that uses a class with a *Dispose* method must specifically call that method to initiate the first-level cleanup code. Still, a programmer may forget to call the *Dispose* method, and resources may be retained until they are fully cleaned up through the *Finalize* method.

## Structures and Modules Versus Classes

In addition to classes, Visual Basic also supports "structures" and "modules." (These are somewhat analogous to the VB 6 "Type" and "code module" features.) These two types are really just classes with syntax rules and default behaviors that differ somewhat from standard classes.

*Structures* implement instances of a value type and always derive from *System. ValueType*. They can never derive from any other base class, nor can a structure be used to derive other structures or classes. The members of a structure cannot specify Protected as an access modifier. Since they are value types, structures are destroyed immediately on disuse; they do not support the *Finalize* destructor. However, they are lightweight and simple to use for basic data constructs. Structures, when they are not too large, experience some performance increase over equivalent classes.

```
Public Structure SimpleStructure
    Public Comment As String
    Public TotalCost As Decimal

    Public Overrides Function ToString( ) As String
        Return Comment & ", " & Format(TotalCost, "$#,##0.00")
```

```
      End Function
   End Structure
```

*Modules* are similar to classes that have the `Public` and `Shared` keyword added to every member by default (although members can be made `Private` as well). Since all members of a module are shared, there is no need to create an instance of the module to access the members. In fact, modules cannot be instantiated. They cannot be used to derive other modules or classes, either. Modules can contain nested classes and structures, but modules themselves cannot be nested in any other type. Modules are commonly used for common procedures and global variables that need to be accessed throughout your application.

```
   Friend Module GenericCode
      Public Function CToF(celsius As Decimal) As Decimal
         ' ----- Convert Celsius to Fahrenheit.
         Return (celsius * 1.8@) + 32@
      End Function
   End Module
```

## Interfaces

Visual Basic implements the object-oriented concept of *interfaces* through the `Interface` keyword. Interfaces define the members of a class but not the implementation. They look a lot like classes, but without the member bodies or `End` constructs (such as `End Sub`). An interface equivalent to the `Person` class defined earlier in this chapter might look like the following:

```
   Interface IPerson
      Event Testing( )
      Sub Test( )
      Property Age( ) As Short
      Property Name( ) As String
   End Interface
```

(By convention, interfaces always begin with the uppercase letter "I.") Interfaces define the public properties, methods, and events of an abstract class. Since interfaces do not support variables, constants, or constructors, some elements of the `Person` class are missing from this interface definition. Also, since all members of an interface are public by definition, the `Public` keyword is not needed on each member.

Classes implement one or more interfaces through the `Implements` keyword. This keyword is used in two contexts within the class: (1) at the beginning of the class to declare which interface(s) will be used in the class, and (2) attached to each member that implements a specific member of an interface. Consider the following code.

```
   Interface IDog
      Sub Bark( )
      Sub ScratchFleas( )
   End Interface

   Interface ICat
      Sub Meow( )
```

```
Sub DestroyFurniture( )
End Interface

Class MixedUpAnimal
    Implements IDog
    Implements ICat

    Public Sub ScratchFleas( ) Implements IDog.ScratchFleas
        ' ----- Add code here.
    End Sub

    Public Sub MakeNoise( ) Implements IDog.Bark, ICat.Meow
        ' ----- Add code here.
    End Sub

    Public Sub Redecorate( ) Implements ICat.DestroyFurniture
        ' ----- Add code here.
    End Sub

    Public Sub ShowOff( )
        ' ----- Add code here.
    End Sub
End Class
```

This code displays various aspects of interface usage.

- A class declares its intention to use an interface immediately, through distinct Implements statements—one for each interface to be used.

- A class may implement multiple interfaces at once.

- When a class implements an interface, it *must* implement all members of the interface, not just some.

- Specific members of an interface are implemented through standard class members, each decorated with a separate Implements keyword followed by the name of the interface and member, as in Implements IDog.ScratchFleas. The implementation's signature must match the interface member's signature.

- A single class member may implement multiple interface members, as long as those members share the same signature with the class member. Each interface member is added to the Implements keyword, separated by commas, as in Implements IDog.Bark, ICat.Meow.

- The class member implementing an instance member may use the same name as the interface member, but it does not have to. The association between a class member and an interface member occurs through the Implements keyword, not through the class member name.

- A class may implement its own members, fully unrelated to any interface members implemented in the class, as is done with the ShowOff procedure in the sample.

While the MixedUpAnimal class implements two distinct interfaces, the term *interface* also describes the complete set of all public members exposed by this class. This dual use of "interface" is generally not a problem, since when discussing the implementation of a specific interface, the name of that interface is usually included in the discussion.

# Inheritance

Visual Basic implements OOP inheritance through the Inherits keyword. When a class inherits from a base class, it takes on all public and protected members of that base class; in a way, the derived class *is* a real implementation of the base class.

As an example of inheritance, consider a simple Employee class.

```
Public Class Employee
    Public FullName As String
    Private currentSalary As Decimal

    Public Property Salary() As Decimal
        ' ----- Salary can be set directly.
    Get
        Return currentSalary
    End Get
    Set(value As Decimal)
        currentSalary = value
    End Set
    End Property

    Public Overridable Sub IncSalary(ByVal raisePercent As Decimal)
        ' ----- Raises given based on a supplied percentage.
        '       The percent should appear as a decimal percentage,
        '       as in 0.03 for a 3% raise.
        currentSalary *= 1@ + raisePercent
    End Sub
End Class
```

This class can be used immediately to manage employee names and salaries. But there may be special salary-related circumstances that apply to specific categories of employees. In this example, all salary increases given to executives include an additional 5 percent increase for a car allowance; secretaries receive an additional 2 percent for an overtime allowance. While distinct classes could be used, inheritance allows all of the classes to still be instances of the Employee class, despite their derived differences.

The IncSalary member in the Employee class includes the Overridable keyword. This keyword allows a derived class to modify the implementation of the base class' member. Here are the definitions for the derived Executive and Secretary classes, each of which overrides the base IncSalary member.

```
Public Class Executive
    Inherits Employee

    Public Overrides Sub IncSalary(ByVal raisePercent As Decimal)
        ' ----- Extra 5% for car allowance.
        Me.Salary *= 1.05@ + raisePercent
    End Sub
End Class

Public Class Secretary
    Inherits Employee
```

```
Public Overrides Sub IncSalary(ByVal raisePercent As Decimal)
    ' ----- Extra 2% for overtime allowance.
    Me.Salary *= 1.02@ + raisePercent
End Sub
End Class
```

The Me keyword will be discussed in more detail below, but in the code it means, "I'm trying to access members of the current class"—in this case, either the Executive or the Secretary class. Since the currentSalary member is private to the Employee class, it can't be accessed directly by the derived classes; all access is made through the public Salary property.

Both derived classes include the statement Inherits Employee, which sets up the inheritance relationship from Employee (the base class) to either Executive or Secretary (the derived classes).

Each derived instance of the IncSalary class includes the Overrides keyword, which states that this member is specifically overriding an overridable member of the base class. A derived class is not required to override an Overridable member, but it may.

Each of these classes can now be used in code, and Visual Basic will call the appropriate class member.

```
Dim worker As New Employee
Dim typist As New Secretary
Dim ceo As New Executive

' ----- Set the initial salaries.
worker.Salary = 30000
typist.Salary = 40000
ceo.Salary = 50000

' ----- Give everyone a 5% raise.
worker.IncSalary(0.05@)
typist.IncSalary(0.05@)
ceo.IncSalary(0.05@)

' ----- Display the new salaries.
MsgBox(worker.Salary)   ' --> Displays 31500, a 5% increase
MsgBox(typist.Salary)   ' --> Displays 42800, a 7% increase
MsgBox(ceo.Salary)      ' --> Displays 55000, a 10% increase
```

The derived classes each have access to all public members of the base class.

```
ceo.FullName = "Bill Fences"
```

Suppose that, in a more complete employee model, there is a derived class for every type of employee. If each of these derived classes implements its own version of IncSalary, then there is no need for any logic to exist in the IncSalary method of the base Employee class. The code could simply leave the Employee. IncSalary method empty. Visual Basic also allows you to define an *abstract member*, a member that has no implementation, only a definition (sort of a single-member interface). Each derived class *must* implement this member to be valid, so VB includes a MustOverride keyword for this purpose.

```
Public MustInherit Class Employee
    ' ---- Define other members, then...
    Public MustOverride Sub IncSalary(ByVal raisePercent As Decimal)
End Class
```

Members added with the MustOverride keyword do not include a body or an end
marker (End Sub, in this case). Visual Basic does not allow a class instance to exist
with any abstract members; this semiabstract Employee class can no longer be used
to create instances directly. The class can only be used to derive other classes. To
state this clearly, the class itself is decorated with the MustInherit keyword.

Any class that contains at least one abstract member is termed an *abstract class*.
There may be situations where all members of a class need to be abstract. Such a
class (called a *pure abstract* class) defines an interface, although it is not a true
Visual Basic Interface.

Consider a Shape class that is designed to model the general properties and actions
of geometric shapes (ellipses, rectangles, trapezoids, etc.). All shapes need a Draw
method, but the implementation varies, depending on the type of shape. Similarly, methods such as Rotate, Translate, and Reflect would each likely require
their own shape-specific logic. This Shape class can be implemented as a pure
abstract class, from which distinct Ellipse, Rectangle, and other shape-specific
classes derive.

```
Public MustInherit Class Shape
    Public MustOverride Sub Draw( )
    Public MustOverride Sub Rotate(ByVal degrees As Single)
    Public MustOverride Sub Translate(ByVal x As Single, _
        ByVal y As Single)
    Public MustOverride Sub Reflect(ByVal slope As Single, _
        ByVal intercept As Single)
End Class
```

Classes can also be defined so that they cannot be used to create new derived
classes. The NotInheritable keyword enables this restriction.

```
Public NotInheritable Class UseThisOne
    ...
End Class
```

Non-inheritable classes may not include any abstract members. Visual Basic also
includes a NotOverridable keyword that can be used to decorate individual
members in a base class.

Classes can be derived at any depth. Class A can be derived into Class B, and
Class B can further be derived into Class C.

Certain rules apply to the inheritance of classes:

- Private members are never inherited.
- Public members are inherited by all derived classes.
- Protected members are inherited by all derived classes, as are Protected
  Friend members.
- Friend members are inherited by all derived classes in the same project as the
  base class, but not by derived classes in another assembly or application.

# MyBase, MyClass, and Me

When working with derived classes, there are times when references to a member may be somewhat ambiguous; a member name may exist in both the derived class and the base class. Visual Basic provides special keywords to help alleviate this ambiguity.

The `MyBase` keyword provides a reference to the base class from within a derived class. If you want to call a member of the base class from within a derived class, you can use the syntax:

```
MyBase.MemberName
```

This will resolve any ambiguity if the derived class also has a member of the same name. The `MyBase` keyword can also be used to create an instance of the base class through its constructor:

```
MyBase.New(...)
```

The `MyBase` keyword cannot be used to access `Private` members of the base class, as they are inaccessible from derived classes.

If a class is derived from a chain of base and derived classes, `MyBase` looks first to the closet "parent" class in the chain for a matching member (including a matching signature). If a match is not found, VB continues up the chain until the *root class*, which is always *System.Object*.

The keywords `Me` and `MyClass` both provide a reference to the local class (the class in which the current code resides), but they exhibit slight differences. Consider a class named `BaseClass` and another derived from it, named `DerivedClass`.

```
Public Class BaseClass
    Public Overridable Function WhereAmI( ) As String
        Return "Base"
    End Function

    Public Sub ShowLocation( )
        MsgBox(Me.WhereAmI( ))
        MsgBox(MyClass.WhereAmI( ))
    End Sub
End Class

Public Class DerivedClass
    Inherits BaseClass
    Public Overrides Function WhereAmI( ) As String
        Return "Derived"
    End Function
End Class
```

Now consider the following code that uses these classes:

```
Dim firstTry As New BaseClass
Dim secondTry As New DerivedClass
Dim useAsBase As BaseClass

useAsBase = firstTry
useAsBase.ShowLocation( )   ' --> Shows "Base", "Base"
```

```
useAsBase = secondTry
useAsBase.ShowLocation( )  ' --> Shows "Derived", "Base"
```

The first call to ShowLocation is made using a variable of type BaseClass that refers to an object of type BaseClass. In this case, both of the calls:

```
Me.WhereAmI( )
MyClass.WhereAmI( )
```

return the same value, because they both call WhereAmI in BaseClass.

However, in the second case, the variable of type BaseClass holds a reference to an object of DerivedClass. In this case, Me refers to an object of type DerivedClass (the secondTry reference), whereas MyClass still refers to the base class BaseClass (the useAsBase reference). When using the Me keyword, the actual object as originally instantiated is used; when using MyClass, the class of the variable that is used to make the method call becomes the controlling class.

## Shadowing and Overloading Members

Visual Basic provides a few additional features that let you provide even more control over which members are used in your base and derived classes.

### Shadowing

*Shadowing* is similar to overriding, but with some very important differences. Consider two classes, BaseClass and DerivedClass:

```
Public Class BaseClass
    Public simpleField As Integer = 1

    Public Overridable Sub TestOverride( )
        MsgBox("BaseClass:TestOverride")
    End Sub

    Public Sub TestShadow( )
        MsgBox("BaseClass:TestShadow")
    End Sub
End Class

Public Class DerivedClass
    Inherits BaseClass

    Public Shadows simpleField As Integer = 2

    Public Overrides Sub TestOverride( )
        MsgBox("DerivedClass:TestOverride")
    End Sub

    Public Shadows Sub TestShadow( )
        MsgBox("DerivedClass:TestShadow")
    End Sub
End Class
```

BaseClass has two methods, TestOverride (with the Overridable keyword) and TestShadow. DerivedClass also defines methods with the same names; in this case, TestOverride includes the Overrides keyword, and TestShadow uses the Shadows keyword. Both fields also have a related public Integer field.

The following code tests the derived class:

```
Dim inUse As DerivedClass = New DerivedClass
inUse.TestOverride( )
inUse.TestShadow( )
MsgBox("Field = " & inUse.simpleField)
```

Because the object reference inUse is to an object of DerivedClass, the calls to the TestOverride and TestShadow methods, as well as to the public variable simpleField, all refer to code in DerivedClass; the output messages are as expected:

```
DerivedClass:TestOverride
DerivedClass:TestShadow
Field = 2
```

The test of the classes working together, though, is a little more interesting:

```
Dim inUse As BaseClass = New DerivedClass
inUse.TestOverride( )
inUse.TestShadow( )
MsgBox("Field = " & inUse.simpleField)
```

In this case, a variable of type BaseClass refers to an object of type DerivedClass. The output this time is:

```
DerivedClass:TestOverride
BaseClass:TestShadow
Field = 1
```

When interacting with base and shadowed members, the type of variable used to reference the members is the deciding factor. In the sample, even though the actual object was of type DerivedClass, the fact that the variable was of type BaseClass caused VB to use the BaseClass version of shadowed features.

Class fields, such as simpleField, can only be shadowed; they cannot be overridden.

One other difference between shadowing and overriding is that a shadow element need not be the same type of element as its base class partner. For instance, the following code is valid.

```
Public Class BaseClass
    Public TheShadowKnows As Integer
End Class

Public Class DerivedClass
    Inherits BaseClass

    Public Shadows Sub TheShadowKnows( )
        MsgBox("This code lacks clarity!")
    End Sub
End Class
```

Shadowing only considers the name of the member, not its type or signature. While allowing members of different types to shadow each other seems like a hazardous practice, it actually has its use. In Visual Basic, your code can include a global variable and a local variable of the same name, but of different data types. This ability is possible because the local variable is shadowing its global namesake. In such a case, references to the variable name in the local procedure always refer to the local variable, not the global variable of the same name. This process is known as *shadowing by scope*.

## Overloading

*Overloading* refers to an item being used in more than one way. Generally, overloading occurs when a class includes multiple methods with the same name but with different signatures. For instance, the *Abs* function in the *System.Math* class includes several versions, but each uses different source and return data types.

```
Overloads Public Shared Function Abs(Decimal) As Decimal
Overloads Public Shared Function Abs(Double) As Double
Overloads Public Shared Function Abs(Int16) As Int16
Overloads Public Shared Function Abs(Int32) As Int32
Overloads Public Shared Function Abs(Int64) As Int64
Overloads Public Shared Function Abs(SByte) As SByte
Overloads Public Shared Function Abs(Single) As Single
```

Each entry includes the Overloads keyword, which tells VB that this function is overloaded. You can create your own overloaded methods. Consider a function that retrieves a current account balance. The account could be identified either by the customer's account number or driver's license number. The method that retrieves the balance might be defined with two different signatures.

```
Overloads Function GetBalance(accountNumber As Long) As Decimal
Overloads Function GetBalance(licenseNumber As String) As Decimal
```

When calling GetBalance, VB decides which version to use based on whether the method is passed a string or a long integer value.

*New in 2005.* The 2005 release of Visual Basic introduced operator overloading to the language. This feature allows a class to define functionality for the standard VB operators, such as the addition operator (+). Operator overloading is discussed in full in Chapter 5.

# 4

# Variables and Data Types

Data manipulation is the heart of any software application. You could choose to process the data the way that your computer's CPU does: bit by bit. But that quickly becomes tedious, so languages like Visual Basic include a variety of *data types*, implementations of data management tools each based on a subset of possible data values. This chapter discusses data types, the data managed by those types, and how they are processed in Visual Basic and .NET.

The term "data types" differs from the more general term "types" used throughout this and other .NET documentation. .NET is built on the concept of the *type*, the basic data construct of .NET, which includes classes, structures, delegates, and other high-level elements used to build applications and pass data around programs. The data types available in .NET are built from these more generalized types, as are your own custom classes. Data types provide a small but essential set of data manipulation tools, grouped by the subset of possible data values managed by each data type.

## Data Types

The .NET *Common Language Runtime* (CLR) includes the *Common Type System* (CTS), which defines the data types that are supported by the CLR. Each .NET-enabled language implements a subset of the CLR data types, although some languages implement all of them (Visual Basic does, starting in 2005).

In .NET, data types are special classes and structures whose instances manipulate a data value that must fall within the limited range of the data type. For instance, the Byte data type can support and manage any 8-bit unsigned integer value, from 0 to 255. It allows no other data values outside of this defined subset, but it handles this subset extremely well. .NET provides data types for those subsets of data that programmers have found essential in software development. These data types make it possible to manipulate virtually any variation of data. For those instances where a predefined .NET data type will not meet your needs, you can use the predefined data types as building blocks to develop your own custom data management class.

The .NET Framework implements nearly 20 of these essential core data types, most designed to manipulate integer or floating point numbers. The native VB data types are wrappers for the core data types. For instance, the VB Integer data type is a wrapper for the *System.Int32* structure. One of the members of the *Int32* structure is *MaxValue*, which returns the maximum numeric value allowed for this data type. Thus, even though *MaxValue* is not officially part of VB, the Integer data type's full dependence on the *Int32* data type allows the following usage:

```
Dim usesInt32 As Integer
MsgBox(usesInt32.MaxValue)    ' Displays 2147483647
```

Before the 2005 release of .NET, only some of the core .NET data types were implemented in Visual Basic. Yet even without specific VB wrappers, the earlier releases of VB.NET still provided access to the unwrapped data types. Since the core data types are simply classes and structures, they can be instantiated just like any other class or structure.

## Value and Reference Types

Data types in Visual Basic fall into two broad categories: (1) *value types* and (2) *reference types*. Value types and reference types differ primarily in how they are stored in memory. The memory allocated to a value type variable contains the actual value. In a statement such as:

```
Dim simpleValue As Integer = 5
```

a memory location is set aside to hold the value of 5. In contrast, the memory storage allocated to a reference type variable stores another memory address location where the real data can be found. It's like a forwarding address at the post office. In a reference type declaration such as:

```
Dim somewhereElse As New MyCustomClass
```

the VB compiler creates an instance of the MyCustomClass class in memory and then sets the value of somewhereElse to the true memory address of that instance. If you are familiar with pointers in languages such as C++, this is Visual Basic's closest equivalent.

In short, value type variables *contain* the data, and reference type variables *point to* the data.

The distinction between value types and reference types has several consequences, one of which is in the way assignments work. Consider the following class, which has a single field:

```
Public Class SimpleClass
    Public Age As Short
End Class
```

and an equivalent structure:

```
Structure SimpleStruct
    Public Age As Short
End Structure
```

Classes are reference types, but structures are value types. The following code illustrates the difference in usage between the two similar yet different types.

```
' ----- Declare two of each type.
Dim refType1 As SimpleClass
Dim refType2 As SimpleClass
Dim valType1 As SimpleStruct
Dim valType2 As SimpleStruct


' ----- First, a demonstration of reference types. Setting
'       refType2 = refType1 causes refType2 to *reference*
'       the same memory location. Further changes made to
'       members of refType1 will impact refType2, and vice
'       versa. They share the same object instance.
refType1 = New SimpleClass
refType1.Age = 20
refType2 = refType1
refType2.Age = 30
Debug.WriteLine(refType1.Age)  ' --> Shows 30
Debug.WriteLine(refType2.Age)  ' --> Shows 30

' ----- Now for value types. Setting valType2 = valType1
'       makes a *copy* of the members of valType1. Any
'       further changes to the members of one variable
'       will have *no* impact on the other.
valType1 = New SimpleStruct
valType1.Age = 20
valType2 = valType1
valType2.Age = 30
Debug.Writeline(valType1.Age)  ' --> Shows 20
Debug.Writeline(valType2.Age)  ' --> Shows 30
```

In a way, both assignments of one variable to the other did the same thing: they copied the value of the right-hand variable to the left-hand. But since the reference type, refType1, had a value of a memory address, that memory address was copied into refType2. Since both variables pointed to the same location in memory where the members were stored, both shared a common set of members.

The assignment of the value type valType1 to valType2 also copied the value of the right-hand variable to the left hand. But the value of valType1 contained its actual members. A distinct copy of those members (only the Age member, in this case) was made for the separate use of valType2.

To clear a reference type, set it to Nothing. Value types always have a value, even if it is zero; they cannot be set to Nothing.

All of the core Visual Basic data types that manage numeric values (such as Integer and Double) are value types. The String data type is a reference type, but it acts like a value type. When you assign a string from one variable to another, you do not get a reference to the first string, as you would expect. That's because the implementation of the String data type always creates a completely new instance of the original string each time an assignment or change is made.

# Visual Basic Data Types: A Reference

Visual Basic implements all of the core .NET data types as of the 2005 edition of the language. These basic data types provide a broad range of features for managing all categories of data. The data types can be arranged into five groups by the type of data managed.

*Boolean Data*
> This single data type provides a single bit of data, either True or False.

*Character Data*
> Visual Basic includes data types that manage either single characters or long strings of characters.

*Date and Time Data*
> A single data type manages both date and time values.

*Floating Point Data*
> The various floating point data types each manage a subset of rational numbers. Some of these data types provide more mathematical accuracy than others.

*Integer Data*
> The integer data types, and there are many, store integer values between a data type-defined minimum and maximum value. Some of these data types support negative numbers.

The remainder of this section includes definitions and commentary on each core data type supplied with the Visual Basic language.

## Boolean data type

*Quick Facts*
> Core .NET Type: *System.Boolean*
>
> Implementation: Value Type (Structure)
>
> Storage Size: 2 bytes
>
> Value Range: True or False

The Boolean data type supports only two possible values: True or False. The VB keywords True and False are used to assign these values to a Boolean variable. You can also assign the result of any logical operation to a Boolean variable.

When a numeric value is converted to Boolean, any nonzero value is converted to True, and zero is converted to False. In the other direction, False is converted to zero, and True is converted to -1. (This differs from other .NET languages, which convert True to 1. Visual Basic uses -1 for reasons of backward compatibility. When sharing Boolean data between components built in different .NET languages, the .NET Framework automatically makes the correct adjustments according to the language in use.)

## Byte data type

*Quick Facts*

Core .NET Type: *System.Byte*

Implementation: Value Type (Structure)

Storage Size: 1 byte

Value Range: 0 to 255 (unsigned)

The Byte data type is the smallest unsigned integer data type supported by Visual Basic. While its range is small, it is especially useful when working with raw binary data.

## Char data type

*Quick Facts*

Core .NET Type: *System.Char*

Implementation: Value Type (Structure)

Storage Size: 2 bytes

Value Range: A character code from 0 to 65,535 (unsigned)

The Char data type stores a single 16-bit Unicode character. All characters in .NET are 16 bits in length, which is sufficient to support double-byte character set (DBCS) languages, such as Japanese. There was no equivalent to the Char data type in pre-.NET versions of Visual Basic.

When using a literal Char value, append the single letter "c" to the value.

```
Dim singleLetter As Char = "A"c
```

A String variable containing a single character is *not* the same as a Char variable holding that same single character. They are distinct data types, and an explicit conversion is required to move data between the two types (when Option Strict is enabled).

## Date data type

*Quick Facts*

Core .NET Type: *System.DateTime*

Implementation: Value Type (Structure)

Storage Size: 8 bytes

Value Range: January 1, 1 AD to December 31, 9999 AD (Gregorian)

Date values are stored as IEEE 64-bit long integers that can represent dates in the range January 1, 1 to December 31, 9999, and times from 0:00:00 to 23:59:59. The actual value is stored internally as the number of "ticks" since midnight on January 1, 1 AD. Each tick represents 100 nanoseconds.

Literal dates must be enclosed in number signs (#).

```
Dim independenceDay As Date = #7/4/1776#
```

## Decimal data type

*Quick Facts*

Core .NET Type: *System.Decimal*

Implementation: Value Type (Structure)

Storage Size: 12 bytes

Value Range: +/-79,228,162,514,264,337,593,543,950,335 with no decimal portion; +/-7.9228162514264337593543950335 with 28 decimal places; the smallest nonzero number is +/-0.0000000000000000000000000001

Values of the Decimal data type are stored as 96-bit signed integers, along with an internal scale factor ranging from 0 to 28, which is applied automatically. This provides a high level of mathematical accuracy for numbers in the valid range, especially currency values.

Literal instances of Decimal data append the letter "D" or the character "@" to the end of the numeric value.

```
Dim startingValue As Decimal = 123.45D
Dim endingValue As Decimal = 543.21@
```

You can also use the "@" character to indicate that a declared variable is of type Decimal.

```
Dim startingValue@ = 123.45D
```

The MaxValue and MinValue members of the Decimal data type provide the range limits.

In pre-.NET implementations of Visual Basic, the Decimal data type was not a true data type; it existed as a subtype to the Variant data type. The .NET version of the Decimal data type is a true data type implementation.

## Double data type

*Quick Facts*

Core .NET Type: *System.Double*

Implementation: Value Type (Structure)

Storage Size: 8 bytes

Value Range: -1.79769313486231E+308 to -4.94065645841247E-324 for negative values; 4.94065645841247E-324 to 1.79769313486232E+308 for positive values

Values of type Double are IEEE 64-bit (8-byte) double-precision signed floating point numbers. They include a large range but also experience some accuracy loss in certain calculations.

Literal instances of Double data append the letter "R" or the character "#" to the end of the numeric value.

```
Dim startingValue As Double = 123.45R
Dim endingValue As Double = 543.21#
```

You can also use the "#" character to indicate that a declared variable is of type Double.

```
Dim startingValue# = 123.45R
```

## Integer data type

*Quick Facts*

Core .NET Type: *System.Int32*

Implementation: Value Type (Structure)

Storage Size: 4 bytes

Value Range: -2,147,483,648 to 2,147,483,647

The Integer data type is a 32-bit signed integer data type. This is the native word size in 32-bit processors, so its use can provide some performance enhancements over other integral data types on those processors.

In pre-.NET versions of Visual Basic, the Integer data type was only 16 bits in size and had a smaller range. The .NET version of Visual Basic includes Short as its 16-bit signed data type.

Literal instances of Integer data optionally append the letter "I" or the character "%" to the end of the numeric value.

```
Dim startingValue As Integer = 123I
Dim endingValue As Integer = 543%
```

You can also use the "%" character to indicate that a declared variable is of type Integer.

```
Dim startingValue% = 123I
```

## Long data type

*Quick Facts*

Core .NET Type: *System.Int64*

Implementation: Value Type (Structure)

Storage Size: 8 bytes

Value Range: -9,223,372,036,854,775,808 to 9,223,372,036,854,775,807

The Long data type is a 64-bit signed integer data type. In pre-.NET versions of Visual Basic, the Long data type was only 32 bits in size and had a smaller range. The .NET version of Visual Basic uses Integer as its 32-bit signed data type.

Literal instances of Long data append the letter "L" or the character "&" to the end of the numeric value.

```
Dim startingValue As Long = 123L
Dim endingValue As Long = 543&
```

You can also use the "&" character to indicate that a declared variable is of type Long.

```
Dim startingValue& = 123L
```

When using the "&" character to identify a Long literal, do not leave a space between the number and the "&" character, as the "&" character alone acts as the string concatenation operator.

## Object data type

*Quick Facts*

Core .NET Type: *System.Object*

Implementation: Reference Type (Class)

Storage Size: 4 bytes

Value Range: Any type can be stored in an Object variable

The Object data type is the universal data type; an Object variable can refer to (point to) data of any other data type. For instance, an Object can refer to Long values, String values, or any other class instance.

```
Dim amazingVariable As Object
amazingVariable = 123L
amazingVariable = "Isn't it great?"
amazingVariable = New MyCustomClass
```

There is a performance penalty when using Object variables. Visual Basic cannot associate the true data's members with the Object variable at compile time; this linking has to be done at runtime, which increases the amount of code required to process object-related methods. This is referred to as *late binding*. Declaring objects as their true type results in *early binding*, where all member links are managed by the compiler. Code such as:

```
Dim lateBound As Object
. . .
lateBound = New MyCustomClass
lateBound.SomeMethod( )
```

requires the application to match up the lateBound variable with MyCustomClass's SomeMethod member at runtime. This is much less efficient than:

```
Dim earlyBound As MyCustomClass
. . .
earlyBound = New MyCustomClass
earlyBound.SomeMethod( )
```

In pre-.NET versions of Visual Basic, the VarType function identified the specific subtype of a Variant value. The VarType function still exists in .NET-enabled Visual Basic; it identifies the true type of the variable or value. The *System.Object* class (and by derivation, all classes in .NET) also includes a *GetType* method that returns information about the true type of the object. Although these tools work with any data type, they are especially useful with objects of type Object.

## SByte data type

*Quick Facts*

Core .NET Type: *System.SByte*

Implementation: Value Type (Structure)

Storage Size: 1 byte

Value Range: -128 to 127

*New in 2005.* The SByte data type is the smallest signed integer data type supported by Visual Basic. It acts as the signed counterpart to the unsigned Byte data type.

The SByte data type is one of four Visual Basic data types, added in the 2005 release of the language, that are not compliant with the minimal Common Language Specification. Components and applications using that standard may not be compatible with applications that use the SByte data type.

## Short data type

*Quick Facts*

Core .NET Type: *System.Int16*

Implementation: Value Type (Structure)

Storage Size: 2 bytes

Value Range: -32,768 to 32,767

The Short data type is a 16-bit signed integer data type. In pre-.NET versions of Visual Basic, the Integer data type was a 16-bit signed data type; the Short data type did not exist in Visual Basic before .NET.

Literal instances of Short data append the letter "S" to the end of the numeric value.

```
Dim startingValue As Short = 123S
```

## Single data type

*Quick Facts*

Core .NET Type: *System.Single*

Implementation: Value Type (Structure)

Storage Size: 4 bytes

Value Range: -3.402823E+38 to -1.401298E-45 for negative values, and 1.401298E-45 to 3.402823E+38 for positive values

Values of type Single are IEEE 32-bit (4-byte) single-precision signed floating point numbers. They include a moderate range but also experience some accuracy loss in certain calculations.

Literal instances of Single data append the letter "F" or the character "!" to the end of the numeric value.

```
Dim startingValue As Single = 123.45F
Dim endingValue As Single = 543.21!
```

You can also use the "!" character to indicate that a declared variable is of type Single.

```
Dim startingValue! = 123.45F
```

## String data type

*Quick Facts*

Core .NET Type: *System.String*

Implementation: Reference Type (Class)

Storage Size: 10 + (2 * *string_length*) bytes

Value Range: 0 to approximately 2 billion Unicode characters

The String data type holds variable-length Unicode character strings of up to approximately 2 billion characters in length.

All strings in .NET are immutable. Once a value is assigned to a string, it cannot be changed. When you modify the contents of a string, the String data type returns a new instance of a string with the modifications.

A String variable containing a single character is *not* the same as a Char variable holding that same single character. They are distinct data types, and an explicit conversion is required to move data between the two types (when Option Strict is enabled).

## UInteger data type

*Quick Facts*

Core .NET Type: *System.UInt32*

Implementation: Value Type (Structure)

Storage Size: 4 bytes

Value Range: 0 to 4,294,967,295 (unsigned)

*New in 2005.* The UInteger data type is a 32-bit unsigned integer data type. It acts as the unsigned counterpart to the signed Integer data type.

The UInteger data type is one of four Visual Basic data types, added in the 2005 release of the language, that are not compliant with the minimal Common Language Specification. Components and applications using that standard may not be compatible with applications that use the UInteger data type.

## ULong data type

*Quick Facts*

Core .NET Type: *System.UInt64*

Implementation: Value Type (Structure)

Storage Size: 8 bytes

Value Range: 0 to 18,446,744,073,709,551,615 (unsigned)

*New in 2005.* The ULong data type is a 64-bit unsigned integer data type. It acts as the unsigned counterpart to the signed Long data type.

The ULong data type is one of four Visual Basic data types, added in the 2005 release of the language, that are not compliant with the minimal Common

Language Specification. Components and applications using that standard may not be compatible with applications that use the ULong data type.

### UShort data type

*Quick Facts*

Core .NET Type: *System.UInt16*

Implementation: Value Type (Structure)

Storage Size: 2 bytes

Value Range: 0 to 65,535 (unsigned)

*New in 2005.* The UShort data type is a 16-bit unsigned integer data type. It acts as the unsigned counterpart to the signed Short data type.

The UShort data type is one of four Visual Basic data types, added in the 2005 release of the language, that are not compliant with the minimal Common Language Specification. Components and applications using that standard may not be compatible with applications that use the UShort data type.

# User-Defined Data Types

While individual variables can potentially meet all of your programming needs, it is often more productive to combine multiple basic data values into logical groups. These *user-defined data types* extend the basic data types with new types of your own choosing.

Pre-.NET versions of Visual Basic supported user-defined data type creation through the Type statement. These structured types were simply groupings of variables with no functionality beyond the ability to set and retrieve the value of each type member. Visual Basic under the .NET Framework greatly expands this feature by allowing code into each structure, as well as other basic .NET elements. Visual Basic 6 types are replaced by the .NET concept of a Structure.

Classes are the basic code and data containers in .NET. Structures are similar to classes, although they have certain limitations that don't apply to classes. One significant difference is that structures implement value types (inherited directly from *System.ValueType*), while classes implement reference types.

To declare a structure, use the Structure statement:

```
[Public|Private|Friend] Structure structureName
    member declarations
End Structure
```

The members of a structure can be fields, properties, methods, shared events, enumerations, or other nested structures. Each member must be declared with an access modifier: Public, Private, or Friend.

The simplest and most common use of structures is to encapsulate related variables, or fields. For instance, a simple structure can be used to define demographic information for a person:

```
Structure Person
    Public Name As String
```

```
      Public Address As String
      Public City As String
      Public State As String
      Public Zip As String
      Public Age As Short
   End Structure
```

A standard declaration defines a variable of type `Person`:

```
Dim onePerson As Person
```

Members of the structure are accessed using the standard "dot" syntax that applies also to classes:

```
onePerson.Name = "Beethoven"
```

More complex structures may include members and properties:

```
Public Structure NameAndState
   ' ----- Public and private fields.
   Public Name As String
   Private theState As String

   Public Function ShowAll( ) As String
      ' ----- A public method. Show all stored values.
      If (theState = "") And (Name = "") Then
         Return "<No Name> from <Nowhere>"
      ElseIf (theState = "") Then
         Return Name & " from <Nowhere>"
      ElseIf (Name = "") Then
         Return "<No Name> from " & theState
      Else
         Return Name & " from " & theState
      End If
   End Function

   Public Property State( ) As String
      ' ----- A public property. Limit state values.
      Get
         Return theState
      End Get
      Set(ByVal value As String)
         If (Len(value) = 2) Then
            theState = UCase(value)
         Else
            Throw New System.ArgumentException( _
               "State limited to 2 characters.", "State")
         End If
      End Set
   End Property
End Structure
```

Instances of the structure can now be created and used just like classes:

```
Dim onePerson As New NameAndState
onePerson.Name = "Donna"
onePerson.State = "CA"
MsgBox(onePerson.ShowAll( ))
```

Structures can be passed as arguments to functions or used as the return type of a function. Although structures are similar to classes, they do not support the following class features:

- Structures cannot explicitly inherit, nor can they be inherited.
- All constructors for a structure must be parameterized.
- Structures cannot define destructors; *Finalize* is never called.
- Member declarations cannot include initializers, nor can they use the As New syntax or specify an initial array size.

For a reference to the object-oriented terminology, see Chapter 3.

## Data Type Conversion

The process of converting a value of one data type to another is called *conversion* or *casting*. A conversion can be applied to a literal value, variable, or expression of a given type. Visual Basic includes several conversion functions that cast data between the basic data types.

```
Dim miniSize As Byte = 6
Dim superSize As Long
superSize = CLng(miniSize)   ' Convert Byte variable to Long
superSize = CLng("12")       ' Convert String literal to Long
```

Casts and conversions can be widening or narrowing. A *widening cast* is one in which the conversion is to a target data type that can accommodate all possible values in the source data type, such as casting from Short to Integer or from Integer to Double. Data is never lost in widening casts. A *narrowing cast* is one in which the target data type cannot accommodate all possible values of the source data type. In this case, data may be lost, and the cast may not succeed.

Visual Basic conversions are made in two ways: implicitly and explicitly. An *implicit conversion* is done by the compiler when circumstances warrant it (and it is legal). For instance, in the statements:

```
Dim smallerData As Integer = 3948
Dim largerData As Long
largerData = smallerData
```

the smallerData value is automatically converted to the larger Long data type used by the largerData variable. The type of implicit conversion that the compiler will do depends in part on the setting of the OptionStrict statement. This statement appears at the top of a source code file, before any class-specific code.

```
Option Strict {On | Off}
```

If Option Strict is On, only widening casts can be implicit; narrowing casts such as:

```
Dim smallerData As Integer
Dim largerData As Long = 3948
smallerData = largerData
```

generate a compile-time error due to the narrowing conversion, even though the sample data could easily fit in the destination variable. *Explicit conversion* is required.

```
smallerData = CInt(largerData)
```

Setting Option Strict to Off permits the implicit conversion, even though the conversion may fail.

In addition to the Option Strict statement, Visual Basic also includes an Option Explicit statement that appears at the start of a source code file.

```
Option Explicit {On | Off}
```

When Option Explicit is On, all variables must be declared (using Dim or a similar declaring keyword) before use. When Option Explicit is Off, VB will automatically add a declaration at compile time for any variable name it encounters that does not already have a declaration. (It won't add new Dim statements to your source code; it will add the declarations silently during the compile process.) Turning this option Off can lead to esoteric bugs that are hard to locate. See the "Option Explicit Statement" entry in Chapter 12 for additional information. The default values for both Option Strict and Option Explicit can be set in the project's properties.

Visual Basic includes conversion functions for the basic data types.

*CBool Function*
> Converts any valid string or numeric expression to Boolean. When a numeric value is converted to Boolean, any nonzero value is converted to True, and zero is converted to False.

*CByte Function*
> Converts any numeric expression in the range of a Byte to Byte, rounding any fractional part.

*CChar Function*
> Converts the first character of a string to the Char data type.

*CDate Function*
> Converts any valid representation of a date or time to Date.

*CDbl Function*
> Converts any numeric expression in the range of a Double to Double.

*CDec Function*
> Converts any numeric expression in the range of a Decimal to Decimal.

*CInt Function*
> Converts any numeric expression in the range of an Integer to Integer, rounding any fractional part.

*CLng Function*
> Converts any numeric expression in the range of a Long to Long, rounding any fractional part.

*CObj Function*
> Converts any expression to an Object. This is useful when you need to treat a value type as a reference type.

*CSByte Function*
> *New in 2005.* Converts any numeric expression in the range of an SByte to SByte, rounding any fractional part.

*CShort Function*

> Converts any numeric expression in the range of a Short to Short, rounding any fractional part.

*CSng Function*

> Converts any numeric expression in the range of a Single to Single.

*CStr Function*

> Converts an expression to its string representation. Boolean values are converted to either "True" or "False." Dates are converted based on the date format defined by the regional settings of the host computer.

*CType Function*

> Provides generalized casting, allowing an object or expression of any type to be converted to another type. It works with all classes, structures, and interfaces. This applies to both the basic data types and custom classes. The function has the following syntax:
>
> ```
> CType(expression, typename)
> ```
>
> For instance, the statement:
>
> ```
> Dim targetNumber As Integer = CType("12", Integer)
> ```
>
> is equivalent to:
>
> ```
> Dim targetNumber As Integer = CInt("12")
> ```
>
> *New in 2005.* The 2005 release of Visual Basic adds operator overloading features, described in Chapter 5. One component of operator overloading is the ability to define CType conversion rules for your own custom classes.

*CUInteger Function*

> *New in 2005.* Converts any numeric expression in the range of a UInteger to UInteger, rounding any fractional part.

*CULong Function*

> *New in 2005.* Converts any numeric expression in the range of a ULong to ULong, rounding any fractional part.

*CUShort Function*

> *New in 2005.* Converts any numeric expression in the range of a UShort to UShort, rounding any fractional part.

# Variables

A *variable* can be defined as an entity that has the following six properties:

*Name*

> A variable's name is used to identify it in code. In VB, a variable name starts with a Unicode alphabetic character or an underscore and is then followed by additional underscore characters or various Unicode characters, such as alphabetic, numeric, formatting, or combined characters. With the introduction of .NET, Microsoft recommends a new set of naming standards for use with variables and other named objects. These naming standards are discussed briefly in the "Naming Conventions" section of Chapter 1.

*Address*

Every variable has an associated memory address, the location where the variable's value is stored. Variables are not guaranteed to maintain a permanent memory address in .NET, so the address of a variable should not be recorded or used.

*Data Type*

The data type of a variable determines the possible values that the variable can assume.

*Value*

The value of a variable is the data content it contains at its memory address. This is also sometimes referred to as the *r-value* of the variable, since it is what appears on the right side of a variable assignment statement. For instance, in the code:

```
Dim targetValue As Integer = 5
```

the statement can be read as "store the *value* of 5 in memory at the address of targetValue." Because it appears on the left side of an assignment operator, the variable (or its memory location) is sometimes called an *l-value*.

*Scope*

The scope of a variable determines where in a program that variable is visible to the code. Variable scope is discussed in more detail later in this chapter.

*Lifetime*

A variable's lifetime determines when and for how long a particular variable exists. It may or may not be visible (that is, be in scope) for that entire period. Variable lifetime is described in more detail later in this chapter.

## Variable Declaration

A *variable declaration* is an association of a variable name with a data type. For non-object variables (value types), declaration is firmly tied to variable instance creation. A declaration such as:

```
Dim createMeNow As Integer
```

creates an Integer variable named createMeNow. This is equivalent to:

```
Dim createMeNow As Integer = New Integer
```

or even:

```
Dim createMeNow As New Integer
```

which emphasizes the creation of a new instance of the variable object.

Multiple variables can be declared within a single statement. Although each variable generally has its own type declaration, this is not a requirement. If a variable lacks an explicit type declaration, then its type is that of the next variable with an explicit type declaration. Thus, in the line:

```
Dim first As Long, second, third As Integer, fourth As String
```

the variables second and third have type Integer. (In VB 6, second would have been Variant.)

Visual Basic permits the initialization of variables in the same line as their declaration. (The assigned value is called an *initializer*.) The statement:

```
Dim alwaysInitialized As Integer = 5
```

declares and creates an `Integer`, and assigns it an initial value of 5. Multiple assignments in a single statement also work.

```
Dim first As Integer = 6, second As Integer = 9
```

When using initializers, each variable must include an explicit data type.

Object variables (reference types) are declared just like their core data type counterparts:

```
Dim newHire As Employee
```

However, this declaration does not create an object variable; the variable's value is equal to `Nothing`. Object creation requires an explicit call to the object's constructor, as in:

```
Dim newHire As New Employee
```

or:

```
Dim newHire As Employee = New Employee
```

or even:

```
Dim newHire As Employee
newHire = New Employee
```

## Variable Scope, Lifetime, and Access Level

Variables have a *scope*, which indicates where in the program the variable is recognized or *visible* to the code.

### Local variables: block-level and procedure-level scope

All variables declared within a function, sub procedure, or property are *local variables*. These variables may be used only within that routine; when the routine is complete, they cease to exist (if they haven't been passed to another variable with a larger scope).

Local variables generally have *procedure-level scope*; they are accessible by every line of code in the procedure. These local variables often appear immediately upon entering the code of the procedure.

```
Public Sub DoTheWork( )
    Dim localInt As Integer
    Dim localEmp As New Employee
```

*Code blocks* are sets of statements contained within an `If` statement, a `For` loop, a `With` statement, or any other similar block of code that has separate starting and ending statements. All statements that appear between the opening statement (`If`, `ElseIf`, `For`, `With`, and so on) and the closing statement (`End If`, `Next`, `End With`, and so on) are part of that code block. Any variable defined within a code block has *block-level scope*; it is only visible within that block of code. Since code blocks can be nested, block-level variables can appear at any depth within the nesting.

```
Public Sub DoTheWork(ByVal fromWhen As Date, ByVal howMuch As Decimal)
    If (fromWhen < Today) Then
        ' ----- This variable is available within the outer-most
        '       If block, which also includes the inner-most block.
        '       It is not available outside the outer-most If block.
        Dim simpleCalculation As Integer

        If (howMuch > 0@) Then
            ' ----- This variable is only available within the
            '       inner-most If block.
            Dim complexCalculation As Integer
        End If
    End If
End Sub
```

Block-level variables cannot be accessed at all outside of their defined block. Consider the following code:

```
If (origValue <> 0) Then
    Dim inverseValue As Decimal
    inverseValue = 1 / origValue
End If
' ----- The next statement will not compile.
MsgBox(CStr(inverseValue))
```

In this code, the variable inverseValue is not recognized outside of the block in which it is defined, so the final line produces a compile-time error.

All local variables, whether procedure-level or block-level in scope, have a *lifetime* of the entire procedure. This means that block-level variables retain their value during the entire procedure's lifetime, even when code outside the block is being executed. In the code:

```
Dim counter As Integer
For counter = 1 To 5
    If (ProcessData(counter) = True) Then
        Dim soFar1 As Integer
        Dim soFar2 As Integer = 0
        soFar1 += 1
        soFar2 += 1
        MsgBox("Status so far: " & soFar1 & ", " & soFar2)
    End If
Next counter
```

the variable soFar1 retains its value from the previous time through the If block. It displays "1" in its first MsgBox use, "2" the second time, and so on. Because the soFar2 variable includes an initializer, it is reset to that value (0, in this case) each time through the block. It always displays "1" in the MsgBox statement.

A procedure can have variables passed to it through its argument list. These variables are always procedure-level in scope.

Local variables can extend their lifetime beyond the execution timeline of the procedure in which they reside. *Static* variables, though local in scope, live for the entire lifetime of the class or module in which they are contained. They are declared with the Static keyword instead of the Dim keyword:

```
Static longLasting As Integer = 0
```

The initializer of a static variable is applied when the class or module is instantiated, not each time the statement is encountered. When you enter a procedure with a static variable, the variable will contain the same value it had the last time the procedure was used. Static variables are not allowed in the procedures of a `Structure`.

### Module-level scope and access levels

All variables declared within a class (or structure or module), but outside of any procedure within that class, have *type-level scope*; they are available to all procedures within the class. However, the scope of these variables can go beyond the type level through the use of an *access modifier*.

Each type-level variable is defined using an access modifier keyword. (You can use `Dim` as well, but as `Dim`'s access level varies between the different module types, this makes the code unclear.) The access modifier grants access in a specific order, with `Public` granting the most generous level of access (see Table 4-1).

*Table 4-1. Access modifiers*

| Access modifier | Description |
|---|---|
| Public | Public variables are accessible to any code that accesses an instance of the class or structure, or that has access to the type containing the variable. If a class has a public variable, and an instance of that class is accessed from a separate project, application, or component, the public variable is fully accessible to that code. |
| Protected | Protected variables are accessible within the confines of a class and can be used in any code derived from that class, but cannot be accessed outside of the class. Protected variables only apply to classes; they are not available to structures or modules. |
| Friend | Friend variables are accessible anywhere within the assembly, but no further. Instances of a class with a friend variable consumed outside of the assembly hide the variable from that external code. Friend variables can be used in classes, structures, and modules. |
| Protected Friend | Using Protected and Friend together grants that variable all the benefits of both; such variables are accessible within the class and all derived classes, and within the assembly, but not outside of it. Protected Friend variables can only be used in classes, not in structures or modules. |
| Private | Private variables are accessible anywhere within a class, structure, or module, but not outside. They are also hidden from the custom members of derived classes. |

Type-level variables have a lifetime that spans the entire lifetime of the class instance, structure instance, or module that contains it. Variables can be marked as `Shared`; they exist without a specific instance of the class, structure, or module being created. These variables have a lifetime that lasts for the entire application's lifetime. All members of a `Module` are shared by default.

# Constants

*Constants* are essentially read-only variables. Once their value is set in code (at compile time), they cannot change. Constants are defined at the local or module level using the `Const` keyword:

```
accessModifier Const name As type = value
```

where *accessModifier* is one of the access modifiers defined earlier. (Access modifiers are not used for constants declared in procedures.) When Option Strict is On, all constant declarations must have a declared type.

# Enumerations

An *enumeration* appears as a group of related integer constants. All members of an enumeration share the same data type, and it must be an integral data type (Byte, Integer, Long, or Short, and also—in 2005 or beyond—SByte, UInteger, ULong, or UShort). The enumeration members are shared and read-only for the lifetime of the application.

```
Public Enum VehicleType As Integer
    bicycle = 2
    tricycle = 3
    passengerCar = 4
    eighteenWheeler = 18
End Enum
```

They are used in code just like constants or variables.

```
Dim whatIDrive As VehicleType
whatIDrive = VehicleType.passengerCar
```

Enumerations are declared at the namespace or module level only; you cannot define an enumeration within a procedure.

# Arrays

The array is a fundamental data structure in many programming languages, including Visual Basic. Arrays store a collection of similar data types or objects. Each *element* has a numbered position, ranging from 0 (the *lower bound*) to the defined *upper bound* of the array.

The following examples show various ways to declare a one-dimensional array:

```
' Implicit constructor: No initial size and no initialization
Dim days() As Integer

' Explicit constructor: No initial size and no initialization
Dim days() As Integer = New Integer() {}

' Implicit constructor: Initial size but no initialization
Dim days(6) As Integer

' Explicit constructor: Initial size but no initialization
Dim days() As Integer = New Integer(6) {}

' Implicit constructor: Initial size implied by initialization
Dim days() As Integer = {1, 2, 3, 4, 5, 6, 7}

' Explicit constructor, Initial size and initialization
Dim days() As Integer = New Integer(6) {1, 2, 3, 4, 5, 6, 7}
```

Array declarations can:

- Call the array's constructor implicitly or explicitly
- Specify an initial size for each dimension or leave the initial size unspecified
- Initialize the elements of the array or not

In VB 6, the programmer could specify both the lower and upper bounds of any array dimension. With .NET, all Visual Basic arrays have a lower bound of zero. The statement:

```
Dim myArray(5) As Integer
```

declares an array with six elements, numbered zero through five.

Arrays can include multiple *dimensions*. The following example declares and initializes a two-dimensional array:

```
Dim rectArray(,) As Integer = {{1, 2, 3}, {4, 5, 6}}
```

The following code displays the contents of this array:

```
Debug.Write(rectArray(0, 0))
Debug.Write(rectArray(0, 1))
Debug.WriteLine(rectArray(0, 2))
Debug.Write(rectArray(1, 0))
Debug.Write(rectArray(1, 1))
Debug.WriteLine(rectArray(1, 2))

' ----- The output is:
123
456
```

Variables and Data Types

The upper bound of any array dimension can be modified using the ReDim statement.

```
ReDim [Preserve] arrayName(newUpperBound)
```

The Preserve qualifier retains any existing values in the array; all array elements are cleared in the absence of this qualifier. When using Preserve, only the last dimension of an array can have its upper bound modified. The number of dimensions in an array cannot be changed.

You can determine the lower and upper bounds of an array dimension using the LBound and UBound functions respectively.

```
Dim smallArray(5) As Integer
MsgBox(UBound(smallArray))  ' Displays "5"
```

Since all array dimensions have a lower bound of zero, the LBound function always returns zero.

# Collections

Visual Basic defines an associative array object called a *collection*. Although similar to an array in that elements appear in a specific order, a collection stores its elements as key-value pairs. Once in a collection, each element can be retrieved by position, by key, or by iterating through the collection one element at a time.

Five of the `Collection` class's members are especially useful.

*Add Method*
Adds an item to the collection. Along with the data itself, you can specify an optional key by which the member can be referenced.

*Clear Method*
Removes all elements from the collection.

*Count Property*
Returns the number of elements in the collection.

*Item Property*
Retrieves an element from the collection either by its index (or ordinal position in the collection) or by its key (if provided when the element was added).

*Remove Method*
Deletes an element from the collection using the element's index or key.

The following code defines a collection of state names, using the state abbreviation as the key.

```
Dim states As New Collection
states.Add("New York", "NY")
states.Add("Michigan", "MI")
```

The elements of this collection can then be iterated using the `For Each...Next` construct.

```
Dim oneState As String
For Each oneState In states
    MsgBox(oneState)
Next oneState
```

Like arrays, collection members are accessible by their index value. The lower bound of a collection is always one (1).

*New in 2005.* The 2005 release of Visual Basic includes a new generics feature that allows collection (and other class) instances to be tied to a specific data type. See Chapter 10 for details on using this new feature.

# Parameters and Arguments

Although procedures are self-contained blocks of code, they often need to interact with data from outside of the procedure. External data can be passed into the procedure through its *parameter list*. This list appears immediately on the declaration line of the procedure itself.

```
Public Function RepeatString(ByVal origText As String, _
        ByVal howManyTimes As Integer) As String
    ' ----- Return a string concatenated to itself many times.
    Dim counter As Integer
    RepeatString = ""
    For counter = 1 To howManyTimes
        RepeatString &= origText
    Next counter
End Function
```

The RepeatString function includes two parameters, origText and howManyTimes. Each parameter includes a data type and a passing method. The passing method is either ByVal ("by value") or ByRef ("by reference"). In .NET, the default parameter passing method is ByVal.

When calling a procedure that has parameters, the values you send from the initiating code are called *arguments*. The following statement includes two arguments in the call to the RepeatString function: a string ("abc") and an integer (5).

```
targetString = RepeatString("abc", 5)
```

Because classes in .NET support overloaded methods, the arguments you send to a procedure must match the parameter signature of one of the overloaded methods. See Chapter 3 for a broader discussion of overloading.

## Passing Arguments

All arguments are passed by value or by reference, depending on whether the ByVal or ByRef keyword is used with a parameter. When data is passed by value, a copy of the source expression or variable is sent to the target procedure. While in that procedure, the parameter acts just like a local variable; it can be examined and modified within the procedure, and it disappears when the procedure is finished. Any changes made to a ByVal parameter in the procedure are not reflected in the source variable. This is clearest when working with value types. Consider the following code.

```
Public Sub ParentRoutine( )
    Dim sourceValue As Integer = 5
    ChildRoutine(sourceValue)
    MsgBox(sourceValue)    ' --> Displays "5"
End Sub

Public Sub ChildRoutine(ByVal incoming As Integer)
    incoming = 10
End Sub
```

Even though sourceValue was passed to ChildRoutine, and its associated parameter incoming was modified, that change did not propagate back to ParentRoutine, since incoming contained only a copy of sourceValue's value.

Objects (reference types) passed into routines ByVal, however, can be modified by the target procedure. More correctly, the *members* of an object can be modified, not the object itself. Objects passed by value pass the memory location of the object, so changes made within that memory area in the target procedure are reflected in the original object. However, you cannot fully replace the object with a new object instance when using ByVal.

```
Public Class DataClass
    Public DataMember As Integer
End Class

Public Class CodeClass
    Public Sub ParentRoutine( )
        Dim sourceValue As New DataClass
        sourceValue.DataMember = 5
```

```
        ChildRoutine(sourceValue)
        MsgBox(sourceValue.DataMember)    ' --> Displays "10"
    End Sub

    Public Sub ChildRoutine(ByVal incoming As DataClass)
        ' ----- This line changes the "real" member.
        incoming.DataMember = 10

        ' ----- But these lines have no impact on sourceValue.
        incoming = New DataClass
        incoming.DataMember = 15
    End Sub
End Class
```

Passing a value type argument to a procedure with a ByRef parameter passes the memory address of the value; changes made in the target procedure are reflected immediately in the source value. (This is true if the source value is a variable; constants and calculated expressions cannot be modified.) Contrast the following code with its ByVal counterpart above.

```
Public Sub ParentRoutine( )
    Dim sourceValue As Integer = 5
    ChildRoutine(sourceValue)
    MsgBox(sourceValue)    ' --> Displays "10"
End Sub

Public Sub ChildRoutine(ByRef incoming As Integer)
    incoming = 10
End Sub
```

Changing ByVal to ByRef made a significant difference. For reference types, the difference is not as noticeable unless you attempt to fully replace the original object in the target procedure. You can do it! This is because the ByRef keyword causes the memory address *of the memory address* of the object to be passed in. If you modify that memory address, you replace the address managed by the source variable. In some languages, this is referred to as a *double pointer*. It's somewhat confusing, but an example should make it clear. Contrast this code with the similar ByVal code shown earlier.

```
Public Class DataClass
    Public DataMember As Integer
End Class

Public Class CodeClass
    Public Sub ParentRoutine( )
        Dim sourceValue As New DataClass
        sourceValue.DataMember = 5
        ChildRoutine(sourceValue)
        MsgBox(sourceValue.DataMember)    ' --> Displays "15"
    End Sub

    Public Sub ChildRoutine(ByRef incoming As DataClass)
        ' ----- This line changes the "real" member.
        incoming.DataMember = 10
```

```
    ' ----- These lines fully replace the object referred
    '        to by sourceValue.
    incoming = New DataClass
    incoming.DataMember = 15
  End Sub
End Class
```

Using ByRef with reference types allows the target procedure to fully replace the original object with a completely new instance of an object.

## Optional Arguments

Visual Basic supports optional parameters through the Optional keyword.

```
Sub Calculate(Optional ByVal silent As Boolean = False)
```

The following rules apply to optional arguments:

- Every optional argument must specify a default value, and this default must be a constant expression (not a variable). This value is used when the calling code does not supply an argument for the optional parameter.

- Every argument following an optional argument must also be optional. All required arguments must appear before the optional arguments in the parameter list.

Pre-.NET versions of VB allowed you to omit the default value, and, if the parameter was of type Variant, you could use the IsMissing function to determine if a value was supplied. This is no longer supported; if an argument is not supplied, the required default value is used instead.

## Parameter Arrays

Normally, a procedure definition specifies a fixed number of parameters. However, the ParamArray ("parameter array") keyword allows the parameter list to be extended beyond the fixed elements. Each call to the procedure can use a different number of parameters beyond any initial required parameters.

Consider a function that takes the average of a number of test scores, but the number of scores may vary.

```
Public Function AverageScore(ByVal ParamArray scores( ) _
      As Single) As Single
  ' ----- Calculate the average score for any number of tests.
  Dim counter As Integer

  AverageScore = 0
  For counter = 0 To UBound(scores)
     AverageScore += scores(counter)
  Next counter
  AverageScore /= UBound(scores) + 1
End Function
```

The call to AverageScore can now include a varied number of arguments.

```
MsgBox(AverageScore(1, 2, 3, 4, 5))  ' --> Displays "3"
MsgBox(AverageScore(1, 2, 3))        ' --> Displays "2"
```

The following rules apply to the use of `ParamArray`:

- A procedure can only have one parameter array, and it must be the last parameter in the parameter list.
- The parameter array must be passed by value, and you must explicitly include `ByVal` in the procedure definition.
- The parameter array must be a one-dimensional array. If the type is not declared, it is assumed to be *System.Object*.

The parameter array is automatically optional. Its default value is an empty one-dimensional array of the parameter array's data type.

# 5

# Operators

Operators are the basic data manipulation tools of any programming language. All data ultimately breaks down into single bits of 0 and 1. And the whole reason a computer exists is to manipulate those single bits of data with basic operators. This chapter discusses the basic operators available in Visual Basic, and how they interact with data.

Operators come in two usage types: unary and binary. Unary operators work on a single operand, while binary operators require two operands. Most operators in Visual Basic are binary operators.

## Arithmetic Operators

The VB arithmetic operators provide basic manipulation of integer and floating point numbers. They could be called "the calculator operators," since most of them appear on even the most basic four-function calculator.

+ *(Addition)*

The addition operator adds numeric expressions together and returns the result.

```
result = expression1 + expression2
```

When used with string operands, the + operator acts like the & string concatenation operator, as described below.

+ *(Unary Plus)*

Usually, the + operator only appears as a binary operator. But it can be used in a unary form. In this usage, when placed immediately before a number or numeric expression, it ensures that the expression retains its sign, either positive or negative. Since expressions retain their sign by default, the unary plus operator is redundant and rarely used.

```
result =+expression
```

*New variation in 2005.* Beginning with the 2005 release of Visual Basic, over-loading this operator may prove useful in some classes.

**- *(Subtraction)***

The subtraction operator deducts the value of one expression from another, returning the difference.

```
result = expression1 - expression2
```

Unlike the addition operator, the subtraction operator cannot be used with string operands.

**- *(Unary Negation)***

The - operator performs double duty as both a unary and binary operator. In its unary form, when placed immediately before a number or numeric expression, it negates the expression, effectively multiplying the expression by -1.

```
result =-expression
```

**\* *(Multiplication)***

The multiplication operator multiplies two numeric expressions together and returns the result.

```
result = expression1 * expression2
```

**/ *(Division)***

The division operator divides one numeric expression into another and returns the result, retaining any decimal remainder. If the second operand is zero (0), a "divide by zero" error occurs.

```
result = expression1 / expression2
```

**\ *(Integer Division)***

The integer division operator works just like the normal division operator, but any decimal remainder is truncated (not rounded) before returning the result. If the second operand is zero (0), a "divide by zero" error occurs.

```
result = expression1 \ expression2
```

This operator always returns a non-decimal data type (such as Short, Integer, or Long), even if the original operands were decimal.

**Mod *(Modulo)***

The modulo operator divides one numeric expression into another and returns only the remainder as a whole number, also known as the modulus. If either of the two source expressions are decimal numbers, they are rounded to integer values prior to the modulo operation. To obtain expected results, explicitly truncate or round decimal expressions before using them as operands. The return value is a nonnegative integral data type.

As an example, the expression:

```
10 Mod 3
```

returns 1, because the remainder of 10 divided by 3 is 1.

```
result = expression1 Mod expression2
```

**^ *(Exponentiation)***

The exponentiation operator raises one numeric expression to the power of the second and returns the result.

```
result = number ^ exponent
```

# Concatenation Operators

Concatenation operators connect two source string expressions together and return a single string joined from the two original strings. Because strings in .NET are immutable, the returned string is always a completely new string instance.

**& *(String Concatenation)***

The string concatenation operator returns a concatenated string from two source string expressions. Any non-string source expression is first converted to a string prior to concatenation (even if `OptionStrict` is set to `On`).

```
result = expression1 & expression2
```

**+ *(Addition)***

When the addition operator is used with string operands, it concatenates the operands instead of adding their values. However, using this operator for concatenation can make the source code unclear, especially when using the new .NET-recommended variable naming conventions. If you mix string and numeric operands, this operator may also cause compile-time or runtime errors, depending on the content of the operands. For the clearest code, use the & concatenation operator instead.

# Logical and Bitwise Operators

Logical operators evaluate one or more expressions and return a Boolean result (`True` or `False`). VB supports six logical operators, many of which can also be used as *bitwise* operators, along with two bitwise-only operators. Bitwise operations work on integral (numeric integer) operands at the bit level and return numeric results. Other languages, such as C#, include distinct logical and bitwise operators, but for historical reasons, VB mostly uses a common set of operators for both types of operations.

If any of the operands are numeric (that is, non-Boolean), a bitwise operation is done instead of a logical operation. In cases where one operand is Boolean and the other is not, the Boolean operand is converted to a number first, using 0 for `False` and -1 for `True`.

In performing some logical operations, the .NET versions of Visual Basic use conditional *short-circuiting*, where complex conditional expressions are only partially evaluated if the final result of the entire expression can be determined without full evaluation. Individual expressions within a larger compound expression are evaluated only until the expression's overall value is known, unless one of the individual expressions involves a call to another function or subroutine. Short-circuiting can occur in logical `AndAlso` operations when the first operand evaluates to `False`, as well as in logical `OrElse` operations when the first operand evaluates to True. When using the more common And and Or operators, no short-circuiting is done.

Boolean operations always use the two Boolean values of True and False. Although Visual Basic's Boolean data type is based on the underlying .NET *System.Boolean* data type, its use in Visual Basic differs from that of other .NET languages. For historical reasons, Visual Basic's True value, when converted to a number, equates to -1. Other .NET languages—specifically C#—use a value of 1 for True. Although .NET resolves this difference through the shared data type, it can become an issue if you use a non-.NET data transfer method (such as a plain text file) to share numeric Boolean data between .NET languages.

And

The And operator performs a logical or bitwise conjunction on the two source operands. In logical operations, it returns True if and only if both operands evaluate to True. If either operand is False, then the result is False. The syntax is:

    result = expression1 And expression2

For example, consider the following statement:

    If (x = 5) And (y < 7) Then

In this case, the code within the Then clause will be executed only if the value of x is 5 *and* the value of y is less than 7.

As a bitwise operator, And returns 1 in a bit position if the compared bits in the same position in both expressions are 1, and it returns 0 in all other cases, as shown in the following table:

| Bit in expression1 | Bit in expression2 | Result |
| --- | --- | --- |
| 0 | 0 | 0 |
| 0 | 1 | 0 |
| 1 | 0 | 0 |
| 1 | 1 | 1 |

For example, the bitwise result of 15 And 179 is 3, as the following binary representation shows:

    00001111 And 10110011 → 00000011

AndAlso

The AndAlso operator works exactly like the logical And operator, but short-circuiting is enabled. If the first operand evaluates to False, the second operand is not evaluated at all, even if that expression includes function calls. Operands are evaluated from left to right. AndAlso does not perform bitwise operations.

Or

The Or operator performs a logical or bitwise disjunction on the two source operands. In logical operations, it returns True if either of the operands evaluates to True. If both operands are False, then the result is False. The syntax is:

    result = expression1 Or expression2

For example, consider the following statement:

```
If (x = 5) Or (y < 7) Then
```

In this case, the code within the Then clause will be executed if either the value of x is 5 *or* the value of y is less than 7.

As a bitwise operator, Or returns 1 in a bit position if either of the compared bits in the same position in the source expressions are 1, and it returns 0 in all other cases, as shown in the following table:

| Bit in expression1 | Bit in expression2 | Result |
|---|---|---|
| 0 | 0 | 0 |
| 0 | 1 | 1 |
| 1 | 0 | 1 |
| 1 | 1 | 1 |

For example, the bitwise result of 150r179 is 191, as the following binary representation shows:

```
00001111 Or 10110011  →  10111111
```

## OrElse

The OrElse operator works exactly like the logical Or operator, but short-circuiting is enabled. If the first operand evaluates to True, the second operand is not evaluated at all, even if that expression includes function calls. Operands are evaluated from left to right. OrElse does not perform bitwise operations.

## Not

The Not operator performs a logical or bitwise negation on a single expression. In logical operations, it returns True if the operand is False, and False if the operand is True. The syntax is:

```
result = Not expression1
```

For example, consider the following statement:

```
If Not IsNumeric(x) Then
```

In this example, the code within the Then clause will be executed if IsNumeric returns False, indicating that x is not a value capable of being represented by a number.

As a bitwise operator, Not simply toggles the value of each bit in the source expression between 0 and 1, as shown in the following table:

| Bit in expression1 | Result |
|---|---|
| 0 | 1 |
| 1 | 0 |

For example, the bitwise result of Not 16 is 239, as the following binary representation shows:

```
Not 00010000  →  11101111
```

Xor

The Xor (an abbreviation for "eXclusive OR") operator performs a logical or bitwise exclusion on the two source operands. In logical operations, it returns True if and only if the two expressions have different truth values. If both expressions are True, or both are False, this operator returns False. If one of the operands is True but the other False, then Xor returns True. The syntax is:

```
result = expression1 Xor expression2
```

As a bitwise operator, Xor returns 1 in a bit position if the compared bits are different from each other, and it returns 0 if they are the same, as shown in the following table:

| Bit in expression1 | Bit in expression2 | Result |
|---|---|---|
| 0 | 0 | 0 |
| 0 | 1 | 1 |
| 1 | 0 | 1 |
| 1 | 1 | 0 |

For example, the result of 15 Xor 179 is 188, as the following binary representation shows:

```
00001111 Xor 10110011  →   10111100
```

---

## Eqv and Imp

Eqv and Imp, two logical and bitwise operators present in VB 6, have been removed from .NET implementations of Visual Basic. Eqv can be replaced with the = (equal to) comparison operator. The expression:

```
expression1 Eqv expression2
```

is the same as the logical comparison:

```
expression1 = expression2
```

Imp can be replaced with a logical expression using the Not and Or operators. For example:

```
expression1 Imp expression2
```

can also be expressed as:

```
(Not expression1) Or expression2
```

If you need more precise replacements using bitwise calculations, see the "Logical and Bitwise Operators" section in Appendix D.

---

<< *(Shift Left)*

*New in 2003.* The << (shift left) operator performs a left shift of the bits in the first operand by the number of bits specified in the second operand. All bits shifted off the left are lost. All bits newly vacated on the right are filled with zeros.

The number of bits you can shift is limited by the number of possible bits in the first operand. Any excess number of shift positions will be ignored. This operator never throws an overflow exception. The syntax is:

```
result = source << bits
```

For example, the bitwise result of 15 << 5 is 224, as the following binary representation shows:

```
00001111 << 5   →   11100000
```

## >> (Shift Right)

*New in 2003.* The >> (shift right) operator performs a right shift of the bits in the first operand by the number of bits specified in the second operand. All bits shifted off the right are lost. All bits newly vacated on the left are filled with the bit value of the leftmost bit position before shifting. When shifting unsigned data values (Byte, UShort, UInteger, ULong), the newly vacated bits on the left are filled with zero (0).

The number of bits you can shift is limited by the number of possible bits in the first operand. Any excess number of shift positions will be ignored. This operator never throws an overflow exception. The syntax is:

```
result = source >> bits
```

For example, the bitwise result of 12 >> 1 is 6, as the following binary representation shows:

```
00001100 >> 1   →   00000110
```

# Assignment Operators

Along with the standard assignment operator (=), many other operators can be turned into assignment operators by simply appending an equals sign to the right of the operator. These converted operators all have the same form:

```
expression1 <operator>= expression2
```

where <operator> is the operator being promoted to an assignment operator. This form is equivalent to:

```
expression1 = expression1 <operator> expression2
```

To illustrate, consider the addition assignment operator. The expression:

```
x += 1
```

is equivalent to:

```
x = x + 1
```

which simply adds 1 to the value of x. Similarly, the expression:

```
s &= "end"
```

is equivalent to:

```
s = s & "end"
```

which concatenates the string "end" to the end of the string s.

All of these "shortcut" assignment operators were introduced with Visual Basic .NET 2002.

= *(Assignment)*

The assignment operator assigns the value or reference of the expression on the right of the assignment operator to the variable on the left. For example, the following assigns y plus an additional value of 5 to x.

```
x = y + 5
```

The assignment operator alone is used to assign both values and references; in previous versions of VB, the Set statement had to be used along with the assignment operator to assign an object reference. The Set keyword is no longer used in this context. Also, the previously optional Let keyword is no longer part of the Visual Basic language.

+=

The addition assignment operator. As an example:

```
totalValue += 1
```

adds 1 to the value of totalValue and assigns the result to totalValue.

-=

The subtraction assignment operator. As an example:

```
totalValue -= 1
```

subtracts 1 from the value of totalValue and assigns the result to totalValue.

*=

The multiplication assignment operator. As an example:

```
totalValue *= 3
```

multiplies the value of totalValue by 3 and assigns the result to totalValue.

/=

The division assignment operator. As an example:

```
totalValue /= 2
```

divides the value of totalValue by 2 and assigns the result to totalValue. If the value to the right of the division assignment operator equates to 0, an error occurs.

\=

The integer division assignment operator. As an example:

```
totalValue \= 2
```

divides the value of totalValue by 2, discards any fractional part, and assigns the result to totalValue. If the value to the right of the integer division assignment operator equates to 0, an error occurs.

^=

The exponentiation assignment operator. As an example:

```
totalValue ^= 2
```

squares the value of totalValue and assigns the result to totalValue.

&=

The concatenation assignment operator. As an example:

```
storyText &= "The End"
```

appends a literal text string to the end of storyText's existing content and assigns this new concatenated string to storyText.

<<=

*New in 2003.* The shift left assignment operator. As an example:

```
dataMask <<= 2
```

shifts the bits of dataMask left two positions and assigns the new value back to dataMask.

>>=

*New in 2003.* The shift right assignment operator. As an example:

```
dataMask >>= 2
```

shifts the bits of dataMask right two positions and assigns the new value back to dataMask.

 Unlike the comparison operators, in which the order of symbols is reversible (that is, >= is the same as =>), the order of the "shortcut" assignment operator symbols is *not* reversible. For example, while:

```
x -= 1
```

decrements x by 1, the expression:

```
x =- 1
```

assigns a value of 1 to the variable x. That is, it really looks like this:

```
x = -1
```

# Comparison Operators

There are three main comparison operators: < (less than), > (greater than), and = (equal to). They can be used individually, or any two operators can be combined with each other to form other comparison operators. The general syntax is:

```
result = expression1 <operator> expression2
```

The result is a Boolean value of True or False.

The following list indicates the condition required with each VB comparison operator to return a value of True.

= *(Equal To)*
True if *expression1* is equal to *expression2*

< *(Less Than)*
True if *expression1* is less than (and not equal to) *expression2*

> *(Greater Than)*
True if *expression1* is greater than (and not equal to) *expression2*

<= *(Less Than or Equal To)*
True if *expression1* is less than or equal to *expression2*

>= *(Greater Than or Equal To)*
   True if *expression1* is greater than or equal to *expression2*

<> *(Not Equal To)*
   True if *expression1* is not equal to *expression2*

Comparison operators can be used with both numeric and string expressions. If one expression is numeric and the other is a string, the string is first converted to a number of type Double (nonnumeric strings throw an exception). If both *expression1* and *expression2* are strings, the "greatest" string is the one that appears second in sort order. The sorting is based on the current character code page in use by the application, the region-specific locale information, and the OptionCompare setting. If that setting is Binary, the comparison is case-sensitive, whereas a setting of Text results in a case-insensitive comparison.

*New in 2005.* There are two "hidden" operators in Visual Basic: IsTrue(*arg*) and IsFalse(*arg*). They return a Boolean value that indicates whether the supplied argument is True or False, respectively. You cannot use them directly in your code, but they do exist, beginning in the 2005 release of Visual Basic, to support operator overloading. This is covered in the "Operator Overloading" section later in this chapter.

## The Like Operator

The Like operator is used to match a string against a pattern. It compares a string expression or literal with a string pattern expression and determines whether they match (the result is True) or not (the result is False). For example:

```
If (testString Like "[A-Z]#") Then
```

matches a capital letter followed by a digit.

For details on the use of this operator, including special characters used in the pattern string, see the "Like Operator" entry in Chapter 12.

# Object Operators

Visual Basic includes five operators that return results based on an operand's object properties.

Is

   The Is operator determines whether two object reference variables refer to the same object instance.

```
result = object1 Is object2
```

   If both *object1* and *object2* refer to the same object instance, the result is True; otherwise, the result is False. You can also use the Is operator to determine if an object variable refers to a valid object. This is done by comparing the object variable to the Nothing keyword:

```
If (customerRecord Is Nothing) Then
```

   The result is True if the object variable does not hold a reference to any object.

IsNot

New in 2005. The IsNot operator is equivalent to the Is operator used with the Not logical operator. The statement:

```
If (customerRecord IsNot Nothing) Then
```

is the same as:

```
If Not (customerRecord Is Nothing) Then
```

There is no functional difference between the two statements. The IsNot operator was added to VB to make such statements more readable.

TypeOf

The TypeOf operator determines if an object variable is of a specific data type. It is always used with the Is operator. (It does not work with the new VB 2005 IsNot operator.) The following statement tests an object variable to see if it is an Integer.

```
If (TypeOf someNumber Is Integer) Then
```

AddressOf

The AddressOf operator returns a procedure delegate that can be used to reference a procedure through a variable. In VB 6, the AddressOf operator returned a *function pointer*, the memory address of the function. While the . NET version of this operator serves a similar purpose, it does not return a memory address. The .NET Framework reserves the right to move objects (including procedures) to new memory locations at any time, so you cannot depend on the memory address.

For details on the AddressOf operator, including usage information, see the *AddressOf Operator* entry in Chapter 12.

GetType

The GetType operator returns a *System.Type* object that contains information about the data type of the operand. You cannot use expressions or variables as operands; you must pass a data type itself. You can use VB data types (like Integer or String), .NET core types (like *System.Int32*), or the name of any class, structure, or similar construct. For example:

```
result = GetType(Integer)
```

returns a *System.Type* object that provides information about the *System.Int32* data type, which is the true data type of the Visual Basic Integer data type.

# Operator Overloading

New in 2005. Although Visual Basic is as powerful as any other .NET language, early versions lacked specific features found in some other .NET languages (just as VB had features absent from those languages). One feature present in C#, but absent in VB, was *operator overloading*, the ability to redefine unary and binary operators and give them special uses when working with specific classes or structures. As of the 2005 release of Visual Basic, operator overloading is now part of the Visual Basic experience.

To perform operator overloading, you simply create a special procedure in your class with the name of the operator, indicate the data type(s) of the operand(s) and the data type of the return value, make it Public and Shared, and it's ready to use. The class (or structure) you put the procedure in is significant. At least one operand for the operator must be of the class data type in which the procedure appears. For the special CType unary operator, either the operand or its return value must use the data type of the class that includes the procedure.

All overloaded operator procedures share a common syntax.

```
Public Shared [otherModifiers] Operator operatorSymbol _
    (ByVal operand1 As dataType[, ByVal operand2 As dataType]) _
    As returnDataType
    ' ----- Statements of the operator procedure.
End Operator
```

As an example, consider a class named LandRegion that defines the boundaries of a piece of land. Since you would like to merge two records together into a larger tract of land using the + addition operator, you define the following procedure in the LandRegion class.

```
Public Shared Operator +(ByVal firstArea As LandRegion, _
    ByVal secondArea As LandRegion) As LandRegion
    ' ----- Merge two land regions together.
    Dim combinedRegion As New LandRegion
    ' ...more code here...
    Return combinedRegion
End Operator
```

Since the routine is Public, it is available to your entire program. Since it is Shared, the routine exists even without the presence of any specific instance of the class (although at least one operand must be of that class). The defined operands must always be passed ByVal. Using this operator is simple.

```
Dim mainCity As New LandRegion
Dim unincorporatedArea As New LandRegion
Dim annexation As LandRegion

' ...fill in mainCity and unincorporatedArea members, then...
annexation = mainCity + unincorporatedArea
```

For binary operators, only one of the operands has to match the enclosing class or structure type.

```
Public Shared Operator +(ByVal wholeOrder As OrderRecord, _
    ByVal orderDetailItem As DetailRecord) As OrderRecord
    ' ----- Append a new product item onto the order.
    ' ...more code here...
End Operator
```

Table 5-1 describes the operators that can be overloaded.

*Table 5-1. Operators that can be overloaded*

| Operator | Description |
|---|---|
| + | Unary Plus operator. It differs from the binary addition operator in that you supply only one operand in the procedure signature. |
| - | Unary Negation operator. It differs from the binary subtraction operator in that you supply only one operand in the procedure signature. |
| Not | Bitwise Negation operator. For overloading, this is a bitwise operation only, not logical. |
| IsTrue | If you overload the Or operator in a class, overloading the IsTrue operator in the same class opens up the use of the OrElse operator with the class. You must also overload the IsFalse operator. The overload procedure's return type must be Boolean. |
| IsFalse | If you overload the And operator in a class, overloading the IsFalse operator in the same class opens up the use of the AndAlso operator with the class. You must also overload the IsTrue operator. The overload procedure's return type must be Boolean. |
| + | Binary Addition operator. It differs from the unary plus operator in that you supply two operands in the procedure signature. |
| - | Binary Subtraction operator. It differs from the unary negation operator in that you supply two operands in the procedure signature. |
| * | Multiplication operator. |
| / | Division operator. |
| \ | Integer Division operator. |
| Mod | Modulo operator. |
| & | Concatenation operator. |
| ^ | Exponentiation operator. |
| << | Shift Left operator. The second operator must use the Integer data type. |
| >> | Shift Right operator. The second operator must use the Integer data type. |
| = | Equal To comparison operator. You must also overload the <> Not Equal To operator. |
| < | Less Than comparison operator. You must also overload the > Greater Than operator. |
| > | Greater Than comparison operator. You must also overload the < Less Than operator. |
| <= | Less Than or Equal To comparison operator. You must also overload the >= Greater Than or Equal To operator. |
| >= | Greater Than or Equal To comparison operator. You must also overload the <= Less Than or Equal To operator. |
| <> | Not Equal To comparison operator. You must also overload the = Equal To operator. |
| And | Bitwise Conjunction operator. For overloading, this is a bitwise operation only, not logical. |
| Or | Bitwise Disjunction operator. For overloading, this is a bitwise operation only, not logical. |
| Xor | Bitwise Exclusion operator. For overloading, this is a bitwise operation only, not logical. |
| Like | Pattern Comparison operator. |
| CType | Unary Conversion operator. Used to convert data from one data type (or class or structure) to another. You must include either the Narrowing or Widening keyword in the definition of the overload, somewhere between the Shared and Operator keywords. These modifiers tell the compiler what type of conversion is allowed. Narrowing conversions may fail if the destination data type cannot support the value of the source data type. Either the operand or the return type of the overload procedure must be of the class or structure that contains the procedure. |

When you overload operators, you can define them to do whatever you want with the source classes in question. In fact, you could create a class where the normal understandings of addition and subtraction were reversed. However, such practices will make the code more difficult to understand and debug.

For further details about operator overloading, see the "Operator Statement" entry in Chapter 12.

## Operator Precedence

If you include more than one operator in a single line of code, you need to know the order in which VB will evaluate them. Otherwise, the results may be completely different from what you intended. For instance, the following statement:

```
x = 5 + 3 * 7
```

could be interpreted as:

```
x = (5 + 3) * 7 ' --> 56
```

or as:

```
x = 5 + (3 * 7) ' --> 26
```

The rule that defines the order in which a language processes operators is known as the *order of precedence*. If the order of precedence results in operations being evaluated in an order other than the intended one, you can explicitly override the order of precedence through the use of parentheses. Indeed, complex (or even relatively simple) expressions should include parentheses to avoid any compiler misinterpretation or human confusion. (By the way, the example, once parentheses are removed, evaluates to 26.)

When multiple operators appear at the same level of evaluation (that is, they are not subgrouped with parentheses), they are processed in a specific order of precedence. In some instances, multiple operators appear at the same level of precedence (as are * and /). They are treated as equals as far as precedence is concerned. The following list indicates the order of precedence in evaluation, from first to last.

1. Exponentiation (^).
2. Negation (-).
3. Multiplication and division (*, /).
4. Integer division (\).
5. Modulo operator (Mod).
6. Addition/concatenation and subtraction (+, -).
7. String concatenation (&).
8. *New in 2003.* Arithmetic bit shift (<<, >>).
9. Comparison and object operators (=, <>, <, <=, >, >=, Like, Is, IsNot, TypeOf); the = operator in this list is the Equal To comparison operator, not the assignment operator. *New in 2005.* The IsNot operator is new in the 2005 release of VB.
10. Logical and bitwise negation (Not).

11. Logical and bitwise conjunction (`And`, `AndAlso`). *New in 2005.* The `AndAlso` operator is new in the 2005 release of VB.

12. Logical and bitwise disjunction (`Or`, `OrElse`, `Xor`). *New in 2005.* The `OrElse` operator is new in the 2005 release of VB.

Since the `AddressOf` and `GetType` operators are implemented like functions, they fall outside of the order of precedence rules for operators.

If multiple operators of the same order of precedence appear at the same level of evaluation, they are processed from left to right.

# 6

# Program Structure

With its tight integration into the .NET Common Language Runtime, Visual Basic owes much of its present personality to .NET. This tie to the .NET Framework and the object-oriented nature of the language itself work together to influence the structure of VB programs. This chapter discusses aspects of Visual Basic program structure in the .NET environment.

## Visual Studio Application Types

The original version of Visual Basic generated applications that were form-focused and included rich features for interaction with the user and the Windows environment. Later releases added support for DLL generation, specifically ActiveX DLLs. With its integration into .NET, Visual Basic compiler can now generate several specific types of output.

*Windows (Forms) Applications*
> In .NET, Windows applications make heavy use of the *System.Windows. Forms* namespace and the control classes contained within it. Although these applications may look like any other non-.NET Windows application, internally they are quite different and are fully managed by the .NET Common Language Runtime.

*Console Applications*
> Back in the days before Windows and other GUI-based platforms, most applications were *console applications*. These wonders of technology interacted with the user through the medium of the $80 \times 24$ character screen display. Such programs generally displayed text on the screen and then waited for keyboard input from the user before continuing. Some systems were able to make use of simple graphic characters and screen positioning to give some semblance of a graphical user interface, but this was generally done by sending special display codes to the basic text display.

Console applications are often procedural in nature; they start at the beginning of the application and run until the end, uninterrupted by external user events like mouse clicks. In this era of Windows applications, console applications exist to provide some basic textual information to the user or to control some service or process that does not logically have a need for a user interface.

*Windows Services*

Windows services are long-running applications that interact directly with the system but not with the user. In fact, they run only within the context of the Windows Service architecture; you cannot start them directly like an EXE file. Even when they run, they belong to the system (in terms of their security profile), not the local user.

*Class Libraries*

Class libraries are more commonly called *dynamic link libraries*, or DLLs. Although not true standalone applications, most applications would be limited without the plethora of available DLLs; the functionality in the .NET Framework Class Library is made available through DLL files. DLLs are loaded at runtime by the applications that use them, and they run in the program space of the controlling application. A special variation of a class library, the *Web Control Library*, is used for ASP.NET server controls.

# Referencing Components and Classes

Applications you develop in Visual Basic will contain custom classes and other .NET types, defined for the specific needs of the application. But you probably want to take advantage of other code already written, such as the classes in the .NET Framework Class Library. Namespaces and classes that you do not write yourself must be specifically identified before they can be used in your code. This is done in two steps.

1. *Reference the assembly that contains the classes you wish to use.* This is done through the References section of the Project Properties for your application. For instance, to use the Windows Forms features of .NET, your application must include a reference to the *System.Windows.Forms.dll* file, which contains the *System.Windows.Forms* assembly and namespace contents. When you create new projects of a specific type (such as a new "Windows Application" project), the typical assemblies you need for that project type are referenced by default.

2. *Specify the class or feature you want to use with its namespace.* For instance, to use the Form class, you must call it *System.Windows.Forms.Form*. Typing this much text quickly becomes a burden, so .NET allows you provide relative names through the use of the Imports statement. For example, the statement:

```
Imports System.Windows.Forms
```

in a code file allows you to use the *Form* class without its full qualification. You can set up global Imports-like settings through the Project Properties. Visual Studio defines several global Imports-like settings for you based on project type.

# Application Entry Points

Any Visual Basic executable—a Windows Forms or Windows console application—has a single application-level entry point, a subroutine named *Main*. *Main* must be a method within one of the application's classes. It must also be:

*A Public Routine*
> In VB 6, *Main* could be either public or private—or it didn't have to exist at all, when a form was set as the startup object. In .NET, it must be public to be visible as an entry point.

*A Shared (Static) Routine*
> Its declaration must include the Shared keyword; this allows it to be called without the need to create an instance of its class. If *Main* resides in a module, it is automatically shared, even without the Shared keyword.

## Using Main in a Standard Class or Module

The *Main* routine can appear in any class in your application, including a Module (which is just a Shared variation of a class). Consider the simple case of a console application, like the one shown in Example 6-1. The example includes a module named StartsHere, which contains the *Main* routine. At runtime, the Common Language Runtime finds the *Main* procedure, displays a message to the console, and then terminates the program.

*Example 6-1. A simple console application*

```
Option Strict On

Imports System

Public Module StartsHere
    Public Sub Main
        Console.WriteLine("This is a console application.")
    End Sub
End Module
```

Since the example uses a Module instead of a Class, the Shared keyword decoration is not necessary on the *Main* routine. The .NET compiler translates this code into a public class and gives it a single method, *Main*, as shown in the ILDASM tree diagram (see Figure 6-1).

The IL code for *Main* also shows that it is marked as the program's entry point (through the .entrypoint text on the third line), and that it is a static (shared) member rather than an instance member.

```
      .method public static void  Main( ) cil managed
{
  .entrypoint
  .custom instance void
      [mscorlib]System.STAThreadAttribute::.ctor( ) = ( 01 00 00 00 )
  // Code size       11 (0xb)
  .maxstack  8
```

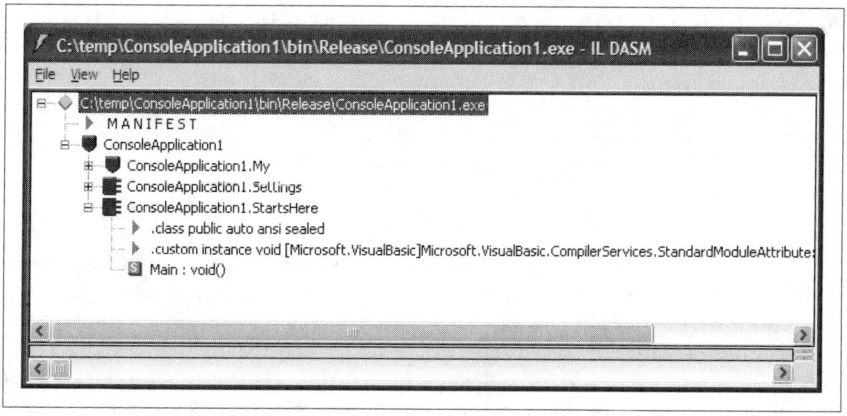

*Figure 6-1. The StartsHere.Main method in ILDASM*

```
IL_0000:  ldstr    "This is a console application."
IL_0005:  call     void [mscorlib]System.Console::WriteLine(string)
IL_000a:  ret
} // end of method StartsHere::Main
```

The Visual Basic compiler and the .NET Common Language Runtime, it would seem, have transformed this simple code module into a self-executing class.

## Using Main in Windows Forms Applications

All forms displayed in Windows Forms applications must be instantiated before use. Visual Basic allows you to specify a Form as the startup object of an application (instead of a standard Class- or Module-based *Main* routine), and you don't have to add the routine yourself. So is it really there? Yes, the framework adds a shared *Main* routine to your class. What does it do? A quick look at the IL gives the answer. (Lines in this presentation have been wrapped for readability.)

```
.method public hidebysig static void  Main( ) cil managed
{
  .entrypoint
  .custom instance void
    [mscorlib]System.STAThreadAttribute::.ctor( ) = ( 01 00 00 00 )
  // Code size       16 (0x10)
  .maxstack  8
  IL_0000:  call     class WindowsApplication1.My.MyProject/
    MyForms WindowsApplication1.My.MyProject::get_Forms( )
  IL_0005:  callvirt instance class WindowsApplication1.Form1
    WindowsApplication1.My.MyProject/MyForms::get_Form1( )
  IL_000a:  call     void
    [System.Windows.Forms]System.Windows.Forms.Application::Run(
    class [System.Windows.Forms]System.Windows.Forms.Form)
  IL_000f:  ret
} // end of method Form1::Main
```

The *Main* routine creates an instance of the form Form1 and then calls the Run method (in the *System.Windows.Forms.Application* class), passing it the instance of the form. This is the normal way to run a Windows Forms application. If you

**Program Structure**

want to create your own *Main* routine in another class that starts a Windows Forms application, it will include this similar basic code.

```
Module StartsHere
   Public Sub Main( )
      Dim startForm As New Form1
      Application.Run(startForm)
   End Sub
End Module
```

*New in 2005.* Visual Basic 2005 includes a new Windows application framework model, a structure that provides events and actions during the startup, running, and shutdown of your application. This feature is enabled or disabled through the Application tab of the Project Properties panel. When this model is enabled, the default *Main* routine resides in a separate special class associated with the application instead of in the default form's class. When creating new Windows Forms applications in Visual Basic 2005, this framework is enabled by default.

# Code File Contents

Visual Basic applications include one or more source code files and possibly some other miscellaneous files (such as ".resx" resource files). These files contain all of the types (classes, structures, enumerations, etc.) of your application. Just as in Visual Basic 6, there is a small declarations section available at the start of each code file, followed by the actual code.

## Declarations Section

The declarations section of a code file includes statements that set up the environment for all the code in that file. This section may include the various Option statements (Option Compare, Option Explicit, Option Strict) and Imports statements that make possible terse class references in the code file. Application-specific and module-specific attributes are defined here as well.

Unlike with VB 6, no global variables, constants, or Declare statements appear in the declarations section.

## Namespaces

All types must appear in namespaces in .NET. By default, all of the code in your application appears in a top-level namespace that has the same name as your project's name. You can override this default in the project property settings or identify a specific namespace for your types by using the Namespace statement. Namespaces can be nested.

```
Namespace Level1
   Namespace Level2
      ' ---- Perhaps put some code here.
   End Namespace
   ' ----- Or even here.
End Namespace
```

All namespaces are public.

*New in 2005.* The new Global keyword provides a way to resolve conflicts in namespace usage. For instance, if your application included a namespace named *MyCompany.System*, and you used the Imports MyCompany statement in your code file, would a reference to "System" mean the .NET-supplied *System* namespace or the *MyCompany.System* namespace? The Global keyword solves the problem. To access the .NET-supplied *System* namespace, reference Global.System, which removes any ambiguity.

## Types

Most of your application is defined through types: the classes, structures, enumerations, interfaces, and so on, of your application. Many types can be nested.

```
Public Class ClassDepth1
    Public Class ClassDepth2
        ' ----- Add code here.
    End Class
    ' ----- And here, too.
End Class
```

Types contain members, mainly the methods, properties, events, and fields of your classes and structures. Members cannot be nested, although members with the same name may appear within different nested types. For instance, if Class A contains Class B, both A and B may include a procedure named ProcessData without conflict.

# The Structure of a Visual Basic Program

Broadly speaking, programs can be either *procedure-driven* or *event-driven*. In a procedure-driven program, program flow is predefined. A classic example is a console application: program flow begins at the program entry point (the *Main* routine) and proceeds along a predictable path until it reaches program termination. But in an event-driven program, program flow is not predetermined and is instead controlled by external events—events initiated by both the user and the system—and possibly by internal code-specified events.

Both types of applications include a starting entry point (the *Main* routine), which can call other functions and subroutines according to the logic needed in the application. Procedure-driven applications are limited to this single entry point. But event-driven applications include many entry points throughout their lifetime (beyond the initial *Main* entry point). These entry points are *event handlers*, which are invoked automatically by the .NET Common Language Runtime in response to user, system, or internal application actions.

The different procedures in your application can be grouped into three broad categories.

*Entry Point Code*
> This procedure type includes the primary entry point (the *Main* routine), as well as all event handlers needed to support the various events for which your application needs to act.

*Custom Procedures*
In these procedures, you often create the main functionality of your application. These procedures are called *methods* within your classes and modules.

*Property Procedures*
These procedures are generally used to get and set the internal values managed by a class.

# Events: The Starting Point

Events can be system generated (such as with *Timer* control events that trigger actions at a specific time or interval) or user generated (as through a mouse click on a command button). You can also include code that forces an event to fire as needed. For instance, a stock monitoring application might generate a *Positive* event when a stock's value goes up and a *Negative* event when its value decreases.

 For a discussion of events and the way in which procedures can be defined to handle events, see Chapter 8.

### Windows Forms events

Windows Forms classes include many special events that fire during the creation and destruction of a form instance. These events appear in the following order:

New Constructor
Load Event
Activated Event
Shown Event (*New in 2005*)
Closing Event
FormClosing Event (*New in 2005*)
Closed Event
FormClosed Event (*New in 2005*)
Deactivate Event

Other form-specific events occur while the form is active on the display. Individual controls also expose events.

### ASP.NET events

ASP.NET exposes a more complex event model, in which events can be trapped at the application, session, and page level. Table 6-1 illustrates the sequence of application, session, and page events for an ASP.NET application.

*Table 6-1. ASP.NET events*

| Event | Type | Description |
|---|---|---|
| Start | Application | Fired when the application starts. The event handler must reside in *global.asax*. |
| Start | Session | Fired when a user session is created. The event handler must reside in *global.asax*. |
| Init | Page | Fired when the page is initialized. |

*Table 6-1. ASP.NET events  (continued)*

| Event | Type | Description |
|-------|------|-------------|
| Load | Page | Fired when the page is loaded. |
| PreRender | Page | Fired when the page is about to be rendered. |
| Unload | Page | Fired when the page is unloaded. |
| Disposed | Page | Fired when the page is released from memory. |
| End | Session | Fired when a user session ends or times out. The event handler must reside in *global.asax*. |
| End | Application | Fired when an application ends. The event handler must reside in *global.asax*. |

Individual controls also expose events.

### Event arguments

When an event is fired, the CLR passes two arguments to the event handler:

*sender*
> An object of type *System.Object* (or some more specific type) that represents the instance of the class raising the event

*e*
> An object of type *System.EventArgs*, or of a type derived from *System.EventArgs*, that contains information about the event

Example 6-2 shows an event handler for a command button's *Click* event in a Windows Forms application.

*Example 6-2. A command button's event handler*

```
Option Strict On

Imports Microsoft.VisualBasic
Imports System
Imports System.Drawing
Imports System.Windows.Forms

Public Class JustAButton
    Inherits System.Windows.Forms.Form

    Friend WithEvents ActionButton As Button

    Private Sub New( )
        ' ----- Form constructor; add the child controls.
        Dim x As Integer
        Dim y As Integer

        ' ----- Configure the button control.
        ActionButton = New Button
        x = CInt(Me.Width/2 - ActionButton.Width / 2)
        y = CInt(Me.Height/2 - ActionButton.Height / 2)
```

*Example 6-2. A command button's event handler (continued)*

```
        Me.ActionButton.Location = New System.Drawing.Point(x, y)
        Me.ActionButton.Text = "Event Information"

        Me.Controls.Add(ActionButton)
    End Sub

    Public Shared Sub Main
        ' ----- The application starts here.
        Application.Run(New JustAButton)
    End Sub

    Private Sub ActionButton_Click(sender As Object, e As EventArgs) _
        Handles ActionButton.Click
        ' ----- This is the button's Click event handler.
        MsgBox(sender.GetType.ToString & vbCrLf & _
            e.GetType.ToString)
    End Sub
End Class
```

When the event is fired, the dialog box shown in Figure 6-2 appears.

*Figure 6-2. A dialog box displaying event information*

The *EventArgs* class itself has no useful members; all of its members are inherited from the *System.Object* class. Most event handlers are passed an instance of the *EventArgs* class, although events with additional useful information to convey will pass an object derived from *EventArgs*, with the extra informational members added. For example, the *Button* and *ImageButton* controls in the *System.Web.UI. WebControls* namespace raise a *Command* event that is fired when the control is clicked. Instead of an instance of the *EventArgs* class, the CLR passes the event handler an instance of the *CommandEventArgs* class. It has the following properties:

*CommandName Property*
> The name of the command to be executed. It corresponds to the *Button* or *ImageButton* control's *CommandName* property.

*CommandArgument Property*
> Any optional arguments passed along with the command.

In some cases, an event's default action can be cancelled. For instance, the *CancelEventArgs* class (derived from *EventArgs*) has a *Cancel* property that, when set to True, cancels the pending action related to the event.

## Calling Routines from Event Handlers

Once processing has been directed to one of your event handlers, it's time to do some work. Of course, you can write every bit of processing code right there in the event-handling routine, but for readability, a divide-and-conquer approach often works better. An event handler can call methods, functions, and procedures, and can set and retrieve property values, all from classes in your own application or from the .NET Framework Class Library. In Example 6-3, the SaveAllData command button's *Click* event demonstrates this approach to event handling by calling SaveDetails, a method in some other part of the code, to do most of the work.

*Example 6-3. Calling an external routine from an event handler*

```
Private Sub SaveAllData_Click(sender As Object, e As EventArgs) _
      Handles SaveAllData.Click
   If SaveDetails() Then
      MsgBox("Data recorded successfully.", vbInformation)
   Else
      MsgBox("Error occurred while saving data.", vbCritical)
   End If
End Sub
```

The SaveDetails method contains all the code to actually save the details, and it can be called from anywhere in the class (or from other classes, if it is public). Placing code in custom procedures not only improves readability of the code, it centralizes the work, making it possible to use the same collection of source code statements from multiple places in your application.

## Writing Custom Procedures

Custom procedures can be added to any class, structure, or module in your application. Visual Basic includes three main types of custom procedures or routines: Functions, Sub procedures, and Properties.

### Functions

A *function* is a collection of related statements and expressions used to perform a particular task. When it completes execution, the function returns a value to the calling routine. If you don't specify an explicit return value for the function, the default value of the return data type is used. If you write a custom function in a class module and declare it as Public, it becomes a class method.

Consider the following simple function, which returns a String data value.

```
Public Function PrepareForSQL(ByVal origText As String) As String
   ' ----- Prepare a string for use in a SQL statement. Any
   '       single quotes must be doubled-up.
   If (Len(origText) = 0) Then
      Return "NULL"
   Else
      Return "'" & Replace(origText, "'", "''") & "'"
   End If
End Function
```

Because functions return values, you can use them as part of an expression in place of a variable or literal value. The following statement includes a custom function as an argument to the VB InStr function.

```
If (InStr(GetCustomerStatusCodes(customerID), "P") > 0) Then
```

This statement is equivalent to this more verbose variation:

```
Dim statusCodes As String
statusCodes = GetCustomerStatusCodes(customerID)
If (InStr(statusCodes, "P") > 0) Then
```

Functions include zero or more arguments, values or references that are passed to the function call for use in that function. For instance, the statement:

```
statusCodes = GetCustomerStatusCodes(customerID)
```

passes the variable customerID to the function. Each argument is of a certain data type, as defined in the parameter list of the function's definition.

```
Public Function GetCustomerStatusCodes( _
    ByVal customerID As Long) As String
```

For full details on the syntax and use of functions, see the entry for the "Function Statement" in Chapter 12.

## Sub procedures

A *Sub procedure* is used just like a function, except it does not return a value. Event handlers are, by definition, Sub procedures, since they do not return values. As with functions, if you write a custom Sub procedure in a class module and declare it as Public, it becomes a class method.

For full details of the syntax and use of Sub procedures, see the entry for the "Sub Statement" in Chapter 12.

## Properties

*Properties* are specialized procedures used to assign and retrieve custom property values. When accessed through code, they look like public variables or constants of a class (fields), but they include logic in their data setting and retrieval code. Properties have two parts.

*Property Accessor*
    Retrieves the value of a property, returning it to the caller. The accessor is defined through the property's Get component.

*Property Mutator*
    Assigns a value to or modifies a property's value. The mutator is defined through the property's Set component.

Properties can be defined as ReadOnly or WriteOnly; when defined with one of these restrictions, the applicable component (Get or Set) is left out of the property definition.

Example 6-4 defines a simple class with a single property.

*Example 6-4. A property*

```
Public Class Person
   Private theName As String

   Public Property Name( ) As String
      Get
         ' ----- Property accessor.
         Return theName
      End Get
      Set(ByVal value As String)
         ' ----- Property mutator.
         If (Trim(value) <> "") Then
            theName = value
         Else
            Throw New System.ArgumentException( _
               "Missing name value.", "Name")
         End If
      End Set
   End Property
End Class
```

While the Name member of the Person class could have just been a public variable for simplicity, using a property made it possible to check for invalid use (an empty name value, in this case).

Internally, properties are implemented as methods. Visual Basic implements each property accessor as a get_*propertyname* method, while each mutator is implemented as a set_*propertyname* method.

*New in 2005.* Normally, the Get and Set components of the Property statement share the same level of accessibility (that is, they both are Public, Friend, or Private). Visual Basic 2005 allows you to specify different access levels for the Get and Set components.

For full details of the syntax and use of Properties, see the entry for the *Property Statement* in Chapter 12.

# 7

# The .NET Framework
# Class Library

With its move to .NET, Visual Basic is now about classes, classes, and more classes. Even something as simple as an Integer is implemented in a class (the *System.Int32* class). As mentioned in Chapter 2, the .NET Framework defines an extensive network of classes and namespaces called the *Framework Class Library* (FCL). This library provides basic application development services, such as core data types, exception handling, and garbage collection, and support for higher-level functionality, such as database interaction, a forms and control package, and a web-based programming system. In total, there are about 200 namespaces containing several thousand classes, interfaces, structures, enumerations, and other items in the .NET Framework Class Library.

The term *Base Class Library* (BCL) refers to an important subset of the larger Framework Class Library. Because most programmers use the whole library without thinking much about whether they are using FCL or BCL, the terms are used interchangeably. You will find the terms sometimes used interchangeably even in this book.

The *System* namespace is at the top of the namespace hierarchy for most namespaces supplied with the .NET Framework, and the *System.Object* class is at the top of the object hierarchy. All types in the .NET Framework Class Library, no matter where they reside in the namespace hierarchy, derive from the *System. Object* class.

The .NET Framework Class Library is sufficiently extensive to require an entire book for itself. This chapter provides just a brief introduction and some examples. This should prepare you to dive into the Class Library documentation supplied with Visual Studio or available through Microsoft's MSDN web site (*http://msdn.microsoft.com*). In parallel with this chapter, you will find documentation for select library elements in Chapter 12, particularly those most useful to VB programmers.

Before becoming intimidated by the size of the Framework Class Library, keep in mind that VB provides wrappers for some elements of the FCL, so we can often just call a VB function rather than resort to accessing the classes in the larger library directly. More generally, while the class library does have much to offer a VB programmer and should not be ignored, it can be studied and used on an "as needed" basis.

*New in 2005.* Beginning with the 2005 release of Visual Basic, a larger number of library features are brought into easier use through the new *My* Namespace feature. This feature takes commonly used FCL activities and wraps them into a smaller, neatly organized hierarchy of tools. For full information on this new feature, see Chapter 13.

Here is a simple example of what the FCL has to offer beyond the basic Visual Basic language syntax. As discussed in Chapter 4, the built-in VB data types are wrappers for corresponding BCL data classes (for reference types) or structures (for value types). This means that your code has access to any special features included with each data type. If we want to verify that a user has entered an integer that lies within the valid range of the Integer data type, we can use code such as the following:

```
Dim userEntry As String
Dim entryValue As Integer
userEntry = InputBox("Enter an integer.")
If IsNumeric(userEntry) Then
    If (CDbl(userEntry) >= entryValue.MinValue) And _
        (CDbl(userEntry) <= entryValue.MaxValue) Then
        entryValue = CInt(userEntry)
    Else
        Debug.WriteLine("Invalid number.")
    End If
Else
    Debug.WriteLine("Non-numeric value.")
End If
```

Visual Basic does not include features that indicate the lower and upper bounds of the Integer data type, but .NET's *Int32* data type does. And since VB's Integer data type is simply a wrapper for the *Int32* data type, VB gets all of its functionality for free, including the *MinValue* and *MaxValue* members. Incidentally, because *MinValue* and *MaxValue* are shared class members, the conditions in the sample code could also have been written as:

```
If IsNumeric(userEntry) Then
    If (CDbl(userEntry) >= Integer.MinValue) And _
        (CDbl(userEntry) <= Integer.MaxValue) Then
```

# The System Namespace

The *System* namespace contains classes for such wide-ranging features as:

- Data types
- Data-type conversions
- Events and event handlers

- Mathematics
- Program invocation
- Application-environment management

It is also the root for almost every other significant Microsoft-supplied .NET class and namespace.

## The System.Convert Class

The *System* namespace defines a class called *Convert*, which implements various data conversion methods. One such method is *ToBoolean*, which includes the following usage variations:

```
Overloads Public Shared Function ToBoolean(Boolean) As Boolean
Overloads Public Shared Function ToBoolean(Byte) As Boolean
Overloads Public Shared Function ToBoolean(Char) As Boolean
Overloads Public Shared Function ToBoolean(DateTime) As Boolean
Overloads Public Shared Function ToBoolean(Decimal) As Boolean
Overloads Public Shared Function ToBoolean(Double) As Boolean
Overloads Public Shared Function ToBoolean(Integer) As Boolean
Overloads Public Shared Function ToBoolean(Long) As Boolean
Overloads Public Shared Function ToBoolean(Object) As Boolean
Overloads Public Shared Function ToBoolean(SByte) As Boolean
Overloads Public Shared Function ToBoolean(Short) As Boolean
Overloads Public Shared Function ToBoolean(Single) As Boolean
Overloads Public Shared Function ToBoolean(String) As Boolean
Overloads Public Shared Function ToBoolean(UInt16) As Boolean
Overloads Public Shared Function ToBoolean(UInt32) As Boolean
Overloads Public Shared Function ToBoolean(UInt64) As Boolean
```

As you can see, there are many *ToBoolean* functions—each one overloaded with a different argument signature—to take care of converting various data types to a Boolean.

Now, just for exercise, consider this block of code:

```
Dim textVersion As String
Dim trueVersion As Boolean
textVersion = "false"
trueVersion = System.Convert.ToBoolean(textVersion)
MsgBox(trueVersion)    ' Displays "False"
```

Because the *System* namespace is always available (or if we are programming outside of Visual Studio, we can import it using the Imports statement), we can omit the *System* qualifier and write:

```
trueVersion = Convert.ToBoolean(textVersion)
```

The built-in VB function *CBool* also performs this conversion.

The *Convert* class contains methods for converting data to the standard Visual Basic data types, as well as to other data types supported by the .NET Framework but not wrapped by Visual Basic. (*New in 2005.* Beginning in the 2005 release, Visual Basic now includes native implementations of all core .NET data types.) The most important of these methods are shown in Table 7-1.

*Table 7-1. Members of the System.Convert class*

| Method | VB equivalent | Description |
|---|---|---|
| ToBoolean | CBool | Converts a value to Boolean |
| ToByte | CByte | Converts a value to an unsigned 8-bit integer Byte |
| ToChar | CChar | Converts a value to a single character Char |
| ToDateTime | CDate | Converts a value to date or time value *DateTime* (Date in Visual Basic) |
| ToDecimal | CDec | Converts a value to a floating point Decimal |
| ToDouble | CDbl | Converts a value to a floating point Double |
| ToInt16 | CShort | Converts a value to a signed 16-bit integer *Int16* (Short in Visual Basic) |
| ToInt32 | CInt | Converts a value to a signed 32-bit integer *Int32* (Integer in Visual Basic) |
| ToInt64 | CLng | Converts a value to a signed 64-bit integer *Int64* (Long in Visual Basic) |
| ToSByte | *New in 2005*: CSByte | Converts a value to a signed 8-bit integer *SByte* (*New in 2005*: SByte in Visual Basic) |
| ToSingle | CSng | Converts a value to a floating point Single |
| ToString | CStr | Converts a value to a character String |
| ToUInt16 | *New in 2005*: CUShort | Converts a value to an unsigned 16-bit integer *UInt16* (*New in 2005*: UShort in Visual Basic) |
| ToUInt32 | *New in 2005*: CUInt | Converts a value to an unsigned 32-bit integer *UInt32* (*New in 2005*: UInteger in Visual Basic) |
| ToUInt64 | *New in 2005*: CULng | Converts a value to an unsigned 64-bit integer *UInt64* (*New in 2005*: ULong in Visual Basic) |

## The System.Array Class

The *System.Array* class contains useful methods for dealing with arrays. For instance, it has a *Sort* method that sorts the elements of an array. The following block of code uses *Array.Sort* to order a list of Integer values.

```
Public Sub SortArray()
    ' ----- Simple array sorting example.
    Dim counter As Integer
    Dim dataToFix() As Integer = {9, 8, 12, 4, 5}

    ' ----- First, show the world the mixed-up mess.
    Console.WriteLine("Unsorted:")
    For counter = 0 To 4
        Console.WriteLine(CStr(dataToFix(counter)))
    Next counter

    ' ----- Yeah! I don't have to Bubble sort by myself.
    Array.Sort(dataToFix)

    ' ----- Display the correct results.
    Console.WriteLine("Sorted:")
    For counter = 0 To 4
        Console.WriteLine(dataToFix(counter))
```

```
        Next counter
    End Sub
```

The output is:

```
Unsorted:
9
8
12
4
5
Sorted:
4
5
8
9
12
```

Some of the more important methods of the *Array* class are shown in Table 7-2.

*Table 7-2. Some members of the System.Array class*

| Method | Description |
| --- | --- |
| BinarySearch | Searches a sorted one-dimensional array for a value |
| IndexOf | Returns the location of the first occurrence of a particular value in a one-dimensional array |
| LastIndexOf | Returns the location of the last occurrence of a particular value in a one-dimensional array |
| Reverse | Reverses the order of the elements in a one-dimensional array or a portion of a one-dimensional array |
| Sort | Sorts a one-dimensional array |

*New in 2005.* Beginning with the 2.0 release of the .NET Framework, *System.Array* now includes features that support the new generics functionality, including a wrapper for read-only, type-specific arrays. For information on using generics, see Chapter 10.

## The System.Math Class

The *System.Math* class includes a number of mathematical methods (such as trigonometric functions), as well as some more useful general numeric methods, such as *Max* and *Min*. For instance, to determine the maximum of two values, use:

```
MsgBox("The maximum of 4 and 7 is " & Math.Max(4, 7))
```

Table 7-3 shows the members of the *Math* class.

*Table 7-3. The members of the System.Math class*

| Topic | Description |
| --- | --- |
| Abs Method | Absolute value |
| Acos Method | Arccosine |
| Asin Method | Arcsine |
| Atan Method | Arctangent; returns the angle with the tangent that is a specified number |

*Table 7-3. The members of the System.Math class (continued)*

| Topic | Description |
|---|---|
| Atan2 Method | Arctangent; returns the angle with the tangent that is the quotient of two specified numbers |
| BigMul Method | Multiplies two large 32-bit integers, returning a 64-bit integer |
| Ceiling Method | Returns the smallest integer greater than or equal to the argument |
| Cos Method | Cosine |
| Cosh Method | Hyperbolic cosine |
| DivRem Method | Returns the modulus, that is, the remainder of a division operation |
| E Field | The natural number $e$ |
| Exp Method | The natural number $e$ raised to a power |
| Floor Method | Returns the largest integer less than or equal to the argument |
| IEEERemainder Method | Returns the remainder of a division operation using an IEEE-defined standard function |
| Log Method | Natural (base $e$) logarithm |
| Log10 Method | Common (base 10) logarithm |
| Max Method | Maximum of two values |
| Min Method | Minimum of two values |
| Pi Field | $\pi$, the ratio of the circumference of a circle to its diameter |
| Pow Method | Exponentiation function |
| Round Method | Rounds a given number to a specified number of decimal places |
| Sign Method | Determines the sign of a number |
| Sin Method | Sine |
| Sinh Method | Hyperbolic sine |
| Sqrt Method | Square root of a value |
| Tan Method | Tangent |
| Tanh Method | Hyperbolic tangent |
| Truncate Method | Returns the integral portion of a number |

## The System.String Class

The *System.String* class implements a set of string manipulation features, including methods for substring isolation, concatenation, replacement, padding, trimming, and so on.

The VB *String* data type is equivalent to the *System.String* class, so the methods of *System.String* apply directly to VB strings, as with the *Insert* method:

```
Dim famousQuote As String = "To be to be"
MsgBox(famousQuote.Insert(6, "or not "))
```

This displays the message, "To be or not to be."

In .NET, strings are immutable. That is, they cannot be modified once they are created. All methods of the *String* class that make changes to strings actually create a new instance of a string that contains the changes.

Table 7-4 shows some significant members of the *System.String* class.

*Table 7-4. Some members of the System.String class*

| Member | Description |
| --- | --- |
| Chars Property | Returns the character at a specific position |
| Compare Method | Compares two string objects |
| CompareTo Method | Compares a string with a designated object |
| Concat Method | Concatenates one or more strings |
| Contains Method | Indicates whether a string contains a certain substring |
| Copy Method | Creates a new copy of an existing string |
| CopyTo Method | Copies characters from a string into a character array |
| Empty Field | A read-only field that represents an empty string |
| EndsWith Method | Indicates whether the end of a string matches a specified string |
| Equals Method | Determines whether a string is equal to another string |
| Format Method | Returns a new string built from a patterned format of one or more data objects |
| IndexOf Method | Returns the position of the first occurrence of a substring within a string |
| IndexOfAny Method | Returns the position within a string of the first occurrence of any character from a given set of characters |
| Insert Method | Inserts a substring into a string |
| Join Method | Concatenates each element of a string array with a specific delimiter between each original string, and returns a new string with the result |
| LastIndexOf Method | Returns the position of the last occurrence of a substring within a string |
| LastIndexOfAny Method | Returns the position within a string of the last occurrence of any character from a given set of characters |
| Length Property | Returns the number of characters in a string |
| PadLeft Method | Right-aligns the characters in a string |
| PadRight Method | Left-aligns the characters in a string |
| Remove Method | Deletes a specified number of characters from a string starting at a specific position |
| Replace Method | Replaces all occurrences of a substring in a string with another substring |
| Split Method | Splits a delimited string into an array of strings |
| StartsWith Method | Indicates whether the beginning of a string matches a particular substring |
| Substring Method | Extracts a substring from a string by position |
| ToCharArray Method | Copies the characters of a string to a character array |
| ToLower Method | Converts a string to lowercase |
| ToUpper Method | Converts a string to uppercase |
| Trim Method | Removes all occurrences of a set of characters (usually whitespace characters) from the beginning and end of a string |
| TrimEnd Method | Removes all occurrences of a set of characters (usually whitespace characters) from the end of a string |
| TrimStart Method | Removes all occurrences of a set of characters (usually whitespace characters) from the beginning of a string |

# The System.Collections Namespace

The *System.Collections* namespace contains classes that implement a variety of collection types, including stacks and queues. A queue is a first-in, first-out data structure. The following code illustrates its use in Visual Basic:

```
Dim textContent As String
Dim wordQueue As New Collections.Queue( )

wordQueue.Enqueue("First")
wordQueue.Enqueue("in")
wordQueue.Enqueue("first")
wordQueue.Enqueue("out")

Do While (wordQueue.Count > 0)
    textContent &= " " & CStr(wordQueue.Dequeue)
Loop
MsgBox(textContent)
```

The output is "First in first out."

The *System.Collections.Stack* class implements a first-in, last-out stack structure, using the standard methods *Push* and *Pop*. See the *Stack Class* entry in Chapter 12 for information on its use.

*New in 2005.* The 2005 release of Visual Basic includes a new generics feature. The collection classes within the *System.Collections* namespace are perfectly suited for use with generics. See Chapter 10 for details on using collections with generics.

# The System.Data Namespace

*System.Data* and its nested namespaces, notably *System.Data.OleDb*, *System. Data.SqlClient*, and *System.Data.OracleClient*, implement the primary database interaction feature of the .NET Framework, ADO.NET. The *OleDb*, *SqlClient*, and *OracleClient* namespaces define data providers that connect to a data source, retrieve data from a data source, write data back to a data source, and execute commands against the data source. The most important class in each of these namespaces is the data adapter class (in the *OleDb* namespace, it's the *OleDbData-Adapter* class; in the *SqlClient* namespace, it's the *SqlDataAdapter* class; *OracleDataAdapter* is its name in the *OracleClient* namespace), which is used to retrieve data from a data source and write it to a dataset. Datasets in ADO.NET include tables, fields, and their interrelations. They are never directly connected to the original data source; datasets are *disconnected*. Any data added to them from a database comes through the connected data adapter.

 ADO.NET is not the same thing as ADO, nor is ADO.NET a new version of ADO. ADO (or ActiveX Data Objects) is a COM-based object model for data access. ADO.NET is an entirely new model for data access that is based on disconnected datasets.

A typical ADO.NET activity involves the retrieval of data from a database, storing the returned records in a dataset. The following function returns a dataset with a single named data table object, based on the records returned from a SQL statement. This example uses the OleDB-focused classes, although the SQL Server or Oracle classes would work the same way.

```
Public Function CreateDataSet(ByVal sqlText As String, _
    ByVal tableName As String) As Data.DataSet
    ' ----- Create a data set/data table from a SQL statement.
    '       The sqlText argument is the actual SQL statement
    '       used to retrieve the records. The tableName argument
    '       gives a meaningful name to the new data set, since
    '       the data set will not extract it from the SQL code.
    Dim dbCommand As OleDb.OleDbCommand
    Dim dbAdaptor As OleDb.OleDbDataAdapter
    Dim dbNewSet As Data.DataSet

    dbCommand = New OleDb.OleDbCommand(sqlText, DBLibrary)
    dbAdaptor = New OleDb.OleDbDataAdapter(dbCommand)
    dbNewSet = New DataSet
    dbAdaptor.Fill(dbNewSet, tableName)
    dbAdaptor = Nothing
    dbCommand = Nothing
    Return dbNewSet
End Function
```

ADO.NET is a robust and feature-rich set of database interfaces. Due to its size and vast number of options, a full discussion is beyond the scope of this book. For a complete treatment, see Bill Hamilton and Matthew MacDonald's book, *ADO. NET in a Nutshell* (O'Reilly Media).

# The System.IO Namespace

The classes in the *System.IO* namespace provide a variety of input/output functionality, such as:

- Manipulating directories (*Directory* class) and files (*File* class)
- Monitoring changes in directories and files (*FileSystemWatcher* class)
- Reading and writing single bytes, multibyte blocks, or characters to and from streams
- Reading and writing characters to and from strings (*StringReader* and *StringWriter*)
- Reading and writing data types and objects to and from streams (*BinaryWriter* and *BinaryReader*)
- Providing random access to files (*FileStream*)

The *System.IO* namespace replaces the functionality found in the COM-based *FileSystemObject* component, a tool commonly used in VBA-based scripting (and part of the Microsoft Scripting Runtime). Chapter 12 includes entries related to the *File* and *Directory* classes of the *System.IO* namespace.

*New in 2005.* With the addition of the *My* Namespace feature, Visual Basic programmers have one more convenient place to accomplish file system-specific tasks. The *My.Computer.FileSystem* object includes many of the most commonly used file system features. See the *FileSystem Object* entry in Chapter 13 for additional usage information.

# The System.Text.RegularExpressions Namespace

The *System.Text.RegularExpressions* namespace contains classes that provide access to the .NET Framework's regular expression engine.

In its simplest form, a regular expression is a text string representing a *pattern* that other strings may or may not match. In more complicated forms, a regular expression is a kind of programming statement. For instance, the expression:

```
s/ab*c/def
```

says to match the given string against the regular expression ab*c (strings that start with ab and end with c). If a match exists, then replace the given string with the string def. Here are some simple regular expressions for pattern matching:

*Single character*
    This is matched only by itself. For example, the letter 'q' matches itself.

*Dot (.)*
    This is matched by any character except the newline character.

*Selection from Character Set*
    A string of characters in square brackets matches any single character from the string of characters. For example, [abc] matches the *single* character a, b, or c. A dash can also be used in the character list; [0-9] matches any single digit. The text [0-9a-z] matches any single digit or any single lowercase character, and [a-zA-Z] matches any single lower-case or uppercase character.

    The ^ symbol negates the match when it appears immediately inside the square brackets. For instance, [^0-9] matches any character *except* a digit.

*Special Match Abbreviations*
    \d matches any single digit; \D matches any single non-digit.

    \w is equivalent to [a-zA-Z_], thus matching any letter or underscore; \W is the negation of \w.

*Asterisk (*)*
    The asterisk matches zero or more repeated instances of the single character preceding the asterisk. For instance, the regular expression \da*\d matches any string beginning with a single digit, continuing with zero or more as and ending with a single digit, as with 01 or 0aaa1.

*Plus Sign (+)*
    The plus sign matches one or more repeated instances of the single character preceding the plus sign. It is similar to the asterisk character, but it requires at least one matching character. For example, the regular expression \da+\d matches any string beginning with a single digit, continuing with one or more as and ending with a single digit, as with 0a1 or 0aaa1, but not 01.

*Question Mark (?)*
    The question mark matches exactly zero or one instances of the single character preceding the question mark. For example, the regular expression \da?\d is matched by any string beginning with a single digit, continuing with zero or one as and ending with a single digit, as with 01 and 0a1.

*General Multiplier*
A set of curly braces with two comma-delimited integer values indicates a repeated match a specific number of times. The format is {x,y}, where x and y are nonnegative integers, and matches if and only if there are at least x but at most y instances of the single character preceding the opening bracket. For example, the regular expression \da{5,10}\d matches any string beginning with a single digit, continuing with at least 5 but at most 10 as and ending with a single digit, as with 0aaaaaa1.

You can leave out one of x or y. Thus, {x,} means "at least x," and {,y} means "at most y."

*Escaped Characters*
Several characters have special meaning within regular expression patterns, such as [ and ?. These characters must be escaped with the backslash character (\) before they can be matched as ordinary non-special characters. For instance, \[ matches an opening bracket, \? matches a question mark, and \\ matches a backslash.

The *System.Text.RegularExpressions* namespace has a *Regex* class, which has objects that represent regular expressions. Here's a simple example of using the *Regex* class.

```
Dim matchPattern As New System.Text.RegularExpressions.Regex( _
    "\da{3,5}\d")
MsgBox(matchPattern.IsMatch("0a1"))      ' Displays False
MsgBox(matchPattern.IsMatch("0aaa1"))    ' Displays True
```

# The System.Windows.Forms Namespace

The *System.Windows.Forms* namespace is the starting point for creating Windows desktop applications. It includes all of the classes that define forms, controls, form-based menus, message boxes, and so on. New forms added to your VB desktop application project are tried directly to the *Form* class from this namespace.

```
Inherits System.Windows.Forms.Form
```

When you drag and drop a *TextBox* control on the form, Visual Studio writes code on your behalf using the classes of the *Windows.Forms* namespace. This code is hidden from view by default, and it is messy when made visible. Fortunately, with Visual Studio doing much of the detail programming for you, Windows Forms application development turns out to be pretty straightforward.

# Other Namespaces

A number of useful second-level namespaces appear nested just below the *System* namespace.

*System.CodeDOM*
Contains classes representing the elements and structure of a source code document.

*System.ComponentModel*
Implement the runtime and design-time behavior of components and controls.

*System.Configuration*
Supports the creation of custom installers for software components.

*System.Data*
Consists mostly of the classes that constitute the ADO.NET architecture, used for database connectivity.

*System.Diagnostics*
Supports the debugging and tracing of applications.

*System.DirectoryServices*
Provides access to Active Directory from managed code.

*System.Drawing*
Provides access to the GDI+ basic graphics functionality. More advanced functionality is provided in the *System.Drawing.Drawing2D*, *System. Drawing.Imaging*, and *System.Drawing.Text* namespaces.

*System.Net*
Provides a simple programming interface to many of the common network protocols, such as FTP and HTTP. The *System.Net.Sockets* namespace provides lower-level network access control.

*System.Reflection*
Contains classes and interfaces that provide a managed view of loaded types, methods, and fields, with the ability to create and invoke types dynamically.

*System.Resources*
Manages generic or culture-specific resources and resource files.

*System.Security*
Provides access to the underlying structure of the .NET Framework security system.

*System.ServiceProcess*
Supports the installation and running of Windows services. Services are long-running executables with no user interface.

*System.Text*
Contains classes representing ASCII, Unicode, UTF-7, and UTF-8 character encodings, as well as abstract base classes for converting blocks of characters to and from blocks of bytes, and more.

*System.Threading*
Provides classes and interfaces that enable multithreaded programming.

*System.Timers*
Provides the Timer component, which allows you to raise an event at a specific interval.

*System.Web and Related Namespaces*
Contains classes and interfaces that enable browser/server communication and allow you to develop ASP.NET applications and web services.

*System.Xml*
Provides standards-based support for processing XML content.

# 8

# Delegates and Events

Because Visual Basic is built on the foundation of the .NET Framework, it is object-oriented. But because it is designed for use in the Microsoft Windows environment, it is also *event-driven*. In standard procedural languages, all statements encountered in the program are processed from beginning to end. The program begins at the start of the *main* routine (or its equivalent) and continues to the end, sometimes taking detours into other routines, but always as dictated by the organization of *main*.

In event-driven programs, a procedure can be called that has no direct or indirect relation to the *main* routine. In fact, very little code within a typical event-driven application is called from *main* or any of its descendants. Most code is called by *events*, user- and system-initiated actions that seek some outlet in your application's code. Events are the natural programming style of any system with multiple user input possibilities (keyboard, mouse, touch screen, the user pressing the system's power button, etc.).

Perhaps you have a program that simulates a cat. Of course you will include a Meow procedure that emits the language of the cat.

```
Public Sub Meow( )
```

Your cat program will need to respond to external stimuli, just like a real cat. This requires events. One such event might be the SteppedOnTail event that, when triggered, calls the Meow method. Other events, such as SeeDog and CraveMilk, might also call the Meow method.

In .NET, any class can respond to a set of events specifically designed for use in that class (or a family of inherited classes). When events are triggered, they call special event-handling routines through a system of *delegates*. Although you will usually implement a single event handler (defined below) for each event of interest, events and event handlers can also exist in many-to-many relationships. One event, when triggered, can call multiple event handlers, and a single event handler can be used for multiple events.

# Delegates

An event needs some way to locate the event handler that will act when the event occurs. In some languages, the location of the handler is identified by its memory address, which is stored in a variable called a *function pointer*. In .NET, the location is stored instead as a *delegate*.

In pre-.NET application development, function pointers allowed you to call a function generically when you didn't know in advance which function you were going to call. For instance, the Windows API includes a function called *EnumFontFamiliesEx* that provides a listing of all installed fonts.

```
Public Declare Function EnumFontFamiliesEx Lib "gdi32" _
    Alias "EnumFontFamiliesExA" ( _
    ByVal hdc As Long, _
    lpLogFont As LOGFONT, _
    ByVal lpEnumFontProc As Long, _
    ByVal lParam As Long, _
    ByVal dw As Long) _
    As Long
```

The API works by calling a routine in your program, once for each font. When you use *EnumFontFamiliesEx*, you pass it the memory address of a *callback* routine to use for each font; you pass this function pointer through the lpEnumFontProc parameter. The callback routine needs to include a specific parameter list signature, as defined in the API's documentation.

```
Public Function EnumFontFamExProc(ByVal lpelfe As Long, _
    ByVal lpntme As Long, ByVal FontType As Long, _
    ByRef lParam As Long) As Long
```

In VB 6, the AddressOf keyword obtains this function pointer, which you then pass to the enumeration API. The problem is that *if any little thing goes wrong, your whole program will crash.* That's because the function pointer is nothing more than a memory address. It can't guarantee that you put all of the ByVal and ByRef keywords in front of the right parameters, or that you even included parameters at all. In fact, there's nothing to stop you from passing any random number as the function pointer. The API doesn't care, until it crashes.

This is where delegates save the day. A .NET delegate isn't just a function pointer; it's a class that includes everything you need to know to call the destination function correctly. It includes complete information about the parameters and return value, and you won't be able to compile your program until you get it all right.

All delegates derive from the *System.Delegate* or *System.MulticastDelegate* classes. The former limits the delegate to a single target event handler, while the latter includes no such limit. Visual Basic uses delegates to bind events to event handlers, and sometimes it seems like a lot of work. Fortunately, Visual Studio links most events and event handlers automatically as you drag-and-drop visual elements.

## Using a Delegate to Call a Method

To call a method using a delegate, use the *Invoke* method of the delegate. To illustrate, consider a class module with a simple method.

```
Public Class SimpleClass
    Public Sub CallMe(ByVal content As String)
        MsgBox(content)
    End Sub
End Class
```

Delegates are one of the many .NET types. Visual Basic includes a `Delegate` keyword that defines delegates. Since the goal is to call the `CallMe` method through a delegate, that delegate must have the same signature as the called method. This small example invokes the delegate from a click on a form, so the delegate's definition appears in the form's class code.

```
Delegate Sub MyDelegate(ByVal s As String)
```

Finally, in the form's *Click* event handler (which works via delegates, but don't think about that now), the call to `CallMe` is made indirectly through a delegate.

```
Private Sub Form1_Click(ByVal sender As System.Object, _
        ByVal e As System.EventArgs) Handles MyBase.Click
    ' ----- Get an instance of the destination class.
    Dim destClass As New SimpleClass()
    Dim theDelegate As MyDelegate

    ' ----- Connect the delegate to its target, the CallMe method.
    theDelegate = New MyDelegate(AddressOf destClass.CallMe)

    ' ----- Make the call.
    theDelegate.Invoke("Display this!")
End Sub
```

It doesn't seem like much, since the code could have just called `destClass.CallMe` directly. But it is much, since the delegate provides generic and indirect access to the target routine for those times when the code needs something generic and indirect. MyDelegate can connect to any target routine, as long as the routine shares the same signature. The Framework Class Library takes advantage of this fact by using a common argument signature for all class events.

## Using a Delegate as a Generic Callback

A delegate is the perfect solution when a generic callback function is needed. The following example implements a simple sorting routine. Usually, sorting routines are limited to a specific type of content, like integers or strings. That's because the sorting routine has to know how to compare the items. But if you could supply a generic "compare function," the sorting routine could sort anything. Or perhaps you need to sort the same type of data (such as an array of integers), but sort the data based on differing comparison standards. It's this second alternative that appears in the example below.

The first step declares the delegate for the common comparison function. Each compare function takes two integers and returns True if they need to be swapped from their current order.

```
Public Delegate Function CompareFunction(ByVal valueOne As Integer, _
    ByVal valueTwo As Integer) As Boolean
```

The two comparison functions take different approaches: one sorts in ascending order, while the other sorts in descending order. As expected, they have the same signature as the delegate.

```
Public Function SortAscending(ByVal valueOne As Integer, _
        ByVal valueTwo As Integer) As Boolean
    If (valueOne > valueTwo) Then Return True Else Return False
End Function

Public Function SortDescending(ByVal valueOne As Integer, _
        ByVal valueTwo As Integer) As Boolean
    If (valueOne < valueTwo) Then Return True Else Return False
End Function
```

Here is the code for the sort routine. It uses the delegate's *Invoke* method to access the comparison function.

```
Public Sub FlexSort(ByVal compareMethod As CompareFunction, _
        ByVal dataValues() As Integer)
    ' ----- Don't tell anyone, but it's a Bubble Sort.
    Dim outer As Integer
    Dim inner As Integer
    Dim swap As Integer

    For outer = 0 To UBound(dataValues)
        For inner = outer + 1 To UBound(dataValues)
            ' ----- Make the generic delegate call here.
            If (compareMethod.Invoke(dataValues(outer), _
                dataValues(inner)) = True) Then
                swap = dataValues(inner)
                dataValues(inner) = dataValues(outer)
                dataValues(outer) = swap
            End If
        Next inner
    Next outer
End Sub
```

The sorting code is tested from a button's *Click* event. Notice that the code does not specifically create a delegate. Since the FlexSort routine's first argument accepts a delegate, and since a delegate is really just a container for a matching function, the delegate gets created anyway by passing the address of a matching function.

```
Private Sub Button1_Click(ByVal sender As System.Object, _
        ByVal e As System.EventArgs) Handles Button1.Click
    ' ----- Click a button, sort some numbers.
    Dim counter As Integer
    Dim dataValues() As Integer = New Integer() {6, 2, 4, 9}
```

```
' ----- First, try it in ascending order.
FlexSort(AddressOf SortAscending, dataValues)
For counter = 0 To 3
    Debug.WriteLine(CStr(dataValues(counter)))
Next counter
Debug.WriteLine("")

' ----- Next, sort them again in descending order.
FlexSort(AddressOf SortDescending, dataValues)
For counter = 0 To 3
    Debug.WriteLine(CStr(dataValues(counter)))
Next counter
End Sub
```

The output is:

```
2
4
6
9

9
6
4
2
```

# Events and Event Binding

An *event* indicates some type of action. This action can be initiated by the user (such as through a mouse click on a command button), by the application code (such as when a change is made to a database record), or by the operating system (such as a timer event). When any action like this occurs, it causes an event to be *raised* or *fired*.

Each event has a *source*. This is the object to which the action is applied, such as the button that was clicked. The source is responsible for alerting the operating system that an event has occurred. It does so by sending an event notification message. For this reason, the event source is often referred to as the *sender*.

An event often has an *event argument*, a means of conveying data that pertains to the event. For instance, the press of a keyboard key generates an event that includes event arguments describing the "key code" of the key, and it also includes information on the state of modifier keys (the Shift, Alt, and Ctrl keys). The event argument is part of the message sent by the event source.

An *event handler* is a procedure that is executed as a result of event notification. The process of associating an event handler with an event is called *binding*.

In .NET applications, event handlers have a consistent procedure signature.

```
Private Sub MyHandler(ByVal sender As System.Object, _
    ByVal e As System.EventArgs)
```

The sender parameter receives the object that initiated the event, while the e parameter receives the event argument. The *System.EventArgs* class is a generic event argument class that doesn't convey any specific argument data at all. Those events that have actual event argument data to convey use for e a class derived from *System.EventArgs* instead.

## Control-Related Events

In Windows Forms applications, controls are a veritable smorgasbord of *built-in events*. For instance, the *TextBox* control has events associated with changing the text in the *TextBox*, pressing a key while the *TextBox* has the focus, clicking or double-clicking on the *TextBox* with the mouse, moving the mouse over the *TextBox*, and more.

The Visual Studio IDE can insert an empty event handler for a control into your source code, complete with the proper event parameters. Once you have added the control to the form, access the source code related to the form. Just above the source code editing area are two drop-down lists. The one to the left provides a list of all controls placed on the form. The drop-down list to the right presents all available events that correspond to the control or source selected in the left drop-down list (Figure 8-1). To add a new event handler, select the control from the list of controls, then select the desired event from the list of events.

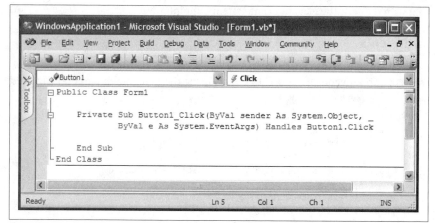

*Figure 8-1. A control event ready to use*

Each control has a *default event*, such as the *Click* event for Command Buttons. As a shortcut, Visual Studio adds an empty default event for a control to your source code when you double-click on the control. For instance, double-clicking a Command Button produces the following code:

```
Private Sub Button1_Click(ByVal sender As System.Object, _
        ByVal e As System.EventArgs) Handles Button1.Click

End Sub
```

The Handles clause at the end of the event signature tells the compiler that this procedure is bound to Button1's *Click* event, *Button1.Click*. Using this clause, it's possible to assign any procedure to handle an event, as long as it has the right signature. Unlike programming in VB 6, you don't have to name your event

Delegates and Events

handler *Control_EventName*; you can give it any name you want, as long as you include the Handles clause.

One common event handler can be used for multiple events. Since every event handler has the same argument signature, you can even share a common event handler for events from different controls or system-defined actions. The Handles clause supports a comma-separated list of the events to handle.

```
Private Sub ManyButtonClicks(ByVal sender As System.Object, _
    ByVal e As System.EventArgs) Handles Button1.Click, _
    Button2.Click, Button3.Click

End Sub
```

It's easy to determine which control triggered the event, since the sender parameter contains a reference to the source object. If your event handler processes events that use different derived classes for the e parameter, use the common *System.EventArgs* class in the parameter signature and then convert the argument to the appropriate class using the CType function. While loading up many events in a single handler is convenient, it should only be done when the events truly result in common functionality. You could send all events for every control on your form to a single handler and use If statements to divide up the work, but that would defeat the elegant event system built into .NET.

## WithEvents

Events aren't limited to controls and forms. Your own custom classes can respond to events, too. Events are added to classes using the Event statement and triggered with the RaiseEvent statement.

```
Public Class ActiveClass
    ' ----- Declare an event.
    Public Event AnEvent(ByVal eventData As Integer)

    Public Sub RaiseTheEvent(ByVal eventData As Integer)
        ' ----- Method to raise the event.
        RaiseEvent AnEvent(eventData)
    End Sub
End Class
```

The class's event is now ready to use. In a Windows Forms class, add a variable of type ActiveClass, including the WithEvents keyword. This keyword enables event handling in the instance of the class.

```
Public WithEvents stuffHappens As ActiveClass
```

This automatically causes the Visual Studio IDE to add the variable name stuffHappens to the left-hand drop-down list above the code window. Selecting this variable causes the right-hand drop-down list to display the events for the class. In this case, the list contains only the AnEvent event. Selecting this event places an empty event shell in the code editor window (edited here to include a MsgBox function).

```
Private Sub stuffHappens_AnEvent(ByVal eventData As Integer) _
    Handles stuffHappens.AnEvent
  MsgBox("Event raised: " & eventData)
End Sub
```

Some code added to a button's *Click* event completes the demonstration.

```
Private Sub Button1_Click(ByVal sender As System.Object, _
    ByVal e As System.EventArgs) Handles Button1.Click
  ' ----- Raise an event in an ActiveClass instance.
  stuffHappens = New ActiveClass()
  stuffHappens.RaiseTheEvent(7)
End Sub
```

The WithEvents keyword approach to event handling has one slight drawback in that the New keyword cannot be used in the declaration, as in:

```
' ----- This doesn't work.
Public WithEvents stuffHappens As New ActiveClass
```

Thus, the object must be instantiated separately from the variable declaration, as demonstrated in the example.

## AddHandler and RemoveHandler

Binding events to event handlers with the Handles keyword is easy, but it's not the only way to use events. Visual Basic also includes the AddHandler statement (and its counterpart, the RemoveHandler statement) to bind an event to an event handler at runtime instead of at design time. For instance, you could connect a button's *Click* event to a handler at runtime. First, create the event handler in the form's code.

```
Private Sub LonelyHandler(ByVal sender As System.Object, _
    ByVal e As System.EventArgs)
  MsgBox("You found me!")
End Sub
```

Add a button named Button1 to the form surface. In the form's *Load* event, add the code that binds the event to the event handler.

```
Private Sub Form1_Load(ByVal sender As Object, _
    ByVal e As System.EventArgs) Handles MyBase.Load
  ' ----- Bind the event to its handler.
  AddHandler Button1.Click, AddressOf Me.LonelyHandler

  ' ----- NOTE: The following would also work:
  '
  '         AddHandler Button1.Click, _
  '             New EventHandler(AddressOf Me.LonelyHandler)
End Sub
```

Run the program and click the button. It works! To remove an existing handler at runtime, use the RemoveHandler statement with a similar syntax to that of AddHandler.

```
RemoveHandler Button1.Click, AddressOf Me.LonelyHandler
```

## Custom Events

*New in 2005.* Sometimes there may be a software need to exhibit more control over the lifetime of an event in your classes. The 2005 release of Visual Basic adds features that let you monitor and take action each time a handler is added to an event, each time a handler is removed from an event, and each time an event is raised. This new feature is called *custom events*.

Using these custom events is easy. In your class definition, simply type:

```
accessModifier Custom Event eventName
```

and press the Enter key. (*accessModifier* is one of the standard access modifiers, like Public, that can be used with events.) Visual Studio provides the outline of the custom event.

```
accessModifier Custom Event eventName As EventHandler
    AddHandler(ByVal value As EventHandler)
        ' ----- Special code when adding handlers.
    End AddHandler

    RemoveHandler(ByVal value As EventHandler)
        ' ----- Special code when removing handlers.
    End RemoveHandler

    RaiseEvent(ByVal sender As Object, ByVal e As System.EventArgs)
        ' ----- Special code when raising the event.
    End RaiseEvent
End Event
```

These event handlers fire when the specific event-related action happens with the *eventName* event.

# 9

# Attributes

*Attributes* are declarative tags that can be used to annotate types (classes, structures, etc.) or type members, thereby modifying their meaning or customizing their behavior. The descriptive information provided by each attribute is stored as metadata in the .NET assembly and can be extracted either at design time or at runtime using a process called *reflection*.

Consider the following example that uses the <WebMethod> attribute.

```
<WebMethod(Description:="Indicates number of visitors to a page")> _
Public Function PageHitCount(baseURL As String) As Integer
```

Ordinarily, public methods of a class can be invoked locally through an instance of that class; they are not treated as members of a web service. The <WebMethod> attribute marks an ordinary class method so that it is callable over the Internet as part of a web service. This <WebMethod> attribute includes a single property, *Description*, which provides the text that will appear on the page describing the web service.

If attributes provide such important software features, why aren't they simply implemented as language elements? The answer is "flexibility." Attributes are stored as metadata in an assembly, rather than as part of its executable code. As an item of metadata, the attribute describes the program element to which it applies and is available for retrieval and examination at design time (when using a tool like Visual Studio that recognizes attributes), at compile time (when the compiler can use attributes to modify, customize, or extend the compiler's basic operation), and at runtime (when it can be used by the Common Language Runtime to modify the code's ordinary runtime behavior).

Since metadata in an assembly can be examined by other applications, third-party tools can take advantage of the attributes included in your code. A third-party tool may make available an attribute previously unavailable with Visual Studio, and you can begin to use its enhanced behavior without having to wait for Microsoft to update the language or the compiler. If these features were implemented as language constructs instead of metadata-generating attributes, this level of flexibility would be difficult or impossible.

The behavior of interface objects (such as Windows Forms controls) in Visual Studio illustrates the importance of attributes. Since Visual Studio offers drag-and-drop placement of controls on forms or web pages, it is necessary for controls to have a design time behavior in addition to their runtime behavior. For instance, when you double-click on a control in Visual Studio (at design time), the code or code template for its default event handler appears. How does Visual Studio know which event handler is the default? An attribute provides the solution. Visual Studio recognizes an attribute named <DefaultEvent>, which provides the control designer with a way to indicate a control's default event. Since the attribute's information is stored in the assembly's metadata, Visual Studio can simply examine the control's metadata to see whether a <DefaultEvent> attribute is attached to a particular event.

The attribute-based system of programming implemented in .NET is extensible. In addition to the attributes predefined by Visual Basic, the .NET Framework, or other vendors, you can define custom attributes that you can then apply to program elements. For an attribute to be meaningful, there must also be software that attempts to detect the presence of the attribute somewhere in your code's lifetime (design time, compile time, runtime) and that acts based on the attribute's settings.

## Syntax and Use

In Visual Basic, an attribute appears within angle brackets (< and >) immediately before the type or type member that it modifies. The attribute name is followed by parentheses, which enclose a comma-delimited list of arguments to be passed to the attribute. For example, the <Obsolete> attribute marks a type or type member as obsolete. One of its optional arguments is a warning message to be passed on to anyone interested. Apply the <Obsolete> attribute with a message as follows:

```
<Obsolete("Don't even think of using this feature.")>
```

If there are no arguments, or none that you wish to include, just use empty parentheses:

```
<Obsolete( )>
```

or remove the parentheses completely:

```
<Obsolete>
```

If more than one attribute is applied to a single program element, the attributes are enclosed in a single set of angle brackets and delimited from one another with commas.

```
<Obsolete, WebMethod> Public Function PageHitCount( _
    baseURL As String) As Integer
```

Each attribute corresponds to a class derived from *System.Attribute*. In fact, the VB compiler actually treats an attribute as an instance of the attribute's class. If you look in the .NET documentation, you will recognize attribute classes by the word "Attribute" on the end of their class names. For instance, the Obsolete attribute comes from the *ObsoleteAttribute* class. It's a good idea to include the word "Attribute" on any attribute classes you create yourself. However, when you use an attribute (within angle brackets), you can omit the trailing word "Attribute" if you want, just to keep things short. The compiler will add "Attribute" back in, if needed.

If the shortened attribute name is a Visual Basic keyword, use the attribute's full class name to prevent a compiler error. For example, the following declaration produces an error because `ParamArray` is a Visual Basic keyword:

```
<ParamArray> scores As Long
```

The following code compiles correctly:

```
<ParamArrayAttribute> scores As Long
```

An attribute's class constructors determine whether any arguments are required. For example, the `<VBFixedString>` attribute corresponds to the *VBFixedStringAttribute* class, which has the following constructor:

```
New(ByVal size As Integer)
```

The `<VBFixedString>` attribute can be used as follows:

```
<VBFixedString(10)> Private customerID As String
```

Attribute constructors can be overloaded. The argument signature you use must correspond to one of the constructor signatures for that attribute.

Arguments passed to an attribute can be *positional* or *named*. Positional arguments appear in the same comma-separated position that is defined in the associated constructor. Named arguments can appear out of order, but they must be preceded by the argument name and the := association operator. Required arguments to a constructor must be positional. Optional arguments can be named or positional, but they must appear after all required arguments. Attribute class properties can be set using named arguments. For instance, the `<WebMethod>` attribute includes a *Description* property that can be set as a named argument.

```
<WebMethod(Description:="Page use counter")> _
Public Function PageHitCount(baseURL As String) As Integer
```

Attributes are evaluated at compile time, when their data is written to the assembly's metadata. This means that only literal values can be passed as arguments to an attribute's constructor, and not variables.

When you use .NET classes in your application, you need to indicate where they reside in the namespace hierarchy, either explicitly with each use or implicitly by using the `Imports` keyword. Since attributes are just classes, you have to indicate their location as well. If an attribute is not in one of the already loaded namespaces (like *System*), you can use `Imports` in the file where you make use of the attribute and set a reference to it in Visual Studio or on the compiler command line.

An attribute immediately precedes the language element to which it applies (and that element's modifiers, like Public), and it must be on the same logical line as that language element. Use the standard line continuation character (the underscore, "_") to join multiple physical lines into a single logical line, if desired.

Attributes can be applied to the following language elements:

Class
Constructor (methods with the name "New")
Delegate
Enum
Event
Field
Interface
Method
Parameter (of a procedure)
Property
Return value (of a procedure)
Structure

For example, the <AttributeUsage> attribute comes before Class statements.

```
<AttributeUsage(AttributeTargets.All)> _
Public Class MyCustomAttrAttribute
```

The <ParamArrayAttribute> attribute comes just before the final parameter in a procedure's parameter list.

```
Public Sub MyProcedure(baseAction As String, _
    <ParamArrayAttribute> actionValues As Long)
```

Attributes that are designed to decorate either an assembly or a module both appear at the top of a source code file (just after any Option or Imports statements). To avoid confusion, these attributes must be prefixed with a modifier (either Assembly: or Module:) indicating the program element to modify. For example:

```
Option Strict On
Imports System.Data.SqlClient
<Assembly: AssemblyDescription("Supplementary data access library")>

Namespace SqlAccess
    ...
```

# Defining a Custom Attribute

An attribute is merely a class that inherits from *System.Attribute*. This section shows you how to build a custom attribute called <DeveloperNote>, which allows a developer to add assorted information (the developer's name, the development date, a comment, and whether the code was written in response to a bug) to a block of code.

1. Define a public class that inherits from *System.Attribute* or from another attribute class derived from *System.Attribute*.

```
Public Class DeveloperNoteAttribute
    Inherits System.Attribute
```

By convention, the name of the class ends with the substring "Attribute."

2. Apply the <AttributeUsage> attribute to the class, which defines the language elements to which the custom attribute can be applied. The attribute's only required argument is one of the following members of the AttributeTargets enumeration:

```
AttributeTargets.All
AttributeTargets.Assembly
AttributeTargets.Class
AttributeTargets.Constructor
AttributeTargets.Delegate
AttributeTargets.Enum
AttributeTargets.Event
AttributeTargets.Field
AttributeTargets.GenericParameter
AttributeTargets.Interface
AttributeTargets.Method
AttributeTargets.Module
AttributeTargets.Parameter
AttributeTargets.Property
AttributeTargets.ReturnValue
AttributeTargets.Struct
```

If an attribute applies to multiple programming elements, but not all elements, the relevant enumeration values can be Or'd together. Since the <DeveloperNote> attribute is pretty generic, it will be applicable to All program elements.

```
<AttributeUsage(AttributeTargets.All, _
    Inherited:=True, _
    AllowMultiple:=True)> _
Public Class DeveloperNoteAttribute
    Inherits System.Attribute
```

The Inherited argument (set to True) allows new attribute classes to be derived from *DeveloperNoteAttribute*. The AllowMultiple argument (set to True) allows the attribute to be applied to the same program element multiple times.

3. Add some protected class members to hold the custom values, like the developer name.

```
Protected developerName As String
Protected codeComment As String
Protected codeRecordDate As Date
Protected dueToBug As Boolean
```

4. Create the class constructor (the New routine), which is called when the attribute is applied to a particular language element. The class constructor defines the attribute's required or positional arguments. At a minimum, the developer using this attribute must to record his or her name, a comment, and a date.

```
Public Sub New(Name As String, Comment As String, _
    DateRecorded As String)
    ' ----- Store the commentary for this program element.
    MyBase.New( )
    developerName = Name
    codeComment = Comment
    codeRecordDate = CDate(DateRecorded)
End Sub
```

The DateRecorded parameter comes into the constructor as a String, not as a
Date. Only certain data types can be used as attribute parameters: integral
data types (Byte, Short, Integer, Long), floating point data types (Single and
Double), Char, String, Boolean, an enumerated type, or *System.Type*. Other
data types, including Date, Decimal, Object, and structured types, cannot be
used as parameters. The new VB 2005 integral data types (SByte, UShort,
UInteger, and ULong) cannot be used, because only Common Language Specification (CLS) compliant data types can be used in attribute definitions, and
these new types do not meet that requirement.

5. Declare properties and fields. The attribute's public properties and fields
correspond to parameters required by the class constructor and to optional
parameters supplied when the attribute is applied to a language element. The
<DeveloperNote> attribute needs a property for each of the three required
constructor arguments, plus one for the optional Bug property.

```
Public Property Name( ) As String
    Get
        Return developerName
    End Get
    Set(ByVal value As String)
        developerName = value
    End Set
End Property

Public Property Comment( ) As String
    Get
        Return codeComment
    End Get
    Set(ByVal value As String)
        codeComment = value
    End Set
End Property

Public Property DateRecorded( ) As Date
    Get
        Return codeRecordDate
    End Get
    Set(ByVal value As Date)
        codeRecordDate = value
    End Set
End Property

Public Property Bug( ) As Boolean
    Get
        Return dueToBug
```

```
      End Get
      Set(ByVal value As Boolean)
         dueToBug = value
      End Set
   End Property
```

That's the whole attribute class with only the most basic of features. The .NET Framework takes care of everything else, including the recording of each custom attribute value in the assembly's metadata. The complete code for the attribute class appears in Example 9-1.

*Example 9-1. The DeveloperNoteAttribute attribute class*

```
Option Strict On
Imports System

Namespace Extensions.CustomAttributes

<AttributeUsage(AttributeTargets.All, _
   Inherited:=True, _
   AllowMultiple:=True)> _
Public Class DeveloperNoteAttribute
   Inherits System.Attribute

   Protected developerName As String
   Protected codeComment As String
   Protected codeRecordDate As Date
   Protected dueToBug As Boolean

   Public Sub New(Name As String, Comment As String, _
         DateRecorded As String)
      ' ----- Store the commentary for this program element.
      MyBase.New( )
      developerName = Name
      codeComment = Comment
      codeRecordDate = CDate(DateRecorded)
   End Sub

   Public Property Name( ) As String
      Get
         Return developerName
      End Get
      Set(ByVal value As String)
         developerName = value
      End Set
   End Property

   Public Property Comment( ) As String
      Get
         Return codeComment
      End Get
      Set(ByVal value As String)
         codeComment = value
      End Set
   End Property
```

*Example 9-1. The DeveloperNoteAttribute attribute class (continued)*

```
Public Property DateRecorded() As Date
    Get
        Return codeRecordDate
    End Get
    Set(ByVal value As Date)
        codeRecordDate = value
    End Set
End Property

Public Property Bug() As Boolean
    Get
        Return dueToBug
    End Get
    Set(ByVal value As Boolean)
        dueToBug = value
    End Set
End Property
End Class

End Namespace
```

# Using a Custom Attribute

The attribute classes included with .NET already have specific uses. Visual Studio and the various .NET compilers take specific actions based on these attributes, such as making a method available on the Internet through the <WebMethod> attribute. But no code yet exists to use the <DeveloperNote> attribute designed above. Not only must you define the custom attribute, you must also develop routines that will identify the attribute and take action as needed.

All attribute properties are stored in .NET assemblies as metadata. This metadata can be accessed programmatically at runtime by using the .NET Framework's reflection classes.

> An assembly's metadata is similar to a COM type library. In addition to its greater accessibility through the .NET Framework's reflection features, assembly metadata is always stored with the assembly. Although COM type libraries can be stored in the EXE or DLL files containing the COM objects, they are most commonly stored in separate files (such as ".tlb" files) that are distinct from the COM objects they describe.

The .NET Framework provides support for reflection through the *System.Type* class and through the features found in the *System.Reflection* namespace. The following code creates a console mode application that uses reflection to extract <DeveloperNote> attribute details from an assembly that uses this custom attribute.

```
Option Strict On

Imports Microsoft.VisualBasic
Imports System
```

```
Imports System.Reflection
Imports System.Text

' ----- We placed the <DeveloperNote> attribute in
'       the Extensions.CustomAttributes namespace.
Imports Extensions.CustomAttributes

Module modComments

Public Sub Main( )
    ' ----- Report on <DeveloperNote> use in an assembly.
    Dim fileToExamine As String
    Dim outputText As String
    Dim assemblyView As System.Reflection.Assembly
    Dim attributeSet( ) As Attribute
    Dim moduleScan As System.Reflection.Module
    Dim moduleSet( ) As System.Reflection.Module

    ' ----- The assembly to examine comes through the command line.
    fileToExamine = Command( )
    If (fileToExamine = "") Then
        Console.WriteLine("Syntax is:" & vbCrLf & _
            "    DevNotes <filename>")
        Exit Sub
    End If

    ' ----- Load the assembly through reflection.
    assemblyView = Reflection.Assembly.LoadFrom(fileToExamine)

    ' ----- Output information on assembly-level attributes.
    attributeSet = Attribute.GetCustomAttributes(assemblyView)
    If (attributeSet.Length > 0) Then
        outputText = PrepareDeveloperNotes(attributeSet)
        If (outputText <> "") Then
            Console.WriteLine(assemblyView.GetName.Name & _
                " Assembly Developer Notes:")
            Console.WriteLine(outputText)
        End If
    End If

    ' ----- Output information on module-level attributes.
    moduleSet = assemblyView.GetModules( )
    For Each moduleScan In moduleSet
        attributeSet = Attribute.GetCustomAttributes(moduleScan)
        If (attributeSet.Length > 0) Then
            outputText = PrepareDeveloperNotes(attributeSet)
            If (outputText <> "") Then
                Console.WriteLine(moduleScan.Name & _
                    " Module Developer Notes:)
                Console.WriteLine(outputText)
            End If
        End If
    Next moduleScan
```

```
    ' ----- Output information on type-level attributes.
    EnumerateTypes(assemblyView)
End Sub

Public Function PrepareDeveloperNotes(attributeSet( ) As Object) _
      As String
    ' ----- Format information about each attribute.
    Dim msg As New StringBuilder
    Dim attributeScan As Attribute
    Dim noteEntry As DeveloperNoteAttribute

    On Error Resume Next

    ' ----- Build the notes.
    For Each attributeScan In attributeSet
        If (TypeOf (attributeScan) Is DeveloperNoteAttribute) Then
            noteEntry = CType(attributeScan, DeveloperNoteAttribute)
            msg.Append("  Developer: " & noteEntry.Name & vbCrLf)
            msg.Append("  Comment: " & noteEntry.Comment & vbCrLf)
            msg.Append("  Date: " & noteEntry.DateRecorded & vbCrLf)
            msg.Append("  Bug: " & noteEntry.Bug & vbCrLf)
        End If
    Next attributeScan

    ' ----- Return the results as an ordinary string.
    Return msg.ToString
End Function

Private Sub EnumerateTypes(assemblyView As Reflection.Assembly)
    ' ----- Process each type in the entire assembly.
    Dim typeScan As Type
    Dim typeSet( ) As Type
    Dim typeCategory As String
    Dim attributeSet( ) As Object
    Dim attributeMsg As String
    Dim methodMsg As String

    ' ----- Retrieve the types for this assembly.
    typeSet = assemblyView.GetTypes( )

    ' ----- Get a friendly name for the type category.
    For Each typeScan In typeSet
        If typeScan.IsClass Then
            typeCategory = "Class"
        ElseIf typeScan.IsValueType Then
            typeCategory = "Structure"
        ElseIf typeScan.IsInterface Then
            typeCategory = "Interface"
        ElseIf typeScan.IsEnum Then
            typeCategory = "Enum"
        Else
            typeCategory = ".NET Type"
        End If
```

```
' ----- Get any type-level attributes.
attributeSet = typeScan.GetCustomAttributes(False)
If (attributeSet.Length > 0) Then
   attributeMsg = PrepareDeveloperNotes(attributeSet)
Else
   attributeMsg = ""
End If


' ----- Get the details for this type's members.
methodMsg = EnumerateTypeMembers(typeScan)

' ----- Display any collected information, if available.
If (methodMsg <> "") Or (attributeMsg <> "") Then
   Console.WriteLine(typeCategory & " " & typeScan.Name & ":")
   If (attributeMsg <> "") Then _
      Console.WriteLine(attributeMsg)
   If (methodMsg <> "") Then _
      Console.WriteLine(methodMsg)
End If
   Next typeScan
End Sub

Private Function EnumerateTypeMembers(typeEntry As Type) As String
   Dim memberInfo As String
   Dim fullInfo As String = ""
   Dim noteDetails As String
   Dim attributeSet( ) As Object
   Dim memberScan As MemberInfo
   Dim memberSet( ) As MemberInfo

   ' ----- Get members of the type.
   memberSet = typeEntry.GetMembers
   For Each memberScan In memberSet
      ' ----- Determine if any attributes are present.
      attributeSet = memberScan.GetCustomAttributes(False)
      If (attributeSet.Length > 0) Then
         ' ----- Determine the member type.
         Select Case memberScan.MemberType
            Case MemberTypes.All
               memberInfo = " All"
            Case MemberTypes.Constructor
               memberInfo = " Constructor"
            Case MemberTypes.Custom
               memberInfo = " Custom method"
            Case MemberTypes.Event
               memberInfo = " Event"
            Case MemberTypes.Field
               memberInfo = " Field"
            Case MemberTypes.Method
               memberInfo = " Method"
            Case MemberTypes.NestedType
               memberInfo = " Nested type"
            Case MemberTypes.Property
               memberInfo = " Property"
```

```
            Case MemberTypes.TypeInfo
                memberInfo = " TypeInfo"
            Case Else
                memberInfo = " Member"
        End Select

        ' ----- Add in the name of the member.
        If (memberScan.Name = ".ctor") Then
            ' ----- Constructor.
            memberInfo = "New" & memberInfo
        Else
            memberInfo = memberScan.Name & memberInfo
        End If

        ' ----- Get the note details.
        noteDetails = PrepareDeveloperNotes(attributeSet)
        If (noteDetails <> "") Then _
            fullInfo &= memberInfo & vbCrLf & noteDetails & vbCrLf
    End If
Next memberScan

' ----- Fully formatted and ready to use.
Return fullInfo
End Function

End Module
```

This program scans an assembly, examining almost everything that can have attributes attached. If it finds attributes attached to an item, it loops through them looking for any that use the <DeveloperNote> attribute. If a match is found, it prints the name of the item and the related developer note details to the console.

The program's entry point, *Main*, first instantiates an *Assembly* object (from the *System.Reflection* namespace) representing the assembly identified on the command line. It then calls the *System.Attribute*'s shared *GetCustomAttributes* method to obtain any attributes associated with the assembly itself. If any exist, they are passed to the PrepareDeveloperNotes method, which looks specifically for DeveloperNoteAttribute entries and formats them for printing.

Back in *Main*, the same process is done for each module contained within the assembly by calling the assembly's *GetModules* method.

The final task displays the developer notes for each type in the assembly. Since the logic is somewhat different, it's all done in the EnumerateTypes routine. This routine gets all the types for the entire assembly through the assembly's *GetTypes* method. Then it scans each type, checking for associated attributes. If it finds them, it documents any developer notes (once again through the PrepareDeveloperNotes function).

Since each type contains members that, in turn, can have <DeveloperNote> attributes, those are displayed as well through the EnumerateTypeMembers routine.

This routine is not that different in its overall structure from the `EnumerateTypes` routine, but there is some interesting code used in the formatting of the member name. If the `memberScan` object represents a constructor, ".ctor" is used for the member name. The routine converts this to the more user-friendly "New."

The program provides a good overview of attribute analysis, although it could be enhanced even more. The `EnumerateTypes` routine could be made a little more generic, and recursion added, allowing it to display attribute information found in nested classes. Another reasonable enhancement would display developer notes associated with parameters belonging to individual methods.

Attributes

# 10

## Generics

The .NET Framework includes several useful collection classes in the *System. Collections* namespace. These classes let you manage groups of objects in many useful ways. For instance, the *System.Collections.Stack* class manages data objects in a last in, first out (LIFO) pancake-style stack. The collection classes work with any type of object or, more accurately, any mixture of objects. A single instance of a collection class can manage integers, strings, employee data objects, Windows Forms instances, and any other type of object you wish to include. But what if you want to only include a single data type? What if you want to *require* that only a single data type be included in a collection instance? Welcome generics!

## What Are Generics?

Visual Basic 2005 includes a new feature named *generics*, built upon features added to Version 2.0 of the .NET Framework. Generics allow you to add enforced strong typing within an otherwise weakly typed type (class, structure, interface, or delegate) or its methods (functions and sub procedures).

Before generics, if you wanted to use the *Stack* class to manage a set of Integer values, and only Integer values, you had a few options.

- Create a brand new collection-type class named IntegerStack that works just like the *Stack* class but is hardcoded to use Integer values only. It would include the *Stack* class's *Push* and *Pop* methods, but they would only deal with Integer value types. While this would solve your problem, it wouldn't be fun to program. You would essentially rewrite all of the code in the existing *Stack* class from scratch. If you later wanted to develop a similar class for strings, you would have to do it all again, this time enforcing the data type to be String.

- Create a new class named IntegerStack that derives from or wraps the functionality of the *Stack* class. This class would have its own new methods that enforce the Integer restriction, but each of those methods would, in turn, call the standard *Stack* class methods. This is a little better, since you wouldn't have to recode the entire *Stack* logic. But you would still have to do it again for String data. And all of this wrapping and type-casting between *System. Object* and Integer can't be that efficient.

- Just use the existing *Stack* class and hope that only integers are used. Unfortunately, this doesn't really solve the problem.

Generics solve this problem by allowing an instance of a class to look like it was written just for a restricted data type. All enforcement occurs at compile time, so the program is also more efficient, since the data does not have to be converted to *System.Object* and back again all the time. Visual Studio also uses the generic definitions to enhance the IntelliSense available when working with generics-enabled types.

Generics are similar to a feature called *templates* in the C++ language, although generics are somewhat easier to use and do not support all of the features available with templates.

# Type Parameters

Consider the following subset of the *Stack* class definition.

```
Public Class StackSubset
    Public Sub Push(ByVal obj As System.Object)
    End Sub
End Class
```

To define this same class using generics, use the new Of keyword.

```
Public Class StackSubset(Of T)
    Public Sub Push(ByVal obj As T)
    End Sub
End Class
```

The T just after Of is a *type parameter*. (You can use another more descriptive name besides T.) This definition says, "In the StackSubset class, the type parameter T is acting kind of like a variable, but for data types. Anywhere it is used within the class, treat it as if it were just some normal type, like Integer or *System. Windows.Forms.Form*."

An instance of the StackSubset class can now be created, specifying a specific data type for the T type parameter.

```
Dim limitedStack As New StackSubSet(Of Integer)
```

This statement creates an instance of the StackSubset class and will only allow Integer objects to be passed as arguments to the class's Push method.

In addition to standard data types such as Integer, the Of clause can be used with any valid type, including interfaces, structures, and so on. If it can be treated as an instance of *System.Object*, you can use it to replace the T type parameter.

Many of the collection classes available to .NET programmers have been modified in 2005 to support a generic type parameter. These new classes are located in the *System.Collections.Generic* namespace. The *Stack* class is one of the collections enabled for generics.

```
Dim pileOfNumbers As New Stack(Of Integer)
```

## Multiple Type Parameters

Some classes may require more than one generic type parameter. The Of keyword supports multiple parameters, each separated by a comma.

```
Public Class SpecialCollection(Of T1, T2)
    Public Sub TakeAction1(ByVal data1 As T1)
    End Sub

    Public Sub TakeAction2(ByVal data1 As T1, ByVal data2 As T2)
    End Sub

    Public Function GetResults() T2
    End Sub
End Class
```

## Constraints

In the class definition:

```
Public Class WorkGroup(Of T)
```

the T type parameter can be assigned to any type when an instance of the class is created. Generics also allow you to place some restrictions or constraints on the set of types used. For instance, if your custom generic class is only designed to work with Windows Forms controls, allowing types like Integer and String could mess things up. Adding an As clause to the type parameter limits the range of data types that can be assigned to T. For example, the class definition:

```
Public Class WorkGroup(Of T As System.Windows.Forms.Control)
```

limits T to the *System.Windows.Forms.Control* class or any class derived from it. The following statements work:

```
Dim anyControls As WorkGroup(System.Windows.Forms.Control)
Dim buttonsOnly As WorkGroup(System.Windows.Forms.Button)
```

but statements using non-*Control* data types do not:

```
' ----- This doesn't work.
Dim buttonsOnly As WorkGroup(Integer)
```

since Integer is not derived from *System.Windows.Forms.Control*.

This use of a *type constraint* to limit the selection of types used for T also applies to interfaces. The statement:

```
Public Class WorkGroup(Of T As Runtime.Serialization.ISerializable)
```

restricts the type-specific use of the WorkGroup class to only those types that implement the *ISerializable* interface.

In addition to these two flavors of type constraints (class and interface), the As clause is also used to establish a *new constraint*. This type of constraint restricts the allowed replacement types to only those types that have a parameterless constructor—that is, a constructor that takes no arguments. To use a new constraint, add the As New clause to the type parameter.

```
Public Class WorkGroup(Of T As New)
```

This enables the class to create new instances of the type replaced by T within the class's source code.

```
Public Class WorkGroup(Of T As New)
    Public Function DoSomeWork( ) As T
        ' ----- Create a new instance of whatever 'T' is.
        Dim result As New T
        ...
        Return result
    End Function
End Class
```

Because the As New clause prepares the class to create an instance of the type defined by the type parameter, you cannot specify any type for the type parameter that includes the MustInherit keyword. Such classes cannot be instantiated, and it would be meaningless (and an error) to use them with the New keyword.

Each defined type parameter can include a different constraint, the same constraint used with other type parameters, or no constraint at all. In this statement, T1 has no constraints placed on it, but the other type parameters do.

```
Public Class WorkGroup(Of T1, T2 As New, T3 As New, _
    T4 As Runtime.Serialization.ISerializable)
```

# Multiple Constraints

A type parameter can specify multiple constraints at the same time, and only classes that meet *all* of the constraints can be used for that parameter. To use multiple constraints, surround the list of constraints with a set of curly braces and separate each constraint by a comma.

```
Public Class WorkGroup(Of T As {New, _
    Runtime.Serialization.ISerializable})
```

This statement restricts the types used for T to only those that implement the *ISerializable* interface *and* include a parameterless constructor. While you can include multiple interface constraints on a single type parameter, each type parameter can include only one class-based type constraint. It would not make sense to include two classes anyway, since Visual Basic does not allow a class to inherit from more than one base class. The New constraint can be used with either class or interface constraints.

# Accessing Type Parameter Members

Consider the following generic class definition.

```
Public Class NoisyClass(Of T)
    Public Sub ShowMe(ByVal theItem As T)
        MsgBox(theItem.ToString( ))
    End Sub
End Class
```

Using this class with an Integer parameter, as in:

```
Dim notSoNoisy As New NoisyClass(Of Integer)
notSoNoisy.ShowMe(5)
```

displays a message box with the integer value, in this case, 5. You can also use other types with the class. For example, the code:

```
Dim notSoNoisy As New NoisyClass(Of System.Exception)
notSoNoisy.ShowMe(New System.Exception)
```

displays "System.Exception: Exception of type 'System.Exception' was thrown." When T includes no class constraints, it becomes the lowest common denominator of all possible substitution types, *System.Object*. The definition:

```
Public Class WorkGroup(Of T)
```

is basically the same as:

```
Public Class WorkGroup(Of T As System.Object)
```

Both definitions work with all types, since all types derive from *System.Object*. When you add a class constraint to a type parameter (or use the default of *System. Object*), any members of that T class type can be used within the generic class definition. For example, consider the following simple class:

```
Public Class ControlLocator(Of T As System.Windows.Forms.Control)
    Public Sub WhereIsIt(ByVal theControl As T)
        MsgBox("Location: " & theControl.Left & ", " & _
            theControl.Top)
    End Sub
End Class
```

Because only types that derive from *System.Windows.Forms.Control* can be used as substitutes for T, all members of *System.Windows.Forms.Control* can be used in all references to T (such as the theControl variable), including the *Left* and *Top* properties.

You can only use members that are related to the type constraints defined for a parameter. If you don't include any type constraints, then you can only use the members of *System.Object*, which appear in every object in .NET. Although the following class definition is slated to work with strings (and the String class's *ToUpper* method), it will not compile, since there is no reference to String in the type parameter's constraints.

```
Public Class UsuallyString(Of T)
    Public Sub ShowUpperCase(ByVal theText As T)
        ' ----- The next line will not compile.
```

```
    MsgBox(theText.ToUpper( ))
  End Sub
End Class
```

Even if you create an instance of this class with a String:

```
Dim usingStringNow As UsuallyString(Of String)
```

the original class definition will not compile because the compiler does not know in advance that you plan to use it with String data.

If you place an interface type constraint on a type parameter, uses of that type parameter can access the members of the interface, as shown in the following code.

```
Public Interface ISimple
  Sub WriteThisCode( )
End Interface

Public Class UsesISimple(Of T As ISimple)
  Public Sub DoTheWork(ByVal theData As T)
    ' ----- Uses the class-specific implementation.
    theData.WriteThisCode( )
  End Sub
End Class
```

If you have multiple type constraints on a type parameter, uses of that parameter can generally access all members of all type constraints. If name conflicts do exist between two constraints (such as a class and interface having a member of the same name), your code will have to cast or convert the typed object to the desired class or interface (using CType or some other method) before calling the conflicting member.

# Generic Methods

Type members (functions and sub procedures) can also be defined with type parameters, whether or not the class in which they appear uses generics. The type parameter information appears between the defined method name and its regular parameter list.

```
Public Sub GenericMessage(Of T As System.Windows.Forms.Control) _
    (ByVal preamble As String, ByVal someObject As T)
  MsgBox(preamble & ": " & someObject.Location.ToString( ))
End Sub
```

All of the multiple parameter, constraint, and member usage rules that apply to generic classes also apply to generic members.

# Nested Generic Types

The type parameters included in a class definition can be used within nested classes:

```
Public Class Level1(Of T1, T2)
  Public Class Level2
```

```
      Public theData As T1
   End Class
End Class
```

However, when you create instances of the outer and inner classes based on different specified parameters, the resulting instances are fully unrelated. For instance, using the Level1 and Level2 classes just defined, the statements:

```
Dim first As New Level1(Integer, Double).Level2
Dim second As Level1(Integer, String).Level2
first.theData = 5
second = first      ' This line will not compile
```

will not compile successfully. Even though the Level2 classes both contain only an Integer public member, they are not compatible because each class is tied to a different set of data types.

Nested types may also include their own type parameters.

```
Public Class Level1(Of T1, T2)
   Public Class Level2(Of T3)
      Public theData As T3
   End Class
End Class
```

# Overloaded Types and Members

Normally, you can only create a single definition of a named class within a namespace. However, you can create multiple class definitions with the same name if they each include a different number of type parameters (zero or more). The following statements define two distinct classes that share a common name.

```
Public Class OverloadedName(Of T1)
End Class

Public Class OverloadedName(Of T1, T2)
End Class
```

The compiler will use the appropriate class definition, depending on the number of type parameters supplied when instantiating that class name.

```
' ----- The compiler will use the (Of T1) definition.
Dim justOne As OverloadedName(Of Integer)
```

Methods can be overloaded in the same way. This type of overloading can be mixed with the standard method of overloading.

```
Public Sub DoSomeWork(Of T)(ByVal data1 As T)
End Sub

Public Sub DoSomeWork(Of T)(ByVal data1 As T, data2 As String)
End Sub

Public Sub DoSomeWork(Of T1, T2)(ByVal data1 As T1, _
      ByVal data2 As T2)
End Sub
```

# 11

# Error Handling in Visual Basic

Even if your source code is completely free of all bugs, application errors may still appear, whether from user data issues, integration problems with third-party components, or unexpected changes in the system environment. This chapter takes a concise look at error-handling techniques in Visual Basic. The terms *exception* and *error* are used synonymously throughout this chapter.

Visual Basic supports the On ErrorGoTo style of error handling that was introduced with the original version of Visual Basic. This type of error handling is referred to as *unstructured error handling*. VB also supports the *structured exception handling* technique familiar to C++ programmers.

## Error Detection and Error Handling

Dealing with errors in your code generally occurs in two steps: *error detecting* and *error handling*. In most cases, you deal with the consequences of an error immediately, merging these two steps into one seamless process. You can also break up the steps, recognizing an error immediately but dealing with it later on in your block of code, or even in a different part of your application. The code location where an error occurs is called the *offending procedure*.

There are two types of errors that can occur in a running program: runtime errors and logic errors. A *runtime error* occurs when the code attempts to perform an operation that is impossible to perform, such as opening a file that does not exist or dividing by zero. Visual Basic automatically takes care of error *detection* of runtime errors because it has no other choice. Proper error *handling* of runtime errors is up to the programmer. Without programmer action, Visual Basic itself handles the error by presenting an error message to the user and then terminating the application, which is, at the very least, a nuisance for the user.

A *logic error* is the production of an unexpected or incorrect result. Consider a function that returns the IQ for an individual based on a set of IQ test scores. A result of 100 is entirely normal and expected. If an individual is very smart, you might expect an IQ in the range of 120 or more. But if the function returns an IQ of -350, that is a logic error, either due to bad code, bad data, or both.

Visual Basic does not provide error detection for logic errors—no computer language does—because to Visual Basic, no error has occurred. However, an unhandled logic error may subsequently result in a runtime error, which Visual Basic will certainly recognize. For instance, code that is intended to retrieve a positive nonzero integer may instead retrieve zero. This is a logic error. If that integer is later used as a denominator in some other part of the application, the seemingly small logic error will become a large runtime problem.

The programmer must anticipate logic errors and provide both error detection and error handling. From this perspective, logic errors are far more serious and much more difficult to deal with than runtime errors. After all, a runtime error won't be completely overlooked—at least Visual Basic will do something about it.

The problem with an overlooked logic error is that it may give the user specious feedback. This is, no doubt, the most insidious behavior a program can produce. In the best-case scenario, a logic error will generate a runtime error at some later time, but tracking down the original logic error source of that runtime error may be a daunting task.

# Runtime Error Handling

Visual Basic supports both unstructured error handling and structured exception handling. This discussion starts with a look at unstructured error handling, the same error-handling support provided in VB 6. You are not required to include any error handling in a VB procedure. If you do include such handling in a procedure, you must include either the structured or unstructured variety; a single procedure cannot include both types of error-handling methods.

## Unstructured Error Handling

Error-handling techniques that revolve around the various On Error... statements are referred to as *unstructured* error-handling techniques. These techniques generally involve the Err object and the Visual Basic call stack.

### The Err object

Visual Basic's built-in error object, called Err, has several useful properties and methods, as shown in Tables 11-1 and 11-2, respectively.

*Table 11-1. Properties of the Err object*

| Property | Description |
| --- | --- |
| Description | A short string describing the error. |
| HelpContext | The numeric context ID for a help topic associated with the error. |
| HelpFile | The fully qualified filename of the associated help file, if available. |

*Table 11-1. Properties of the Err object (continued)*

| Property | Description |
| --- | --- |
| LastDLLError | The return code from a call made to a function in an external DLL. This property may change value at any time, so it is wise to store the current value in a variable immediately upon return from the DLL call. VB does not raise errors based on the return value of a DLL function, since it cannot know which return values indicate errors. |
| Number | The error number of the error. |
| Source | A string that indicates the object that generated the error. When the error is generated within your application, the Source property is the project programmatic ID. For class-initiated errors, it is in the format *project.class*. When the error is generated by an external COM component, the Source property returns the programmatic ID of that component, generally in the form *application.object*. |

*Table 11-2. Methods of the Err object*

| Method | Description |
| --- | --- |
| Clear | Clears the values of all properties of the Err object. Its syntax is:<br>`Err.Clear( )`<br>The Clear method is called implicitly when any of the following statements are executed: a Resume statement; an Exit Sub, Exit Function, or Exit Property statement; a Try...Catch...Finally statement; or an On Error statement. |
| Raise | Causes Visual Basic to generate a runtime error and sets the properties of the Err object to the values given by the parameters of the Raise method. Its syntax is:<br>`Err.Raise(Number[, Source[, Description[, _`<br>`    HelpFile[, HelpContext]]]])`<br>where all but the first named argument is optional. Each parameter corresponds to the property of the same name. |

## Dealing with runtime errors

Visual Basic detects a runtime error as soon as it occurs, sets the properties of the Err object, and directs the flow of execution to a location that the programmer has specified by the most recent On Error statement. This location can be one of the following:

- The line of code immediately following the line that caused the error
- Another labeled location within the offending procedure
- Any enabled error handler within the current procedure's call stack
- *New in 2005.* In Windows Forms applications, the error handler associated with the *My.Application.UnhandledException* event

If none of these methods exist or are enabled (and no structured exception handlers are in use), VB issues an error message and terminates the application. The remainder of this section describes each option in more detail.

**Inline error handling.** Code execution will be "redirected" to the line following the offending line of code if the most recent On Error statement is:

```
On Error Resume Next
```

This is referred to as *inline error handling.* The following example demonstrates this type of error handling in the process of renaming a file. The code specifically examines any error number (Err.Number) generated by the Rename function.

```
Dim oldName As String
Dim newName As String

On Error Resume Next

' ----- Prompt the user for the old and new names.
oldName = InputBox("Enter the file name to rename.")
newName = InputBox("Enter the new file name.")

' ----- Rename the file.
Err.Clear()
Rename("c:\" & oldName, "c:\" & newName)

' ----- Deal with any error.
If (Err.Number = 53) Then
    ' ----- File not found error.
    MsgBox("File '" & oldName & "' not found.")
    Exit Sub
ElseIf (Err.Number <> 0) Then
    ' ----- All other errors.
    MsgBox("Error " & Err.Number & ": " & Err.Description)
    Exit Sub
End If
```

**Centralized error handling.** *Centralized error handling* keeps error detection and error handling in the same procedure, but it places all error-handling code in a common location within that procedure. This is especially useful when code detection for a common set of errors occurs multiple times throughout a large procedure. Execution is redirected to the central error-handling code block using the statement:

```
On Error GoTo label
```

This is outlined in the following code template:

```
Public Sub Example()
    On Error GoTo ErrorHandler

    ' ----- If a run-time error occurs here, Visual Basic
    '       directs execution to the ErrorHandler label.
    Exit Sub

ErrorHandler:
    ' ----- Code can be placed here to handle errors directly.
    '       Err.Number, Err.Description, and Err.Source can be
    '       examined here.
End Sub
```

Once the On Error GoTo ErrorHandler statement is executed, the error handler beginning at the label ErrorHandler is *active.* There are several possibilities for dealing with the error. The most common possibility is simply to handle the error in the active error handler, perhaps by displaying an error message asking the user to take corrective action.

Another common approach is to pass information about an error to the calling procedure through parameters or through the return value of the offending function. For instance, if a function is designed to rename a file, the function might return an integer error code indicating the success or failure of the operation. This method is quite common among the Win32 API functions. In particular, the error code might be 0 for success, -1 if the file does not exist, -2 if the new filename is invalid, and so on.

A third possibility is to pass the error to the calling procedure by invoking the Err. Raise method within the active error handler:

```
Err.Raise(Err.Number, Err.Source, Err.Description, _
    Err.HelpFile, Err.HelpContext)
```

This triggers the next procedure up in the call stack to process the error using its own active error handler. This process is called *regenerating* or *reraising* the error. If that procedure does not have an active error handler, the raised error continues up the call stack until it finds a procedure with an active error handler.

**No enabled error handler.** When you first enter any procedure, error handling is disabled in that procedure until the code encounters some sort of On Error or structured exception-handling statement. Using On Error GoTo *label* enables centralized error handling, but what if you want to turn off the central error-handling block code? The following statement takes just such an action, restoring the error-handling state to what it was when you first entered the procedure.

```
On Error GoTo 0
```

Without an enabled error handler, all errors cause execution to move up the call stack to the next procedure, continuing up until an enabled exception handler is found. A lack of exception handlers causes Visual Basic to display an error message and terminate the application.

A third variation of the On Error statement disables an error handler from inside of an error handler:

```
On Error GoTo -1
```

This statement can be used within a block of error-handling code. It causes the procedure to forget that it is in an error handler; Resume statements will have no impact after using this statement. To reinstate error handling, you must use another On Error statement.

*New in 2005.* Visual Basic 2005 adds support for a global, central error-handling routine. This feature is only available in Windows Forms applications, and it is accessed through the *My.Application.UnhandledException* event. The actual procedure for this event is found in the application's *ApplicationEvents.vb* file, which is hidden from the Solution Explorer view by default. (Click the *Show All Files* button in the Solution Explorer to display this and other hidden files.) The event procedure has the following form.

```
Namespace My
    Class MyApplication
        Private Sub MyApplication_UnhandledException( _
            ByVal sender As Object, _
```

```
            ByVal e As UnhandledExceptionEventArgs) _
            Handles Me.UnhandledException
      ' ----- Special error handling code goes here.
      End Sub
   End Class
End Namespace
```

This special event handler is ignored when running your application within the Visual Studio IDE.

## Structured Exception Handling

*Structured exception handling* uses the Try...Catch...Finally construct to handle local errors. This is a much more object-oriented approach, involving objects of the *System.Exception* class and its derived classes.

The syntax of the Try...Catch...Finally construct is:

```
Try
      tryStatements

[Catch [exception [As type]] [When expression]
      catchStatements
[Exit Try]]

[Catch [exception [As type]] [When expression]
      catchStatements]
. . .
[Catch [exception [As type]] [When expression]
      catchStatements]

[Finally
      finallyStatements]
End Try
```

The *tryStatements* (which are required) constitute the Try block and are the statements that are monitored for errors by VB. Error handling is *active* within the Try block.

The Catch blocks (you can include zero or more of these) contain code that is executed in response to VB "catching" a particular type of error within the Try block. Thus, the Catch blocks consist of the error handlers for the Try block.

The *exception* [As *type*] and [When *expression*] clauses are referred to as *filters*. An *exception* is either a variable of type *System.Exception* or one of its derived classes. It is by using one of these derived classes that you can narrow the scope of a Catch clause to a specific error. The clause:

```
Catch ex As Exception
```

will catch any exception for handling within that Catch block. The clause:

```
Catch ex As DivideByZeroException
```

catches divide-by-zero division errors, but no others. The *DivideByZeroException* class is one of the classes derived from *System.Exception*.

The When filter is typically used with user-defined errors. For instance, the code in the following Try block raises an error if the user does not enter a number.

```
Dim userInput As String
Try
    userInput = InputBox("Enter a number.")
    If Not IsNumeric(userInput) Then Err.Raise(1)
Catch When Err.Number = 1
    MsgBox("Supplied data was non-numeric.")
End Try
```

The following code will not catch an error, since no true error is generated:

```
Dim testNumber As Integer
Try
    testNumber = 5
Catch When testNumber = 5
    ' ----- Execution will never come here.
    MsgBox(testNumber & " is not right.")
End Try
```

The Finally clause in a Try statement includes any code that must be executed, whether an error occurs or not. This final code can be used for cleanup in the event of an error.

The Exit Try statement can appear anywhere within a Try...Catch...Finally block to jump out of the statement immediately. Any remaining Finally clause statements are skipped.

As with unstructured error handling, VB may pass an error up the call stack when using structured exception handling. This happens in the following situations:

- An error occurs within a Try block that is not handled by one of the Catch blocks.

- An error occurs outside any Try block.

## Exception classes

The following list includes many of the common exception types derived from the *System.Exception* class. Classes are indented under the class from which they are derived.

```
Exception
    ApplicationException
    SystemException
        AccessException
            FieldAccessException
            MethodAccessException
            MissingMemberException
                MissingFieldException
                MissingMethodException
        AppDomainUnloadedException
        AppDomainUnloadInProgressException
        ArgumentException
            ArgumentNullException
            ArgumentOutOfRangeException
```

```
        DuplicateWaitObjectException
    ArithmeticException
        DivideByZeroException
        NotFiniteNumberException
        OverflowException
    ArrayTypeMismatchException
    BadImageFormatException
    CannotUnloadAppDomainException
    ContextMarshalException
    CoreException
        ExecutionEngineException
        IndexOutOfRangeException
        StackOverflowException
    ExecutionEngineException
    FormatException
    InvalidCastException
    InvalidOperationException
    MulticastNotSupportedException
    NotImplementedException
    NotSupportedException
        PlatformNotSupportedException
    NullReferenceException
    OutOfMemoryException
    RankException
    ServicedComponentException
    TypeInitializationException
    TypeLoadException
        EntryPointNotFoundException
    TypeUnloadedException
    UnauthorizedAccessException
    WeakReferenceException
URIFormatException
```

In general, the derived classes provide no additional class members; it is the class instance itself that provides the information needed to distinguish between different types of errors. (It is possible to access the exception class for an error even when you are using the On Error unstructured error-handling methods. The Err object includes a GetException method that returns an instance of the exception class related to the error.)

Some of the derived classes do include additional information that can be useful to your error-processing actions. For instance, the *ArgumentException* class includes a ParamName property that returns the name of the parameter that causes the exception. The following example demonstrates its use.

```
Sub CopyAnImportantFile( )
    Dim sourceFile As String = "c:\temp.txt"
    Dim destFile As String = "I am not a file path!"
    Try
        FileCopy(sourceFile, destFile)
    Catch ex As ArgumentException
        MsgBox(ex.Message & " Parameter: " & e.ParamName)
    End Try
End Sub
```

The *System.Exception* class includes several important members, as listed in Table 11-3.

*Table 11-3. Members of the System.Exception class*

| Member | Description |
| --- | --- |
| Data | Property. *New in 2005.* A dictionary collection used to add additional information to custom exceptions. |
| Message | Property. A string containing the error message. |
| Source | Property. A string that describes the application or object that threw the exception. Generally the application's programmatic ID, the COM programmatic ID, or a *project.class* name for in-class errors. |
| StackTrace | Property. A string that contains the stack trace immediately before the exception was thrown. |
| TargetSite | Property. The name of the method that threw the exception. |
| ToString | Method. Obtains the name of the exception as a string and possible additional information about the current error. |

The following example displays the type of content you can except from these class properties. It generates an *ArgumentNullException* exception manually, which is handled two procedures further up the call stack.

```
Public Sub Level1Routine( )
    Dim info As String
    Try
        Level2Routine( )
    Catch ex As Exception
        info = "Message: " & ex.Message & vbCrLf & _
            "Source: " & ex.Source & vbCrLf & _
            "Stack: " & ex.StackTrace & vbCrLf & _
            "Target: " & ex.TargetSite.Name & vbCrLf & _
            "ToString: " & ex.ToString
        Debug.WriteLine(info)
    End Try
End Sub

Sub Level2Routine( )
    Level3Routine( )
End Sub

Public Sub Level3Routine( )
    Throw New ArgumentNullException( )
End Sub
```

In Level3Routine, an *ArgumentNullException* is thrown using the Throw statement, passing a new instance of the exception up the call stack. The output from the call to Level1Routine is as follows (slightly formatted for readability):

```
Message: Value cannot be null.
Source: WindowsApplication1
Stack:  at WindowsApplication1.Form1.Level3Routine( )
            in C:\temp\Form1.vb:line 26
        at WindowsApplication1.Form1.Level2Routine( )
            in C:\temp\Form1.vb:line 22
```

```
        at WindowsApplication1.Form1.Level1Routine( )
            in C:\temp\Form1.vb:line 10
Target: Level3Routine
ToString: System.ArgumentNullException: Value cannot be null.
        at WindowsApplication1.Form1.Level3Routine( )
            in C:\temp\Form1.vb:line 26
        at WindowsApplication1.Form1.Level2Routine( )
            in C:\temp\Form1.vb:line 22
        at WindowsApplication1.Form1.Level1Routine( )
            in C:\temp\Form1.vb:line 10
```

# Dealing with Logic Errors

Logic errors occur most often from conflicts between data and code. A function expects the user to enter a date in string format; the user enters his name instead. A block of code requires a number of 1 to 100; the database field somehow contains -5 instead. Invalid user data entry, unexpected results from external data sources, and good data turned bad by problematic algorithms in the code work against the application—and against the user.

Since so many logic errors stem from issues with the data being manipulated by the application, it makes sense to focus on detecting and correcting data issues. There are two key places in any application where data error detection is most useful: (1) when the data comes into the program and (2) when the data is just about to be processed by the program. Although data comes from many different sources (users, files, Internet connections, database queries), this section discusses user-entered data.

Consider the following function, which retrieves a number from the user.

```
Public Function GetSomeData( ) As Integer
   ' ----- Retrieve a number from 1 to 100 only.
   Dim userEntry As Integer

   userEntry = CInt(InputBox("Enter an integer from 1 to 100."))
   Return userEntry
End Sub
```

Visual Basic sure makes the coding of such user interaction easy. But what happens when the user enters "101" in the InputBox's text field, or "123456," or even "abc?" To protect the program against bad data, this code needs to detect the potential logic error immediately, *when the data is entering the program*. The GetSomeData routine can be corrected by adding some simple data confirmation code.

```
Public Function GetSomeData( ) As Integer
   ' ----- Retrieve a number from 1 to 100 only.
   Dim userEntry As String

   Do While True
      ' ----- Prompt the user for the number.
      userEntry = InputBox("Enter an integer from 1 to 100.")
```

```
' ----- Check for valid input.
If (IsNumeric(userEntry) = False) Or _
        (InStr(userEntry, ".") > 0) Then
    MsgBox("Entry was non-numeric or decimal. Try again.")
ElseIf (Val(userEntry) < 1) Or (Val(userEntry) > 100) Then
    MsgBox("Entry must range from 1 to 100. Try again.")
Else
    ' ----- Looks like good data.
    Return CInt(userEntry)
End If
    Loop
End Function
```

That takes care of the invalid data. This function could even be modified to use either structured exception handling or unstructured error handling by manually raising errors.

```
Public Function GetSomeData( ) As Integer
    ' ----- Retrieve a number from 1 to 100 only.
    Dim userEntry As String

    On Error GoTo ErrorHandler

TryEntryAgain:
    ' ----- Prompt the user for the number.
    userEntry = InputBox("Enter an integer from 1 to 100.")

    ' ----- Check for valid input.
    If (IsNumeric(userEntry) = False) Or _
            (InStr(userEntry, ".") > 0) Then
        Err.Raise(1, Nothing, _
            "Entry was non-numeric or decimal. Try again.")
    ElseIf (Val(userEntry) < 1) Or (Val(userEntry) > 100) Then
        Err.Raise(2, Nothing, _
            "Entry must range from 1 to 100. Try again.")
    End If

    ' ----- Looks like good data.
    Return CInt(userEntry)
    Exit Function

ErrorHandler:
    ' ----- Something happened. Show the error.
    MsgBox(Err.Description)
    Resume TryEntryAgain
End Function
```

In most cases, detecting error issues right when they occur is best. This gives the user a chance to correct the error right away, before the errant content can cause any damage. But sometimes it makes sense to postpone analysis of the incoming data for just a little while, until just before it is used. This is most often the case on a data-entry form with many input fields. Consider the data-entry form in Figure 11-1.

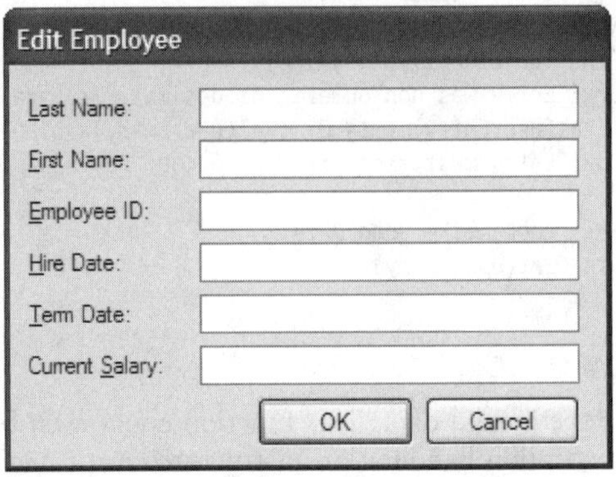

*Figure 11-1. Form in need of data verification*

This type of form generally has code to send the user-supplied data to a database record. You could monitor every data-entry field for valid data, perhaps when each field lost the input focus, and throw up a warning message if anything was out of place. But this would quickly become tiresome to the user. In forms such as this, it's better to wait until the user is finished with all data entry and then verify the data *just before using it*—or just before storing it in the database. The OKButton button's Click event is the perfect place to confirm all data at once and only then warn the user of data conflicts and issues.

```
Private Sub OKButton_Click(ByVal sender As System.Object, _
      ByVal e As System.EventArgs) Handles OKButton.Click
   ' ----- Confirm and save the data before closing the form.
   If (VerifyData( ) = False) Then Exit Sub
   If (SaveData( ) = False) Then Exit sub
   Me.Close( )
End Sub
```

On this particular form, the VerifyData routine would check for the following data issues.

1. All fields other than *Date of Termination* are required.

2. For new records, the *Employee ID* must not already exist in the database.

3. *Date of Hire* and *Date of Termination* (when supplied) must be valid dates.

4. If *Date of Termination* appears, it must occur chronologically after *Date of Hire*.

5. *Current Salary* must be a valid number and should fall within some reasonable parameters, such as not falling below some minimum salary value stored in the database.

# Error Constants

The sample code in the previous section demonstrated the Err.Raise method being used for custom error reporting. Since .NET already uses this same method to indicate predefined system errors, there needs to be some way to confirm that your code's custom error numbers do not conflict with system-defined error numbers. Visual Basic defines a constant, vbObjectError, that assists in the selection of custom error-code values. This constant represents the minimum error code you should use for your own custom error messages. The recommended range is from vbObjectError to vbObjectError + 65535. If your application interacts with COM components, you should start your error codes with vbObjectError + 512, since COM components often use the first 512 values in this range for their own error codes.

# II

# Reference

This section consists of two very long but useful chapters. Chapter 12, *The Language Reference*, which contains an alphabetic reference of VB language elements, documents the following:

- Statements, such as `AddHandler` and `Structure...End Structure`.

- Procedures, such as `AppActivate` and `Rename`. Many of these were classified as statements in pre-.NET versions of Visual Basic, but now they are methods of one class or another, usually within the *Microsoft.VisualBasic* namespace. The official documentation often describes them as functions, but since they don't return values, they are described here as procedures.

- Functions, such as `Format` and `IsReference`.

- Compiler directives, such as `#Const` and `#If`.

- Visual Basic classes and their members. Apart from the *My* Namespace objects, the two intrinsic objects available in Visual Basic are the *Collection* class and the *Err* object.

- Selected classes in the .NET Framework Class Library, along with their members. Documentation of Framework Class Library entries, however, is highly selective; classes and their members appear here either because they replace language elements that were present in VB 6, or because they provide much-needed functionality that supplements existing language elements.

- Attributes, such as `<AttributeUsage>` and `<VBFixedString>`. Of the dozens of attributes available in the .NET Framework, this chapter includes only those of greatest interest to the VB programmer.

Most operators, such as the addition operator (+), are documented separately in Chapter 5. Also, certain language features reference predefined constants and enumeration values. Some of the more useful and interesting constants and enumerations are listed in Appendix C.

Chapter 13, *The 'My' Reference*, includes an alphabetic reference of all major nodes in the *My* Namespace hierarchy. It specifically documents the following:

- Objects, which include the major nodes of the hierarchy.
- Properties, used for setting and retrieving values. Many properties are read-only, and many provide access to consistent system and environment information.
- Methods, which take a specific useful action.
- Events, of which there are only a few supported through the *My* Namespace feature.

When you're looking for a particular language element but don't quite remember what it's called, an alphabetic reference is of little value. Appendix A provides just such a category-based lookup. In a similar way, the *My* Namespace hierarchy isn't always easy to visualize when its elements are sorted alphabetically. Therefore, Appendix B includes all *My* Namespace nodes listed hierarchically.

# 12

# The Language Reference

This chapter documents the major Visual Basic language elements. The elements are arranged alphabetically; see Appendix A for a listing by category.

Several different types of language elements appear in this chapter.

*Functions*

The entry for each function includes basic syntax information, with the details of parameters and return values. This is followed by a functional description and usage information (in the "Description" and "Usage at a Glance" sections). Many function entries also include source code examples.

Each VB function is, in fact, a method, since it is a member of a particular class in the *Microsoft.VisualBasic* (or other) namespace. Each entry identifies the class in which the function appears.

Visual Basic supports both named and positional arguments for most functions, procedures, and methods. Functions, procedures, or methods that accept parameter arrays as arguments don't accept named arguments if the ParamArray parameter is present. Some functions are actually resolved at compile time (the data-conversion functions fall into this category) and do not accept named arguments. To use named arguments, consider the syntax of the Mid function, which has two required arguments and one optional argument.

```
Mid(str As String, start As Long[, length As Long])
```

Using positional arguments, you might call the function as follows:

```
smallPart = Mid(wholeString, 12, 10)
```

The same function call using named arguments might appear as follows:

```
smallPart = Mid(start:=12, str:=wholeString, length:=10)
```

Since most functions accept named arguments, the entries in this chapter only indicate when a function or procedure does not support named arguments.

The "Version Differences" section found in some entries documents changes in usage for the entry between the different versions of Visual Basic, including Visual Basic 6.0, Visual Basic .NET 2002, Visual Basic .NET 2003, and Visual Basic 2005.

*Procedures*

Procedures are functions that don't return a value to the caller. Except for the absence of a return value, the same information is presented for procedures as for functions.

*Statements*

Visual Basic statements are not class members, do not support named arguments, and do not return a value. Aside from these three differences, the same information is presented for statements as for procedures and functions.

*Directives*

Visual Basic directives provide instruction to the VB compiler or to a .NET development environment such as Visual Studio. Like statements, they are not class members, do not support named arguments, and do not return a value. In general, the same information is presented for directives as for statements.

*Classes and Objects*

Entries for classes and objects identify the namespace to which the class belongs and indicate whether the class is directly creatable. If a class is creatable, a new instance of that class can be created by using the New keyword, as in:

```
Dim unitedStates As New Collection
```

In some cases, the entry for the class or object also includes a summary listing of the class's members.

*Class Members (Properties, Methods, and Events)*

Class members of particular interest or importance have their own separate entries. These entries generally contain the same level of detail as function entries.

*Attributes*

Attributes are classes derived from *System.Attribute* that allow you to store information with an assembly's metadata. This chapter includes only those attributes that Visual Basic programmers are most likely to use. Each attribute entry includes information about the attribute, its constructor, and its properties. Attribute properties can be used as optional named arguments in the constructor.

# #Const Directive

## Syntax

```
#Const constantName = expression
```

*constantName (required)*
Name of the compiler constant

*expression (required; literal expression)*
Any combination of literal values, other conditional compiler constants defined with the #Const directive, and arithmetic or logical operators except Is and IsNot

## Description

The #Const directive defines a conditional compiler constant. By using compiler constants to create code blocks that are included in the compiled application only when a particular condition is met, you can create more than one version of the application using the same source code. This is a two-step process.

1. Define the conditional compiler constant through the #Const directive, the project properties, or command-line compiler switches (see Appendix H).

2. Evaluate the constant with a #If...Then directive block. If a particular compiler constant is referenced in a #If...Then directive but is not defined, it has value of Nothing.

A conditional compiler constant can be assigned any string, numeric, or logical value returned by an expression. The expression can only consist of literals, operators other than Is and IsNot, and other conditional compiler constants.

When the compiler evaluates the condition of a #If...Then directive, its block of code is compiled as part of the application only when the evaluated expression is True.

## Usage at a Glance

- You can use any arithmetic or logical operator in the expression except Is and IsNot.

- You cannot use constants defined with the standard Const statement in the expression.

- You cannot use regular Visual Basic functions or variables in the expression.

- Setting a compiler constant to Nothing is the same as not defining it.

- Constants defined with #Const can only be used in conditional code blocks, not in standard VB code.

- You can place the #Const directive anywhere within a source file. If placed outside of all types, the defined constant is visible throughout the source file, but it is not visible to any other source files in the project. If placed in a type, the scope of the constant is that type. If placed in a procedure, the scope is that procedure and all called procedures.

- The #Const directive must be the first statement on a line of code. It can be followed only by a comment. The colon, which is used to combine multiple statements on a single logical line, cannot be used with compiler directives.

- Conditional compiler constants help you debug your code, as well as provide a way to create more than one version of your application. For instance, you can include code that only operates when run in debug mode. The code can be left in your final version and does not compile unless running in the debugger. Therefore, you don't need to keep adding and removing debugging code.

- Conditional compiler constants may be defined in terms of other conditional compiler constants. In this sample, the Flags constant will have a value of 2.

```
#Const Flag1 = 1
#Const Flag2 = 1
#Const Flags = Flag1 + Flag2
```

- A conditional compiler constant can be defined at the command line using the /define or /d switch.

- Constants defined by #Const are evaluated at compile time and therefore do not return information about the system on which the application is running.

- The Visual Basic compiler includes several predefined compiler constants for your use. See the "Conditional Compilation Constants" section of Appendix H for a listing of these constants.

### See Also
#If...Then...#Else Directive

---

## #If...Then...#Else Directive

### Syntax

```
#If expression Then
    statements
[#ElseIf expression Then
    [statements]]
[#Else
    [statements]]
#End If
```

*expression (required)*
An expression made up of literals, operators, and conditional compiler constants that evaluates to True or False

*statements (required for #If block)*
One or more lines of code or compiler directives

### Description

The #If...Then...#Else directive defines blocks of code that are only included in the compiled application when a particular condition is met or not met, allowing you to create more than one version of the application using the same source code.

Conditionally including a block of code is a two-step process:

1. Define the conditional compiler constant through the #Const directive, the project properties, or command-line compiler switches (see Appendix H).

2. Evaluate the constant with a #If...Then directive block. If a particular compiler constant is referenced in a #If...Then directive but is not defined, it has value of Nothing.

Only code blocks with expressions that evaluate to True are included in the executable. You can use the #Else statement to include code when none of the conditions are met. Use the #ElseIf portion any number of times to evaluate more conditions.

Conditional compilation blocks can be used to include or exclude debugging code. Such code can be excluded from a release compilation of the project. They can also be used to conditionally include code in different editions of your application. For instance, your project may result in two outputs, one with limited features available at a lower price to your customers and one with more advanced features.

### Usage at a Glance

- Unlike the normal If...Then statement, you cannot use a single-line version of the #If...Then statement.

- All expressions are evaluated using Option Compare Text, regardless of the setting of Option Compare.

- If a conditional compiler constant is undefined, comparing it to Nothing, 0, False, or an empty string ("") returns True.

- The Visual Basic compiler includes several predefined compiler constants for your use. See the "Conditional Compilation Constants" section of Appendix H for a listing of these constants.

### Example

```
#Const UseAdvancedSet = True
Private monitoredSet As Object

Public Sub MonitorCorrectSet( )
#If UseAdvancedSet = True Then
   monitoredSet = New MyObject.AdvancedSet
#Else
   monitoredSet = New MyObject.BasicSet
#End If
End Sub
```

Only one of the assignment statements will appear in the compiled output; for the line that is not included, it will be as if the source code never included it at all.

### See Also

#Const Directive

---

## #Region...#End Region Directive

### Syntax

```
#Region "identifierString"
...code goes here
#End Region
```

*identifierString (required)*
    The title of the code block

## Description

The #Region...#End Region directive marks a block of code as an expandable and collapsible region in the Visual Studio editor.

## Usage at a Glance

- Code blocks delineated with the #Region...#End Region directive are collapsed by default.
- *identifierString* identifies the region when it is collapsed.
- Multiline directives (such as #If) cannot be split across a #Region or #End Region boundary.

# Abs Function

## Class

System.Math

## Syntax

```
Dim result As type = Math.Abs(value)
```

*type (required; signed numeric type)*
One of the following data types: Decimal, Double, Integer, Long, SByte, Single, or Short

*value (required; expression of type type)*
A number with the absolute value that is to be returned

## Description

The *Abs* function returns the absolute value of *value*. The source and return data type are always the same.

## Usage at a Glance

- This is a shared member of the *System.Math* class, so it can be used without an instance.
- If Option Strict is Off, you will be able to pass string representations of numbers to the *Abs* function. Use the IsNumeric function to confirm that the string contains a valid number.

## Example

This sample returns the difference between two integers, regardless of their order.

```
Public Function IntegerDiff(ByVal first As Integer, _
    ByVal second As Integer) As Integer
  Return Math.Abs(second - first)
End Function
```

## Version Differences

In VB 6, Abs is an intrinsic VB function. In the .NET platform, it is a member of the *System.Math* class and not directly part of the VB language.

## Acos Function

### Class
System.Math

### Syntax
```
Dim result As Double = Math.Acos(d)
```
*d (required; Double)*
A cosine, a number between -1 and 1 inclusive

### Description
The *Acos* function returns the arccosine of *d* in radians, between 0 and π.

### Usage at a Glance
- If *d* is out of range (less than -1 or greater than 1), *Acos* returns *System.Double. NaN*.
- This is a shared member of the *System.Math* class, so it can be used without an instance.
- To convert from radians to degrees, multiply by 180/π.

### Version Differences
The *Acos* function did not exist in VB 6.

### See Also
Asin Function, Atan Function, Atan2 Function

## AddHandler Statement

### Syntax
```
AddHandler nameOfEventSender, AddressOf nameOfEventHandler
```
*nameOfEventSender (required)*
The name of a class or object instance and its event, such as *Button1.Click*

*nameOfEventHandler (required)*
The name of a subroutine that is to serve as the event handler for *nameOfEventSender*

### Description
The AddHandler statement binds an event handler to an event.

## Usage at a Glance

The AddHandler and RemoveHandler statements can be used to dynamically add and remove event-notification handlers at runtime. By contrast, the Handles keyword establishes an event-notification handler at compile time.

## Example

Chapter 8 includes examples of using event handlers.

## Version Differences

Visual Basic 2005 includes a new Custom Events statement that impacts the use of the AddHandler statement. See the *Custom Event Statement* entry in this chapter for additional information.

## See Also

Custom Event Statement, RemoveHandler Statement

# AddressOf Operator

## Syntax

```
AddressOf procedureName
```

*procedureName* (required)
The name of a procedure or method to be referenced as a delegate

## Description

The AddressOf operator returns a procedure delegate instance that references a specific procedure. Common uses of this operator include the following:

- To bind event handlers to events through the AddHandler statement:

  ```
  AddHandler Form1.Click, AddressOf Me.Form1_Click
  ```

- To create delegate objects, as in:

  ```
  Dim holdDelegate As Delegate = _
      New Delegate(AddressOf someClass.SomeMethod)
  ```

- To pass the address of a callback function to a Win32 API function:

  ```
  Call TypicalAPI(1, AddressOf MyCallbackRoutine)
  ```

## Version Differences

In VB 6, the procedure must reside in a standard code module, a restriction no longer enforced with .NET.

# AppActivate Procedure

## Class

Microsoft.VisualBasic.Interaction

## Syntax

```
AppActivate({ title | processID })
```

*title*  *(required if processID missing; String)*
The name of the application as currently shown in the application's title bar

*processID*  *(required if title missing; Integer)*
The task ID returned from the Shell function

## Description

The AppActivate procedure activates a window based on its caption or process ID.

## Usage at a Glance

- When activating an application by *title*, AppActivate performs a case-insensitive search on all top-level windows for a match. If an exact match is found, the window is activated. If no match is found, then the window captions are searched for a prefix match (*title* matches the beginning of the window caption). For example, the *title* "My Program" matches "My Program-MyDocument.xyz." If a prefix match is found, the window is activated. If multiple prefix matches are found, there is no way to predict which matching window will be activated.

- The window state (Maximized, Minimized, or Normal) of the activated application is not affected by AppActivate.

- If a matching application cannot be found, an error occurs.

- AppActivate searches only top-level windows.

- The Shell function returns an Integer value representing the process ID of the new application. This value can be passed directly to the AppActivate procedure.

- Several years ago, Microsoft changed their recommended method of naming window captions. The new standard places the document name first, followed by the application name, as in "Untitled.doc - Microsoft Word." This can make it more difficult to locate a window by caption.

- AppActivate is often used to give the focus to a particular window before keystrokes are sent to it using the SendKeys statement.

## Example

```
Public Function ActivateAppByTitle(ByVal theTitle As String) _
    As Boolean
' ----- Return success flag.
On Error GoTo ErrorHandler

AppActivate(theTitle)
Return True

ErrorHandler:
MsgBox ("Application " & theTitle & " could not be activated.")
Return False
End Function
```

## Version Differences

In VB 6, AppActivate has an optional Boolean parameter, *wait*, which postpones activation until the local program has the focus. In .NET, *wait* is not supported.

## See Also

SendKeys Statement, Shell Function

# Application Class

## Namespace

System.Windows.Forms

## Creatable

No

## Description

The Application class provides a diverse range of functionality, including support for multithreaded programming, access to the system registry, and support for subclassing (intercepting messages sent to application windows). It also includes a variety of informational functions, such as properties to retrieve the company name, to retrieve the application's executable path, and to retrieve the application's name and version. Members of the Application class are shared and do not require an object instance for use.

The following table lists some of the more useful and interesting members of the Application class. Those marked with an asterisk (*) have separate entries in this chapter.

| Member | Description |
| --- | --- |
| AddMessageFilter Method | Adds a special filter procedure to a thread's message queue. |
| ApplicationExit Event | Fires when an application is being shut down. |
| CompanyName Property * | Gets the company name as stored in the assembly. |
| CurrentCulture Property | Retrieves an object that describes the active culture-specific information. |
| CurrentInputLanguage Property | Retrieves an object that describes the user-interface input language. |
| DoEvents Method * | Allows the application to process pending messages in the message queue. |
| EnableRTLMirroring Method | *New in 2005.* Enables automatic right-to-left mirroring when displaying text. |
| ExecutablePath Property * | Returns the full path of the current application. |
| Exit Method | Exits the application gracefully. |
| ExitThread Method | Exits the current thread gracefully. |
| Idle Event | Fires when the application is about to enter an idle state. |
| OpenForms Property | *New in 2005.* The collection of open forms in the application. |
| ProductName Property * | Gets the product name as stored in the assembly. |
| ProductVersion Property * | Gets the product version information as stored in the assembly. |
| RemoveMessageFilter Method | Removes a previously added message filter. |
| Run Method * | Starts a new thread and message loop. |
| StartupPath Property | Gets the path of the application that started the current process. |
| ThreadExit Event | Fires when a thread is about to shut down. |

## Version Differences

Beginning with Visual Basic 2005, the *My.Application* object provides simplified access to many application-specific features and informational properties.

Application.CompanyName Property, Application.DoEvents Method, Application.
ExecutablePath Property, Application.ProductName Property, Application.Product-
Version Property

## Application.CompanyName Property

### Class
System.Windows.Forms.Application

### Syntax
```
Dim result As String = Application.CompanyName
```

### Description
The *CompanyName* property gets the company name for the application as recorded
in the assembly. It is set using the <AssemblyCompany> attribute of the assembly, which
normally appears in the *AssemblyInfo.vb* file. Its syntax is:
```
<Assembly: AssemblyCompany("company")>
```
where *company* is the company name. This is a read-only property.

### Version Differences
Visual Basic 2005 includes the *My.Application.Info.CompanyName* property, which
provides similar functionality.

### See Also
Application Class, Application.ProductName Property, Application.ProductVersion
Property

## Application.DoEvents Method

### Class
System.Windows.Forms.Application

### Syntax
```
Application.DoEvents()
```

### Description
The *DoEvents* method allows the application to process events and messages waiting
in its message queue. Some processor-intensive activities in your application may
prevent user-related input and output events from occurring in a timely manner. The
*DoEvents* method processes pending events.

### Usage at a Glance
- While *DoEvents* can be indispensable for increasing the responsiveness of your
  application, its use should be limited, since it significantly impacts performance.
  For example, here are the results of a test that counted the number of seconds

required to iterate a simple For...Next loop one million times, with and without an included *DoEvents* method call.

| | |
|---|---|
| Without `DoEvents` | 0.01 seconds |
| With `DoEvents` | 49.26 seconds |

- If most of a procedure's processing occurs inside of a processor-intensive loop, one way to avoid too many calls to *DoEvents* is to call it conditionally every 10, 100, or 1000 iterations. The following code calls *DoEvents* once for every 1000 iterations:

```
Dim soFar As Long = 0
For soFar = 1 To 1000000
    If ((soFar Mod 1000) = 0) Then DoEvents
Next soFar
```

- Calling *DoEvents* from within event calls may cause pseudo-recursion issues, as the event handler may be called again due to a separate message in the message queue.

## Example

The following example demonstrates the usefulness of the *DoEvents* method. When the GetBusy command button is clicked, it begins a very busy and infinite process. Normally, clicks on the TakeABreak command button would be blocked by the activity, but the *DoEvents* method makes its use possible.

```
' ----- Assumes a form with two buttons, GetBusy and TakeABreak.
Private iterationsSoFar As Long
Private interruptFlag As Boolean

Private Sub GetBusy_Click(ByVal sender As System.Object, _
        ByVal e As System.EventArgs) Handles GetBusy.Click
    interruptFlag = False
    Do While (interruptFlag = False)
        iterationsSoFar += 1
        DoEvents( )
    Loop
    MsgBox("Loop interrupted after " & iterationsSoFar & _
        " iterations.")
End Sub

Private Sub TakeABreak_Click(ByVal sender As System.Object, _
        ByVal e As System.EventArgs) Handles TakeABreak.Click
    ' ----- Stop the work.
    interruptFlag = True
End Sub
```

## Version Differences

Visual Basic 2005 adds an equivalent *My.Application.DoEvents* method.

## See Also

Application Class

## Application.ExecutablePath Property

### Class
System.Windows.Forms.Application

### Syntax
```
Dim result As String = Application.ExecutablePath
```

### Description
The *ExecutablePath* property returns the complete path of the executable file for the application. This is a read-only property.

### Version Differences
- The *ExecutablePath* property in the .NET Framework corresponds to the *App.Path* property in VB 6.
- Visual Basic 2005 includes the *My.Application.Info.DirectoryPath* property and other members of the *My.Application.Info* object that provide similar information.

### See Also
Application Class

---

## Application.ProductName Property

### Class
System.Windows.Forms.Application

### Syntax
```
Dim result As String = Application.ProductName
```

### Description
The *ProductName* property gets the product name of the application as recorded in the assembly. It is set using the <AssemblyProduct> attribute of the assembly, which normally appears in the *AssemblyInfo.vb* file. Its syntax is:
```
<Assembly: AssemblyProduct("product")>
```
where *product* is the product name. This is a read-only property.

### Version Differences
- This property corresponds to the *App.ProductName* property in VB 6.
- Visual Basic 2005 includes the *My.Application.Info.ProductName* property, which provides similar functionality.

### See Also
Application Class, Application.CompanyName Property, Application.ProductVersion Property

# Application.ProductVersion Property

## Class
System.Windows.Forms.Application

## Syntax
```
Dim result As String = Application.ProductVersion
```

## Description
The *ProductVersion* property gets the product version information for the application as recorded in the assembly. It is set using the `<AssemblyVersion>` attribute of the assembly, which normally appears in the *AssemblyInfo.vb* file. Its syntax is:

```
<Assembly: AssemblyVersion("major.minor.build.revision")>
```

where `major`, `minor`, `build`, and `revision` are the numeric parts of the version number. This is a read-only property.

The version number is normally a set of four numbers that represent the major, minor, build, and revision components of the version number. The default value is "1.0.*," which indicates that Visual Studio maintains default build and revision numbers.

## Version Differences
- This property corresponds to the *App.Major*, *App.Minor*, and *App.Revision* properties in VB 6.
- Visual Basic 2005 includes the *My.Application.Info.Version* property, which provides similar functionality.

## See Also
Application Class, Application.CompanyName Property, Application.ProductName Property

# Application.Run Method

## Class
System.Windows.Forms.Application

## Syntax
```
Application.Run(mainForm)
```
*mainForm (required; Windows.Forms.Form)*
   The form to use as the main form of the new application on the current thread

Other syntax variations are available.

## Description
The *Run* method starts a new application on the current thread, specifying the main form to display and use as the basis of the application. This is a common way of starting a Windows Forms application.

## Example

```
Module GeneralCode
    Public Sub Main( )
        ' ----- Starts the application.
        Application.Run(New Form1)
    End Sub
End Module
```

## Version Differences

Visual Basic 2005 includes new features that let you show the main form of an application with a syntax more familiar to VB 6 developers. See the *My.Forms Object* entry in Chapter 13 for additional information.

## See Also

Application Class

# Array Class

## Namespace

System

## Creatable

Yes

## Description

The *Array* object implements an ordered list of objects, numbered from 0 to a specified upper bound. Arrays can include multiple dimensions, each of which has its own range. Although the *Array* class is a distinct .NET class, it is wrapped by Visual Basic as its own array implementation; any standard VB array can take advantage of the *Array* class features.

The following table lists some of the more useful and interesting members of the *Array* class. Those marked with an asterisk (*) have separate entries in this chapter.

| Member | Description |
| --- | --- |
| BinarySearch Method * | Searches for an element in a sorted array dimension |
| Clear Method | Sets a range of array elements to their default content value |
| Clone Method | Creates a copy of an array, although reference type elements in the new array refer to the same objects as those in the old array |
| Copy Method * | Copies elements of one array into another existing array |
| GetValue Method | Retrieves a single value from an array |
| IndexOf Method * | Finds the first occurrence of a value in a range of array elements |
| IsReadOnly Property | Indicates whether the array is read-only or not |
| LastIndexOf Method * | Finds the last occurrence of a value in a range of array elements |
| Length Property | Identifies the full number of elements in all dimensions |
| Rank Property | Identifies the number of dimensions |
| Reverse Method * | Reverses the order of a range of array elements |

| Member | Description |
| --- | --- |
| SetValue Method | Sets a single value in an array |
| Sort Method * | Sorts a range of elements in an array |

### Version Differences

Arrays in VB 6 were an intrinsic part of the language and were not associated with the larger set of functionality available through the *System.Array* class.

## Array.BinarySearch Method

### Class

System.Array

### Syntax

```
Dim result As Integer = Array.BinarySearch(array, value[, comparer])
```

or:

```
Dim result As Integer = Array.BinarySearch(array, index, _
    length, value[, comparer])
```

*array* *(required; any array)*
The one-dimensional array to be searched

*value* *(required in syntax 1; any)*
The value to search for in *array*

*index* *(required in syntax 2; Integer)*
The array element at which the search is to start

*length* *(required in syntax 2; Integer)*
The number of array elements to be searched

*comparer* *(optional; IComparer interface)*
A class implementing the *IComparer* interface that determines how two items are compared for equality

### Description

The *BinarySearch* method returns the zero-based ordinal position of the first element that matches *value* in *array*. The dimension or range being searched must already be sorted. This method uses a binary search algorithm.

If nameSet is an array of names in alphabetical order, then the code:

```
Array.BinarySearch(nameSet, "steve")
```

returns the position of the first element with the name "steve." If no match is found, *BinarySearch* returns the negative number whose bitwise complement is the index of the first element that is larger than "steve."

### Usage at a Glance

- The array must be a one-dimensional array sorted in ascending order.
- If *value* is not found in the array, the method returns a negative number, which is the bitwise complement of the index of the first element that is larger than *value*.

To change this negative value into an index you can use, use the Not operator, as in the following code fragment:

```
position = Array.BinarySearch(someArray, valueToFind)
If (position >= 0) Then
    MsgBox(position)
Else
    MsgBox(position & vbCrLf & Not position)
End If
```

- If an array contains Boolean values, the method fails to correctly identify the position of the first False value in the array.

- By default, the *System.Collections.Comparer* class is used to compare *value* with the members of *array*. It performs case-sensitive comparisons.

- In addition to the *Comparer* class, you can also pass an instance of the *System. Collections.CaseInsensitiveComparer* class as the *comparer* argument. It provides for case-insensitive comparisons. For example:

```
Dim someStates() As String = {"Alaska", "ALASKA", _
    "Michigan", "MICHIGAN", "New York", "NEW YORK"}
Dim searchState As String
Dim position As Integer
Dim toCompare As New CaseInsensitiveComparer

searchState = "MICHIGAN"
position = Array.BinarySearch(someStates, searchState, toCompare)
```

The value of position will be 2.

### See Also

Array Class, Array.IndexOf Method, Array.LastIndexOf Method, Array.Sort Method

## Array.Copy Method

### Class

System.Array

### Syntax

```
Array.Copy(sourceArray, destinationArray, length)
```

or:

```
Array.Copy(sourceArray, sourceIndex, destinationArray, _
    destinationIndex, length)
```

*sourceArray*  (required; any array)
  The source array to be copied

*sourceIndex*  (required in syntax 2; Integer or Long)
  The index in *sourceArray* at which copying begins

*destinationArray* (required; any array)
  The destination array for the copied array items

*destinationIndex  (required in syntax 2; Integer or Long)*
    The index in *destinationArray* where the first element is to be copied

*length  (required; Integer or Long)*
    The number of elements to copy

## Description

The *Copy* method makes a copy of all or part of an array. Since arrays are reference types, setting one array variable equal to another simply assigns a new reference to the same array. Consider the following code:

```
Dim mainArray( ) As Integer = {1, 2, 3}
Dim otherArray( ) As Integer
otherArray = mainArray
otherArray(0) = 10
MsgBox(mainArray(0))    ' Displays 10
```

Since changes to otherArray impacted mainArray, the two arrays are clearly the same.

The *Copy* method makes a true copy of the elements, not simply a new reference to the same array. For arrays of value types, the new elements will be truly distinct. For arrays of reference types, the new elements can still impact the original reference data.

## Usage at a Glance

- The first syntax copies a range of values from the beginning of *sourceArray* to the beginning of *destinationArray*. The second syntax copies a range of values from anywhere in *sourceArray* to anywhere in *destinationArray*.

- *sourceArray* and *destinationArray* must have the same number of dimensions.

- *length* is the total number of elements to be copied. If sampleArray is a two-by-two array (four total elements), the statement:

    ```
    Array.Copy(sampleArray, 0, targetArray, 0, 3)
    ```

    copies elements (0,0), (0,1), and (1,0) from sampleArray to targetArray.

- To copy all elements, use UBound(sourceArray)+1 as an argument to *length*.

- If *sourceArray* and *destinationArray* are the same, and *destinationIndex* lies within the range of values being copied (that is, if the source and target ranges overlap), no data will be lost. The method behaves as if it copies *length* elements from *sourceArray* to a temporary buffer, then copies from the temporary buffer to *destinationArray*.

## Example

This sample is similar to the code shown above in the "Description" section comments, but it uses the *Copy* method instead of a direct assignment.

```
Dim mainArray( ) As Integer = {1, 2, 3}
Dim otherArray( ) As Integer
ReDim otherArray(UBound(mainArray) + 1)
Array.Copy(mainArray, otherArray, UBound(mainArray) + 1)
otherArray(0) = 10
MsgBox(mainArray(0))    ' Displays 1
```

## Version Differences

Since arrays were not reference types in VB 6, you could simply create a copy of an existing array through assignment, thus eliminating the need for a *Copy* method.

Array Class, Array.Sort Method

## Array.IndexOf Method

### Class
System.Array

### Syntax
```
Dim result As Integer = Array.IndexOf(array, _
    value[, startIndex[, count]])
```
*array* *(required; any array)*
The array to be searched.

*value* *(required; any)*
The object to be searched for in the array.

*startIndex* *(optional; Integer)*
The index at which to begin the search. If omitted, the search begins with the first element of the array.

*count* *(optional; Integer)*
The number of items to search. If omitted, the search continues to the end of the array.

### Description
The *IndexOf* method returns the index of the first occurrence of *value* in *array*, or -1 if *value* was not found within the range searched.

### Usage at a Glance
* *array* must be a one-dimensional array.
* Specifying a *count* value that goes past the end of the array results in an error.

### Example
The following code searches for a value in an Integer array:
```
Dim counter As Integer
Dim dataSet(99999) As Integer
For counter = 0 To 99999
    dataSet(counter) = CInt(Rnd( ) * 100000)
Next counter
MsgBox(Array.IndexOf(dataSet, 36500))
```

### See Also
Array Class, Array.LastIndexOf Method

## Array.LastIndexOf Method

### Class
System.Array

## Syntax

```
Dim result As Integer = Array.LastIndexOf(array, _
    value[, startIndex[, count]])
```

*array* *(required; any array)*
  The array to be searched.

*value* *(required; any)*
  The object that is searched for in the array.

*startIndex* *(optional; Integer)*
  The index at which to begin the search. If omitted, the search begins with the last element of the array.

*count* *(optional; Integer)*
  The number of items to search. If omitted, the search continues to the beginning of the array. This count moves backward. If *startIndex* is 6 and *count* is 3, items 6, 5, and then 4 are examined.

## Description

The *LastIndexOf* method returns the index of the last occurrence of *value* in *array*, or -1 if *value* was not found within the range searched.

## Usage at a Glance

- *array* must be a one-dimensional array.

- The *LastIndexOf* method has the same syntax as the *IndexOf* method and works the same way as *IndexOf*, except that it searches from the end of the array and returns the largest index of a matching element.

- Specifying a *count* value that goes past the beginning of the array results in an error.

## Example

See the example for the *Array.IndexOf Method* entry, as the use of the *LastIndexOf* method is identical.

## See Also

Array Class, Array.IndexOf Method

---

# Array.Reverse Method

## Class

System.Array

## Syntax

```
Array.Reverse(array[, startindex, endindex])
```

*array* *(required; any array)*
  The array to be reversed

*startIndex* *(optional; Integer)*
  The index at which to start the reversal process

*endIndex* *(optional; Integer)*
  The index at which to end the reversal process

## Description

The *Reverse* method reverses a portion of, or all of, the elements of an array.

## Example

```
Dim counter As Integer
Dim dataSet( ) As Integer = {1, 2, 3, 4, 5}
Array.Reverse(dataSet, 1, 3)
For counter = 0 To 4
    Debug.Write(dataSet(counter))
Next counter
```

This code prints the sequence 14325, which is the original array 12345 with the middle section from index 1 to index 3 reversed.

## See Also

Array Class, Array.Sort Method

# Array.Sort Method

## Class

System.Array

## Syntax

```
Array.Sort(array[, comparer])
Array.Sort(array, index, length[, comparer])
Array.Sort(keys, items[, comparer])
Array.Sort(keys, items, index, length[, comparer])
```

*array*  *(required in syntax 1 and 2; any array)*
The array of objects to be sorted.

*keys*  *(required in syntax 3 and 4; any array)*
The array of keys to use for sorting. This array is also sorted.

*items*  *(required in syntax 3 and 4; any array)*
A parallel array of values to be sorted in the order of *keys*, their corresponding keys.

*index*  *(required in syntax 2 and 4; Integer)*
The index at which to start the sort.

*length*  *(required in syntax 2 and 4; Integer)*
The number of items to include in the sort.

*comparer*  *(optional; IComparer interface)*
An object implementing the *IComparer* interface to be used for sorting. If omitted, then the sort uses the *IComparable* implementation of each element (either from *array* or *keys*).

## Description

The *Sort* method sorts a portion of, or all of, an entire one-dimensional array, with an optionally specified key array and an optionally specified *IComparer* interface.

**Example**

```
Public Sub SortArray( )
   ' ----- Start with the unsorted data.
   Dim counter As Integer
   Dim dataSet( ) As Integer = {9, 8, 12, 4, 5}
   For counter = 0 To 4
      Console.Write(CStr(dataSet(counter)) & " ")
   Next counter
   Console.WriteLine("")

   ' ----- Sort and display the data.
   System.Array.Sort(dataSet)
   Console.WriteLine("Sorted:")
   For counter = 0 To 4
      Console.Write(CStr(dataSet(counter)) & " ")
   Next counter
   Console.WriteLine("")
End Sub
```

The output is:

```
9 8 12 4 5
Sorted:
4 5 8 9 12
```

**See Also**

Array Class, Array.Reverse Method

# Asc, AscW Functions

**Class**

Microsoft.VisualBasic.Strings

**Syntax**

```
Dim result As Integer = Asc(string)
Dim result As Integer = AscW(string)
```

*string* *(required; String or Char)*
   Any expression that evaluates to a non-empty string

**Description**

The Asc and AscW functions return the character code for the first character of the string passed to them. All other characters in the string are ignored. The range for the returned value is 0 to 255 on Single Byte Character Set values, and -32768 to 32767 on Double Byte Character Set values. The AscW version always uses the larger range.

**Usage at a Glance**

The Asc version uses the active code page of the current thread; the AscW function always uses the general Unicode character set.

## Example

```
Dim charCode As Integer

If Len(sampleString) > 0 Then
    charCode = Asc(sampleString)
    If (charCode < Asc("A")) Or (charCode > Asc("Z")) Then
        MsgBox("The first character must be uppercase.")
    End If
End If
```

## See Also

Chr, ChrW Functions

# AssemblyVersion Attribute

## Class

System.Reflection.AssemblyVersionAttribute

## Applies To

Assembly

## Constructor

```
New(version)
```

*version (required; String)*
    The version of the assembly

## Properties

*Version (String)*
    Read-only. Value from the *version* constructor parameter.

## Description

The <AssemblyVersion> attribute specifies the version of the assembly. The version is represented as a four-part number, as follows:

*major.minor.build.revision*

Ordinarily, the .NET runtime considers a difference in any one of these four-part numbers to indicate a different version.

A wildcard character (*) in any of the four positions indicates that an assembly can be used with clients requesting any value for the wildcard element. For example, if the version is set to "1.0.*," the assembly can be used for clients requesting Version 1.0.1681.0, 1.0.1723.0, and 1.0.1723.2.

> In Visual Studio, the <AssemblyVersion> attribute is automatically added to the *AssemblyInfo.vb* file, and its value is set to "1.0.*."

## Version Differences

Beginning with Visual Basic 2005, the *My.Application.Info.Version* property returns the assembly version information for the active application.

# Asin Function

## Class
System.Math

## Syntax
```
Dim result As Double = Math.Asin(d)
```
*d* (required; *Double*)
A sine, a number from -1 to 1 inclusive

## Description
The *Asin* function returns the arcsine of *d* in radians, between $\pi/2$ and $\pi/2$.

## Usage at a Glance
- If *d* is out of range, the function returns *System.Double.NaN*.
- This is a shared member of the *System.Math* class, so it can be used without an instance.
- To convert from radians to degrees, multiply by $180/\pi$.

## Version Differences
The *Asin* function did not exist in VB 6.

## See Also
Acos Function, Atan Function, Atan2 Function

# Atan Function

## Class
System.Math

## Syntax
```
Dim result As Double = Math.Atan(d)
```
*d* (required; *Double*)
A number representing a tangent

## Description
The *Atan* function returns the arctangent in radians of *d*, in the range $\pi/2$ to $\pi/2$.

## Usage at a Glance
- If *d* is out of range, the function returns *System.Double.NaN*.
- This is a shared member of the *System.Math* class, so it can be used without an instance.
- To convert radians to degrees, multiply radians by $180/\pi$.
- Arctangent is not the cotangent. Arctangent is the inverse trigonometric function of the tangent; cotangent is the reciprocal of the tangent.

### Version Differences

In VB 6, Atan is an intrinsic VB function. In the .NET platform, it is a member of the *System.Math* class and not directly part of the VB language.

### See Also

Acos Function, Asin Function, Atan2 Function

---

## Atan2 Function

### Class

System.Math

### Syntax

```
Dim result As Double = Math.Atan2(y, x)
```

*x* (required; Double)
    The x-coordinate of a point

*y* (required; Double)
    The y-coordinate of a point

### Description

The *Atan2* function returns the arctangent of the ratio $x/y$ in radians. This is the angle in the Cartesian plane formed by the x-axis and a vector starting from the origin (0,0) and terminating at the point $(x, y)$. More specifically, the return value satisfies the following:

- For $(x, y)$ in quadrant 1, $0 < result < \pi/2$.
- For $(x, y)$ in quadrant 2, $\pi/2 < result < \pi$.
- For $(x, y)$ in quadrant 3, $\pi < result < \pi/2$.
- For $(x, y)$ in quadrant 4, $\pi/2 < result < 0$.

### Usage at a Glance

This is a shared member of the *System.Math* class, so it can be used without an instance.

### Version Differences

The *Atan2* function does not exist in VB 6.

### See Also

Acos Function, Asin Function, Atan Function

---

## AttributeUsage Attribute

### Class

System.AttributeUsageAttribute

## Applies To

Class

## Constructor

```
New(validOn)
```

*validOn  (required; AttributeTargets enumeration)*
Indicates the program elements to which a custom attribute can be applied. One of the following *System.AttributeTargets* enumeration values: All, Assembly, Class, Constructor, Delegate, Enum, Event, Field, Interface, Struct, Method, Module, Parameter, Property, or ReturnValue. Multiple values can be Or'd together to indicate an attribute to be used for many element types.

## Properties

*AllowMultiple (Boolean)*
Indicates whether the attribute can be used more than once on a single program element. Its default value is False.

*Inherited (Boolean)*
Indicates whether the attribute is automatically inherited by derived classes and overridden members. Its default value is True.

*ValidOn (AttributeTargets enumeration)*
Read-only. Value from the *validOn* constructor parameter.

## Description

The <AttributeUsage> attribute defines the program elements to which a custom attribute can be applied. Its use is required when defining a custom attribute class.

## Example

Chapter 9 discusses the use of the <AttributeUsage> attribute in the design of new custom attributes.

---

# Beep Procedure

## Class

Microsoft.VisualBasic.Interaction

## Syntax

```
Beep( )
```

## Description

The Beep procedure sounds a tone through the computer's speaker.

## Usage at a Glance

The frequency and duration of the tone depend on the computer's hardware. The user can also mute all system sounds, and some users may be limited in their ability to hear the generated tone.

## Example
```
Public Sub Main( )
    DoSomeLongFunction( )
    Beep( )
    MsgBox("Finished!")
End Sub
```

# Call Statement

## Syntax
```
[Call] procedureName([argumentList])
```
*procedureName (required)*
The name of the subroutine being called

*argumentList (optional)*
A comma-delimited list of arguments to pass to the subroutine being called

## Description
The Call statement passes execution control to a procedure, function, or dynamic-link library (DLL) procedure or function.

## Usage at a Glance
- Use of the Call keyword is optional.
- *argumentList*, if present, must always be enclosed in parentheses.
- If you use Call to call a function, the function's return value is discarded.

## Example
```
Call SomeProcedure(True, importantData)

...later...

Public Sub SomeProcedure(ByVal silentFlag As Boolean, _
    ByVal workData As Integer)
    ...
End Sub
```

## Version Differences
- In VB 6, calls to subroutines only included parentheses around the argument list when the Call keyword was included. In .NET, parentheses are required whenever arguments are present.
- In VB 6, when calling an external routine defined using the Declare statement, you could override the defined method of passing an argument by specifying the ByVal or ByRef keywords before the argument in the Call statement. In .NET, you cannot change the argument-passing method from the defined setting.

## See Also
CallByName Function

# CallByName Function

## Class
Microsoft.VisualBasic.Interaction

## Syntax
```
Dim result As Object = CallByName(objectRef, procName, _
    useCallType, args())
```
*objectRef*  *(required; Object)*
    A reference to the object containing the property or method being accessed.
*procName*  *(required; String)*
    The name of the property or method to call or access.
*useCallType*  *(required; CallType enumeration)*
    The type of procedure being accessed. One of the following *Microsoft.VisualBasic.*
    *CallType* enumeration values. Each member also has an equivalent Visual Basic
    intrinsic constant.

| Value | VB constant | Description |
|-------|-------------|-------------|
| Method | vbMethod | The called procedure is a method. |
| Get | vbGet | The called procedure retrieves a property value. |
| Set | vbSet | The called procedure sets the value of a property. |

*args*  *(optional; any)*
    One or more comma-delimited arguments (a ParamArray argument) representing
    the arguments required by the procedure being called. This may also be an array
    of argument objects.

## Description
The CallByName function provides a method for calling a class member by name. It
calls any property accessor (get or set) or method and returns that member's return
value, if available. The member name is sent as a string instead of as a design-time
compiled member.

Since *procName* is a string expression, it is possible to call routines dynamically at
runtime using the name of the members.

## Usage at a Glance
- The return type of CallByName is the return type of the called member.
- *procName* is not case-sensitive.
- The performance of CallByName is inferior to calling members through direct
  object member access.

## Example
The following example uses a parameter array to call the Multiply method of a class
named EasyMath:

```
Module GeneralCode
   Public Sub TestCallByName( )
      Dim mathTester As New EasyMath
      Dim testArguments( ) As Double = {1.0#, 2.0#, 3.0#}

      MsgBox(CallByName(mathTester, "Multiply", _
         CallType.Method, testArguments))     ' Displays "6"
   End Sub
End Module

Public Class EasyMath
   Public Function Multiply(ByVal sourceValues( ) As Double) _
         As Double
      Dim operationResult As Double = 1.0#
      Dim counter As Integer

      For counter = 0 To UBound(sourceValues)
         operationResult *= sourceValues(counter)
      Next counter
      Return operationResult
   End Function
End Class
```

## See Also

Call Statement

---

# CBool Function

## Syntax

```
Dim result As Boolean = CBool(expression)
```

*expression* *(required; String or Numeric)*
Any numeric expression or a string representation of a numeric value. The string values "True" and "False" are also supported.

## Description

The CBool function converts *expression* to the Boolean data type.

## Usage at a Glance

- When a numeric value is converted to Boolean, any nonzero value is converted to True, and zero is converted to False.

- If the expression to be converted is a string, the string must be capable of being evaluated as a number, or it must be "True" and "False." Any other string generates a runtime error.

- You can check the validity of a numeric expression prior to using the CBool function by using the IsNumeric function.

- This function does not support named arguments.

# CByte Function

## Syntax

```
Dim result As Byte = CByte(expression)
```

*expression* (required; *String or Numeric*)
Any expression in the valid range of the Byte data type

## Description

The CByte function converts *expression* to the Byte data type.

## Usage at a Glance

- An expression that evaluates outside the valid range of the target data type results in a runtime error. Nonnumeric expressions also generate an error.
- This function does not support named arguments.

## Example

```
Dim targetNumber As Byte
If IsNumeric(stringNumber) Then
    targetNumber = CByte(stringNumber)
End If
```

## See Also

CSByte Function

# CChar Function

## Syntax

```
Dim result As Char = CChar(expression)
```

*expression* (required; *String*)
Any string expression

## Description

The CChar function converts the first character of a string to the Char data type.

## Usage at a Glance

- Use the ChrW function to convert a numeric code to its corresponding Char data type.
- This function does not support named arguments.

## Example

```
MsgBox(CChar("abc"))     ' Displays "a"
MsgBox(CChar("56"))      ' Displays "5"
```

## See Also

Chr, ChrW Functions

# CDate Function

## Syntax

    Dim result As Date = CDate(*expression*)

*expression* (required; String or Numeric)
  Any valid representation of a date and time

## Description

The CDate function converts *expression* to the Date data type. The interpretation of the date components in the expression is based on the locale setting of the local computer.

## Usage at a Glance

- The supported date range of the Date data type is from January 1, 1 AD to December 31, 9999 AD in the Gregorian calendar.
- You can check that a date expression is valid using the IsDate function.
- Passing an empty string to CDate generates an error.
- This function does not support named arguments.
- The CDate function makes some guesses about how to interpret invalid date formats so they are still usable. For example, on systems that use the "m/d/yyyy" date component arrangement, a source expression of "30/12/97" will still result in December 30, 1997, since CDate understands that "30" is an invalid month, but "12" is valid. This can cause problems if your code expects an error to be generated from this input.
- The CDate function guesses the century if a two-digit year is supplied. It sometimes places it in the previous century and sometimes in the current century. In general, two-digit years under 30 appear in the current century, while those 30 and beyond appear in the previous century.
- If you do not specify a year, the CDate function uses the year from the current date on your computer.

## See Also

DateValue Function, TimeValue Function

# CDbl Function

## Syntax

    Dim result As Double = CDbl(*expression*)

*expression* (required; Numeric or String)
  Any expression in the valid range of the Double data type

## Description

The CDbl function converts *expression* to the Double data type.

### Usage at a Glance

- An expression that evaluates outside the valid range of the target data type results in a runtime error. Nonnumeric expressions also generate an error.

- In most cases, the numeric conversion functions are a better choice than the Val function when converting a string, as the conversion functions take into account the system's regional settings. However, Val converts empty strings to zero without error.

- Use IsNumeric to test whether *expression* evaluates to a number.

- This function does not support named arguments.

### Example

```
Dim targetNumber As Double
If IsNumeric(stringNumber) Then
    targetNumber = CDbl(stringNumber)
End If
```

### See Also

CSng Function, Val Function

---

## CDec Function

### Syntax

```
Dim result As Decimal = CDec(expression)
```

*expression*  (required; Numeric or String)
  Any expression in the valid range of the Decimal data type

### Description

The CDec function converts *expression* to the Decimal data type.

### Usage at a Glance

- An expression that evaluates outside the valid range of the target data type results in a runtime error. Nonnumeric expressions also generate an error.

- In most cases, the numeric conversion functions are a better choice than the Val function when converting a string, as the conversion functions take into account the system's regional settings. However, Val converts empty strings to zero without error.

- Use IsNumeric to test whether *expression* evaluates to a number.

- This function does not support named arguments.

### Example

```
Dim targetNumber As Decimal
If IsNumeric(stringNumber) Then
    targetNumber = CDec(stringNumber)
End If
```

### Version Differences

The Decimal data type replaces the VB 6 Currency data type, and it is appropriate for high-precision numbers.

### See Also

Val Function

## Ceiling Function

### Class

System.Math

### Syntax

```
Dim result As Double = Math.Ceiling(d)
```

*d (required; Double)*
   Any valid number

### Description

The *Ceiling* function returns the smallest integer greater than or equal to the argument *d*.

### Example

```
MsgBox(Math.Ceiling(12.1))     ' Displays 13
MsgBox(Math.Ceiling(12.5))     ' Displays 13
MsgBox(Math.Ceiling(-12.5))    ' Displays -12
MsgBox(Math.Ceiling(-12.8))    ' Displays -12
```

### Usage at a Glance

This is a shared member of the *System.Math* class, so it can be used without an instance.

### Version Differences

The *Ceiling* function did not exist in VB 6.

### See Also

Floor Function

## ChDir Procedure

### Class

Microsoft.VisualBasic.FileSystem

### Syntax

```
ChDir(path)
```

*path (required; String)*
   The path of the directory to set as the new default or "current" directory

## Description
The ChDir procedure changes the current working (default) directory.

## Usage at a Glance
- *path* can be either an absolute path or a relative path from the current directory.
- Changing the default directory does not change the default drive; it only changes a particular drive's default directory.
- If the root of a drive is already the current directory, and you try to change to a parent directory (".."), no error occurs and the directory is not changed.
- An error occurs if the specified path does not exist.
- Networked drives can only be used with ChDir if they have been mapped to a local drive letter and that drive letter is used in *path*.

## Example
```
ChDir("c:\My Documents\My Folder\")
ChDir("..")  ' Uses the current directory's parent
```

## Version Differences
- ChDir was a statement in VB 6; it is now a procedure (a method of the *FileSystem* class) and requires parentheses around the *path* argument.
- Visual Basic 2005 includes a *My.Computer.FileSystem.CurrentDirectory* property that provides similar functionality.

## See Also
ChDrive Procedure, CurDir Function

---

# ChDrive Procedure

## Class
Microsoft.VisualBasic.FileSystem

## Syntax
```
ChDrive(drive)
```
*drive* *(required; String or Char)*
   The letter of the drive (A–Z) to set as the new default drive

## Description
The ChDrive procedure changes the current working (default) disk drive.

## Usage at a Glance
- Only the first character of *drive* is considered. If a zero-length string is supplied, the drive is not changed.
- The current directory is unaffected by the ChDrive procedure.
- Since ChDrive only considers the first letter of the *drive* string, it is not valid to supply a UNC path (such as \\*ServerName\ShareName*).
- Use the CurDir function to determine the current drive and directory.

## Example

The following example implements one method of testing for a valid drive using the ChDrive procedure.

```
Public Function IsAvailableDrive(newDrive As String) As Boolean
    ' ----- Check for the existence of a logical drive.
    Dim currentDrive As String

    ' ----- Save the current setting.
    On Error Resume Next
    currentDrive = Microsoft.VisualBasic.Left(CurDir( ), 1)

    ' ----- Change to the proposed drive. If an error occurs,
    '       then assume the drive doesn't exist.
    Err.Clear( )
    ChDrive(newDrive)
    If (Err.Number = 0) Then
        IsAvailableDrive = True
    Else
        IsAvailableDrive = False
    End If

    ' ----- Restore the previous settings.
    ChDrive(currentDrive)
End Function
```

## Version Differences

- ChDrive was a statement in VB 6; it is now a procedure (a method of the *FileSystem* class) and requires parentheses around the *drive* argument.
- Visual Basic 2005 includes a *My.Computer.FileSystem.CurrentDirectory* property that provides related functionality.

## See Also

ChDrive Procedure, CurDir Function

# Choose Function

## Class

Microsoft.VisualBasic.Interaction

## Syntax

```
Dim result As Object = Choose(index, item_1[, item_2[..., item_n]])
```

*index  (required; Double)*
An expression that evaluates to the 1-based index of the object to choose from the list

*item_1 to item_n  (required; any)*
A comma-delimited list of values from which to choose or a ParamArray object that includes the items

## Description

The Choose function programmatically selects an object from a predefined list of objects (which are passed as parameters to the function) based on its ordinal position in the list.

## Usage at a Glance

- The item parameters can be variables, constants, literals, expressions, or function calls. Each item may be of a different type; the return value will be of type Object.
- If the rounded value of *index* does not correspond to an item in the list, the function returns Nothing.
- If *index* is not a whole number, it is rounded before being used.
- All item parameters are fully evaluated before they are considered as results for the Choose function. If they contain function calls, those functions will be called, even in the items that are not returned by the function. For instance, in the statement:

```
result = Choose(methodToUse, ProcessFile(tempFileName), _
    ProcessFile(mainFileName))
```

  both calls to ProcessFile will always be performed, regardless of the value of methodToUse. However, at most, only one return value from among the function calls will be returned from the Choose function, and possibly none will be.
- This function does not support named arguments.
- By providing *item_1* through *item_n* in the form of a ParamArray, the list of values can be expanded or contracted programmatically at runtime.

## Version Differences

- In VB 6, *item_1* through *item_n* must only take the form of a comma-delimited list. In .NET, these arguments can also take the form of a ParamArray.
- In VB 6, an error occurs if *index* falls outside the range of choices. In .NET, this condition results in a return value of Nothing.

## See Also

Switch Function

---

# Chr, ChrW Functions

## Class

Microsoft.VisualBasic.Strings

## Syntax

```
Dim result As Char = Chr(charCode)
Dim result As Char = ChrW(charCode)
```

*charCode (required; Integer)*
    An expression that evaluates to a character code

## Description

The Chr and ChrW functions return the character represented by *charCode*.

## Usage at a Glance

- The Chr version uses the active code page of the current thread; the ChrW function always uses the general Unicode character set.
- The following table lists some of the more commonly used character codes that are supplied in the call to the Chr function:

| Code | Constant | Description |
|------|----------|-------------|
| 0 | vbNullChar | Used as a string terminator in many languages, such as with C and C++ |
| 8 | vbBack | The backspace character |
| 9 | vbTab | The tab character |
| 10 | vbLf | The linefeed character |
| 13 | vbCr | The carriage return character |
| 34 | ControlChars.Quote | The quotation mark |

## Version Differences

- The VB 6 ChrB function is no longer supported.
- The VB 6 version of the Chr function returns a String; the .NET version returns a Char.

## See Also

Asc, AscW Functions

# CInt Function

## Syntax

```
Dim result As Integer = CInt(expression)
```

*expression* (required; Numeric or String)
Any expression in the valid range of the Integer data type

## Description

The CInt function converts *expression* to the Integer data type; any fractional portion of *expression* is rounded.

## Usage at a Glance

- An expression that evaluates outside the valid range of the target data type results in a runtime error. Nonnumeric expressions also generate an error.
- In most cases, the numeric conversion functions are a better choice than the Val function when converting a string, as the conversion functions take into account the system's regional settings. However, Val converts empty strings to zero without error.
- Use IsNumeric to test whether expression evaluates to a number.
- This function does not support named arguments.

- CInt differs from the Fix and Int functions, which truncate, rather than round, the fractional part of a number. Also, Fix and Int always return the same data type as what was passed in.

## Example

```
Dim targetNumber As Integer
If IsNumeric(stringNumber) Then
    targetNumber = CInt(stringNumber)
End If
```

## Version Differences

The CInt function under .NET most closely corresponds to the VB 6 CLng function, since both return 32-bit integers.

## See Also

CLng Function, CShort Function, CUInt Function

---

# Class...End Class Statement

## Syntax

```
[accessModifier] [Shadows] [MustInherit | NotInheritable]_
    Class name [(Of typeParamName)]
    [Inherits baseClass]
    [Implements interfaceName[, interfaceName...]]
    [statements]
End Class
```

accessModifier *(optional)*
Specifies the scope and accessibility of the class. One of the following access levels:

| Access level | Description |
| --- | --- |
| Public | The class is publicly accessible anywhere, both inside and outside of the project. |
| Private | The class is accessible within the type in which it is defined. |
| Protected | The class is accessible only to the type in which it is defined and to derived instances of that type. |
| Friend | The class is accessible only within the project that contains the structure definition. |
| Protected Friend | Combines the access features of Protected and Friend. |

If omitted, the Friend access level is used.

Shadows *(optional)*
Indicates that the class shadows an identically named element in a base class.

MustInherit *(optional)*
This class can only be used as a base class for another derived class definition. Objects of this base class cannot be created.

`NotInheritable` *(optional)*

    This class can only be used to create objects. It cannot be used as a base class for another derived class.

*name* *(required)*

    The name of the class.

*typeParamName* *(optional; any)*

    Adds type parameter placeholders that will later enforce strong typing when the class is used. The `Of` clause implements generics, which are fully described in Chapter 10. If generics will not be used, this clause can be excluded.

*baseClass* *(optional)*

    Indicates that the class inherits from another class.

*interfaceName* *(optional)*

    Indicates that the class implements the members of one or more interfaces.

*statements* *(required)*

    Code that defines the members of the class.

## Description

The `Class...End Class` statement defines a class and its members. Class members include fields, methods, properties, events, and other types.

## Usage at a Glance

- If the `Inherits` or `Implements` statements appear in a class module, they must appear before any other statements in the module. If both are used, the `Inherits` keyword must appear before the `Implements` keyword.

- Class members are declared as `Public`, `Private`, `Protected`, `Friend`, or `Protected Friend`. The `Dim` keyword is equivalent to `Private` when used for members.

- To add a custom constructor within a class module, define a subroutine called *New*. The *New* subroutine (like any other method) can be overloaded.

- To add a destructor within a class module, override the *Finalize* method from the base *System.Object* class, from which all classes inherit.

  ```
  Protected Overrides Sub Finalize( )
      ' ----- Add other code here, and also call...
      MyBase.Finalize( )
  End Sub
  ```

  Destructors cannot be overloaded.

- The `Shadows` keyword has the following meaning: if this class is derived from a base class and if *name* is used in the base class as the name of any element type (property, method, constant, enum, etc.), then any use of *name* in classes derived from the class *name* refers to the *name* class rather than the *name* element in the base class. For more on shadowing, see Chapter 4.

- For more information on classes and object-oriented programming practices, see Chapter 3.

- One class property can be assigned as the default property using the `Default` keyword with its definition.

- The `Me` or `MyClass` keywords can be used within the `Class...End Class` construct to reference the class.

### Version Differences

- The Class...End Class construct is new to VB under .NET. In VB 6, each class was defined in its own class source code file. The syntax and functionality differences between them are significant.

- Visual Basic 2005 adds support for generics to classes, as discussed in Chapter 10.

### See Also

Property Statement, Structure...End Structure Statement

---

## Clipboard Class

### Namespace

System.Windows.Forms

### Creatable

No

### Description

The *Clipboard* class represents the Windows Clipboard, an object that allows data to be shared across processes. The members of the *Clipboard* class allow data to be placed in, and retrieved from, the Clipboard.

### Version Differences

Visual Basic 2005 introduces the new *My.Computer.Clipboard* object, which encapsulates many convenient clipboard-related features. Please refer to the "Clipboard Object" entry in Chapter 13 for information on using the new features.

---

## CLng Function

### Syntax

```
Dim result As Long = CLng(expression)
```

*expression* (required; Numeric or String)
Any expression in the valid range of the Long data type

### Description

The CLng function converts *expression* to the Long data type; any fractional portion of *expression* is rounded.

### Usage at a Glance

- An expression that evaluates outside the valid range of the target data type results in a runtime error. Nonnumeric expressions also generate an error.

- In most cases, the numeric conversion functions are a better choice than the Val function when converting a string, as the conversion functions take into account the system's regional settings. However, Val converts empty strings to zero without error.

- Use IsNumeric to test whether *expression* evaluates to a number.

---

- This function does not support named arguments.

- CLng differs from the Fix and Int functions, which truncate, rather than round, the fractional part of a number. Also, Fix and Int always return the same data type as what was passed in.

### Example

```
Dim targetNumber As Long
If IsNumeric(stringNumber) Then
    targetNumber = CLng(stringNumber)
End If
```

### Version Differences

The CLng function under .NET returns a 64-bit integer; the VB 6 CLng function returned a 32-bit integer.

### See Also

CInt Function, CShort Function, CULng Function

## CLSCompliant Attribute

### Class

System.CLSCompliantAttribute

### Applies To

All elements

### Constructor

```
New(isCompliant)
```

*isCompliant* (required; Boolean)
    Indicates whether the program element is CLS-compliant

### Property

*IsCompliant (Boolean)*
    Read-only. Value from the *isCompliant* constructor parameter.

### Description

The <CLSCompliant> attribute indicates whether the program element complies with the Common Language Specification (CLS). If the <CLSCompliant> attribute is not present, the VB compiler does not enforce CLS compliance. This can prevent other languages from successfully accessing components written in VB.

If a particular program element is marked as CLS-compliant, it is assumed that all contained program elements are CLS-compliant as well, unless they are explicitly marked otherwise.

By default, Visual Studio adds the <CLSCompliant> attribute to the *AssemblyInfo.vb* file and sets its value to True.

# CObj Function

## Syntax

```
Dim result As Object = CObj(expression)
```

*expression* *(required; any)*
  Any expression

## Description

The CObj function converts any expression that can be interpreted as an object to the Object data type.

## Usage at a Glance

- The operation of the CObj function is possible because all .NET data types derive from Object.
- Once a data type is converted to type Object, you can display its value by calling its *ToString* method:

  ```
  Dim strongFlag As Boolean = True
  Dim weakData As Object = CObj(strongFlag)
  MsgBox(weakData.ToString())    ' Displays "True"
  ```
- Variables can be assigned to Object variables using direct assignment as well.

  ```
  Dim strongData As New SomeClass
  Dim weakData As Object
  weakData = strongData
  ```
- This function does not support named arguments.

## Example

The following code stores strongly typed data as an Object:

```
Dim strongData As New SomeClass
Dim weakData As Object
weakData = CObj(strongData)
```

## Version Differences

The CObj function did not exist in VB 6. The closest equivalent in VB 6 was CVar, which converted a data type to a Variant.

---

# Collection Class

## Namespace

Microsoft.VisualBasic

## Creatable

Yes

## Syntax

```
Dim result As [New] Collection
```

---

## Description

A Collection object allows you to store members of any data type, including mixed types, as a named group and to retrieve each one using a unique key.

Collection objects are a form of associative array, where each member is indexed by a meaningful and unique key. The Collection object is discussed in more detail in Chapter 4.

The following table lists some of the more useful and interesting members of the Collection class. Those marked with an asterisk (*) have separate entries in this chapter.

| Member | Description |
| --- | --- |
| Add Method * | Adds a new item to the collection |
| Clear Method | Removes all items from the collection |
| Contains Method | Indicates whether the collection includes an item with a specific key |
| Count Property * | Returns the number of items currently found in the collection |
| Item Property * | Retrieves an item from the collection by position or by key |
| Remove Method * | Removes an item from the collection |

## Usage at a Glance

- You can use a Collection object to store data of any data type, including object types and even other Collection objects.

- The first member in a collection is stored at ordinal position 1, not at 0, as is done with arrays.

- A highly efficient method of enumerating the members of a collection is to use the ForEach...Next statement, as the following example shows:

```
Dim unitedStates As New Collection
Dim scanState As String

' ----- Build the list of states.
unitedStates.Add("Alabama", "AL")
unitedStates.Add("Alaska", "AK")
...and so on...

' ----- Process each state.
For Each scanState In unitedStates
    MsgBox(scanState)    ' Displays full name of state
Next scanState
```

- The Collection class is implemented specifically within the Visual Basic portion of the .NET Framework. Other collection classes can be found in the *System. Collections* namespace.

## Example

This example shows the basic use of the Collection class.

```
Public Sub TestCollection( )
    Dim miscItems As New Collection
    Dim displayText As string
```

```
' ----- Add each item with a key, but with different types.
miscItems.Add("am", "second")   ' Adds a String
miscItems.Add(25, "third")      ' Adds an Integer
miscItems.Add("I"c, "first")    ' Adds a Char

' ----- Now play them back in order.
displayText = miscItems("first") & " " & _
   miscItems("second") & " " & miscItems("third")
MsgBox(displayText)        ' Displays "I am 25"
End Sub
```

### Version Differences

Visual Basic 2005 adds support for generics to several collection-style classes. Generics are discussed in Chapter 10.

### See Also

Array Class, Hashtable Class, Queue Class, Stack Class

---

## Collection.Add Method

### Class

Microsoft.VisualBasic.Collection

### Syntax

```
objectVariable.Add(item[, key[, before[, after]]])
```

*objectVariable (required; Collection)*
The instance of a Collection to which an item is to be added.

*item (required; any)*
The new item to add to the collection.

*key (optional; String)*
A unique string expression that specifies a key that can be used, instead of a positional index, to access a member of the collection.

*before (optional; Object)*
The existing collection member immediately before which the new member will be inserted. If *after* is used, this argument must be left blank. Either a numeric position or a key (String).

*after (optional; Object)*
The existing collection member immediately after which the new member will be inserted. If *before* is used, this argument must be left blank. Either a numeric position or a key (String).

### Description

The *Add* method adds an object to a collection with an optional search key and, optionally, at a specific ordinal position. The new item may be of any type, and that type need not match the type of items already in the collection (unless using the new Visual Basic 2005 generics feature).

### Usage at a Glance

- If you do not specify a *before* or *after* value, the member is appended to the end of the collection (in index order).

- If you do not specify a *key* value, you will only be able to access the item by position or by iteration using the For Each...Next statement.

- The *before* or *after* argument can refer to an index or a key. For instance, consider the following code:

```
Dim someNames As New Collection( )
someNames.Add("Donna", "111")
someNames.Add("Steve", "222")
someNames.Add("Bill", "333", "222")
MsgBox(someNames.Item(2))
```

This code adds "Bill" just before "Steve." The following statement could also be used to achieve the same ordering of items.

```
someNames.Add("Bill", "333", 2)
```

- Key values must be unique, or an error occurs.

- You can use named parameters to add items.

```
unitedStates.Add(Key:="MT", Item:="Montana")
```

### Version Differences

Visual Basic 2005 adds support for generics to several collection-style classes. Generics are discussed in Chapter 10.

### See Also

Collection Class, Collection.Count Property, Collection.Item Property, Collection. Remove Method

---

## Collection.Count Property

### Class

Microsoft.VisualBasic.Collection

### Syntax

```
Dim result As Integer = objectVariable.Count
```

*objectVariable* (required; Collection)
 The instance of a Collection for which items are to be counted

### Description

The *Count* property returns the number of items currently contained in a collection.

### Usage at a Glance

Collections are 1-based; this differs from arrays, which are 0-based. Collection items range from 1 to the value returned by the Count property.

## Example

```
For counter = 1 To someCollection.Count
    oneItem = someCollection.Item(counter)
    ...more code here...
Next counter
```

## Version Differences

Visual Basic 2005 adds support for generics to several collection-style classes. Generics are discussed in Chapter 10.

## See Also

Collection Class, Collection.Add Method, Collection.Item Property, Collection. Remove Method

# Collection.Item Property

## Class

Microsoft.VisualBasic.Collection

## Syntax

```
objectVariable.Item(index)
```

*objectVariable (required; Collection)*
    The instance of a Collection from which an item is to be retrieved

*index (required; Integer or String)*
    Either the 1-based ordinal position (Integer) or the unique key (String) of an item in the collection

## Description

The *Item* property retrieves an item from a collection based on its position or its unique key.

## Usage at a Glance

- The *Contains* method of the Collection class can tell you whether the collection includes an item with a specific key.
- The *Item* property is the default member of the Collection object; the "Item" member name can be omitted when retrieving items from a collection. The following two lines are functionally identical:

```
typicalItem = ordinaryCollection.Item(6)
typicalItem = ordinaryCollection(6)
```

## Version Differences

Visual Basic 2005 adds support for generics to several collection-style classes. Generics are discussed in Chapter 10.

## See Also

Collection Class, Collection.Add Method, Collection.Count Property, Collection. Remove Method

# Collection.Remove Method

## Class
Microsoft.VisualBasic.Collection

## Syntax
```
objectVariable.Remove(index)
```
*objectvariable  (required; Collection)*
    The instance of a Collection from which an item is to be removed

*index  (required; Integer or String)*
    Either the 1-based ordinal position (Integer) or the unique key (String) of an item in the collection

## Description
The *Remove* method removes an item from a collection based on its position or its unique key.

## Usage at a Glance
- Members of the collection that follow the removed member are automatically moved by one ordinal position; no gaps are left in the collection. This also means that the ordinal positions of many members may change during a deletion.
- If you are deleting multiple members of a collection by numeric index value, you should delete them backwards—from highest index value to lowest—since the collection is reindexed after each deletion.
- The *Clear* method of the Collection class removes all items immediately.

## Version Differences
Visual Basic 2005 adds support for generics to several collection-style classes. Generics are discussed in Chapter 10.

## See Also
Collection Class, Collection.Add Method, Collection.Count Property, Collection.Item Property

---

# ColorDialog Class

## Namespace
System.Windows.Forms

## Creatable
Yes

## Description
The *ColorDialog* class represents a common dialog box for selecting a color. The *ColorDialog* class has properties that let you configure, display, and retrieve the results from this dialog box, from which the user selects a single color.

The following list discusses the more interesting members of the *ColorDialog* class.

*AllowFullOpen Property*
> Configures the dialog box so that the user can define custom colors (True) or not (False). The default is True.

*AnyColor Property*
> Configures the dialog box so that all available basic colors are displayed (True), or so that only a subset of these colors is displayed (False). The default is False.

*Color Property*
> Upon successful use of the dialog box by the user, this property returns the selected color, an instance of the *System.Drawing.Color* class. This class provides access to the color in several ways. Distinct *R*, *G*, and *B* properties indicate the color components. The *Name* property returns a preconfigured name for the color—or its numeric equivalent if no name is assigned. There are also flags that provide more details about the color, such as *IsKnownColor*, *IsNamedColor*, and *IsSystemColor*.

*CustomColors Property*
> An array of integer values used to define the custom colors that will be shown in the dialog box.

*Reset Method*
> Resets the dialog box, setting all options and custom colors to their default values, and setting the selected color to black.

*ShowDialog Method*
> Presents the dialog box to the user.

*SolidColorOnly Property*
> For systems displaying 256 colors or less, this property, when True, restricts the dialog box to solid colors only.

## Example

The following code asks the user for a color and displays that color:

```
Dim colorSelect As New ColorDialog( )
If (colorSelect.ShowDialog( ) = DialogResult.OK) Then
    Console.WriteLine(colorSelect.Color.ToString( ))
    Console.WriteLine(colorSelect.Color.Name)
Else
    Console.WriteLine("No color chosen.")
End If
```

Here is a typical example of what is returned by this code:

```
Color [A=255, R=80, G=156, B=218]
ff509cda
```

## Version Differences

The public interfaces used for this *ColorDialog* class and the related VB 6 Common-Dialog control are quite different.

## See Also

FontDialog Class

# COMClass Attribute

## Class
Microsoft.VisualBasic.COMClassAttribute

## Applies To
Class

## Constructor
```
New([classID[, interfaceID[, eventID]]][, interfaceShadows])
```
*classID* (optional; String)
> The class identifier (CLSID) globally unique identifier (GUID) that uniquely identifies the COM class.

*interfaceID* (optional; String)
> The interface identifier (IID) GUID that uniquely identifies the class's default COM interface.

*eventID* (optional; String)
> The event identifier GUID that uniquely identifies an event.

*interfaceShadows* (optional; Boolean)
> Indicates whether the COM interface name is the same as the name of another member of the class or the base class. If omitted, the default value is False.

## Properties
*ClassID (String)*
> Read-only. Set by the *classID* class constructor parameter.

*EventID (String)*
> Read-only. Set by the *interfaceID* class constructor parameter.

*InterfaceID (String)*
> Read-only. Set by the *eventID* class constructor parameter.

*InterfaceShadows (Boolean)*
> Indicates whether the COM interface name is the same as the name of another member of the class or the base class. Set by the *interfaceShadows* class constructor parameter.

## Description
The <COMClass> attribute adds metadata to a class that exposes a .NET class as a COM object. You can supply the attribute with a class identifier, an interface identifier, and an event identifier. All are GUIDs that can be generated by using the *guidgen.exe* utility. Using this attribute ensures that the COM component retains the same GUIDs even when it is recompiled.

## Example
The example defines a simple class named Contact that includes the <COMClass> attribute. The GUIDs are in standard registry format except for the absence of the opening and closing braces.
```
<COMClass(Contact.ClassID, Contact.InterfaceID, Contact.EventID)> _
Public Class Contact
```

```
    Friend Const ClassID As String = _
        "C7BA6669-DCFB-43d6-9A74-B1BCC6EE467B"
    Friend Const InterfaceID As String = _
        "72663B50-6A44-46e7-83B6-F1A4F149FF5F"
    Friend Const EventID As String = _
        "BD2C0D5E-C0D7-4e1e-A9E8-AD29C8003D4B"

    Private contactName As String
    Private contactCity As String
    Private contactState As String
    Private contactZip As String

    Public Property Name() As String
        Get
            Return contactName
        End Get
        Set(ByVal value As String)
            contactName = value
        End Set
    End Property

    Public Sub New()
        MyBase.New()
    End Sub
End Class
```

### See Also

MarshalAs Attribute

---

## Command Function

### Class

Microsoft.VisualBasic.Interaction

### Syntax

```
Dim result As String = Command()
```

### Description

The Command function returns the arguments used when launching an application created with Visual Basic.

### Usage at a Glance

- Command returns a string containing everything entered on the command line after the executable filename. If there are no arguments available to return, the function returns an empty string.

- Command returns an unparsed string containing the command-line arguments. Use the Split function to break the argument list up by spaces for easier processing.

    ```
    Dim eachArgument() As String
    eachArgument = Split(Command(), " ")
    ```

- The shared *GetCommandLineArgs* method of the *System.Environment* class returns a string array with a first element that is the program filename, and with remaining elements that are the command-line arguments.

- During the development phase, you can pass arguments to your program using the *Command line arguments* text box, found in the *Debug* section of the application's Property Pages.

## Example

The following example parses the command-line arguments, reporting them to the console. It looks for a minus (-) or slash (/) sign at the start of an argument and considers everything after a colon to be additional information for the argument. Given the command-line arguments:

```
-d:50 -f -g -k
```

the program outputs the following text to the console:

```
Option d, with parameter = 50
Option f
Option g
Option k
```

The source code is as follows:

```
' Uses: Imports MVB = Microsoft.VisualBasic

Public Sub ParseCommandLine()
    ' ----- Parse and display each argument.
    Dim eachArgument() As String
    Dim counter As Integer
    Dim optionText As String
    Dim paramText As String
    Dim colonPos As Integer

    ' ----- Put the arguments in an array.
    eachArgument = Split(Command(), " ")
    For counter = 0 To eachArgument.Length - 1
        optionText = eachArgument(counter)
        If (MVB.Left(optionText, 1) = "-") Or _
            (MVB.Left(optionText, 1) = "/") Then
            ' ----- Found a valid argument. Remove the - or /.
            optionText = Mid(optionText, 2)

            ' ----- See if there is a parameter.
            paramText = ""
            colonPos = InStr(optionText, ":")
            If (colonPos > 0) Then
                paramText = Mid(optionText, colonPos + 1)
                optionText = MVB.Left(optionText, colonPos - 1)
            End If

            ' ----- Report on the option.
            If (paramText = "") Then
                Console.WriteLine("Option " & optionText)
            Else
                Console.WriteLine("Option " & optionText & _
                    ", with parameter = " & paramText)
```

```
        End If
      End If
    Next counter
  End Sub
```

## Version Differences

Visual Basic 2005 includes a new *My.Application.CommandLineArgs* property that returns a collection of the command-line arguments, with each argument as a separate item in the collection.

# Const Statement

## Syntax

```
[accessModifier] Const [Shadows] name [As type] = value
```

*accessModifier (optional)*
Specifies the scope and accessibility of the constant. One of the following access levels:

| Access level | Description |
|---|---|
| Public | The constant is publicly accessible anywhere, both inside and outside of the project. |
| Private | The constant is accessible only within the defining type. |
| Protected | The constant is accessible only to the code in the defining type or to one of its derived types. |
| Friend | The constant is accessible only within the project that contains the constant definition. |
| Protected Friend | Combines the access features of Protected and Friend. |

If omitted, the Public access level is used. The access modifier is excluded when the Const statement is used within a procedure.

Shadows *(optional)*
Indicates that the constant shadows an identically named element in a base class. The Shadows keyword is excluded when the Const statement is used within a procedure.

*name (required)*
The name of the constant.

*type (optional; Type)*
The data type of the constant; it can be Boolean, Byte, Char, Date, Decimal, Double, Integer, Long, Object, SByte, Short, Single, String, UInteger, ULong, UShort, or the name of any enumerated type.

*value (required; any)*
A literal, constant, or an expression made up of literals, constants, and the arithmetic or logical operators, except Is and IsNot. Any of the conversion functions (such as CByte) are allowed, as is AscW.

## Description

The Const statement defines a constant value within a class, structure, or procedure. These constants are also referred to as *symbolic constants*.

## Usage at a Glance

- If Option Strict is On, the As *type* clause is required.
- Constants are inherently shared, static, and read-only.
- Multiple constants can be defined through the same Const statement by separating the definitions with commas. Each definition requires its own As clause.
- If you are building a large application with many different modules, you may find your code easier to maintain if you create a single separate code module to hold your Public constants.
- If two or more constants with integral values make up a set of constants, you should consider defining them through an enumerated data type using the Enum statement.

## Example

```
Private Const MY_CONSTANT As Double = 3.1417#
```

## See Also

Dim Statement, Enum Statement

---

# Continue Statement

## Syntax

```
Continue { Do | For | While }
```

## Description

*New in 2005.* The Continue statement immediately jumps to the next iteration of a Do... Loop, For...Next, For Each...Next, or While...End While loop construct. The second keyword of the Continue statement matches the first word of the loop construct.

## Usage at a Glance

- If you have nested loops of the same type, the Continue statement goes to the next iteration of the innermost loop (of the same type).
- Continue Do is used for Do...Loop statements; Continue For is used for For...Next and For Each...Next statements; Continue While is used for While...End While statements.
- Using the Continue statement may cause a loop to exit if the next iteration would normally have caused an exit of the loop.

## Version Differences

The Continue statement is new with Visual Basic 2005.

## See Also

Do...Loop Statement, For...Next Statement, For Each...Next Statement, While...End While Statement

---

# Cos Function

## Class
System.Math

## Syntax
```
Dim result As Double = Math.Cos(d)
```
*d* (*required; Double*)
An angle expressed in radians

## Description
The *Cos* function returns the cosine of an angle, the ratio of the length of the side adjacent to the angle divided by the length of the hypotenuse, in the range of -1 to 1 inclusive.

## Usage at a Glance
- This is a shared member of the *System.Math* class, so it can be used without an instance.
- To convert degrees to radians, multiply degrees by $\pi/180$.
- To convert radians to degrees, multiply radians by $180/\pi$.

## Version Differences
In VB 6, Cos is an intrinsic VB function. In the .NET platform, it is a member of the *System.Math* class and not directly part of the VB language.

## See Also
Cosh Function, Sin Function, Tan Function

---

# Cosh Function

## Class
System.Math

## Syntax
```
Dim result As Double = Math.Cosh(value)
```
*value* (*required; Double*)
An angle expressed in radians.

## Description
The *Cosh* function returns the hyperbolic cosine of an angle.

## Usage at a Glance
This is a shared member of the *System.Math* class, so it can be used without an instance.

---

## Version Differences
The *Cosh* function did not exist in VB 6.

## See Also
Cos Function, Sinh Function, Tanh Function

---

# CreateObject Function

## Class
Microsoft.VisualBasic.Interaction

## Syntax
```
Dim result As Object = CreateObject(progID[, serverName])
```
*progID (required; String)*
> The programmatic class identifier (ProgID) of the object to create. The ProgID is defined in the system registry and usually takes the form *library.class* or *application.class*.

*serverName (optional; String)*
> The name of the server on which the object resides. If omitted, the default value is an empty string ("") which indicates that the local server is to be used.

## Description
The CreateObject function creates an instance of an ActiveX or COM server and returns a new object from that instance. Once created, that object's members can be accessed and used.

## Usage at a Glance
- If your project does not include a reference to the object's definition, you must declare the object variable type as Object.
- If an instance of the ActiveX object is already running, CreateObject may start a new server instance when it creates the object.
- CreateObject can only be used to create instances of COM or ActiveX objects; it cannot be used to instantiate .NET components.
- This function does not support named arguments.
- When using a variable of type *System.Object* to receive the result of the CreateObject function, the new object will be *late bound*. Late binding is inherently less robust in terms of performance than *early binding*.

The *serverName* parameter allows you to specify a remote system as the source of the new object instance. This code block demonstrates a possible use of this parameter:
```
Dim primarySystem As String
Dim secondarySystem As String
Dim customer As Object

primarySystem = "MainServer"
secondarySystem = "BackupServer"
```

```
    If IsOnline(primarySystem) Then
        customer = CreateObject("Sales.Customer", primarySystem)
    Else
        customer = CreateObject("Sales.Customer", secondarySystem)
    End If
```

- To obtain an object instance from an already running ActiveX server, use the GetObject function instead.

- If an object is registered as a single-instance object (an out-of-process ActiveX EXE), only one instance of the object can be created at a time. Each time you call CreateObject to create this object, you will obtain a reference to the same instance of the object.

- Always set the instance variable to Nothing when you are finished, so that all required cleanup code can run in a timely manner.

## Example

The following code records the time required to access a Microsoft Excel application object, both by early-binding and late-binding methods.

```
Public Sub TestBinding()
    ' ----- Compare early and late binding.
    Dim startingTime As Double
    Dim message As String
    Dim excelAppLate As Object
    Dim excelAppEarly As Excel.Application

    ' ----- Calculate time for late binding.
    startingTime = DateAndTime.Timer
    excelAppLate = CreateObject("Excel.Application")
    excelAppLate = Nothing
    message = "Late Bound: " & _
        (DateAndTime.Timer - startingTime) & vbCrLf

    ' ----- Calculate time for early binding.
    startingTime = DateAndTime.Timer
    excelAppEarly = Excel.Application
    excelAppEarly = Nothing
    message &= "Early Bound: " & _
        (DateAndTime.Timer - startingTime)

    MsgBox (message, MsgBoxStyle.OKOnly, "Late and Early Binding")
End Sub
```

## See Also

GetObject Function

## CSByte Function

## Syntax

```
    Dim result As SByte = CSByte(expression)
```

*expression (required; String or Numeric)*
    Any expression in the valid range of the SByte data type

## Description

*New in 2005.* The CSByte function converts *expression* to the SByte data type.

## Usage at a Glance

- An expression that evaluates outside the valid range of the target data type results in a runtime error. Nonnumeric expressions also generate an error.
- Use IsNumeric to test whether *expression* evaluates to a number.
- This function does not support named arguments.

## Example

```
Dim targetNumber As SByte
If IsNumeric(stringNumber) Then
    targetNumber = CSByte(stringNumber)
End If
```

## Version Differences

The CSByte function is new in the 2005 version of VB.

## See Also

CByte Function

# CShort Function

## Syntax

```
Dim result As Short = CShort(expression)
```

*expression* (required; Numeric or String)
   Any expression in the valid range of the Short data type

## Description

The CShort function converts *expression* to the Short data type; any fractional portion of *expression* is rounded.

## Usage at a Glance

- An expression that evaluates outside the valid range of the target data type results in a runtime error. Nonnumeric expressions also generate an error.
- In most cases, the numeric conversion functions are a better choice than the Val function when converting a string, as the conversion functions take into account the system's regional settings. However, Val converts empty strings to zero without error.
- Use IsNumeric to test whether *expression* evaluates to a number.
- This function does not support named arguments.
- CShort differs from the Fix and Int functions, which truncate, rather than round, the fractional part of a number. Also, Fix and Int always return the same data type as what was passed in.

**Example**

```
Dim targetNumber As Short
If IsNumeric(stringNumber) Then
    targetNumber = CShort(stringNumber)
End If
```

**Version Differences**

The CShort function is new to VB under .NET. However, it corresponds directly to the VB 6 CInt function, since both return 16-bit integers.

**See Also**

CInt Function, CLng Function, CUShort Function

---

## CSng Function

**Syntax**

```
Dim result As Single = CSng(expression)
```

*expression* *(required; Numeric or String)*
Any expression in the valid range of the Single data type.

**Description**

The CSng function converts *expression* to the Single data type.

**Usage at a Glance**

- An expression that evaluates outside the valid range of the target data type results in a runtime error. Nonnumeric expressions also generate an error.
- In most cases, the numeric conversion functions are a better choice than the Val function when converting a string, as the conversion functions take into account the system's regional settings. However, Val converts empty strings to zero without error.
- Use IsNumeric to test whether *expression* evaluates to a number.
- This function does not support named arguments.

**Example**

```
Dim targetNumber As Single
If IsNumeric(stringNumber) Then
    targetNumber = CSng(stringNumber)
End If
```

**See Also**

CDbl Function

---

## CStr Function

**Syntax**

```
Dim result As String = CStr(expression)
```

*expression  (required; any)*
> Any numeric, date, string, or Boolean expression—or most any other object

## Description

The CStr function returns a string representation of *expression*.

## Usage at a Glance

- If *expression* is Boolean, the function returns one of the strings "True" or "False." For an expression that can be interpreted as a date, the return value is a string representation of that date, in the "short date" format of the host computer. For a numeric expression, the return value is a string representing the number.
- An uninitialized date variable passed to CStr returns "12:00:00AM."
- This function does not support named arguments.
- Objects in .NET include a *ToString* method, which can also be used to convert the object's value to a string format.

## See Also

CChar Function, Str Function

---

# CType Function

## Syntax

```
Dim result As typename = CType(expression, typename)
```

*expression  (required; any)*
> The value to be converted. This can be any data, object, structure, or interface type.

*typename  (required)*
> The data type, object type, structure, or interface to which *expression* is to be converted. This can be virtually anything that can appear after the As clause of a Dim statement.

## Description

The CType function converts an expression or object to the specified type.

## Usage at a Glance

- If *expression* cannot be converted to the new data type (perhaps due to incompatibility of the types), an error occurs.
- CType can perform the same conversions as the individual conversion functions. For example, the last two lines in this code are equivalent:

```
Dim booleanString As String = "True"
Dim realBoolean As Boolean
realBoolean = CBool(booleanString)
realBoolean = CType(booleanString, Boolean)
```

- This function does not support named arguments.

- CType is often used to convert an object between its derived and base types. It is also used to restore an object back to its true type from an instance of type Object.

- Assignment of a derived object to its parent object type can be done implicitly. However, assignments in the opposite direction (from base to descendant) need to be cast with CType if Option Strict is On.

### Example

Each list item added to a Windows Forms *ListBox* control includes an object of any type that is used to both display the text and store custom user data. Internally, it is stored as Object. When you retrieve the data object for a single list entry, you must convert it to the original type before using its members.

This example defines a simple form with a *ListBox*. When an item is selected, the data associated with the selected item is cast back to a TeamDetails object.

```
Public Class BaseballTeams
    Inherits System.Windows.Forms.Form

    ' ----- Define a simple class to store in the list.
    Protected Class TeamDetails
        Public TeamName As String
        Public Members As Integer
        Public Sub New(ByVal fullName As String, _
                ByVal totalMembers As Integer)
            ' ----- Simple constructor.
            TeamName = fullName
            Members = totalMembers
        End Sub
        Public Overrides Function ToString() As String
            ' ----- Properly displays information in list box.
            Return TeamName & " (" & Members & ")"
        End Function
    End Class

    Private Sub BaseballTeams_Load(ByVal sender As System.Object, _
            ByVal e As System.EventArgs) Handles MyBase.Load
        ' ----- Add some basic teams.
        TeamNames.Items.Add(New TeamDetails("Tokyo Giants", 18))
        TeamNames.Items.Add(New TeamDetails("Seattle Mariners", 20))
    End Sub

    Private Sub TeamNames_SelectedIndexChanged( _
            ByVal sender As System.Object, ByVal e As _
            System.EventArgs) Handles TeamNames.SelectedIndexChanged
        ' ----- To display the details, we must convert the type.
        Dim selectedTeam As TeamDetails

        selectedTeam = CType(TeamNames.SelectedItem, TeamDetails)
        MsgBox("Team = " & selectedTeam.TeamName & vbCrLf & _
            "Members = " & selectedTeam.Members)
    End Sub
End Class
```

## Version Differences

- The CType function was not present in VB 6.

- Visual Basic 2005 adds features that let you define custom CType conversions for use with your own types. These features are part of the operator overloading additions, and they are described in Chapter 5.

## See Also

CBool Function, CByte Function, CChar Function, CDate Function, CDbl Function, CDec Function, CInt Function, CLng Function, CObj Function, CSByte Function, CShort Function, CSng Function, CStr Function, CUInt Function, CULong Function, CUShort Function

# CUInt Function

## Syntax

```
Dim result As UInteger = CUInt(expression)
```

*expression*  *(required; Numeric or String)*
Any expression in the valid range of the UInteger data type

## Description

*New in 2005.* The CUInt function converts *expression* to the UInteger data type; any fractional portion of *expression* is rounded.

## Usage at a Glance

- An expression that evaluates outside the valid range of the target data type results in a runtime error. Nonnumeric expressions also generate an error.

- In most cases, the numeric conversion functions are a better choice than the Val function when converting a string, as the conversion functions take into account the system's regional settings. However, Val converts empty strings to zero without error.

- Use IsNumeric to test whether *expression* evaluates to a number.

- This function does not support named arguments.

- CUInt differs from the Fix and Int functions, which truncate, rather than round, the fractional part of a number. Also, Fix and Int always return the same data type as what was passed in.

## Example

```
Dim targetNumber As UInteger
If IsNumeric(stringNumber) Then
    targetNumber = CUInt(stringNumber)
End If
```

## Version Differences

The CUInt function is new in the 2005 version of VB.

## See Also

CInt Function, CULng Function, CUShort Function

# CULng Function

## Syntax

```
Dim result As ULong = CULng(expression)
```

*expression* (required; Numeric or String)
Any expression in the valid range of the ULong data type

## Description

*New in 2005.* The CULng function converts *expression* to the ULong data type; any fractional portion of *expression* is rounded.

## Usage at a Glance

- An expression that evaluates outside the valid range of the target data type results in a runtime error. Nonnumeric expressions also generate an error.
- In most cases, the numeric conversion functions are a better choice than the Val function when converting a string, as the conversion functions take into account the system's regional settings. However, Val converts empty strings to zero without error.
- Use IsNumeric to test whether *expression* evaluates to a number.
- This function does not support named arguments.
- CULng differs from the Fix and Int functions, which truncate, rather than round, the fractional part of a number. Also, Fix and Int always return the same data type as what was passed in.

## Example

```
Dim targetNumber As ULong
If IsNumeric(stringNumber) Then
    targetNumber = CULng(stringNumber)
End If
```

## Version Differences

The CULng function is new in the 2005 version of VB.

## See Also

CLng Function, CUInt Function, CUShort Function

# CUShort Function

## Syntax

```
Dim result As UShort = CUShort(expression)
```

*expression* (required; Numeric or String)
Any expression in the valid range of the UShort data type

## Description

*New in 2005.* The CUShort function converts *expression* to the UShort data type; any fractional portion of *expression* is rounded.

## Usage at a Glance

- An expression that evaluates outside the valid range of the target data-type results in a runtime error. Nonnumeric expressions also generate an error.

- In most cases, the numeric conversion functions are a better choice than the Val function when converting a string, as the conversion functions take into account the system's regional settings. However, Val converts empty strings to zero without error.

- Use IsNumeric to test whether *expression* evaluates to a number.

- This function does not support named arguments.

- CUShort differs from the Fix and Int functions, which truncate, rather than round, the fractional part of a number. Also, Fix and Int always return the same data type as what was passed in.

## Example

```
Dim targetNumber As UShort
If IsNumeric(stringNumber) Then
    targetNumber = CUShort(stringNumber)
End If
```

## Version Differences

The CUShort function is new in the 2005 version of VB.

## See Also

CShort Function, CUInt Function, CULng Function

---

# CurDir Function

## Class

Microsoft.VisualBasic.FileSystem

## Syntax

```
CurDir([drive])
```

*drive* (optional; String or Char)
The letter of the drive (A to Z) from which to return the current directory

## Description

The CurDir function returns the current directory of a particular drive or of the default drive.

## Usage at a Glance

- If no drive is specified or if *drive* is a zero-length string (""), CurDir returns the path for the current working (default) drive.

- Since CurDir only considers the first letter of the *drive* string, it's not possible to supply a UNC path (such as \\*ServerName\ShareName*).

## Version Differences

Visual Basic 2005 includes a *My.Computer.FileSystem.CurrentDirectory* property that provides related functionality.

## See Also

ChDir Procedure, ChDrive Procedure, MkDir Procedure, RmDir Procedure

---

# Custom Event Statement

## Syntax

```
[accessModifier] [Shadows] Custom Event name As delegateName _
    [Implements implementsList]
    AddHandler(ByVal value As delegateName)
        [statements]
    End AddHandler
    RemoveHandler(ByVal value As delegateName)
        [statements]
    End RemoveHandler
    RaiseEvent(delegateSignature)
        [statements]
    End RaiseEvent
End Event
```

*accessModifier (optional)*
Specifies the scope and accessibility of the custom event. One of the following access levels:

| Access level | Description |
|---|---|
| Public | The custom event is publicly accessible anywhere, both inside and outside of the project. |
| Private | The custom event is accessible only within the defining type. |
| Protected | The custom event is accessible only to the code in the defining type or to one of its derived types. |
| Friend | The custom event is accessible only within the project that contains the custom event definition. |
| Protected Friend | Combines the access features of Protected and Friend. |

If omitted, the Public access level is used.

*Shadows (optional)*
Indicates that the custom event shadows an identically named element in a base class.

*name (required)*
The name of the custom event.

*implementsList (optional)*
Comma-separated list of the interface members implemented by this custom event.

*delegateName* *(required)*
> A delegate with an argument signature that is used as the argument signature of this custom event.

*value* *(required)*
> The name of the accessor argument. By convention, this argument is named "value." The argument is always of type *delegateName*.

*statements* *(optional)*
> Program code to be executed within the AddHandler, RemoveHandler, and RaiseEvent accessors.

*delegateSignature* *(optional; any)*
> A comma-delimited list of parameters to be supplied to the custom event as arguments when the event is raised. This argument list must match the one defined by *delegateName*.
>
> *delegateSignature* uses the following syntax and parts:
>
> > [ByVal | ByRef] *varname*[( )] [As *argtype*]

ByVal *(optional)*
> The argument is passed by value; the local copy of the variable is assigned the value of the argument. ByVal is the default method of passing variables.

ByRef *(optional)*
> The argument is passed by reference; the local variable is a reference to the argument being passed. All changes made to the local variable will also be reflected in the calling argument.

*varname* *(required)*
> The name of the argument.

*argtype* *(optional; Type)*
> The data type of the argument. Any valid .NET data type can be used.

## Description

*New in 2005.* The Custom Event statement defines a custom event that the containing type can raise at any time using the RaiseEvent statement. As event handlers for this event are added, removed, or called (raised), one the three accessors (AddHandler, RemoveHandler, and RaiseEvent) is called respectively, immediately before the actual related action occurs. This allows the designer of the event to exert more control over the lifetime of the event.

## Usage at a Glance

- To handle events, an object must be declared with the WithEvents keyword.
- To declare an event without the additional AddHandler, RemoveHandler, and RaiseEvent accessors, use the standard Event statement. See the *Event Statement* entry in this chapter for more information.

## Version Differences

The Custom Event statement is new with Visual Basic 2005.

## See Also

Event Statement

# DateAdd Function

## Class
Microsoft.VisualBasic.DateAndTime

## Syntax
```
Dim result As Date = DateAdd(interval, number, dateValue)
```
*interval  (required; String or DateInterval enumeration)*

A String expression or *Microsoft.VisualBasic.DateInterval* enumeration item indicating which part of the date to adjust. The following table lists both the string and enumeration choices. Some intervals allow partial (decimal) values to be added to the date.

| String | DateInterval | Description |
|--------|--------------|-------------|
| d | Day | Day, to the nearest whole day |
| y | DayOfYear | Day, to the nearest whole day |
| h | Hour | Hour, to the nearest millisecond |
| n | Minute | Minute, to the nearest millisecond |
| m | Month | Month, to the nearest whole month |
| q | Quarter | Quarter (of a year), to the nearest whole quarter |
| s | Second | Second, to the nearest millisecond |
| w | Weekday | Day, to the nearest whole day |
| ww | WeekOfYear | Week, to the nearest whole week |
| yyyy | Year | Year, to the nearest whole year |

*number  (required; Double)*

An expression denoting the number of time intervals by which to alter the original date, either positive (to add value) or negative (to subtract value).

*dateValue  (required; Date or date expression)*

The starting date to which the interval is to be added or subtracted.

## Description
The DateAdd function adds or subtracts a component date or time value to a starting date and returns the new date. For instance, you can calculate the date 178 months before today's date, or the date and time 12,789 minutes from now.

## Usage at a Glance
- The DateAdd function has a built-in calendar algorithm to prevent it from returning an invalid date. For example, you can add 10 minutes to 31 December 1999 23:55, and DateAdd automatically recalculates all elements of the date to return a valid date, in this case, 1 January 2000 00:05. Proper adjustments are made for leap years.

- You can check that a date is valid using the IsDate function.

- To add a number of days to *dateValue*, use either the day of the year ("y" or DateInterval.DayOfYear), the day ("d" or DateInterval.Day), or the weekday ("w" or DateInterval.Weekday).

- DateAdd generates an error if the computed date falls outside the valid range of the Date data type.
- The Date data type also includes members that let you manipulate the date in ways that are similar to the DateAdd function.

## Example

```
DateAdd(DateInterval.Day, 120, #3/3/2005#)    ' Returns 7/1/2005
```

## Version Differences

VB 6 lacks the *DateInterval* enumeration and therefore only accepts a string for the *interval* argument.

## See Also

DateDiff Function

# DateDiff Function

## Class

Microsoft.VisualBasic.DateAndTime

## Syntax

```
Dim result As Long = DateDiff(interval, date1, date2[, _
    dayOfWeek[, weekOfYear]])
```

*interval* (required; String or DateInterval enumeration)

A string expression or *Microsoft.VisualBasic.DateInterval* enumeration item indicating which part of the date to report in the return value. The following table lists both the string and enumeration choices.

| String | DateInterval | Description |
| --- | --- | --- |
| d | Day | The difference in days |
| y | DayOfYear | The difference in days |
| h | Hour | The difference in hours |
| n | Minute | The difference in minutes |
| m | Month | The difference in months |
| q | Quarter | The difference in quarters |
| s | Second | The difference in seconds |
| w | Weekday | The difference in weeks, based on counting individual days |
| ww | WeekOfYear | The difference in weeks, based on full calendar weeks |
| yyyy | Year | The difference in years |

*date1* (required; Date)

The first date from which to calculate the difference.

*date2* (required; Date)

The second date from which to calculate the difference. To return a positive result, this date should occur after *date1*.

*dayOfWeek* *(optional; FirstDayOfWeek enumeration)*
Indicates the first day of the week. One of the following *Microsoft.VisualBasic.* *FirstDayOfWeek* enumeration members: Sunday, Monday, Tuesday, Wednesday, Thursday, Friday, Saturday, or System (to use the regional default). If omitted, Sunday is used.

*weekOfYear* *(optional; FirstWeekOfYear enumeration)*
Indicates which week counts as the first week of a given year. One of the following *Microsoft.VisualBasic.FirstWeekOfYear* enumeration members.

| Value | Description |
|---|---|
| System | Uses the system-defined value |
| Jan1 | Uses the week in which January 1 appears |
| FirstFourDays | Uses the first week of the year that has at least four days in it |
| FirstFullWeek | Uses the first week of the year that has a full seven days in it |

If omitted, Jan1 is used.

## Description

The DateDiff function calculates the number of time intervals between two dates. For example, you can use the function to determine how many days there are between January 1, 1980, and May 31, 1998.

## Usage at a Glance

- To calculate the number of days between *date1* and *date2*, you can use the *DateInterval* constants Day or DayOfYear or the string literals "d" or "y."

- When *interval* is Weekday or "w," DateDiff returns the number of weeks between the two dates based on the number of days between the two dates. When *interval* is Week or "ww," DateDiff returns the number of weeks by first considering the full weeks in which *date1* and *date2* appear and then counting based on the first day of each of these weeks. The *dayOfWeek* parameter is significant in this calculation.

- In the calculation, the interval is determined by subtracting *date1* from *date2*. If *date1* appears before *date2* in chronological order, the return value will be positive; if *date1* appears after *date2* in chronological order, the return value will be negative.

- The expression DateDiff("yyyy", #12/31/2005#, #1/2/2006#) returns 1, even though only two days have elapsed. Similar results occur for related differences in other intervals.

- DateDiff considers the four quarters of the year to be January 1 to March 31, April 1 to June 30, July 1 to September 30, and October 1 to December 31.

## Version Differences

- VB 6 lacks the *DateInterval* enumeration and therefore only accepts a string for the *interval* argument.

- VB 6 supports a number of constants beginning with vb... (such as vbSunday) as values for the *dayOfWeek* and *weekOfYear* arguments. While these are still supported in .NET, the new *FirstDayOfWeek* and *FirstWeekOfYear* enumerations are preferred.

DateAdd Function

# DatePart Function

## Class

Microsoft.VisualBasic.DateAndTime

## Syntax

```
DatePart(interval, dateValue[, firstDayOfWeekValue[, _
    firstWeekOfYearValue]])
```

*interval* (required; String or DateInterval enumeration)
A String expression or *Microsoft.VisualBasic.DateInterval* enumeration item indicating which part of the date to return. The following table lists both the string and enumeration choices.

The Language
Reference

| String | DateInterval | Description |
| --- | --- | --- |
| d | Day | The day of the month, from 1 to 31 |
| y | DayOfYear | The day of the year, from 1 to 366 |
| h | Hour | The hour of the day, from 0 to 23 |
| n | Minute | The minute of the hour, from 0 to 59 |
| m | Month | The month of the year, from 1 to 12 |
| q | Quarter | The quarter of the year, from 1 to 4 |
| s | Second | The second of the minute, from 0 to 59 |
| w | Weekday | The day of the week, from 1 to 7; the value 1 is normally used for Sunday, but it may differ based on the *firstDayOfWeekValue* parameter |
| ww | WeekOfYear | The week number of the year, from 1 to 53; the *firstWeekOfYearValue* parameter impacts this value |
| yyyy | Year | The year of the Gregorian calendar, from 1 AD to 9999 AD |

*dateValue* (required; Date or date expression)
The date from which to extract a component.

*firstDayOfWeekValue* (optional; FirstDayOfWeek enumeration)
Indicates the first day of the week. One of the following *Microsoft.VisualBasic.FirstDayOfWeek* enumeration members: Sunday, Monday, Tuesday, Wednesday, Thursday, Friday, Saturday, or System (to use the regional default). If omitted, Sunday is used.

*firstWeekOfYearValue* (optional; FirstWeekOfYear enumeration)
Indicates which week counts as the first week of a given year. One of the following *Microsoft.VisualBasic.FirstWeekOfYear* enumeration members.

| Value | Description |
| --- | --- |
| System | Uses the system-defined value |
| Jan1 | Uses the week in which January 1 appears |

| Value | Description |
|---|---|
| FirstFourDays | Uses the first week of the year that has at least four days in it |
| FirstFullWeek | Uses the first week of the year that has a full seven days in it |

If omitted, Jan1 is used.

## Description

The DatePart function returns an individual component of the date or time (such as the month or the second) from a date or time value.

## Usage at a Glance

- DatePart replicates the functionality of the distinct Year, Month, Day, Hour, Minute, and Second functions.
- You can check that a date expression is valid using the IsDate function.

## Version Differences

- VB 6 lacks the *DateInterval* enumeration and therefore only accepts a string as the *interval* argument.
- VB 6 supports a number of constants beginning with vb... (such as vbSunday) as values for the *firstDayOfWeekValue* and *firstWeekOfYearValue* arguments. While these are still supported in .NET, the new *FirstDayOfWeek* and *FirstWeekOfYear* enumerations are preferred.

## See Also

DateSerial Function, DateString Property, DateValue Function

---

# DateSerial Function

## Class

Microsoft.VisualBasic.DateAndTime

## Syntax

```
Dim result As Date = DateSerial(year, month, day)
```

*year  (required; Integer)*
The year, a number between 1 and 9999, inclusive

*month  (required; Integer)*
The month, a number between 1 and 12, inclusive

*day  (required; Integer)*
The day, a number between 1 and 31, inclusive

## Description

The DateSerial function returns a Date with the value that is specified by the three date components.

## Usage at a Glance

- If the month or day value exceeds its normal limits in either a positive or negative direction, `DateSerial` adjusts the date accordingly. For example, if you try `DateSerial(2005, 1, 35)`—January 35, 2005—`DateSerial` returns February 4, 2005.

- If any of the parameters exceed the range of the `Integer` data type, a runtime error occurs.

- `DateSerial` handles two-digit years in the same way as other Visual Basic date functions. A year argument between 0 and 29 is taken to be in the current century; year arguments between 30 and 99 are taken to be in the previous century.

## See Also

DatePart Function, DateString Property, DateValue Function, TimeSerial Function

---

# DateString Property

## Class

Microsoft.VisualBasic.DateAndTime

## Syntax

```
Dim result As String = DateAndTime.DateString
```

or:

```
DateAndTime.DateString = newDate
```

*newDate* *(required in second syntax; String)*
A date in string format used to set the current system date

## Description

The `DateString` property gets or sets the current system date. The first syntax returns a string representing the current system date in the "MM-dd-yyyy" format. The second syntax sets the current system date using a string that is in a culture-independent format.

## Usage at a Glance

- The first syntax always returns a date in the format "MM-dd-yyyy."
- The string in the second syntax must use one of the following date formats: "M-d-yyyy," "M-d-y," "M/d/yyyy," or "M/d/y."
- See the *Format Function* entry for details on custom date formats.
- To get or set the current system time as a `String`, use the `TimeString` property.
- To access the current system date as a `Date`, use the `Today` property.
- The security settings of the active user may prevent the system date and time from being altered.

## Version Differences

The `DateString` property is new to VB under .NET. It is a replacement for the VB 6 `Date` statement, which sets the system date, and the `Date` and `Date$` functions, which retrieve the system date.

## See Also

Format Function, Now Property, TimeString Property, Today Property

---

# DateValue Function

## Class

Microsoft.VisualBasic.DateAndTime

## Syntax

```
Dim result As Date = DateValue(stringDate)
```

*stringDate* *(required; String)*
A string containing any valid date format

## Description

The `DateValue` function converts *stringDate* to the `Date` data type, setting any time component to midnight. The interpretation of the date components in the expression is based on the locale setting of the local computer.

## Usage at a Glance

- The supported date range of the `Date` data type is from January 1, 1 AD to December 31, 9999 AD in the Gregorian calendar.
- You can check that a date is valid using the `IsDate` function.
- If *stringDate* includes time information as well as date information, the time information is ignored. However, if only time information is passed to `DateValue`, an error is generated.
- The `DateValue` function guesses the century if a two-digit year is supplied. It sometimes places it in the previous century and sometimes in the current century. In general, two-digit years under 30 appear in the current century, while those 30 and beyond appear in the previous century.

## See Also

CDate Function, DatePart Function, DateSerial Function, DateString Property

---

# Day Function

## Class

Microsoft.VisualBasic.DateAndTime

## Syntax

```
Dim result As Integer = Day(dateValue)
```

*dateValue (required; Date)*
The source date from which to extract the day

## Description

The Day function returns a value from 1 to 31, representing the day of the month of the supplied date.

## Usage at a Glance

With Option Strict set to On, the source value must first be converted to a Date data type. You can use the CDate function for this purpose. The IsDate function can also be used to confirm that the source expression is a valid date.

## See Also

DatePart Function, Month Function, WeekdayName Function, Year Function

# DDB Function

## Class

Microsoft.VisualBasic.Financial

## Syntax

DDB(*cost, salvage, life, period*[, *factor*])

*cost (required; Double)*
The initial cost of the asset.

*salvage (required; Double)*
The value of the asset at the end of *life*.

*life (required; Double)*
Length of life of the asset.

*period (required; Double)*
Period for which the depreciation is to be calculated.

*factor (optional; Double)*
The rate at which the asset balance declines. If omitted, 2.0 is used by default (double-declining method).

## Description

The DDB function returns a Double representing the depreciation of an asset for a specific time period. This is done using the double-declining balance method or another method that you specify using the *factor* argument.

The double-declining balance method calculates depreciation at a differential rate, which varies inversely with the age of the asset. Depreciation is highest at the beginning of an asset's life and declines over time.

## Usage at a Glance

- The *life* and *period* arguments must be specified in the same time units. For instance, both must be expressed in units of months, or both must be years.
- All arguments must be positive numbers.

- The double-declining balance depreciation method calculates depreciation at a higher rate in the initial period and a decreasing rate in subsequent periods.
- The DDB function uses the following formula to calculate depreciation for a given period:

$$depreciation \ / \ period = ((cost - salvage) * factor) \ / \ life$$

## Example

```
Dim initialCost As Double = 2000
Dim salvageValue As Double = 50
Dim usefulLife As Double = 12
Dim totalDepreciation As Double = 0
Dim periodScan As Double
Dim thisPeriodDepr As Double

For periodScan = 1 To 12
    thisPeriodDepr = DDB(initialCost, salvageValue, _
        usefulLife, periodScan)
    totalDepreciation += thisPeriodDepr
    Console.WriteLine("Month " & periodScan & ": " & _
        thisPeriodDepr)
Next periodScan

Console.WriteLine("Total: " & totalDepreciation)
```

## Debug Class

### Namespace
System.Diagnostics

### Creatable
No

### Description
The *Debug* class is used to send messages to the Output Window (called the Immediate Window in VB 6). The *Debug* class can also send output to other targets (such as text files) referred to as *listeners*. See the *Debug.Listeners Property* entry for additional information. The *Debug* class also allows you to check program logic with assertions.

Because the *Debug* class's members are shared, you do not need to instantiate a *Debug* object before accessing its members. The following code fragment, for instance, illustrates a call to the *Debug* object's *WriteLine* method:

```
Debug.WriteLine(soFar & " iterations through the loop")
```

The following table lists some of the more useful and interesting members of the *Debug* class. Those marked with an asterisk (*) have separate entries in this chapter.

| Member | Description |
| --- | --- |
| Assert Method * | Tests a condition and reports problems |
| AutoFlush Property | Indicates whether written data should be flushed to the output stream automatically |
| Close Method | Flushes and closes each listener (except the Output Window) |

| Member | Description |
| --- | --- |
| Fail Method | Sends an error message to the listeners |
| Flush Method | Flushes all pending data to the listeners |
| Indent Method | Increases the current indent level |
| IndentLevel Property | Indicates the current indent level |
| IndentSize Property | Identifies the number of spaces for each indent level |
| Listeners Property * | Lists the collection of listeners |
| Unindent Method | Decreases the current indent level |
| Write Method * | Writes text to the debug listeners |
| WriteIf Method * | Conditionally writes text to the debug listeners |
| WriteLine Method * | Writes full-line text to the debug listeners |
| WriteLineIf Method * | Conditionally writes full-line text to the debug listeners |

## Usage at a Glance

The *Debug* class features only work in the design-time environment; the statement has no effect in a compiled application. You do have to remove *Debug*-related features from your code before release.

## Version Differences

The VB 6 Debug object had only two methods: Assert and Print. The .NET *Assert* method is similar to the VB 6 method of the same name, except that the .NET version displays a message if an expression is False, while the VB 6 version suspends program execution. In .NET, the VB 6 Print method is removed, replaced by the *Write*, *WriteIf*, *WriteLine*, and *WriteLineIf* methods.

## See Also

Debug.Assert Method, Debug.Write Method, Debug.WriteLine Method

# Debug.Assert Method

## Class

System.Diagnostics.Debug

## Syntax

```
Debug.Assert(booleanExpression[, string1[, string2]])
```

*booleanExpression* (required; Boolean)
Expression that evaluates to a Boolean value

*string1* (optional; String)
String to output if *booleanExpression* is False

*string2* (optional; String)
Additional detail text to output if *booleanExpression* is False

## Description

The *Assert* method outputs messages to the debug listeners if a condition fails.

## Usage at a Glance

- *Assert* is typically used to test an expression that should evaluate to True.
- The *Debug* class features only work in the design-time environment; the statement has no effect in a compiled application. You do not have to remove *Debug*-related features from your code before release.
- If neither string is supplied, the current call stack is output on failure.

## Version Differences

The .NET *Assert* method is similar to the VB 6 method of the same name, except that the .NET version displays a message if an expression is False, while the VB 6 version suspends program execution.

## See Also

Debug Class

---

# Debug.Listeners Property

## Class

System.Diagnostics.Debug

## Syntax

```
Dim result As TraceListenerCollection = Debug.Listeners
```

## Description

The *Listeners* property retrieves a collection of all *TraceListener* objects that monitor the debug output. Each listener is a destination for all trace and debug information created by the application.

## Usage at a Glance

While all *Debug* class features work within the development environment, they are disabled by default in code compiled for release. They must be specifically enabled if you wish to use them in a compiled application.

## Example

The following code adds a text file output method to the collection of listeners. As a result, all *Debug.Write* and similar methods will not only send the output to the Output Window (the default listener) but also to the text file.

```
' ----- Uses "Imports System.IO" above.

' ----- Define a new listener object.
Dim fileTrace As New TextWriterTraceListener( )

' ----- Since the listener is generic and doesn't have any
'         specific destination, the code needs to create the
'         destination and associate it with the listener. In
'         this case, the destination will be a file stream.
Dim debugStream As FileStream = New FileStream("c:\log.txt", _
```

```
        FileMode.Append, FileAccess.Write)
    fileTrace.Writer = New StreamWriter(debugStream)

    ' ----- Now the listener is ready to be used.
    Debug.Listeners.Add(fileTrace)

    ' ----- These Debug statements will go to the new file, and
    '         also to the Output Window.
    Debug.WriteLine("We are busy debug statements;")
    Debug.WriteLine("we go to two places at once.")

    ' ----- Test complete. Close all opened resources.
    Debug.Listeners.Remove(fileTrace)
    fileTrace.Close( )
    debugStream.Close( )

    ' ----- This Debug statement goes only to the Output Window.
    Debug.WriteLine("I'm not really that busy.")
```

### See Also

Debug Class

## Debug.Write Method

### Class

System.Diagnostics.Debug

### Syntax

```
Debug.Write(output[, category])
```

*output*  (required; *String or Object*)

The string to be sent to the debug listener outputs. For Objects, the *ToString* method is used to access the string content.

*category*  (optional; *String*)

A category name used to group output messages; the text is attached to the beginning of *output*.

### Description

The *Write* method prints text to the Output Window and other debug listeners when an application runs in the design-time environment.

### Usage at a Glance

The *Debug* class features only work in the design-time environment; the statement has no effect in a compiled application. You do not have to remove *Debug*-related features from your code before release.

### See Also

Debug Class, Debug.WriteIf Method, Debug.WriteLine Method, Debug.WriteLineIf Method

# Debug.WriteIf Method

## Class
System.Diagnostics.Debug

## Syntax
Debug.WriteIf(*condition, output*[, *category*])

*condition (required; Boolean)*
Condition that must evaluate to True before output is sent to the debug listeners.

*output (required; String or Object)*
The string to be sent to the debug listener outputs. For Objects, the *ToString* method is used to access the string content.

*category (optional; String)*
A category name used to group output messages; the text is attached to the beginning of *output*.

## Description
The *WriteIf* method prints text to the Output Window and other debug listeners when an application runs in the design-time environment, provided that *condition* is True.

## Usage at a Glance
The *Debug* class features only work in the design-time environment; the statement has no effect in a compiled application. You do not have to remove *Debug*-related features from your code before release.

## See Also
Debug Class, Debug.Write Method, Debug.WriteLine Method, Debug.WriteLineIf Method

# Debug.WriteLine Method

## Class
System.Diagnostics.Debug

## Syntax
Debug.WriteLine(*output*[, *category*])

*output (required; String or Object)*
The string to be sent to the debug listener outputs. For Objects, the *ToString* method is used to access the string content.

*category (optional; String)*
A category name used to group output messages; the text is attached to the beginning of *output*.

## Description
The *WriteLine* method prints text to the Output Window and other debug listeners, followed by a line break, when an application runs in the design-time environment.

### Usage at a Glance

The *Debug* class features only work in the design-time environment; the statement has no effect in a compiled application. You do not have to remove *Debug*-related features from your code before release.

### See Also

Debug Class, Debug.Write Method, Debug.WriteIf Method, Debug.WriteLineIf Method

---

## Debug.WriteLineIf Method

### Class

System.Diagnostics.Debug

### Syntax

```
Debug.WriteLineIf(condition, output[, category])
```

*condition* *(required; Boolean)*
    Condition that must evaluate to True before output is sent to the debug listeners.

*output* *(required; String or Object)*
    The string to be sent to the debug listener outputs. For Objects, the *ToString* method is used to access the string content.

*category* *(optional; String)*
    A category name used to group output messages; the text is attached to the beginning of *output*.

### Description

The *WriteLineIf* method prints text to the Output Window and other debug listeners, followed by a line break, when an application runs in the design-time environment, provided that *condition* is True.

### Usage at a Glance

The *Debug* class features only work in the design-time environment; the statement has no effect in a compiled application. You do not have to remove *Debug*-related features from your code before release.

### See Also

Debug Class, Debug.Write Method, Debug.WriteIf Method, Debug.WriteLine Method

---

## Declare Statement

### Syntax

```
[accessModifier] [Shadows] Declare [Ansi | Unicode | Auto] _
    {Sub | Function} name Lib "libname" [Alias "aliasname"] _
    [([arglist])] [As type]
```

*accessModifier (optional)*

Specifies the scope and accessibility of the declaration. One of the following access levels:

| Access level | Description |
|---|---|
| Public | The declaration is publicly accessible anywhere, both inside and outside of the project. |
| Private | The declaration is accessible only within the defining type. |
| Protected | The declaration is accessible only to the code in the defining type or to one of its derived types. |
| Friend | The declaration is accessible only within the project that contains the declaration definition. |
| Protected Friend | Combines the access features of Protected and Friend. |

If omitted, the Public access level is used.

Shadows *(optional)*

Indicates that the declaration shadows an identically named element in a base class.

Ansi *(optional)*

Converts all strings to ANSI values. This is the default if none of the string translation modifiers are used.

Unicode *(optional)*

Converts all strings to Unicode values.

Auto *(optional)*

Converts the strings according to .NET rules based on the name of the method (or the alias name, if specified).

*name (required)*

Any valid procedure name. Dynamic-link library (DLL) procedure and function names are case-sensitive. If the *aliasname* argument is used, *name* represents the name by which the function or procedure is referenced in your code, while *aliasname* represents the true name of the routine as found in the DLL.

*libname (required; String)*

The name of the DLL or code resource that contains the declared procedure.

*aliasname (optional; String)*

Indicates the true name of the procedure or function in the DLL, as opposed to the local name identified through *name*. If the true procedure or function name conflicts with a Visual Basic or .NET keyword or reserved word, use this feature to supply a nonconflicting name.

*arglist (optional)*

A comma-delimited list of parameters defined by the DLL function or procedure. Each comma-delimited parameter includes a parameter name and a data type.

*arglist* uses the following syntax and parts:

```
[ByVal | ByRef] varname[()] [As argtype]
```

ByVal *(optional)*

The argument is passed by value to the DLL. ByVal is the default method of passing variables.

ByRef *(optional)*
> The argument is passed by reference to the DLL. All changes made to the argument in the DLL procedure will be reflected in the original variable.

*varname (required)*
> The name of the argument, although it may vary from the parameter name given by the designer of the DLL.

*argtype (optional; Type)*
> The data type of the argument. Any valid .NET data type can be used. Visual Basic does not examine the DLL at compile time to see if this data type is correct.

*type (optional; Type)*
> Data type of the value returned by a DLL function. Arrays cannot be returned, but an Object containing an array is valid.

## Description

The Declare statement is used at the module level to declare references to external procedures in DLLs.

## Usage at a Glance

- The data type of each parameter, and also the data type of the return value, may differ in name between .NET and the DLL. For instance, 16-bit signed integers may be known as "Integer" in the DLL, but they should be declared as Short in the Declare parameter list.

- The number and type of arguments included in *arglist* are checked each time the procedure is called.

- You can use the # symbol at the beginning of *aliasname* to denote that *aliasname* is, in fact, the ordinal position of a procedure within the DLL or code library. In this case, all characters following the # sign must be numeric. For example:

```
Friend Declare Function GetForegroundWindow Lib "user32" _
    Alias "#237" ( ) As Long
```

- DLL entry points are case-sensitive. Either *name* or *aliasname* (whichever one represents the true name of the DLL procedure) must correspond in case exactly to the routine as it is defined in the external DLL. If you aren't sure how the routine name appears in the DLL, use the *DumpBin.exe* utility to view its export table. For instance, the following command displays the export table of *advapi32.dll*, one of the Windows system files:

```
dumpbin /exports c:\windows\system32\advapi32.dll
```

- *libname* can include an optional path that identifies precisely where the external library is located. If the path is not included along with the library name, VB searches the current directory, the Windows directory, the Windows system directory, and the directories in the path, in that order.

- If the external library is one of the major Windows system DLLs (such as *Kernel32.dll* or *User32.dll*), *libname* can consist of only the root filename, rather than the complete filename and extension.

- One of the most common uses of the Declare statement is to make routines in the Win32 API accessible to your programs. For more on this topic, see *Win32 API Programming with Visual Basic* by Steven Roman (O'Reilly Media).

- The .NET Framework also defines a <DllImport> attribute that provides similar functionality.
- In many cases, you can use routines available in the .NET Base Class Library or Framework Class Library instead of calling procedures in the Win32 API.

### Example

The following example retrieves the handle of a window from its title bar caption. This is done using the *FindWindow* API function.

```
Friend Declare Function FindWindow Lib "user32" _
    Alias "FindWindowA" (ByVal lpClassName As String, _
    ByVal lpWindowName As String) As Integer

Private Sub ShowWindowHandle( )
    MsgBox(FindWindow(vbNullString, "Document - WordPad"))
End Sub
```

### Version Differences

- In VB 6, it is possible to declare the data type of an argument as Any, which suspends type checking by the VB runtime engine. In .NET, this usage is not supported.
- In VB 6, if ByVal or ByRef is not specified, an argument is passed to the calling procedure by reference. In .NET, arguments are passed by value, by default.
- In VB 6, it is possible to override the method in which an argument is passed to an external function within the call itself by specifying either ByVal or ByRef before the argument. In .NET, this usage is not permitted.
- Due to data-type changes between VB 6 and VB under .NET, some data-type changes may be required in the Declare statement. For instance, parameters declared as Integer in VB 6 are declared as Short in .NET.

---

## DefaultMember Attribute

### Class

System.Reflection.DefaultMemberAttribute

### Applies To

Class, Struct, or Interface

### Constructor

New(*memberName*)

*memberName* (required; String)
   The name of the default member

### Properties

*MemberName (String)*
   Read-only. The name of the default member. Its value is set by the constructor's *memberName* parameter.

## Description

The <DefaultMember> attribute defines the default member of a structure, class, or interface. The default member is the member executed by the *Type* object's *Invoke-Member* method when a null string is supplied as the method's *name* argument.

The Visual Basic Default keyword (part of the Property statement syntax) is ultimately translated by the Visual Basic compiler into the <DefaultMember> attribute. Visual Basic, however, requires that default members be parameterized. The use of the Default keyword allows you to specify a particular array element without having to explicitly reference the member name. For instance, if the Items property is the default member of CampSite, the statement:

```
CampSite.Items(10) = "Sleeping bag"
```

is functionally identical to:

```
CampSite(10) = "Sleeping bag"
```

Because the <DefaultMember> attribute, unlike the Default keyword, does not have to refer to a parameterized property, you can use the <DefaultMember> attribute to define default members that are not parameterized. However, this does not allow you to omit a reference to that member in code when using instances of the object. For instance, if the default member of the CashRegister object is a member named TotalValue, you cannot reference it implicitly, as follows:

```
CashRegister = 10
```

You can, however, invoke that member using the *Type.InvokeMember* method without explicitly naming it.

The <DefaultMember> attribute and Default keyword are different in one other important respect. If you use <DefaultMember> rather than Default to define a parameterized property as the default member of a class, at runtime, Visual Basic will be unable to resolve implicit references to the member. The sole capability that the <DefaultMember> attribute affords you is the ability to *explicitly* invoke a default member using the *Type.InvokeMember* method.

If you use both the Default keyword and the <DefaultMember> attribute in the same class definition, even if both reference the same member, an error occurs.

 If *memberName* is not a member of the class, structure, or interface, the <DefaultMember> attribute is ignored, and no error is raised.

## Example

```
Option Strict

Imports System
Imports System.Reflection

<DefaultMember("GetName")> _
Public Class Contact
    Private contactName As String
    Private contactCity As String
    Private contactComments() As String
```

```
Public Sub New()
    Me.New("John Doe", "Anywhere, U.S.A.")
End Sub

Public Sub New(ByVal fullName As String, _
        ByVal homeCity As String)
    MyBase.New()
    contactName = fullName
    contactCity = homeCity
End Sub

Public Property Name() As String
    Get
        Return contactName
    End Get
    Set(ByVal value As String)
        contactName = value
    End Set
End Property

Public Property Comments(index As Integer) As String
    Get
        Return contactComments(index)
    End Get
    Set(ByVal value As Integer)
        contactComments(index) = value
    End Set
End Property

Public Function GetName() As String
    Return contactName
End Function

Public Function GetCity() As String
    Return contactCity
End Function
End Class

Module GeneralCode
    Public Sub Main
        Dim useContact As New Contact
        Dim contactType As Type = GetType(Contact)
        Dim bindings As BindingFlags = BindingFlags.Instance Or _
        BindingFlags.Public Or BindingFlags.InvokeMethod

        ' ----- The first two lines will produce the same result.
        Console.WriteLine(contactType.InvokeMember("", bindings, _
            Nothing, useContact, Nothing))
        Console.WriteLine(contactType.InvokeMember("GetName", _
            bindings, Nothing, useContact, Nothing))
        Console.WriteLine(contactType.InvokeMember("GetCity", _
            bindings, Nothing, useContact, Nothing))
    End Sub
End Module
```

# Delegate Statement

## Syntax

```
[accessModifier] [Shadows] Delegate { Sub | Function } name _
    [(Of typeParamList)] [([argList])] [As type]
```

accessModifier *(optional)*
Specifies the scope and accessibility of the delegate. One of the following access levels:

| Access level | Description |
|---|---|
| Public | The delegate is publicly accessible anywhere, both inside and outside of the project. |
| Private | The delegate is accessible only within the defining type. |
| Protected | The delegate is accessible only to the code in the defining type or to one of its derived types. |
| Friend | The delegate is accessible only within the project that contains the delegate definition. |
| Protected Friend | Combines the access features of Protected and Friend. |

If omitted, the Public access level is used.

Shadows *(optional)*
Indicates that the delegate shadows an identically named element in a base class.

name *(required)*
The name of the delegate. It need not match the target procedure or function name.

typeParamList *(optional)*
Adds type parameter placeholders that will later enforce strong typing when the delegate is used. The Of clause implements generics, which are fully described in Chapter 10. If generics will not be used, this clause can be excluded.

argList *(optional; any)*
The argument list specific to this delegate. It must have the same signature as the target procedure or function, although the names of each argument need not match.

type *(optional; any)*
The return type of the function-associated delegate. The As clause is only used for function parameters; it is excluded when defining a procedure delegate.

## Description

The Delegate statement declares the parameters and return type of a delegate. The syntax is similar to that used to declare subroutines and functions.

## Usage at a Glance

- Any procedure with an argument list and return type that match that of a declared delegate class can be used to create an instance of this delegate class.
- For more information on delegates, see Chapter 8.

## Example

Consider the following class definition:

```
Public Class SimpleClass
    Public Sub SimpleMethod(ByVal onlyArg As String)
        MsgBox(onlyArg)
    End Sub
End Class
```

A delegate can be defined that carries the same signature as the SimpleMethod procedure.

```
Delegate Sub MatchingDelegate(ByVal anyArg As String)
```

The following code uses the delegate to call the SimpleClass.SimpleMethod member:

```
Private Sub Button1_Click(ByVal sender As Object, _
        ByVal e As System.EventArgs) Handles Button1.Click
    ' ----- Call a method through a delegate.
    Dim classInstance As New SimpleClass
    Dim theDelegate As MatchingDelegate

    ' ----- Define the delegate, passing the address of the
    '       object's method, which has a matching signature.
    theDelegate = New MatchingDelegate(AddressOf _
        classInstance.SimpleMethod)

    ' ----- Use Invoke to call the method.
    theDelegate.Invoke("test")
End Sub
```

## Version Differences

- Delegates are new to VB under .NET.
- Visual Basic 2005 adds support for generics to delegates. See Chapter 10 for information on using generics.

## See Also

Function Statement, Sub Statement

---

# DeleteSetting Procedure

## Class

Microsoft.VisualBasic.Interaction

## Syntax

```
DeleteSetting(appname[, section[, key]])
```

*appname* (required; String)

The name of the application branch to be deleted or that contains the setting to be deleted.

*section* (optional; String)

The name of the application's subkey that is to be deleted or that contains the key to be deleted. This can be a single key or a relative registry path, with path components separated by backslashes.

*key* (optional; String)

The name of the value entry to delete.

## Description

The DeleteSetting procedure deletes a complete application settings branch, one of its subkeys, or a single value entry within a subkey. All of these settings values are stored in the Windows registry.

## Usage at a Glance

- You cannot use DeleteSetting to delete entries from registry keys that are not subkeys of HKEY_CURRENT_USER\Software\VB and VBA ProgramSettings.

- *section* is a relative path (similar to that used to describe the directories on a hard drive) used to navigate from the application key to the subkey to be deleted. For example, to delete the value entry named TestKey in the registry key HKEY_CURRENT_USER\Software\VB and VBA ProgramSettings\RegTester\BranchOne\BranchTwo, you would use:

      DeleteSetting("RegTester", "BranchOne\BranchTwo", "TestKey")

- If *key* is supplied, only the value entry named *key* and its associated value are deleted. If *key* is omitted, the subkey named *section* is deleted. If *section* is omitted, the entire application branch named *appname* is deleted.

- DeleteSetting cannot be used to delete the default value (i.e., the unnamed value entry) belonging to any key. If you are using only the VB registry functions, though, this is not a serious limitation, since SaveSetting does not allow you to create a default value.

- Care should be used with this function, since it will allow you to delete entries created by other Visual Basic applications.

- If the key or branch to be deleted does not exist, an error occurs.

- The .NET Framework includes registry-related features that provide more flexibility than the VB "Settings" functions. These features are found in the *Registry* and *RegistryKey* classes of the *Microsoft.Win32* namespace.

## Version Differences

Visual Basic 2005 includes several new features that let you manage the settings used by an application. Although they are not compatible with the older VB "Settings" functions, they provide a richer set of features. These features are located in the *My.Settings* object. The *My.Computer.Registry* object also provides access to convenient registry-related features.

## See Also

GetAllSettings Function, GetSetting Function, SaveSetting Procedure

# Dim Statement

## Syntax

```
[accessModifier] [[Shared] [Shadows] | [Static]] [ReadOnly] _
    [Dim] [WithEvents] name[([subscripts])] _
    [As [New] type] [= expression]
```

*accessModifier (optional)*

Specifies the scope and accessibility of the variable(s). For variables defined within a procedure or code block, no access modifier is permitted; all procedure-level and block-level variables have procedure-level or block-level scope. For all module-level variables, one of the following access levels may be used in place of the Dim keyword:

| Access level | Description |
| --- | --- |
| Public | The variable(s) are publicly accessible anywhere, both inside and outside of the project. |
| Private | The variable(s) are accessible only within the defining type. |
| Protected | The variable(s) are accessible only to the code in the defining type or to one of its derived types. |
| Friend | The variable(s) are accessible only within the project that contains the variable definition. |
| Protected Friend | Combines the access features of Protected and Friend. |

If omitted in a declaration at the module level (and the Dim keyword is used instead), the Public access level is used.

Shared *(optional)*

Indicates that the variables are shared variables instead of instance variables. Shared variables may be accessed without a particular instance of the object. Shared variables are also known as *static variables*, but they are different from Static variables used within procedures. The Shared keyword is only valid in module-level declarations.

Shadows *(optional)*

Indicates that the variables shadow identically named elements in a base class. The Shadows keyword is only valid in module-level declarations.

Static *(optional)*

Indicates that the variables have a lifetime that lasts for the lifetime of the object that contains the variable, although their scope is limited to the procedure or code block in which they are defined. The Static keyword is only valid in procedure-level or block-level declarations.

ReadOnly *(optional)*

Indicates that the variable(s) are read-only beyond their initial setting through *expression*; they are functionally equivalent to Const fields. Static variables cannot be ReadOnly.

Dim *(optional)*

The Dim keyword is required unless one of the following keywords is used: Public, Private, Friend, Protected, Protected Friend, or Static. When one of those keywords appears, Dim is always excluded.

WithEvents *(optional)*

Indicates that the object will respond to, and process events through, event handlers. When using the WithEvents keyword, the As clause must appear, and the data type may not be an array. The WithEvents keyword is only valid in module-level declarations.

*name (required)*

The name of the variable.

*subscripts (optional)*

The dimensions of an array variable, with up to 60 comma-delimited dimensions. Each dimension has the format:

    [[0 To] *upper*]

which indicates the upper bound of the array dimension. The optional 0 To clause is for clarity only; all array dimensions have a lower bound of zero. All dimensions can be left blank to allow the array to be dimensioned by *expression*, or later through a ReDim statement. You can indicate the number of dimensions without indicating the range of each dimension by using commas only, without an *upper* value for each dimension.

New *(optional)*

Creates an instance of an object and assigns it to *name*.

*type (optional unless* OptionStrict *is* On; *any)*

The data type of *name*. If omitted, the data type is set to Object. If the New keyword is used, *type* may be followed by constructor parameters in parentheses.

*expression (optional)*

Any expression that provides the initial value to assign to the variable; cannot be used if an As New clause is used.

## Description

The Dim statement declares and allocates storage space in memory for variables. The Dim statement is used either at the module level or the procedure level to declare variables of a particular data type.

## Usage at a Glance

- If you use WithEvents, the variable cannot be of type Object.
- If *type* does not expose any events, the WithEvents keyword generates a compiler error.
- Reference types have an initial value of Nothing, unless the New keyword is used to assign an initial value, or *expression* is used to assign an initial value.
- Multiple variables may be declared with the same Dim statement; each variable is separated from the others by a comma. If one of the variables is not given an explicit type declaration, then its type is that of the next variable with an explicit type declaration. For example, in the line:

      Dim first As Long, second, third, fourth As Integer

the variables second and third are of type Integer, as is fourth. In VB 6, the variables second and third would have been of type Variant.

More than one variable can be assigned a value in a single Dim statement:

```
Dim first As Integer = 6, second As Integer = 9
```

- Variables that are not explicitly initialized by the Dim statement have the following default values:

| Data type | Initial value |
|---|---|
| All numeric types | 0 |
| Boolean | False |
| Date | January 1, 1 AD, 12:00:00 AM |
| Object | Nothing |
| String | Nothing |

- Local variables can have *procedure-level scope* or *block-level scope*. A variable that is declared within a Visual Basic procedure but not within a code block has procedure-level scope: its scope consists of the procedure in which it is declared. If a variable is declared inside a *code block* (a statement that contains subordinate statements, as with an If or For statement), then the variable has block-level scope: it is visible only within that block. However, block-level variables have a lifetime of the entire procedure. Once set, their value is retained even when the block is exited.

- There are several ways to declare and assign an initial value to a one-dimensional array:

```
'Implicit constructor: No initial size and no initialization
Dim sampleArray() As Integer

'Explicit constructor: No initial size and no initialization
Dim sampleArray() As Integer = New Integer() {}

'Implicit constructor: Initial size but no initialization
Dim sampleArray(6) As Integer

'Explicit constructor: Initial size but no initialization
Dim sampleArray() As Integer = New Integer(6) {}

'Implicit constructor: Initial size implied by initialization
Dim sampleArray() As Integer = {1, 2, 3, 4, 5, 6, 7}

'Explicit constructor, Initial size and initialization
Dim sampleArray() As Integer = New Integer(6) {1, 2, 3, 4, 5, 6, 7}
```

- To declare a multidimensional array, use one of the following sample templates:

```
' Two-dimensional array of unknown size
Dim sampleArray(,) As Integer

' Two-dimensional array of unknown size
Dim sampleArray(,) As Integer = New Integer(,) {}
```

```
' Two-dimensional array of size 3 by 2
Dim sampleArray(3, 2) As Integer

' Two-dimensional array of size 3 by 2
Dim sampleArray(,) As Integer = New Integer(3, 2) {}

' Two-dimensional array of size 3 by 2, initialized
Dim sampleArray(,) As Integer = {{1, 4}, {2, 5}, {3, 6}}

' Two-dimensional array of size 3 by 2, initialized
Dim sampleArray(,) As Integer = _
    New Integer(3, 2) {{1, 4}, {2, 5}, {3, 6}}
```

- There is no limit to the number of object variables that can refer to the same instance using the WithEvents keyword; they will all respond to that object's events.

- Using Option Explicit On requires that each variable used in your code have a declaration. Enforcing this requirement can greatly reduce potential errors in your code.

- Static variables retain their value between calls to the procedure in which they are declared, although a Static variable's scope is limited to the procedure in which it is created. A static variable's initial value is set by *expression*. This initial assignment only occurs when the variable is first created as part of the object instance creation process.

- A type's constructor is called when you use the New keyword on a declaration. You may include constructor parameters after *type*. If no parameters are supplied, the default parameterless constructor is used.

- If you attempt to iterate an array (such as with the For Each...Next statement) that has not yet been dimensioned, an error occurs.

## Version Differences

- There are some syntax and functionality differences between the VB 6 and the .NET versions of the Dim statement.

- In VB 6, all variables that do not specifying a data type are of type Variant. In .NET, such variables are of type Object.

- When multiple variables are declared in a single Dim statement in VB 6, variables without a specific data type are cast as Variant. In .NET, such variables are assigned to the data type of the next variable (in the same statement) that has a declared data type.

- .NET adds the ability to assign an initial value to a variable in the Dim statement.

- In VB 6, all variables defined within a procedure have procedure-level scope. In .NET, variables defined in code blocks (such as loops) have block-level scope.

- VB 6 supports fixed-length strings; .NET does not include this feature.

- In VB 6, arrays could be either fixed-length or dynamic. In .NET, all arrays are dynamic.

- VB 6 allows you to set the lower bound of an array dimension to a nonzero value. The lower bound of all .NET array dimensions is zero.
- In VB 6, it was possible to define a procedure as Static; all variables within a Static procedure would be Static. In .NET, the use of the Static keyword with Function or Sub statements is not supported.

### See Also

Private Keyword, Public Keyword, ReDim Statement, Static Statement, WithEvents Keyword

## Dir Function

### Class

Microsoft.VisualBasic.FileSystem

### Syntax

```
Dim result As String = Dir([pathname[, attributes]])
```

*pathname* (optional; String)
A filename or directory, with optional wildcard characters * and ? in the filename component.

*attributes* (optional; FileAttribute enumeration)
One or more of the following *Microsoft.VisualBasic.FileAttribute* enumeration values, added or Or'd together, specifying the file attributes to be matched:

| Value | Description |
| --- | --- |
| Normal | Normal file (one that has neither the Hidden nor the System flag set) |
| ReadOnly | Read-only flag set on file |
| Hidden | Hidden file |
| System | System file |
| Volume | Volume label; must be used without any other attributes or enumeration values |
| Directory | Directory or folder |
| Archive | Archive flag set on file |

If omitted, but *pathname* is supplied, Normal is used.

### Description

The Dir function returns the name of a single file or directory matching the pattern and attribute mask passed to the function. One or both of the arguments must be supplied the first time the Dir function is called; this call returns the first match based on the supplied arguments. Subsequent calls do not include any arguments and return the next match based on the original use of the function. When there are no more matches, Dir returns an empty string.

### Usage at a Glance

- If *attributes* is not specified, files matching *pathname* are returned regardless of the attributes defined for those files.
- You can use the wildcard characters * and ? within *pathname* to return multiple files.

- Using Volume for *attributes* returns the volume label for the drive specified by *pathname* instead of a matching filename.

- In previous versions of Visual Basic, the Dir function was commonly used to determine whether a particular file existed. Although it can still be used for this purpose, the *System.IO.File.Exists* method is more straightforward. In Visual Basic 2005, the *My.Computer.FileSystem.FileExists* method also checks for the existence of a file.

- The Dir function returns filenames in the order in which they appear in the file-allocation table.

- The Dir function saves its state between invocations. This means that the function cannot be called recursively. For example, if the function returns the name of the directory, you cannot then call the Dir function to iterate the files in that directory and then return to the original directory.

- If you are calling the Dir function to return the names of one or more files, you must provide an explicit file specification. For instance, if you want to retrieve the names of all files in the *Windows* directory, the function call:

  ```
  fileMatch = Dir("C:\windows", FileAttribute.Normal)
  ```

  fails. Instead, the Dir function must be called with *pathname* defined as follows:

  ```
  fileMatch = Dir("C:\windows\*.*", FileAttribute.Normal)
  ```

## Example

```
Private Sub Button1_Click(ByVal sender As System.Object, _
    ByVal e As System.EventArgs) Handles Button1.Click
' ----- Add all matching files to the list.
Dim matchingFile As String

ListBox1.Items.Clear( )
matchingFile = Dir(TextBox1.Text)
Do While (matchingFile <> "")
    ListBox1.Items.Add(matchingFile)
    matchingFile = Dir( )
Loop
End Sub
```

## Version Differences

Visual Basic 2005 includes a *My.Computer.FileSystem.GetDirectoryInfo* method that provides related functionality. The *My.Computer.FileSystem.FileExists* method can be used to test for the existence of a file.

# DirectCast Function

## Syntax

```
Dim result As typename = DirectCast(expression, typename)
```

*expression (required; any)*
    The value to be converted. This can be any data, object, structure, or interface type.

*typename (required; Type)*
    The data type, object type, structure, or interface to which *expression* is to be converted. This can be virtually anything that can appear after the As clause of a

`Dim` statement. However, this type must have an inheritance relationship with the type of *expression*.

## Description

The `DirectCast` function converts an expression or object to the specified type. The original type of *expression* must have an inheritance relationship with the new type, or an error occurs.

## Usage at a Glance

- The cast will fail if the source and target data types do not have an inheritance relationship—that is, one does not eventually derive from the other. The cast may also fail if it is a narrowing cast and `Option Strict` is `On`.
- This function does not support named arguments.

## Version Differences

- The `DirectCast` function is new to VB under .NET.
- Visual Basic 2005 includes a new `TryCast` function that includes slightly different functionality.

## See Also

CType Function, TryCast Function

---

# Directory Class

## Namespace

System.IO

## Creatable

No

## Description

The *Directory* class has a number of members that allow you to retrieve information about directories, to move and delete a directory, and to create a new directory. All of the members of the *Directory* class are shared methods, so they can be called without instantiating any objects. For example, use the following statement to call the *Create-Directory* method:

```
Directory.CreateDirectory("C:\projects\project1")
```

The following table lists some of the more useful and interesting members of the *Directory* class. Those marked with an asterisk (*) have separate entries in this chapter.

| Member | Description |
| --- | --- |
| CreateDirectory Method * | Creates a new directory |
| Delete Method * | Deletes an existing directory |
| Exists Method * | Tests a directory to see if it exists |
| GetCreationTime Method * | Gets the original creation date and time of a directory |
| GetCurrentDirectory Method | Gets the directory used for the "current" directory, from which all relative paths derive |

| Member | Description |
|---|---|
| GetDirectories Method * | Gets an array of all directories within a parent directory |
| GetDirectoryRoot Method * | Gets the drive root of a given directory |
| GetFiles Method * | Gets an array of all files within a parent directory |
| GetFileSystemEntries Method * | Gets an array of all files and directories within a parent directory |
| GetLastAccessTime Method | Gets the date and time that a directory was last accessed |
| GetLastWriteTime Method | Gets the date and time that a directory was last modified |
| GetLogicalDrives Method * | Gets an array of all logical drives on the local system |
| GetParent Method * | Gets the parent directory of a given directory |
| Move Method * | Moves a directory to a new location |
| SetCurrentDirectory Method | Selects the directory used for the "current" directory, from which all relative paths derive |

## Version Differences

- The *Directory* object loosely corresponds to the *Folder* object in the *FileSystem Object* object model, part of the Microsoft Scripting Runtime Library and often used in VBScript and ASP-based web development. There is, however, a significant difference in the members of each class, and, in some cases, methods with similar functionality have different names.

- Visual Basic 2005 includes a *My.Computer.FileSystem* object that provides directory management functionality.

## See Also

File Class

# Directory.CreateDirectory Method

## Class

System.IO.Directory

## Syntax

```
Directory.CreateDirectory(path)
```

*path* (required; String)
    The path of the new directory

## Description

The *CreateDirectory* method creates a new directory based on a supplied path.

## Usage at a Glance

- *path* can be an absolute or a relative path. For example:

```
' ----- Absolute path.
Directory.CreateDirectory("C:\Temp")

' ----- Relative path.
Directory.CreateDirectory("..\Chapter2")
```

- If needed, *CreateDirectory* creates all directories down the line to the final directory. For example, the code:

  ```
  Directory.CreateDirectory("c:\NewDirectory\NewSubDirectory")
  ```

  creates the *NewDirectory* directory if it does not exist and then creates the *NewSubDirectory* directory if it does not exist.
- *path* can be either a path on the local system, the path of a mapped network drive, or a UNC path.
- The *CreateDirectory* method does not raise an error if the directory to be created already exists.

### Version Differences

Visual Basic 2005 includes a *My.Computer.FileSystem.CreateDirectory* method that provides similar functionality.

## Directory.Delete Method

### Class

System.IO.Directory

### Syntax

```
Directory.Delete(path[, recursive])
```

*path* (required; String)
: The path of the directory to delete.

*recursive* (optional; Boolean)
: Indicates whether the directory and its entire contents (including nested subdirectories) are to be deleted if the directory is not empty. Its default value is False.

### Description

The *Delete* method deletes an existing directory, with all of its contents if requested.

### Usage at a Glance

- If *path* does not exist, a runtime error occurs.
- If *recursive* is set to False and the directory is not empty, a runtime error occurs.
- *path* can be either an absolute path or a relative path from the current directory.
- *path* can be either a path on the local system, the path of a mapped network drive, or a UNC path.
- *path* cannot contain wildcard characters.
- The *Delete* method permanently deletes directories and their contents. It doesn't move them to the Recycle Bin.
- Care must be taken when setting *recursive* to True, especially since no prompting is done before the deletion occurs.

### Version Differences

Visual Basic 2005 includes a *My.Computer.FileSystem.DeleteDirectory* method that provides similar functionality.

# Directory.Exists Method

## Class

System.IO.Directory

## Syntax

```
Dim result As Boolean = Directory.Exists(path)
```

*path* (required; String)
: The path of the directory whose existence is to be determined

## Description

The *Exists* method indicates whether a given directory exists (True) or not (False).

## Usage at a Glance

- *path* can be either an absolute path or a relative path from the current directory.
- *path* can be either a path on the local system, the path of a mapped network drive, or a UNC path.
- *path* cannot contain wildcard characters.

## Version Differences

Visual Basic 2005 includes a *My.Computer.FileSystem.DirectoryExists* method that provides similar functionality.

---

# Directory.GetCreationTime Method

## Class

System.IO.Directory

## Syntax

```
Dim result As Date = Directory.GetCreationTime(path)
```

*path* (required; String)
: A valid path to be examined for a creation time

## Description

Indicates the date and time when a given directory was first created

## Usage at a Glance

- *path* can be either an absolute path or a relative path from the current directory.
- *path* can be either a path on the local system, the path of a mapped network drive, or a UNC path.
- *path* cannot contain wildcard characters.

## Version Differences

Visual Basic 2005 includes a *My.Computer.FileSystem.GetDirectoryInfo* method that provides access to detailed information about a directory.

---

# Directory.GetDirectories Method

## Class
System.IO.Directory

## Syntax
```
Dim result( ) As String = Directory.GetDirectories(path[, _
    searchPattern[, searchOption]])
```
*path* (required; String)
  A valid path to a directory.
*searchPattern* (optional; String)
  A directory specification, optionally including the wildcard characters * and ?.
*searchOption* (optional; SearchOption enumeration)
  *New in 2005.* One of the following *Microsoft.VisualBasic.FileIO.SearchOption* enumeration members:

| Member | Description |
|---|---|
| AllDirectories | The method returns information about all nested subdirectories. |
| TopDirectoryOnly | The method returns information about the topmost directory only. |

If omitted, TopDirectoryOnly is used.

## Description
The *GetDirectories* method returns an array of strings, with each string containing the name of one subdirectory of the specified main directory, optionally matching a pattern. The results can optionally include all nested subdirectories.

## Usage at a Glance
- *path* can be either an absolute path or a relative path from the current directory.
- *path* can be either a path on the local system, the path of a mapped network drive, or a UNC path.
- *path* cannot contain wildcard characters, but *searchPattern* can.
- If *searchPattern* is specified, the method returns only those directories with names that match the string, which can contain wildcard characters. Otherwise, *GetDirectories* returns the names of all the subdirectories in the *path* directory.
- If the directory specified by *path* has no subdirectories, or if no directories match *searchPattern*, an empty array is returned.

## Example
The following code displays all top-level subdirectories of *c:\* with names that start with the letter P:
```
Dim thePDirectories( ) As String
Dim counter As Integer
thePDirectories = Directory.GetDirectories("c:\", "P*")
For counter = 0 To UBound(thePDirectories)
```

```
        Console.WriteLine(thePDirectories(counter))
    Next counter
```

### Version Differences

- The *searchOption* parameter is new with Visual Basic 2005.
- Visual Basic 2005 includes a *My.Computer.FileSystem.GetDirectories* method that provides similar functionality.

### See Also

Directory.GetFiles Method, Directory.GetFileSystemEntries Method

---

## Directory.GetDirectoryRoot Method

### Class

System.IO.Directory

### Syntax

```
Dim result As String = Directory.GetDirectoryRoot(path)
```

*path  (required; String)*
    A valid path to a directory

### Description

The *GetDirectoryRoot* method returns the name of the root directory of the drive on which *path* resides. For example, the code:

```
Directory.GetDirectoryRoot("c:\Program Files\MyCompany")
```

returns the string "C:\" as the root directory.

### Usage at a Glance

- *path* can be either an absolute path or a relative path from the current directory.
- *path* can be either a path on the local system, the path of a mapped network drive, or a UNC path. For example, the code:

    ```
    Directory.GetDirectoryRoot("\\SomeServer\C\SomeFolder")
    ```

    returns "\\SomeServer\C," and if the directory \\*SomeServer\C\SomeFolder* maps to the local "Z" drive, then:

    ```
    Directory.GetDirectoryRoot("Z:\temp")
    ```

    returns Z:\.
- *path* cannot contain wildcard characters.

### Version Differences

Visual Basic 2005 includes a *My.Computer.FileSystem.GetDirectoryInfo* method that provides access to detailed information about a directory.

### See Also

Directory.GetParent Method

---

# Directory.GetFiles Method

## Class
System.IO.Directory

## Syntax
```
Dim result( ) As String = Directory.GetFiles(path[, _
    searchPattern[, searchOption]])
```
*path (required; String)*
A valid path to a directory

*searchPattern (optional; String)*
A file specification, optionally including the wildcard characters * and ?

*searchOption (optional; SearchOption enumeration)*
*New in 2005.* One of the following *Microsoft.VisualBasic.FileIO.SearchOption* enumeration members:

| Member | Description |
|---|---|
| AllDirectories | The method returns information about all nested subdirectories. |
| TopDirectoryOnly | The method returns information about the top-most directory only. |

If omitted, TopDirectoryOnly is used.

## Description
The *GetFiles* method returns an array of strings, with each string containing the name of one file from the specified main directory, optionally matching a pattern. The results can optionally include all nested subdirectories.

## Usage at a Glance
- *path* can be either an absolute path or a relative path from the current directory.
- *path* can be either a path on the local system, the path of a mapped network drive, or a UNC path.
- *path* cannot contain wildcard characters, but *searchPattern* can.
- If *searchPattern* is specified, the method returns only those files with names that match the string, which can contain wildcard characters. Otherwise, the function returns the names of all the files in the *path* directory.
- If the directory specified by *path* has no files, or if no files match *searchPattern*, an empty array is returned.

## Example
The following code displays all files in *c:\* that have the ".txt" extension:
```
Dim allTextFiles( ) As String
Dim counter As Integer
allTextFiles = Directory.GetFiles("c:\", "*.txt")
For counter = 0 To UBound(allTextFiles)
    Console.WriteLine(allTextFiles(counter))
Next counter
```

### Version Differences
- The *searchOption* parameter is new with Visual Basic 2005.
- Visual Basic 2005 includes a *My.Computer.FileSystem.GetFiles* method that provides similar functionality.

### See Also
Directory.GetDirectories Method, Directory.GetFileSystemEntries Method

---

## Directory.GetFileSystemEntries Method

### Class
System.IO.Directory

### Syntax
```
Dim result( ) As String = Directory.GetFileSystemEntries(path[, _
    searchPattern])
```
*path* (required; String)
: A valid path to a directory

*searchpattern* (optional; String)
: A file specification, optionally including the wildcard characters * and ?.

### Description
The *GetFileSystemEntries* method returns a string array with the names of all files and directories in the specified directory, optionally matching a pattern.

### Usage at a Glance
- *path* can be either an absolute path or a relative path from the current directory.
- *path* can be either a path on the local system, the path of a mapped network drive, or a UNC path.
- *path* cannot contain wildcard characters, but *searchPattern* can.
- If the directory specified by *path* has no files or subdirectories, or if no files or subdirectories match *searchPattern*, an empty array is returned.
- This method combines the functionality of the *GetDirectories* and *GetFiles* methods.

### Version Differences
Visual Basic 2005 includes a *My.Computer.FileSystem* object that provides access to detailed information about files and directories.

### See Also
Directory.GetDirectories Method, Directory.GetFiles Method

## Directory.GetLogicalDrives Method

**Class**

System.IO.Directory

**Syntax**

```
Dim result( ) As String = Directory.GetLogicalDrives( )
```

**Description**

The *GetLogicalDrives* method returns an array of strings, with each element containing the root directory of each logical drive on the local system.

**Usage at a Glance**

In the case of a mapped network drive, *GetLogicalDrives* returns the letter to which the drive is mapped. For instance, if the directory *\\SomeServer\C\SomeFolder* is mapped to the "Z" drive, then *GetLogicalDrives* will return "Z:\" for this logical drive.

**Example**

```
Dim allDrives( ) As String
Dim counter As Integer
allDrives = Directory.GetLogicalDrives( )
For counter = 0 To UBound(allDrives)
    Console.WriteLine(allDrives(counter))
Next counter
```

Typical output for this code looks like the following:

```
A:\
C:\
D:\
E:\
F:\
G:\
```

**Version Differences**

Visual Basic 2005 includes a *My.Computer.FileSystem.Drives* property that provides similar functionality.

## Directory.GetParent Method

**Class**

System.IO.Directory

**Syntax**

```
Dim result As DirectoryInfo = GetParent(path)
```

*path (required; String)*
　　A valid path to a directory

## Description

The *GetParent* method returns a *DirectoryInfo* object representing the parent directory of *path*.

## Usage at a Glance

- *path* can be either an absolute path or a relative path from the current directory.
- *path* can be either a path on the local system, the path of a mapped network drive, or a UNC path.
- *path* cannot contain wildcard characters.
- The *DirectoryInfo* object contains many useful members, including informational properties and directory manipulation tools.

## Version Differences

Visual Basic 2005 includes *My.Computer.FileSystem.GetDirectoryInfo* and *My.Computer.FileSystem.GetParentPath* methods that, when used together, provide one method of achieving similar functionality.

## See Also

Directory.GetDirectoryRoot Method

---

# Directory.Move Method

## Class

System.IO.Directory

## Syntax

```
Directory.Move(sourceDirName, destDirName)
```

*sourceDirName  (required; String)*
    The name of the directory to be moved

*destDirName  (required; String)*
    The location to which the source directory and its contents are to be moved

## Description

The *Move* method moves a directory and all its contents, including nested subdirectories and their files, to a new location.

## Usage at a Glance

- *sourceDirName* and *destDirName* can be either absolute paths or relative paths from the current directory. *destDirName* must include the name to be assigned to the moved directory. This allows you to change the directory name as you move it.
- *sourceDirName* and *destDirName* can be either paths on the local system, the paths of a mapped network drive, or UNC paths.
- Neither *sourceDirName* nor *destDirName* can contain wildcard characters.
- If the directory indicated by *destDirName* already exists, an error occurs.

## Example

The statement:

```
Directory.Move("c:\folder1", "c:\folder2")
```

moves *folder1* to *folder2* in the root of the C drive. That is, it moves all items found within *folder1* to a new directory named *folder2* and removes the original *folder1*.

## Version Differences

Visual Basic 2005 includes a *My.Computer.FileSystem.MoveDirectory* method that provides similar functionality.

## See Also

Directory.Delete Method

---

# Do...Loop Statement

## Syntax

```
Do [{While | Until} condition]
    [statements]
    [Exit Do]
    [statements]
    [Continue Do]
    [statements]
Loop
```

or:

```
Do
    [statements]
    [Exit Do]
    [statements]
    [Continue Do]
    [statements]
Loop [{While | Until} condition]
```

*condition (optional; Boolean)*
An expression that is reevaluated each pass through the loop

*statements (optional)*
Program statements to execute while (or until) *condition* is True

## Description

The Do...Loop statement repeatedly executes program code while (or until) a given condition remains True. When used with the While clause, the loop block is executed each time *condition* evaluates to True; when used with the Until clause, the loop block is executed until *condition* evaluates to True. Once the sustaining condition is no longer met, the entire loop is exited. The Exit Do statement can be used at any time to exit the Do loop early.

If the condition appears at the top of the loop construct, the code within the loop might execute zero or more times, depending on the evaluation result of *condition*.

---

When the condition appears at the bottom of the loop construct, the code within the loop always executes at least once.

*New in 2005.* The Continue Do statement can be used at any time to immediately jump back to the top of the loop and attempt to process the next iteration. The *condition* is reevaluated immediately upon reaching the top of the loop (or the bottom, if the condition is located there).

### Usage at a Glance

- You can create an infinite loop by leaving out the While and Until clauses completely.

  ```
  Do
      [statements]
  Loop
  ```

  Such loops should generally include Exit statements so that the loop can eventually be exited.

- A *condition* of Nothing is treated as False.

- You can nest Do...Loop statements within each other.

### Version Differences

Visual Basic 2005 includes the Continue Do statement.

### See Also

While...End While Statement

---

# E Field

### Class

System.Math

### Syntax

```
Dim result As Double = Math.E
```

### Description

The *E* field returns the approximate value of the irrational number *e*, the base of the natural logarithms, approximately 2.71828182845905.

### Usage at a Glance

This is a shared member of the *System.Math* class, so it can be used without an instance.

### Version Differences

The *E* Field is new to VB under .NET.

### See Also

PI Field

# End Statement

## Syntax

```
End
End AddHandler
End Class
End Enum
End Function
End Get
End If
End Interface
End Module
End Namespace
End Property
End RaiseEvent
End RemoveHandler
End Select
End Set
End Structure
End Sub
End SyncLock
End Try
End Using
End With
End While
```

## Description

Ends an application, a procedure, or a block of code.

## Usage at a Glance

* The End statement is used as follows:

| Statement | Description |
|---|---|
| End | Terminates program execution. |
| End AddHandler | *New in 2005*. Marks the end of an AddHandler block in a Custom Event definition.. |
| End Class | Marks the end of a class definition. |
| End Enum | Marks the end of a series of enumerated constants. |
| End Function | Marks the end of a Function procedure. |
| End Get | Marks the end of a Property Get definition. |
| End If | Marks the end of an If...Then...Else statement. |
| End Interface | Marks the end of an Interface definition. |
| End Module | Marks the end of a code Module. |
| End Namespace | Marks the end of a Namespace definition. |
| End Property | Marks the end of a Property definition. |
| End RaiseEvent | *New in 2005*. Marks the end of a RaiseEvent block in a Custom Event definition. |
| End RemoveHandler | *New in 2005*. Marks the end of a RemoveHandler block in a Custom Event definition. |

| Statement | Description |
| --- | --- |
| End Select | Marks the end of a SelectCase statement. |
| End Set | Marks the end of a Property Set definition. |
| End Structure | Ends the definition of a Structure (user-defined type). |
| End Sub | Marks the end of a Sub procedure. |
| End SyncLock | Terminates synchronization code in a SyncLock block. |
| End Try | Marks the end of a Try...Catch...Finally statement. |
| End Using | *New in 2005.* Marks the end of a Using statement. |
| End With | Marks the end of a With statement. |
| End While | Marks the end of a While statement. |

- When used alone, the End statement wraps calls to the private *FileSystem.Close-AllFiles* function, as well as to the *System.Environment* object's Exit method, making it a relatively safe statement for terminating an application. However, it does not release resources not automatically handled by the garbage collector, and it does not automatically call *Finalize* destructors.

## Version Differences

- In VB 6, the End statement used by itself was to be avoided, since it terminated program execution abruptly without performing normal cleanup operations. In .NET, End is much safer and is not to be avoided.
- A number of the End statements, such as End Namespace, are new to .NET.
- The End While statement replaces the VB 6 Wend statement to terminate a While loop.
- The 2005 version of VB introduces the End Using, End AddHandler, End RaiseEvent, and End RemoveHandler statements.

## See Also

Exit Statement

# Enum Statement

## Syntax

```
accessModifier Enum [Shadows] name [As type]
memberName [= constantExpression]
memberName [= constantExpression]
    ...
End Enum
```

*accessModifier (optional)*

Specifies the scope and accessibility of the enumeration. One of the following access levels:

| Access level | Description |
| --- | --- |
| Public | The enumeration is publicly accessible anywhere, both inside and outside of the project. |
| Private | The enumeration is accessible only within the defining type. This level cannot be used for namespace-level enumerations. |

| Access level | Description |
| --- | --- |
| Protected | The enumeration is accessible only to the code in the defining type or to one of its derived types. This level cannot be used for namespace-level enumerations. |
| Friend | The enumeration is accessible only within the project that contains the enumeration definition. |
| Protected Friend | Combines the access features of Protected and Friend. This level cannot be used for namespace-level enumerations. |

If omitted, the Public access level is used when declared within types, and Friend is used when declared within namespaces.

Shadows *(optional)*
Indicates that the enumeration shadows an identically named element in a base class.

*name (required)*
The name of the enumerated data type.

*type (optional; integral type)*
The data type of the enumeration. All enumerated members must be integer-based; possible values are Byte, Integer, Long, SByte, Short, UInteger, ULong, and UShort. If omitted, the default type is Integer.

*memberName (required)*
The name of a member of the enumerated data type.

*constantExpression (optional; integral type)*
The value to be assigned to *memberName*.

## Description

The Enum statement defines an enumerated data type. All of the members and related values of the data type are defined by the *memberName* entries.

## Usage at a Glance

- The Enum statement can appear at the namespace level and within types such as classes, but not within members such as procedures.

- *constantExpression* can be either a negative or a positive number. It can also be another member of an enumerated data type or an expression that includes integers, constants, and enumerated data types. The rules that apply to assigning values to constants also apply to enumeration members. See the *Const Statement* entry in this chapter for more information.

- If you assign a floating point value to *constantExpression*, it is automatically rounded and converted to an integer only if Option Strict is Off; otherwise, it generates a compiler error.

- If *constantExpression* is omitted, the value assigned to *memberName* is 0 if it is the first expression in the enumeration. Otherwise, its value is 1 greater than the value of the preceding *memberName*.

- The values assigned to *memberName* entries cannot be modified at runtime.

- Once you define an enumerated type, you can use *name* as you would any other data type. Enumerated data type members appear as value types.

- The compiler does not enforce range restrictions on variables declared using enumerated data types. If an enumeration includes entries for integer values 1 through 5, your code can still assign a value of 10 to the variable, even though 10 does not represent one of the enumerated values.

- Individual values of an enumerated type can be used in your program just like normal constants, except that they must be prefaced with the name of the enumeration.

- If you want to retrieve or display the name of an enumerated member rather than its value, you can use the member's *ToString* method. For example:

```
Public Module GeneralCode
    Public Enum WorkDayTypes
        Weekday = 0
        Weekend = 1
        Holiday = 2
        Floating = 3
        Personal = 4
        Vacation = 5
    End Enum

    Public Sub TestEnum( )
        Dim dayType As WorkDayTypes = WorkDayTypes.Vacation
        MsgBox(dayType.ToString( ))  ' Displays "Vacation"
    End Sub
End Module
```

## Example

```
Public Enum AnnualQuarter
    FirstQuarter = 1
    SecondQuarter = 2
    ThirdQuarter = 3
    FourthQuarter = 4
End Enum
```

## Version Differences

- In VB 6, members of an enumeration can be accessed without having to qualify them with the name of the enumeration to which they belong. In .NET, this behavior is not permitted; the members of an enumeration can only be accessed by referring to the name of their enumeration.

- In VB 6, all enumerated members are of type Long. .NET allows you to define the integral data type of the enumeration's members.

- In VB 6, members of a public enumeration can be hidden from the Object Browser by adding a leading underscore to the member name. For example, in the enumeration:

```
Public Enum Primes
    [_x0] = 0
    x1 = 1
    x2 = 3
End Enum
```

the constant _x0 is hidden in IntelliSense and the Object Browser unless the Object Browser's "Show Hidden Members" option is selected. In .NET, a leading underscore does not hide a member.

## Environ Function

### Class
Microsoft.VisualBasic.Interaction

### Syntax
```
Dim result As String = Environ(expression)
```
*expression  (required; String, or a numeric expression)*
    If *expression* is a string, it must be the name of an environment variable; if *expression* is numeric, it must be the 1-based ordinal number of the environment variable within the environment table.

### Description
The Environ function returns the value assigned to an operating-system environment variable.

### Usage at a Glance
- A zero-length string ("") is returned if *expression* does not exist in the operating system's environment-string table or if there is no environment string in the position specified by *expression*.

- If *expression* is numeric, both the name and the value of the variable are returned. An equals sign (=) is used to separate them. For example, the function call Environ(1) might return the string "TEMP=C:\WINDOWS\TEMP."

- Environment variables are defined through various system startup files and relevant registry entries.

### Example
```
Public Sub LoadEnvironmentStrings()
    ' ----- Store all environment strings internally.
    Dim environmentEntries As New Collection
    Dim oneEntry As String
    Dim counter As Integer
    Dim parts As String()

    ' ----- Scan through each valid environment variable.
    counter = 1
    Do
        ' ----- Get the next entry.
        oneEntry = Environ(counter)
        If (oneEntry = "") Then Exit Do
        counter = counter + 1

        ' ----- Get the name and value parts.
        parts = Split(oneEntry, "=")
```

```
' ----- Store the variable in the collection.
If (UBound(parts) = 0) Then
    environmentEntries.Add("(undefined)", parts(0))
Else
    environmentEntries.Add(parts(1), parts(0))
End If
Loop
MsgBox("Loaded " & environmentEntries.Count & " variable(s).")
End Sub
```

### Version Differences

- In VB 6, the Environ function retrieved environmental variables and their values only from the environment-string table. In .NET, the function retrieves values from both the environment-string table and the system registry.

- In VB 6, the function could be called using either the *envString* named argument (if the argument was the name of an environment variable) or the *number* named argument (if the number represented the ordinal position of the variable in the environment table). VB.NET replaces these with a single named argument, *expression*.

- Visual Basic 2005 adds the new *My.Application.GetEnvironmentVariable* method, which provides related functionality.

## EOF Function

### Class

Microsoft.VisualBasic.FileSystem

### Syntax

```
Dim result As Boolean = EOF(fileNumber)
```

*fileNumber* (required; Integer)
Any valid file number of a file opened with FileOpen

### Description

The EOF function indicates whether the current position within an open file is at the end of the file (True) or not (False). This function applies to files opened for binary, random, or sequential input.

### Usage at a Glance

- *fileNumber* must represent a file that is currently open.

- If a file is opened for binary access, you cannot successfully use EOF with the Input procedure. Instead, use LOF and Loc. If you want to use EOF, you must use FileGet rather than Input. In this case, EOF returns False until the previous FileGet procedure is unable to read an entire record.

- When appending data to files, the current file position will always be the end of the file, since the position marker is placed just after the most recently written data.

## Example

```
Dim oneLine As String
Dim fileID As Integer = FreeFile()

FileOpen(fileID, "c:\data.txt", OpenMode.Input, OpenAccess.Read)
Do While Not EOF(fileID)
    oneLine = LineInput(fileID)
    Console.WriteLine(oneLine)
Loop
FileClose(fileID)
```

## Version Differences

In Visual Basic 2005, the *My.Computer.FileSystem* object provides more robust access to file management features.

## See Also

LOF Function

---

# Erase Statement

## Syntax

```
Erase arrayList
```

*arrayList (required)*
A list of one or more comma-delimited array variable names to clear

## Description

The Erase statement releases an array object and all of its items. This is equivalent to setting the array variable to Nothing.

## Usage at a Glance

- The Erase statement causes all memory allocated to arrays to be released.
- Once you use Erase to clear an array, it must be redimensioned with ReDim before being used again.

## See Also

Dim Statement, ReDim Statement

---

# Erl Property

## Class

Microsoft.VisualBasic.Information

## Syntax

```
Erl
```

## Description

The Erl property indicates the line number on which an error occurred.

---

## Usage at a Glance

- Erl returns the line number only if one has been provided in the source code.
- If the error occurs on a line that does not have a line number, Erl returns 0.
- Erl is not affected by compiler settings. Compiling with the /debug- switch does not prevent Erl from accurately reporting the line number.
- Line numbers—numeric labels followed by a colon—are rarely used in modern VB code.

## Version Differences

In VB 6, line numbers are distinct from labels and do not require any colon or other symbol (other than whitespace) to separate them from source code on the same lines. In .NET VB code, line numbers are labels that must be followed by a colon.

## See Also

Err Object

# Err Object

## Class

Microsoft.VisualBasic.ErrObject

## Creatable

No

## Description

The Err object supplies information about a single runtime error in a Visual Basic program. It also lets you generate errors manually. Because the Err object is a shared object with global scope, you do not need to create an instance of it to use its features.

When an error is generated in your application—whether it is handled or not—Visual Basic populates the properties of the Err object with the details of the error. You can also generate custom errors through this object, to be handled by other parts of your code or by external assemblies that make use of your components.

When your program reaches an Exit statement (such as Exit Function), a Resume statement, or another On Error statement, the Err object is cleared and its properties reinitialized. This can also be done explicitly using the *Err.Clear* method.

The following table lists some of the more useful and interesting members of the Err object. Those marked with an asterisk (*) have separate entries in this chapter.

| Member | Description |
|---|---|
| Clear Method * | Resets all the properties of the Err object. |
| Description Property * | The text description for the active error. |
| Erl Property | Provides the line number of the active error; equivalent to the intrinsic Visual Basic Erl property. See the *Erl Property* entry in this chapter for additional information.. |
| GetException Method * | Returns an instance of a *System.Exception* object related to the active error, an object more commonly used with the new structured exception handling features of VB. |
| HelpContext Property * | A related help context ID within an online help file, related to the active error. |

| Member | Description |
| --- | --- |
| HelpFile Property * | The path to an online help file, related to the active error. |
| LastDLLError Property * | The return value of the most recent DLL function call. |
| Number Property * | The numeric code of the active error (the "error code"). |
| Raise Method * | Forces a specific error to occur immediately. |
| Source Property * | The name of the application, project, or class that generated the active error. |

### Usage at a Glance

- The Err object is not a collection; it contains information about only the most recent error, if one occurred.
- For a full description of error handling in Visual Basic, see Chapter 11.

### See Also

Erl Property, Err.Description Property, Err.HelpContext Property, Err.HelpFile Property, Err.Number Property, Err.Source Property

# Err.Clear Method

### Class

Microsoft.VisualBasic.ErrObject

### Syntax

```
Err.Clear( )
```

### Description

The *Clear* method explicitly resets all the properties of the Err object after an error has been handled.

### Usage at a Glance

- Use the *Clear* method at your convenience when you want to make sure that an error contained in the Err object is truly a new error and not a leftover error from an earlier block of code.
- The Err object is automatically reset when any Resume, On Error, or Exit statement is executed.

### Example

```
On Error Resume Next
Err.Clear( )
Call ErrorProneRoutineWithNoHandler( )
If (Err.Number <> 0) Then
    ' ----- The generated error must have come from the
    '        subroutine call, since the Clear( ) method
    '        set Err.Number to 0.
    MsgBox ("The Error : " & Err.Description & vbCrLf _
        & " was generated in " & Err.Source & ".")
End If
```

Err Object, Err.Raise Method

## Err.Description Property

### Class
Microsoft.VisualBasic.ErrObject

### Syntax
```
Dim result As String = Err.Description
```

### Description
The *Description* property gets or sets a general text description of a runtime error.

### Usage at a Glance
- When a runtime error occurs, the *Description* property is automatically assigned the standard description of the error.
- While you can assign the *Description* property directly, the *Err.Raise* method is a better way to assign the values of a custom error.
- You can override a standard error description by assigning your own description to the *Description* property for both VB errors and application-defined errors.

### See Also
Err Object, Err.Number Property, Err.Source Property

## Err.GetException Method

### Class
Microsoft.VisualBasic.ErrObject

### Syntax
```
Dim result As System.Exception = Err.GetException( )
```

### Description
The *GetException* method returns the *System.Exception* object associated with the current error.

### Usage at a Glance
- If there is no exception, the method returns `Nothing`.
- An *Exception* object is automatically supplied when using structured exception handling (the `Try...Catch...Finally` statement), but the traditional Visual Basic error-handling code relies on the `Err` object. The *GetException* method lets you use elements of both types of error handling.

The Language Reference

### Version Differences

The *GetException* method is new to VB under .NET.

### See Also

Err Object, Exception Class

---

## Err.HelpContext Property

### Class

Microsoft.VisualBasic.ErrObject

### Syntax

```
Dim result As Integer = Err.HelpContext
```

### Description

The *HelpContext* property gets or sets the ID number of the online help page associated with the active error, as found in the help file indicated by the *Err.HelpFile* property.

### Usage at a Glance

- When a runtime error occurs, the *HelpContext* property is automatically assigned for standard Visual Basic and .NET errors.

- While you can assign the *HelpContext* property directly, the *Err.Raise* method is a better way to assign the values of a custom error.

- When errors occur that have both the *HelpFile* and *HelpContext* properties set, the user can press the F1 key from the standard Visual Basic error dialog box to view the related online help. You can also use these values to manually display online help related to an error.

- Help context IDs can be assigned to online help file pages as part of the design process for these files. See the documentation supplied with your online help development tool for information on setting these IDs.

### See Also

Err Object, Err.HelpFile Property

---

## Err.HelpFile Property

### Class

Microsoft.VisualBasic.ErrObject

### Syntax

```
Dim result As String = Err.HelpFile
```

### Description

The *HelpFile* property gets or sets the path to the online help file associated with the active error.

---

## Usage at a Glance

- When a runtime error occurs, the *HelpFile* property is automatically assigned for standard Visual Basic and .NET errors.

- While you can assign the *HelpFile* property directly, the *Err.Raise* method is a better way to assign the values of a custom error.

- When errors occur that have both the *HelpFile* and *HelpContext* properties set, the user can press the F1 key from the standard Visual Basic error dialog box to view the related online help. You can also use these values to manually display online help related to an error.

## See Also

Err Object, Err.HelpContext Property

---

# Err.LastDLLError Property

## Class

Microsoft.VisualBasic.ErrObject

## Syntax

```
Dim result As Integer = Err.LastDLLError
```

## Description

The *LastDLLError* property is a read-only property that contains the return code of the most recently called external DLL function.

## Usage at a Glance

- Only direct calls to a Windows system DLL function from VB code will assign a value to the *LastDLLError* property.

- No error or exception is raised when Visual Basic sets the *LastDllError* property. You must manually examine this field when appropriate.

- The *LastDLLError* property is only used by system DLLs, such as *kernel32.dll*. Therefore, errors that occur within DLLs you may have created will not cause an error code to be assigned to the property.

- Some DLL calls to the Windows API return 0 to denote a successful function call, and others return 0 to denote an unsuccessful call.

## See Also

Err Object

---

# Err.Number Property

## Class

Microsoft.VisualBasic.ErrObject

## Syntax

```
Dim result As Integer = Err.Number
```

## Description

The *Number* property gets or sets the numeric error code for the active error.

## Usage at a Glance

- When a runtime error occurs, the *Number* property is automatically assigned the numeric code of the error.
- While you can assign the *Number* property directly, the *Err.Raise* method is a better way to assign the values of a custom error.
- Many COM and OLE errors include an OLE-specific error flag in the error code. Use the following code snippet to get the true error code after an OLE-related error.

```
Dim trueError As Integer
If ((Err.Number And vbObjectError) = vbObjectError) Then
    trueError = Err.Number - vbObjectError
End If
```

## See Also

Err Object, Err.Description Property, Err.Source Property

---

# Err.Raise Method

## Class

Microsoft.VisualBasic.ErrObject

## Syntax

```
Err.Raise(number[, source[, description[, helpFile, helpContext]]])
```

*number*  (required; Integer)
　　A numeric code for a particular error

*source*  (optional; String)
　　The name of the project, application, or class responsible for generating the error

*description*  (optional; String)
　　A useful description of the error

*helpFile*  (optional; String)
　　The fully qualified path to a Microsoft Windows help file containing online help or reference material about the error

*helpContext*  (optional; Integer)
　　The context ID within *helpFile*

## Description

The *Raise* method generates a runtime error, specifying the details of the error, including optional online help file information.

## Usage at a Glance

- If you supply any of the *number*, *source*, *description*, *helpFile*, or *helpContext* arguments when you call the *Err.Raise* method, they are supplied as values to the *Number*, *Source*, *Description*, *HelpFile*, and *HelpContext* properties of the Err

---

object, respectively. Refer to the entries of the individual properties in this chapter for additional information.

- Visual Basic errors are in the range 0 to 65535. The range 0 to 512 is reserved for system errors; the range 513 to 65535 is available for user-defined errors. When setting the *Number* property to your own error code, add the vbObjectError constant to your error code.

- The *Raise* method does not reinitialize the Err object prior to assigning the values you pass in as arguments. Any Err object property values not explicitly assigned through the *Raise* method are retained.

### Version Differences

Although the Error statement is still included in the .NET version of Visual Basic, it should not be used. Use the *Err.Raise* method instead.

### See Also

Err Object, Err.Clear Method

## Err.Source Property

### Class

Microsoft.VisualBasic.ErrObject

### Syntax

```
Dim result As String = Err.Source
```

### Description

The *Source* property gets or sets the project, application, or class name responsible for generating the active error.

### Usage at a Glance

- When a runtime error occurs, the *Source* property is automatically assigned the name of the originator of the error.

- While you can assign the *Source* property directly, the *Err.Raise* method is a better way to assign the values of a custom error.

- The *Source* property is usually in the format *project.class*.

### See Also

Err Object, Err.Description Property, Err.Number Property

## Error Statement

### Syntax

```
Error errorNumber
```

*errorNumber* (optional; Integer)
    Any valid numeric error code

## Description

The `Error` statement raises an error.

## Usage at a glance

The `Error` statement is included only for backward compatibility; instead, if you're using unstructured error handling, you should use the `Err.Raise` method and the `Err` object. You can also use structured exception handling with the `Try...Catch...Finally` construct.

## See Also

Err.Raise Method, Try...Catch...Finally Statement

---

# ErrorToString Function

## Class

Microsoft.VisualBasic.Conversion

## Syntax

```
Dim result As String = ErrorToString([errorNumber])
```

*errorNumber* (optional; *Integer*)
    A numeric error code

## Description

The `ErrorToString` function returns the error message or description corresponding to a particular error code. If no error code is supplied, the message for the most recent runtime error is returned instead; this is generally the same as the *Err.Description* property.

## Usage at a Glance

- If no error code is supplied, and there have been no runtime errors, a blank string is returned.

- If the supplied error code is not recognized as a valid error, a generic message indicating an application-specific error is returned.

## See Also

Err.Description Property

---

# Event Statement

## Syntax

```
[accessModifier] [Shadows] Event name ([arglist]) _
    [Implements implementsList]
```

or:

```
[accessModifier] [Shadows] Event name As delegateName _
    [Implements implementsList]
```

*accessModifier* *(optional)*

Specifies the scope and accessibility of the event. One of the following access levels:

| Access level | Description |
| --- | --- |
| Public | The event is publicly accessible anywhere, both inside and outside of the project. |
| Private | The event is accessible only within the defining type. |
| Protected | The event is accessible only to the code in the defining type or to one of its derived types. |
| Friend | The event is accessible only within the project that contains the event definition. |
| Protected Friend | Combines the access features of Protected and Friend. |

If omitted, the Public access level is used.

Shadows *(optional)*

Indicates that the event shadows an identically named element in a base class.

*name* *(required)*

The name of the event.

*arglist* *(optional; any)*

A comma-delimited list of parameters to be supplied to the event as arguments when the event is fired.

*arglist* uses the following syntax and parts:

    [ByVal | ByRef] *varname*[( )] [As *argtype*]

ByVal *(optional)*

The argument is passed by value; the local copy of the variable is assigned the value of the argument. ByVal is the default method of passing variables.

ByRef *(optional)*

The argument is passed by reference; the local variable is a reference to the argument being passed. All changes made to the local variable will also be reflected in the calling argument.

*varname* *(required)*

The name of the argument, although event handlers need not retain this name.

*argtype* *(optional; Type)*

The data type of the argument. Any valid .NET data type can be used.

*implementsList* *(optional)*

Comma-separated list of the interface members implemented by this event.

*delegateName* *(optional)*

*New in 2005.* A delegate with an argument signature that is used as the argument signature of this event.

## Description

The Event statement defines an event that the containing type can raise at any time using the RaiseEvent statement. Events can appear within classes, structures, and modules.

## Usage at a Glance

- To handle events, an object variable must be declared with the WithEvents keyword.
- All events for forms and controls in the .NET Framework's Windows Forms package share a common argument signature:

  ```
  Public Event name (ByVal sender As Object, _
      ByVal e As System.EventArgs)
  ```

- VB events do not return a value; however, you can use the ByRef keyword in *arglist* to return data from the event through a parameter.

## Example

The following example implements a simple class with one event, which is triggered through the UpdateRecords procedure.

```
Friend Class EventLadenClass
    Public Event StatusChanged(ByVal message As String)

    Public Sub UpdateRecords()
        RaiseEvent StatusChanged("Records are being updated.")
    End Sub
End Class
```

## Version Differences

- Visual Basic 2005 adds the As *delegateName* clause to the Event statement, a new way of indicating the argument signature for an event.
- Visual Basic 2005 adds a Custom Event statement that includes greater control over the lifetime of an event. See the "Custom Event Statement" entry in this chapter for additional information.

## See Also

Custom Event Statement, RaiseEvent Statement

---

# Exception Class

## Namespace

System

## Creatable

Yes

## Description

The *System.Exception* class and its inherited (child) classes represent runtime exceptions. When errors occur in the context of a Try...Catch...Finally statement, an *Exception* object is made available that describes the exception or runtime error.

The following table lists some of the more useful and interesting members of the *Exception* class.

| Member | Description |
| --- | --- |
| GetBaseException Method | Exceptions may actually be a chain of related exceptions. This method returns the *Exception* object that represents the "root cause" of the exception chain. |
| HelpFile Property | A path to the online help file related to the exception. |
| InnerException Property | Exceptions may actually be a chain of related exceptions. This property returns the *Exception* object that caused the active exception event. |
| Message Property | The text of the error message. |
| Source Property | The name of the application, project, or class that caused the exception. |
| StackTrace Property | A string that lists all methods currently on the stack. This information is presented in a human-readable format. |
| TargetSite Property | The name of the method that threw the exception. |

The *System.Exception* class is the base class for a substantial collection of derived exception classes. Each class represents a specific exception that can occur in the lifetime of an application. Chapter 11 includes a hierarchical listing of the derived exception classes.

### Usage at a Glance

In the Catch clause of a Try...Catch...Finally statement, you can trap the generic *Exception* object, or you can trap a specific exception object descendant if you expect a certain type of error.

### Version Differences

The *Exception* class, along with structured exception handling, is new to Visual Basic under the .NET platform.

### See Also

Err Object

---

## Exit Statement

### Syntax

```
Exit Do
Exit For
Exit Function
Exit Property
Exit Select
Exit Sub
Exit Try
Exit While
```

### Description

The various Exit statements prematurely exit a block of code.

### Usage at a Glance

The Exit statement is used as follows:

| Statement | Description |
|---|---|
| Exit Do | Exits a Do...Loop statement. If the statement appears in nested Do...Loop loops, only the innermost loop is exited. Program execution continues with the first line of code after the exited loop. |
| Exit For | Exits a For...Next or a For Each...Next loop. If the statement appears in nested For loops of any type, only the innermost loop is exited. Program execution continues with the first line of code after the exited loop. |
| Exit Function | Exits the current function and returns control to the calling procedure. |
| Exit Property | Exits the current property (either Get or Set) and returns control to the calling procedure. |
| Exit Select | Exits a Select Case construct. If the statement appears in nested Select Case blocks, only the innermost block is exited. Program execution continues with the first line of code after the exited block. |
| Exit Sub | Exits the current sub procedure and returns control to the calling procedure. |
| Exit Try | Exits a Try...Catch block. Program execution proceeds with the Finally block if it is present or, otherwise, with the statement following the End Try statement. |
| Exit While | Exits a While...End While statement. If the statement appears in nested While...End While loops, only the innermost loop is exited. Program execution continues with the first line of code after the exited loop. |

### See Also

Continue Statement, End Statement

## Exp Function

### Class

System.Math

### Syntax

```
Dim result As Double = Math.Exp(d)
```

d *(required; Double)*
 Any valid numeric expression

### Description

The *Exp* function returns the natural number *e* raised to the power *d*.

### Usage at a Glance

- The maximum value for *d* is 709.782712893.
- *Exp* is the inverse of the *Log* function.
- This is a shared member of the *System.Math* class, so it can be used without an instance.

### Version Differences

In VB 6, Exp is an intrinsic VB function. In the .NET platform, it is a member of the *System.Math* class and not directly part of the VB language.

### See Also

Log Function, Log10 Function, E Field, Pow Function

# File Class

## Namespace

System.IO

## Creatable

No

## Description

The *File* class has a number of members that allow you to retrieve information about files, and to move and delete files. All of the members of the *File* class are shared methods, so they can be called without instantiating any objects.

The following table lists some of the more useful and interesting members of the *File* class. Those marked with an asterisk (*) have separate entries in this chapter.

| Member | Description |
| --- | --- |
| AppendText Method | Opens an existing text file, ready to add additional text to the end of the file |
| Copy Method | Copies an existing file to a new location |
| Create, CreateText Methods | Opens a new file for output |
| Delete Method | Deletes an existing file |
| Exists Method * | Tests a file path to see if it exists |
| GetAttributes Method | Retrieves the attributes for a given file |
| GetCreationTime Method | Retrieves the date and time that a file was originally created |
| GetLastAccessTime Method | Retrieves the date and time that a file was last accessed |
| GetLastWriteTime Method | Retrieves the date and time that a file was last written |
| Move Method | Moves an existing file to a new location |
| Open, OpenRead, OpenText, OpenWrite Methods | Opens an existing file for input or output |
| SetAttributes Method | Modifies the attributes of an existing file |

## Version Differences

Visual Basic 2005 includes a *My.Computer.FileSystem* object that provides file management functionality.

## See Also

Directory Class

---

# File.Exists Method

## Class

System.IO.File

## Syntax

```
Dim result As Boolean = File.Exists(path)
```

*path  (required; String)*
The file path to test for existence

## Description
The *Exists* method indicates whether a file exists (`True`) or not (`False`).

## Usage at a Glance
- *path* can be either an absolute path or a relative path from the current directory.
- *path* can be either a path on the local system, the path of a mapped network drive, or a UNC path.
- *path* cannot contain wildcard characters.

## Version Differences
Visual Basic 2005 includes a *My.Computer.FileSystem.FileExists* method that provides similar functionality.

## See Also
Directory.Exists Method

---

# FileAttr Function

## Class
Microsoft.VisualBasic.FileSystem

## Syntax
```
Dim result As OpenMode = FileAttr(fileNumber)
```
*fileNumber  (required; Integer)*
Any valid file number of a file opened with `FileOpen`

## Description
The `FileAttr` function indicates the file-access mode for a file opened using the `FileOpen` procedure. One of the *Microsoft.VisualBasic.OpenMode* enumeration values from the following table:

| Value | Description |
| --- | --- |
| Input | Sequential record input |
| Output | Sequential record output |
| Random | Random access within a binary or text file |
| Append | Sequential record output, starting from the end of the file |
| Binary | Access to formatted binary data |

## Version Differences
- In VB 6, `FileAttr` included a superfluous *returnType* parameter that is no longer required in .NET.
- In Visual Basic 2005, the *My.Computer.FileSystem* object provides more robust access to file management features.

FileOpen Procedure

## FileClose Procedure

### Class
Microsoft.VisualBasic.FileSystem

### Syntax
```
FileClose([fileNumber[, fileNumber[..., fileNumber]])
```
*fileNumber* *(optional; Integer)*
  One or more file numbers, for files opened with `FileOpen`, which are to be closed

### Description
The `FileClose` procedure closes one or more files previously opened with the `FileOpen` procedure. To close multiple files, include them as multiple comma-delimited arguments.

### Usage at a Glance
- If no *fileNumber* values are included, all open files are closed.
- If the file you are closing was opened for `Output` or `Append`, the remaining data in the I/O buffer is written to the file. The memory buffer is then reclaimed.
- When the `FileClose` procedure is executed, the file number used is freed for further use.

### Version Differences
- `FileClose` is new to VB under .NET. It replaces the `Close` statement in VB 6.
- In Visual Basic 2005, the *My.Computer.FileSystem* object provides more robust access to file management features.

### See Also
FileOpen Procedure, Reset Procedure

## FileCopy Procedure

### Class
Microsoft.VisualBasic.FileSystem

### Syntax
```
FileCopy(source, destination)
```
*source* *(required; String)*
  The path of the file to be copied

*destination* *(required; String)*
  The path and name of the new target file

## Description

The FileCopy procedure copies an existing file to a new location, optionally giving the file a new name.

## Usage at a Glance

- The *source* and *destination* may contain absolute or relative paths, but they must always contain the old and new filenames. *destination* must include the filename; it cannot be the destination directory only.
- You cannot copy a file that is currently open.
- FileCopy raises errors on failure instead of returning an error code.
- If the *destination* file already exists, it will be overwritten without warning.

## Version Differences

Visual Basic 2005 includes a *My.Computer.FileSystem.CopyFile* method that provides similar functionality.

## See Also

Rename Procedure

---

# FileDateTime Function

## Class

Microsoft.VisualBasic.FileSystem

## Syntax

```
Dim result As Date = FileDateTime(pathName)
```

*pathName* (required; String)
The file from which to retrieve the date and time information

## Description

The FileDateTime function retrieves the most recent modification date, which may be the same as the creation date, for an existing file.

## Usage at a Glance

- *pathName* can be either an absolute path or a relative path from the current directory.
- An error occurs if the file does not exist.
- The *File* class, discussed elsewhere in this chapter, includes distinct members that specifically retrieve either the creation date and time or the last modification date and time for a given file.

## Version Differences

Visual Basic 2005 includes a *My.Computer.FileSystem* object that provides file management functionality.

## See Also

File Class, File.Exists Method

---

# FileGet, FileGetObject Procedures

## Class
Microsoft.VisualBasic.FileSystem

## Syntax

```
FileGet(fileNumber, value[, recordNumber[, dataFlag]])
FileGetObject(fileNumber, value[, recordNumber[, dataFlag]])
```

*fileNumber (required; Integer)*
Any valid file number of a file opened with FileOpen.

*value (required; multiple data types)*
Variable in which to place retrieved data. May be one of the following data types: Object, Short, Integer, Single, Double, Decimal, Byte, Boolean, Date, *System.Array*, or String.

*recordNumber (optional; Integer)*
The 1-based location at which reading begins, either a record number (for Random mode) or a byte number (for Binary mode). If omitted, it defaults to 1, which indicates the next available record in the file should be used.

*dataFlag (optional; Boolean)*
New in 2005. This flag is only used when *value* is of type *System.Array* or String. For *System.Array* data, the flag indicates whether the array is dynamic (True) or not (False). For strings, the flag indicates whether the string is fixed in size (True) or not (False). If omitted, this field defaults to False.

## Description
The FileGet and FileGetObject procedures read data from an open file into a variable. For files open in Random mode, the data is read from a record position. For Binary files, the data is read from a byte position in the file. FileGet and FileGetObject are identical in functionality, but using FileGetObject may reduce compile-time data-conversion issues when working with Object data values.

## Usage at a Glance
- The number of bytes read is governed by the data type of *value*. When strings are written using FilePut or FilePutObject, a length descriptor is included in the output, unless *dataFlag* is set to True, which writes out a fixed-length string. When reading back such fixed-length strings, set the *dataFlag* argument to True and preload the string with the right number of characters before calling this function.

- When a record or a number of bytes is read from a file using FileGet, the file pointer automatically moves to the record or byte following the one just read. You can therefore read all data sequentially from a Random or Binary file by omitting *recordNumber*, as this snippet shows:

```
Dim oneChar As Char
Dim fileID As Integer = FreeFile()

FileOpen(fileID, "c:\data.txt", OpenMode.Binary, OpenAccess.Read)
Do While (Loc(fileID) <> LOF(fileID))
    FileGet(fileID, oneChar)
```

```
        ' ----- Do something with oneChar...
        Loop
        FileClose(fileID)
```

- FileGet is most commonly used to read data from files written with the FilePut function.

## Version Differences

- The FileGet and FileGetObject procedures are new with .NET. They are replacements for the Get statement in VB 6, which has a syntax similar to that of FileGet.
- The *dataFlag* argument in both the FileGet and the FileGetObject functions is new with Visual Basic 2005.
- In Visual Basic 2005, the *My.Computer.FileSystem* object provides more robust access to file-management features.

## See Also

FileOpen Procedure, FilePut, FilePutObject Procedures

---

## FileLen Function

### Class

Microsoft.VisualBasic.FileSystem

### Syntax

```
Dim result As Long = FileLen(pathName)
```

*pathName (required; String)*
　　The name and path of the file to examine for its length

### Description

The FileLen function retrieves the length of a disk file in bytes.

### Usage at a Glance

- *pathName* can be either an absolute path or a relative path from the current directory.
- An error occurs if the file does not exist.
- FileLen returns the length of a file as it was last recorded in the directory's record of files. Changes made to the file while actively open may not be reflected in this number. For files currently being modified by your application, use the LOF function instead.

### Version Differences

In Visual Basic 2005, the *My.Computer.FileSystem* object provides more robust access to file management features.

### See Also

LOF Function

# FileOpen Procedure

## Class
Microsoft.VisualBasic.FileSystem

## Syntax
```
FileOpen(fileNumber, fileName, mode[, access[,_
    share[, recordLength]]])
```

*fileNumber* (required; Integer)
Any valid file number of a file opened with FileOpen.

*fileName* (required; String)
The name and path of the file to open.

*mode* (required; OpenMode enumeration)
The file access mode. One of the following *Microsoft.VisualBasic.OpenMode* enumeration values:

| Value | Description |
|-------|-------------|
| Append | Sequential output of data to an existing file, starting from the end of the current file contents |
| Binary | Reading and writing of binary data |
| Input | Sequential input of data from a file |
| Output | Sequential output of data to a file |
| Random | Random access of records within a file, each of a specified length |

*access* (optional; OpenAccess enumeration)
Specifies the allowable file operations. One of the following *Microsoft.VisualBasic. OpenAccess* enumeration values:

| Value | Description |
|-------|-------------|
| Default | Same as ReadWrite |
| Read | Allows reading of data from the file |
| ReadWrite | Allows reading of data from, or writing of data to, the file |
| Write | Allows writing of data to the file |

If omitted, ReadWrite is used.

*share* (optional; OpenShare enumeration)
Indicates how the file will interact with external processes while in use by the current process. One of the following *Microsoft.VisualBasic.OpenShare* enumeration values:

| Value | Description |
|-------|-------------|
| Default | Same as LockReadWrite |
| LockRead | External processes are blocked from reading the file |
| LockReadWrite | External processes are blocked from reading or writing the file |
| LockWrite | External processes are blocked from writing the file |
| Shared | External processed are permitted to read and write the file |

If omitted, `LockReadWrite` is used.

*recordLength (optional; Integer)*
The length of each record (for Random mode), or the size of the input/output buffer (for sequential modes). This value may not exceed 32,767. If omitted, it defaults to -1, which indicates no specific record or buffer size.

## Description

Opens or creates a file for reading or writing

## Usage at a Glance

- There are three modes of file access: sequential, binary, and random. The Input, Output, and Append access modes are sequential access modes. *Sequential access* is for text files consisting of individual Unicode characters and control codes. Most of the file-manipulation functions (`LineInput`, `Print`, `PrintLine`, and so on) apply to files opened for sequential access. *Random access* (used with Random mode) is used with files that have a structure—files that consist of records, each of which is made up of the same set of fields. For instance, a record might contain name, address, and employee ID number fields. *Binary access* (used with Binary mode) is for files where each byte in the file is accessible independently.

- *fileName* may be either an absolute path or a relative path from the current directory. The file may reside on a local drive or a remote drive.

- A new file is created if the specified file does not exist when opened in Append, Binary, Output, or Random mode. The file must exist when opened in Input mode.

- Always use the `FreeFile` function to retrieve an available file number before calling the `FileOpen` function.

- You can open an already opened file using a different file number in Binary, Input, and Random modes. However, you must close a file opened using Append or Output before you can open it with a different file number.

## Example

The following example opens a random access data file, adds two records, and then retrieves some of the written data.

```
Option Strict Off
Module GeneralCode
    Structure Person
        <VBFixedString(10)> Public Name As String
        Public Age As Short
    End Structure

    Public Sub ManageData( )
        ' ----- Simple record management.
        Dim onePerson As New Person
        Dim fileID As Integer = FreeFile( )

        ' ----- Create the file.
        FileOpen(fileID, "c:\data.txt", OpenMode.Random, _
            OpenAccess.ReadWrite, OpenShare.Default, Len(onePerson))
```

```
' ----- Write out two records.
onePerson.Name = "Donna"
onePerson.Age = 20
FilePut(fileID, onePerson, 1)

onePerson.Name = "Steve"
onePerson.Age = 30
FilePut(fileID, onePerson, 2)

' ----- Get the first record back. MsgBox displays:
'          "Donna is 20"
FileGet(fileID, onePerson, 1)
MsgBox(onePerson.Name & " is " & onePerson.Age)

        FileClose(fileID)
    End Sub
End Module
```

Since random access files require a fixed record length, the `<VBFixedString(10)>` attribute has been included in the structure to ensure that the Name field is a constant size.

### Version Differences

- The FileOpen procedure is new to VB under .NET. It is a replacement for the VB 6 Open statement.

- In Visual Basic 2005, the *My.Computer.FileSystem* object provides more robust access to file-management features.

### See Also

FileClose Procedure, FileGet, FileGetObject Procedures, FilePut, FilePutObject Procedures

---

## FilePut, FilePutObject Procedures

### Class

Microsoft.VisualBasic.FileSystem

### Syntax

```
FilePut(fileNumber, value[, recordNumber[, dataFlag]])
FilePutObject(fileNumber, value[, recordNumber[, dataFlag]])
```

*fileNumber (required; Integer)*
    Any valid file number of a file opened with FileOpen.

*value (required; multiple data types)*
    Variable or data to be written to the file. May be one of the following data types: Object, Short, Integer, Single, Double, Decimal, Byte, Boolean, Date, *System.Array*, or String.

*recordNumber (optional; Integer)*
    The 1-based location at which writing begins, either a record number (for Random mode) or a byte number (for Binary mode). If omitted, it defaults to -1, which indicates the next available record in the file should be used.

*dataFlag* *(optional; Boolean)*

New in 2005. This flag is only used when *value* is of type *System.Array* or String. For *System.Array* data, the flag indicates whether the array is dynamic (True) or not (False). For strings, the flag indicates whether the string is fixed in size (True) or not (False). If omitted, this field defaults to False.

## Description

The FilePut and FilePutObject procedures write data to an open file. For files open in Random mode, the data is written as a record. For Binary files, the data is written as a stream of bytes. FilePut and FilePutObject are identical in functionality, but using FilePutObject may reduce compile-time data conversion issues when working with Object data values.

## Usage at a Glance

- If you have opened a file in Random mode, it is important to ensure that the record length specified in the *recordLength* argument of the FileOpen procedure matches the actual length of the data being written. If the length of the data being written is less than that specified by the *recordLength* argument, the space up to the end of the record will be padded. If the actual data length is more than that specified, an error occurs.

- If you open the file in Binary mode, the *recordLength* argument of the FileOpen procedure has no effect. When you use FilePut to write data to the disk, the data is written contiguously, and no padding is placed between records.

- Records written with FilePut and FilePutObject are normally read using FileGet and FileGetObject.

## Example

The following code writes the letters A–Z to a file:

```
Dim oneChar As Char
Dim counter As Integer
Dim fileID As Integer = FreeFile( )

FileOpen(fileID, "c:\data.txt", OpenMode.Binary)
For counter = Asc("A") To Asc("Z")
    oneChar = Chr(counter)
    FilePut(fileID, oneChar)
Next counter
FileClose(fileID)
```

## Version Differences

- The FilePut and FilePutObject procedures are new to .NET. They are almost direct replacements for the VB 6 Put statement.

- The *dataFlag* argument in both the FilePut and the FilePutObject functions is new with Visual Basic 2005.

- In Visual Basic 2005, the *My.Computer.FileSystem* object provides more robust access to file-management features.

**See Also**
FileClose Procedure, FileGet, FileGetObject Procedures, FileOpen Procedure

## FileWidth Procedure

### Class
Microsoft.VisualBasic.FileSystem

### Syntax
```
FileWidth(fileNumber, recordWidth)
```
*fileNumber  (required; Integer)*
Any valid file number of a file opened with FileOpen.

*recordWidth  (required; Integer)*
A number between 0 and 255 that indicates the output line width. Use 0 for unlimited length lines.

### Description
The FileWidth procedure specifies a virtual file width when working with files opened with the FileOpen function. This line width can range from 1 to 255 characters. A setting of zero removes any line width limitations.

### Version Differences
- The FileWidth procedure is new to VB under .NET.
- In Visual Basic 2005, the *My.Computer.FileSystem* object provides more robust access to file management features.

**See Also**
FileOpen Procedure

## Filter Function

### Class
Microsoft.VisualBasic.Strings

### Syntax
```
Dim result As String() = Filter(source, match[, include[, compare]])
```
*source  (required; String array or Object array)*
An array containing values to be filtered.

*match  (required; String)*
The substring of characters to find in the elements of the source array.

*include  (optional; Boolean)*
If True (the default value), Filter includes all matching values in the returned array; if False, Filter includes all non-matching values.

*compare (optional; CompareMethod enumeration)*

Indicates the text comparison method. One of the following *Microsoft.Visual-Basic.CompareMethod* enumeration values:

| Value | Description |
| --- | --- |
| Binary | Performs a binary (case-sensitive) comparison |
| Text | Performs a text (case-insensitive) comparison |

If omitted, Binary is used.

## Description

The Filter function produces an array of matching (or non-matching) values from an array of source values.

## Usage at a Glance

- If no matches are found, Filter returns an empty array.
- Although the Filter function is primarily a string function, you can also filter numeric values. To do this, specify a *source* of type Object and populate this array with numeric values. Then assign the string representation of the numeric value you wish to filter onto the *match* parameter. The returned array contains string representations of the filtered numbers. For example:

```
Dim sourceArray( ) As Object = _
    {123, 222, 444, 139, 1, 12, 98, 908, 845, 22, 3, 9, 11}

Dim targetArray( ) As String = Filter(sourceArray, "1")
```

returns an array containing five elements: 123, 139, 1, 12, and 11.

## See Also

Partition Function

---

# Fix Function

## Class

Microsoft.VisualBasic.Conversion

## Syntax

```
Dim result As type = Fix(number)
```

*number (required; any numeric expression)*

The number to be processed. Uses one of the following data types: Double, Single, Decimal, Integer, Long, Short, or Object. If Object is used, the value must evaluate to a number. The return data type always matches the data type of *number*.

## Description

The Fix function returns the integer portion of a number, with any fractional part truncated.

## Usage at a Glance

- Fix truncates numbers; it does not round. For example, Fix(100.9) returns 100.

- Even for negative source values, Fix simply truncates the fractional portion. For example, Fix(-10.9) returns -10.

- A source of Nothing returns Nothing.

- The Int and Fix functions work identically with positive numbers. However, for negative numbers, Fix returns the first negative integer *greater than* the source value, while Int returns the first negative integer *less than* that value. For example, Fix(-10.1) returns -10, while Int(-10.1) returns -11.

## See Also

Int Function, Round Function

# Flags Attribute

## Class

System.Flags

## Applies To

Enum

## Constructor

New( )

## Properties

None defined

## Description

The <Flags> attribute indicates that an enumerated type should be treated as a set of flags that can be added together, rather than as a set of mutually exclusive values.

# Floor Function

## Class

System.Math

## Syntax

Math.Floor(*d*)

*d* (required; Double)
Any valid number

## Description

The *Floor* function returns the largest integer less than or equal to the argument *d*.

### Example
```
MsgBox(Math.Floor(12.9))      ' Displays 12
MsgBox(Math.Floor(-12.1))     ' Displays -13
```

### Usage at a Glance
This is a shared member of the *System.Math* class, so it can be used without an instance.

### Version Differences
The *Floor* function did not exist in VB 6.

### See Also
Ceiling Function

---

# FontDialog Class

### Namespace
System.Windows.Forms

### Creatable
Yes

### Description
The *FontDialog* class represents a common dialog box for selecting or saving a font. The *FontDialog* class has properties that let you configure, display, and retrieve the results from this dialog box, from which the user selects a font.

The following list discusses the more interesting members of the *FontDialog* class.

*Color Property*
> Sets or retrieves the color of the font, an instance of *System.Drawing.Color*. Colors can be set by their RBG value or by common names assigned to the more typical colors (like "Red").

*Font Property*
> Sets or retrieves the font chosen by the user, an instance of *System.Drawing.Font*. The *Font* class has a number of members, including:

> *Bold, Italic, Strikeout, and Underline Properties*
>> Boolean properties for basic attributes of the font.

> *FontFamily Property*
>> A *FontFamily* object associated with the font. Use the *Name* property to get the name of the font family.

> *Name Property*
>> Returns the face name of the font as a String.

> *SizeInPoints Property*
>> Returns the size of the font, in points, as a Single.

> *Style Property*
>> Returns a *FontStyle* constant that contains information about the style of the font. The *FontStyle* constants are Bold, Italic, Regular, Strikeout, and Underline, and they can be combined using a bitwise Or operation.

---

*MaxSize, MinSize Properties*
Limits the font size that the user can specify for the font.

*ShowApply Property*
Indicates whether the dialog box has an Apply button. The default is False.

*ShowColor Property*
Indicates whether the dialog box shows the font-color-choice controls. (The default is False.)

*ShowEffects Property*
Indicates whether the dialog box shows the strikethrough and underline options. (The default is True.)

## Example

The following code displays the Font dialog box and then displays the user's choice of font family.

```
Public Sub FontTest( )
    Dim selectFont As New FontDialog
    selectFont.ShowDialog( )
    MsgBox(selectFont.Font.FontFamily.Name)
End Sub
```

## Version Differences

The public interfaces used for this *FontDialog* class and the related VB 6 Common-Dialog control are quite different.

## See Also

ColorDialog Class

# For...Next Statement

## Syntax

```
For counter [As datatype] = start To end [Step step]
    [statements]
    [Exit For]
    [statements]
    [Continue For]
[statements]
Next [counter]
```

*counter  (required in For clause; numeric variable)*
A variable that serves as the loop counter.

*datatype  (optional)*
New in 2003. The data type of *counter* when including the declaration in the For clause.

*start  (required; numeric expression)*
The starting value of *counter* for the first iteration of the loop.

*end  (required; numeric expression)*
The maximum limit of *counter* (or minimum limit, if *step* is negative) during its iterations.

*step* *(optional; numeric expression)*
  The amount by which *counter* is to be incremented or decremented on each iteration of the loop. If omitted, the default value is 1.

*statements* *(optional)*
  Lines of program code to execute within the loop.

## Description

The For...Next statement defines a loop that executes a given number of times, as determined by a loop counter.

To use the For...Next loop, you must assign a numeric value to a counter variable. This counter is either incremented or decremented automatically with each iteration of the loop. In the For statement, you specify the value that is to be assigned to the counter initially and the maximum value the counter will reach for the block of code to be executed. The Next statement marks the end of the loop. The Exit For statement can be used at any time to exit the loop immediately.

*New in 2005.* The Continue For statement can be used at any time to immediately jump back to the top of the loop and attempt to process the next iteration. The *counter* variable is adjusted by *step* and is reevaluated immediately upon reaching the top of the loop.

## Usage at a Glance

- Normally, *counter* is an integral data type. However, it can be any data type that supports the following operators: less than or equal to (<=), greater than or equal to (>=), addition (+), and subtraction (-). Beginning with Visual Basic 2005, this can include any class or structure, as long as these operators have been overloaded to support the specified class. *counter* cannot be a Boolean variable or an array element.

- The values for *start*, *end*, and *step* can be positive, negative, or zero. They are evaluated only the first time through the loop. If you change their values in the loop's code, it has no impact on the number of iterations.

- If *end* is less than *start* and no Step keyword is used, or the step counter is positive, the For...Next loop is ignored and execution commences with the first line of code immediately following the Next statement.

- If *start* and *end* are equal and *step* is 1, the loop will execute once.

- The For...Next loop can contain any number of Exit For statements. When the Exit For statement is executed, program execution continues with the first line of code immediately following the Next statement.

- For...Next loops can be nested, as shown here:

```
For eachDay = 1 to 365
    For eachHour = 0 to 23
        For eachMinute = 0 to 59
        ...code here...
        Next eachMinute
    Next eachHour
Next eachDay
```

- You should avoid changing the value of *counter* in the code within the loop, as this can lead to unexpected results.

- Once the loop has finished executing, the value of *counter* is officially undefined. That is, you should not make any assumptions about its value outside of the For... Next loop, and you should not use it unless you first reinitialize it.

## Example

The following code adds up all of the values in an array.

```
Public Function SumArray(ByVal sourceArray() As Integer) As Integer
    Dim counter As Integer
    Dim newTotal As Integer = 0

    For counter = LBound(sourceArray) To UBound(sourceArray)
        newTotal += sourceArray(counter)
    Next counter
    Return counter
End Function
```

The following code block does the same thing, but in reverse order.

```
For counter = UBound(sourceArray) To LBound(sourceArray) Step -1
    newTotal += sourceArray(counter)
Next counter
```

## Version Differences

- Visual Basic .NET 2003 adds the As clause to the For statement for inline counter declaration.
- Visual Basic 2005 includes the Continue For statement.

## See Also

For Each...Next Statement

---

# For Each...Next Statement

## Syntax

```
For Each element [As datatype] In group
    [statements]
    [Exit For]
    [statements]
    [Continue For]
    [statements]
Next [element]
```

*element* (required; any)
: An object variable to which the current element from the group is assigned. Its data type must be compatible with the data elements in *group*.

*datatype* (optional)
: *New in 2003*. The data type of *element* when including the declaration in the For Each clause.

*group* (required; IEnumerable interface)
: A collection or array of elements to iterate. The object must implement the *System.Collections.IEnumerable* interface.

*statements (optional)*
　　Lines of program code to execute within the loop.

## Description

Defines a loop that iterates through all items in a collection or array. *element* and *group* must be of compatible data types. The code within the loop is executed once for each element in *group*, with *element* being assigned to each successive element within *group*, one assignment per pass. The Exit For statement can be used at any time to exit the loop immediately.

*New in 2005.* The Continue For statement can be used at any time to immediately jump back to the top of the loop and attempt to process the next iteration. The *element* variable is assigned the next element in *group* upon reaching the top of the loop.

## Usage at a Glance

- The For Each...Next code block is executed only if *group* contains at least one element. If *group* is an empty collection or an array that has not yet been initialized, an error occurs.

- All *statements* are executed for each *element* in *group* in turn, until either there are no more elements in *group* or the loop is exited prematurely using the Exit For statement. Program execution then continues with the line of code following Next.

- For Each...Next loops can be nested, but each *element* must be unique, as in:

```
For Each groupScan In bigCollectionOfItems
    For Each subScan In groupScan.DetailItems
        ...processing code goes here...
    Next subScan
Next groupScan
```

## Version Differences

- In VB 6, *element* had to be a variable of type Variant. .NET removes this restriction; *element* can be a strongly typed data type or the more generic *System.Object* type.

- Visual Basic .NET 2003 adds the As clause to the For Each statement for inline counter declaration.

- Visual Basic 2005 includes the Continue For statement.

## See Also

For...Next Statement

---

# Format Function

## Class

Microsoft.VisualBasic.Strings

## Syntax

```
Dim result As String = Format(expression[, style])
```

*expression* (required; Object)
The date, time, or numeric content to be formatted.

*style* (optional; String)
A named or user-defined format expression, as described below. If omitted, the default value is "General Number" for numbers or "General Date" for dates and times.

## Description

The Format function formats a date, time, or numeric expression according to a predefined format, or through a user-defined set of format rules, and returns the resulting string. The Format function examines the source *expression* to determine if it is a date/time or a number and then applies this source against the supplied *style*.

The following table shows the available predefined numeric formats:

| Numeric format text | Description |
| --- | --- |
| General Number or G or g | Displays a basic number with no digits grouping in the mantissa. |
| Currency or C or c | Displays a number as currency, using settings defined by the in-effect locale. |
| Fixed or F or f | Displays a number with two digits to the right of the decimal point. |
| Standard or N or n | Same as Fixed but includes digits grouping in the mantissa. |
| Percent | Displays a number as a percent, with a trailing percent sign (%) and two digits to the right of the decimal point. The source value is first multiplied by 100. |
| E or e | Displays a number in scientific notation. |
| D or d | Displays a number using the decimal (base-10) system. |
| X or x | Displays a number using the hexadecimal (base-16) system. |
| Yes/No | Displays "No" for zero and "Yes" for all other values. |
| True/False | Displays "False" for zero and "True" for all other values. |
| On/Off | Displays "Off" for zero and "On" for all other values. |

The following table shows the available predefined date and time formats. Those formats identified as "locale-specific" format the date or time based on the in-effect locale settings.

| Date/time format text | Description |
| --- | --- |
| General Date or G | Displays a locale-specific date and time; typically equivalent to Short Date and Long Time used together |
| Long Date or Medium Date or D | Locale-specific long date format |
| Short Date or d | Locale-specific short date format |
| Long Time or Medium Time or T | Locale-specific long time format |
| Short Time or t | Locale-specific short time format |
| f | Locale-specific long date and short time format |
| F | Locale-specific long date and long time format |
| g | Locale-specific short date and short time format |
| M or m | Full month name plus the day of the month, as in "August 23" |
| R or r | Date and time, adjusted to Greenwich Mean Time, and in the sample format "Tue, 23 Aug 2005 17:33:11 GMT" |

| Date/time format text | Description |
| --- | --- |
| s | Formats the date and time in a format that allows for easy sorting: "2005-08-23T17:33:11" |
| u | Adjusts the date and time to Greenwich Mean Time and then formats the result for easy sorting: "2005-08-23 17:33:11Z" |
| U | Adjusts the date and time to Greenwich Mean Time, and then formats the result using the locale-specific long date and long time format |
| Y or y | Full month name, a comma, and then the year, as in "August, 2005" |

User-defined *style* formats allow for more flexibility in the output. The user-defined numeric format can include up to four semicolon delimited sections, although only one is required. Each section applies to a different type of number.

- Section 1 applies to all positive numbers and any numbers not formatted by one of the other three sections.
- Section 2 applies to negative numbers.
- Section 3 applies to a value of zero.
- Section 4 applies to a value of Nothing.

If you leave a section blank, it will use the format in the first section, the one used for positive numbers. For example, the format string:

```
"#.00;;#,##"
```

does not define a format for negative numbers or Nothing values. These will use the format for positive values.

Each user-defined numeric section uses the following format codes:

| Numeric format code | Description |
| --- | --- |
| 0 | Displays a digit, or "0" if no digit is defined in that position in the source. Used to add leading or trailing zeros. |
| # | Displays a digit, or nothing if no digit is defined in that position in the source. |
| . | Inserts the locale-specific decimal separator. |
| % | Inserts the percent sign and treats the number as a percent, multiplying it by 100 before formatting. |
| , | Inserts the locale-specific thousands separator or digits grouping symbol. This only needs to be included once per format section. For example, a format of "#,##0" formats one million as "1,000,000." |
| : | Inserts the locale-specific time separator. |
| / | Inserts the locale-specific date separator. |
| E+, e+, E-, or e- | Formats the number in scientific notation. The "-" versions include a negative sign before negative exponents; the "+" versions also include a plus sign before positive exponents. |
| -, +, $, (, ) | Inserts any of these literal characters in the output. Any other character you wish to insert must be preceded (or escaped) by a backslash (\). Use \\ to insert a backslash. |
| "any text" | Any text between quotation marks appears as is. |

User-defined dates only include a single section. The user-defined date and time formats use the following format codes:

| Date/time format code | Description |
|---|---|
| : | Inserts the locale-specific time separator. |
| / | Inserts the locale-specific date separator. |
| % | If your user-defined date format would otherwise include only a single letter, prepend that letter with the percent sign so that the format is not confused with the predefined date formats that use the same single letters. |
| d | Day of the month with no leading zero. |
| dd | Two-digit day of the month, with a leading zero if needed. |
| ddd | Abbreviated locale-specific day of the week, as in "Tue." |
| dddd | Full locale-specific day of the week, as in "Tuesday." |
| M | Month of the year with no leading zero. |
| MM | Two-digit month of the year, with a leading zero if needed. |
| MMM | Abbreviated locale-specific month name, as in "Aug." |
| MMMM | Full locale-specific month name, as in "August." |
| gg | The period or era string, as in "A.D." |
| h | Hour of the day with no leading zero, using a 12-hour clock. |
| hh | Two-digit hour of the day, with a leading zero if needed, using a 12-hour clock. |
| H | Hour of the day with no leading zero, using a 24-hour clock. |
| HH | Two-digit hour of the day, with a leading zero if needed, using a 24-hour clock. |
| m | Minutes of the time with no leading zero. |
| mm | Two-digit minutes of the time, with a leading zero if needed. |
| s | Seconds of the time with no leading zero. |
| ss | Two-digit seconds of the time, with a leading zero if needed. |
| f | Fractions of a second. Use multiple "f" characters for more digits. For example, "s.fff" displays thousandths of a second. Uppercase or lowercase "f" will work. |
| t | Displays "A" for prenoon times or "P" for noon and beyond. |
| tt | Displays "AM" for prenoon times or "PM" for noon and beyond. |
| y | Displays the last two digits of the year, removing any leading zero if needed. |
| yy | Displays the last two digits of the year, adding a leading zero if needed. |
| yyy | Same as "yyyy." |
| yyyy | Displays the full year, up to four digits. |
| z | Displays the local offset from Greenwich Mean Time with no leading zeros. This value may include a negative sign. |
| zz | Displays the local offset from Greenwich Mean Time as a two-digit number, with a leading zero if needed. This value may include a negative sign. |
| zzz | Displays the local offset from Greenwich Mean Time in time format, as in "-7:00." This value may include a negative sign. |

## Usage at a Glance

Unlike the Str function, the Format function removes the leading space normally reserved for the sign from positive numbers.

## Version Differences

The predefined and user-defined format codes available to the Format function in VB 6 differ significantly from those available in .NET. This is especially true for the codes used for months and minutes.

## See Also

FormatCurrency, FormatNumber, FormatPercent Functions, FormatDateTime Function

---

# FormatCurrency, FormatNumber, FormatPercent Functions

## Class

Microsoft.VisualBasic.Strings

## Syntax

```
Dim result As String = FormatCurrency(expression[, _
    numDigitsAfterDecimal[, includeLeadingDigit[, _
    useParensForNegativeNumbers[, groupDigits]]]])

Dim result As String = FormatNumber(expression[, _
    numDigitsAfterDecimal[, includeLeadingDigit[, _
    useParensForNegativeNumbers[, groupDigits]]]])

Dim result As String = FormatPercent(expression[, _
    numDigitsAfterDecimal[, includeLeadingDigit[, _
    useParensForNegativeNumbers[, groupDigits]]]])
```

Several parameters use the *Microsoft.VisualBasic.TriState* enumeration, which has the following members:

| Value | Description |
|---|---|
| True | Use the "true" or enabled setting. |
| False | Use the "false" or disabled setting. |
| UseDefault | Use the default regional setting for this parameter. |

*expression (required; Object)*
> The number or numeric expression to be formatted.

*numDigitsAfterDecimal (optional; Integer)*
> The number of digits the formatted string should contain after the decimal point. If omitted, 1 is used, which indicates that the default regional settings should be used.

*includeLeadingDigit (optional; TriState enumeration)*
> Indicates whether the formatted string is to have a 0 before floating point numbers between 1 and -1. If omitted, UseDefault is used.

*useParensForNegativeNumbers (optional; TriState enumeration)*
> Indicates whether parentheses should be placed around negative numbers. If omitted, UseDefault is used.

---

*groupDigits (optional; TriState enumeration)*
Determines whether digits in the returned string should be grouped using the delimiter specified in the computer's regional settings. For example, in the United States region, the value 1000000 is returned as "1,000,000" if *groupDigits* is True. If omitted, UseDefault is used.

## Description

The FormatCurrency, FormatNumber, and FormatPercent functions are used to format decimal numbers using common formats. FormatCurrency returns the number formatted as currency based on the regional settings; FormatNumber returns the number in a standard decimal format; and FormatPercent returns the number formatted as a percentage (first multiplying the number by 100).

## Usage at a Glance

- In the FormatCurrency function, the position of the currency symbol in relation to the currency value is defined by the computer's regional settings.
- These three functions first appeared in VBScript Version 2 as "light" alternatives to the Format function, which had originally been left out of VBScript due to its size.

## See Also

Format Function, FormatDateTime Function

---

# FormatDateTime Function

## Class

Microsoft.VisualBasic.Strings

## Syntax

```
Dim result As String = FormatDateTime(expression[, dateFormat])
```

*expression (required; Date)*
The date to be formatted.

*dateFormat (optional; DateFormat enumeration)*
Defines the format of the date to return. One of the following *Microsoft.Visual-Basic.DateFormat* enumeration values.

| Value | Description |
|-------|-------------|
| GeneralDate | Displays the date and time using the "Short Date" and "Long Time" formats together. Either the date or time may be omitted if unset. |
| LongDate | Displays the date using the regionally defined "Long Date" format. |
| ShortDate | Displays the date using the regionally defined "Short Date" format. |
| LongTime | Displays the time using the regionally defined "Long Time" format. |
| ShortTime | Displays the time using a 24-hour format of "hh:mm." |

If omitted, GeneralDate is used.

## Description

The *FormatDateTime* function formats a date or time expression based on the computer's regional settings.

## Usage at a Glance

The following two statements are identical:

```
niceDate = FormatDateTime(sourceDate, DateFormat.LongDate)
niceDate = Format(sourceDate, "Long Date")
```

## See Also

Format Function, FormatCurrency, FormatNumber, FormatPercent Functions

---

# FreeFile Function

## Class

Microsoft.VisualBasic.FileSystem

## Syntax

```
Dim result As Integer = FreeFile()
```

## Description

The `FreeFile` function returns the next available file number for use with the `FileOpen` procedure.

## Usage at a Glance

- It is good programming practice to always use `FreeFile` to obtain a file number for use with the `FileOpen` procedure, even for a given file number previously used with another file that is now closed.

- The number returned by `FreeFile` always represents the next available unopened file number. After retrieving this file number, you should immediately call the `FileOpen` procedure, particularly if your file access code resides in a multi-threaded application or component. Failure to do so may cause the same handle to be assigned to two different variables, so that one of the calls to `FileOpen` fails.

## Example

This example shows that file numbers should be used immediately. The following code is correct.

```
Dim fileNum1 As Integer
Dim fileNum2 As Integer

fileNum1 = FreeFile()
FileOpen(fileNum1, "c:\file1.txt", OpenMode.Input)

fileNum2 = FreeFile()
FileOpen(fileNum2, "c:\file2.txt", OpenMode.Input)
```

The following code, however, is incorrect, since `fileNum1` and `fileNum2` will likely be assigned the same file number.

```
Dim fileNum1 As Integer
Dim fileNum2 As Integer

fileNum1 = FreeFile( )
fileNum2 = FreeFile( )

FileOpen(fileNum1, "c:\file1.txt", OpenMode.Input)
' ----- The next line will generate an error.
FileOpen(fileNum2, "c:\file2.txt", OpenMode.Input)
```

## Version Differences

In Visual Basic 2005, the *My.Computer.FileSystem* object provides more robust access to file management features.

## See Also

FileOpen Procedure

---

# Friend Keyword

## Description

The Friend keyword is used to set the access level for various types and type members. By including this keyword, the associated type or member can be accessed by the entire assembly or application but not by other assemblies that may interact with the type or member.

When combined with the Protected keyword, the related element takes on all aspects of both the Protected and Friend keywords.

The Friend keyword can be used with the following statements:

Class Statement
Const Statement (but not for local constants)
Declare Statement
Delegate Statement
Dim Statement (but not for local variables)
Enum Statement
Event Statement
Function Statement
Interface Statement
Module Statement
Property Statement
Structure Statement
Sub Statement

By default, classes, modules, structures, and interfaces have Friend access.

## See Also

For the statements listed above, see the related entries elsewhere in this chapter for usage information. For information on using the Friend keyword as a statement, see the entry for the *Dim Statement*.

Private Keyword, Protected Keyword, Public Keyword

# Function Statement

## Syntax

```
[accessModifier] [procModifier] [Shared] [Shadows] _
    Function name [(Of typeParamList)] ([arglist]) _
    [Implements implementsList | Handles eventList] [As type]
    [statements]
    [name = expression]
    [Exit Function | Return expression]
    [statements]
End Function
```

accessModifier *(optional)*

Specifies the scope and accessibility of the function. One of the following access levels:

| Access level | Description |
| --- | --- |
| Public | The function is publicly accessible anywhere, both inside and outside of the project. |
| Private | The function is accessible only within the defining type. |
| Protected | The function is accessible only to the code in the defining type or to one of its derived types. |
| Friend | The function is accessible only within the project that contains the function definition. |
| Protected Friend | Combines the access features of Protected and Friend. |

If omitted, the Public access level is used.

procModifier *(optional)*

One of the keywords shown in the following table:

| Keyword | Description |
| --- | --- |
| Overloads | Indicates that more than one declaration of this function exists, each with a different argument signature |
| Overrides | For derived classes, indicates that the function overrides a function with the same name and argument signature in the base class |
| Overridable | Indicates that the function can be overridden in a derived class |
| NotOverridable | Indicates that the function cannot be overridden in a derived class |
| MustOverride | Indicates that the function must be overridden in a derived class |

Shared *(optional)*

Indicates that the function is shared and not an instance function. Shared functions may be called without a particular instance of the type in which they appear. Shared functions are also known as *static functions*.

Shadows *(optional)*

Indicates that the function shadows an identically named element in a base class.

name *(required)*

The name of the function.

*typeParamName  (optional; any)*
> Adds type parameter placeholders that will later enforce strong typing when the function is used. The Of clause implements generics, which are fully described in Chapter 10. If generics will not be used, this clause can be excluded.

*arglist  (optional; any)*
> A comma-delimited list of parameters to be supplied to the function as arguments from the calling routine.
>
> *arglist* uses the following syntax and parts:
> > [Optional] [ByVal | ByRef] [ParamArray] *varname*[( )] _
> >     [As *argtype*] [= *defaultValue*]

> Optional *(optional)*
> > Flags an argument as optional; optional arguments need not be supplied by the calling routine. All arguments following an optional argument must also be optional. A ParamArray argument cannot be optional.

> ByVal *(optional)*
> > The argument is passed by value; the local copy of the variable is assigned the value of the argument. ByVal is the default method of passing variables.

> ByRef *(optional)*
> > The argument is passed by reference; the local variable is a reference to the argument being passed. All changes made to the local variable will also be reflected in the calling argument.

> ParamArray *(optional)*
> > The argument is an optional array containing an arbitrary number of elements. It can only be used as the last element of the argument list, and it cannot be modified by either the ByRef or Optional keywords. If Option Strict is on, the array type must also be specified.

> *varname  (required)*
> > The name of the argument as used in the local function.

> *argtype  (optional; Type)*
> > The data type of the argument. Any valid .NET data type can be used.

> *defaultValue  (optional; any)*
> > For optional arguments, indicates the default value to be supplied when the calling routine does not supply the value. When the Optional keyword is used, this default value is required.

*implementsList  (optional)*
> Comma-separated list of the interface members implemented by this function.

*eventList  (optional)*
> Comma-separated list of the events handled by this function. Each event is in the form *eventVariable.eventMember*, where *eventVariable* is a variable declared with the WithEvents keyword, and *eventMember* is an event member of that variable.

*type  (optional; Type)*
> The return data type of the function.

*statements  (optional)*
> Program code to be executed within the function.

*expression  (optional)*
> The value to return from the function to the calling procedure.

## Description

The `Function` statement defines a function, including all arguments and the return value. Functions can appear within classes, structures, and modules. To call a function, specify its name, followed by any arguments in parentheses.

```
result = SomeFunction(12, "second argument")
```

The return value can be assigned to a variable, immediately used as a parameter for another function, or ignored by using the `Call` keyword.

```
Call SomeFunction(12, "second argument")
```

## Usage at a Glance

- Functions cannot be nested; that is, you cannot define one function inside another function. (This restriction applies to all procedures.)

- `Overloads` and `Shadows` cannot be used in the same declaration.

- Any number of `Exit Function` or `Return` statements can be placed within the function. When these statements are encountered, execution continues with the line of code immediately following the call to the function. If a value has not been assigned to the function when the `Exit Function` statement executes, the function will return the default initialization value of the data type specified for the return value of the function. If the data type of the function is an object reference, the exited function returns `Nothing`.

- The return value of a function is passed back to the calling procedure by either assigning a value to the function name or by using the `Return` statement. The `Return` statement also exits the function; assigning the return value to the function name does not exit the function.

- To return arrays of any type from a procedure, follow *type* with parentheses:

  ```
  Public Function BuildIntArray( ) As Integer( )
  ```

- The names of a function's parameters become the function's named arguments.

## Version Differences

- There are several syntax and functionality differences in the declaration of a function between VB 6 and the .NET version of VB.

- In VB 6, arguments to functions are passed by reference if no passing method is specified. In .NET, the default is to pass by value.

- If a parameter array is used in VB 6, it is an array of variants. In .NET, all parameter arrays are either of type `Object` or of some other specified type.

- In VB 6, optional arguments do not require that you specify a default value. Instead, the `IsMissing` function is used to determine whether the optional argument is supplied. In .NET, you must assign a default value to an optional argument.

- Visual Basic 2005 adds support for generics to functions, as discussed in Chapter 10.

## See Also

Sub Statement

# FV Function

## Class
Microsoft.VisualBasic.Financial

## Syntax
```
Dim result As Double = FV(rate, nPer, pmt[, pv [, due]])
```
*rate*  *(required; Double)*
The interest rate per period.

*nPer*  *(required; Double)*
The number of payment periods in the annuity.

*pmt*  *(required; Double)*
The payment made in each period.

*pv*  *(optional; Double)*
The present value of the loan or annuity. Defaults to 0.

*due*  *(optional; DueDate enumeration)*
A value indicating when payments are due, from the *Microsoft.VisualBasic. DueDate* enumeration. *DueDate.EndOfPeriod* indicates that payments are due at the end of the payment period; *DueDate.BegOfPeriod* indicates that payments are due at the beginning of the period. If omitted, the default value is *DueDate. EndOfPeriod*.

## Description
The FV function calculates the future value of an annuity (either an investment or loan) based on a regular number of payments of a fixed value and a static interest rate over the period of the annuity.

## Usage at a Glance
- The time units used for the number of payment periods, the rate of interest, and the payment amount must be the same. For instance, if you state the payment period in months, you must also express the interest rate as a monthly rate and indicate the amount paid per month.
- The rate is supplied as a decimal percent. For example, 10% is stated as 0.1. If you are calculating using monthly periods, you must also divide the annual rate by 12. For example, a 10% per annum rate equates to .00833 per period.
- The *pv* argument is most commonly used as the initial value of a loan.
- Payments made against a loan or added to the value of savings are expressed as negative numbers.

## See Also
IPmt Function, NPer Function, NPV Function, PPmt Function, PV Function, Rate Function

# GetAllSettings Function

## Class
Microsoft.VisualBasic.Interaction

## Syntax
```
Dim result(,) As String = GetAllSettings(appname, section)
```
*appname* *(required; String)*
    The name of the application branch to be retrieved.

*section* *(required; String)*
    The name of the application's subkey that is to be retrieved. This can be a single key or a relative registry path, with path components separated by backslashes.

## Description
The GetAllSettings function returns the registry value entry names and their corresponding values for the specified application and section, all as a two-dimensional array. For each entry in the first dimension, entry (*x*, 0) contains the name, and entry (*x*, 1) contains its value.

## Usage at a Glance
- GetAllSettings works exclusively with the subkeys of HKEY_CURRENT_USER\Software\VB and VBA ProgramSettings.

- *section* is a relative path (similar to that used to describe the directories on a hard drive) used to navigate from the application key to the subkey to be accessed. For example, to access the HKEY_CURRENT_USER\Software\VB and VBA ProgramSettings\RegTester\BranchOne\BranchTwo section, you would use:

    ```
    GetAllSettings("RegTester", "BranchOne\BranchTwo")
    ```

- A call to GetAllSettings will return only the value entry names and data belonging to the final registry key specified by the *section* argument. If that key itself has one or more subkeys, the data for those subkeys will not be retrieved by the function.

- If either *appname* or *section* do not exist, GetAllSettings returns Nothing.

- Although the registry supports multiple data types, the GetAllSettings function only supports string values.

- GetAllSettings cannot be used to access the default value (i.e., the unnamed value entry) belonging to any section. If you're using only the VB registry functions, though, this isn't a serious limitation, since SaveSetting does not allow you to create a default value.

- Data saved with SaveSetting is placed in the registry on a per-user basis.

- The .NET Framework includes registry-related features that provide more flexibility than the VB "Settings" functions. These features are found in the *Registry* and *RegistryKey* classes of the *Microsoft.Win32* namespace.

## Version Differences
Visual Basic 2005 includes several new features that let you manage the settings used by an application. Although they are not compatible with the older VB "Settings" func-

tions, they provide a richer set of features. These features are located in the *My.Settings* object. The *My.Computer.Registry* object also provides access to convenient registry-related features.

### See Also

DeleteSetting Procedure, GetSetting Function, SaveSetting Procedure

## GetAttr Function

### Class

Microsoft.VisualBasic.FileSystem

### Syntax

```
Dim result As FileAttribute = GetAttr(pathname)
```

*pathname (required; String)*
   The file or directory from which to obtain the attribute details

### Description

The GetAttr function retrieves the current set of attributes for a specific file. The return value is the sum of one or more of the following *Microsoft.VisualBasic.FileAttribute* enumeration values (each of which has a related intrinsic Visual Basic constant):

| Enumeration | Constant | Value | Description |
|---|---|---|---|
| Normal | vbNormal | 0 | Normal file (the absence of other attributes) |
| ReadOnly | vbReadOnly | 1 | Read-only file |
| Hidden | vbHidden | 2 | Hidden file |
| System | vbSystem | 4 | System file |
| Directory | vbDirectory | 16 | Directory or folder |
| Archive | vbArchive | 32 | File has changed since last backup |

### Usage at a Glance

- *pathname* can be either an absolute or relative path to a file. It can exist on the local or remote drive and can use the drive-letter or UNC path format.
- An error occurs if *pathname* is invalid or cannot be found.
- You can check if a particular attribute has been set by performing a bitwise And comparison of the GetAttr return value with the attribute constant. For example:

```
If ((GetAttr("myfile.txt") And vbReadOnly) = 0) then
    MsgBox("The file is Read-Write")
Else
    MsgBox("The file is Read-Only")
End If
```

### Version Differences

Visual Basic 2005 includes *My.Computer.FileSystem.GetDirectoryInfo* and *My.Computer.FileSystem.GetFileInfo* methods that provide access to related functionality.

SetAttr Procedure

## GetChar Function

### Class
Microsoft.VisualBasic.Strings

### Syntax
```
Dim result As Char = GetChar(str, index)
```
str  *(required; String)*
  The string from which to extract the character

index  *(required; Integer)*
  Position of the character to extract (1-based)

### Description
The GetChar function returns the character that is at position *index* within a given string.

### Usage at a Glance
If *index* exceeds the number of character positions in *str*, an error occurs.

### Version Differences
The GetChar function did not exist in VB 6.

### See Also
InStr Function, Left Function, Mid Function, Right Function

## GetObject Function

### Class
Microsoft.VisualBasic.Interaction

### Syntax
```
Dim result As Object = GetObject([pathname][, class])
```
pathname  *(optional; String)*
  The full path and name of the COM or ActiveX object.

class  *(optional; String)*
  The class's programmatic identifier (ProgID) of the object to obtain. The ProgID is defined in the system registry and usually takes the form *library.class* or *application.class*.

### Description
The GetObject function obtains an ActiveX or COM object from an already-running instance of that server. Once created, that object's members can be accessed and used.

### Usage at a Glance

- Although both *pathname* and *class* are optional, at least one parameter must be supplied.

- In situations where you cannot create a project-level reference to an ActiveX object, you can use the GetObject function to assign an object reference from an external ActiveX object to an object variable.

- GetObject is used when there is already a current instance of the ActiveX object; to create the first instance, use the CreateObject function.

- If you specify *pathname* as a zero-length string, GetObject will return a new instance of the object—unless the object is registered as single instance, in which case, the current instance will be returned.

- An error is generated if *pathname* is not specified and no current instance of the object can be found.

- When using a variable of type *System.Object* to receive the result of the GetObject function, the new object will be *late bound*. Late binding is inherently lest robust in terms of performance than is *early binding*.

- If an object is registered as a single-instance object (an out-of-process ActiveX EXE), only one instance of the object can be created at a time. Each time you call GetObject to create this object, you will obtain a reference to the same instance of the object.

- You cannot use GetObject to obtain a reference to a class created with Visual Basic 6 or earlier.

### See Also

CreateObject Function

## GetSetting Function

### Class

Microsoft.VisualBasic.Interaction

### Syntax

```
GetSetting(appname, section, key[, default])
```

*appname*  (required; String)
: The name of the application branch to be retrieved.

*section*  (required; String)
: The name of the application's subkey to be retrieved. This can be a single key or a relative registry path, with path components separated by backslashes.

*key*  (required; String)
: The name of the value entry to retrieve.

*default*  (optional; String)
: The value to return if no setting can be found. If omitted, the default value is an empty string ("").

## Description

The GetSetting function returns a single value from a specified section of your application's entry in the HKEY_CURRENT_USER\Software\VB and VBA ProgramSettings\ branch of the registry. If a matching entry is not found, or if any portion of the path to the entry is not found, *default* is returned instead.

## Usage at a Glance

- *section* is a relative path (similar to that used to describe the directories on a hard drive) used to navigate from the application key to the subkey to be accessed. For example, to access the value entry named TestKey in the registry key HKEY_CURRENT_USER\Software\VB and VBA ProgramSettings\RegTester\BranchOne\BranchTwo, you would use:

      GetSetting("RegTester", "BranchOne\BranchTwo", "TestKey")

- Although the registry supports multiple data types, the GetSetting function only supports string values.

- You cannot use GetSetting to access entries from registry keys that are not subkeys of HKEY_CURRENT_USER\Software\VB and VBA ProgramSettings.

- GetSetting cannot be used to access the default value (i.e., the unnamed value entry) belonging to any key. If you're using only the VB registry functions, though, this isn't a serious limitation, since SaveSetting does not allow you to create a default value.

- Data saved with SaveSetting is placed in the registry on a per-user basis.

- The .NET Framework includes registry-related features that provide more flexibility than the VB "Settings" functions. These features are found in the *Registry* and *RegistryKey* classes of the *Microsoft.Win32* namespace.

## Version Differences

Visual Basic 2005 includes several new features that let you manage the settings used by an application. Although they are not compatible with the older VB "Settings" functions, they provide a richer set of features. These features are located in the *My.Settings* object. The *My.Computer.Registry* object also provides access to convenient registry-related features.

## See Also

DeleteSetting Procedure, GetAllSettings Function, SaveSetting Procedure

---

# GetType Operator

## Syntax

    Dim result As System.Type = GetType(typename)

*typename  (required; any type)*
  The name of a type

## Description

The GetType operator returns information about a particular type or instance, such as the name, base type, reference or value type status, COM-related GUID, namespace, and so on.

## Usage at a Glance

- Passing an instance variable to GetType generates a compiler error.
- If you don't know the name of the type about which you'd like to get information, but you do have an object instance of that type, you can retrieve a *System.Type* object using the *Type.GetType* method.

## Version Differences

The GetType operator is new to VB under .NET.

## See Also

CType Function

# Global Keyword

## Syntax

```
Global[.namespace...]
```

*namespace (required)*
> The name of a top-level namespace, such as *System* or *Microsoft*, followed by additional namespace and type qualifiers

## Description

*New in 2005.* The Global keyword provides a way to specify, without ambiguity, a namespace from the topmost level of the namespace hierarchy.

Normally, specifying a full namespace is unambiguous. However, it is possible to create situations where conflicts arise. Consider the following code.

```
Imports MyCompany
Namespace MyCompany.System.Configuration
   Public Class Configuration
      ' ----- Class code here.
   End Class
End Namespace
Namespace MyCompany.MyProgram
   Public Module GeneralCode
      Public Sub SomeRoutine( )
         ' ----- This next line is ambiguous.
         Dim whichOne As System.Configuration.Configuration
      End Sub
   End Module
End Namespace
```

The Dim statement in this code is ambiguous because there are now two *System.Configuration* namespaces: one at the top and one within the MyCompany namespace, both of which contain a *Configuration* class.

To resolve this conflict, use the Global keyword to specify a full namespace from the very top of the hierarchy. Global appears just before all top-level namespaces. The two classes in this example can each be specified using the Global keyword as follows:

- *Global.System.Configuration.Configuration*
- *Global.MyCompany.System.Configuration.Configuration*

## Version Differences

The Global keyword is new in Visual Basic 2005.

## See Also

Continue Statement, On Error Statement

---

# GoTo Statement

## Syntax

```
GoTo label
```

*label (required)*
A source-code label that appears somewhere in the current procedure

## Description

The GoTo statement passes execution to a specified line within a procedure.

## Usage at a Glance

- GoTo can branch only to lines within the procedure where it appears.
- The GoTo statement cannot jump into one of the following block constructs from a location outside of that block: For...Next, For Each...Next, SyncLock...End SyncLock, Try...Catch...Finally, Using...End Using, or With...End With.
- Within a Try...Catch...Finally statement, a GoTo statement can be used to jump out of the entire statement only from the Try or Catch blocks, not from the Finally block.
- Within a Try...Catch...Finally statement, a GoTo statement can be used to jump from a Catch block to the Try block, but no other inter-block jumps are permitted. Jumps are allowed within the same block.
- GoTo is frequently used to control program flow within a procedure, a technique that often produces highly unreadable "spaghetti code." Great care and restraint should be taken when using the GoTo statement.

## Version Differences

Prior to the 2005 release of Visual Basic, the GoTo statement was sometimes used to skip a portion of a loop and continue immediately with the next iteration.

```
For counter = 1 To 10
    ' some code here
    If (someCondition) Then GoTo NextIteration
    ' some more code here

NextIteration:
    ' ----- This label is only used to iterate.
Next counter
```

In Visual Basic 2005, the new Continue keyword provides a better method for jumping to the next iteration of a loop.

```
For counter = 1 To 10
    ' some code here
    If (someCondition) Then Continue For
```

```
' some more code here
Next counter
```

## See Also
Continue Statement, On Error Statement

# Guid Attribute

## Class
System.Runtime.InteropServices.GuidAttribute

## Applies To
Assembly, Class, Delegate, Enum, Interface, Struct

## Constructor
```
New(guid)
```
*guid (required; String)*
The GUID to be assigned to the program element

## Properties
*Value (String)*
Read-only. Value from the *guid* constructor parameter.

## Description
The <Guid> attribute assigns an explicit Globally Unique Identifier (GUID) to a program element when an automatically generated GUID is undesirable. The <Guid> attribute is used for COM interop. A GUID can be generated by a utility named *guidgen.exe*, which is included with Visual Studio.

Assigning a GUID to a program element, rather than allowing Visual Studio to do it automatically, ensures that it remains constant over successive recompilations of the source code. Because COM uses GUIDs to permanently identify program elements, inadvertently changing a GUID may cause COM to fail to recognize a component. Visual Studio automatically adds the <Guid> attribute to each *AssemblyInfo.vb* file to ensure that, should a type library be generated for a particular project, its library identifier (LibID) will remain unchanged when the project is recompiled.

# Handles Keyword

## Syntax
```
Handles name.event
```
*name (required)*
The name of the object with the event that the procedure is handling
*event (required)*
The name of the event member that the procedure is handling

## Description

The Handles statement defines a procedure as the event handler for a particular class or type event.

## Usage at a Glance

- The Handles keyword is used to define event handlers for events trapped by an object defined with the WithEvents keyword.
- The Handles keyword can only be used with a Sub procedure declaration, since an event handler must be a procedure rather than a function.
- The Handles keyword must be on the same logical line as the procedure declaration.
- A single Handles keyword can be followed by multiple comma-delimited *event* entries. This is done when a single event handler is used for multiple events.
- The WithEvents and Handles keywords are designed to define event handlers at compile time. If you want to define event handlers dynamically at runtime, use the AddHandler and RemoveHandler statements.
- By convention, event handlers take the form *objectname_eventname*. For example, the default event handler name for the Click event of an object named Button1 is Button1_Click. Although this convention is traditional and in common use, you are not required to follow it.

## Example

If you add a command button to a new form, the form initialization code generated by Visual Studio includes the following statement:

```
Friend WithEvents Button1 As System.Windows.Forms.Button
```

The WithEvents keyword allows the events of this control to be processed by event handlers. The default procedure template used to handle this button's *Click* event looks like the following:

```
Private Sub Button1_Click(ByVal sender As System.Object, _
    ByVal e As System.EventArgs) Handles Button1.Click
    ' ----- Custom code goes here.
End Sub
```

The Handles clause in this code is what links Button1's *Click* event with the event handler code.

## Version Differences

- The Handles keyword is new to VB under .NET. In VB 6, the link between an object and its event handler was handled automatically and transparently by Visual Basic, based on the name of the event-handling procedure.
- Visual Basic 2005 includes a new Custom Event feature that gives the developer more control over the lifetime of an event.

## See Also

WithEvents Keyword

# Hashtable Class

## Namespace
System.Collections

## Creatable
Yes

## Description
The *Hashtable* class implements a hash-based dictionary of value pairs. A hashtable represents a collection of *values* that are indexed by *keys*; these values and keys are associated in a dictionary of key/value pairs. A *hashing function* is used to speed up access to each pair. In .NET, both the values and the keys are objects of any type. The *Hashtable* class is somewhat more flexible than the standard VB `Collection` class.

The following table lists some of the more useful and interesting members of the *Hashtable* class. Those marked with an asterisk (*) have separate entries in this chapter.

| Member | Description |
|---|---|
| Add Method * | Adds a key/value pair to a hashtable |
| Clear Method * | Removes all items from the hashtable |
| Clone Method | Makes a distinct copy of the hashtable and its members |
| Contains Method | Identical to the *Hashtable.ContainsKey* method |
| ContainsKey Method * | Indicates whether a specific key is in the hashtable |
| ContainsValue Method * | Indicates whether a specific value is in the hashtable |
| CopyTo Method * | Copies hashtable elements to an existing array |
| Count Property | Indicates the number of items currently in the hashtable |
| IsReadOnly Property | Indicates whether the hashtable is read-only or not |
| Item Property * | Retrieves a value from the hashtable based on its key |
| Keys Property * | Retrieves the collection of all keys in the hashtable |
| Remove Method * | Removes a value/key pair from the hashtable |
| Values Property * | Retrieves the collection of all values in the hashtable |

## Example
This example makes use of a simple hashtable.

```
' ----- Build a simple hashtable.
Dim nameHash As New Hashtable( )
nameHash.Add("Be", "Beethoven")
nameHash.Add("Ch", "Chopin")
nameHash.Add("Mo", "Mozart")

' ----- Select and remove items.
MsgBox(nameHash.Item("Be"))     ' Displays "Beethoven"
nameHash.Remove("Ch")           ' Removes "Chopin"
MsgBox(nameHash.Count)          ' Displays 2
nameHash.Clear( )
```

## Hashtable.Add Method

### Class
System.Collections.Hashtable

### Syntax
```
hashtableVariable.Add(key, value)
```
*key* (required; any)
   The key to be used to access the newly added value

*value* (required; any)
   The new value to be added to the hashtable

### Description
The *Add* method adds a key/value pair to the hashtable.

### Usage at a Glance
- *key* must be unique or a runtime error occurs. *value* does not need to be unique.
- Keys are immutable. Once added, a particular key cannot be changed during the lifetime of the hashtable except by removing it through the *Remove* or *Clear* method and then adding it once again. Values associated with keys can be changed through the *Item* property.
- The *Item* property can also be used to add new members to the hashtable.
- To ensure that a key is unique when calling the *Add* method, use the *ContainsKey* method.

### See Also
Hashtable Class, Hashtable.ContainsKey Method, Hashtable.Item Property

## Hashtable.ContainsKey Method

### Class
System.Collections.Hashtable

### Syntax
```
Dim result As Boolean = hashtableVariable.ContainsKey(key)
```
*key* (required; any)
   The key to search for among the hashtable entries

### Description
The *ContainsKey* method indicates whether a given key is contained in the hashtable (True) or not (False).

## Usage at a Glance

The *Contains* method is identical in functionality to the *ContainsKey* method.

## See Also

Hashtable Class, Hashtable.ContainsValue Method

# Hashtable.ContainsValue Method

## Class

System.Collections.Hashtable

## Syntax

```
Dim result As Boolean = hashtableVariable.ContainsValue(value)
```

*value* (required; any)
The value to search for among the hashtable entries

## Description

The *ContainsValue* method indicates whether a given value is contained in the hashtable (True) or not (False).

## See Also

Hashtable Class, Hashtable.ContainsKey Method

# Hashtable.CopyTo Method

## Class

System.Collections.Hashtable

## Syntax

```
hashtableVariable.CopyTo(array, arrayIndex)
```

*array* (required; array of DictionaryEntry)
Array to which to copy the hashtable's key/value pairs

*arrayIndex* (required; Integer)
The index of the first zero-based array element to receive a hashtable pair.

## Description

The *CopyTo* method copies hashtable key/value pairs into an existing array, starting at a specified array index. The array must use the *DictionaryEntry* structure for its type; this structure includes members for both keys and values.

## Usage at a Glance

- The array must be sized to accommodate the elements of the hashtable prior to calling the *CopyTo* method.

- Elements are copied from the hashtable to *array* in the same order in which the hashtable is iterated.

## Example

The sample code copies hashtable pairs to an array.

```
Dim nameTable As New Hashtable
Dim stateArray( ) As DictionaryEntry

' ----- Build the hashtable.
nameTable.Add("Ch", "Chopin")
nameTable.Add("Mo", "Mozart")
nameTable.Add("Be", "Beethoven")

ReDim stateArray(nameTable.Count - 1)
nameTable.CopyTo(stateArray, 0)
```

## See Also

Hashtable Class, Hashtable.Keys Property

---

# Hashtable.Item Property

## Class

System.Collections.Hashtable

## Syntax

```
Dim result As Object = hashtableVariable.Item(key)
```

*key* *(required; any)*
The key with the related value that is to be retrieved

## Description

The *Item* property returns the hashtable value associated with a particular key.

## Usage at a Glance

- *Item* is the default property of the *Hashtable* class, so ".Item" is optional. The following two lines are equivalent.

  ```
  resultObject = myHashtable.Item("abc")
  resultObject = myHashtable("abc")
  ```

- The *Item* property can be used to add or update values. The statement:

  ```
  myHashtable.Item("abc") = sourceObject
  ```

  either updates the value associated with the key "abc" (if it already exists in the hashtable) or adds it as a new item with the key "abc" (if it does not yet exist in the hashtable).

- If *key* does not exist in the hashtable when you attempt to retrieve a value, the *Item* property returns Nothing.

- To guard against inadvertently adding a member to the hashtable when you intend to modify an existing value, call the *ContainsKey* method to test the key.

- You can also retrieve individual members of the *Hashtable* object by iterating it using the For Each...Next statement. Each iteration of the loop returns a *Dictionary-Entry* object containing a single key/value pair.

**See Also**

Hashtable Class

---

# Hashtable.Keys Property

**Class**

System.Collections.Hashtable

**Syntax**

```
Dim result As ICollection = hashtableVariable.Keys
```

**Description**

The *Keys* property returns a collection of the keys contained in a hashtable. The returned object exposes the *ICollection* interface, so any feature that uses this interface can use the returned set of keys.

**See Also**

Hashtable Class, Hashtable.Values Property

---

# Hashtable.Remove Method

**Class**

System.Collections.Hashtable

**Syntax**

```
hashtableVariable.Remove(key)
```

*key* (required; any)
  The key with the key/value pair that is to be removed

**Description**

The *Remove* method removes an element from a hashtable based on its key.

**Usage at a Glance**

- If *key* is not found in the hashtable, the hashtable remains unchanged, and no error occurs.
- For cases in which you need to know whether the call to the *Remove* method will actually remove an entry, call the *ContainsKey* method beforehand to make sure that the key you want to remove exists.

**See Also**

Hashtable Class

## Hashtable.Values Property

### Class
System.Collections.Hashtable

### Syntax
```
Dim result As ICollection = hashtableVariable.Values
```

### Description
The *Values* property returns a collection of the values contained in a hashtable. The returned object exposes the *ICollection* interface, so any feature that uses this interface can use the returned set of values.

### See Also
Hashtable Class, Hashtable.Keys Property

## Hex Function

### Class
Microsoft.VisualBasic.Conversion

### Syntax
```
Dim result As String = Hex(number)
```
*number* (required; numeric or string value)
A number, or a string that can be interpreted as a number. Nonintegral numbers are rounded before conversion.

### Description
The Hex function returns a string that represents the hexadecimal value of a numeric expression.

### Usage at a Glance
- Nonintegral numbers are rounded before conversion to hexadecimal format. An Empty value results in "0." A value of Nothing generates an error.
- The hexadecimal result is limited to 16 digits. Numbers larger than this limit result in an overflow error.
- If the source value is a string, it may appear in hexadecimal format. Such strings begin with the standard "&H" hexadecimal prefix for Visual Basic, as in "&H10" for a decimal value of 16.

### Version Differences
The Visual Basic 6 version of the Hex function only handled up to eight hex digits. The .NET version handles up to 16 digits.

Oct Function

# Hour Function

## Class
Microsoft.VisualBasic.DateAndTime

## Syntax
```
Dim result As Integer = Hour(timeValue)
```
*timeValue* *(required; Date)*
> The source date from which to extract the hour

## Description
The Hour function returns a value from 0 to 23, representing the hour of the supplied date or time.

## Usage at a Glance
- With Option Strict set to On, the source value must first be converted to a Date data type. You can use the CDate function for this purpose. The IsDate function can also be used to confirm that the source expression is a valid date.
- The Hour function always returns an hour value using a 24-hour clock.

## Example
The following statement displays "13."
```
MsgBox(Hour(#1:33:00 PM#))
```

## See Also
DatePart Function, Minute Function, Second Function

# IEEERemainder Function

## Class
System.Math

## Syntax
```
Dim result As Double = Math.IEEERemainder(x, y)
```
*x* *(required; Double)*
> A numerator in a division expression

*y* *(required; Double)*
> A nonzero denominator in a division expression

## Description
The *IEEERemainder* function returns the remainder after dividing *x* by *y*.

### Usage at a Glance

- VB has a built-in Mod operator that also returns the remainder upon division.
- The *IEEERemainder* function complies with the remainder operation as defined in Section 5.1 of ANSI/IEEE Std 754-1985; IEEE Standard for Binary Floating-Point Arithmetic; Institute of Electrical and Electronics Engineers, Inc; 1985.
- This is a shared member of the *System.Math* class, so it can be used without an instance.

### Example

```
MsgBox(Math.IEEEremainder(4, 3))      ' Displays 1
```

### Version Differences

The *IEEERemainder* function did not exist in VB 6.

### See Also

Mod Operator

---

# If...Then...Else Statement

### Syntax

```
If condition [Then]
    [statements]
[ElseIf condition [Then]
    [statements]] ...
[Else
    [statements]]
End If
```

Or:

```
If condition Then [statements] [Else [statements]]
```

*condition* (required; Boolean)

An expression to be evaluated. If True, the related *statements* section executes.

*statements* (optional)

Program code to be executed if *condition* is True. The *statements* in the Else section only execute if no other section does. In the single-line syntax, multiple statements may be separated by colons.

### Description

Executes a statement or block of statements based on the Boolean (True or False) value of an expression. If a given *condition* is True, the statements following that condition are executed. If no *condition* evaluates to True, the statements following the Else statement are executed.

### Usage at a Glance

- Any number of ElseIf clauses and related *statements* blocks may appear. In some cases, a Select Case statement may be a better alternative than numerous End If statements.
- In the block form, one End If clause ends the entire statement. ElseIf clauses do not have their own End If.

- The ElseIf and Else blocks are optional. If both are used, the Else block must appear last.
- If *condition* returns Null, it will be treated as False.
- *condition* can use the Is and TypeOf operators to test for object type, as follows:

      If (TypeOf *objectName* Is *objectType*) Then

- *statements* are required when using the single-line form of If in which there is no Else clause.
- Indentation is important for the readability of If blocks, especially in nested If statements. The set of statements within each new If...Else...EndIf block should be indented, and it is automatically indented by the Visual Studio IDE.
- It is permissible to write a statement such as:

      If someValue Then ...

  where someValue is an Integer variable. The statement works because Visual Basic interprets all nonzero values as equal to the Boolean True and all zero values as False. However, if Option Strict is On, statements such as these will generate a compiler error. One of the following two statements will restore the condition to its Boolean form.

      If (someValue <> 0) Then

  or:

      If CBool(someValue) Then

- Logical comparison operators can be included in the *condition* expression, allowing you to make decisions based on the outcome of more than one individual element. For instance, using the Or operator, you can create conditions like:

      If (x = 0) Or (x = 2) Then

  Parentheses may be included to improve readability and to enforce a specific expression analysis order.

### See Also

IIf Function, Select Case Statement

---

# IIf Function

### Class

Microsoft.VisualBasic.Interaction

### Syntax

    Dim result As Object = IIf(*expression*, *truePart*, *falsePart*)

*expression* *(required; Boolean)*
: Expression to be evaluated

*truePart* *(required; any value or expression)*
: Expression or value to return if *expression* is True

*falsePart* *(required; any value or expression)*
: Expression or value to return if *expression* is False

## Description

The IIf function returns one of two results, depending on whether *expression* evaluates to True or False.

## Usage at a Glance

- The IIf function, as shown in the syntax listed above, is generally equivalent to:

```
If expression Then
    Return truePart
Else
    Return falsePart
End If
```

- *truePart* and *falsePart* can be variables, constants, literals, expressions, or function calls. *expression* can also be built from many complex elements, as long as it ultimately results in a Boolean value.

- Both *truePart* and *falsePart* are fully evaluated before they are considered as results for the IIf statement. If they contain function calls, those functions will be called, even in the part that is not returned by the IIf function. For instance, in the statement:

```
result = IIf(tempOnly, ProcessFile(tempFileName), _
    ProcessFile(mainFileName))
```

both calls to ProcessFile will always be performed, regardless of the value of tempOnly. However, the return value from only one of the calls will be returned from the IIf function.

## See Also

If...Then...Else Statement

---

# Implements Keyword

## Syntax

```
Implements interfaceName.interfaceMember[, ...]
```

*interfaceName* *(required)*
: The name of the interface being implemented by a class or structure. This interface must appear in the related Implements statement used at the start of the class or structure.

*interfaceMember* *(required)*
: The name of the interface member being implemented by a local member of the current class or structure.

## Description

The Implements keyword indicates that a specific class or structure member provides the implementation for a member defined in an interface. This keyword appears as part of the implementation member definition.

## Usage at a Glance

- The Implements keyword can only be used in a class or structure in which the Implements statement has also been used to associate the matching interface to the class or structure.

- The Implements keyword must be on the same logical line as the property, function, procedure, or event definition that implements the interface member.

- The implementing member must have the same argument and return type signature, and be of the same member type, as the interface member.

- Classes and structures that implement interfaces must implement all members declared in the interface.

## Example

See the example in the *Implements Statement* entry.

## Version Differences

- The Implements keyword is new to VB under .NET. Its addition means that the implementation of a class or structure member does not have to use the name defined by the interface. This differs from the VB 6 practice, which required that class members that implemented an interface definition have the form *interfaceName_membername*.

- VB 6 does not allow derived classes to implement events defined in interfaces. The .NET version of Visual Basic removes this restriction.

## See Also

Implements Statement, Interface...End Interface Statement

---

# Implements Statement

## Syntax

```
Implements interfaceName[, interfaceName...]
```

*interfaceName* (required)

The name of the interface that a class or structure implements. This name may include the namespace of the interface, as in *namespace.interface*.

## Description

The Implements statement specifies that a class or structure will implement an interface defined. The Implements statement appears on the line immediately following the Class clause, or immediately after the Inherits line if the class definition includes an Inherits statement:

```
Friend Class ClassWithAPurpose
    Implements IPurpose
    ...
```

or:

```
Friend Class ClassWithAPurpose
    Inherits ClassWithLimitedPurpose
    Implements IPurpose
    ...
```

A single class may implement multiple interfaces.

## Usage at a Glance

- Any interface specified by the Implements statement must have all of its members fully implemented by the class or structure where the Implements statement appears. However, if you do not wish to support one interface member, the implementation procedure can simply raise a *NotImplementedException* exception.

- The Implements statement cannot be used with code modules; it is used only in class and structure definitions.

- Each class or structure member that implements a member of an interface uses the Implements keyword as part of its definition.

- Traditionally, once a public interface is implemented, it should not be changed. Any additional functionality should be provided by defining additional interfaces.

- VB under .NET provides only single inheritance using the Inherits statement. However, a single class can implement multiple interfaces at the same time.

## Example

```
Friend Interface IAnimal
    ReadOnly Property Name() As String
    Function GetFood() As String
    Function GetNoise() As String
End Interface

Friend Class Wolf
    Implements IAnimal

    Public ReadOnly Property Name() As String _
        Implements IAnimal.Name
        Get
            Return "Wolf"
        End Get
    End Property

    Public Function GetFood() As String Implements IAnimal.GetFood
        Return "caribou, salmon, other fish"
    End Function

    Public Function GetNoise() As String Implements IAnimal.GetNoise
        Return "howl"
    End Function
End Class

Module GeneralCode
    Public Sub TestAnimal()
        Dim loneWolf As IAnimal=New Wolf
        MsgBox(loneWolf.GetNoise())
        loneWolf = Nothing
    End Sub
End Module
```

### Version Differences

In VB 6, the Implements statement does not support events; any events publicly declared in an interface are ignored. VB under .NET allows interface events to be implemented in classes and structures.

### See Also

Implements Statement, Interface...End Interface Statement

## Imports Statement

### Syntax

```
Imports [aliasName =] namespace[.element]
```

*aliasName (optional)*
: The name by which the namespace or element must be referenced within the source-code file that contains the Imports statement

*namespace (required)*
: The name of the namespace being imported

*element (optional)*
: The name of an element in the namespace

### Description

The Imports statement makes a namespace or parts of a namespace available to the current module without additional qualification.

### Usage at a Glance

- A single Imports statement can import only one namespace or element.
- A module can have as many Imports statements as needed.
- Imports statements are used to import names from other projects and assemblies, as well as from namespaces in the current project.
- Imports statements must be placed in a module before references to any types (classes, structures, etc.).
- *namespace* must be a fully qualified namespace name, even if you use the compiler option /rootnamespace or supply a value for the "Root namespace" in the project's Properties dialog in Visual Studio.
- If *aliasName* is absent from an Imports statement, types in that namespace can be referenced without qualification. If *aliasName* is present in an Imports statement, types in that namespace must be qualified with *aliasName* in order to be accessible without full qualification. The name *aliasName* must not be assigned to any other member within the module.
- If *element* is specified, it can be the name of an enumeration, structure, class, or module within the namespace. If specified, this restricts importation to members of that element only.

- You do not have to use the Imports statement to import namespaces into an ASP. NET application. Instead, you can import a namespace into an ASP.NET application in a number of ways:
  - By creating an "<add namespace>" directive in a *web.config* configuration file. For example:

    ```
    <compilation>
        <namespaces>
            <add namespace="System.IO" />
            ...
        </namespaces>
    ```

    imports the *System.IO* namespace within the scope defined in the *web.config* file.
  - By adding an "@ Import" directive to *global.asax*. For example:

    ```
    <%@ Import namespace="System.IO" %>
    ```

    imports the *System.IO* namespace for the ASP.NET application.
  - By adding an "@ Import" page directive. This has the same form as the *global. asax* directive and must appear at the beginning of the page.

### Example

```
Imports MVB = Microsoft.VisualBasic
```

### See Also

Namespace Statement

## Inherits Statement

### Syntax

```
Inherits className
```

*className (required)*
The name of the inherited (base) class

### Description

The Inherits statement specifies the name of the class from which a new class is being derived; it specifies the base class of the current class. The statement appears immediately after the Class statement or the Interface statement.

### Usage at a Glance

- The Inherits statement must be the first line of code in the class or interface. It can be preceded only by blank lines and comments.
- Visual Basic does not support simultaneous inheritance from multiple classes in a derived class. There can be only a single Inherits statement in a class definition.
- Interfaces support either single or multiple inheritance from other interfaces. Use a comma used to delimit multiple base interfaces:

  ```
  Interface IPerson
      Property Name As String
  ```

```
End Interface

Interface IEmployee
    Property SSN As String
End Interface

Interface ISalaried
    Inherits IPerson, IEmployee

    Property Salaried As Boolean
    Property Salary As Decimal
End Interface
```

### See Also

Class Statement, Interface...End Interface Statement

---

## Input Procedure

### Class

Microsoft.VisualBasic.FileSystem

### Syntax

```
Input(fileNumber, value)
```

*fileNumber* *(required; Integer)*
: Any valid file number of a file opened with FileOpen

*value* *(required; any)*
: The destination object into which data from the file will be stored

### Description

The Input procedure reads delimited data from a file into a variable. This statement is used to read files created using the Write and WriteLine procedures. Those procedures output data as comma-delimited fields with quotation marks around strings.

### Usage at a Glance

- Data read by Input has usually been written using the Write and WriteLine procedures.

- Use this statement with files that have been opened in Input or Binary mode only.

- An error occurs if the data type of *value* cannot store the data being read by the Input procedure.

- The Input procedure removes quotation marks that it finds around strings before storing the data in *value*.

- After the Input procedure reads *value*, it advances the file pointer to the next unread variable or, if the file contains no additional delimited data, to the end of the file.

- An error occurs if the end of the file is reached during the operation.

- The Input procedure assigns string or numeric data to *value* without modification. However, other types of data can be modified as shown in the following table:

| Data | Value assigned to variable |
|------|----------------------------|
| Delimiting comma or blank line | "" (empty string) |
| #FALSE# | False |
| #TRUE# | True |
| #yyyy-mm-dd hh:mm:ss# | Date or time |

#TRUE# and #FALSE# are case-sensitive.

- Use the EOF function to determine whether the end of the file has been reached.
- Use the Write and WriteLine procedures to write data to a file, since they delimit data fields correctly. This ensures that the data can be read correctly with the Input procedure.

## Example

If the file *c:\data.txt* contains the following data:

```
"one", "two", "three"
```

then the following code will print each string on a separate line in the Output window:

```
Dim oneValue As String
Dim fileID As Integer = FreeFile()

FileOpen(fileID, "c:\data.txt", OpenMode.Input)
Do While Not EOF(fileID)
    Input(fileID, oneValue)
    Console.WriteLine(oneValue)
Loop
FileClose(fileID)
```

## Version Differences

- The Input procedure differs syntactically from its VB 6 counterpart. The VB 6 version supported multiple input values in a single statement, among other changes.
- In VB 6, if *value* is numeric and the data read from the file is not numeric, *value* is initialized to the default value for its type. In .NET, this generates an error.
- In addition to the standard data types, VB 6 also recognizes Empty, Null, and Error types. In .NET, these are not supported.
- In Visual Basic 2005, the *My.Computer.FileSystem* object provides more robust access to file management features.

## See Also

Write, WriteLine Procedures

# InputBox Function

## Class

Microsoft.VisualBasic.Interaction

## Syntax

```
Dim result As String = InputBox(prompt[, title[, _
    defaultResponse[, xpos[, ypos]]]])
```

*prompt  (required; String)*
> A message displayed in the body of the dialog box that usually emphasizes the type of data to be entered. May include line termination characters.

*title  (optional; String)*
> The text to display in the title bar of the dialog box. If omitted or blank, the name of the application is used.

*defaultResponse  (optional; String)*
> String to be displayed in the text box when the dialog box first opens. This may be an empty string.

*xpos  (optional; Numeric)*
> The distance in twips from the left-hand side of the screen to the left-hand side of the dialog box. If omitted, the dialog box is centered horizontally.

*ypos  (optional; Numeric)*
> The distance in twips from the top of the screen to the top of the dialog box. If omitted, the dialog box is positioned vertically about one-third of the way down from the top of the screen.

## Description

The InputBox function displays a dialog box containing a prompt for the user, a text box for entering data, and OK and Cancel buttons. When the user clicks OK, the function returns the contents of the text box. If the user clicks the Cancel button, an empty string ("") is returned.

## Usage at a Glance

- It is not possible to distinguish between a click on the OK button with a blank text field and a click on the Cancel button.

- *prompt* can contain approximately 1,000 characters, including nonprinting characters such as the intrinsic vbCrLf constant.

- If you are omitting one or more of the optional arguments and are using subsequent arguments, you must use a comma to signify the missing parameter. For example, the following code fragment displays a prompt and a default string in the text box; default values will be used for the title and for dialog box positioning.

  ```
  Dim userResponse As String
  userResponse = InputBox("Enter the data", , "The Data")
  ```

- InputBox always returns a string. Your code is responsible for converting it to the required data type before use.

MsgBox Function

---

# InputString Function

## Class
Microsoft.VisualBasic.FileSystem

## Syntax
```
Dim result As String = InputString(fileNumber, charCount)
```
*fileNumber* (required; Integer)
   Any valid file number of a file opened with `FileOpen`

*charCount* (required; Integer)
   Number of characters to read from the file

## Description
The `InputString` function reads data from a file into a string variable, up to *charCount* characters in length.

## Usage at a Glance
- `InputString` should only be used with files opened in Input or Binary modes.
- `InputString` begins reading from the current read position in the file.
- `InputString` returns all the characters it reads, regardless of their type. This includes spaces, carriage returns, line feeds, commas, end-of-file markers, unprintable characters, and so on.
- Once the function finishes reading *charCount* characters, it advances the current file position *charCount* characters.
- `InputString` is often used with data written to a file using the `Print`, `PrintLine`, or `FilePut` procedures.
- If a read of *charCount* characters moves past the end of the file, an error occurs.

## Example
If the file *c:\data.txt* contains the data:
```
abcdefghijklmnopq
```
the following code reads the characters, three at a time:
```
Dim oneLine As String
Dim counter As Long
Dim fileID As Integer = FreeFile()

FileOpen(fileID, "c:\data2.txt", OpenMode.Input)
For counter = 1 To LOF(fileID) \ 3
    oneLine = InputString(fileID, 3)
    Console.WriteLine(oneLine)
Next counter
FileClose(fileID)
```

## Version Differences

- The new InputString function corresponds to the VB 6 Input, Input$, InputB, and InputB$ functions.
- The order of parameters is reversed between the VB 6 and .NET versions. In VB 6, the first parameter is *charCount* and the second is *fileNumber*.
- In Visual Basic 2005, the *My.Computer.FileSystem* object provides more robust access to file management features.

## See Also

FilePut, FilePutObject Procedures, Print, PrintLine Procedures

---

# InStr Function

## Class

Microsoft.VisualBasic.Strings

## Syntax

```
Dim result As Integer = InStr([start, ]string1, string2[, compare])
```

*start*  (optional; Integer)
   The 1-based starting position for the search. If omitted, 1 is used.

*string1*  (required; String)
   The string being searched.

*string2*  (required; String)
   The substring to be found within *string2*.

*compare*  (optional; CompareMethod enumeration)
   The type of string comparison. One of the following *Microsoft.VisualBasic. CompareMethod* enumeration values.

| Value | Description |
|---|---|
| Binary | Performs a binary (case-sensitive) comparison |
| Text | Performs a text (case-insensitive) comparison |

If omitted, the setting specified through the Option Compare statement is used.

## Description

The InStr function finds the 1-based starting position of *string2* within *string1*, optionally skipping the first few characters. If a match is not found, zero is returned.

## Usage at a Glance

If *string2* is empty or Nothing, the value of *start* is returned.

## See Also

InStrRev Function

# InStrRev Function

## Class
Microsoft.VisualBasic.Strings

## Syntax
```
Dim result As Integer = InStrRev(stringCheck, stringMatch[, _
    start[, compare]])
```
*stringCheck  (required; String)*
    The string being searched.

*stringMatch  (required; String)*
    The substring to be found within *stringCheck*.

*start  (optional; Numeric)*
    The 1-based starting position for the search. If omitted, -1 is used, which indicates the last character of the string. Although the counting is done from the left end of the string, the search uses the character at that position and proceeds to the left.

*compare  (optional; CompareMethod enumeration)*
    The type of string comparison. One of the following *Microsoft.VisualBasic. CompareMethod* enumeration values.

| Value | Description |
|-------|-------------|
| Binary | Performs a binary (case-sensitive) comparison |
| Text | Performs a text (case-insensitive) comparison |

If omitted, Binary is used.

## Description
Finds the 1-based starting position of the last occurrence of *stringMatch* within *stringCheck*, optionally skipping the last few characters. If a match is not found, zero is returned. The search is done from the specified character position (the last character by default) and proceeds toward the left, the beginning of the string.

## Usage at a Glance
- The syntax of InStrRev is different from InStr.
- While InStr searches a string from left to right, InStrRev searches a string from right to left.

## Example
This example uses both InStr and InStrRev to highlight the different results produced by each.
```
Dim bigString As String = _
    "I like the functionality that InStrRev gives."
MsgBox(InStr(bigString, "th"))      ' Displays 8
MsgBox(InStrRev(bigString, "th"))   ' Displays 26
```

See Also
InStr Function

# Int Function

### Class
Microsoft.VisualBasic.Conversion

### Syntax
```
Dim result As type = Int(number)
```
*number* *(required; any numeric expression)*
> The number to be processed. The data type of *number* is one of Double, Single, Decimal, Integer, Long, Short, or Object. If Object, the value must evaluate to a number. The return data type always matches the data type of *number*.

### Description
The Int function returns the whole number that is less than or equal to the source value.

### Usage at a Glance
- Int truncates numbers; it does not round. For example, Int(100.9) returns 100.
- If the source value is negative, Int returns the first negative integer less than or equal to that value. For example, Int(-10.1) returns -11.
- A source of Nothing returns Nothing.
- The Int and Fix functions work identically with positive numbers. However, for negative numbers, Fix returns the first negative integer *greater than* the source value, while Int returns the first negative integer *less than* that value. For example, Fix(-10.1) returns -10, while Int(-10.1) returns -11.
- Int is not the same as the CInt function. CInt casts the number passed to it as an Integer data type, while Int returns the same data type that was passed to it.

### See Also
CInt Function, Fix Function, Round Function

# Interface...End Interface Statement

### Syntax
```
[accessModifier] [Shadows] Interface name [(Of typeParamList)]
    [statements]
End Interface
```
*accessModifier* *(optional)*
> Specifies the scope and accessibility of the interface. One of the following access levels:

| Access level | Description |
| --- | --- |
| Public | The interface is publicly accessible anywhere, both inside and outside of the project. |
| Private | The interface is accessible within the type in which it is defined. |
| Protected | The interface is accessible only to the type in which it is defined and to derived instances of that type. |
| Friend | The interface is accessible only within the project that contains the interface definition. |
| Protected Friend | Combines the access features of Protected and Friend. |

If omitted, the Friend access level is used.

Shadows *(optional)*
Indicates that the interface shadows an identically named element in a base class.

*name (required)*
The name of the interface.

*typeParamList (optional)*
Adds type parameter placeholders that will later enforce strong typing when the interface is used through its class implementation. The Of clause implements generics, which are fully described in Chapter 10. If generics will not be used, this clause can be excluded.

*statements (optional)*
Code that defines the interface members that derived classes must implement.

## Description

The Interface...End Interface statement defines a virtual base class along with its members. The members of an interface include sub procedures, functions, properties, and events. All members are automatically public within the interface.

Interfaces are implemented by derived classes and structures using the Implements statement.

## Usage at a Glance

- By convention, interface names generally begin with the capital letter I.
- The interface definition (*statements*) may contain the following elements:

Inherits *statement*
Indicates that *name* inherits some of its properties and methods from another interface. Its syntax is:

Inherits *interfaceName*[, *interfaceName*...]
where *interfacename* is the name(s) of the interface(s) from which *name* inherits.

*Property definitions*
Property definitions take the form:

[Default] [ReadOnly | WriteOnly] Property *procname*([*arglist*]) As *type*

where *procname* is the name of the property, with its defined *arglist* and return *type*. Default indicates that *procname* is the interface's default member. The ReadOnly and WriteOnly keywords limit the accessors of the property.

*Function definitions*
Functions are defined as:

```
Function membername([arglist]) As type
```

where *membername* is the name of the function, *arglist* defines the number and type of arguments that can be passed to the function, and *type* indicates the function's return value.

*Procedure definitions*
Procedures are defined as:

```
Sub membername[(arglist)]
```

where *membername* is the name of the procedure, and *arglist* specifies the number and type of arguments that can be passed to the procedure.

*Event definitions*
Events are defined as:

```
Event membername[(arglist)]
```

where *membername* is the name of the event, and *arglist* defines the number and type of arguments that are passed to an event handler whenever the event is fired.

- In each case, the syntax of the statement is different from the "standard" implementation syntax. Access modifiers, for instance, are not permitted as a part of interface member definitions (since they would all be Public), nor are End statements, such as End Function, End Sub, or End Property.

- The *name* interface cannot inherit from an interface with an access type that is more restrictive than its own. For example, if *name* is a Public interface, it cannot inherit from a Friend interface.

- Classes and structures that implement the interface must implement all of its members, and each member implementation must include the interface's signature for that member.

- An interface can have only one default property. This includes properties defined in base interfaces, as well as in the interface itself.

## Version Differences

- The Interface...End Interface construct is new to VB under .NET. In VB 6, an interface was defined by creating a class module with members that had no implementation.

- Visual Basic 2005 adds support for generics to interfaces, as discussed in Chapter 10.

## See Also

Implements Keyword, Implements Statement

# IPmt Function

## Class

Microsoft.VisualBasic.Financial

## Syntax

```
Dim result As Double = IPmt(rate, per, nPer, pv[, fv[, due]])
```

*rate (required; Double)*
  The interest rate per period.

*per (required; Double)*
  The period for which a payment is to be computed.

*nPer (required; Double)*
  The total number of payment periods.

*pv (required; Double)*
  The present value of a series of future payments.

*fv (optional; Double)*
  The future value or cash balance after the final payment. If omitted, the default value is 0.

*due (optional; DueDate enumeration)*
  A value indicating when payments are due, from the *Microsoft.VisualBasic. DueDate* enumeration. *DueDate.EndOfPeriod* indicates that payments are due at the end of the payment period; *DueDate.BegOfPeriod* indicates that payments are due at the beginning of the period. If omitted, the default value is *DueDate. EndOfPeriod.*

## Description

The IPmt function computes the interest payment for a given period of an annuity, based on regular fixed payments and a fixed interest rate. An annuity is a series of fixed cash payments made over a period of time. It can be either a loan or an investment.

## Usage at a Glance

- The value of *per* ranges from 1 to *nPer*.

- If *pv* and *fv* represent liabilities, their values are negative; if they represent assets, their values are positive.

- *rate* and *nPer* must be expressed in the same time unit. That is, if *nPer* reflects the number of monthly payments, *rate* must be the monthly interest rate.

- The rate is supplied as a decimal percent. For example, 10% is stated as 0.1.

## Example

The ComputeSchedule function accepts a loan amount, an annual interest rate, and a number of payment months. It uses the IPmt and PPmt functions to calculate the interest and principal per month, and it returns an array of all interest and principal payments.

```
Public Structure PaymentData
    Public WhichPayment As Integer
    Public Interest As Double
    Public Principal As Double
End Structure

Public Function ComputeSchedule(ByVal amount As Double, _
    ByVal rate As Double, ByVal periods As Integer) _
    As PaymentData( )
```

```
Dim periodScan As Integer
Dim allPayments(0 To periods - 1) As PaymentData

For periodScan = 1 To periods
   With allPayments(periodScan - 1)
      .WhichPayment = periodScan
      .Interest = IPmt(rate / 12, periodScan, periods, -amount)
      .Principal = PPmt(rate / 12, periodScan, periods, -amount)
   End With
Next periodScan

   Return allPayments
End Function
```

### See Also

FV Function, NPer Function, NPV Function, Pmt Function, PPmt Function, PV Function, Rate Function

# IRR Function

### Class

Microsoft.VisualBasic.Financial

### Syntax

```
Dim result As Double = IRR(valueArray( )[, guess])
```

*valueArray( ) (required; array of Double)*
   An array of cash flow values.

*guess  (optional; Double)*
   Estimated value to be returned by the function. If omitted, a value of 0.1 is used.

### Description

The IRR function calculates the internal rate of return for a series of periodic cash flows (payments and receipts). The internal rate of return is the interest rate generated by an investment consisting of payments and receipts that occur at regular intervals. It is generally compared to a "hurdle rate," or a minimum return, to determine whether a particular investment should be made.

### Usage at a Glance

- *valueArray* must be a one-dimensional array that contains at least one negative value (a payment) and at least one positive value (a receipt).

- Individual members of *valueArray* are interpreted sequentially, from first to last.

- IRR begins with *guess* and uses iteration to obtain an internal rate of return that is accurate to within 0.00001 percent. If this cannot be done within 20 iterations, the function fails. If it fails, try a different value for *guess*.

- Each element of *valueArray* represents a payment or a receipt that occurs at a regular time interval. If this is not the case, IRR will return erroneous results.

# Is Operator

## Syntax

```
Dim result As Boolean = object1 Is { object2 | Nothing }
```

*object1* *(required; Object or any reference type)*
  An object or instance for comparison

*object2* *(required; Object or any reference type)*
  An object or instance for comparison

## Description

The Is operator compares two object references and indicates whether they refer to the same underlying instance (True) or not (False). It is most often used with If...Then... Else statements, as in:

```
If (someVariable Is someOtherVariable) Then
    ' ----- Equivalent-specific code here.
End If
```

Comparing a variable with Nothing tests whether an instance has not yet been assigned to that variable.

```
If (someVariable Is Nothing) Then
    ' ----- The variable is undefined.
End If
```

## Usage at a Glance

- Both *object1* and *object2* must be reference-type variables. This includes string variables, object variables, and array variables. You can call the IsReference function to ensure that both *object1* and *object2* are reference types.

- The Is operator can be used with the TypeOf operator to determine if an object reference is of a specific type.

- The Is operator reports that uninitialized reference types are equal. For example, the following comparison equates to True:

```
Dim emptyForm As Windows.Forms.Form
Dim ordinaryString As String
If (emptyForm Is ordinaryString) Then MsgBox("Same")
    ' ----- The MsgBox will indeed appear.
```

## Version Differences

In .NET, strings and arrays are reference types. In VB 6, strings and arrays are not reference types and, therefore, cannot be used with the Is operator.

## See Also

IsNot Operator, TypeOf Operator

# IsArray Function

## Class
Microsoft.VisualBasic.Information

## Syntax
```
Dim result As Boolean = IsArray(varName)
```
*varName* *(required; any variable)*
A variable that may be an array

## Description
The IsArray function indicates whether a variable is an array (True) or not (False).

## Usage at a Glance
- Due to the nature of .NET objects, it is not always obvious that an Object variable contains an array, since an entire array can be assigned to a simple Object variable. Calling array-specific functions like UBound or trying to access array elements on a variable that is not an array will generate an error. If there is doubt as to the nature of a variable, it should first be tested using the IsArray function.
- An uninitialized array returns False. For example:
```
Dim unusedArray( ) As String
MsgBox(IsArray(unusedArray))    ' Displays "False"
```
- Array-like data structures, such as the Collection object, are not true arrays and return False when passed to the IsArray function.

## Example
The following code displays "True," even though the Object variable was not initially declared as an array.
```
Dim multipleData( ) As Integer = {1, 2}
Dim singleData As Object
singleData = multipleData
MsgBox(IsArray(singleData))    ' Displays "True"
```

## Version Differences
In VB 6, the IsArray function returns True when passed an uninitialized array. In .NET, it returns False.

## See Also
Array Class

# IsDate Function

## Class
Microsoft.VisualBasic.Information

### Syntax

```
Dim result As Boolean = IsDate(expression)
```

*expression* *(required; any)*
  Expression containing a date or time

### Description

The `IsDate` function determines if an expression can be interpreted as a date without error (`True`) or not (`False`).

### Usage at a Glance

- Uninitialized `Date` variables return `True`.

- `IsDate` uses the regional settings of the local system to determine if the value is recognizable as a date. What is a legal date format on one machine may fail on another.

### See Also

CDate Function

---

## IsDBNull Function

### Class

Microsoft.VisualBasic.Information

### Syntax

```
Dim result As Boolean = IsDBNull(expression)
```

*expression* *(required; any)*
  The expression to be evaluated against *System.DBNull*

### Description

The `IsDBNull` function determines whether *expression* evaluates to *System.DbNull* (`True`) or not (`False`).

### Usage at a Glance

- *DbNull* is not the same as `Nothing` or an empty string. *DbNull* is used to denote a missing or nonexistent value, and it is used primarily in the context of database field values.

- Because of the way that VB deals with expressions containing *DBNull*, you cannot simply compare a variable to *DBNull*, as in:

    ```
    If (someVariable = DbNull) Then
    ```

  You must make the comparison using the `IsDbNull` function.

    ```
    If (IsDBNull(someVariable) = True) Then
    ```

### Version Differences

- The `IsDBNull` function is new with VB under .NET.

- Visual Basic 2005 includes a new *IsNullOrEmpty* method as part of the `String` data type that may better meet your needs.

---

# IsError Function

## Class

Microsoft.VisualBasic.Information

## Syntax

```
Dim result As Boolean = IsError(expression)
```

*expression*  (required; Object)
An object variable that may be a *System.Exception* object

## Description

The IsError function indicates whether an object is an instance of the *System.Exception* class or one of its derived classes (True) or not (False).

## Example

The following example shows how a single object may or may not be an *Exception* object. However, the method of indicating the error is nonstandard and is only used here as a demonstration.

```
Public Sub TestForError()
    Dim testValue As Object = "You can't increment a string!"
    Dim testResult As Object

    ' ----- Perform the test.
    testResult = IncrementTest(testValue)
    If (IsError(testResult) = True) Then
        MsgBox(testResult.Message)
    Else
        MsgBox(testResult)
    End If
End Sub

Public Function IncrementTest(ByVal testValue As Object) As Object
    ' ----- Increment the value, but only if it is possible.
    If (IsNumeric(testValue) = True) Then
        Return testValue + 1
    Else
        Return New System.InvalidOperationException
    End If
End Function
```

## Version Differences

In VB 6, the IsError function takes a Variant argument and determines if its subtype is vbError. It is often used with the CVErr function to determine if the value returned from a function is an error. In .NET, the IsError function is used to test whether an object is an instance of the *Exception* class or one of its derived classes.

## See Also

Exception Class

## IsNot Operator

### Syntax

```
Dim result As Boolean = object1 IsNot { object2 | Nothing }
```

*object1 (required; Object or any reference type)*
    An object or instance for comparison

*object2 (required; Object or any reference type)*
    An object or instance for comparison

### Description

*New in 2005.* The IsNot operator compares two object references and indicates whether they refer to a different underlying instance (True) or the same instance (False). It is most often used with If...Then...Else statements, as in:

```
If (someVariable IsNot someOtherVariable) Then
   ' ----- Non-equivalent-specific code here.
End If
```

Comparing a variable with Nothing tests whether an instance has already been assigned to that variable.

```
If (someVariable IsNot Nothing) Then
   ' ----- The variable is already defined.
End If
```

The IsNot operator is the negation of the Is operator. Before Visual Basic 2005, the functionality of the IsNot operator had to be done with the Not operator.

```
If Not (someVariable Is Nothing) Then
   ' ----- The variable is already defined.
End If
```

### Usage at a Glance

- Both *object1* and *object2* must be reference-type variables. This includes string variables, object variables, and array variables. You can call the IsReference function to ensure that both *object1* and *object2* are reference types.

- The IsNot operator can be used with the TypeOf operator to determine if an object reference is not of a specific type.

- The IsNot operator reports that uninitialized reference types are equal. For example, the following comparison equates to True:

```
Dim emptyForm As Windows.Forms.Form
Dim ordinaryString As String
If (emptyForm IsNot ordinaryString) Then MsgBox("Different")
   ' ----- The MsgBox will not appear.
```

### Version Differences

- The IsNot operator is new with Visual Basic 2005.

- In .NET, strings and arrays are reference types. In VB 6, strings and arrays are not reference types and, therefore, cannot be used with the IsNot operator.

### See Also

Is Operator, TypeOf Operator

# IsNothing Function

## Class
Microsoft.VisualBasic.Information

## Syntax
```
Dim result As Boolean = IsNothing(expression)
```
*expression (required; any)*
The expression to compare with Nothing

## Description
The `IsNothing` function determines whether *expression* evaluates to Nothing (True) or not (False). The line:
```
If IsNothing(someObject) Then
```
is equivalent to:
```
If (someObject Is Nothing) Then
```

## Version Differences
- The `IsNothing` function is new with VB under .NET.
- Visual Basic 2005 includes a new *IsNullOrEmpty* method as part of the String data type that may better meet your needs.

## See Also
Is Operator, IsNot Operator, Nothing Keyword

---

# IsNumeric Function

## Class
Microsoft.VisualBasic.Information

## Syntax
```
Dim result As Boolean = IsNumeric(expression)
```
*expression (required; any)*
The expression to be examined for numeric content

## Description
The `IsNumeric` function determines whether *expression* can be evaluated as a number (True) or not (False).

---

# IsReference Function

## Class
Microsoft.VisualBasic.Information

## Syntax

```
Dim result As Boolean = IsReference(expression)
```

*expression* *(required; any)*

The expression to be examined

## Description

The IsReference function determines if *expression* contains reference type data (True) or value type data (False).

## Usage at a Glance

- IsReference returns True if *expression* is an array, since an array is a reference type.
- Just because a variable has been declared to be of type Object does not mean that the IsReference function will return True when that variable is passed to it as an argument. Consider the following code:

```
Dim generalData As Object
MsgBox(IsReference(generalData))          ' Displays "True"

generalData = New Employee
MsgBox(IsReference(generalData))          ' Displays "True"

generalData = 3
MsgBox(IsReference(generalData))          ' Displays "False"

generalData = "This is a string"
MsgBox(IsReference(generalData))          ' Displays "True"
```

The IsReference function returns True only if an Object variable is Nothing, or if its true data content is a reference type.

## Version Differences

The IsReference function is new with VB in .NET.

---

# Join Function

## Class

Microsoft.VisualBasic.Strings

## Syntax

```
Dim result As String = Join(sourceArray, [delimiter])
```

*sourceArray* *(required; String or Object array)*

Array with elements that are to be concatenated.

*delimiter* *(optional; String)*

String used to delimit the individual values in the new joined string. If omitted, the space character ("") is used. *delimiter* may be an empty string ("").

## Description

The Join function concatenates an array of strings or string expressions into a delimited string using a specified delimiter.

## Usage at a Glance

- If you want to concatenate numeric or other nonstring values in *sourceArray*, use an Object array.
- The *delimiter* can be of any length. Include a zero-length string to concatenate the array elements together without any delimiter.

## See Also

Split Function

---

# Kill Procedure

## Class

Microsoft.VisualBasic.FileSystem

## Syntax

```
Kill(pathname)
```

*pathname* *(required; String)*
    The file or files to be deleted

## Description

The Kill procedure deletes one or more files. The supplied *pathname* may include the * and ? wildcard characters in the filename component.

## Usage at a Glance

- *pathname* can be a relative or absolute path, either to a local or remote file.
- If the file is open or is set to read-only, an error occurs.
- The file or files are permanently deleted; they are not placed in the Recycle Bin. Visual Basic 2005 adds a new *My.Computer.FileSystem.DeleteFile* method that includes an option for the Recycle Bin.
- Use the RmDir procedure to delete directories.

## Version Differences

Visual Basic 2005 includes a *My.Computer.FileSystem.DeleteFile* method that provides similar functionality.

## See Also

RmDir Procedure

---

# LBound Function

## Class

Microsoft.VisualBasic.Information

## Syntax

```
Dim result As Integer = LBound(array[, rank])
```

*array  (required; any array)*
    An array with a lower bound that is to be determined.

*rank  (optional; Integer)*
    The dimension to assess for a lower bound. If omitted, it defaults to 1.

## Description

The LBound function returns the lower limit of the specified dimension of an array. In .NET, all array dimensions have a lower bound of zero, so this function always return zero.

## Usage at a Glance

- If *array* is uninitialized, LBound generates a runtime error. Compare *array* to Nothing to prevent this error:

  ```
  If (someArray IsNot Nothing) Then
      ' ----- OK to use LBound
  ```

- Since VB.NET does not allow you to change the lower bound of an array, the LBound function appears to be superfluous except for reasons of backward compatibility. However, as the .NET Framework may someday support variable lower bounds, its use is still warranted.

## Version Differences

- In VB 6, with its ability to alter the lower bound of an array, the use of LBound was essential. As of the 2005 release of VB, its use under .NET is optional.

- The 2005 release of Visual Basic supports a new array declaration syntax that restores the VB 6 style "*lower* To *upper*" syntax, as in:

  ```
  Dim someArray(0 To 5) As String
  ```

  However, the specified lower bound must still be 0.

## See Also

UBound Function

---

# LCase Function

## Class

Microsoft.VisualBasic.Strings

## Syntax

```
Dim result As type = LCase(value)
```

*type  (required)*
    One of the following data types: Char or String

*value  (required; expression of type type)*
    A valid string expression or a character

## Description

The LCase function converts a string or character to lowercase.

## Usage at a Glance

- LCase only affects uppercase letters; all other characters in *value* are unaffected.
- LCase returns Nothing if *value* contains Nothing.
- LCase returns the same data type as *value*.

## See Also

UCase Function

# Left Function

## Class

Microsoft.VisualBasic.Strings

## Syntax

```
Dim result As String = Left(str, length)
```

*str* (required; String)
   The string to be processed

*length* (required; Long)
   The number of characters to return from the left portion of the string

## Description

The Left function returns a string containing the leftmost *length* characters of *str*.

## Usage at a Glance

- If *length* is 0, a zero-length string is returned.
- If *length* is greater than the length of *str*, *str* is returned.
- If *length* is less than zero or is Nothing, an error is generated.
- If *str* is Nothing, Left returns Nothing.
- Because of naming conflicts, you may have to preface this function with the name of the *Microsoft.VisualBasic* namespace.
- Use the Len function to determine the overall length of *str*.

## See Also

Mid Function, Right Function

# Len Function

## Class

Microsoft.VisualBasic.Strings

## Syntax

```
Dim result As Integer = Len(expression)
```

*expression* (required; any)
   Any valid variable name, object, or expression

## Description

The Len function returns the number of characters within a string or the storage size in bytes for a given variable.

## Usage at a Glance

- If *expression* contains Nothing, Len returns 0.

- For string variables, Len returns the number of characters in the string. For all other types, Len returns the number of bytes required to store the content.

- If *expression* is an array, you must also specify a valid subscript. Len cannot be used to determine the total number of elements in, or the total size of, an array.

- Len cannot accurately report the number of bytes required to store structures that contain variable-length strings. If you need to know how many bytes of storage space will be required by a structure that includes string members, you can fix the length of the strings by using the <VBFixedString(*length*)> attribute in the Structure statement. For details, see the *Structure...End Structure Statement* entry.

- For strings, Len is functionally similar to the String data type's Length public instance method, although there are some differences for empty and nonstandard strings.

## See Also

Structure...End Structure Statement, VBFixedString Attribute

# Like Operator

## Syntax

```
Dim result As Boolean = string Like pattern
```

*string* (required; *String*)
  The string to be tested against *pattern*

*pattern* (required; *String*)
  A series of characters used as rules by which *string* is evaluated

## Description

The Like operator indicates whether *string* matches *pattern* (True) or not (False). In general, characters match themselves; a pattern of "abc" matches a string of "abc." But there are a few special characters that enable generic pattern matching.

| Character | Meaning |
|---|---|
| ? | Matches any single character |
| * | Matches zero or more characters |
| # | Matches any single digit (0–9) |
| [*list*] | Matches any single character in *list* |
| [!*list*] | Matches any single character except those in *list* |

The characters are used together to form patterns. For instance, the pattern "a?###" matches the letter a followed by any single character and then followed by three digits.

The *list* character in square brackets may include a simple set of characters, like "[3kd]," but it can also use the hyphen (-) character to specify a range, such as "[a-m0-9]," which specifies the lowercase letters a through m or the digits 0 through 9. Use a hyphen at the beginning or end of *list* to match the hyphen character.

To use special characters, such as #, as normal characters, enclose them in square brackets.

## Usage at a Glance

- If either *string* or *pattern* is Nothing, then *result* will be Nothing.

- The default comparison method for the Like operator is binary (case sensitive). This can be overridden using the OptionCompare statement. The overall sort order is based on the code page currently being used, as determined by the Windows regional settings.

- The exclamation point, when used outside of square brackets, matches itself.

- Different written languages place different priorities on particular characters in relation to sort order. Therefore, the same program using the same data may yield different results when run on machines in different parts of the world, depending upon the locale settings of the systems.

- Regular expressions provide an even more powerful method for searching and comparing strings. You can use regular expressions through the .NET Framework's *System.Text.RegularExpressions.RegEx* class.

## Example

The following example matches a U.S. Social Security number, which is three groups of digits, 3, 2, and 4 digits, respectively. The groups are separated by hyphens.

```
Public Function IsSSN(ByVal testText As String) As Boolean
    If (testText Like "###-##-####") Then
        Return True
    Else
        Return False
    End if
End Function
```

# LineInput Function

## Class

Microsoft.VisualBasic.FileSystem

## Syntax

```
Dim result As String = LineInput(fileNumber)
```

*filenumber* (required; Integer)
Any valid file number of a file opened with FileOpen

## Description

The LineInput function returns a single line of text from a file opened in Input mode. Single lines are delimited by carriage returns (vbCr) or carriage return/line-feed pairs (vbCrLf). The line-delimiting characters are not included in the returned string.

## Usage at a Glance

- After reading a line, the file pointer advances to the first character after the end of the line, or to the end of file if there are no more lines.

- Data read with the LineInput function is normally written to the source file with the Print and PrintLine procedures.

## Example

The following code reads all of the lines in a text file and sends them to the Output window:

```
Dim fileID As Integer = FreeFile( )
FileOpen(fileID, "c:\data.txt", OpenMode.Input, OpenAccess.Read)
Do While Not EOF(fileID)
    Console.WriteLine(LineInput(fileID))
Loop
FileClose(fileID)
```

## Version Differences

- The LineInput function differs syntactically from the LineInput statement used in VB 6.

- In Visual Basic 2005, the *My.Computer.FileSystem* object provides more robust access to file-management features.

## See Also

Print, PrintLine Procedures

---

# Loc Function

## Class

Microsoft.VisualBasic.FileSystem

## Syntax

```
Dim result As Long = Loc(fileNumber)
```

*fileNumber (required; Integer)*
   Any valid file number of a file opened with FileOpen

## Description

The Loc function indicates the current 0-based position within an open file.

## Usage at a Glance

- For files opened in Binary mode, Loc returns the position of the last byte read or written. For files opened in Random mode, Loc returns the record number of the last record read or written. For files opened in Input or Output modes (sequential), Loc returns the current byte position in the file, divided by 128.

- For sequential files, the return value of Loc is not consistent and should not be used.

- The current position in the file cannot be changed using the Loc function.

## Version Differences

In Visual Basic 2005, the *My.Computer.FileSystem* object provides more robust access to file-management features.

## See Also

FileOpen Procedure, LOF Function, Seek Function

---

# Lock Procedure

## Class

Microsoft.VisualBasic.FileSystem

## Syntax

```
Lock(fileNumber[, record])
```

or:

```
Lock(fileNumber[, fromRecord, toRecord])
```

*fileNumber* *(required; Integer)*
 Any valid file number of a file opened with FileOpen

*record* *(optional; Long)*
 The 1-based record or byte number at which to commence the lock

*fromRecord* *(optional; Long)*
 The first 1-based record or byte number to lock

*toRecord* *(optional; Long)*
 The last 1-based record or byte number to lock

## Description

The Lock procedure prevents another process from accessing a record, section, or whole file until it is unlocked by the Unlock procedure. Use the Lock procedure in situations where multiple programs or more than one instance of your program may need read-and-write access to the same data file.

## Usage at a Glance

- If only the *fileNumber* argument is included, the entire file is locked.

- *record* is interpreted as a record number in Random files and as a byte number in Binary files.

- The Lock procedure locks an entire file opened in Input or Output (sequential) mode, regardless of any record number arguments.

- Attempting to access a locked file or portion of a file generates a "Permission denied" error.

- The matching Unlock procedure must include the same arguments.

- You must take care to remove all file locks with the Unlock procedure before either closing a file or ending the application; otherwise, you can leave the file in an unstable state. Where appropriate, error-handling code must correctly unlock any locks that are no longer necessary.

## Version Differences

- In VB 6, the *fromRecord* argument can be left blank to lock all records up to *toRecord*. This syntax is not supported in .NET.

- In the VB 6 Lock statement, you can separate the *fromRecord* and *toRecord* arguments with the To keyword. In the .NET Lock procedure, this syntax is not supported.

- In Visual Basic 2005, the *My.Computer.FileSystem* object provides more robust access to file-management features.

## See Also

Unlock Procedure

---

# LOF Function

## Class

Microsoft.VisualBasic.FileSystem

## Syntax

```
Dim result As Long = LOF(fileNumber)
```

*fileNumber (required; Integer)*
Any valid file number of a file opened with FileOpen

## Description

The LOF function returns the size of an open file in bytes.

## Usage at a Glance

LOF works only on an open file; if you need to know the size of a file that isn't open, use the FileLen function.

## Example

The following example shows how to use the LOF function to prevent reading past the end of a file in binary mode:

```
Dim oneChar As Char
Dim fileID As Integer = FreeFile( )

FileOpen(fileID, "c:\data.txt", OpenMode.Binary, OpenAccess.Read)
Do While (Loc(fileID) < LOF(fileID))
   FileGet(fileID, oneChar)
   Console.WriteLine(Loc(fileID) & ": " & oneChar)
Loop
FileClose(fileID)
```

## Version Differences

In Visual Basic 2005, the *My.Computer.FileSystem* object provides more robust access to file-management features.

## See Also

FileLen Function, FileOpen Procedure

---

# Log Function

## Class
System.Math

## Syntax
```
Dim result As Double = Math.Log(d)
```
or:
```
Dim result As Double = Math.Log(a, newBase)
```
*d, a (required; Double)*
　　A numeric expression greater than zero
*newBase (required; Double)*
　　The base of the logarithm

## Description
The *Log* function returns the natural (base *e*) logarithm of a given number (the first syntax), or the logarithm of a given number in a specified base (the second syntax).

## Usage at a Glance
- The *Log* function is the inverse of the *Exp* function.
- This is a shared member of the *System.Math* class, so it can be used without an instance.
- You can calculate base-*n* logarithms for any number, *x*, by dividing the natural logarithm of *x* by the natural logarithm of *n*:
  ```
  Logn(x) = Log(x) / Log(n)
  ```
  For example, you can replicate the Log10 function using this method:
  ```
  Static Function Log10(ByVal x As Double) As Double
      Return Log(x) / Log(10#)
  End Function
  ```
- The inverse trigonometric functions, which are not intrinsic to VB, can be computed using the value returned by the *Log* function. The functions and their formulas are:

  *Inverse hyperbolic sine*
  ```
  HArcsin(x) = Log(x + Sqrt(x * (x + 1)))
  ```
  *Inverse hyperbolic cosine*
  ```
  HArccos(x) = Log(x + Sqrt(x * (x - 1)))
  ```
  *Inverse hyperbolic tangent*
  ```
  HArctan(x) = Log((1 + x) / (1 - x)) / 2
  ```
  *Inverse hyperbolic secant*
  ```
  HArcsec(x) = Log((Sqrt(-x * (x + 1)) + 1) / x)
  ```
  *Inverse hyperbolic cosecant*
  ```
  HArccosec(x) = Log((Sign(x) * _
      Sqrt(x * x + 1) + 1) / x)
  ```
  *Inverse hyperbolic cotangent*
  ```
  HArccotan(x) = Log((x + 1) / (x - 1)) / 2
  ```

Exp Function, Log10 Function

## Log10 Function

### Class
System.Math

### Syntax
```
Dim result As Double = Math.Log10(d)
```
*d  (required; Double)*
A numeric expression greater than zero

### Description
The *Log10* function returns the common (base 10) logarithm of a given number.

### Usage at a Glance
- The common logarithm satisfies the equation:
  ```
  10^Log10(x) = x
  ```
- This is a shared member of the *System.Math* class, so it can be used without an instance.

### Version Differences
The *Log10* function did not exist in VB 6.

### See Also
Exp Function, Log Function

## LSet Function

### Class
Microsoft.VisualBasic.Strings

### Syntax
```
Dim result As String = LSet(source, length)
```
*source  (required; String)*
The string to be left-aligned

*length  (required; Integer)*
The length of the returned string

### Description
The LSet function left-aligns a string.

### Usage at a Glance

- If the length of *source* is greater than or equal to *length*, the function returns only the leftmost *length* characters.

- If the length of *source* is less than *length*, spaces are added to the right of the returned string so that its length becomes *length*.

### Version Differences

- In VB 6, LSet was implemented as a kind of assignment statement. Because it is implemented as a function in .NET, its syntax is completely different.

- In VB 6, LSet could be used only with fixed-length strings. In .NET, LSet works with all string data.

### See Also

RSet Function

## LTrim Function

### Class

Microsoft.VisualBasic.Strings

### Syntax

```
Dim result As String = LTrim(str)
```

str  *(required; String)*
    A valid string expression

### Description

The LTrim function removes any leading spaces from *str*.

### Usage at a Glance

If *str* is Nothing, LTrim returns Nothing.

### See Also

RTrim Function, Trim Function

## MarshalAs Attribute

### Class

System.Runtime.InteropServices.MarshalAsAttribute

### Applies To

Field, Parameter, ReturnValue

### Constructor

```
New(unmanagedType)
```

*unmanagedType (required; UnmanagedType enumeration)*
Indicates the unmanaged COM data type to which the data is to be converted. One of the *UnmanagedType* enumeration members (see below).

## Properties

*Value (UnmanagedType enumeration)*
The unmanaged COM data type that the managed .NET data is to be marshaled as. Defined through the constructor's *unmanagedType* parameter. One of the *UnmanagedType* enumeration members (see below).

## Fields

*ArraySubType (UnmanagedType enumeration)*
The subtype of an array of type *ByValArray* or *LPArray*. It is used when an array contains strings. This allows the runtime to correctly marshal a string array to COM. One of the *UnmanagedType* enumeration members (see below).

*MarshalCookie (String)*
An undefined field that can be used to pass user-defined data to a custom marshaler. The value of the MarshalCookie field as passed to the custom marshaler's *GetInstance* method.

*MarshalType (String)*
The fully qualified name of a custom marshaler. It is required if the *Value* property is set to `CustomMarshaler`.

*MarshalTypeRef (Type)*
Implements the *MarshalType* value as a *Type* rather than as a string.

*SafeArraySubType (VarEnum enumeration)*
The data type of a SafeArray. One of the *System.Runtime.InteropServices. VarEnum* enumeration values:

| Value | Description |
| --- | --- |
| VT_ARRAY | A SAFEARRAY pointer |
| VT_BLOB | A length-prefixed collection of bytes |
| VT_BLOB_OBJECT | A VT_BLOB containing an object |
| VT_BOOL | A Boolean value |
| VT_BSTR | A string of type BSTR |
| VT_BYREF | A value passed by reference |
| VT_CARRAY | A C-style array |
| VT_CF | Clipboard format |
| VT_CLSID | A class identifier (CLSID) |
| VT_CY | A currency value |
| VT_DATE | A date or time value |
| VT_DECIMAL | A decimal value |
| VT_DISPATCH | An IDispatch pointer |
| VT_EMPTY | No specified value |
| VT_ERROR | An SCODE value |
| VT_FILETIME | A FILETIME value |
| VT_HRESULT | An HRESULT value |
| VT_I1 | A signed 8-bit integer |

| Value | Description |
|---|---|
| VT_I2 | A signed 16-bit integer |
| VT_I4 | A signed 32-bit integer |
| VT_I8 | A signed 64-bit integer |
| VT_INT | An integer value |
| VT_LPSTR | A null-terminated string |
| VT_LPWSTR | A null-terminated Unicode string |
| VT_NULL | A null reference (Nothing) |
| VT_PTR | A pointer |
| VT_R4 | A floating point value |
| VT_R8 | A double value |
| VT_RECORD | A user-defined type |
| VT_SAFEARRAY | A SAFEARRAY |
| VT_STORAGE | A named storage entry |
| VT_STORED_OBJECT | Storage containing an object |
| VT_STREAM | A named stream |
| VT_STREAMED_OBJECT | A stream containing an object |
| VT_UI1 | An unsigned 8-bit integer |
| VT_UI2 | An unsigned 16-bit integer |
| VT_UI4 | An unsigned 32-bit integer |
| VT_UI8 | An unsigned 64-bit integer |
| VT_UINT | An unsigned integer |
| VT_UNKNOWN | An IUnknown pointer |
| VT_USERDEFINED | A user-defined type |
| VT_VARIANT | A VARIANT far pointer |
| VT_VECTOR | A simple counted array |
| VT_VOID | A C-style void |

*SafeArrayUserDefinedSubType (Type)*
> The user-defined type of the SAFEARRAY. This field is used only when the value of the SafeArraySubType field is VT_UNKNOWN, VT_DISPATCH, or VT_RECORD.

*SizeConst (Integer)*
> The number of elements in a fixed-length array.

*SizeParamIndex (Short)*
> Indicates which zero-based parameter contains a count of array elements.

## Description

The <MarshalAs> attribute defines the correct type conversion between managed and unmanaged data. Unmanaged types are defined by the following *System.Runtime. InteropServices.UnmanagedType* enumeration values.

| Value | Description |
|---|---|
| AnsiBStr | An ANSI BSTR (a character string whose first byte indicates the string length). |
| AsAny | Dynamic type determination at runtime. |
| Bool | 4-byte Boolean (True <> 0, False = 0). |

| Value | Description |
|---|---|
| BStr | A Unicode BSTR (a character string with first two bytes that indicate the string length). |
| ByValArray | An array passed by value. An array that is a field in a structure must have this attribute. The SizeConst field must be set to the number of array elements, and the ArraySubType field can optionally be set to the unmanaged data type of the array. |
| ByValTStr | An inline fixed-length character array within a structure. The character type is determined by the *CharSet* argument of the containing structure's <StructLayout> attribute. |
| Currency | A COM Currency data type. Used with the .NET Decimal data type. |
| CustomMarshaler | A custom marshaler class. The class is defined by the MarshalType or MarshalTypeRef field. Additional information can be passed to the custom marshaler by the MarshalCookie field. |
| Error | An HRESULT value. The native .NET type should be a 4-byte signed or unsigned integer. |
| FunctionPtr | A function pointer. |
| I1 | A 1-byte signed integer. |
| I2 | A 2-byte signed integer. |
| I4 | A 4-byte signed integer. |
| I8 | An 8-byte signed integer. |
| IDispatch | A COM IDispatch pointer. |
| Interface | A COM interface pointer. |
| IUnknown | A COM IUnknown pointer. |
| LPArray | A C-style array. Its length is indicated by the SizeConst and SizeParamIndex fields. Optionally, the ArraySubType field can indicate the unmanaged type of string elements within the array. |
| LPStr | An ANSI (single-byte) character string. |
| LPStruct | A pointer to a structure. |
| LPTStr | A platform-dependent character string (ANSI on Windows 9x, Unicode on Windows NT/2000/XP). LPTStr is supported only for platform invoke and not for COM interop. |
| LPWStr | A Unicode (double-byte) character string. |
| R4 | A 4-byte floating point number. |
| R8 | An 8-byte floating point number. |
| SafeArray | A SafeArray (a self-describing array that includes information on its type, dimension, and bounds). |
| Struct | A C-style structure used to marshal .NET formatted classes and value types. |
| SysInt | A platform-dependent integer (4 bytes on 32-bit Windows, 8 bytes on 64-bit Windows). |
| SysUInt | The hardware's natural-sized unsigned integer. |
| TBStr | A length-prefixed, platform-dependent character string (ANSI in Windows 9x, Unicode on Windows NT/2000/XP). |
| U1 | A 1-byte unsigned integer. |
| U2 | A 2-byte unsigned integer. |
| U4 | A 4-byte unsigned integer. |
| U8 | An 8-byte unsigned integer. |
| VariantBool | A 2-byte OLE-defined Boolean value (True = -1, False = 0). |
| VBByRefStr | Allows Visual Basic to change a string in unmanaged code and reflect the change in managed code. |

## See Also

COMClass Attribute

# Max Function

### Class
System.Math

### Syntax
```
Dim result As type = Math.Max(val1, val2)
```
*type* *(required)*
One of the following data types: Byte, Decimal, Double, Integer, Long, SByte, Single, Short, UInteger, ULong, or UShort

*val1, val2* *(required; any valid numeric expression of type type)*
Two valid numbers to be compared

### Description
The *Max* function returns the maximum of *val1* and *val2*.

### Usage at a Glance
- If Option Strict is Off and the two values have different numeric data types, the narrower data type is automatically converted to the wider data type before use in the function.
- This is a shared member of the *System.Math* class, so it can be used without an instance.

### Version Differences
The *Max* function did not exist in VB 6.

### See Also
Min Function

---

# Me Keyword

### Syntax
```
Me
```

### Description
The Me keyword represents a reference to the current class from within the class.

### Usage at a Glance
- Me is an explicit reference to the current class or type as defined by the Class... EndClass construct or similar construct.
- Me is particularly useful when passing an instance of the current class as a parameter to a routine outside the class.

### Example
This example shows how the Me keyword can be used to access class elements masked by local variables with the same name.

```
Public Class TestClass
    Private sampleData As Integer

    Private Sub CheckTheData( )
        Dim sampleData As String = "abc"
        Me.sampleData = 5
        MsgBox(sampleData)          ' Displays "abc"
        MsgBox(Me.sampleData)       ' Displays "5"
    End Sub
End Class
```

### See Also

MyBase Keyword, MyClass Keyword

---

## Mid Function

### Class

Microsoft.VisualBasic.Strings

### Syntax

```
Dim result = String = Mid(str, start[, length])
```

*str* *(required; String)*
> The expression from which to return a substring

*start* *(required; Long)*
> The starting position of the substring

*length* *(optional; Long)*
> The length of the substring to extract

### Description

The Mid function returns a substring of a specified length from a given string.

### Usage at a Glance

- If *str* contains Nothing, Mid returns Nothing.
- If *start* is greater than the length of *str*, a zero-length string is returned. An error occurs if *start* is less than zero.
- If *length* is omitted, or if selecting *length* characters would exceed the length of the string, all characters from *start* to the end of *str* are returned.
- Use the Len function to determine the total length of *str*.
- The Mid function corresponds to the String data type's *Substring* method. In the following code, the two assignments to the twoOnly variable are identical.

  ```
  Dim twoOnly As String
  Dim threeNumbers As String = "One Two Three"
  twoOnly = Mid(threeNumbers, 5, 3)
  twoOnly = threeNumbers.Substring(4, 3)
  ```

  The *Substring* method uses a zero-based index to determine the starting position of the substring.

## Example

The following example extracts the final directory name from a file path. For instance, in the path *c:\folder1\folder2\file.txt*, the function returns "folder2."

```
Public Function FinalDirectory(ByVal filePath As String) As String
    ' ----- Return the last directory name.
    Dim lastSlash As Integer
    Dim nextSlash As Integer

    ' ----- Check for missing data.
    If (Trim(filePath) = "") Then Return ""

    ' ----- Don't accept UNC paths.
    If (VisualBasic.Left(filePath, 1) = "\") Then Return ""

    ' ----- Find the slashes that surround the directory.
    lastSlash = InStrRev(filePath, "\")
    nextSlash = InStrRev(filePath, "\", lastSlash - 1)
    If (nextSlash = 0) Then Return ""

    ' ----- Extract and return the name.
    Return Mid(filePath, nextSlash + 1, lastSlash - nextSlash - 1)
End Function
```

## See Also

Left Function, Mid Function, Right Function

---

# Mid Statement

## Syntax

Mid(*target*, *start*[, *length*]) = *expression*

*target* (required; String)
: The name of the string variable to be modified

*start* (required; Long)
: The position within *target* at which the replacement begins

*length* (optional; Long)
: The number of characters in *target* to replace

*expression* (required; String)
: The string used to replace characters within *target*

## Description

The Mid statement replaces a section of a string with characters from another string.

## Usage at a Glance

- If you omit *length*, as many characters of *string* as can fit into *target* are used.
- If *start* + *length* is greater then the portion of *target* to be replaced, *string* is truncated to fit in the same space as that portion of *target*. The length of *target* is not altered by the Mid statement.
- If *start* is less than zero, an error occurs.

- If *string* is Nothing, a runtime error occurs.
- VB includes the Replace function, which enhances the functionality of the Mid statement by allowing you to specify the number of times a replacement is carried out in the same string.
- Because it is a statement, this version of Mid does not accept named arguments. Mid is implemented by the compiler rather than by the String data type.

### See Also

Mid Function

## Min Function

### Class

System.Math

### Syntax

```
Dim result As type = Math.Min(val1, val2)
```

*type* (required)
One of the following data types: Byte, Decimal, Double, Integer, Long, SByte, Single, Short, UInteger, ULong, or UShort

*val1, val2* (required; expressions of type type)
Two valid numbers to be compared

### Description

The *Min* function returns the minimum of *val1* and *val2*.

### Usage at a Glance

- If Option Strict is Off and the two values have different numeric data types, the narrower data type is automatically converted to the wider data type before use in the function.
- This is a shared member of the *System.Math* class, so it can be used without an instance.

### Version Differences

The *Min* function did not exist in VB 6.

### See Also

Max Function

## Minute Function

### Class

Microsoft.VisualBasic.DateAndTime

## Syntax

```
Dim result As Integer = Minute(timeValue)
```

*timeValue* *(required; Date)*
    The source date from which to extract the minute

## Description

The Minute function returns a value from 0 to 59, representing the minute of the supplied date or time.

## Usage at a Glance

With Option Strict set to On, the source value must first be converted to a Date data type. You can use the CDate function for this purpose. The IsDate function can also be used to confirm that the source expression is a valid date.

## See Also

DatePart Function, Hour Function, Second Function

---

# MIRR Function

## Class

Microsoft.VisualBasic.Financial

## Syntax

```
Dim result As Double = MIRR(valueArray( ), financeRate, reinvestRate)
```

*valueArray( )* *(required; array of Double)*
    An array of cash-flow values

*financeRate* *(required; Double)*
    The interest rate paid as the cost of financing.

*reinvestRate* *(required; Double)*
    The interest rate received on gains from a cash investment.

## Description

The MIRR function calculates the modified internal rate of return, the rate calculated from a series of payments and receipts that are financed at different rates.

## Usage at a Glance

* *valueArray* must be a one-dimensional array that contains at least one negative value (a payment) and at least one positive value (a receipt). The order of elements within the array should reflect the order in which payments and receipts occur.

* The rates are supplied as a decimal percent. For example, 10% is stated as 0.1.

* Each element of *valueArray* represents a payment or a receipt that occurs at a regular time interval. If this is not the case, MIRR will return erroneous results.

## See Also

IRR Function

# MkDir Procedure

## Class
Microsoft.VisualBasic.FileSystem

## Syntax
```
MkDir(path)
```
*path (required; String)*
The name of the directory to be created

## Description
The `MkDir` procedure creates a new directory on a drive.

## Usage at a Glance
- *path* can be a relative or absolute path, either of a new local or remote directory.
- An error occurs if the specified directory already exists.
- `MkDir` does not automatically make the new directory the current working (default) directory.

## Version Differences
Visual Basic 2005 includes a *My.Computer.FileSystem.CreateDirectory* method that provides similar functionality.

## See Also
RmDir Procedure

---

# Mod Operator

## Syntax
```
Dim result As type = number1 Mod number2
```
*type (required)*
One of the following data types: `Byte`, `Decimal`, `Double`, `Integer`, `Long`, `Single`, or `Short`

*number1 (required; any valid numeric expression)*
A numerator in a division expression

*number2 (required; any valid numeric expression)*
A nonzero denominator in a division expression

## Description
The `Mod` operator returns the modulus, that is, the remainder when *number1* is divided by *number2*. This return value is a nonnegative integral data type.

## Usage at a Glance
- Floating point numbers are rounded to integers before the division.
- If *number1* or *number2* is `Nothing`, an error occurs.

---

- The Mod operator returns the data type of *number1* and *number2* if they are the same type, or the widest data type of *number1* and *number2* if they are different.

## Example

```
MsgBox(10 Mod 3)    ' returns 1
```

## Version Differences

The Mod operator can be overloaded beginning in the 2005 edition of Visual Basic. The custom overload can assign any logic or restrictions on its use.

## See Also

IEEERemainder Function

---

# Module...End Module Statement

## Syntax

```
[accessModifier] Module name
    [statements]
End Module
```

*accessModifier* (optional)
Specifies the scope and accessibility of the module. One of the following access levels:

| Access level | Description |
| --- | --- |
| Public | The module is publicly accessible anywhere, both inside and outside of the project. |
| Friend | The module is accessible only within the project that contains the module definition. |

If omitted, the Friend access level is used.

*name* (required)
The name of the code module.

*statements* (optional)
Code that defines the members of the module.

## Description

The Module...End Module statement defines a code block as a code module. A module is similar to a class where every member is Shared by default. Modules may contain fields, properties, methods, events, and other types.

## Usage at a Glance

- Modules may not be nested, nor may modules inherit from any other type.
- Since all members of a module are essentially Shared, modules cannot be instantiated as objects.

## Version Differences

The Module statement is new to VB under .NET, but the idea of a module was always part of Visual Basic. VB 6 placed each code module in a separate BAS file, which rendered beginning and ending statements unnecessary. A single VB source code file in .NET, on the other hand, can contain multiple code modules and other types.

### See Also
Class...End Class Statement

## Month Function

### Class
Microsoft.VisualBasic.DateAndTime

### Syntax
```
Dim result As Integer = Month(dateValue)
```
*dateValue (required; Date)*
The source date from which to extract the month

### Description
The Month function returns a value from 1 to 12, representing the month of the supplied date.

### Usage at a Glance
With Option Strict set to On, the source value must first be converted to a Date data type. You can use the CDate function for this purpose. The IsDate function can also be used to confirm that the source expression is a valid date.

### See Also
DatePart Function, Day Function, MonthName Function, Year Function

## MonthName Function

### Class
Microsoft.VisualBasic.DateAndTime

### Syntax
```
Dim result As String = MonthName(month[, abbreviate])
```
*month (required; Integer)*
The ordinal number of the month, from 1 to 13 (that's right, 13).

*abbreviate (optional; Boolean)*
A flag to indicate if an abbreviated month name should be returned. The default value is False.

### Description
The MonthName function returns the name of a given month, based on the current regional settings in effect. For example, a *month* of 1 in an English-speaking region returns "January," or "Jan" if *abbreviate* is set to True.

## Usage at a Glance

- The *month* value must be an integer; it cannot be a date. Use the Month function to obtain a month number from a date.

- Some regional calendar systems support 13 months. A 13th month is only supported under such calendars; when a 12-month calendar is in effect, a value of 13 returns an empty string.

- If *month* has a fractional portion, it is rounded before use.

- MonthName with *abbreviate* set to False is the equivalent of Format(dateValue,"MMMM").

- MonthName with *abbreviate* set to True is the equivalent of Format(dateValue,"MMM").

## See Also

Month Function, WeekdayName Function

# MsgBox Function

## Class

Microsoft.VisualBasic.Interaction

## Syntax

```
Dim result As MsgBoxResult = MsgBox(prompt[, buttons[, title]])
```

*prompt* *(required; String)*
The text of the message to display in the message dialog box.

*buttons* *(optional; MsgBoxStyle enumeration)*
One or more constants (either added or Or'd together) that set various display and action properties of the dialog box. The constants are taken from the *Microsoft.VisualBasic.MsgBoxStyle* enumeration:

| Enumeration member | Value | Description |
|---|---|---|
| OKOnly | 0 | Buttons: Display OK button only |
| OKCancel | 1 | Buttons: Display OK and Cancel buttons |
| AbortRetryIgnore | 2 | Buttons: Display Abort, Retry, and Ignore buttons |
| YesNoCancel | 3 | Buttons: Display Yes, No, and Cancel buttons |
| YesNo | 4 | Buttons: Display Yes and No buttons |
| RetryCancel | 5 | Buttons: Display Retry and Cancel buttons |
| Critical | 16 | Icon: Display Critical Message icon |
| Question | 32 | Icon: Display Warning Query icon |
| Exclamation | 48 | Icon: Display Warning Message icon |
| Information | 64 | Icon: Display Information Message icon |
| DefaultButton1 | 0 | Default Button: Default to first button |
| DefaultButton2 | 256 | Default Button: Default to second button |
| DefaultButton3 | 512 | Default Button: Default to third button |

| Enumeration member | Value | Description |
|---|---|---|
| DefaultButton4 | 768 | Default Button: Default to fourth button |
| ApplicationModal | 0 | Modality: Response required to continue application |
| SystemModal | 4096 | Modality: Response required to continue application, and the message box appears on top of all other windows |

If omitted, this parameter defaults to OKOnly.

*title (optional; String)*
The title displayed in the title bar of the message dialog box. If omitted, the name of the application or project is used.

### Description

The MsgBox function displays a dialog box containing a message, buttons, and an optional icon. A value indicating the button clicked by the user is returned by the function, one of the *Microsoft.VisualBasic.MsgBoxResult* enumeration values:

| Enumeration member | Value | Button clicked |
|---|---|---|
| OK | 1 | OK |
| Cancel | 2 | Cancel |
| Abort | 3 | Abort |
| Retry | 4 | Retry |
| Ignore | 5 | Ignore |
| Yes | 6 | Yes |
| No | 7 | No |

If the message box contains a Cancel button, the Esc key simulates a click on that button. The Enter key simulates a click on the currently highlighted button.

### Usage at a Glance

- *prompt* can contain approximately 1,024 characters, including special characters such as the vbCrLf constant.
- *Application modality* means that the user cannot access other parts of the application until a response to the message box has been given.
- *System modality* used to mean that all applications were suspended until the message box was closed. However, this functionality was only supported in Microsoft Windows 3.x and earlier. In newer versions of Windows, using system modality causes the message box to "stay on top" of all application windows.
- The message box is always displayed in the center of the screen.
- If your application is to run out-of-process on a remote machine, you should remove all MsgBox functions, since they will not appear on the user's workstation but on the monitor of the remote system.
- MsgBox should never be used in ASP.NET applications.
- The *System.Windows.Forms.MessageBox* class provides enhanced message box functionality, including the ability to specify online help information.

## Version Differences

In VB 6, the MsgBox function includes a *helpFile* parameter and a *context* parameter, both used with online help files. These two parameters are not supported in .NET.

## See Also

InputBox Function

---

# MTAThread Attribute

## Class

System.MTAThreadAttribute

## Applies To

Method

## Constructor

New( )

## Properties

None defined

## Description

The <MTAThread> attribute indicates that the application to which the program element belongs uses the *multithreaded apartment* model for COM interop. The attribute should be applied to the application's *Main* method or subroutine. This attribute only applies to applications that use COM interop.

The <MTAThread> attribute is similar to setting a *System.Threading.Thread* object's *ApartmentState* property to *ApartmentState.MTA*. The difference is that the <MTAThread> attribute creates a multithreaded apartment at startup, while setting the property does it only from the point that the property is set.

## See Also

STAThread Attribute

---

# MyBase Keyword

## Syntax

MyBase

## Description

The MyBase keyword provides a reference to the base class from within a derived class. If you want to call a member of the base class from within a derived class, you can use the syntax:

MyBase.*MemberName*

where *MemberName* is the name of the member. This will resolve any ambiguity if the derived class also has a member of the same name.

---

## Usage at a Glance

- `MyBase` will call through the chain of inherited classes until it finds a callable implementation. For example, in the code:

```
Public Class TestClass
    ...
End Class

Public Class TestClass2
    Inherits TestClass

    Public Function ShowType() As Type
        Return MyBase.GetType
    End Function
End Class
```

the call to `ShowType` is eventually resolved as a call to *Object.GetType*, since all classes are ultimately derived from the *System.Object* class.

- `MyBase` cannot be used to call `Private` class members in the base class.
- `MyBase` cannot be used to call base class members marked as `MustOverride`.
- `MyBase` is commonly used to call an overridden member from the member that overrides it in the derived class.
- The `MyBase` keyword can be used to call the constructor of the base class to instantiate a member of that class, as in:

```
MyBase.New(...)
```

## Version Differences

The `MyBase` keyword is new to VB under .NET.

## See Also

Me Keyword, MyClass Keyword

---

# MyClass Keyword

## Syntax

```
MyClass
```

## Description

The `MyClass` keyword provides a reference to the class in which the keyword is used.

## Usage at a Glance

- When using `MyClass` (as opposed to `Me`) to qualify a method invocation, as in:

```
MyClass.IncSalary()
```

the method is treated as if declared using the `NotOverridable` keyword. Regardless of the type of the object at runtime, the method called is the one declared in the class containing this statement (and not in any derived classes). The upcoming example illustrates this difference between `MyClass` and `Me`.

- `MyClass` cannot be used with shared members.

---

## Example

The following code defines a base class and a derived class, each of which has an IncSalary method.

```
Public Class BaseClass
    Public Overridable Function SuperSize _
        (ByVal startValue As Long) As Long
    ' ----- Double it!
        Return startValue * 2
    End Function

    Public Sub ShowSuperSize(ByVal startValue As Long)
        MsgBox(Me.SuperSize(startValue))
        MsgBox(MyClass.SuperSize(startValue))
    End Sub
End Class

Public Class DerivedClass
    Inherits BaseClass

    Public Overrides Function SuperSize _
        (ByVal startValue As Long) As Long
    ' ----- Triple it!
        Return startValue * 3
    End Function
End Class
```

Consider the following code, placed in a form module:

```
Dim testWithBase As New BaseClass( )
Dim testWithDerived As New DerivedClass( )

Dim pointToTest As BaseClass

pointToTest = testWithBase
pointToTest.ShowSuperSize(100)   ' Shows 200, 200

pointToTest = testWithDerived
pointToTest.ShowSuperSize(100)   ' Shows 300, 200
```

The first call to ShowSuperSize is made using a variable of type BaseClass that refers to an object of type BaseClass. In this case, both calls:

```
Me.ShowSuperSize
MyClass.ShowSuperSize
```

return the same value, because they both call BaseClass.SuperSize.

However, in the second case, the variable of type BaseClass holds a reference to an object of type DerivedClass. In this case, Me refers to an object of type DerivedClass, whereas MyClass still refers to BaseClass. So the statement:

```
Me.ShowSuperSize(100)
```

returns 300, while:

```
MyClass.ShowSuperSize(100)
```

returns 200.

**Version Differences**

The My Class keyword is new to VB under .NET.

**See Also**

Me Keyword, MyBase Keyword

---

## Namespace Statement

**Syntax**

```
Namespace name
    component types
End Namespace
```

*name (required)*

The name of the namespace, either a single namespace component or a hierarchy section of namespaces, as in SomeCompany.SomeApplication

*component types (required)*

The elements that are being declared as part of the namespace, including enumerations, structures, interfaces, classes, delegates, modules, and other nested namespaces

**Description**

The Namespace statement declares a namespace and specifies the items in the namespace.

**Usage at a Glance**

- Namespaces are used in the .NET Framework as an organized method of exposing program components to other programs and applications.
- Namespaces are always Public, although types defined within a namespace can have varying levels of declared access.

---

## New Keyword

**Syntax**

```
New type[(arglist)]
```

*type (required; any)*

The data type of the newly created object.

*arglist (optional; any)*

A list of comma-delimited parameters sent to the constructor *type*. If using a default constructor that has no parameters, *arglist* can be left off completely.

**Description**

The New keyword creates a new instance of *type*. The New keyword is often used in assignment statements or to create a new onetime instance to pass as a parameter to a function.

```
someVariable = New InterestingClass
```

---

New instances of objects are also created as part of the Dim statement syntax. See the *Dim Statement* entry in this chapter for additional information.

A completely different use of the New keyword is in the building of constructors. If you create a class Sub procedure and give it the name New, it becomes a class constructor.

### Usage at a Glance

- The New keyword is only used with reference types.

- A type's constructor is called when you use the New keyword on a declaration. You may include constructor parameters after *type*. If no parameters are supplied, the default parameterless constructor is used.

### See Also

Dim Statement, Sub Statement

## Nothing Keyword

### Syntax

```
Nothing
```

### Description

The Nothing keyword represents an undefined instance of an object. Reference types that have not yet been assigned an instance have a value of Nothing.

Value types never have a value of Nothing; they always have a value assigned. Assigning Nothing to a value type assigns that variable the default value for that type. For instance, in the statement:

```
Dim unassignedValue As Integer = Nothing
```

the unassignedValue variable is assigned zero, the default value for Integer variables.

### Usage at a Glance

- To test a value for Nothing, do not use the equals comparison operator (=). Instead, use the IsNothing function or the Is operator.

  ```
  If (IsNothing(someVariable) = True) Then...
  ```

  ```
  If (someVariable Is Nothing) Then...
  ```

### See Also

Is Operator, IsNot Operator, IsNothing Function

## Now Property

### Class

Microsoft.VisualBasic.DateAndTime

### Syntax

```
Dim result As Date = Now
```

## Description

The Now property returns the current system date and time.

## Usage at a Glance

- The Now property is read-only.

- The Now property is a wrapper for the Date data type's *Now* shared property. As a result, calls to the *Date.Now* property may offer a slight performance improvement over calls to the *DateAndTime.Now* property.

## See Also

Today Property

---

# NPer Function

## Class

Microsoft.VisualBasic.Financial

## Syntax

```
Dim result As Double = NPer(rate, pmt, pv [, fv [, due]])
```

*rate  (required; Double)*
> The interest rate per period.

*per  (required; Double)*
> The period for which a payment is to be computed.

*pv  (required; Double)*
> The present value of a series of future payments.

*fv  (optional; Double)*
> The future value or cash balance after the final payment. If omitted, the default value is 0.

*due  (optional; DueDate enumeration)*
> A value indicating when payments are due, from the *Microsoft.VisualBasic.DueDate* enumeration. *DueDate.EndOfPeriod* indicates that payments are due at the end of the payment period; *DueDate.BegOfPeriod* indicates that payments are due at the beginning of the period. If omitted, the default value is *DueDate.EndOfPeriod.*

## Description

The NPer function determines the number of payment periods for an annuity, based on regular fixed payments and a fixed interest rate. An annuity is a series of fixed cash payments made over a period of time. It can be either a loan or an investment.

## Usage at a Glance

- If *pv* and *fv* represent liabilities, their value is negative; if they represent assets, their value is positive.

- *rate* and *pmt* must be expressed in the same time unit. That is, if *pmt* reflects the monthly payment amount, *rate* must be the monthly interest rate.

- The rate is supplied as a decimal percent. For example, 10% is stated as 0.1.

---

## Example

This sample displays the amount of time needed to pay off a credit card. It uses the NPer function to determine the length of time required.

```
Public Sub HowLongToPay()
    ' ----- Detail the extent of a debt.
    Dim interestRate As Double
    Dim currentBalance As Double
    Dim monthlyPayment As Double
    Dim totalPeriods As Integer

    Try
        currentBalance = CDbl(InputBox("Credit card balance."))
        monthlyPayment = CDbl(InputBox("Monthly payment."))
        interestRate = CDbl(InputBox("Monthly interest rate " & _
            "(use 0.05 for 5%)."))
        totalPeriods = CInt(NPer(interestRate, -monthlyPayment, _
            currentBalance, 0#, DueDate.BegOfPeriod))

        MsgBox("Your credit card balance will be paid in " & _
            totalPeriods & " months. That's " & _
            Int(totalPeriods / 12) & " years and " & _
            (totalPeriods Mod 12) & " months.")
    Catch e As System.Exception
        MsgBox("Unable to compute period because of error " & _
            e.Message)
    End Try
End Sub
```

## See Also

FV Function, IPmt Function, NPV Function, Pmt Function, PPmt Function, PV Function, Rate Function

# NPV Function

## Class

Microsoft.VisualBasic.Financial

## Syntax

```
Dim result As Double = NPV(rate, valueArray())
```

*rate* *(required; Double)*
  The discount rate over the period, expressed as a decimal percent

*valueArray()* *(required; array of Double)*
  An array of cash-flow values

## Description

The NPV function calculates the net present value of an investment based on a series of periodic variable cash-flow events (payments and receipts) and a discount rate. The *net present value* is the value today of a series of future cash-flow events discounted at some rate back to the first day of the investment period.

## Usage at a Glance

- The discount rate is stated as a decimal percent. For example, 10% is stated as 0.1.
- *valueArray* is a one-dimensional array that must contain at least one negative value (a payment) and one positive value (a receipt).
- The NPV investment begins one period before the date of the first cash-flow value and ends with the last cash-flow value in the array.
- NPV requires future cash flows. If the first cash-flow occurs at the beginning of the first period, the first value must be added to the value returned by NPV and must not be included in *valueArray*.
- NPV is like the PV function, except that PV allows cash flows to begin either at the beginning or the end of a period and requires that cash flows be fixed throughout the investment.

## See Also

FV Function, IPmt Function, NPer Function, Pmt Function, PPmt Function, PV Function, Rate Function

---

# Obsolete Attribute

## Class

System.ObsoleteAttribute

## Applies To

Class, Struct, Enum, Constructor, Method, Property, Field, Event, Interface, and Delegate (all program elements except parameters and return values)

## Constructors

New([*message*[, *error*]])

*message* (optional; String)
> Provides relevant information concerning the obsolete element, including possible workarounds.

*error* (optional; Boolean)
> Indicates whether the compiler generates an error if the program element is used. If omitted, the value defaults to False.

## Properties

*IsError (Boolean)*
> Read-only. Value from the *error* constructor parameter.

*Message (String)*
> Read-only. Value from the *message* constructor parameter.

## Description

The <Obsolete> attribute indicates that the program element is obsolete and no longer valid for use.

# Oct Function

## Class
Microsoft.VisualBasic.Conversion

## Syntax
```
Dim result As String = Oct(number)
```
*number  (required; numeric or string value)*
> A number, or a string that can be interpreted as a number. Nonintegral numbers are rounded before conversion.

## Description
The Oct function returns a string that represents the octal value of a numeric expression.

## Usage at a Glance
- Nonintegral numbers are rounded before conversion to octal format. An empty value results in "0." A value of Nothing generates an error.
- The octal result is limited to 22 digits. Numbers larger than this limit result in an overflow error.
- If the source value is a string, it may appear in octal format. Such strings begin with the standard "&O" octal prefix for Visual Basic, as in "&O10" for a decimal value of 8.

## Version Differences
The Visual Basic 6 version of the Oct function only handled up to 11 octal digits. The .NET version handles up to 22 digits.

## See Also
Hex Function

---

# Of Keyword

## Syntax
```
(Of typeParamList)
```
*typeParamList  (required; any)*
> Adds type parameter placeholders that will later enforce strong typing when the related construct is used.

## Description
The Of keyword enables generics, the use of type parameters in a language construct, such as a class definition. Type parameters are used as placeholders for strongly typed data, to be enforced when the related construct is instantiated.

Generics are fully described in Chapter 10, complete with examples.

## Usage at a Glance

Type parameters added with the Of keyword cannot be used with Common Language Specification (CLS) compliant components.

## Version Differences

Generics and the Of keyword are new with Visual Basic 2005.

## See Also

Class...End Class Statement, Delegate Statement, Function Statement, Interface...End Interface Statement, Structure Statement, Sub Statement

---

## On Error Statement

```
On Error { GoTo { label | 0 | -1 } | Resume Next }
```

*label (required, unless 0 or -1 used)*
    A valid label within the procedure

## Description

The On Error statement enables or disables error handling within a procedure. Error handling is performed either by using a Try...Catch...Finally statement or with an On Error statement. The On Error statement has several variations.

On Error GoTo *label*

    When an error occurs, execution continues within the procedure at the line marked with *label*. A Resume statement can be used within that block of code to return to the errant section of code.

On Error GoTo 0

    Disables error handling in the current procedure. This is the same as if no error handlers were ever enabled in the procedure in the first place.

On Error GoTo -1

    Used inside of an error handler to make the code forget that it is inside of an error handler. It says, "Forget that the error ever happened, but don't Resume me back to the earlier part of the code; leave me here."

On Error Resume Next

    When an error occurs, execution continues with the line that follows the errant line. The Err object can be examined for the error details.

## Usage at a Glance

- If you have no error handling in your procedure, or if error handling is disabled, the VB runtime engine will trace back through the call stack until a procedure is reached where error handling is enabled. In that case, the error will be handled by that procedure. However, if no error handler can be found in the call stack, a runtime error occurs, and program execution is halted. (*New in 2005.* Visual Basic 2005 also allows you to include a global error handler that catches errors not caught by another error handler.)

- Use of the On Error Resume Next statement can cause legitimate errors to go unnoticed. Use it with care.

- The following code demonstrates the typical use of the On Error statement.

```
Sub SomeProcedure( )
    On Error Goto ErrorHandler
    ' ... other code goes here ...

CleanupCode:
    ' ... cleanup code goes here ...
    Exit Sub

ErrorHandler:
    ' ... error handling code goes here ...
    Resume CleanupCode
End Sub
```

If cleanup code isn't required within the procedure, the CleanupCode section can be removed (keep the Exit Sub statement), and the error handler can use Resume Next or Exit Sub to complete the error.

- If the calling procedure is responsible for handling the error, the following type of code will do minimal error handling before reporting the error up the call stack.

```
Sub SomeProcedure( )
    On Error Goto ErrorHandler
    ' ... other code goes here ...

    ' ... cleanup code goes here ...
    Exit Sub

ErrorHandler:
    ' ... minimal error handling code goes here ...
    Err.Raise ...   ' passes the error up
    Exit Sub
End Sub
```

- For more information on both unstructured error handling and structured exception handling, see Chapter 11.

### See Also

Err Object

## OpenFileDialog Class

### Namespace

System.Windows.Forms

### Creatable

Yes

### Description

The *OpenFileDialog* class represents a common dialog box for selecting or opening a file. The *OpenFileDialog* class has properties that let you configure, display, and retrieve the results from this dialog box, from which the user selects a single file or multiple files. The dialog box does not open the file(s); it only indicates the file(s) to be opened.

The following list discusses the more interesting members of the *OpenFileDialog* class.

*AddExtension Property*
> Indicates whether the dialog box should automatically add the default file extension to the user-supplied file name. The default value is `True`.

*CheckFileExists Property*
> Indicates whether a warning message should be displayed if the user enters the name of a file that does not exist. The default value is `True`.

*DefaultExt Property*
> Defines the default file extension. The string should consist of the file extension only, without a leading period.

*FileName Property*
> Returns the fully qualified file name—the file name with its complete path and extension. If no file is selected, the property returns an empty string.

*FileNames Property*
> Returns an array of fully qualified file names (with complete paths and extensions) for the files selected by the user. If no file is selected, the property returns an empty array. This property returns a single-element array if the *Multiselect* property is `False` and the user selects a file.

*Filter Property*
> Used to configure a filter string that indicates the types of files (by extension) to display in the dialog box. These types appear in the "Files of type" drop-down control on the dialog box. A single item consists of a file description, a vertical bar, and the file extension (usually "*." plus the file extension). If there are multiple extensions in a single item, they are separated by semicolons. If there are multiple items, they are separated by vertical bars. For example, the following code fragment assigns a filter string for text files and VB source code files:

```
Dim openPrompt As New OpenFileDialog
openPrompt.Filter = _
    "Text files (*.txt; *.vb)|*.txt;*.vb|" & _
    "Visual Basic files (*.vb)|*.vb|" & _
    "All files (*.*)|*.*"
```

*FilterIndex Property*
> Indicates the selected 1-based position in the *Filter* property's item list. The default is 1. If the user selects a different filter, this property is updated to reflect that change.

*InitialDirectory Property*
> Indicates the initial directory to use when first displaying the dialog.

*Multiselect Property*
> Indicates whether the user is allowed to select more than one file.

*OpenFile Method*
> Opens the file selected by the user, returning a *Stream* object. The file is opened in read-only mode.

*ReadOnlyChecked Property*
> Indicates whether the Read Only checkbox is selected on the dialog box. The default is `False`.

*RestoreDirectory Property*
> Indicates whether the current working (default) directory is restored before the dialog box closes. The default value is `False`.

*ShowDialog Method*

Displays the dialog box to the user. Once the user has dismissed the dialog box, the *FileName* and *FileNames* properties can be used to get the user's selection(s).

*ShowReadOnly Property*

Indicates whether the Read Only checkbox should appear on the dialog box.

*Title Property*

Sets the title of the dialog box.

## Example

The following code asks the user for one or more files and then displays the filenames in the Output window.

```
Dim selectFile As New OpenFileDialog
Dim counter As Integer
selectFile.Multiselect = True
If (selectFile.ShowDialog() = DialogResult.OK) Then
    For counter = 0 To UBound(selectFile.FileNames)
        Console.WriteLine(selectFile.FileNames(counter))
    Next counter
End If
```

## Version Differences

The public interfaces used for this *OpenFileDialog* class and the related VB 6 CommonDialog control are quite different.

## See Also

SaveFileDialog Class

---

# Operator Statement

## Syntax

```
Public [Overloads] Shared [Shadows] [Widening | Narrowing] _
    Operator symbol (operand1[, operand2]) [As type]
    [statements]
    Return expression
    [statements]
End Function
```

Overloads *(optional)*

Indicates that more than one declaration of this overloaded operator exists, each with a different argument signature.

Shadows *(optional)*

Indicates that the overloaded operator shadows an identically named element in a base class.

Widening *(optional)*

Indicates that the use of the overloaded operator will never result in the loss of data due to a change in data types.

Narrowing *(optional)*

Indicates that the use of the overloaded operator may possibly result in the loss of data, due to a change in data types.

*symbol* *(required)*

The operator to overload. One of the following operator symbols:

- Unary: +, -, IsFalse, IsTrue, Not, CType
- Binary: +, -, *, /, \, &, ^, >>, <<, = (comparison), <>, >, >=, <, <=, And, Like, Mod, Or, Xor

*operand1* *(required; any)*

The first operand used with the operator. For binary operators, this operand appears to the left of the operator. It has the form:

    [ByVal] *operandName* As *operandType*

where *operandName* is the name of the operand as used in the operator procedure, and *operandType* is the data type as it is used in the operator.

*operand2* *(optional; any)*

The second operand used with the binary operator. This operand appears to the right of the operator. It has the form:

    [ByVal] *operandName* As *operandType*

where *operandName* is the name of the operand as used in the operator procedure, and *operandType* is the data type as it is used in the operator. Its data type may or may not match the data type of *operand1* or of the return *type*.

*type* *(optional; Type)*

The return data type of the operator. This may or may not match the data type of the operand(s).

*statements* *(optional)*

Program code to be executed within the procedure.

*expression* *(optional)*

The value of type *type* to return from the procedure to the calling procedure as a result of the operation.

## Description

*New in 2005.* The Operator statement defines an overloaded operator. Normally, the standard Visual Basic operators can only be used with the built-in data types as defined by the VB compiler. The Operator statement allows you to define new uses for these standard operators.

Operators are fully described, with examples, in the "Operator Overloading" section of Chapter 5.

## Usage at a Glance

- All overloaded operators are Public and Shared. They can be used without a specific instance of the type.
- At least one of the operands must be of the type that contains the overloaded operator definition. When overloading the CType operator, either the operand or the return value must be of that containing data type.
- Certain pairs of operators must be overloaded as a matched set:
  - = and <>
  - > and <
  - >= and <=
  - IsTrue and IsFalse

- The IsTrue and IsFalse operators must return data of type Boolean.
- The << and >> operators must use Integer for the data type of *operand2*.
- The And, Or, Not, and Xor operators overload the bitwise versions of these operators, not the logical versions.
- The AndAlso operator requires that And and IsFalse also be overloaded. Likewise, the OrElse operator requires that Or and IsTrue also be overloaded.

### Version Differences
Operator overloading is new in Visual Basic 2005.

### See Also
Sub Statement

## Option Compare Statement

### Syntax
```
Option Compare {Binary | Text}
```

### Description
The Option Compare statement is used to set the default method for comparing string data within a source code file.

### Usage at a Glance
- A default project-wide setting for Option Compare can be set in the project properties within Visual Studio. The Option Compare statement, when used in a source code file, takes precedence over the project setting.
- When OptionCompare is not used in a file, and there is no project-wide setting, the default comparison method is Binary.
- When OptionCompare is used, it must appear at the start of the module's declarations section, before any types.
- *Binary comparison*—the default text comparison method in Visual Basic—uses the internal binary code of each character to determine the sort order of the characters. Binary comparisons are case sensitive.
- *Text comparison* uses the locale settings of the current system to determine the sort order of the characters. Text comparison is case insensitive.

### See Also
Option Explicit Statement, Option Strict Statement

## Option Explicit Statement

### Syntax
```
Option Explicit [On | Off]
```

## Description

Use the `Option Explicit` statement to generate a compile-time error whenever a variable that has not been declared is used in a source code file.

## Usage at a Glance

- A default project-wide setting for `Option Explicit` can be set in the project properties within Visual Studio. The `Option Explicit` statement, when used in a source code file, takes precedence over the project-wide setting.

- The `Option Explicit` statement must appear in the declarations section of a source code file, before any types.

- In source code files where the `Option Explicit` statement is not used, any undeclared variables are automatically cast as `Object`.

- The default action of `Option Explicit` is `On`, so that:

  ```
  Option Explicit
  ```

  is equivalent to:

  ```
  Option Explicit On
  ```

- It is considered good programming practice to always enable `Option Explicit`. The following example shows why.

  ```
  1:   Dim variable As Integer
  2:   variable = 100
  3:   variable = varable + 50
  4:   MsgBox variable
  ```

  In this code snippet, an integer variable, `variable`, has been declared. However, because the name of the variable has been mistyped on line 3, the message box shows its value as only 100 instead of 150. This is because `varable` is assumed to be an undeclared variable with an initial value of 0. If the `Option Explicit On` statement had been used, the code would not have compiled, and `varable` would have been highlighted as the cause.

- For an ASP.NET page, use the `@PAGE` directive, rather than `Option Explicit`, to require variable declaration. Its syntax is:

  ```
  <%@ Page Language="VB" Explicit=true/false %>
  ```

  By default, `Explicit` is true in ASP.NET pages.

  You can also use the `<system.web>` section of the *web.config* file to require variable declaration for an entire virtual directory or an ASP.NET application by adding an explicit attribute to the `compilation` tag. Its syntax is:

  ```
  <compilation explicit="true/false">
  ```

  In both cases, true corresponds to `Option Explicit On`, and false corresponds to `Option Explicit Off`.

## See Also

Option Compare Statement, Option Strict Statement

---

# Option Strict Statement

## Syntax

```
Option Strict [On | Off]
```

## Description

Use the Option Strict statement to allow or prevent VB from making any *implicit* data type conversions that are *narrowing* in a source code file. Option Strict On disallows all implicit narrowing conversions, while the Off setting permits them. Narrowing conversions may involve data loss. For example:

```
Dim bigNumber As Long = 2455622
Dim smallNumber As Integer = bigNumber
```

converts a Long to an Integer. Even though in this case, no data loss would result from the narrowing, Option Strict On still does not allow the conversion and would instead generate a compiler error.

## Usage at a Glance

- A default project-wide setting for Option Strict can be set in the project properties within Visual Studio. The Option Strict statement, when used in a source code file, takes precedence over the project-wide setting.

- If the Option Strict statement is not present in a module, it defaults to Off.

- The default action for Option Strict is On, so that:

  ```
  Option Strict
  ```

  is equivalent to the statement:

  ```
  Option Strict On
  ```

- The Option Strict statement must appear in the declarations section of a module, before any types.

- Option Strict On implies Option Explicit On.

- Explicit narrowing conversions, such as those using the CInt function, are not affected by Option Strict. However, if data loss does occur as a result of an explicit conversion, a runtime error may still occur.

- When Option Strict is On, literals must often be cast to a specific data type before use. For example, the statement:

  ```
  Dim someMoney As Decimal = 10.32
  ```

  generates a compiler error because 10.32 is interpreted as a Double, and implicit conversions from Double to Decimal are not allowed. You can correct this compiler error with a statement like:

  ```
  Dim someMoney As Decimal = 10.32D
  ```

- Setting Option Strict On is highly recommended.

- For an ASP.NET page, use the @Page directive, rather than Option Strict, to control strict type checking. Its syntax is:

  ```
  <%@ Page Language="VB" Strict=true|false %>
  ```

  By default, Strict is false in ASP.NET pages.

  You can also use the <system.web> section of the *web.config* file to control strict type checking for an entire virtual directory or an ASP.NET application by adding a strict attribute to the compilation tag. Its syntax is:

  ```
  <compilation strict="true|false">
  ```

  In both cases, true corresponds to Option Strict On, and false corresponds to Option Strict Off.

**Version Differences**

The Option Strict statement did not exist in VB 6.

**See Also**

Option Compare Statement, Option Explicit Statement

---

# Out Attribute

**Class**

System.Runtime.InteropServices.OutAttribute

**Applies To**

Parameter

**Constructor**

```
New( )
```

**Properties**

None defined

**Description**

The <Out> attribute defines an outbound parameter, a variation of a ByRef parameter. Memory allocation for ByRef parameters is managed by the caller of the procedure; parameters with the <Out> attribute applied have their memory allocation managed by the procedure itself. No value comes in from the caller; a return value only goes out through the parameter. This makes <Out> parameters far more efficient in remoting (calls across machines) and in web method calls.

**Usage at a Glance**

Although you can define an out parameter using the <Out> attribute, the Visual Basic compiler does not enforce it. If you fail to assign a value to the out parameter, or if you indicate that the parameter is to be passed by value rather than by reference, the compiler does not generate an error. Care must be taken to ensure that all <Out> parameters are passed ByRef, and that they are explicitly assigned a value before the method exits.

**Example**

```
Imports System
Imports System.Runtime.InteropServices

Public Class Person
    Public Name As String
    Private standardAge As Integer
    Dim standardHeight As Integer
    Dim standardWeight As Integer

    Public Sub New(fullName As String)
        ' ----- Perhaps the initial fields would come from a
        '       database, but here they are just hard-coded.
```

```
            Name = fullName
            standardAge = 26
            standardHeight = 73
            standardWeight = 185
        End Sub

        Public Sub GetStats(<Out> ByRef currentAge As Integer, _
            <Out> ByRef currentHeight As Integer, _
            <Out> ByRef currentWeight As Integer)
            currentAge = standardAge
            currentHeight = standardHeight
            currentWeight = standardWeight
        End Sub
    End Class

    Module GeneralCode
        Public Sub Main( )
            Dim mrTypical As New Person("John Doe")
            Dim hisAge As Integer
            Dim hisHeight As Integer
            Dim hisWeight As Integer

            mrTypical.GetStats(hisAge, hisHeight, hisWeight)
            MsgBox(mrTypical.Name & " is " & hisHeight & " inches tall.")
        End Sub
    End Module
```

## ParamArray Attribute

### Class
System.ParamArrayAttribute

### Applies To
Parameter

### Constructor
New( )

### Properties
None defined

### Description
The <ParamArray> attribute indicates that the parameter represents a parameter array, which can support a variable number of arguments.

The same effect is achieved by using the ParamArray keyword in a function or subroutine declaration. In fact, the ParamArray keyword is converted into the <ParamArray> attribute during a compile.

If you do use the attribute, it must appear as <ParamArrayAttribute> rather than as <ParamArray>, since ParamArray is a Visual Basic keyword.

## Partial Keyword

### Syntax

```
Partial Class className
    [statements]
End Class
```

or:

```
Partial Structure structureName
    [statements]
End Structure
```

These two syntax examples show only the minimal grammar for the Class and Structure statements, for demonstration of the Partial keyword only.

### Description

The Partial keyword allows a single class or structure definition to be divided into multiple source code files. At least one of the class or structure portions must include the Partial keyword.

For syntax details on using the Partial keyword in context, see the *Class...End Class Statement* and the *Structure...End Structure Statement* entries elsewhere in this chapter.

### Example

This example shows a class divided into two distinct files. The first source code file includes the following code.

```
Public Class Customer
    ...statements...
End Class
```

The second source code file includes this code.

```
Public Partial Class Customer
    ...more statements...
End Class
```

If desired, the Partial keyword could be added to both class component definitions.

### Version Differences

The Partial keyword was introduced with Visual Basic 2005.

### See Also

Class...End Class Statement, Structure...End Structure Statement

## Partition Function

### Class

Microsoft.VisualBasic.Interaction

### Syntax

```
Dim result As String = Partition(number, start, stop, interval)
```

*number*  *(required; Long)*
> Number to evaluate against the intervals.

*start*  *(required; Long)*
> Start of the range. Must be nonnegative.

*stop*  *(required; Long)*
> End of the range. Must be greater than *start*.

*interval*  *(required; Long)*
> Size of each interval into which the range is partitioned.

## Description

The Partition function returns a string that describes which interval contains *number*. The format returned is x:y, where x is the start of the range, and y is the end of the range.

## Usage at a Glance

- Partition returns a range formatted with enough leading spaces so that there are the same number of characters to the left and right of the colon as there are characters in *stop*, plus one. This ensures that the interval text will be handled properly during any sort operations.

- If *number* is outside of the range of *start*, the range reported is :y, where y is start - 1, and no value exists before the colon.

- If *number* is outside the range of *end*, the range reported is x:, where x is end + 1, and no value exists after the colon.

- If *interval* is 1, the range is *number:number*, regardless of the *start* and *stop* arguments. For example, if *interval* is 1, *number* is 100, and *stop* is 1000, Partition returns 100:100.

- The Partition function is useful in creating histograms, which give the number of integers from a collection that fall into various ranges.

## Example

The code:

```
Dim counter As Integer
For counter = -1 To 110 \ 5
    Console.WriteLine(CStr(counter * 5) & " is in interval " & _
        Partition(counter * 5, 0, 100, 10))
Next counter
```

produces the following output:

```
-5 is in interval    : -1
0 is in interval    0:  9
5 is in interval    0:  9
10 is in interval   10: 19
15 is in interval   10: 19
20 is in interval   20: 29
25 is in interval   20: 29
30 is in interval   30: 39
35 is in interval   30: 39
40 is in interval   40: 49
45 is in interval   40: 49
50 is in interval   50: 59
```

```
 55 is in interval  50: 59
 60 is in interval  60: 69
 65 is in interval  60: 69
 70 is in interval  70: 79
 75 is in interval  70: 79
 80 is in interval  80: 89
 85 is in interval  80: 89
 90 is in interval  90: 99
 95 is in interval  90: 99
100 is in interval 100:100
105 is in interval 101:
110 is in interval 101:
```

### Version Differences

- The Partition function did not exist in VB 6, although it was available in Microsoft Access.

## PI Field

### Class
System.Math

### Syntax
```
Dim result As Double = Math.PI
```

### Description
The *PI* field returns the approximate value of the irrational number π, approximately 3.14159265358979.

### Usage at a Glance
This is a shared member of the *System.Math* class, so it can be used without an instance.

### Version Differences
The *PI* field is new to VB under .NET.

### See Also
E Field

## Pmt Function

### Class
Microsoft.VisualBasic.Financial

### Syntax
```
Dim result As Double = Pmt(rate, nPer, pv[, fv[, due]])
```

*rate  (required; Double)*
> The interest rate per period.

*nPer  (required; Double)*
> The total number of payment periods.

*pv  (required; Double)*
> The present value of a series of future payments.

*fv  (optional; Double)*
> The future value or cash balance after the final payment. If omitted, the default value is 0.

*due  (optional; DueDate enumeration)*
> A value indicating when payments are due, from the *Microsoft.VisualBasic.DueDate* enumeration. *DueDate.EndOfPeriod* indicates that payments are due at the end of the payment period; *DueDate.BegOfPeriod* indicates that payments are due at the beginning of the period. If omitted, the default value is *DueDate.EndOfPeriod*.

## Description

The Pmt function calculates the periodic payment for an annuity, based on regular fixed payments and a fixed interest rate. An annuity is a series of fixed cash payments made over a period of time. It can be either a loan or an investment.

## Usage at a Glance

- If *pv* and *fv* represent liabilities, their value is negative; if they represent assets, their value is positive.
- *rate* and *nPer* must be expressed in the same time unit. That is, if *nPer* reflects the number of monthly payments, *rate* must be the monthly interest rate.
- The rate is supplied as a decimal percent. For example, 10% is stated as 0.1.

## Example

See the example for the *IPmt Function* entry, which employs a similar syntax.

## See Also

FV Function, IPmt Function, NPer Function, NPV Function, PPmt Function, PV Function, Rate Function

---

# Pow Function

## Class

System.Math

## Syntax

```
Dim result As Double = Math.Pow(x, y)
```

*x  (required; Double)*
> The base number to be raised to a power

*y  (required; Double)*
> The exponent by which to raise the base number

## Description

The *Pow* function returns the base *x* raised to the power (exponent) *y*.

## Usage at a Glance

- This is a shared member of the *System.Math* class, so it can be used without an instance.
- Visual Basic also includes an intrinsic ^ exponentiation operator that performs the same function.

## Version Differences

The *Pow* function did not exist in VB 6.

## See Also

Exp Function

---

# PPmt Function

## Class

Microsoft.VisualBasic.Financial

## Syntax

```
Dim result As Double = PPmt(rate, per, nPer, pv[, fv[, due]])
```

*rate* *(required; Double)*
  The interest rate per period.

*per* *(required; Double)*
  The period for which a payment is to be computed.

*nPer* *(required; Double)*
  The total number of payment periods.

*pv* *(required; Double)*
  The present value of a series of future payments.

*fv* *(optional; Double)*
  The future value or cash balance after the final payment. If omitted, the default value is 0.

*due* *(optional; DueDate enumeration)*
  A value indicating when payments are due, from the *Microsoft.VisualBasic. DueDate* enumeration. *DueDate.EndOfPeriod* indicates that payments are due at the end of the payment period; *DueDate.BegOfPeriod* indicates that payments are due at the beginning of the period. If omitted, the default value is *DueDate. EndOfPeriod.*

## Description

The PPmt function computes the principal payment for a given period of an annuity, based on regular fixed payments and a fixed interest rate. An annuity is a series of fixed cash payments made over a period of time. It can be either a loan or an investment.

## Usage at a Glance

- The value of *per* ranges from 1 to *nPer*.

- If *pv* and *fv* represent liabilities, their value is negative; if they represent assets, their value is positive.

- *rate* and *nPer* must be expressed in the same time unit. That is, if *nPer* reflects the number of monthly payments, *rate* must be the monthly interest rate.

- The rate is supplied as a decimal percent. For example, 10% is stated as 0.1.

## Example

See the example for the *IPmt Function* entry.

## See Also

FV Function, IPmt Function, NPer Function, NPV Function, Pmt Function, PV Function, Rate Function

---

# Print, PrintLine Procedures

## Class

Microsoft.VisualBasic.FileSystem

## Syntax

```
Print(fileNumber, output)
PrintLine(fileNumber[, output])
```

*fileNumber* (required; Integer)
   Any valid file number of a file opened with `FileOpen`

*output* (required for `Print`; any)
   A comma-delimited list of expressions, or a `ParamArray`, to be written to the file

## Description

The `Print` and `PrintLine` procedures output formatted data to a disk file opened in `Append` or `Output` mode. The `PrintLine` version also appends line termination characters.

In addition to standard data, output can include the `SPC` and `TAB` functions, discussed in their own entries in this chapter.

## Usage at a Glance

- The `Print` and `PrintLine` procedures use the locale settings for the system to format dates, times, and numbers.

- The `Print` and `PrintLine` procedures are often used to output data in a human-readable format, not necessarily for reprocessing by a software application.

## Example

The following code writes some simple formatted data using the `PrintLine` procedure and the `TAB` function.

```
Dim fileID As Integer = FreeFile()
FileOpen(fileID, "c:\data.txt", OpenMode.Output, OpenAccess.Write)
PrintLine(fileID, "          1          2")
PrintLine(fileID, "12345678901234567890")
```

```
PrintLine(fileID, "--------------------")
PrintLine(fileID, 1, TAB(10), 10)
PrintLine(fileID, 100, TAB(10), 1000)
FileClose(fileID)
```

This code generates the following output.

```
          1         2
12345678901234567890
--------------------
1         10
100       1000
```

### Version Differences

- There are many syntactical differences between the VB 6 Print statement and the .NET Print procedure.

- The PrintLine procedure is new with .NET as a partial replacement for the VB 6 Print statement.

- In Visual Basic 2005, the *My.Computer.FileSystem* object provides more robust access to file-management features.

### See Also

Write, WriteLine Procedures

---

## Private Keyword

### Description

The Private keyword is used to set the access level for various types and type members. By including this keyword, the associated type or member can only be accessed within its declaration context. For instance, members within a class that use the Private keyword can only be accessed within that class's code.

The Private keyword can be used with the following statements:

> Class Statement
> Const Statement (but not for local constants)
> Declare Statement
> Delegate Statement
> Dim Statement (but not for local variables)
> Enum Statement
> Event Statement
> Function Statement
> Interface Statement
> Property Statement
> Structure Statement
> Sub Statement

By default, fields and constants declared within classes have Private access.

### See Also

For the statements listed above, see the related entries elsewhere in this chapter for usage information. For information on using the Private keyword as a statement, see the entry for the *Dim Statement*.

---

## Property Statement

### Syntax

```
[Default] [accessModifier] [propModifier] [Shared] [Shadows] _
    [ReadOnly | WriteOnly] Property name [(ByVal arglist)] _
    [As type] [Implements implementsList]
    [subAccessModifier] Get
        [statements]
        [Exit Property | Return expression]
        [statements]
    End Get
    [subAccessModifier] Set(ByVal value As type)
        [statements]
        [Exit Property]
        [statements]
    End Set
End Property
```

Default *(optional)*

Indicates that the property is the default property. Both a Get and a Set block must be defined for default properties. Only one property in a class definition can be the default.

accessModifier *(optional)*

Specifies the primary scope and accessibility of the property. This setting can be further restricted in the Get or Set blocks, beginning with Visual Basic 2005. One of the following access levels:

| Access level | Description |
| --- | --- |
| Public | The property is publicly accessible anywhere, both inside and outside of the project. |
| Private | The property is accessible only within the defining type. The default property of a class cannot be Private. |
| Protected | The property is accessible only to the code in the defining type or to one of its derived types. |
| Friend | The property is accessible only within the project that contains the property definition. |
| Protected Friend | Combines the access features of Protected and Friend. |

If omitted, the Public access level is used.

procModifier *(optional)*

One of the keywords shown in the following table:

| Keyword | Description |
| --- | --- |
| Overloads | Indicates that more than one declaration of this property exists, each with a different argument signature |
| Overrides | For derived classes, indicates that the property overrides a property with the same name and argument signature in the base class |
| Overridable | Indicates that the property can be overridden in a derived class |

| Keyword | Description |
| --- | --- |
| NotOverridable | Indicates that the property cannot be overridden in a derived class |
| MustOverride | Indicates that the property must be overridden in a derived class |

Shared *(optional)*

Indicates that the property is shared and not an instance property. Shared properties may be called without a particular instance of the type in which they appear. Shared properties are also known as *static properties.*

Shadows *(optional)*

Indicates that the property shadows an identically named element in a base class.

ReadOnly *(optional)*

Indicates that the property is read-only. The Get block must be supplied; the Set block must be absent.

WriteOnly *(optional)*

Indicates that the property is write-only. The Set block must be supplied; the Get block must be absent.

*name (required)*

The name of the property.

*arglist (optional; any)*

A comma-delimited list of parameters to be supplied to the property as arguments from the calling routine. The value assigned to the property from the calling procedure is not included in this argument list.

*arglist* uses the following syntax and parts:

```
[Optional] ByVal [ParamArray] varname[()] _
    [As argtype] [= defaultValue]
```

Optional *(optional)*

Flags an argument as optional; optional arguments need not be supplied by the calling routine. All arguments following an optional argument must also be optional. A ParamArray argument cannot be optional.

ByVal *(required)*

The argument is passed by value; the local copy of the variable is assigned the value of the argument. ByVal is the default method of passing variables. All arguments passed to properties must be passed by value.

ParamArray *(optional)*

The argument is an optional array containing an arbitrary number of elements. It can only be used as the last element of the argument list and cannot be modified by the Optional keyword. If Option Strict is on, the array type must also be specified.

*varname (required)*

The name of the argument as used in the local property.

*argtype (optional; Type)*

The data type of the argument. Any valid .NET data type can be used.

*defaultValue (optional; any)*

For optional arguments, indicates the default value to be supplied when the calling routine does not supply the value. When the Optional keyword is used, this default value is required.

*type (optional; Type)*

The return data type of the property. It is also the data type of the value assigned to the property by the calling procedure, as processed by the Set block of the property. The default data type is Object.

*implementsList (optional)*

Comma-separated list of the interface members implemented by this property.

*subAccessModifier (optional)*

*New in 2005.* This sub-access modifier allows one portion of the property to impose a more restrictive access level than is used for the other portion. If both a Get and a Set block are defined, one of them can also include a sub-access modifier. This modifier is one of the following keywords: Private, Protected, Friend, or Protected Friend. It has the same impact as the modifier used for the property's *accessModifier*, but it must be more restrictive than that modifier.

*statements (optional)*

Program code to be executed within the property.

*expression (optional)*

The value to return from the Get block of the property to the calling procedure.

*value (required)*

The value assigned to the property from the calling procedure. By tradition, this parameter is always named "value."

## Description

The Property statement declares a class property, including distinct assignment (Set) and retrieval (Get) accessors. Properties can appear within classes, structures, or modules.

## Usage at a Glance

- Overloads and Shadows cannot be used in the same property declaration.

- In the Get block, the property value can be returned either by using the Return statement or by assigning the value to a variable with a name that is the same as the property.

- The Default keyword can be used only with parameterized properties. Typically, these are properties that either return collection items or are implemented as property arrays.

- A Property Get procedure is used like a function; its return value can be assigned or used just like a function's return value.

  ```
  Dim someValue = someClass.SomeProperty
  ```

- The calling routine assigns a value to a property through a standard assignment statement. The assigned value becomes the *value* argument in the Set block.

  ```
  someClass.SomeProperty = someValue
  ```

- If an Exit Property or Return statement is used, the property procedure exits and program execution continues with the statement following the call to the property. Any number of Exit Property or Return statements can appear in a property.

- The value managed by a property is usually a Private variable within the class or type. This adheres to accepted object-oriented techniques by protecting the property value from accidental modification with invalid data.

```
Private hiddenSalary As Decimal
Public Property Salary() As Decimal
    Get
        Return hiddenSalary
    End Get
    Set(ByVal value As Decimal)
        hiddenSalary = value
    End Set
End Property
```

- Typically, *arglist* is only used in the case of property arrays. This entry's example shows such a use for the Wage property.
- The class constructor is often used to set properties to their initial values.

## Example

The example code illustrates a class that has a simple property and a property array.

```
Public Enum WageCategory
    Rate = 0
    Overtime = 1
    Differential = 2
End Enum

Public Class Employee
    ' ----- Simple class with two public properties.
    Dim empName As String
    Dim wagesByType(0 To 2) As Decimal

    Public Property Name() As String
        Get
            Return empName
        End Get
        Set(ByVal value As String)
            empName = value
        End Set
    End Property

    Public Property Wage(wageType As WageCategory) As Decimal
        Get
            Return wagesByType(wageType)
        End Get
        Set(ByVal value As Decimal)
            wagesByType(wageType) = value
        End Set
    End Property
End Class

Module GeneralCode
    Public Sub TestEmployeeClass()
        Dim oneEmployee As New Employee

        oneEmployee.Name = "Bill"
        oneEmployee.Wage(WageCategory.Rate) = 15@
        oneEmployee.Wage(WageCategory.Overtime) = 15@ * 1.5@
        oneEmployee.Wage(WageCategory.Differential) = 15@ * 0.1@.1@
```

```
      Console.WriteLine(oneEmployee.Name)
      Console.Writeline(oneEmployee.Wage(WageCategory.Rate))
      oneEmployee = Nothing
   End Sub
End Module
```

## Version Differences

- VB 6 includes `Property Get` and `Property Set` features for its classes, but the syntax used in VB 6 is significantly different from the syntax used in .NET.

- VB 6 support distinct `Property Set` and `Property Let` accessors. VB under .NET eliminates the `Property Let` accessor.

- Visual Basic 2005 adds *subAccessModifier* to the `Get` and `Set` block definitions, allowing separate visibility for the two portions of the property.

## See Also

Function Statement, Sub Statement

# Protected Keyword

## Description

The `Protected` keyword is used to set the access level for classes and class members. By including this keyword, the associated class or member can be accessed by the entire class, and by all derived classes, but not by any other code.

Declaring a class module as `Protected` limits all of the class's members to Protected access (or stronger, if the member has further specific access restrictions).

When combined with the `Friend` keyword, the related element takes on all aspects of both the `Protected` and `Friend` keywords.

The `Protected` keyword can be used with the following statements:

> Class Statement
> Const Statement (but not for local constants)
> Declare Statement
> Delegate Statement
> Dim Statement (but not for local variables)
> Enum Statement
> Event Statement
> Function Statement
> Interface Statement
> Property Statement
> Structure Statement
> Sub Statement

Even among these statements, the `Protected` keyword is only valid in the context of a class definition.

## Example

Consider the following class declaration.

```
Public Class MainClass
   Protected internalData As String
End Class
```

Then, within `MainClass` or any of its derived classes in any project, the `internalData` variable can be accessed directly:

```
Public Class LaterClass
    Inherits MainClass

    Public Sub Test( )
        MsgBox(internalData)
    End Sub
End Class
```

However, code that uses `MainClass`, but does not derive from it, cannot use the variable.

```
Dim intruderAlert As New MainClass
' ----- The following line will not compile.
intruderAlert.internalData = "Secret"
```

### Version Differences

The `Protected` keyword is new to VB under .NET.

### See Also

For the statements listed above, see the related entries elsewhere in this chapter for usage information. For information on using the `Protected` keyword as a statement, see the entry for the *Dim Statement*.

Friend Keyword, Private Keyword, Public Keyword

---

## Public Keyword

### Description

The `Public` keyword is used to set the access level for various types and type members. By including this keyword, the associated type or member can be used by virtually any code within the current assembly, or within other assemblies if the code has been configured for external access.

The `Public` keyword can be used with the following statements:

> Class Statement
> Const Statement (but not for local constants)
> Declare Statement
> Delegate Statement
> Dim Statement (but not for local variables)
> Enum Statement
> Event Statement
> Function Statement
> Interface Statement
> Property Statement
> Structure Statement
> Sub Statement

By default, methods and properties declared within classes have `Public` access, as do all structure members.

For the statements listed above, see the related entries elsewhere in this chapter for usage information. For information on using the Public keyword as a statement, see the entry for the *Dim Statement*.

Friend Keyword, Private Keyword, Protected Keyword

# PV Function

## Class

Microsoft.VisualBasic.Financial

## Syntax

```
Dim result As Double = PV(rate, nPer, pmt[, fv [, due]])
```

*rate* (required; Double)
    The interest rate per period.

*nPer* (required; Double)
    The total number of payment periods.

*pmt* (required; Double)
    The payment made in each period.

*fv* (optional; Double)
    The future value or cash balance after the final payment. If omitted, the default value is 0.

*due* (optional; DueDate enumeration)
    A value indicating when payments are due, from the *Microsoft.VisualBasic.DueDate* enumeration. *DueDate.EndOfPeriod* indicates that payments are due at the end of the payment period; *DueDate.BegOfPeriod* indicates that payments are due at the beginning of the period. If omitted, the default value is *DueDate.EndOfPeriod*.

## Description

The PV function calculates the present value of an annuity (either an investment or loan), based on a regular number of future payments of a fixed value and a fixed interest rate. The *present value* is the current value of a future stream of equal cash-flow events discounted at some fixed interest rate.

## Usage at a Glance

- The time units used for the number of payment periods, the rate of interest, and the payment amount must be the same. If you state the payment period in months, you must also express the interest rate as a monthly rate and the amount paid as a per-month payment.

- Payments made against a loan or added to the value of savings are expressed as negative numbers.

- The rate is supplied as a decimal percent. For example, 10% is stated as 0.1. If you are calculating using monthly periods, you must also divide the annual rate by 12. For example, 10% per annum equates to a rate per period of .00833.

FV Function, IPmt Function, NPer Function, NPV Function, Pmt Function, PPmt Function, Rate Function

# QBColor Function

## Class
Microsoft.VisualBasic.Information

## Syntax
```
Dim result As Integer = QBColor(color)
```
*color* (required; *Integer*)
A whole number between 0 and 15

## Description
The QBColor function returns a value representing the RGB ("red, green, blue") system color code.

## Usage at a Glance
- The source *color* value is one of the following values:

| Value | Description |
|-------|-------------|
| 0 | Black |
| 1 | Blue |
| 2 | Green |
| 3 | Cyan |
| 4 | Red |
| 5 | Magenta |
| 6 | Yellow |
| 7 | White |
| 8 | Gray |
| 9 | Light Blue |
| 10 | Light Green |
| 11 | Light Cyan |
| 12 | Light Red |
| 13 | Light Magenta |
| 14 | Light Yellow |
| 15 | Bright White |

- The RGB function allows much more flexibility than the QBColor function, which is a remnant of the older QBasic programming language.
- Visual Basic now contains a wide range of intrinsic color constants that can be used to assign colors directly to the color properties of objects. These colors are members of the *System.Drawing.Color* structure.

RGB Function

## Queue Class

### Namespace

System.Collections (standard version)

System.Collections.Generic (generic version)

### Creatable

Yes

### Description

A *Queue* object implements a "first in, first out" (FIFO) data structure. Items are added in a line (queue), with new items placed at the end of the line. Only the item at the beginning of the line can be removed. Its real-world counterpart is a line for the ticket counter at a movie theater.

The queue includes features for adding items (*Enqueue*), removing items (*Dequeue*), and counting the items in the queue (*Count*), among other features. Objects of any type may be added to the queue.

The following table lists some of the more useful and interesting members of the *Queue* class. Those marked with an asterisk (*) have separate entries in this chapter.

| Member | Description |
| --- | --- |
| Clear Method | Removes all items from the queue |
| Clone Method | Makes a distinct copy of the queue and its members |
| Contains Method * | Indicates whether a specific object is in the queue |
| CopyTo Method * | Copies queue elements to an existing array |
| Count Property | Indicates the number of items currently in the queue |
| Dequeue Method * | Removes and returns the beginning item in the queue |
| Enqueue Method * | Adds a new item to the end of the queue |
| IsReadOnly Property | Indicates whether the queue is read-only or not |
| Peek Method * | Returns the beginning queue item without removing it |
| ToArray Method * | Copies the queue to a new array |

### Example

This sample code shows the basic use of the queue.

```
' ----- Add some basic items to a queue.
Dim nameQueue As New Queue
nameQueue.Enqueue("Chopin")
nameQueue.Enqueue("Mozart")
nameQueue.Enqueue("Beethoven")
```

```
' ----- Examine and return the items.
MsgBox(nameQueue.Peek( ))      ' Displays "Chopin"
MsgBox(nameQueue.Dequeue( ))   ' Displays "Chopin"
MsgBox(nameQueue.Dequeue( ))   ' Displays "Mozart"

' ----- Remove the remaining items.
MsgBox(nameQueue.Count)      ' Displays 1 (for Beethoven)
nameQueue.Clear( )
```

### Version Differences

Visual Basic 2005 adds support for generics to several collection-style classes, including the *Queue* class. The version of the *Queue* class that supports generics appears in the *System.Collections.Generic* namespace. Generics are discussed in Chapter 10.

### See Also

Collection Class, Hashtable Class, Stack Class

---

## Queue.Contains Method

### Class

System.Collections.Queue (standard version)

System.Collections.Generic.Queue (generic version)

### Syntax

```
Dim result As Boolean = queueVariable.Contains(obj)
```

*obj* (required; any)
The object to search for in the queue

### Description

The *Contains* method indicates whether a given object is somewhere in the queue (True) or not (False).

### Usage at a Glance

- *obj* must correspond exactly to an item in the queue for the method to return True.
- String comparison is case sensitive and is not affected by the setting of Option Compare.

### Version Differences

Visual Basic 2005 adds support for generics to queues, as discussed in Chapter 10.

### See Also

Queue Class

# Queue.CopyTo Method

## Class

System.Collections.Queue (standard version)

System.Collections.Generic.Queue (generic version)

## Syntax

```
queueVariable.CopyTo(array, index)
```

*array*  *(required; compatible array)*
Array to which to copy the queue's objects

*index*  *(required; Integer)*
The index of the first zero-based array element to receive a queue member

## Description

The *CopyTo* method copies the queue elements into an existing array, starting at a specified array index.

## Usage at a Glance

- The array can be of any data type that is compatible with the queue elements. An array of Integer can accept Short queue elements but not String elements.

- The array must be sized to accommodate the elements of the queue prior to calling the *CopyTo* method.

## Example

The sample code copies queue items to an array.

```
Dim nameQueue As New Queue
Dim nameArray( ) As Object

' ----- Build the queue.
nameQueue.Enqueue("Chopin")
nameQueue.Enqueue("Mozart")
nameQueue.Enqueue("Beethoven")

' ----- Size the array and copy elements.
ReDim nameArray(nameQueue.Count - 1)
nameQueue.CopyTo(nameArray, 0)
```

## Version Differences

Visual Basic 2005 adds support for generics to queues, as discussed in Chapter 10.

## See Also

Queue Class, Queue.ToArray Method

# Queue.Dequeue Method

## Class
System.Collections.Queue (standard version)
System.Collections.Generic.Queue (generic version)

## Syntax
```
Dim result As Object = queueVariable.Dequeue( )
```

## Description
The *Dequeue* method removes the beginning item from the queue and returns it as an Object.

## Usage at a Glance
*Dequeue* generates an error if applied to an empty queue. Use the *Count* property to check for items in the queue.

## Version Differences
Visual Basic 2005 adds support for generics to queues, as discussed in Chapter 10.

## See Also
Queue Class, Queue.Peek Method


# Queue.Enqueue Method

## Class
System.Collections.Queue (standard version)
System.Collections.Generic.Queue (generic version)

## Syntax
```
queueVariable.Enqueue(obj)
```
*obj* (required; any)
    The item to place in the queue

## Description
The *Enqueue* method places an object at the end of the queue.

## Version Differences
Visual Basic 2005 adds support for generics to queues, as discussed in Chapter 10.

## See Also
Queue Class, Queue.Dequeue Method

## Queue.Peek Method

### Class
System.Collections.Queue (standard version)
System.Collections.Generic.Queue (generic version)

### Syntax
```
Dim result As Object = queueVariable.Peek( )
```

### Description
The *Peek* method returns the beginning item in the queue as an Object, but it does not remove it from the queue.

### Usage at a Glance
The *Peek* method is similar to the *Queue* object's *Dequeue* method, except that it leaves the queue intact.

### Version Differences
Visual Basic 2005 adds support for generics to queues, as discussed in Chapter 10.

### See Also
Queue Class, Queue.Dequeue Method

---

## Queue.ToArray Method

### Class
System.Collections.Queue (standard version)
System.Collections.Generic.Queue (generic version)

### Syntax
```
Dim result( ) As Object = queueVariable.ToArray( )
```

### Description
The *ToArray* method creates an array of type Object, copies the elements of the queue in order into the array, and then returns the array. The array need not be created in advance.

### Usage at a Glance
The beginning item in the queue becomes array element zero.

### Version Differences
Visual Basic 2005 adds support for generics to queues, as discussed in Chapter 10.

### See Also
Queue Class, Queue.CopyTo Method

# RaiseEvent Statement

## Syntax

```
RaiseEvent eventName[(argList)]
```

*eventName (required)*

The name of the event to raise

*argList (optional)*

A comma-delimited list of arguments, each of which has its accepted data type defined by the original event definition

## Description

The RaiseEvent statement causes a specific event to fire, passing any required arguments expected by the event handler(s).

## Usage at a Glance

- *eventName* must already be defined within the same module as the RaiseEvent statement.

- *argList* must correctly match the number and data type of parameters defined in the Event statement that defined the target event, and it must be surrounded by parentheses.

- To allow the client code to handle the event being fired, the client object variable must be declared using the WithEvents keyword.

- RaiseEvent is not asynchronous. When you call the RaiseEvent statement in your class code, your class code will not continue executing until the event has been either handled by the client or ignored (if the client is not handling the events raised by the class).

- For more information about implementing your own custom events, see Chapter 8.

## Example

The following code uses an event to notify the calling code when something important occurs (in this case, having some processing limit exceeded). The event handler can return a status code through one of its parameters. The instance of the object with the event must be declared with the WithEvents keyword.

```
Public Class Transact
    ' ----- Define the event with two arguments.
    Public Event Status(ByVal Message As String, _
        ByRef Cancel As Boolean)

    Public Function UpdateRecords(ByRef level As Integer) As Boolean
        ' ----- Pretend to process real records.
        Dim cancelNow As Boolean = False

        If (level > 1000) Then
            RaiseEvent Status("Is value too high?", cancelNow)
            If cancelNow Then
                Console.WriteLine("Abandoning operation...")
                Exit Function
```

```
            Else
                level = 1000
            End If
        End If
        Console.WriteLine(level)
    End Function
End Class

Module GeneralCode
    ' ----- Declare the object that has an event.
    Public WithEvents workObject As New Transact

    Public Sub Main
        workObject.UpdateRecords(1100)
    End Sub

    Private Sub CheckForProblem(ByVal problemPrompt As String, _
        ByRef cancelNow As Boolean) Handles workObject.Status
        If (MsgBoxResult.Yes = MsgBox(problemPrompt, _
        MsgBoxStyle.YesNo Or MsgBoxStyle.Question)) Then _
            cancelNow = True
    End Sub
End Module
```

**Version Differences**

Visual Basic 2005 includes a new Custom Event declaration that provides for additional management of event-related activities.

**See Also**

Event Statement

---

# Randomize Procedure

**Class**

Microsoft.VisualBasic.VBMath

**Syntax**

```
Randomize([number])
```

*number* (optional; Double)

A number used to initialize the random-number generator

**Description**

The Randomize procedure initializes the random-number generator with an optional "seed."

**Usage at a Glance**

- Randomize uses *number* as a new seed value to initialize the pseudorandom-number generator used by the Rnd function. If you do not supply *number*, the value of the system timer will be used as the new seed value.

- Repeatedly passing the same number to Randomize does not cause Rnd to repeat the same sequence of random numbers.

- If you need to repeat a sequence of random numbers, you should call the Rnd function with a negative number as an argument immediately prior to using Randomize with any numeric argument.

### See Also

Rnd Function

---

## Rate Function

### Class

Microsoft.VisualBasic.Financial

### Syntax

```
Dim result As Double = Rate(nPer, pmt, pv[, fv[, due[, guess]]])
```

nPer  *(required; Double)*
: The total number of payment periods.

pmt  *(required; Double)*
: The payment amount per period.

pv  *(required; Double)*
: The present value of a series of future payments.

fv  *(optional; Double)*
: The future value or cash balance after the final payment. If omitted, the default value is 0.

due  *(optional; DueDate enumeration)*
: A value indicating when payments are due, from the *Microsoft.VisualBasic. DueDate* enumeration. *DueDate.EndOfPeriod* indicates that payments are due at the end of the payment period; *DueDate.BegOfPeriod* indicates that payments are due at the beginning of the period. If omitted, the default value is *DueDate. EndOfPeriod.*

guess  *(optional; Double)*
: An estimate of the value to be returned by the function. If omitted, its value defaults to 0.1 (that is, 10%).

### Description

The Rate function calculates the interest rate for an annuity that consists of fixed payments over a known duration. An annuity is a series of fixed cash payments made over a period of time. It can be either a loan or an investment.

### Usage at a Glance

- If *pv* and *fv* represent liabilities, their value is negative; if they represent assets, their value is positive.

- The function works using iteration. Starting with *guess*, the function cycles through the calculation until the result is accurate to within 0.00001 percent. If a

---

result can't be found after 20 tries, it fails. If it fails, a different value for *guess* can be used.

- The value returned is the per-period rate. If you calculate the monthly rate, multiply by 12 to obtain the annual percentage rate.

### See Also

FV Function, IPmt Function, NPer Function, NPV Function, Pmt Function, PV Function, NPV Function

---

## ReDim Statement

### Syntax

```
ReDim [Preserve] name(boundList)[, name(boundList)...]
```

Preserve *(optional)*
: Preserves existing data within an array when changing the range of the last array dimension.

*name* *(required)*
: The name of the variable.

*boundList* *(required; numeric)*
: Comma-delimited list of ranges for each dimension in the array. Each comma-delimited element has the following syntax:

```
[0 To] upper
```

where upper specifies the new upper bound of the array dimension. The lower bound of each array dimension is always zero. The number of array dimensions must be the same as the dimensions declared in the original Dim statement for the variable.

### Description

The ReDim statement is used within a procedure to resize and reallocate storage space for an array. This statement sets new upper bounds in each dimension of the existing array. The original array dimensions for an array variable were defined through the Dim statement or an equivalent statement. Only the range of each dimension can change using the ReDim statement; the number of dimensions cannot be changed. If the Preserve keyword is included, only the last array dimension's range can be adjusted.

### Usage at a Glance

- There is no limit to the number of times you can redimension a dynamic array with the ReDim statement.
- The number of dimensions cannot be changed, nor can the data type of the array.
- If you do not use the Preserve keyword, you can resize any or all of the dimensions.
- You can redimension an array in a called procedure if you pass the array to the procedure by reference. For example:

```
Public Sub WorkProcedure()
    Dim someArray() As Integer = {1, 2, 3, 4, 5, 6, 7, 8, 9, 10}
    Dim oneElement As Integer
```

```
ResizeArray(someArray)

' ----- The following loop will output all 16 elements of
'        the array (0 to 15), including those assigned in
'        the ResizeArray procedure.
For Each oneElement In someArray
   Console.WriteLine(oneElement)
Next oneElement
End Sub

Public Sub ResizeArray(ByRef arrayToChange( ) As Integer)
   ReDim Preserve arrayToChange(15)
   arrayToChange(10) = 20
   arrayToChange(11) = 50
   arrayToChange(12) = 80
   arrayToChange(13) = 90
   arrayToChange(14) = 100
   arrayToChange(15) = 200
End Sub
```

- If the ReDim Preserve statement is used to reduce the number of array elements, the data in the discarded elements is lost.
- Redimensioning an array, particularly a large string array, can be expensive in terms of an application's performance. Frequent redimensioning, as with:

```
ReDim Preserve nameSet(UBound(nameSet) + 1)
```

can noticeably degrade your application. You may experience better results if you "pool" the allocation of array elements, redimensioning a block (of say 50 or 100) at once, and not redimensioning again until that block is fully used.

## Version Differences

- VB 6 allowed the initial declaration of an array to use the ReDim statement instead of the Dim statement. With .NET, VB requires separate Dim and ReDim statements for the initial and subsequent allocation actions.
- In VB 6, only arrays declared without an explicit number of elements, such as:

```
Dim vntData( ) As Variant
```

were dynamic arrays and could be redimensioned using ReDim. In .NET, all arrays are dynamic.
- VB 6 allowed both the upper and lower bound of each array dimension to change. In .NET, since the lower bound of every dimension is always zero, it cannot be changed.
- VB 6 permitted changes in the number of array dimensions with the ReDim statement, as long as the Preserve keyword wasn't used. .NET does not support this type of change.
- Visual Basic 2005 adds an optional lower bound "0 To" clause in each array dimension, for clarity:

```
ReDim someArray(0 To 5)
```

Although this appears to specify the lower bound, that lower bound must always be zero.

---

See Also
Dim Statement

---

# Rem Statement

## Syntax

```
Rem comment
' comment
```

*comment (optional)*
A textual comment to place within the code

## Description

Use the Rem statement or an apostrophe (') to place remarks within the code. The comment may appear on a line by itself or at the end of a logical statement line.

*New in 2005.* Visual Basic 2005 includes a new *XML Comments* feature that lets you decorate your class members with special XML-formatted comments. Visual Studio recognizes and uses these comments to enhance the development environment. To use XML comments, place the insertion point on a blank line in your code, just above a method definition, then type three single-quote marks. Immediately, even before pressing the Enter key, the following template appears.

```
''' <summary>
'''
''' </summary>
''' <param name="sender"></param>
''' <param name="e"></param>
''' <remarks></remarks>
```

Once these parts are filled in with the appropriate content, Visual Studio uses the information to display more verbose IntelliSense details concerning the related method. It also exports the XML content to a documentation file during the compile of the assembly.

## Usage at a Glance

- Text or code commented out using the Rem statement or the apostrophe (') is not compiled into the final program and, therefore, does not add to the size of the executable.

- If you use the Rem statement on the same line as program code, a colon is required after the program code and before the Rem statement. For example:

```
Set activeDoc = New AppDoc: Rem Define the object
                            Rem reference.
```

The colon is not necessary when using the apostrophe as the comment marker:

```
Set activeDoc = New AppDoc  ' Define the object reference.
```

- Apostrophes held within quotation marks are not treated as comment markers:

```
quotedString = "'This string contains single quotes!'"
```

The Language Reference

- The Visual Studio development environment contains block-comment and block-uncomment buttons on the Text Editor toolbar, which allow you to comment or uncomment a selection of many rows of code at once.
- You cannot use line-continuation characters ("_") with comments.

### Version Differences
- VB 6 allowed comment lines to be connected with the line-continuation character ("_"). In .NET, each comment line must include its own Rem keyword or apostrophe (').
- XML comments are new with Visual Basic 2005.

## RemoveHandler Statement

### Syntax
```
RemoveHandler nameOfEventSender, AddressOf nameOfEventHandler
```
*nameOfEventSender (required)*
The name of a class or object instance and its event, such as *Button1.Click*

*nameOfEventHandler (required)*
The name of a subroutine to remove from the set of active event handlers for *nameOfEventSender*

### Description
The RemoveHandler statement removes a previous binding of an event handler to an event.

### Usage at a Glance
The AddHandler and RemoveHandler statements can be used to add and remove event notification handlers dynamically at runtime. By contrast, the Handles keyword establishes an event notification handler for the lifetime of an object.

### Example
Chapter 8 includes examples of using event handlers.

### Version Differences
Visual Basic 2005 includes a new Custom Event statement that impacts the use of the RemoveHandler statement. See the *Custom Event Statement* entry in this chapter for additional information.

### See Also
AddHandler Statement, Custom Event Statement

## Rename Procedure

### Class
Microsoft.VisualBasic.FileSystem

## Syntax

```
Rename(oldpath, newpath)
```

*oldpath  (required; String)*
: The name and optional path of the file or directory to be renamed

*newpath  (required; String)*
: The new name and optional path to give to the file

## Description

The Rename procedure renames a file or directory.

## Usage at a Glance

- If *oldpath* does not exist or is currently in use, or if *newpath* already exists or contains an invalid path, an error occurs.
- If *newpath* and *oldpath* include different directory paths, the file or directory will be renamed *and* moved to the new location. Directories cannot be moved from one drive to another using this method.
- Path information included in *newpath* and *oldpath* can include relative or absolute paths and can use the drive-letter or UNC format.
- Wildcard characters cannot be used.

## Version Differences

- The Rename procedure is new to VB under .NET.
- Visual Basic 2005 includes *My.Computer.FileSystem.RenameFile* and *My.Computer. FileSystem.RenameDirectory* methods that provide similar functionality.

## See Also

FileCopy Procedure

---

# Replace Function

## Class

Microsoft.VisualBasic.Strings

## Syntax

```
Dim result As String = Replace(expression, find, replacement _
    [, start[, count[, compare]]])
```

*expression  (required; String)*
: The complete string containing the substring to be replaced.

*find  (required; String)*
: The substring to be found by the function.

*replacement  (required; String)*
: The new substring that will replace occurrences of the *find* substring.

*start  (optional; Integer)*
: The character position in *expression* at which the search for *find* begins. Any characters before this position are not even returned. If omitted, the search begins with the first character.

*count (optional; Integer)*
  The number of instances of *find* to replace. If omitted, all instances are replaced.

*compare (optional; CompareMethod constant)*
  The method used to compare *find* with *expression*; its value can be *CompareMethod.Binary* (for case-sensitive comparison) or *CompareMethod.Text* (for case-insensitive comparison). If omitted, *CompareMethod.Binary* is used.

## Description

The Replace function replaces a given number of instances of a specified substring in another string. The starting position for replacement and a maximum number of replacements can be specified.

## Usage at a Glance

- Setting the *replacement* argument to an empty string removes all occurrences of *find* from the original string.

- The String data type also has a public instance Replace method, which replaces all occurrences of a character or string with another. Its syntax is:

  `someString.Replace(oldValue, newValue)`

  where *oldValue* is a String or Char value containing the text to be replaced, and *newValue* is a String or Char value containing the replacement text.

## See Also

InStr Function, InStrRev Function, Mid Statement

---

# Reset Procedure

## Class

Microsoft.VisualBasic.FileSystem

## Syntax

    Reset( )

## Description

The Reset procedure closes all files that have been opened using the FileOpen procedure.

## Usage at a Glance

- The contents of any current file buffers are written to disk by the Reset procedure immediately prior to Reset closing the respective files.

- The Reset procedure is functionally equivalent to the FileClose procedure used with no arguments.

- The Reset procedure is generally used as a last resort, closing all files if your program is terminating abnormally. Normally, you should write code to close each open file using the FileClose procedure.

In Visual Basic 2005, the *My.Computer.FileSystem* object provides more robust access to file management features.

**See Also**

FileClose Procedure, FileOpen Procedure

---

# Resume Statement

**Syntax**

```
Resume [Next | label]
```

*label (required)*
A source code label that appears somewhere in the current procedure

**Description**

The Resume statement is used to continue program execution when an error-handling routine is complete. Resume can take any of the forms shown in the following list:

Resume

Program execution continues with the source-code line that caused the error. That line may be a call to another subroutine where the actual error occurred but that contained no error-handling code of its own.

Resume Next

Program execution continues with the source-code line immediately following the one that caused the error. The line that caused the error may be a call to another subroutine where the actual error occurred but that contained no error-handling code of its own; that line is still skipped, and the subroutine call is not repeated.

Resume *label*

Program execution continues at the specified label, which must appear in the same procedure as the error handler.

**Usage at a Glance**

- You can only use the Resume statement in an error-handling section of code.

- An error-handling section of code does not have to contain a Resume statement. That code may decide to exit the current routine altogether. In that case, it issues an Exit Sub or similar statement instead of a Resume statement.

**Version Differences**

VB 6 supported a "Resume 0" syntax that was identical to a plain "Resume" statement. The "Resume 0" syntax has been removed in .NET.

**See Also**

Err Object, On Error Statement

# Return Statement

## Syntax

In a subroutine or Set property accessor:

    Return

In a function or property Get accessor:

    Return returnValue

*returnValue (required; any)*
    The return value of the function

## Description

The Return statement returns control to the calling procedure from a sub procedure, property, or function. When used from functions and property Get accessors, it also returns an associated value to the calling procedure.

## Usage at a Glance

- If the Return statement appears in a function or in the Get component of a property, it must specify a return value.

- Return causes program flow to leave the active procedure and return to the calling procedure; any statements in the function or subroutine that follow Return are not executed.

- Return is identical in operation to the Exit Sub statement; it prematurely transfers control from a procedure to the calling routine. It is also similar to the Exit Function statement; while it prematurely transfers control out of the function, it also allows a particular value to be returned by the function.

## Example

```
Public Sub AddAndDisplayNumbers( )
    Dim returnedValue As Double = GetNumbers( )
    MsgBox("The sum of values is " & returnedValue)
End Sub

Public Function GetNumbers( ) As Double
    ' ----- Prompts for up to 10 numbers and returns the sum.
    Dim counter As Integer = 1
    Dim userInput As String
    Dim sumOfNumbers As Double = 0#

    Do
        ' ----- Get the number from the user.
        userInput = InputBox("Enter number " & counter & ":", "Sum")
        If (userInput = "") Then Exit Do

        ' ----- Check for valid input.
        If IsNumeric(userInput) Then
            sumOfNumbers += CDbl(userInput)
            counter = counter + 1
        End If
    Loop While (counter <= 10)
```

```
'  ----- All added and ready to return.
    Return sumOfNumbers
End Function
```

## Version Differences

In VB 6, the Return statement was used in a block of code accessed through a GoSub statement. The GoSub statement is no longer supported in VB under .NET, and the Return statement now serves a different purpose.

## See Also

Exit Statement

---

# RGB Function

## Class

Microsoft.VisualBasic.Information

## Syntax

```
Dim result As Integer = RGB(red, green, blue)
```

*red* (required; Integer)
    A number between 0 and 255, inclusive

*green* (required; Integer)
    A number between 0 and 255, inclusive

*blue* (required; Integer)
    A number between 0 and 255, inclusive

## Description

The RGB function returns a system color code, with combined red, green, and blue components, that can be assigned to object color properties.

## Usage at a Glance

- The RGB color value represents the relative intensity of the red, green, and blue components of a pixel that produces a specific color on the display.
- The RGB function assumes any argument greater than 255 to be 255.
- The following table demonstrates how the individual color values combine to create certain colors:

| Color | Red | Green | Blue |
|-------|-----|-------|------|
| Black | 0 | 0 | 0 |
| Blue | 0 | 0 | 255 |
| Green | 0 | 255 | 0 |
| Red | 255 | 0 | 0 |
| White | 255 | 255 | 255 |

- The RGB value is calculated using the following formula:
    $$RGB = red + (green * 256) + (blue * 65536)$$

- Visual Basic now contains a wide range of intrinsic color constants that can be used to assign colors directly to the color properties of objects. These colors are members of the *System.Drawing.Color* structure.

**See Also**

QBColor Function

---

# Right Function

## Class

Microsoft.VisualBasic.Strings

## Syntax

```
Dim result As String = Right(str, length)
```

*str* *(required; String)*
The string to be processed

*length* *(required; Integer)*
The number of characters to return from the rightmost portion of the string

## Description

The Right function returns a string containing the rightmost *length* characters of *str*.

## Usage at a Glance

- If *length* is zero, a zero-length string is returned.
- If *length* is greater than the length of *str*, *str* is returned.
- If *length* is less than zero or is Nothing, an error is generated.
- If *str* contains Nothing, Right returns Nothing.
- Because of naming conflicts, you may have to preface this function with the name of the *Microsoft.VisualBasic* namespace.
- Use the Len function to determine the total length of *str*.

## Example

The following example uses the Right function to ensure that a directory path ends with a "\" character.

```
Public Function ProperDirectory(origPath As String) As String
    If (Right(origPath, 1) = "\") Then
        Return origPath
    Else
        Return origPath & "\"
    End If
End Function
```

## See Also

Left Function, Mid Function

# RmDir Procedure

## Class

Microsoft.VisualBasic.FileSystem

## Syntax

```
RmDir(path)
```

*path (required; String)*
The directory to be deleted

## Description

The RmDir procedure removes an empty directory from a drive.

## Usage at a Glance

- *path* can be a relative or absolute path, either of a local or remote directory.
- If the directory contains any files or subdirectories, an error occurs.
- The directory is permanently deleted; it is not placed in the Recycle Bin. Visual Basic 2005 includes a new *My.Computer.FileSystem.DeleteDirectory* method that includes an option for the Recycle Bin.
- The RmDir procedure only deletes empty directories. Visual Basic 2005 includes a new *My.Computer.FileSystem.DeleteDirectory* method that includes an option to delete all subordinate items.
- Use the Kill procedure to delete files.

## Version Differences

Visual Basic 2005 includes a *My.Computer.FileSystem.DeleteDirectory* method that provides similar functionality but with a few additional options.

## See Also

Kill Procedure, MkDir Procedure

The Language Reference

---

# Rnd Function

## Class

Microsoft.VisualBasic.VBMath

## Syntax

```
Dim result As Single = Rnd[(number)]
```

*number (optional; Single)*
The pseudorandom-number generator seed value. The following list describes how the Rnd function interprets *number*.

| Number | Rnd generates |
| --- | --- |
| Negative | The same number each time, using *number* as the seed number |
| Positive | The next random number in the current sequence |

| Number | Rnd generates |
|---|---|
| Zero | The most recently generated number |
| Not Supplied | The next random number in the current sequence |

### Description
The Rnd function returns a random number between 0 and 1, inclusive.

### Usage at a Glance
- Before calling the Rnd function, you should use the Randomize procedure to initialize the random-number generator.
- The standard formula for producing random numbers in a given range is:

  ```
  result = Int((highest - lowest + 1) * Rnd() + lowest)
  ```

  where *lowest* is the lowest required number in the range and *highest* is the highest.

### Example
The following example returns an array of 100 random numbers.

```
Public Function GenerateRandomNumbers() As Single()
    Dim results As Single(0 To 99)
    Dim counter As Integer

    Randomize()
    For counter = 0 To 99
        results(counter) = Rnd()
    Next counter
    Return results
End Function
```

### See Also
Randomize Procedure

## Round Function

### Class
System.Math

### Syntax
```
Dim result As type = Math.Round(value[, mode])
```
or
```
Dim result As type = Math.Round(value, digits[, mode])
```
*type* (required)
  One of the following data types: Decimal or Double.

*value* (required; any expression of type type)
  A number to be rounded.

*mode* *(optional; MidpointRounding enumeration)*
New in 2005. Indicates how to round numbers found at the halfway point between two rounding options, from the *System.MidpointRounding* enumeration. The AwayFromZero value rounds in the opposite direction of zero, while ToEven rounds toward the nearest even number (in the least significant decimal place). If not supplied, ToEven is used by default.

*digits* *(optional; Integer)*
The number of places to include after the decimal point and at which to perform the rounding.

## Description

The *Round* function rounds a given number to a specified number of decimal places.

## Usage at a Glance

- *digits* can be any whole number between 0 and 28.
- This is a shared member of the *System.Math* class, so it can be used without an instance.
- If *value* contains fewer decimal places than *digits*, *Round* does not pad the return value with trailing zeros.

## Version Differences

- The named parameters of the *Round* function differ in VB 6 and in the .NET Framework. In VB 6, the named arguments are *number* and *numDigitsAfterDecimal*. In .NET, they are *value* and *digits*.
- The *mode* parameter was added in the 2005 release of the .NET Framework.

## See Also

Fix Function, Int Function

---

# RSet Function

## Class

Microsoft.VisualBasic.Strings

## Syntax

```
Dim result As String = RSet(source, length)
```

*source* *(required; String)*
The string to be right aligned

*length* *(required; Integer)*
The length of the returned string

## Description

The RSet function right aligns a string.

### Usage at a Glance

- If the length of *source* is greater than or equal to *length*, the function returns only the leftmost *length* characters.
- If the length of *source* is less than *length*, spaces are added to the left of the returned string so that its length becomes *length*.

### Version Differences

- In VB 6, RSet was implemented as a kind of assignment statement. Because it is implemented as a function in .NET, its syntax is completely different.
- In VB 6, RSet could be used only with fixed-length strings. In .NET, RSet works with all string data.

### See Also

LSet Function

---

## RTrim Function

### Class

Microsoft.VisualBasic.Strings

### Syntax

```
Dim result As String = RTrim(str)
```

*str* *(required; String)*
A valid string expression

### Description

The RTrim function removes any trailing spaces from *str*.

### Usage at a Glance

If *string* contains Nothing, RTrim returns Nothing.

### See Also

LTrim Function, Trim Function

---

## SaveFileDialog Class

### Namespace

Windows.Forms

### Creatable

Yes

### Description

The *SaveFileDialog* class represents a common dialog box for selecting or saving a file. The *SaveFileDialog* class has properties that let you configure, display, and retrieve the results from this dialog box, from which the user selects a single file. The dialog does not create or update the file; it only indicates the file to be modified.

The following list discusses the more interesting members of the *SaveFileDialog* class.

*AddExtension Property*
> Indicates whether the dialog box should automatically add the default file extension to the user-supplied file name. The default value is True.

*DefaultExt Property*
> Defines the default file extension. The string should consist of the file extension only, without a leading period.

*FileName Property*
> Returns the fully qualified file name—the file name with its complete path and extension. If no file is selected, the property returns an empty string.

*Filter Property*
> Used to configure a filter string that indicates the types of files (by extension) to display in the dialog box. These types appear in the "Save as type" drop-down control on the dialog box. A single item consists of a file description, a vertical bar, and the file extension (usually "*." plus the file extension). If there are multiple extensions in a single item, they are separated by semicolons. If there are multiple items, they are separated by vertical bars. For example, the following code fragment assigns a filter string for text files and VB source code files:

```
Dim savePrompt As New SaveFileDialog
savePrompt.Filter = _
    "Text files (*.txt; *.vb)|*.txt;*.vb|" & _
    "Visual Basic files (*.vb)|*.vb|" & _
    "All files (*.*)|*.*"
```

*FilterIndex Property*
> Indicates the selected 1-based position in the *Filter* property's item list. The default is 1. If the user selects a different filter, this property is updated to reflect that change.

*InitialDirectory Property*
> Indicates the initial directory to use when first displaying the dialog.

*OverwritePrompt Property*
> Indicates whether a confirmation dialog box should appear automatically when the user selects an existing file. The default value is True.

*RestoreDirectory Property*
> Indicates whether the current working (default) directory is restored before the dialog box closes. The default value is False.

*ShowDialog Method*
> Displays the dialog box to the user. Once the user has dismissed the dialog box, the *FileName* property can be used to get the user's selection.

*Title Property*
> Sets the title of the dialog box.

## Example

The following code prompts the user for a filename to save.

```
Dim selectFile As New SaveFileDialog
selectFile.OverwritePrompt = True
```

```
If (selectFile.ShowDialog( ) = DialogResult.OK) Then
    Console.WriteLine(selectFile.FileName)
End If
```

### Version Differences

The public interfaces used for this *SaveFileDialog* class and the related VB 6 Common-Dialog control are quite different.

### See Also

OpenFileDialog Class

---

## SaveSetting Procedure

### Class

Microsoft.VisualBasic.Interaction

### Syntax

```
SaveSetting(appname, section, key, setting)
```

*appname  (required; String)*
The name of the application branch to be updated.

*section  (required; String)*
The name of the application's subkey to be updated. This can be a single key or a relative registry path, with path components separated by backslashes.

*key  (required; String)*
The name of the value entry to update.

*setting  (required; String)*
The value to assign to the specified key value entry.

### Description

The SaveSetting procedure creates or updates a single value in a specified section of your application's entry in the HKEY_CURRENT_USER\Software\VB and VBA ProgramSettings\ branch of the registry.

### Usage at a Glance

- The function writes a value within the KEY_CURRENT_USER\Software\VB and VBA ProgramSettings section of the registry.

- If the *appname*, *section*, or *key* entries are not found in the registry, they are automatically created.

- *section* is a relative path (similar to that used to describe the directories on a hard drive) used to navigate from the application key to the subkey to be updated. For example, to update the value entry named TestKey in the registry key HKEY_CURRENT_USER\Software\VB  and  VBA  ProgramSettings\RegTester\BranchOne\ BranchTwo, you would use:

    ```
    SaveSetting("RegTester", "BranchOne\BranchTwo", "TestKey", "test")
    ```

- Although the registry supports multiple data types, the GetSetting function only supports string values. All settings are written to the registry as REG_SZ entries.

---

- If the setting cannot be saved, a runtime error occurs.

- Since `SaveSetting` saves data on a per-user basis, it should not be used to save configuration settings that apply to all users, such as hardware configuration values.

- You cannot use `SaveSetting` to update entries from registry keys that are not subkeys of `HKEY_CURRENT_USER\Software\VB` and `VBA ProgramSettings`.

- `SaveSetting` does not allow you to write to the default value of a registry key. Attempting to do so produces a runtime error. This isn't a serious limitation, since the other Visual Basic "Settings" functions do not allow you to retrieve the default value of a registry key.

- The .NET Framework includes registry-related features that provide more flexibility than the VB "Settings" functions. These features are found in the *Registry* and *RegistryKey* classes of the *Microsoft.Win32* namespace.

### Version Differences

Visual Basic 2005 includes several new features that let you manage the settings used by an application. Although they are not compatible with the older VB "Settings" functions, they provide a richer set of features. These features are located in the *My. Settings* object. The *My.Computer.Registry* object also provides access to convenient registry-related features.

### See Also

DeleteSetting Procedure, GetAllSettings Function, GetSetting Function

---

# ScriptEngine Property

### Class

Microsoft.VisualBasic.Globals

### Syntax

```
Dim result As String = Globals.ScriptEngine
```

### Description

The `ScriptEngine` property returns the name of the script engine or programming language currently in use. In Visual Basic, this property always returns "VB."

### Usage at a Glance

- The `ScriptEngine` is a read-only property.

- A number of scripting engines support a `ScriptEngine` property, which allows you to determine the programming language used for a particular block of code. The following table lists some commonly supported values:

| Language | Property value |
|---|---|
| Microsoft Jscript | JScript |
| VB for .NET | VB |
| VBScript | VBScript |

### Version Differences

The ScriptEngine property is new to .NET and is not supported in VB 6.

### See Also

ScriptEngineBuildVersion Property, ScriptEngineMajorVersion Property, ScriptEngine-MinorVersion Property

## ScriptEngineBuildVersion Property

### Class

Microsoft.VisualBasic.Globals

### Syntax

```
Dim result As Integer = Globals.ScriptEngineBuildVersion
```

### Description

The ScriptEngineBuildVersion property returns the build number of the Visual Basic language engine.

### Version Differences

The ScriptEngineBuildVersion property is new to .NET and is not supported in VB 6.

### See Also

ScriptEngine Property, ScriptEngineMinorVersion Property, ScriptEngineMajorVersion Property

## ScriptEngineMajorVersion Property

### Class

Microsoft.VisualBasic.Globals

### Syntax

```
Dim result As Integer = Globals.ScriptEngineMajorVersion
```

### Description

The ScriptEngineMajorVersion property returns the major version number of the Visual Basic language engine.

### Usage at a Glance

This property returns 7 in the 2002 and 2003 releases of Visual Basic; the 2005 release of VB returns 8.

### Version Differences

The ScriptEngineMajorVersion property is new to .NET and is not supported in VB 6.

ScriptEngine Property, ScriptEngineBuildVersion Property, ScriptEngineMinorVersion Property

## ScriptEngineMinorVersion Property

### Class
Microsoft.VisualBasic.Globals

### Syntax
```
Dim result As Integer = Globals.ScriptEngineMinorVersion
```

### Description
The `ScriptEngineMinorVersion` property returns the minor version number of the Visual Basic language engine.

### Usage at a Glance
This property returns 0 in the 2002 release of Visual Basic, 1 in the 2003 release, and 0 in the 2005 release.

### Version Differences
The `ScriptEngineMinorVersion` property is new to .NET and is not supported in VB 6.

### See Also
ScriptEngine Property, ScriptEngineBuildVersion Property, ScriptEngineMajorVersion Property

## Second Function

### Class
Microsoft.VisualBasic.DateAndTime

### Syntax
```
Dim result As Integer = Second(timeValue)
```
*timeValue (required; Date)*
The source date from which to extract the second

### Description
The `Second` function returns a value from 0 to 59, representing the second of the supplied date or time.

### Usage at a Glance
With `Option Strict` set to `On`, the source value must first be converted to a `Date` data type. You can use the `CDate` function for this purpose. The `IsDate` function can also be used to confirm that the source expression is a valid date.

The Language Reference

DatePart Function, Hour Function, Minute Function

---

## Seek Function

### Class
Microsoft.VisualBasic.FileSystem

### Syntax
```
Dim result As Long = Seek(fileNumber)
```
*fileNumber (required; Integer)*
  Any valid file number of a file opened with FileOpen

### Description
The Seek function returns the current 1-based position within an open file. This position represents the next place that data will be either written or read. For files open in Random mode, this is the next record number; for files open in other modes, this is the byte position.

### Version Differences
In Visual Basic 2005, the *My.Computer.FileSystem* object provides more robust access to file management features.

### See Also
Loc Function, Seek Procedure

---

## Seek Procedure

### Class
Microsoft.VisualBasic.FileSystem

### Syntax
```
Seek(fileNumber, position)
```
*filenumber (required; Integer)*
  Any valid file number of a file opened with FileOpen

*position (required; Long)*
  The new 1-based position within the file, to be used for the next read or write operation

### Description
The Seek procedure moves the current position within an open file such that the next data read or written will be at the 1-based location *position*. For files open in Random mode, this is the next record number; for files open in other modes, this is the byte position.

---

## Usage at a Glance

- The use of a record number in any subsequent `FileGet` or `FilePut` procedure overrides the position set by the `Seek` procedure.

- *position* can be set to a value that is well beyond the end of the file. The file size will be automatically increased as needed during the next write operation.

- A runtime error occurs if *position* is 0 or negative.

- Unwritten records in a data file are generally padded with spaces. For example, if you open a brand new data file, perform a seek operation to record number 10, and then write a new record, the preceding nine records will be padded as needed.

## Version Differences

In Visual Basic 2005, the *My.Computer.FileSystem* object provides more robust access to file management features.

## See Also

Seek Function

---

# Select Case Statement

## Syntax

```
Select Case testExpression
   [Case expressionList-n
       [statements-n]] ...
   [Case Else
       [elseStatements]]
End Select
```

*testExpression* (required)

Any expression whose value determines which block of code within the larger `Select Case` statement is executed. The expression must evaluate to one of the core Visual Basic data types or `Object`.

*expressionList-n* (required)

Comma-delimited list of expressions to compare with *testExpression*. Each comma-delimited part uses one syntax from the following table:

| Expression list syntax | Description |
| --- | --- |
| *expression* | *testExpression* is compared with *expression*. If they match, the related *statements* are executed. |
| *expression1* To *expression2* | *testExpression* is compared with an inclusive range from *expression1* to *expression2*. If they match, the related *statements* are executed. |
| Is *op expression* | *testExpression* is compared with *expression* by using a specific comparison operator. If they match, the related *statements* are executed. *op* may be one of the following comparison operators: =, <>, <, <=, >, or >=. If "Is =" is used, it can be replaced with just "Is." |

*statements-n (optional)*

Program statements to execute if a match is found between *testExpression* and the related *expressionList* entry.

*elseStatements (optional)*

Program statements to execute if none of the other *expressionList* sections resulted in a match.

## Description

The Select Case statement allows for conditional execution of code, typically out of three or more available code blocks, based on some condition. Use the Select Case statement as an alternative to complex If...Then...Else statements.

## Usage at a Glance

- Any number of Case clauses can be included in the Select Case statement.

- If a match between *testExpression* and any part of a particular *expressionList* is found, the program statements related to the matched *expressionList* will be executed. When program execution encounters the next Case clause or the End Select clause, execution continues with the statement immediately following the End Select clause.

- If multiple Case clauses are True, only the statements belonging to the first true Case clause are executed.

- If used, the Case Else clause must be the last Case clause. Program execution will only encounter the Case Else clause—and thereby execute the *elseStatements* section—if all other *expressionList* comparisons fail.

- Use the To keyword to specify a range of values. The lower value must precede the To clause, and the higher value must follow it. Failure to do this does not generate a syntax error. Instead, it causes the comparison of the expression with *testExpression* to always fail, so that the related section of code is never executed.

- Select Case statements can be nested.

- The Case Else clause is optional, but it should be included if you must take some action when all other Case clauses fail.

- The Is keyword used in the Select Case statement is not the same as the Is comparison operator.

- Multiple conditions in a single Case statement are evaluated separately, not together; they are connected with a logical Or, not a logical And. For example, the statement:

  ```
  Case Is > 20, Is < 40
  ```

  will evaluate to True whenever the value of *testExpression* is greater than 20. In this case, the second comparison is never evaluated; it is evaluated only when *testExpression* is under 20. A *testExpression* value of 60 evaluates to True in this case.

## Example

The following example uses Select Case in response to a MsgBox function:

```
Select Case MsgBox("Backup file before changing?", vbYesNoCancel)
    Case vbYes
        ' ----- Do something.
```

```
      Case vbNo
         ' ----- Do something.
      Case vbCancel
         ' ----- Do something.
   End Select
```

**See Also**

If...Then...Else Statement

---

# Send, SendWait Methods

## Class

System.Windows.Forms.SendKeys

## Syntax

```
SendKeys.Send(keys)
```

or:

```
SendKeys.SendWait(keys)
```

*keys  (required; String)*
   String that describes the keystrokes to send to the active window

## Description

The *Send* and *SendWait* methods simulate the typing of one or more keys in the active window. With *SendKeys.Send*, further execution continues without waiting for the keys to be processed. With *SendKeys.SendWait*, further execution is suspended until the keystrokes have been processed.

To send plain text, simply include that text in the *keys* argument. For instance, using "abc" for the *keys* argument will send the characters a, b, and c, one at a time, to the active window. To have the Shift key held down with a key, precede that key with a plus sign (+). To use the Control key with another key, precede that key with the caret (^). To use the Alt key with another key, precede that key with the percent sign (%). To use one of these special keys with multiple other keys, enclose those other keys in parentheses. For instance, "+(abc)" sends a, b, and c with the Shift key held down.

You can repeat a key multiple times by using the syntax "{*key count*}" (that is, the character, then a space, and then a numeric value, all within braces). For example, "{a 25}" will send the "a" key 25 times.

These methods support several special keys, such as the Left Arrow key. Also, some standard keys must be enclosed in a set of braces to be recognized as standard keys. The following table lists all of these special keys and special-use standard keys.

| To include | Use this text |
| --- | --- |
| Backspace | {BACKSPACE} or {BS} or {BKSP} |
| Break | {BREAK} |
| Caps Lock | {CAPSLOCK} |
| Caret (^) | {^} |
| Clear | {CLEAR} |

| To include | Use this text |
|---|---|
| Close Brace (}) | {}} |
| Close Bracket (]) | {]} |
| Close Parenthesis (")") | {)} |
| Delete | {DELETE} or {DEL} |
| Down Arrow | {DOWN} |
| End | {END} |
| Enter | ~ |
| Escape | {ESCAPE} or {ESC} |
| F1 through F16 | {F1} through {F16} |
| Help | {HELP} |
| Home | {HOME} |
| Insert | {INSERT} or {INS} |
| Keypad Add | {ADD} |
| Keypad Divide | {DIVIDE} |
| Keypad Enter | {ENTER} |
| Keypad Multiply | {MULTIPLY} |
| Keypad Subtract | {SUBTRACT} |
| Left Arrow | {LEFT} |
| Num Lock | {NUMLOCK} |
| Open Brace ({) | {{} |
| Open Bracket ([) | {[} |
| Open Parenthesis (" (") | {(} |
| Page Down | {PGDN} |
| Page Up | {PGUP} |
| Percent Sign (%) | {%} |
| Plus (+) | {+} |
| Print Screen | {PRTSC} |
| Return | {RETURN} |
| Right Arrow | {RIGHT} |
| Scroll Lock | {SCROLLLOCK} |
| Tab | {TAB} |
| Tilde (~) | {~} |
| Up Arrow | {UP} |

## Usage at a Glance

- *Send* and *SendWait* will only work directly with applications designed to run in Microsoft Windows.
- You may find that some keys or key combinations cannot be sent successfully. For example, you cannot send the Print Screen key to any application. Also, you cannot send the Alt+Tab key combination ("%{Tab}").
- Because of the event-driven nature of Windows, and because the user can change to a different active window at any time, there is no guarantee that the keys you intend to send to a window will ever arrive at that window.

## Example

The following program uses the Notepad application to add some text to the clipboard.

```
Dim notepadID As Integer

' ----- Start and activate the Notepad.
notepadID = Shell("notepad.exe", AppWinStyle.NormalFocus)
AppActivate(notepadID)
Windows.Forms.Application.DoEvents()

' ----- Add some text.
SendKeys.SendWait("+visual +basic~")
SendKeys.SendWait("{- 12}~")
SendKeys.SendWait("+it's fun{!}")

' ----- Select all text with Control+A, then copy with Control+C.
SendKeys.SendWait("^(a)")
SendKeys.SendWait("^(c)")

' ----- Quit Notepad.
SendKeys.SendWait("%{F4}")
SendKeys.SendWait("n")

' ----- See if we copied the text correctly.
MsgBox(My.Computer.Clipboard.GetText())
```

## Version Differences

Visual Basic 2005 includes the *My.Computer.Keyboard.SendKeys* method, which provides equivalent functionality.

## See Also

AppActivate Procedure

---

# SetAttr Procedure

## Class

Microsoft.VisualBasic.FileSystem

## Syntax

```
SetAttr(pathname, attributes)
```

*pathname  (required; String)*
> The file or directory whose attribute details are to be set.

*attributes  (required; FileAttribute enumeration)*
> One or more of the following *Microsoft.VisualBasic.FileAttribute* enumeration values, added or Or'd together. Each member also has a related Visual Basic intrinsic constant that can be used instead.

| Enumeration | Constant | Description |
| --- | --- | --- |
| Normal | vbNormal | · Normal file (the absence of other attributes) |
| ReadOnly | vbReadOnly | Read-only file |
| Hidden | vbHidden | Hidden file |
| System | vbSystem | System file |
| Archive | vbArchive | File has changed since the last backup |

## Description

The SetAttr procedure modifies the attributes of a file or directory.

## Usage at a Glance

- *pathname* can be either an absolute or relative path to a file. It can exist on the local or remote drive and can use the drive-letter or UNC path format.
- An error occurs if *pathname* is invalid or cannot be found.
- Attempting to set the attributes of an open file generates a runtime error.
- Setting file attributes clears any attributes that are not included in the *attributes* argument. For example, if *somefile.txt* is a read-only file, the statement:

  ```
  SetAttr("somefile.txt", vbArchive)
  ```

  sets the archive attribute but clears the read-only attribute. To retain a file's attributes while setting new ones, first retrieve its attributes using the GetAttr function.
- The *FileAttribute.Directory* enumeration member cannot be applied to a file or directory; it can only be set by the operating system.

## Version Differences

Visual Basic 2005 includes *My.Computer.FileSystem.GetDirectoryInfo* and *My. Computer.FileSystem.GetFileInfo* methods that provide access to related functionality.

## See Also

GetAttr Function

---

# Shadows Keyword

## Description

The Shadows keyword identifies a type member in a derived class that masks another member of the same name, as found in the base class.

When a member of a derived class has the same name as a member of the same type in the base class, and the keywords Overridable and Overrides are used appropriately, then the derived class member overrides the base class member. Any reference to the member using a derived class object refers to the implementation in the derived class.

Shadowing works in a similar way but allows any member type to "override" any other member type. For example, a method can "override" a property, or a constant can "override" a delegate. For a complete discussion of shadowing, see the "Shadowing and Overloading Members" section of Chapter 3.

### Version Differences

The Shadows keyword is new to VB under .NET.

---

## Shared Keyword

### Description

The Shared keyword indicates that a type member is a *shared member* instead of an *instance member*. Shared members are available without creating an instance of the type; instance members can only be used through an instance. Consider the following simple class:

```
Friend Class ClassForSharing
    Public Shared sharedValue As Integer
    Public unsharedValue As Integer
End Class
```

The following code block shows how to access each member.

```
Dim realInstance As New ClassForSharing
ClassForSharing.sharedValue = 5
realInstance.unsharedValue = 10
```

Shared members are indirectly shared among all instances of the class, even though they exist apart from all instances.

The Shared keyword can be used with the following statements:

Dim Statement
Event Statement
Function Statement
Operator Statement
Property Statement
Sub Statement

By default, all of these members are instance members unless qualified with the Shared keyword.

### See Also

For the statements listed above, see the related entries elsewhere in this chapter for usage information.

---

## Shell Function

### Class

Microsoft.VisualBasic.Interaction

### Syntax

```
Dim result As Integer = Shell(pathName[, style[, wait[, timeout]]])
```

*pathName* *(required; String)*
   The name and path of the program to start.

*style* (optional; *AppWinStyle enumeration*)

The style of the new application's window and whether it receives the focus automatically when starting up. One of the following *Microsoft.VisualBasic. AppWinStyle* enumeration values:

| Value | Description |
|---|---|
| Hide | The new application window is hidden and does not receive the focus. |
| NomalFocus | The new application window is displayed normally and immediately receives the focus. |
| MinimizedFocus | The new application window is minimized but does receive the focus. |
| MaximizedFocus | The new application window is maximized and immediately receives the focus. |
| MinimizedNoFocus | The new application window is minimized and does not receive the focus. |
| MaximizedNoFocus | The new application window is maximized but does not receive the focus. |

If omitted, the default value is MinimizedFocus.

*wait* (optional; *Boolean*)

Indicates whether to wait for the *pathName* application to finish execution before continuing execution of subsequent code (True) or not (False). If omitted, the default value is False.

*timeout* (optional; *Integer*)

If *wait* is True, this argument indicates the number of milliseconds to wait for the *pathName* application to terminate before the Shell function times out. If omitted, the default value is -1, which indicates that the Shell function should never time out.

## Description

The Shell function launches another application and, if successful, returns that application's task or process ID.

## Usage at a Glance

- *pathName* can be a relative or absolute path on a local or remote drive.

- *pathName* can include, after the application name, any command-line arguments and switches required by the application. For example:

      Call Shell("notepad.exe c:\data.txt", AppWinStyle.NormalFocus)

  launches Notepad, which then loads the file *c:\data.txt*.

- If the application named in *pathName* executes successfully, Shell returns the Windows task ID of the program. (The task ID is also known as the process ID (PID), a unique 32-bit value used to identify each running process.) This value can be used as an argument to the AppActivate procedure. The process ID is also required by a number of Win32 API functions.

- If the application named in *pathName* fails to execute, a runtime error occurs.

- The file launched by Shell must be executable. That is, it must be a file with an extension that is .EXE or .COM (an executable file), .BAT (a batch file), or .PIF (a DOS shortcut file). You cannot use Shell to launch web pages or other URL-based resources. It also cannot be used to launch applications by association. Using "MyDocument.txt" for *pathName* will not start Notepad.

- *Wait* determines whether the Shell function operates synchronously (True) or asynchronously (False). The default is False; control returns immediately to the application, and the code continues executing as soon as the process ID is known. If True, the Shell function returns only when the *pathName* application is closed or, if *timeout* is not -1, when the timeout period has expired.

- If the *pathName* application exits before the Shell function returns, the return value of Shell will be 0.

- Setting *wait* to True and leaving *timeout* at its default value of -1 creates the possibility that control will never return from the *pathName* application to the initiating application.

### Version Differences
The *wait* and *timeout* arguments are new to .NET. They are not supported by VB 6.

### See Also
AppActivate Procedure

---

## Sign Function

### Class
System.Math

### Syntax
```
Dim result As Integer = Sign(value)
```
*value* (required; any signed numeric type)
A numeric expression of one of the following data types: Decimal, Double, Integer, Long, SByte, Single, or Short

### Description
The *Sign* function determines the sign of a number. It returns 1 for negative numbers, 1 for positive numbers, or 0 for zero.

### Usage at a Glance
- This is a shared member of the *System.Math* class, so it can be used without an instance.

- Use the CBool function instead of the *Sign* function to evaluate a logic truth value.

### Version Differences
The name of this function has changed since VB 6. In VB 6, its name was Sgn, and it was an intrinsic VB function. In .NET, it is named *Sign*, and it is a member of the *System.Math* class.

### See Also
Abs Function

# Sin Function

### Class
System.Math

### Syntax
```
Dim result As Double = Sin(a)
```
*a* *(required; Double)*
    An angle expressed in radians

### Description
The *Sin* function returns the sine of an angle, the ratio of two sides of a right triangle, in the range -1 to 1.

### Usage at a Glance
- The ratio is determined by dividing the length of the side opposite the angle by the length of the hypotenuse.
- This is a shared member of the *System.Math* class, so it can be used without an instance.
- To convert degrees to radians, multiply degrees by $\pi/180$.
- To convert radians to degrees, multiply radians by $180/\pi$.

### Version Differences
In VB 6, Sin is an intrinsic VB function. In the .NET platform, it is a member of the *System.Math* class and not directly part of the VB language.

### See Also
Cos Function, Tan Function

---

# Sinh Function

### Class
System.Math

### Syntax
```
Dim result As Double = Math.Sinh(value)
```
*value* *(required; Double)*
    An angle expressed in radians

### Description
The *Sinh* function returns the hyperbolic sine of an angle.

### Usage at a Glance
This is a shared member of the *System.Math* class, so it can be used without an instance.

### Version Differences

The *Sinh* function did not exist in VB 6.

### See Also

Cosh Function, Tanh Function

---

## SLN Function

### Class

Microsoft.VisualBasic.Financial

### Syntax

```
Dim result As Double = SLN(cost, salvage, life)
```

*cost* *(required; Double)*
: The initial cost of the asset

*salvage* *(required; Double)*
: The value of the asset at the end of its useful life

*life* *(required; Double)*
: The length of the useful life of the asset

### Description

The SLN function computes the straight-line depreciation of an asset for a single period. Each period receives an equal depreciation share.

### Usage at a Glance

- The function uses a very simple formula to calculate depreciation:

  ```
  depreciation = (cost - salvage) / life
  ```

- All arguments must be positive numeric values.

### See Also

DDB Function, SYD Function

---

## Space Function

### Class

Microsoft.VisualBasic.Strings

### Syntax

```
Dim result As String = Space(number)
```

*number* *(required; Integer)*
: The number of spaces required

### Description

The Space function creates a string containing *number* spaces.

## Usage at a Glance

- While *number* can be zero (in which case, the function returns the empty string), a runtime error occurs if *number* is negative.
- One of the custom constructors for the String data type can also be used to create a string of spaces. The following statement creates a new string with 10 spaces.

```
Dim blankString As New String(" "c, 10)
```

## See Also

SPC Function, StrDup Function

---

# SPC Function

## Class

Microsoft.VisualBasic.FileSystem

## Syntax

```
Dim result As SPCInfo = SPC(count)
```

*count* (required; Short)
The number of spaces to insert before outputting the next data value

## Description

The SPC function inserts spaces between expressions in a Print or PrintLine procedure.

## Usage at a Glance

- SPC is generally only useful with the Print or PrintLine procedures.
- If the SPC function moves the current position past the end of the output width, *count* is first reduced using the formula *count* Mod *width*. In some cases, this may still bring the print position to the next line.
- Use the TAB function to format data in columns, starting at specific positions on each line.

## Version Differences

In Visual Basic 2005, the *My.Computer.FileSystem* object provides more robust access to file management features.

## See Also

Print, PrintLine Procedures, TAB Function

---

# Split Function

## Class

Microsoft.VisualBasic.Strings

## Syntax

```
Dim result() As String = Split(expression[, delimiter[, _
    limit[, compare]]])
```

*expression* (required; String)
A string to be broken up into multiple strings.

*delimiter* (optional; String)
The character used to delimit the substrings in *expression*. If omitted, the space character is used.

*limit* (optional; Integer)
The maximum number of strings to return. If omitted, -1 is used, which indicates that no limit is imposed.

*compare* (optional; CompareMethod enumeration)
Indicates the text comparison method. One of the following *Microsoft.Visual-Basic.CompareMethod* enumeration values:

| Value | Description |
| --- | --- |
| Binary | Performs a binary (case-sensitive) comparison |
| Text | Performs a text (case-insensitive) comparison |

If omitted, Binary is used.

## Description

The Split function splits a string into multiple smaller strings using *delimiter* to determine where to divide the string, and it returns the results as an array of strings.

## Usage at a Glance

- If *expression* is a zero-length string, Split returns an empty array.
- If *delimiter* is not found in *expression*, Split returns the entire string in element 0 of the returned array.
- Once one less than *limit* has been reached, the remainder of the string is placed, unprocessed, into the final element of the returned array.
- Strings are written to the returned array in the order in which they appear in *expression*.
- The setting of *compare* impacts how *delimiter* is compared with the text of *expression*.

## See Also

Join Function

# Sqrt Function

## Class

System.Math

## Syntax

```
Dim result As Double = Sqrt(d)
```

*d* (required; Double)
Any numeric expression greater than or equal to 0

## Description

The *Sqrt* function calculates the square root of a given number, *d*.

## Usage at a Glance

This is a shared member of the *System.Math* class, so it can be used without an instance.

## Version Differences

The name of this function has changed since VB 6. In VB 6, its name was Sqr, and it was an intrinsic VB function. In .NET, it is named *Sqrt*, and it is a member of the *System.Math* class.

## See Also

Pow Function

---

# Stack Class

## Namespace

System.Collections (standard version)

System.Collections.Generic (generic version)

## Creatable

Yes

## Description

The *Stack* object implements a "last in, first out" (LIFO) data structure. Items are added to the top of the stack, and new items are placed "on top" of the previously added items. Only the current topmost item can be removed. A real-life parallel would be a stack of books or a stack of pancakes.

The stack includes features for adding items (*Push*), removing items (*Pop*), and counting the items in the stack (*Count*), among other features. Objects of any type may be added to the stack.

The following table lists some of the more useful and interesting members of the *Stack* class. Those marked with an asterisk (*) have separate entries in this chapter.

| Member | Description |
| --- | --- |
| Clear Method | Removes all items from the stack |
| Clone Method | Makes a distinct copy of the stack and its members |
| Contains Method * | Indicates whether a specific object is on the stack |
| CopyTo Method * | Copies stack elements to an existing array |
| Count Property | Indicates the number of items currently on the stack |
| IsReadOnly Property | Indicates whether the stack is read-only or not |
| Peek Method * | Returns the top stack item without removing it |
| Pop Method * | Removes and returns the top item on the stack |
| Push Method * | Adds a new item to the top of the stack |
| ToArray Method* | Copies the stack to a new array |

## Example

This sample code shows the basic use of the stack.

```
' ----- Add some basic items to a stack.
Dim nameStack As New Stack
nameStack.Push("Chopin")
nameStack.Push("Mozart")
nameStack.Push("Beethoven")

' ----- Examine and return the items.
MsgBox(nameStack.Peek())    ' Displays "Beethoven"
MsgBox(nameStack.Pop())     ' Displays "Beethoven"
MsgBox(nameStack.Pop())     ' Displays "Mozart"

' ----- Remove the remaining items.
MsgBox(nameStack.Count)     ' Displays 1 (for Chopin)
nameStack.Clear()
```

## Version Differences

Visual Basic 2005 adds support for generics to several collection-style classes, including the *Stack* class. The version of the *Stack* class that supports generics appears in the *System.Collections.Generic* namespace. Generics are discussed in Chapter 10.

## See Also

Collection Class, Hashtable Class, Queue Class

---

# Stack.Contains Method

## Class

System.Collections.Stack (standard version)

System.Collections.Generic.Stack (generic version)

## Syntax

```
Dim result As Boolean = stackVariable.Contains(obj)
```

*obj* (required; any)
: The object to search for on the stack

## Description

The *Contains* method indicates whether a given object is somewhere on the stack (True) or not (False).

## Usage at a Glance

- *obj* must correspond exactly to an item on the stack for the method to return True.
- String comparison is case-sensitive and is not affected by the setting of the OptionCompare statement.

## Version Differences

Visual Basic 2005 adds support for generics to stacks, as discussed in Chapter 10.

---

Stack Class

---

## Stack.CopyTo Method

### Class
System.Collections.Stack (standard version)

System.Collections.Generic.Stack (generic version)

### Syntax
```
stackVariable.CopyTo(array, index)
```
*array  (required; compatible array)*
   Array to which to copy the stack's objects

*index  (required; Integer)*
   The index of the first zero-based array element to receive a stack member

### Description
The *CopyTo* method copies the stack elements into an existing array, starting at a specified array index.

### Usage at a Glance
- The array can be of any data type that is compatible with the stack elements. An array of Integer can accept Short stack elements but not String elements.
- The array must be sized to accommodate the elements of the stack prior to calling the *CopyTo* method.

### Example
The sample code copies stack items to an array.
```
Dim nameStack As New Stack
Dim nameArray( ) As Object

' ----- Build the stack.
nameStack.Push("Chopin")
nameStack.Push("Mozart")
nameStack.Push("Beethoven")

' ----- Size the array and copy elements.
ReDim nameArray(nameStack.Count - 1)
nameStack.CopyTo(nameArray, 0)
```

### Version Differences
Visual Basic 2005 adds support for generics to stacks, as discussed in Chapter 10.

### See Also
Stack Class, Stack.ToArray Method

---

# Stack.Peek Method

## Class
System.Collections.Stack (standard version)
System.Collections.Generic.Stack (generic version)

## Syntax
```
Dim result As Object = stackVariable.Peek( )
```

## Description
The *Peek* method returns the top item on the stack as an Object, but does not remove it from the stack.

## Usage at a Glance
The *Peek* method is similar to the *Stack* object's *Pop* method, except that it leaves the stack intact.

## Version Differences
Visual Basic 2005 adds support for generics to stacks, as discussed in Chapter 10.

## See Also
Stack Class, Stack.Pop Method

---

# Stack.Pop Method

## Class
System.Collections.Stack (standard version)
System.Collections.Generic.Stack (generic version)

## Syntax
```
Dim result As Object = stackVariable.Pop( )
```

## Description
The *Pop* method removes the top item from the stack and returns it as an Object.

## Usage at a Glance
*Pop* generates an error if applied to an empty stack. Use the *Count* property to check for items on the stack.

## Version Differences
Visual Basic 2005 adds support for generics to stacks, as discussed in Chapter 10.

## See Also
Stack Class, Stack.Peek Method

# Stack.Push Method

## Class
System.Collections.Stack (standard version)

System.Collections.Generic.Stack (generic version)

## Syntax
```
stackVariable.Push(obj)
```
*obj* *(required; any)*
    The item to place on the stack

## Description
The *Push* method places an object on the top of the stack.

## Version Differences
Visual Basic 2005 adds support for generics to stacks, as discussed in Chapter 10.

## See Also
Stack Class, Stack.Pop Method

# Stack.ToArray Method

## Class
System.Collections.Stack (standard version)

System.Collections.Generic.Stack (generic version)

## Syntax
```
Dim result( ) As Object = stackVariable.ToArray( )
```

## Description
The *ToArray* method creates an array of type Object, copies the elements of the stack in order into the array, and then returns the array. The array need not be created in advance.

## Usage at a Glance
The top item on the stack becomes array element zero.

## Version Differences
Visual Basic 2005 adds support for generics to stacks, as discussed in Chapter 10.

## See Also
Stack Class, Stack.CopyTo Method

# STAThread Attribute

## Class
System.STAThreadAttribute

## Applies To
Method

## Constructor
New( )

## Properties
None defined

## Description
The <STAThread> attribute indicates that the application to which the program element belongs uses the *single-threaded apartment* model for COM interop. The attribute should be applied to the application's *Main* method or subroutine. This attribute only applies to applications that use COM interop.

The <STAThread> attribute is similar to setting a *System.Threading.Thread* object's *ApartmentState* property to *ApartmentState.STA*. The difference is that the <STAThread> attribute creates a single-threaded apartment from startup, while setting the property does it only from the point that the property is set.

## See Also
MTAThread Attribute

---

# Static Statement

## Description
The Static statement is used at the procedure level to define a local variable with a value that is retained for the lifetime of the object in which it appears, even when the variable goes out of scope (that is, even when the procedure's code is not currently being executed).

The Static statement is actually a variation of the Dim statement. For more information on the syntax and use of the Static statement, see the *Dim Statement* entry elsewhere in this chapter.

## See Also
Dim Statement

---

# Stop Statement

## Syntax
```
Stop
```

---

## Description

The Stop statement suspends program execution.

## Usage at a Glance

- There is no limit to the number and position of Stop statements within procedures.

- The Stop statement acts like a breakpoint—placing the program in break mode and highlighting the current line in the development environment—allowing you to step through the code line by line.

- Stop is intended primarily for use in the design-time environment, where it suspends program execution without terminating it. In the runtime environment, Stop invokes the debugger.

- Unlike the End statement, Stop does not explicitly close any open files or clear any variables, except in a compiled executable.

## See Also

End Statement

## Str Function

### Class

Microsoft.VisualBasic.Conversion

### Syntax

```
Dim result As String = Str(number)
```

*number* *(required; Object)*
Any valid numeric expression or an expression that can be converted to a number

### Description

The Str function converts *number* from a number to a string.

### Usage at a Glance

- If *number* cannot be converted to a string, a runtime error occurs. To prevent this, check *number* with the IsNumeric function first.

- If the return value is positive, the Str function always includes a leading space in the returned string for the sign of *number*.

- Use the LTrim function to remove the leading space that the Str function adds to the start of the returned string.

- The CStr and Format functions are often a better choice than the Str function. The CStr function does not add a leading space for the sign of a positive number. Both the CStr and the Format functions are internationally aware, recognizing locale-specific decimal delimiters.

### See Also

CStr Function, Format Function

# StrComp Function

## Class

Microsoft.VisualBasic.Strings

## Syntax

```
Dim result As Integer = StrComp(string1, string2[, compare])
```

*string1* *(required; String)*
  Any string expression.

*string2* *(required; String)*
  Any string expression.

*compare* *(optional; CompareMethod constant)*
  Indicates the text comparison method. One of the following *Microsoft.Visual-Basic.CompareMethod* enumeration values:

| Value | Description |
|-------|-------------|
| Binary | Performs a binary (case-sensitive) comparison |
| Text | Performs a text (case-insensitive) comparison |

If omitted, the current Option Compare method in effect is used.

## Description

The StrComp function determines whether two strings are equal and, if not, which of the two strings has the greater value. The following table identifies the return values.

| Scenario | Return value |
|----------|--------------|
| string1 < string2 | -1 |
| string1 = string2 | 0 |
| string1 > string2 | 1 |
| *string1* or *string2* is Null | Null |

## Usage at a Glance

- Using the comparison operators <, <=, >, and >= to compare strings performs a character-by-character binary comparison.
- The StrComp function can provide a significant performance improvement (in the neighborhood of 30 percent to 70 percent) over the comparison operators.

## See Also

StrConv Function, StrDup Function, StrReverse Function

---

# StrConv Function

## Class

Microsoft.VisualBasic.Strings

## Syntax

```
Dim result As String = StrConv(str, conversion[, localeID])
```

*str* (required; String)

The string expression to convert.

*conversion* (required; VbStrConv enumeration)

The type of conversion to perform. One or more of the following *Microsoft.Visual-Basic.VbStrConv* enumeration values (multiple constants can be Or'd together):

| Value | Description |
|---|---|
| UpperCase | Converts the entire string to uppercase. |
| LowerCase | Converts the entire string to lowercase. |
| ProperCase | Capitalizes only the first letter of each word. |
| Wide | Widens supported characters from their narrow equivalents. |
| Narrow | Narrows supported characters from their wide equivalents. |
| Katakana | Converts *hiragana* characters to *katakana*. |
| Hiragana | Converts *katakana* characters to *hiragana*. |
| LinguisticCasing | Uses linguistic rules for casing. To use this, Or this constant together with UpperCase or LowerCase. |
| None | Performs no conversion; returns the original string. |
| SimplifiedChinese | Converts traditional Chinese characters to simplified Chinese. |
| TraditionalChinese | Converts simplified Chinese characters to traditional Chinese. |

*localeID* (optional; Integer)

The locale identifier to use for the conversion.

## Description

The StrConv function performs a special character conversion on *str*, and returns the converted version.

## Usage at a Glance

- You can combine multiple *VbStrConv* constants together by adding or Or'ing them together, as long as they are not mutually exclusive in meaning. For instance, the following pair is valid:

  ```
  VbStrConv.UpperCase Or VbStrConv.Wide
  ```

  but the following statement is not:

  ```
  VbStrConv.UpperCase Or VbStrConv.LowerCase
  ```

- *VbStrConv.Katakana* and *VbStrConv.Hiragana* can only be used with Japanese locales.

- *VbStrConv.Wide* and *VbStrConv.Narrow* can only be used with Asian locales.

- When determining the start of a new word to convert to proper case, StrConv recognizes the following characters as word separators (with their decimal ASCII values in parentheses): Null (0), Horizontal Tab (9), Line Feed (10), Vertical Tab (11), Form Feed (12), Carriage Return (13), and Space (32).

- If you convert to proper case, StrConv converts the first letter of each word to uppercase, regardless of whether that word is significant. The string "this is the time" becomes "This Is The Time," even though "the" ordinarily would not be capitalized.

## Version Differences

Two *conversion* values supported in VB 6, vbUnicode and vbFromUnicode, have no equivalent in .NET. The function can no longer be used to convert ASCII to Unicode or Unicode to ASCII.

## See Also

StrComp Function, StrDup Function, StrReverse Function

---

# StrDup Function

## Class

Microsoft.VisualBasic.Strings

## Syntax

```
Dim result As String = StrDup(number, character)
```

*number* (required; Integer)
> The number of times to duplicate the first character in a string.

*character* (required; String, Char, or Object)
> The content with the first character that is to be duplicated. If the data type is Object, it must contain a String or Char value, and Object will be returned instead of String.

## Description

The StrDup function returns a string that consists of the first character of *character* duplicated *number* times.

## Version Differences

The StrDup function is new to .NET. It can be used as a partial replacement for the VB 6 String function.

## See Also

Space Function

---

# StrReverse Function

## Class

Microsoft.VisualBasic.Strings

## Syntax

```
Dim result As String = StrReverse(expression)
```

*expression* (required; String)
> The string whose characters are to be reversed

## Description

The StrReverse function returns a string that is the reverse of the string passed to it. For example, if the string "and" is passed to it as an argument, StrReverse returns the string "dna."

---

## Structure...End Structure Statement

### Syntax

```
[accessModifier] [Shadows] Structure name [(Of typeParamName)]
    [Implements interfaceName[, interfaceName...]]
    statements
End Structure
```

*accessModifier (optional)*

Specifies the scope and accessibility of the structure. One of the following access levels:

| Access level | Description |
| --- | --- |
| Public | The structure is publicly accessible anywhere, both inside and outside of the project. |
| Private | The structure is accessible within the type in which it is defined. |
| Protected | The structure is accessible only to the type in which it is defined and to derived instances of that type. |
| Friend | The structure is accessible only within the project that contains the structure definition. |
| Protected Friend | Combines the access features of Protected and Friend. |

If omitted, the Friend access level is used.

*Shadows (optional)*

Indicates that the structure shadows an identically named element in a base class.

*name (required)*

The name of the structure.

*typeParamName (optional; any)*

Adds type parameter placeholders that will later enforce strong typing when the structure is used. The Of clause implements generics, which are fully described in Chapter 10. If generics will not be used, this clause can be excluded.

*interfaceName (optional)*

Indicates that the structure implements the members of one or more interfaces.

*statements (required)*

Code that defines the members of the structure. Structures must contain at least one instance member.

### Description

The Structure...End Structure statement is used to declare structures, also known as user-defined types. Structures are similar to classes, but they are value types rather than reference types. Although you can create an instance of a structure, you cannot derive another structure or class from it.

## Usage at a Glance

- The members of a structure can be fields, properties, methods, events, or types. Each member must be declared with an access modifier.

- You cannot assign a structure member an initial value as part of its declaration. The initial values of structure members can be set in the structure's constructor.

- If a structure member is an array, it cannot be explicitly dimensioned in its definition.

- Although structures are similar to classes, they cannot explicitly inherit, nor can they be inherited. All constructors for a structure must be parameterized, and structures cannot define destructors.

## Example

The simplest and most common use of structures is to encapsulate related variables, as in this sample code:

```
Structure Person
    Public Name As String
    Public Address As String
    Public City As String
    Public State As String
    Public Zip As String
    Public Age As Short
End Structure
```

An instance of Person is declared as:

```
Dim personRecord As Person
```

As with classes, structure members use the "dot" syntax:

```
personRecord.Name = "Beethoven"
```

## Version Differences

- The Structure...EndStructure construct is new to VB under .NET. It replaces the Type...EndType construct in VB 6. The syntax and functionality differences between the two are significant.

- VB 6 user-defined types are groupings of basic data types. .NET structures are objects, similar to classes, with similar OOP features.

- Visual Basic 2005 adds support for generics to structures, as discussed in Chapter 10.

## See Also

Class...End Class Statement

---

# Sub Statement

## Syntax

```
[accessModifier] [procModifier] [Shared] [Shadows] _
    Sub name [(Of typeParamName)] ([arglist]) _
    [Implements implementsList | Handles eventList]
    [statements]
```

```
    [Exit Sub | Return]
    [statements]
End Sub
```

*accessModifier* *(optional)*

Specifies the scope and accessibility of the procedure. One of the following access levels:

| Access level | Description |
| --- | --- |
| Public | The procedure is publicly accessible anywhere, both inside and outside of the project. |
| Private | The procedure is accessible only within the defining type. |
| Protected | The procedure is accessible only to the code in the defining type or to one of its derived types. |
| Friend | The procedure is accessible only within the project that contains the procedure definition. |
| Protected Friend | Combines the access features of Protected and Friend. |

If omitted, the Public access level is used.

*procModifier* *(optional)*

One of the keywords shown in the following table:

| Keyword | Description |
| --- | --- |
| Overloads | Indicates that more than one declaration of this subroutine exists, each with a different argument signature |
| Overrides | For derived classes, indicates that the subroutine overrides a subroutine with the same name and argument signature in the base class |
| Overridable | Indicates that the subroutine can be overridden in a derived class |
| NotOverridable | Indicates that the subroutine cannot be overridden in a derived class |
| MustOverride | Indicates that the subroutine must be overridden in a derived class |

Shared *(optional)*

Indicates that the subroutine is shared and not an instance subroutine. The shared subroutine may be called without a particular instance of the type in which it appears. Shared subroutines are also known as *static subroutines*.

Shadows *(optional)*

Indicates that the subroutine shadows an identically named element in a base class.

*name* *(required)*

The name of the subroutine. If you use the name "New," the procedure will be a constructor. If you use the name "Finalize" and include the Overrides keyword, the procedure will be a destructor.

*typeParamName* *(optional; any)*

Adds type parameter placeholders that will later enforce strong typing when the procedure is used. The Of clause implements generics, which are fully described in Chapter 10. If generics will not be used, this clause can be excluded.

*arglist (optional; any)*

A comma-delimited list of parameters to be supplied to the procedure as arguments from the calling routine.

*arglist* uses the following syntax and parts:

```
[Optional] [ByVal | ByRef] [ParamArray] varname[()] _
    [As argtype] [= defaultValue]
```

Optional *(optional)*

Flags an argument as optional; optional arguments need not be supplied by the calling routine. All arguments following an optional argument must also be optional. A ParamArray argument cannot be optional.

ByVal *(optional)*

The argument is passed by value; the local copy of the variable is assigned the value of the argument. ByVal is the default method of passing variables.

ByRef *(optional)*

The argument is passed by reference; the local variable is a reference to the argument being passed. All changes made to the local variable will also be reflected in the calling argument.

ParamArray *(optional)*

The argument is an optional array containing an arbitrary number of elements. It can only be used as the last element of the argument list and cannot be modified by either the ByRef or Optional keywords. If Option Strict is on, the array type must also be specified.

*varname (required)*

The name of the argument as used in the local procedure.

*argtype (optional; Type)*

The data type of the argument. Any valid .NET data type can be used.

*defaultValue (optional; any)*

For optional arguments, indicates the default value to be supplied when the calling routine does not supply the value. When the Optional keyword is used, this default value is required.

*implementsList (optional)*

Comma-separated list of the interface members implemented by this procedure.

*eventList (optional)*

Comma-separated list of the events handled by this procedure. Each event is in the form *eventVariable.eventMember*, where *eventVariable* is a variable declared with the WithEvents keyword, and *eventMember* is an event member of that variable.

*statements (optional)*

Program code to be executed within the procedure.

## Description

The Sub statement defines a subroutine, including all arguments. Subroutines can appear within classes, structures, or modules. To call a subroutine, specify its name, followed by any arguments in parentheses.

```
SomeSubroutine(12, "second argument")
```

## Usage at a Glance

- Subroutines cannot be nested; you cannot define one subroutine inside another subroutine.
- Overloads and Shadows cannot be used in the same declaration.
- Any number of ExitSub or Return statements can be placed within the subroutine. When these statements are encountered, execution continues with the line of code immediately following the call to the subroutine.
- The names of a procedure's parameters become the procedure's named arguments.

## Version Differences

- There are several syntax and functionality differences in the declaration of a procedure between VB 6 and the .NET version of VB.
- In VB 6, arguments to procedures are passed by reference if no passing method is specified. In .NET, the default is to pass by value.
- If a parameter array is used in VB 6, it is an array of variants. In .NET, all parameter arrays are either of type Object or of some other strong type.
- In VB 6, parentheses only surrounded the arguments of a procedure call when the Call keyword was used. In .NET, parentheses always surround the arguments.
- In VB 6, optional arguments do not require that you specify a default value. Instead, the IsMissing function is used to determine whether the optional argument is supplied. In .NET, you must assign a default value to an optional argument.
- Visual Basic 2005 adds support for generics to subroutines, as discussed in Chapter 10.

## See Also

Function Statement

---

# Switch Function

## Class

Microsoft.VisualBasic.Interaction

## Syntax

```
Dim result As Object = Switch(expr_1, value_1[, _
    expr_2, value_2[..., expr_n, value_n]])
```

*expr_1 to expr_n  (required; Boolean)*
A number of expressions to be evaluated.

*value_1 to value_n (required; Object)*
A number of expressions from which one is returned if the associated expression is the first one to evaluate to True.

Instead of using a comma-delimited list of expressions and values, all expressions and values can be stored in a ParamArray object, with elements in the same order that they would appear in the argument list.

---

## Description

The Switch function evaluates a list of expressions and, on finding the first expression to evaluate to True, returns an associated value.

## Usage at a Glance

- At least one expression/value pair must be included, and they must always appear in pairs.

- Expressions are evaluated from left to right.

- If none of the expressions is True, the Switch function returns Nothing.

- The parameters can be variables, constants, literals, expressions, or function calls. Each value parameter may be of a different type; the return value will be of type Object.

- All parameters are fully evaluated before they are considered as conditions or results for the Switch function. If they contain function calls, those functions will be called, even in the items that are not returned by the function. For instance, in the statement:

  ```
  result = Switch(useTempFile, ProcessFile(tempFileName), _
      True, ProcessFile(mainFileName))
  ```

  both calls to ProcessFile will always be performed, regardless of the value of useTempFile. However, at most, only one return value from among the function calls will be returned from the Switch function, and possibly none.

- This function does not support named arguments.

- By providing all parameters in the form of a ParamArray, the list of values can be expanded or contracted programmatically at runtime.

## Example

This example returns a string based on a selection of numeric ranges.

```
rangeText = Switch(currentValue < 0, "Negative", _
    currentValue > 0, "Positive", True, "Neutral")
```

## See Also

Choose Function

---

# SYD Function

## Class

Microsoft.VisualBasic.Financial

## Syntax

```
Dim result As Double = SYD(cost, salvage, life, period)
```

cost *(required; Double)*
: The initial cost of the asset

salvage *(required; Double)*
: The value of the asset at the end of its useful life

*life (required; Double)*
The length of the useful life of the asset

*period (required; Double)*
The period whose depreciation is to be calculated

## Description

The SYD function computes the sum-of-years' digits depreciation of an asset for a specified period. The sum-of-years' digits method allocates a larger amount of the depreciation in the earlier years of the asset.

## Usage at a Glance

- *life* and *period* must be expressed in the same time unit. For example, if *life* represents the life of the asset in years, *period* must be a particular year for which the depreciation amount is to be computed.

- All arguments must be positive numeric values.

- To calculate the depreciation for a given period, SYD uses the formula:

  (Cost-Salvage)*((Life-Period + 1)/(Life*(Life + 1)/2))

## See Also

DDB Function, SLN Function

---

# SyncLock Statement

## Syntax

```
SyncLock lockObject
    [code]
End SyncLock
```

*lockObject (required; any)*
The variable or instance to be locked; it is used as a gatekeeper for the enclosed code

*code (optional)*
Any Visual Basic source code that needs to be protected from simultaneous use by separate threads

## Description

The SyncLock statement prevents multiple threads of execution in the same process from accessing a block of code at the same time.

## Usage at a Glance

- *lockObject* cannot be set to Nothing.

- If *lockObject* is a shared object, all instances with access to that object are blocked until the SyncLock block exits. If it is an instance object, only threads using that particular instance are blocked.

- You may not jump into a SyncLock block using a GoTo statement. You may jump out of the block; the lock will be properly released.

- The SyncLock statement wraps a call to the .NET Framework's *System.Threading. Monitor* class's *Enter* and *Exit* methods.

- .NET includes a number of other synchronization mechanisms, all of which are located in the *System.Threading* namespace.

## Version Differences
The SyncLock statement is new to VB under .NET.

# SystemTypeName Function

## Class
Microsoft.VisualBasic.Information

## Syntax
```
SystemTypeName(vbName)
```
*vbName* *(required; String)*
The name of a Visual Basic data type

## Description
The SystemTypeName function returns the fully qualified type name of the Common Type System (CTS) data type that corresponds to a particular Visual Basic data type. For instance, passing the name "Date" to this function returns "System.DateTime."

## Usage at a Glance
- If *vbName* is not a valid Visual Basic data type, the function returns Nothing.
- To determine the CTS data type of a particular variable, pass the variable as an argument to the TypeName function and then pass that function's return value as an argument to the SystemTypeName function. For example:
```
trueType = SystemTypeName(TypeName(someVariable))
```

## Version Differences
The SystemTypeName function is new to VB under .NET.

## See Also
TypeName Function, VbTypeName Function

# TAB Function

## Class
Microsoft.VisualBasic.FileSystem

## Syntax
```
Dim result As TABInfo = TAB([column])
```
*column* *(optional; Short)*
A column position to which the insertion point will move before outputting the next data value

## Description

The TAB function is used with the Print and PrintLine procedures to move the text-insertion point to a given 1-based column, or to the start of the next print zone, before outputting additional data.

## Usage at a Glance

- TAB is generally only useful with the Print and PrintLine procedures.
- The TAB function does not actually insert any tab (ASCII 9) characters; instead, it fills the space from the end of the last expression to column *column* (or to the start of the next print zone) with space characters.
- If the *column* argument is omitted, the text-insertion point will be moved to the beginning of the next print zone.
- The value of *column* determines the behavior of the insertion point:

| Value of column | Position of insertion point |
| --- | --- |
| Current column > *column* | Moves one line down to the *column* column. |
| *column* > Output Width | Uses the formula *column* Mod *width*. If the result is less than the current insertion point, the insertion point will move down one line; otherwise, the insertion point will remain on the same line. |
| < 1 | Column 1 |

- The width of the output is indicated by the FileWidth procedure.

## Version Differences

In Visual Basic 2005, the *My.Computer.FileSystem* object provides more robust access to file management features.

## See Also

SPC Function

# Tan Function

## Class

System.Math

## Syntax

```
Dim result As Double = Tan(a)
```

*a* (required; *Double*)
  An angle expressed in radians

## Description

The *Tan* function returns the tangent of an angle, the ratio of two sides of a right triangle.

## Usage at a Glance

- The returned ratio is derived by dividing the length of the side opposite the angle by the length of the side adjacent to the angle.
- This is a shared member of the *System.Math* class, so it can be used without an instance.
- To convert degrees to radians, multiply degrees by $\pi/180$.
- To convert radians to degrees, multiple radians by $180/\pi$.

## Version Differences

In VB 6, Tan is an intrinsic VB function. In the .NET platform, it is a member of the *System.Math* class and not directly part of the VB language.

## See Also

Cos Function, Sin Function, Tanh Function

# Tanh Function

## Class

System.Math

## Syntax

```
Dim result As Double = Math.Tanh(value)
```
*value* (required; Double)
    An angle expressed in radians

## Description

The *Tanh* function returns the hyperbolic tangent of an angle.

## Usage at a Glance

This is a shared member of the *System.Math* class, so it can be used without an instance.

## Version Differences

The *Tanh* function did not exist in VB 6.

## See Also

Cosh Function, Sinh Function, Tan Function

# ThreadStatic Attribute

## Class

System.ThreadStaticAttribute

## Applies To

Field

## Constructor

New( )

## Properties

None defined

## Description

The <ThreadStatic> attribute specifies that the value of a static field is not shared across threads, so that each thread in the application has its own version of the field. In the absence of this attribute, a static field is shared across all threads.

## Example

The example illustrates the use of the <ThreadStatic> attribute by creating a second thread and having both threads increment a static field. With the <ThreadStatic> attribute, the variable's value is maintained on a per-thread basis. If you remove the <ThreadStatic> attribute and recompile the source, the variable is maintained on a per-application basis.

```
Option Strict On

Imports Microsoft.VisualBasic
Imports System
Imports System.Threading

Public Class ThreadingTest
   <ThreadStatic> Private Shared keepCount As Integer

   Public Shared Sub Main( )
      ' ----- Start the second thread.
      Dim otherThread As New Thread(AddressOf SecondThread)
      otherThread.Start

      ' ----- Do the primary thread's work.
      IncrementCount("T1,1:")
      DelayLoop(2000)
      IncrementCount("T1,2:")
      DelayLoop(2000)
      IncrementCount("T1,3:")
   End Sub

   Private Shared Sub SecondThread( )
      ' ----- Do the second thread's work.
      IncrementCount("T2,1:")
      DelayLoop(2000)
      IncrementCount("T2,2:")
      DelayLoop(2000)
      IncrementCount("T2,3:")
   End Sub

   Private Shared Sub IncrementCount(ByVal statusText As String)
      ' ----- Increment the thread-specfic static counter.
      keepCount += 1
```

```
      Console.WriteLine(statusText & keepCount)
   End Sub

   Private Shared Sub DelayLoop(ByVal milliSecs As Integer)
      ' ----- Wait a while.
      System.Threading.Thread.Sleep(milliSecs)
   End Sub
End Class
```

## Throw Statement

### Syntax

```
Throw exception
```

*exception  (required; Exception or derived from Exception)*
   A *System.Exception* object representing the exception being thrown

### Description

The Throw statement initiates an exception that can be handled using either structured exception handling (with a Try...Catch...Finally statement) or unstructured error handling (with an On Error statement).

### Example

```
Dim positiveNumber As Integer
Try
   ' ----- Throw an exception if the user enters anything other
   '        than a positive number.
   positiveNumber = CInt(InputBox("Enter number of items."))
   If (positiveNumber <= 0) Then
      Throw New Exception("Entry must be a positive number.")
   End If
Catch ex As Exception
   MsgBox(ex.Message)
End Try
```

### Version Differences

The Throw statement is new to VB under .NET.

### See Also

Exception Class, Try...Catch...Finally Statement

## TimeOfDay Property

### Class

Microsoft.VisualBasic.DateAndTime

### Syntax

```
Dim result As Date = DateAndTime.TimeOfDay
```

or:

```
DateAndTime.TimeOfDate = newTime
```

*newTime  (required in second syntax; Date)*
    A time used to set the current system time

## Description

The `TimeOfDay` property gets or sets the current system time of day. The first syntax returns a Date representing the current system time, with the date set to January 1, 1 AD. The second syntax sets the current system time using a Date; any date component of that value is ignored.

## Usage at a Glance

- The `TimeOfDay` property includes the date January 1, 1 AD, along with the current system time. Use one of the date formatting features to exclude this date when presenting the date for display:

```
MsgBox(Format(TimeOfDay, "Long Time"))
MsgBox(FormatDateTime(TimeOfDay, DateFormat.LongTime))
```

- The security settings of the active user may prevent the system date and time from being altered.

## See Also

Now Property

---

# Timer Property

## Class

Microsoft.VisualBasic.DateAndTime

## Syntax

```
Dim result As Double = DateAndTime.Timer
```

## Description

The `Timer` property returns the number of seconds since midnight.

## Usage at a Glance

- The `Timer` property is useful as a seed value for the `Randomize` procedure:

```
Randomize Timer
```

- The `Timer` property is useful for measuring the time taken to execute a procedure or block of code:

```
Dim startTime As Double
Dim counter As Integer
startTime = Timer
For counter = 1 To 100
    Console.WriteLine("Hello")
Next counter
MsgBox("Time Taken = " & Timer - startTime & " Seconds")
```

However, this type of code will sometimes fail, since the second reading of the `Timer` property may sometimes be less than the first. This occurs when the first reading occurs before midnight, but the second one is after midnight.

## Version Differences

- In VB 6, `Timer` was classified as a function; it is a read-only property in .NET. Also, the VB 6 version returned a `Single`, while the .NET version returns a `Double`.
- The 2005 release of VB includes a new *My.Computer.Clock.TickCount* property, which returns the number of milliseconds since midnight.

# TimeSerial Function

## Class

Microsoft.VisualBasic.DateAndTime

## Syntax

```
Dim result As Date = TimeSerial(hour, minute, second)
```

*hour* *(required; Integer)*
    The hour, a number between 0 and 23, inclusive

*minute* *(required; Integer)*
    The minute, a number between 0 and 59, inclusive

*second* *(required; Integer)*
    The second, a number between 0 and 59, inclusive

## Description

The `TimeSerial` function returns a `Date` with the value that is specified by the three time components.

## Usage at a Glance

- The *hour* argument requires a 24-hour clock format.
- If an element exceeds its normal limits in either a positive or negative direction, `TimeSerial` adjusts the time accordingly. For example, if you specify `TimeSerial(11, 35, 82)`—11:35:82—`TimeSerial` returns 11:36:22.
- If any of the parameters exceed the range of the `Integer` data type, a runtime error occurs.

## See Also

DateSerial Function, TimeOfDay Property, TimeString Property, TimeValue Function

# TimeString Property

## Class

Microsoft.VisualBasic.DateAndTime

## Syntax

```
Dim result As String = DateAndTime.TimeString
```

or:

```
DateAndTime.TimeString = newTime
```

*newTime  (required in second syntax; String)*
    A time in string format used to set the current system time

### Description

The `TimeString` property gets or sets the current system time. The first syntax returns a string representing the current system time in the "HH:mm:ss" format, which uses a 24-hour clock. The second syntax sets the current system time using a string that is in any system-recognized time format.

### Usage at a Glance

- The first syntax always returns a time in the format "HH:mm:ss."
- See the *Format Function* entry for details on custom time formats.
- To get or set the current system date as a `String`, use the `DateString` property.
- To access the current system time as a `Date`, use the `TimeOfDay` property.
- The security settings of the active user may prevent the system date and time from being altered.

### Version Differences

The `TimeString` property is new to VB under .NET.

### See Also

TimeOfDay Property, TimeSerial Function, TimeValue Function

---

## TimeValue Function

### Class

Microsoft.VisualBasic.DateAndTime

### Syntax

```
Dim result As Date = TimeValue(stringTime)
```

*stringTime  (required; String)*
    A string containing any valid time format

### Description

The `TimeValue` function converts *stringDate* to the `Date` data type, setting any date component to January 1, 1 AD. The interpretation of the time components in the expression is based on the locale setting of the local computer.

### Usage at a Glance

If *stringTime* is invalid or `Nothing`, a runtime error is generated.

### Version Differences

In VB 6, `TimeValue` returns the time only. Under .NET, the function also returns the base date of January 1, 1 AD.

---

DateValue Function, TimeOfDay Property, TimeSerial Function, TimeString Property

## Today Property

### Class
Microsoft.VisualBasic.DateAndTime

### Syntax
```
Dim result As Date = DateAndTime.Today
```
or:
```
DateAndTime.Today = newDate
```
*newDate* *(required in syntax 2; Date)*
   A date used to set the current system date

### Description
The Today property gets or sets the current system date. The first syntax returns a Date representing the current system date, with the time set to midnight. The second syntax sets the current system date using a Date; any time component of that value is ignored.

### Usage at a Glance
- Older versions of Microsoft Windows, such as Windows 95, limit the system date to between January 1, 1980 and December 31, 2099.
- The security settings of the active user may prevent the system date and time from being altered.

### See Also
Now Property

## Trim Function

### Class
Microsoft.VisualBasic.Strings

### Syntax
```
Dim result As String = Trim(str)
```
*str* *(required; String)*
   Any valid string expression

### Description
The Trim function removes both leading and trailing spaces from *str*.

### Usage at a Glance
- If *str* is Nothing, the Trim function returns Nothing.
- Trim is equivalent to calling both the RTrim and LTrim functions.

In VB 6, the function's single named argument is *string*. In .NET, its single named argument is *str*.

**See Also**

LTrim Function, RTrim Function

---

## Try...Catch...Finally Statement

**Syntax**

```
Try
    [tryStatements]
[Catch [exception [As type]] [When expression]
    [catchStatements]
    [Exit Try]...]
[Finally
    [finallyStatements]]
End Try
```

*tryStatements (optional)*
Program code to be executed and monitored for exceptions.

*exception  (optional; System.Exception or a derived type)*
The exception to catch. If *exception* is omitted, or if it is *System.Exception*, all exceptions will be caught. However, if *exception* is omitted, no information about the exception will be accessible within the Catch block.

*type  (optional)*
The data type of the exception to be handled by the Catch block. Its value can be *System.Exception* (to handle all possible exceptions) or any class derived from *System.Exception* (to handle only exceptions of that specific type). If omitted, its value defaults to *System.Exception*.

*expression  (optional; Boolean)*
Defines a condition under which the error matching *exception* is to be handled by the Catch block. If *expression* is True, the related Catch block is entered.

*catchStatements  (optional)*
Program code to be executed when a general or specific exception occurs.

*finallyStatements  (optional)*
Program code to be executed upon leaving the Try...Catch...Finally statement for any reason, whether there was an exception or not.

**Description**

The Try...Catch...Finally statement enables structured exception handling for a specific block of code. If an error or exception occurs in the *tryStatements* block of code, that exception is compared with the *exception* defined by each Catch clause. If a match is found (and the optional When *expression* also matches), the related *catchStatements* are processed. In all cases, the *finallyStatements* are executed just before exiting the Try statement, even if the Try statement is exited through a Return statement or any other method.

## Usage at a Glance

- The `Try` statement can include any number of `Catch` blocks.

- The `ExitTry` statement is used to break out of any portion of a `Try...Catch...Finally` block. The *finallyStatements* block is still executed. `Exit Try` is not permitted in the *finallyStatements* block.

- If multiple `Catch` clauses match a triggered exception, only the first matching `Catch` block is executed. This means that `Catch` blocks should be ordered from most specific to most general, with a `Catch` block handling errors of type *System. Exception* occurring last.

- If an error occurs within *tryStatements* that is not handled by a `Catch` block, the error is passed up the VB call stack to the next error handler, either structured or unstructured, that can handle the exception.

## Example

The code in the following `Try` block will raise an error if the user does not enter a number. The `Catch` block will catch this error.

```
Dim numerator As Decimal
Dim denominator As Decimal
Dim quotient As Decimal
Dim badData As Boolean = False
Try
    numerator = CInt(InputBox("Enter the numerator."))
    denominator = CInt(InputBox("Enter the denominator."))
    quotient = numerator / denominator
Catch ex As System.Exception
    ' ----- Probably a divide by zero error.
    MsgBox(ex.Message)
    badData = True
End Try
If (badData = False) Then MsgBox("Quotient = " & quotient)
```

## Version Differences

Structured exception handling using the `Try...Catch...Finally` construct is new to VB under .NET. It provides an alternate method of monitoring and processing errors, in addition to the unstructured `On Error` handling methods long a part of VB.

## See Also

On Error Statement, Using Statement

---

# TryCast Function

## Syntax

```
Dim result As typename = TryCast(expression, typename)
```

*expression (required; any)*

The value to be converted. This can be any data, object, structure, or interface type.

*typename (required)*
> The data type, object type, structure, or interface to which *expression* is to be converted. This can be virtually anything that can appear after the As clause of a Dim statement. However, this type must have an inheritance relationship with the type of *expression*.

## Description

*New in 2005.* The TryCast function converts an expression or object to the specified type. The original type of *expression* must have an inheritance relationship with the new type, or an error occurs.

## Usage at a Glance

- The cast will fail if the source and target data types do not have an inheritance relationship, that is, if one does not eventually derive from the other.
- The cast may fail if it is a narrowing cast and Option Strict is On. Under such conditions, Nothing is returned.
- The TryCast function works like DirectCast, but it returns Nothing instead of generating an error on a narrowing failure.
- This function does not support named arguments.

## Version Differences

The TryCast function is new to Visual Basic 2005.

## See Also

CType Function, DirectCast Function

---

# TypeName Function

## Class

Microsoft.VisualBasic.Information

## Syntax

```
Dim result As String = TypeName(varName)
```

*varName (required; any)*
> The variable, instance, or expression to assess

## Description

The TypeName function returns the name of the data type for *varName*. The possible return values are:

| String returned | Variable contents |
|---|---|
| Boolean | Boolean value (True or False) |
| Byte | 8-bit binary value |
| Char | 16-bit character value |
| Date | 64-bit date and time value |
| DBNull | Missing or nonexistent data |

| String returned | Variable contents |
|---|---|
| Decimal | 96-bit fixed point numeric value |
| Double | 64-bit floating point numeric value |
| Integer | 32-bit integer value |
| Long | 64-bit integer value type |
| Nothing | Object with no instance; uninitialized string; undimensioned array |
| Object | Unspecialized object; instance of `System.Object` |
| Short | 16-bit integer value |
| Single | 32-bit floating point numeric value |
| String | String of 16-bit characters |
| Anything else | The name of the class or structure used to create an instance of `varName` |

## Usage at a Glance

- If `varName` is an array, the returned name is followed by a set of empty parentheses, as in "Integer( )."

- This function returns the immediate type used for `varName`; it does not return the derived class name. If it did, the function would always return "Object."

- Only the type name is returned by `TypeName`; the namespace is not included.

## Example

```
Dim genericObject As Object
genericObject = New Employee
MsgBox(TypeName(genericObject))    ' Displays: Employee

genericObject = 100
MsgBox(TypeName(genericObject))    ' Displays: Integer

genericObject = Nothing
MsgBox(TypeName(genericObject))    ' Displays: Nothing
```

## Version Differences

- In VB 6, the following code fragment:

  ```
  Dim strVar As String
  MsgBox(TypeName(strVar))
  ```

  returns "String." In .NET, this same code displays "Nothing," since the string has not yet been assigned an instance.

- In VB 6, `TypeName` cannot be used with user-defined data types; this use is supported in .NET.

- In VB 6, passing an uninitialized array to the `TypeName` function returns the type name plus parentheses. In .NET, it returns "Nothing."

- In VB 6, a variable with a type that is not declared is reported as "Variant;" in .NET, it is "Object."

## See Also

VarType Function

# TypeOf Operator

## Syntax

```
Dim result As Boolean = TypeOf varName Is typeName
```

or:

```
Dim result As Boolean = TypeOf varName IsNot typeName
```

*varName (required; any)*
The variable, instance, or expression to compare with a data type

*typeName (required)*
The class, interface, structure, or other type name against which to compare *varName*

## Description

The TypeOf operator indicates whether an instance of data is of a specific type (True) or not (False). It is always used with the Is or IsNot keyword, followed by a valid .NET type. It is most often used with If...Then...Else statements, as in:

```
If (TypeOf someVariable Is Integer) Then
    ' ----- Integer-specific code here.
End If
```

*New in 2005.* Visual Basic 2005 introduced a new IsNot keyword that negates the Boolean result of the TypeOf operator.

```
If (TypeOf someVariable IsNot Integer) Then
    ' ----- Non-Integer-specific code here.
End If
```

Before 2005, the equivalent of this syntax required the use of the Not operator.

```
If Not (TypeOf someVariable Is Integer) Then
    ' ----- Non-Integer-specific code here.
End If
```

## Version Differences

Visual Basic 2005 includes a new IsNot keyword. It was not available in earlier versions of VB for .NET or in VB 6.

## See Also

Is Operator, IsNot Operator

---

# UBound Function

## Class

VisualBasic.Information

## Syntax

```
Dim result As Integer = UBound(array[, rank])
```

*array (required; any)*
An array with an upper bound that is to be determined.

---

*rank*  *(optional; Integer)*
The dimension to assess for an upper bound. If omitted, it defaults to 1.

## Description
The UBound function returns the upper limit of the specified dimension of an array.

## Usage at a Glance
- If *array* is uninitialized, UBound generates a runtime error. Compare *array* to Nothing to prevent this error:

  ```
  If (someArray IsNot Nothing) Then
      ' ----- OK to use UBound
  ```

- Since the lower bound of .NET arrays is always 0, the number of items in an array dimension is always UBound(*array, rank*) + 1.

## Version Differences
The 2005 release of Visual Basic supports a new array declaration syntax that restores the VB 6 style "*lower* To *upper*" syntax, as in:

```
Dim someArray(0 To 5) As String
```

However, the specified lower bound must still be 0.

## See Also
LBound Function

---

# UCase Function

## Class
Microsoft.VisualBasic.Strings

## Syntax

```
Dim result As type = UCase(value)
```

*type*  *(required)*
One of the following data types: Char or String

*value*  *(required; expression of type type)*
A valid string expression or a character

## Description
The UCase function converts a string or character to uppercase.

## Usage at a Glance
- UCase only affects lowercase letters; all other characters in *value* are unaffected.
- UCase returns Nothing if *value* contains Nothing.
- UCase returns the same data type as *value*.

## See Also
LCase Function, StrConv Function

## Unlock Procedure

### Class
Microsoft.VisualBasic.FileSystem

### Syntax
```
Unlock(fileNumber[, record])
```
or:
```
Unlock(fileNumber[, fromRecord, toRecord])
```
*fileNumber* *(required; Integer)*
> Any valid file number of a file opened with FileOpen

*record* *(required; Long)*
> The 1-based record or byte number at which to commence lock removal

*fromRecord* *(required; Long)*
> The first 1-based record or byte number to unlock

*toRecord* *(required; Long)*
> The last 1-based record or byte number to unlock

### Description
The Unlock procedure removes record, section, or file locks previously set using the Lock procedure. Locks are used in situations where multiple programs or more than one instance of the same program may need read-and-write access to the same data file.

### Usage at a Glance
- If only the *fileNumber* argument is included, the entire file is unlocked.
- *record* is interpreted as a record number in Random files and as a byte number in Binary files.
- The Unlock procedure unlocks an entire file opened in Input or Output (sequential) mode, regardless of any record number arguments.
- The matching Lock procedure must include the same arguments.
- All file locks should be removed with the Unlock procedure before either closing a file or ending the application; otherwise, you can leave a file in an unstable state. Where appropriate, error-handling code must correctly unlock any locks that are no longer necessary.

### Version Differences
- In VB 6, the *fromRecord* argument can be left blank to unlock all records up to *toRecord*. This syntax is not supported in .NET.
- In the VB 6 Unlock statement, you can separate the *fromRecord* and *toRecord* arguments with the To keyword. In the .NET Unlock procedure, this syntax is not supported.
- In Visual Basic 2005, the *My.Computer.FileSystem* object provides more robust access to file management features.

Lock Procedure

# Using...End Using Statement

## Syntax

```
Using resourceExpression...
    [statements]
End Using
```

*resourceExpression* (required)
One or more resources to be allocated and used within the Using block. Multiple resources are separated by commas. Resource expressions are similar to what you would see in a Dim statement, either:

*resourceName* As *type*[(*arguments*)]
or:

*resourceName* As *type* = *expression*
where *resourceName* is the instance name to use, *type* is the data type of the resource instance, *arguments* are the constructor arguments for the data type (if required), and *expression* is an expression that evaluates to an instance of *type*.

*statements* (optional)
Program code to execute using the allocated resource(s).

## Description

*New in 2005.* The Using...End Using block construct is used to execute a series of statements on one or more resource objects, and to have those objects automatically release all of their allocated resources when the block is left in any way. The Using statement is basically a formal method of ensuring that the object's *Dispose* method is called when the object is no longer needed.

## Usage at a Glance

- Each object in *resourceExpression* must implement the *IDisposable* interface.
- The *Dispose* method for each allocated resource object will always be called when the code exits the block, even if the block is exited abnormally due to an exception.
- You cannot jump into or out of a Using block using the GoTo statement. If you need to exit a block early, you can place a label on the End Using line and use a GoTo statement to jump to that line.
- The various *resourceExpression* objects cannot be assigned a new instance while in the Using block.
- You can nest Using blocks. If there are no conditions on the allocation of the nested objects, including those multiple objects in the original Using clause will achieve the same purpose as nesting.
- If the requested resource cannot be allocated, it will be set to Nothing.

## Version Differences

The Using...End Using statement is new with Visual Basic 2005.

With...End With Statement

## Val Function

### Class

Microsoft.VisualBasic.Conversion

### Syntax

```
    Dim result As Double = Val(expression)
```

or

```
    Dim result As Integer = Val(charExpression)
```

*expression* *(required; String or Object)*
    Any string representation of a number

*charExpression* *(required; Char)*
    Any valid character

### Description

The Val function converts a string or object representation of a number to the Double data type. A second variation converts a Char data type to its Integer equivalent.

### Usage at a Glance

- Only digits at the start of the string expression are examined for conversion; conversion stops at the first nonnumeric character. All whitespace is removed before conversion. An empty string converts to zero.
- &O and &H (the octal and hexadecimal prefixes) are recognized by the Val function.
- Currency symbols, such as $ and £, and delimiters, such as commas, are not recognized by the Val function.
- The Val function only recognizes the period (.) as a decimal delimiter; regional settings are ignored.
- The conversion functions, such as the CDbl function, consider regional settings.

### See Also

CDbl Function

## VarType Function

### Class

Microsoft.VisualBasic.Information

### Syntax

```
    Dim result As VariantType = VarType(varName)
```

*varName* *(required; any)*
    The variable, instance, or expression to test

## Description

The VarType function indicates the data type of an expression or instance, returning one of the following *Microsoft.VisualBasic.VariantType* enumeration values. Visual Basic also defines intrinsic constants for many of the members.

| Enumeration value | Intrinsic constant | Description |
|---|---|---|
| Array | vbArray | An array of data. |
| Boolean | vbBoolean | Boolean data type (True or False). |
| Byte | vbByte | Byte data type. |
| Char | vbChar | Char data type. |
| Currency | vbCurrency | Currency data type. This entry is for backward compatibility. The .NET Decimal data type replaces the VB 6 Currency data subtype. |
| DataObject | | Data objects. |
| Date | vbDate | Date data type. |
| Decimal | vbDecimal | Decimal data type. |
| Double | vbDecimal | Double data type. |
| Empty | vbEmpty | Null reference. |
| Error | | *System.Exception* instance. |
| Integer | vbInteger | Integer data type. |
| Long | vbLong | Long data type. |
| Null | vbNull | Null object; *DBNull*. |
| Object | vbObject | Object, uninitialized string, uninitialized array, object of a nonspecific type; Nothing. |
| Short | | Short data type. |
| Single | vbSingle | Single data type. |
| String | vbString | String data type. |
| UserDefinedType | vbUserDefinedType | A structure instance. |
| Variant | vbVariant | Variant data type. This entry is for backward compatibility. The .NET Object data type replaces the VB 6 Variant data type. |

## Usage at a Glance

- If *varName* is a dimensioned array, the VarType function returns *VariantType.Array* and the data type of the array elements, combined using a bitwise Or operation. You can test for an array with a code fragment, such as the following:

```
If ((VarType(someVariable) And VariantType.Array) = _
    VariantType.Array) Then
```

  You can extract the data type of the array with the following code fragment:

```
VarType(someVariable) And Not VariantType.Array
```

- All object variables, whether late bound or early bound, return *VariantType.Object*.
- Data types that are members of the base class library but do not directly map to one of the core data types listed in the *VariantType* enumeration (such as UInt16 or even UInteger) return *VariantType.UserDefinedType*.

## Version Differences

- You could not pass a user-defined data type to `VarType` in VB 6. This use is supported in .NET.
- In VB 6, using the `VarType` function on an object returned the data type of its default property. In .NET, all objects, including objects that have default properties, return *VariantType.Object*.

## See Also

TypeName Function

---

# VBFixedArray Attribute

## Class

Microsoft.VisualBasic.VBFixedArrayAttribute

## Applies To

Field

## Constructor

New(*upper1*[, *upper2*])

*upper1 (required; Integer)*
The upper limit of the array's first dimension

*upper2 (optional; Integer)*
The upper limit of the array's second dimension

## Properties

*Bounds (array of Integer)*
The upper bounds of a particular dimension of the array. The first dimension is represented by *VBFixedArrayAttribute*.Bounds(0). The upper boundary of the array dimension can be retrieved by calling the `UBound` function.

*Length (Integer)*
The total number of elements in all dimensions of the array.

## Description

The `<VBFixedArray>` attribute defines a fixed array. This attribute can be used in defining fixed arrays within structures, particularly structures that are passed to Win32 API functions, and for defining fixed-length structures used by VB file input and output functions.

---

# VBFixedString Attribute

## Class

Microsoft.VisualBasic.VBFixedStringAttribute

## Applies To
Field

## Constructor
New(*length*)

*length  (required; Integer)*
 The length of the string

## Properties
*Length (Integer)*
 Read-only. Value from the *length* constructor parameter.

## Description
The <VBFixedString> attribute identifies a fixed-length string. It is the rough equivalent of the VB 6 declaration:

```
Dim sFixed As String * length
```

This attribute can be used to define fixed-length strings within structures, particularly structures that are to be passed to Win32 API functions. It is also useful when defining fixed-length strings to be written to, and read from, random access files.

## Example
This example creates a random access file, which must contain fixed-length records, and uses the <VBFixedString> attribute to create a fixed-length string of 10 characters. This ensures that all records will be a uniform length. Without the <VBFixedString> attribute, the code would generate runtime errors (*IOException*) due to the invalid record length.

```
' Assumes "Option Strict Off"
Structure Person
    <vbFixedString(10)> Public Name As String
    Public Age As Short
End Structure

Public Sub BuildFile( )
    Dim onePerson As New Person
    Dim outputFile As Integer = FreeFile( )

    FileOpen(outputFile, ".\person.txt", OpenMode.Random, _
        OpenAccess.ReadWrite, OpenShare.Default, Len(onePerson))

    onePerson.Name = "John"
    onePerson.Age = 31
    FilePut(outputFile, onePerson, 1)

    onePerson.Name = "Jane"
    onePerson.Age = 27
    FilePut(outputFile, onePerson, 2)

    FileGet(outputFile, onePerson, 1)
    Console.WriteLine(Trim(onePerson.Name) & " is " & onePerson.Age)
    FileClose(outputFile)
End Sub
```

## VbTypeName Function

### Class
Microsoft.VisualBasic.Information

### Syntax
```
VbTypeName(urtName)
```
*urtName* *(required; String)*
> The name of a Common Type System data type

### Description
The VbTypeName function returns the name of the Visual Basic data type wrapper that corresponds to a particular Common Type System (CTS) data type. For instance, passing "DateTime" returns the text "Date."

### Usage at a Glance
- If *urtName* is not a valid CTS data type or does not correspond to a Visual Basic data type, the function returns Nothing.
- To determine the VB data type of a particular variable, call the variable's *GetType* method to retrieve a *Type* object and then call the *Type* object's *ToString* method to retrieve its data type name. This string can then be passed to the VbTypeName function. For example:
  ```
  vbName = VbTypeName(someVariable.GetType( ).ToString( ))
  ```

### Version Differences
The VbTypeName function is new to VB under .NET.

### See Also
SystemTypeName Function, TypeName Function

---

## WebMethod Attribute

### Class
System.Web.Services.WebMethodAttribute

### Applies To
Method

### Constructors
```
New([[[[enableSession], transactionOption], cacheDuration], _
bufferResponse])
```
*enableSession* *(optional; Boolean)*
> Indicates whether session state is enabled for the web method call (True) or not (False). If omitted, the default value is False.

*transactionOption  (optional; TransactionOption enumeration)*

Indicates whether the web method supports transactions. One of the following *System.EnterpriseServices.TransactionOption* enumeration values: Disabled, NotSupported, Supported, Required, and RequiresNew. A web method must participate as the root object of a transaction. Because of this, Supported and NotSupported are both equivalent to NotSupported, and Required and RequiresNew are both equivalent to RequiresNew. If omitted, the default value is Disabled.

*cacheDuration  (optional; Integer)*

Indicates the number of seconds the response to the web method request should be stored in the cache. If omitted, the default value is 0, which indicates that responses to web methods are not cached.

*bufferResponse  (optional; Boolean)*

Indicates whether the response to the web method request is buffered (True) or not (False). If omitted, the default value is True.

## Properties

*BufferResponse (Boolean)*

Value from the *bufferResponse* constructor parameter.

*CacheDuration (Integer)*

Value from the *cacheDuration* constructor parameter.

*Description (String)*

Provides a description for the web service that is displayed in the Service Description page and the Web Service Help page. Its default value is an empty string.

*EnableSession (Boolean)*

Read-only. Value from the *enableSession* constructor parameter.

*MessageName (String)*

Identifies the public name by which the web method is invoked by clients. Since web methods do not support overloading, the property provides a method for identifying overloaded methods that share the same name. Its default value is the name of the web method.

*TransactionOption (TransactionOption enumeration)*

Read-only. Value from the *transactionOption* constructor parameter.

## Description

The <WebMethod> attribute marks a method within a web service as a web method callable from a web client. The method and the class to which it belongs must be public and must be part of an ASP.NET application.

# WebService Attribute

## Class

System.Web.Services.WebServiceAttribute

## Applies To

Class

## Constructor

New( )

## Properties

*Description (String)*

A textual description of the web service. The description is displayed in the Service Description page and the Web Service Help page.

*Name (String)*

The name to be assigned to the web service. Ordinarily, the web service name corresponds to the name of the class. However, the *Name* property of the <WebService> attribute is used instead of the class name as the name of the web service.

*Namespace (String)*

The web service's namespace. During development, the namespace *http://tempuri. org/* is used by default. However, a unique namespace should be assigned to any production web service. Although the namespace for a web service resembles a URL, it need not point to any valid Internet resource.

## Description

The <WebService> attribute is used to assign a namespace and a description to an ASP. NET web service. Each web service must also include the "@ WebService" directive.

## Example

The example uses an ".asmx" file with the following contents:

```
<%@ WebService Language="VB" Class="HelloWebService"
    Codebehind="Hello.asmx.vb" %>
```

It has the following code-behind file:

```
Option Strict

Imports System.Web.Services

<WebService(Name:="Hello", _
    Description:="Displays a greeting to the user.", _
    Namespace:="http://www.oreilly.com/VbNet")> _
Public Class HelloWebService
    <WebMethod> Public Function SayHello(ToWhom As String) As String
        Return "Hello, " & ToWhom
    End Function
End Class
```

## See Also

WebMethod Attribute

---

# Weekday Function

## Class

Microsoft.VisualBasic.DateAndTime

## Syntax

```
Dim result As Integer = Weekday(dateValue[, dayOfWeek])
```

*dateValue  (required; Date)*
The source date from which to extract the weekday.

*dayOfWeek (optional; FirstDayOfWeek enumeration)*
Indicates the first day of the week. One of the following *Microsoft.VisualBasic.*
*FirstDayOfWeek* enumeration members: Sunday, Monday, Tuesday, Wednesday,
Thursday, Friday, Saturday, or System (to use the regional default). If omitted,
Sunday is used.

## Description

The Weekday function returns a value indicating the day of the week. A value of 1 indicates the first day of the week; 7 is the last day. These numbers are interpreted based
on the definition of the first day of the week. By default, Sunday is the first day of the
week.

## Usage at a Glance

If passing a date literal as *dateValue*, the Weekday function requires that all four digits of
the year be present.

## Example

Since the code:

```
Weekday(#11/7/2005#, FirstDayOfWeek.Sunday)
```

returns 2; the date November 7, 2005 is a Monday.

## Version Differences

The named parameters of the function have changed from *date* and *firstDayOfWeek* in
VB 6 to *dateValue* and *dayOfWeek* in .NET respectively.

## See Also

DatePart Function, Day Function, WeekdayName Function

---

# WeekdayName Function

## Class

Microsoft.VisualBasic.DateAndTime

## Syntax

```
Dim result As String = WeekdayName(weekday[, abbreviate[, _
    firstDayOfWeekValue]])
```

*weekday  (required; Long)*
The ordinal number of the weekday, from 1 (first) to 7 (last).

*abbreviate  (optional; Boolean)*
Specifies whether to return the full day name or an abbreviation. The default
value is False.

*firstDayOfWeekValue (optional; FirstDayOfWeek constant)*
Indicates the first day of the week. One of the following *Microsoft.VisualBasic.*
*FirstDayOfWeek* enumeration members: Sunday, Monday, Tuesday, Wednesday,
Thursday, Friday, Saturday, or System (to use the regional default). If omitted,
System is used.

### Description

The WeekdayName function returns the name of the indicated weekday.

### Usage at a Glance

- *weekday* must be a number between 1 and 7, or the function generates an error.
- The *weekday* argument must be an Integer, not a Date. Use the Weekday function to obtain a weekday from a date. The setting used for the first day of the week should be identical in both functions.

### See Also

MonthName Function, Weekday Function

---

## While...End While Statement

### Syntax

```
While condition
    [statements]
    [Exit While]
    [statements]
    [Continue While]
    [statements]
End While
```

*condition* (required; Boolean)
>   An expression that is reevaluated each pass through the loop

*statements* (optional)
>   Program statements to execute while *condition* remains True

### Description

The While...End While statement repeatedly executes program code while a given condition remains True. The loop block is executed each time *condition* evaluates to True; the entire loop is skipped once *condition* evaluates to False. The Exit While statement can be used at any time to exit the While statement early.

*New in 2005.* The Continue While statement can be used at any time to immediately jump back to the top of the loop and attempt to process the next iteration. The *condition* is reevaluated immediately upon reaching the top of the loop.

### Usage at a Glance

- A Nothing condition is evaluated as False.
- You can nest While...End While loops within each other.
- The While...End While statement is a subset of the more flexible Do...Loop statement.

### Version Differences

- In VB 6, the ending clause that accompanies the While construct is Wend; in .NET, it is EndWhile.
- Visual Basic 2005 includes the Continue While statement.

Do...Loop Statement

---

# With...End With Statement

## Syntax

```
With object
    [statements]
End With
```

*object* *(required; Object)*
A previously declared object variable or instance

*statements* *(optional)*
Program code to execute against *object*

## Description

The With...End With block construct is used to execute a series of statements on an object without having to qualify each use with the object name itself.

## Usage at a Glance

- A member of *object* is referenced within a With block by omitting the object name and simply leading with a period and the member name.

- With statements can be nested, but only the object referenced in the inner block's With clause can be used without qualification by the code in the inner block.

- You cannot jump into or out of a With block using the GoTo statement. If you need to exit a block early, you can place a label on the End With line and use a GoTo statement to jump to that line.

- *object* cannot be assigned a new instance while in the With block.

## Example

```
Public Structure Point
    Public x As Integer
    Public y As Integer
End Structure

Public Sub TestPoint( )
    Dim samplePoint As Point
    With samplePoint
        .x = 10      ' Refers to samplePoint.x
        .y = 100     ' Refers to samplePoint.y
    End With
    MsgBox(samplePoint.x)
End Sub
```

## See Also

Using...End Using Statement

# WithEvents Keyword

## Description
The WithEvents keyword enables event management on an instance variable. For more information on using the WithEvents keyword, see the *Dim Statement* entry elsewhere in this chapter.

## See Also
Dim Statement, Handles Keyword

# Write, WriteLine Procedures

## Class
Microsoft.VisualBasic.FileSystem

## Syntax
```
Write(fileNumber, output)
WriteLine(fileNumber[, output])
```

*fileNumber*  (required; Integer)
Any valid file number of a file opened with FileOpen

*output*  (required for Write; any)
A comma-delimited list of expressions, or a ParamArray, to be written to the file

## Description
The Write and WriteLine procedures write data to a sequential file. The WriteLine version also appends line termination characters.

## Usage at a Glance
- *output* can be a ParamArray array containing values to be written to the file indicated by *fileNumber*.
- The following table describes how the Write and WriteLine procedures handle certain types of data, regardless of the locale, to allow files to be read universally:

| Data type | Data written to file |
|---|---|
| Numeric | Decimal separator is always written as a period (.) |
| Boolean | #TRUE# or #FALSE# |
| Date | #yyyy-mm-dd hh:mm:ss# (uses a 24-hour clock) |
| Null | #NULL# |
| Error | #ERROR errorcode# |

- The Write and WriteLine procedures automatically delimit output fields with commas and surround string data with quotation marks.
- Data written to a file using the Write and WriteLine procedures is often read using the Input procedure.

- If no *output* arguments are supplied to the WriteLine procedure, only the line termination characters are written.
- These procedures do not support named arguments.

### Version Differences
- There are many syntactical differences between the VB 6 Write statement and the .NET Write procedure.
- The WriteLine procedure is new with .NET as a partial replacement for the VB 6 Write statement.
- In Visual Basic 2005, the *My.Computer.FileSystem* object provides more robust access to file management features.

### See Also
Input Procedure, Print, PrintLine Procedures

## Year Function

### Class
Microsoft.VisualBasic.DateAndTime

### Syntax
```
Dim result As Integer = Year(dateValue)
```
*dateValue* *(required; Date)*
    The source date from which to extract the year

### Description
The Year function returns a value representing the year of the supplied date.

### Usage at a Glance
With OptionStrict set to On, the source value must first be converted to a Date data type. You can use the CDate function for this purpose. The IsDate function can also be used to confirm that the source expression is a valid date.

### See Also
DatePart Function, Day Function, Month Function

# 13

# The 'My' Reference

The *My* Namespace feature is one of many productivity enhancements introduced with Visual Basic 2005 that bring additional ease of use to .NET. It collects many of the commonly used features of the existing Framework Class Library and bundles them into an ordered hierarchy, simplifying the syntax of those features where possible. More than just a quick lookup or a list of shortcuts, *My* takes many complex Framework classes and simplifies them for VB programmers.

This chapter includes a reference entry for each member of the *My* Namespace hierarchy. Each entry includes the following descriptive components:

*Location*
Identifies the position of the entry within the *My* hierarchy.

*Syntax*
Demonstrates the basic usage and syntax of the entry, with descriptions for all programmer-supplied values.

*Description*
Provides general information on the entry and its use.

*Public Members*
For entries that represent entire objects, this component identifies some or all of the more useful public members of that object. Some objects have separate entries in this chapter for each member within the object.

*Usage at a Glance*
Identifies issues that may impact the use of this entry in your source code.

*Example*
Many entries include a short example that demonstrates common usage for the entry.

*Related Framework Entries*

Most of the entries in the *My* hierarchy are derived from other parts of the Framework Class Library. This component identifies those root sources and additional library features that provide identical or related functionality.

*See Also*

Identifies related elements in the *My* hierarchy that are also defined in this chapter.

The *My* Namespace feature includes many hierarchy branches. Some branches, and also some members within each branch, are only available for use in certain types of applications. For instance, the *My.Response* object is only available in ASP.NET applications. Other members provide different types of functionality, depending on the project type. All of these limitations are discussed within each entry.

Some entries are only valid in Windows Forms applications, specifically those Windows forms applications that have the "application framework" enabled. This feature, introduced in Visual Basic 2005, provides a simplified method of starting up and ending Windows Forms applications, at least from the point of view of the source code. These features are enabled through the project's Application Properties panel. To access the project's properties, select the *Properties* command in Visual Studio's *Project* menu or double-click on the *My Project* entry in Visual Studio's Solution Explorer. On this panel, use the *Enable application framework* field to toggle the use of this feature.

Some members within the *My* hierarchy are more commonly used than others. Some of the less commonly used features are hidden from Visual Studio's IntelliSense feature by default. To view these entries, select the *All* tab from the IntelliSense listing that appears while typing the entry's parent in your source code.

Some features within the *My* hierarchy may be limited for use by the current set of security permissions in effect for the active user, application, or thread of execution. Permissions are found in the *System.Security.Permissions* namespace.

See Appendix B for a hierarchical listing of all entries discussed in this chapter.

The 'My' Reference

---

## AllUsersApplicationData Property

### Location

My.Computer.FileSystem.SpecialDirectories.AllUsersApplicationData

### Syntax

```
Dim result As String = My.Computer.FileSystem. _
    SpecialDirectories.AllUsersApplicationData
```

### Description

The *AllUsersApplicationData* property returns a string that contains the full path name to the "application data" directory shared by all users on the local workstation. Usually, this directory is found at *C:\Documents and Settings\All Users\ApplicationData*, but it may vary from system to system.

## Usage at a Glance

- This property is read-only.
- This directory contains files and directories used to manage application-specific data that is shared by all authorized users of the workstation.
- This path may not be defined in some cases. In such cases, use of this property generates an exception.
- The returned path will never have a backslash "\" character at the end.

## Related Framework Entries

- Microsoft.VisualBasic.MyServices.SpecialDirectoriesProxy.AllUsersApplication-Data Property
- Microsoft.VisualBasic.FileIO.SpecialDirectories.AllUsersApplicationData Property

## See Also

CurrentUserApplicationData Property, Desktop Property, MyDocuments Property, MyMusic Property, MyPictures Property, ProgramFiles Property, Programs Property, SpecialDirectories Object, Temp Property

# AltKeyDown Property

## Location

My.Computer.Keyboard.AltKeyDown

## Syntax

```
Dim result As Boolean = My.Computer.Keyboard.AltKeyDown
```

## Description

The *AltKeyDown* property that indicates the current state of the Alt key, whether down (True) or up (False)

## Usage at a Glance

- This property is read-only.
- This property is only valid in non-server applications.
- For systems with two Alt keys, this setting indicates whether either Alt key is pressed. To examine the state of a specific Alt key during a control event, perform a bitwise comparison of the control's *ModifierKeys* property with the *Keys.LMenu* or *Keys.RMenu* enumeration value.

## Related Framework Entries

- Microsoft.VisualBasic.Devices.Keyboard.AltKeyDown Property
- System.Windows.Forms.Control.ModifierKeys Property
- System.Windows.Forms.Keys Enumeration

## See Also

CtrlKeyDown Property, Keyboard Object, ShiftKeyDown Property

# Application Object

## Location

My.Application

## Description

The *Application* object provides access to features and information about the currently running application or DLL library.

## Public Members

The following members of the *My.Application* object have their own entries elsewhere in this chapter.

- ApplicationContext Property
- ChangeCulture Method
- ChangeUICulture Method
- CommandLineArgs Property
- Culture Property
- Deployment Property
- DoEvents Method
- GetEnvironmentVariable Method
- Info Object (My.Application)
- IsNetworkDeployed Property
- Log Object (My.Application)
- MinimumSplashScreenDisplayTime Property
- NetworkAvailabilityChanged Event (My.Application)
- OpenForms Property
- Run Method
- SaveMySettingsOnExit Property
- Shutdown Event
- SplashScreen Property
- Startup Event
- StartupNextInstance Event
- UICulture Property
- UnhandledException Event

## Related Framework Entries

- Microsoft.VisualBasic.ApplicationServices.ApplicationBase Class
- Microsoft.VisualBasic.ApplicationServices.ConsoleApplicationBase Class
- Microsoft.VisualBasic.ApplicationServices.WindowsFormsApplicationBase Class

## See Also

Info Object (My.Application)

# ApplicationContext Property

## Location
My.Application.ApplicationContext

## Syntax
```
Dim result As System.Windows.Forms.ApplicationContext = _
    My.Application.ApplicationContext
```

## Description
The *ApplicationContext* property returns an object of type *System.Windows.Forms. ApplicationContext* for the active thread. This object provides features that let you monitor and interact with the closing activities of the current thread of execution. For instance, you can force the exit of the current thread based on conditions you determine.

## Public Members
The returned *ApplicationContext* object includes the following notable public members.

| Member | Description |
| --- | --- |
| ExitThread | Method. Forces the current application thread to exit. |
| MainForm | Property. Identifies the "main" Windows form within the running application thread. |
| OnMainFormClosed | Method. This method is called when the main application form (as defined through the *MainForm* property) closes. By default, this method causes the thread to exit. |
| ThreadExit | Event. Called just before the active thread exits so that any closing activities can be performed. |

## Usage at a Glance
This property is only valid in Windows Forms applications.

## Related Framework Entries
- Microsoft.VisualBasic.ApplicationServices.WindowsFormsApplicationBase. ApplicationContext Property
- System.Windows.Forms.ApplicationContext Class

## See Also
Application Object

---

# AssemblyName Property

## Location
My.Application.Info.AssemblyName

## Syntax
```
Dim result As String = My.Application.Info.AssemblyName
```

### Description

The *AssemblyName* property returns the name of the assembly file for the application, first removing the extension. This file contains the manifest for the assembly.

### Usage at a Glance

- This property is read-only.
- Any file extension, such as ".exe" or ".dll," is first removed before reporting the assembly name through this property.

### Related Framework Entries

- Microsoft.VisualBasic.ApplicationServices.AssemblyInfo.AssemblyName Property
- System.Reflection.AssemblyName.Name Property

### See Also

DirectoryPath Property, Info Object (My.Application), LoadedAssemblies Property

---

## Audio Object

### Location

My.Computer.Audio

### Description

Use the *Audio* object to play system sound files and other sound files through the system speakers.

### Public Members

The following members of the *My.Computer.Audio* object have their own entries elsewhere in this chapter.

- Play Method
- PlaySystemSound Method
- Stop Method

### Usage at a Glance

This object and its members are only valid in non-server applications.

### Related Framework Entries

- Microsoft.VisualBasic.Devices.Audio Class

### See Also

Computer Object

---

## AvailablePhysicalMemory Property

### Location

My.Computer.Info.AvailablePhysicalMemory

---

### Syntax

```
Dim result As ULong = My.Computer.Info.AvailablePhysicalMemory
```

### Description

The *AvailablePhysicalMemory* property returns the total amount of free bytes of physical memory on the local computer.

### Usage at a Glance

- This property is read-only.
- This property only works on platforms that make the information available. This includes Windows XP, Windows 2000 Professional, Windows Server 2003, Windows 2000 Server, or any later versions of these systems.
- An exception is thrown if, for any reason, the application is unable to determine the current status of memory on the system.

### Related Framework Entries

- Microsoft.VisualBasic.Devices.ComputerInfo.AvailablePhysicalMemory Property

### See Also

AvailableVirtualMemory Property, Info Object (My.Computer), TotalPhysicalMemory Property, TotalVirtualMemory Property

---

## AvailableVirtualMemory Property

### Location

My.Computer.Info.AvailableVirtualMemory

### Syntax

```
Dim result As ULong = My.Computer.Info.AvailableVirtualMemory
```

### Description

The *AvailableVirtualMemory* property returns the total amount of free bytes of virtual address space on the local computer.

### Usage at a Glance

- This property is read-only.
- This property only works on platforms that make the information available. This includes Windows XP, Windows 2000 Professional, Windows Server 2003, Windows 2000 Server, or any later versions of these systems.
- An exception is thrown if, for any reason, the application is unable to determine the current status of memory on the system.

### Related Framework Entries

- Microsoft.VisualBasic.Devices.ComputerInfo.AvailableVirtualMemory Property

AvailablePhysicalMemory Property, Info Object (My.Computer), TotalPhysical-
Memory Property, TotalVirtualMemory Property

---

# ButtonsSwapped Property

## Location
My.Computer.Mouse.ButtonsSwapped

## Syntax
```
Dim result As Boolean = My.Computer.Mouse.ButtonsSwapped
```

## Description
On most systems, the left mouse button performs selection, while the right mouse
button performs context-specific actions. The *ButtonsSwapped* property indicates
whether the functionality normally assigned to each button has been reversed (True) or
not (False).

## Usage at a Glance
- This property is read-only.
- This property is only valid in non-server applications.
- An exception is thrown if the computer does not have an installed mouse.

## Related Framework Entries
- Microsoft.VisualBasic.Devices.Mouse.ButtonsSwapped Property
- System.Windows.Forms.SystemInformation.MouseButtonsSwapped Property

## See Also
Mouse Object, WheelExists Property, WheelScrollLines Property

---

# CapsLock Property

## Location
My.Computer.Keyboard.CapsLock

## Syntax
```
Dim result As Boolean = My.Computer.Keyboard.CapsLock
```

## Description
The *CapsLock* property indicates the current state of the Caps Lock key, whether on
(True) or off (False).

## Usage at a Glance

- This property is read-only.
- This property is only valid in non-server applications.

## Related Framework Entries

- Microsoft.VisualBasic.Devices.Keyboard.CapsLock Property

## See Also

Keyboard Object, NumLock Property, ScrollLock Property

---

# ChangeCulture Method

## Location

My.Application.ChangeCulture

## Syntax

```
My.Application.ChangeCulture(cultureName)
```

*cultureName (required; String)*
> The name of the culture to use. This parameter includes a two-letter lowercase language code, optionally followed by a hyphen and a two-letter uppercase country or region code. These codes are defined as ISO standards. For instance, the culture for the English language with no specified region is "en," while English in the United States is defined as "en-US." Setting this parameter to the empty string ("") indicates the default "invariant" culture. See the *System.Globalization. CultureInfo Class* entry in the Visual Studio documentation for a full listing of all possible culture name values.

## Description

The *ChangeCulture* method modifies the active culture settings used by the active thread to format and manage certain display elements. The culture setting controls the formatting of dates, times, numbers, currency values, letter casing, and the sorting and comparison of text strings. For instance, this setting controls the default order of the month, day, and year values when formatting dates. Although the culture setting includes a language code, it is not used to determine the user interface language.

## Usage at a Glance

An exception is thrown if an invalid culture name is used.

## Related Framework Entries

- Microsoft.VisualBasic.ApplicationServices.ApplicationBase.ChangeCulture Method
- System.Globalization.CultureInfo Class
- System.Threading.Thread.CurrentCulture Property

## See Also

Application Object, ChangeUICulture Method, Culture Property

# ChangeUICulture Method

## Location

My.Application.ChangeUICulture

## Syntax

```
My.Application.ChangeUICulture(cultureName)
```

*cultureName (required; String)*
　　The name of the culture to use. This parameter includes a two-letter lowercase language code, optionally followed by a hyphen and a two-letter uppercase country or region code. These codes are defined as ISO standards. For instance, the culture for the English language with no specified region is "en," while English in the United States is defined as "en-US." Setting this parameter to the empty string ("") indicates the default "invariant" culture. See the *System.Globalization.CultureInfo Class* entry in the Visual Studio documentation for a full listing of all possible culture name values.

## Description

The *ChangeUICulture* method modifies the active user-interface culture settings used by the active thread to correctly locate display resources. An application may include different display strings and other resources that vary by culture or language. This setting causes the application to automatically select the appropriate set of resources.

## Usage at a Glance

- An exception is thrown if an invalid culture name is used.
- The use of this method impacts the application's interaction with the Resource Manager and alters the behavior of the *My.Resources* object.

## Related Framework Entries

- Microsoft.VisualBasic.ApplicationServices.ApplicationBase.ChangeUICulture Method
- System.Globalization.CultureInfo Class
- System.Threading.Thread.CurrentUICulture Property

## See Also

Application Object, ChangeCulture Method, InstalledUICulture Property, Resources Object, UICulture Property

---

# ClassesRoot Property

## Location

My.Computer.Registry.ClassesRoot

## Syntax

```
Dim result As Microsoft.Win32.RegistryKey = _
    My.Computer.Registry.ClassesRoot
```

### Description

The *ClassesRoot* property returns a *Microsoft.Win32.RegistryKey* object that refers to the HKEY_CLASSES_ROOT location in the Windows registry. This entry point is used primarily to store ActiveX class-specific information and Windows file associations.

### Usage at a Glance

- This property is read-only.
- You must have sufficient security permissions to read or write keys and values in the registry.

### Example

The following example displays all of the sub-elements of the HKEY_CLASSES_ROOT registry key element in a listbox control. The example assumes that you are using this code on a form with a defined ListBox1 control.

```
ListBox1.DataSource = _
    My.Computer.Registry.ClassesRoot.GetSubKeyNames( )
```

### Related Framework Entries

- Microsoft.VisualBasic.MyServices.RegistryProxy.ClassesRoot Property
- Microsoft.Win32.Registry.ClassesRoot Property

### See Also

CurrentConfig Property, CurrentUser Property, DynData Property, GetValue Method, LocalMachine Property, PerformanceData Property, Registry Object, SetValue Method, Users Property

## Clear Method

### Location

My.Computer.Clipboard.Clear

### Syntax

```
My.Computer.Clipboard.Clear( )
```

### Description

The *Clear* method removes all data from the system clipboard.

### Usage at a Glance

- This method is only valid in non-server applications.
- Security restrictions in place for the active user may limit access to the system clipboard.

### Related Framework Entries

- Microsoft.VisualBasic.MyServices.ClipboardProxy.Clear Method
- System.Windows.Forms.Clipboard.Clear Method

# Clipboard Object

## Location
My.Computer.Clipboard

## Description
Use the *Clipboard* object to add data to, and retrieve data from, the system clipboard.

## Public Members
The following members of the *My.Computer.Clipboard* object have their own entries elsewhere in this chapter.

- Clear Method
- ContainsAudio Method
- ContainsData Method
- ContainsFileDropList Method
- ContainsImage Method
- ContainsText Method
- GetAudioStream Method
- GetData Method
- GetDataObject Method
- GetFileDropList Method
- GetImage Method
- GetText Method
- SetAudio Method
- SetData Method
- SetDataObject Method
- SetFileDropList Method
- SetImage Method
- SetText Method

## Usage at a Glance
- This object and its members are only valid in non-server applications.
- The lifetime of clipboard data is beyond the control of your application. Data that you place on the clipboard may persist even after your application is closed. Also, other applications may replace data you add with different data, even if your application is still active.
- The clipboard only holds one set of data at a time, normally in a single format. The most common formats are those defined through the *System.Windows.Forms. DataFormats* enumeration. To store multiple formats on the clipboard at the same time, use the *My.Computer.Clipboard.SetDataObject* method.

- Only threads using the single-threaded apartment (STA) mode can access the clipboard remotely. An exception is raised when accessing the clipboard remotely using other modes.
- A class must be serializable (with the *ISerializable* interface) before its data can be added to the clipboard.

**Related Framework Entries**
- Microsoft.VisualBasic.MyServices.ClipboardProxy
- Microsoft.VisualBasic.VariantType.DataObject
- System.Windows.Forms.Clipboard
- System.Windows.Forms.DataFormats

**See Also**
Computer Object

## Clock Object

**Location**
My.Computer.Clock

**Description**
Use this object to access features related to timing and the system clock.

**Public Members**
The following members of the *My.Computer.Clock* object have their own entries elsewhere in this chapter.
- GmtTime Property
- LocalTime Property
- TickCount Property

**Related Framework Entries**
- Microsoft.VisualBasic.Devices.Clock Object

**See Also**
Computer Object

## Close Method

**Location**
TextFieldParser.Close

**Syntax**
```
Dim fileParser As FileIO.TextFieldParser
' ...later...
fileParser.Close()
```

### Description

The *Close* method closes the file represented by a *TextFieldParser* object and ends the active parsing process.

### Usage at a Glance

You must close the *TextFieldParser* object when finished with it. Use the object's *Close* method or create the object instance with the Using keyword. See the *TextFieldParser Object* entry in this chapter for an example.

### Related Framework Entries

- Microsoft.VisualBasic.FileIO.TextFieldParser.Close Method

### See Also

EndOfData Property, ReadFields Method, ReadLine Method, ReadToEnd Method, TextFieldParser Object

---

## CombinePath Method

The 'My' Reference

### Location

My.Computer.FileSystem.CombinePath

### Syntax

```
Dim result As String = _
    My.Computer.FileSystem.CombinePath(baseDirectory, relativePath)
```

*baseDirectory (required; String)*
> The first path to be combined; an absolute path, either in UNC or drive-letter format

*relativePath (required; String)*
> The second path to be combined; a relative path

### Description

The *CombinePath* method combines an absolute path component with a relative path component and returns a properly concatenated and formatted version. The concatenation properly inserts backslashes in the right places.

### Usage at a Glance

An exception is thrown if one or both of the paths are malformed. Neither the two input paths nor the final output path need exist, but they all must be in a valid format.

### Example

The following example combines a root directory path and a relative path component into a single formatted path.

```
Dim finalPath As String
finalPath = My.Computer.FileSystem.CombinePath _
    (My.Computer.FileSystem.SpecialDirectories.MyDocuments, _
    "Business\Expenses.txt")
```

### Related Framework Entries

- Microsoft.VisualBasic.MyServices.FileSystemProxy.CombinePath Method
- Microsoft.VisualBasic.FileIO.FileSystem.CombinePath Method
- System.IO.Path.Combine Method

### See Also

FileSystemObject, GetName Method, GetParentPath Method

---

## CommandLineArgs Property

### Location

My.Application.CommandLineArgs

### Syntax

```
Dim result As System.Collections.ObjectModel.ReadOnlyCollection( _
    Of String) = My.Application.CommandLineArgs
```

### Description

The *CommandLineArgs* property returns a collection of each space-delimited argument from the command-line text used to initiate the application. This collection includes the arguments only; the application path used to start the application is not included. The *System.Environment.CommandLine* property, on the other hand, includes the application path.

### Usage at a Glance

- This property is read-only.
- If your application is configured to run as a single instance only, this property will always return the command-line arguments for the initial instance. To view the arguments for subsequent instances, use the *My.Application.StartupNextInstance* event and examine the *CommandLine* property of the second parameter (e) for that event.

### Example

The following example looks for the argument "/?" and takes action when found.

```
Private Sub CheckCommandOptions( )
    Dim scanArg As String

    For Each scanArg In My.Application.CommandLineArgs
        If (scanArg = "/?") Then
            ' ----- Show application usage.
            MsgBox("syntax: PrintInColor.exe [filename]")
            End
        End If
    Next scanArg
End Sub
```

### Related Framework Entries

- Microsoft.VisualBasic.ApplicationServices.ConsoleApplicationBase.Command-LineArgs Property
- Microsoft.VisualBasic.ApplicationServices.StartupEventArgs.CommandLine Property
- System.Environment.CommandLine Property

### See Also

Application Object, GetEnvironmentVariable Method

---

# CommentTokens Property

### Location

TextFieldParser.CommentTokens

### Syntax

```
Dim fileParser As FileIO.TextFieldParser
' ...later...
Dim result As String( ) = fileParser.CommentTokens
```

or:

```
fileParser.CommentTokens = setOfTokens
```

*setOfTokens (required; String array)*

An array of the character or multicharacter values that, when appearing at the start of a line in the input file being parsed by a *TextFieldParser* object, indicate that the line should be considered as a comment. Any array elements with zero-length strings are ignored.

### Description

The *CommentTokens* property sets or retrieves the comment tokens used with a *TextFieldParser* object. Each comment token is a string of one or more characters. As each line of the input file is read by the parser, a comparison is done between each token and the first few characters of the input line. If there is a token match, the whole line is considered to be a comment line, and no fields are extracted from the line.

### Usage at a Glance

- The *CommentTokens* property is valid with either fixed-width or delimited input files.
- You must close the *TextFieldParser* object when finished with it. Use the object's *Close* method or create the object instance with the Using keyword. See the *TextFieldParser Object* entry in this chapter for an example.
- Tokens assigned to the *CommentTokens* property may not include whitespace characters.

### Example

The following example sets two comment tokens for the input file: "//" and "REM."

```
Dim scanInput As Microsoft.VisualBasic.FileIO.TextFieldParser
' ...later...
scanInput.CommentTokens = New String( ) {"//", "REM"}
```

**Related Framework Entries**

- Microsoft.VisualBasic.FileIO.TextFieldParser.CommentTokens Property

**See Also**

Delimiters Property, FieldWidths Property, PeekChars Method, TextFieldParser Object

---

## CompanyName Property

### Location

My.Application.Info.CompanyName

### Syntax

```
Dim result As String = My.Application.Info.CompanyName
```

### Description

The *CompanyName* property returns the company name as defined in the informational section of the assembly.

### Usage at a Glance

- This property is read-only.
- An exception occurs if the company name attribute, *AssemblyCompanyAttribute* (or <AssemblyCompany>), is undefined in the active assembly.

### Related Framework Entries

- Microsoft.VisualBasic.ApplicationServices.AssemblyInfo.CompanyName Property
- System.Diagnostics.FileVersionInfo.CompanyName Property

### See Also

Copyright Property, Description Property, Info Object (My.Application), Product-Name Property, Title Property, Trademark Property

---

## Computer Object

### Location

My.Computer

### Description

Use the *Computer* object to access many features and objects related to the local computer.

---

## Public Members

The following members of the *My.Computer* object have their own entries elsewhere in this chapter.

- Audio Object
- Clipboard Object
- Clock Object
- FileSystem Object
- Info Object (My.Computer)
- Keyboard Object
- Mouse Object
- Name Property (My.Computer)
- Network Object
- Ports Object
- Registry Object
- Screen Property

## Related Framework Entries

- Microsoft.VisualBasic.Devices.Computer Class
- Microsoft.VisualBasic.Devices.ServerComputer Class

## See Also

My Namespace

---

# ContainsAudio Method

## Location

My.Computer.Clipboard.ContainsAudio

## Syntax

```
Dim result As Boolean = My.Computer.Clipboard.ContainsAudio( )
```

## Description

The *ContainsAudio* method indicates whether the system clipboard contains audio data (True) or not (False).

## Usage at a Glance

- This method is only valid in non-server applications.
- Security restrictions in place for the active user may limit access to the system clipboard.

## Related Framework Entries

- Microsoft.VisualBasic.MyServices.ClipboardProxy.ContainsAudio Method
- System.Windows.Forms.Clipboard.ContainsAudio Method

Clipboard Object, ContainsData Method, ContainsFileDropList Method, ContainsImage Method, ContainsText Method, GetAudioStream Method, SetAudio Method

---

## ContainsData Method

### Location
My.Computer.Clipboard.ContainsData

### Syntax
```
Dim result As Boolean = My.Computer.Clipboard.ContainsData(format)
```
*format (required; String)*
The name of the data type to look for on the clipboard

### Description
The *ContainsData* method indicates whether the system clipboard contains the named custom format of data (True) or not (False).

### Usage at a Glance
- This method is only valid in non-server applications.
- Security restrictions in place for the active user may limit access to the system clipboard.

### Example
The following example checks the clipboard for data in the "MozartMusic" format.
```
If My.Computer.Clipboard.ContainsData("MozartMusic") Then
    MsgBox("Found classical music.")
End If
```

### Related Framework Entries
- Microsoft.VisualBasic.MyServices.ClipboardProxy.ContainsData Method
- System.Windows.Forms.Clipboard.ContainsData Method

### See Also
Clipboard Object, ContainsAudio Method, ContainsFileDropList Method, ContainsImage Method, ContainsText Method, GetData Method, SetData Method

---

## ContainsFileDropList Method

### Location
My.Computer.Clipboard.ContainsFileDropList

### Syntax
```
Dim result As Boolean = My.Computer.Clipboard.ContainsFileDropList( )
```

## Description

The *ContainsFileDropList* method indicates whether the system clipboard contains a list of file paths (True) or not (False).

### Usage at a Glance
- This method is only valid in non-server applications.
- Security restrictions in place for the active user may limit access to the system clipboard.

### Related Framework Entries
- Microsoft.VisualBasic.MyServices.ClipboardProxy.ContainsFileDropList Method
- System.Windows.Forms.Clipboard.ContainsFileDropList Method

### See Also

Clipboard Object, ContainsAudio Method, ContainsData Method, ContainsImage Method, ContainsText Method, GetFileDropList Method, SetFileDropList Method

---

# ContainsImage Method

### Location
My.Computer.Clipboard.ContainsImage

### Syntax
```
Dim result As Boolean = My.Computer.Clipboard.ContainsImage()
```

### Description

The *ContainsImage* method indicates whether the system clipboard contains image data (True) or not (False).

### Usage at a Glance
- This method is only valid in non-server applications.
- Security restrictions in place for the active user may limit access to the system clipboard.

### Related Framework Entries
- Microsoft.VisualBasic.MyServices.ClipboardProxy.ContainsImage Method
- System.Windows.Forms.Clipboard.ContainsImage Method

### See Also

Clipboard Object, ContainsAudio Method, ContainsData Method, ContainsFileDropList Method, ContainsText Method, GetImage Method, SetImage Method

---

# ContainsText Method

### Location
My.Computer.Clipboard.ContainsText

## Syntax

```
Dim result As Boolean = My.Computer.Clipboard.ContainsText([format])
```

*format (optional; TextDataFormat enumeration)*
The specific type of text to be checked for on the clipboard. One of the following *System.Windows.Forms.TextDataFormat* enumeration values.

| Value | Description |
|---|---|
| *Not supplied* | Any type of text |
| CommaSeparatedValue | Comma-separated fields of data in one or more records |
| Html | HTML format |
| Rtf | Rich Text Format |
| UnicodeText | 16-bit Unicode character text |

## Description

The *ContainsText* method indicates whether the system clipboard contains text data (True) or not (False), for either general text or a specific type of text.

## Usage at a Glance

- This method is only valid in non-server applications.
- If the format parameter is missing, this method checks for any type of text on the system clipboard.
- Security restrictions in place for the active user may limit access to the system clipboard.

## Related Framework Entries

- Microsoft.VisualBasic.MyServices.ClipboardProxy.ContainsAudio Method
- System.Windows.Forms.Clipboard.ContainsAudio Method

## See Also

Clipboard Object, ContainsAudio Method, ContainsData Method, ContainsFile-DropList Method, ContainsImage Method, GetText Method, SetText Method

---

# CopyDirectory Method

## Location

My.Computer.FileSystem.CopyDirectory

## Syntax

```
My.Computer.FileSystem.CopyDirectory(source, _
    destination[, overwrite])
```

or:

```
My.Computer.FileSystem.CopyDirectory(source, _
    destination, showUI[, onUserCancel])
```

*source (required; String)*
The path of the directory to be copied.

---

*destination (required; String)*

The path of the new directory. New copies of the files contained within *source* will be stored directly within *destination*.

*overwrite (optional; Boolean)*

Indicates whether existing files at the destination should be overwritten (True) or not (False). If this parameter is missing from the first syntax, it defaults to False.

*showUI (required in syntax 2; UIOption enumeration)*

Indicates whether error or progress dialog windows should appear during the copy. One of the following *Microsoft.VisualBasic.FileIO.UIOption* enumeration values.

| Value | Description |
| --- | --- |
| OnlyErrorDialogs | Only shows error dialog boxes; does not display progress |
| AllDialogs | Shows progress and error dialogs |

If this parameter is missing, OnlyErrorDialogs is used by default.

*onUserCancel (optional; UICancelOption enumeration)*

The progress window includes a Cancel button. When pressed, the method takes action based on this parameter. One of the following *Microsoft.VisualBasic. FileIO.UICancelOption* enumeration values.

| Value | Description |
| --- | --- |
| DoNothing | Aborts the copy but returns no information indicating that the copy was cancelled |
| ThrowException | Throws an exception |

If this parameter is missing, ThrowException is used by default.

## Description

The *CopyDirectory* method copies the indicated directory and all files within it to a new location. *destination* is the new final directory; new copies of the files contained within the *source* directory will appear directly within the *destination* directory.

## Usage at a Glance

- If the destination directory, though valid, does not exist, it will be created.

- If a destination directory of the same name already exists, files already found in the destination will be overwritten (when requested) as needed; files without name conflicts will remain. In other words, the source and destination files will be merged.

- An exception is thrown if the source or destination parameters are missing or invalid.

- An exception is thrown if the source directory does not exist or a file to be overwritten is in use.

- An exception is thrown if the user lacks sufficient file access permissions.

- An exception is thrown if the source and destination are the same or the source contains the destination.

## Example

The following example moves a directory to a new parent directory.

```
My.Computer.FileSystem.CopyDirectory( _
    "C:\Templates\Documents", "C:\Archive")
```

## Related Framework Entries

- Microsoft.VisualBasic.FileIO.FileSystem.CopyDirectory Method
- Microsoft.VisualBasic.MyServices.FileSystemProxy.CopyDirectory Method

## See Also

CopyFile Method, CreateDirectory Method, DeleteDirectory Method, DeleteFile Method, FileSystem Object, MoveDirectory Method, MoveFile Method, RenameDirectory Method, RenameFile Method

---

# CopyFile Method

## Location

My.Computer.FileSystem.CopyFile

## Syntax

```
My.Computer.FileSystem.CopyFile(source, destination[, overwrite])
```

or:

```
My.Computer.FileSystem.CopyFile(source, destination, _
    showUI[, onUserCancel])
```

*source (required; String)*
The path of the file to be copied.

*destination (required; String)*
The path of the new destination file.

*overwrite (optional; Boolean)*
Indicates whether an existing file at the destination should be overwritten (True) or not (False). If this parameter is missing from the first syntax, it defaults to False.

*showUI (required in syntax 2; UIOption enumeration)*
Indicates whether error or progress dialog windows should appear during the copy. One of the following *Microsoft.VisualBasic.FileIO.UIOption* enumeration values.

| Value | Description |
| --- | --- |
| OnlyErrorDialogs | Only shows error dialog boxes; does not display progress |
| AllDialogs | Shows progress and error dialogs |

If this parameter is missing, OnlyErrorDialogs is used by default.

*onUserCancel (optional; UICancelOption enumeration)*

The progress window includes a Cancel button. When pressed, the method takes action based on this parameter. One of the following *Microsoft.VisualBasic. FileIO.UICancelOption* enumeration values.

| Value | Description |
|---|---|
| DoNothing | Aborts the copy but returns no information indicating that the copy was cancelled |
| ThrowException | Throws an exception |

If this parameter is missing, ThrowException is used by default.

## Description

The *CopyFile* method copies the indicated file to a new location.

## Usage at a Glance

- If the destination directory, though valid, does not exist, it will be created.
- An exception is thrown if the source or destination parameters are missing or invalid.
- An exception is thrown if the source file does not exist or is in use, or if a file to be overwritten is in use.
- An exception is thrown if the user lacks sufficient file access permissions.

## Example

The following example copies a file to a new location, overwriting any existing file with the same name.

```
My.Computer.FileSystem.CopyFile( _
    "C:\Templates\project.txt", "C:\NewProject\project.txt", True)
```

## Related Framework Entries

- Microsoft.VisualBasic.FileIO.FileSystem.CopyFile Method
- Microsoft.VisualBasic.MyServices.FileSystemProxy.CopyFile Method
- System.IO.File.Copy Method

## See Also

CopyDirectory Method, CreateDirectory Method, DeleteDirectory Method, Delete-File Method, FileSystem Object, MoveDirectory Method, MoveFile Method, RenameDirectory Method, RenameFile Method

---

# Copyright Property

## Location

My.Application.Info.Copyright

## Syntax

```
Dim result As String = My.Application.Info.Copyright
```

## Description

The *Copyright* property returns the copyright owner notice as defined in the informational section of the assembly.

## Usage at a Glance

- This property is read-only.
- An exception occurs if the copyright attribute, *AssemblyCopyrightAttribute* (or `<AssemblyCopyright>`), is undefined in the active assembly.

## Related Framework Entries

- Microsoft.VisualBasic.ApplicationServices.AssemblyInfo.Copyright Property
- System.Diagnostics.FileVersionInfo.LegalCopyright Property

## See Also

CompanyName Property, Description Property, Info Object (My.Application), ProductName Property, Title Property, Trademark Property

---

# CreateDirectory Method

## Location

My.Computer.FileSystem.CreateDirectory

## Syntax

```
My.Computer.FileSystem.CreateDirectory(path)
```

*path (required; String)*
The path of the new directory to be created

## Description

The *CreateDirectory* method creates a new empty directory.

## Usage at a Glance

- If the directory already exists, no error occurs.
- Any nonexistent directories between the top of the file system and the destination directory to be created will also be created.
- An exception is thrown if the path parameter is missing or invalid.
- An exception is thrown if the user lacks sufficient file access permissions.

## Related Framework Entries

- Microsoft.VisualBasic.FileIO.FileSystem.CreateDirectory Method
- Microsoft.VisualBasic.MyServices.FileSystemProxy.CreateDirectory Method
- System.IO.Directory.CreateDirectory Method

CopyDirectory Method, CopyFile Method, DeleteDirectory Method, DeleteFile Method, FileSystem Object, MoveDirectory Method, MoveFile Method, RenameDirectory Method, RenameFile Method

## CtrlKeyDown Property

### Location
My.Computer.Keyboard.CtrlKeyDown

### Syntax
```
Dim result As Boolean = My.Computer.Keyboard.CtrlKeyDown
```

### Description
The *CtrlKeyDown* property indicates the current state of the Control key, whether down (True) or up (False).

### Usage at a Glance
- This property is read-only.
- This property is only valid in non-server applications.
- For systems with two Control keys, this setting indicates whether either Control key is pressed. To examine the state of a specific Control key during a control event, perform a bitwise comparison of the control's *ModifierKeys* property with the *Keys.LControlKey* or *Keys.RControlKey* enumeration value.

### Related Framework Entries
- Microsoft.VisualBasic.Devices.Keyboard.CtrlKeyDown Property
- System.Windows.Forms.Control.ModifierKeys Property
- System.Windows.Forms.Keys Enumeration

### See Also
AltKeyDown Property, Keyboard Object, ShiftKeyDown Property

## Culture Property

### Location
My.Application.Culture

### Syntax
```
Dim result As System.Globalization.CultureInfo = _
    My.Application.Culture
```

### Description
The *Culture* property returns a *System.Globalization.CultureInfo* object that indicates the active culture settings used by the active thread to format and manage certain

The 'My' Reference

display elements. The culture setting controls the formatting of dates, times, numbers, currency values, letter casing, and the sorting and comparison of text strings. For instance, this setting controls the default order of the month, day, and year values when formatting dates. Although the culture setting includes a language code, it is not used to determine the user interface language.

### Related Framework Entries

- Microsoft.VisualBasic.ApplicationServices.ApplicationBase.Culture Property
- System.Globalization.CultureInfo Class
- System.Threading.Thread.CurrentCulture Class

### See Also

Application Object, ChangeCulture Method, InstalledUICulture Property, UICulture Property

---

## CurrentConfig Property

### Location

My.Computer.Registry.CurrentConfig

### Syntax

```
Dim result As Microsoft.Win32.RegistryKey = _
    My.Computer.Registry.CurrentConfig
```

### Description

The *CurrentConfig* property returns a *Microsoft.Win32.RegistryKey* object that refers to the HKEY_CURRENT_CONFIG location in the Windows registry. This entry point is used primarily to store device-specific settings for the local computer.

### Usage at a Glance

- This property is read-only.
- You must have sufficient security permissions to read or write keys and values in the registry.

### Example

The following example displays all of the sub-elements of the HKEY_CURRENT_CONFIG registry key element in a listbox control. The example assumes that you are using this code on a form with a defined ListBox1 control.

```
ListBox1.DataSource = My.Computer.Registry. _
    CurrentConfig.GetSubKeyNames( )
```

### Related Framework Entries

- Microsoft.VisualBasic.MyServices.RegistryProxy.CurrentConfig Property
- Microsoft.Win32.Registry.CurrentConfig Property

ClassesRoot Property, CurrentUser Property, DynData Property, GetValue Method, LocalMachine Property, PerformanceData Property, Registry Object, SetValue Method, Users Property

## CurrentDirectory Property

### Location

My.Computer.FileSystem.CurrentDirectory

### Syntax

```
Dim result As String = My.Computer.FileSystem.CurrentDirectory
```

or:

```
My.Computer.FileSystem.CurrentDirectory = path
```

*path (required; String)*

The full or relative path to a valid directory to use as the new "current" directory

### Description

The *CurrentDirectory* property returns the full path to the "current" directory, the directory used when referring to files with relative path names. This property can also set the current directory to a new path.

### Usage at a Glance

- An exception is thrown if the user lacks sufficient privileges to examine the file system, or at least the specified part of the file system.

- An exception is thrown when setting this property if the supplied path is invalid.

### Example

This sample code shows the basic functionality of the *CurrentDirectory* property.

```
My.Computer.FileSystem.CurrentDirectory = "c:\Windows\System32"
My.Computer.FileSystem.CurrentDirectory = ".."   ' Up one level
MsgBox(My.Computer.FileSystem.CurrentDirectory)
   ' ----- Displays "c:\WINDOWS"
```

### Related Framework Entries

- Microsoft.VisualBasic.MyServices.FileSystemProxy.CurrentDirectory Method
- Microsoft.VisualBasic.FileIO.FileSystem.CurrentDirectory Method
- System.IO.Directory.GetCurrentDirectory Method

### See Also

Drives Property, FileSystem Object, FindInFiles Method, GetDirectories Method, GetDirectoryInfo Method, GetDriveInfo Method, GetFileInfo Method, GetFiles Method, GetTempFileName Method

The 'My' Reference

# CurrentPrincipal Property

## Location
My.User.CurrentPrincipal

## Syntax
```
Dim result As System.Security.Principal.IPrincipal = _
    My.User.CurrentPrincipal
```

## Description
The *CurrentPrincipal* property gets or sets the current role-based security principal (the security context, with access to user and role information) using the *System.Security.Principal.IPrincipal* interface. In most Windows applications, this interface will exist through an instance of *Security.Principal.WindowsPrincipal*. However, other custom principal formats are possible.

## Usage at a Glance
- An exception is thrown if you attempt to update this property without sufficient permissions.
- In ASP.NET applications, the security information refers to the user associated with the current HTTP request.

## Example
The following example obtains the user name. This example checks if the application is using Windows or custom authentication and uses that information to parse the *My.User.Name* property.
```
Public Function GetCurrentUserName( ) As String
    If TypeOf My.User.CurrentPrincipal Is _
            System.Security.Principal.WindowsPrincipal Then
        ' ----- Windows username = "domain\user".
        Return Mid(My.User.Name, Instr(My.User.Name, "\") + 1)
    Else
        ' ----- Some other custom type of user.
        Return My.User.Name
    End If
End Function
```

## Related Framework Entries
- Microsoft.VisualBasic.ApplicationServices.User.CurrentPrincipal Property
- Microsoft.VisualBasic.ApplicationServices.WebUser.CurrentPrincipal Property
- System.Security.Principal.GenericPrincipal
- System.Security.Principal.IPrincipal Interface
- System.Security.Principal.WindowsPrincipal

## See Also
InitializeWithWindowsUser Method, IsAuthenticated Property, IsInRole Method, Name Property (My.User), User Object

## CurrentUser Property

### Location

My.Computer.Registry.CurrentUser

### Syntax

```
Dim result As Microsoft.Win32.RegistryKey = _
    My.Computer.Registry.CurrentUser
```

### Description

The *CurrentUser* property returns a *Microsoft.Win32.RegistryKey* object that refers to the HKEY_CURRENT_USER location in the Windows registry. This entry point is used primarily to store application and system settings specific to the current Windows user.

### Usage at a Glance

- This property is read-only.
- You must have sufficient security permissions to read or write keys and values in the registry.

### Example

The following example displays all of the sub-elements of the HKEY_CURRENT_USER registry key element in a listbox control. The example assumes that you are using this code on a form with a defined ListBox1 control.

```
ListBox1.DataSource = My.Computer.Registry. _
    CurrentUser.GetSubKeyNames( )
```

### Related Framework Entries

- Microsoft.VisualBasic.MyServices.RegistryProxy.CurrentUser Property
- Microsoft.Win32.Registry.CurrentUser Property

### See Also

ClassesRoot Property, CurrentConfig Property, DynData Property, GetValue Method, LocalMachine Property, PerformanceData Property, Registry Object, SetValue Method, Users Property

---

## CurrentUserApplicationData Property

### Location

My.Computer.FileSystem.SpecialDirectories.CurrentUserApplicationData

### Syntax

```
Dim result As String = My.Computer.FileSystem. _
    SpecialDirectories.CurrentUserApplicationData
```

## Description

The *CurrentUserApplicationData* property returns the full path name to the "application data" folder for the current user on the local workstation. Usually, this directory is found at *C:\Documents and Settings\user\ApplicationData*, but it may vary from system to system.

## Usage at a Glance

- This property is read-only.
- This folder contains files and directories used to manage application-specific data for a specific authorized user.
- This path may not be defined in some cases. In such cases, use of this property generates an exception.
- The returned path will never have a backslash "\" character at the end.

## Related Framework Entries

- Microsoft.VisualBasic.MyServices.SpecialDirectoriesProxy.CurrentUserApplicationData Property
- Microsoft.VisualBasic.FileIO.SpecialDirectories.CurrentUserApplicationData Property

## See Also

AllUsersApplicationData Property, Desktop Property, MyDocuments Property, MyMusic Property, MyPictures Property, ProgramFiles Property, Programs Property, SpecialDirectories Object, Temp Property

---

# DefaultFileLogWriter Property

## Location

My.Application.Log.DefaultFileLogWriter

My.Log.DefaultFileLogWriter

## Syntax

For client applications:

```
Dim result As Microsoft.VisualBasic.Logging. _
    FileLogTraceListener = _
    My.Application.Log.DefaultFileLogWriter
```

For ASP.NET applications:

```
Dim result As Microsoft.VisualBasic.Logging. _
    FileLogTraceListener = My.Log.DefaultFileLogWriter
```

## Description

The *DefaultFileLogWriter* property returns an object of type *Microsoft.VisualBasic. Logging.FileLogTraceListener* that identifies the current trace listener used by the logging system.

## Usage at a Glance

- This property is read-only.

- Diagnostic content written using the various *Debug.Write* methods is not sent to the trace listeners.

- This property is only valid in client and ASP.NET applications. For client applications, use *My.Application.Log.DefaultFileLogWriter*. For ASP.NET applications, use *My.Log.DefaultFileLogWriter*.

## Related Framework Entries

- Microsoft.VisualBasic.Logging.FileLogTraceListener Class
- Microsoft.VisualBasic.Logging.Log.DefaultFileLogWriter Property

## See Also

Log Object (My), Log Object (My.Application), TraceSource Property, WriteEntry Method, WriteException Method

---

# DeleteDirectory Method

## Location

My.Computer.FileSystem.DeleteDirectory

## Syntax

```
My.Computer.FileSystem.DeleteDirectory(path, onDirectoryNotEmpty)
```

or:

```
My.Computer.FileSystem.DeleteDirectory(path, showUI, _
    recycle[, onUserCancel])
```

*path (required; String)*
The path to the directory to be deleted.

*onDirectoryNotEmpty (required in syntax 1; DeleteDirectoryOption enumeration)*
Indicates the action to take if the directory is not empty. One of the following *Microsoft.VisualBasic.FileIO.DeleteDirectoryOption* enumeration values.

| Value | Description |
|---|---|
| DeleteAllContents | Deletes all subordinate items. |
| ThrowIfDirectoryNonEmpty | Throws an exception. The *Data* property of the *Exception* object lists the blocking items. |

If this parameter is missing, DeleteAllContents is used by default.

*showUI (optional; UIOption enumeration)*
Indicates whether error or progress dialog windows should appear during the delete. One of the following *Microsoft.VisualBasic.FileIO.UIOption* enumeration values.

| Value | Description |
|---|---|
| OnlyErrorDialogs | Only shows error dialog boxes; does not display progress |
| AllDialogs | Shows progress and error dialogs |

If this parameter is missing, OnlyErrorDialogs is used by default.

*recycle (optional; RecycleOption enumeration)*
Indicates the state of the directory after it has been deleted. One of the following *Microsoft.VisualBasic.FileIO.RecycleOption* enumeration values.

| Value | Description |
|---|---|
| DeletePermanently | Permanently deletes the directory and its contents |
| SendToRecycleBin | Moves the directory to the Recycle Bin |

If this parameter is missing, DeletePermanently is used by default.

*onUserCancel (optional; UICancelOption enumeration)*
The progress window includes a Cancel button. When pressed, the method takes action based on this parameter. One of the following *Microsoft.VisualBasic. FileIO.UICancelOption* enumeration values.

| Value | Description |
|---|---|
| DoNothing | Aborts the deletion but returns no information indicating that the deletion was cancelled |
| ThrowException | Throws an exception |

If this parameter is missing, ThrowException is used by default.

## Description

The *DeleteDirectory* method deletes the indicated directory and all of its contents.

## Usage at a Glance

- Visual Basic includes an RmDir procedure that also deletes directories. However, that procedure fails if the directory is not empty.
- An exception is thrown if the path parameter is missing, invalid, or refers to a file.
- An exception is thrown if the directory does not exist or is in use (including any of its contents).
- An exception is thrown if the user lacks sufficient file access permissions.

## Example

The following example permanently deletes a directory and its contents.

```
My.Computer.FileSystem.DeleteDirectory( _
    ("C:\OldFiles", DeleteAllContents)
```

## Related Framework Entries

- Microsoft.VisualBasic.FileIO.FileSystem.DeleteDirectory Method
- Microsoft.VisualBasic.MyServices.FileSystemProxy.DeleteDirectory Method
- System.IO.Directory.Delete Method

CopyDirectory Method, CopyFile Method, CreateDirectory Method, DeleteFile Method, FileSystem Object, MoveDirectory Method, MoveFile Method, Rename-Directory Method, RenameFile Method

## DeleteFile Method

### Location

My.Computer.FileSystem.DeleteFile

### Syntax

```
My.Computer.FileSystem.DeleteFile(path[, showUI, _
   recycle[, onUserCancel]])
```

*path (required; String)*
:   The path to the file to be deleted.

*showUI (optional; UIOption enumeration)*
:   Indicates whether error or progress dialog windows should appear during the delete. One of the following *Microsoft.VisualBasic.FileIO.UIOption* enumeration values.

| Value | Description |
|---|---|
| OnlyErrorDialogs | Only shows error dialog boxes; does not display progress |
| AllDialogs | Shows progress and error dialogs |

If this parameter is missing, OnlyErrorDialogs is used by default.

*recycle (optional; RecycleOption enumeration)*
:   Indicates the state of the file after it has been deleted. One of the following *Microsoft.VisualBasic.FileIO.RecycleOption* enumeration values.

| Value | Description |
|---|---|
| DeletePermanently | Permanently deletes the file |
| SendToRecycleBin | Moves the file to the Recycle Bin |

If this parameter is missing, DeletePermanently is used by default.

*onUserCancel (optional; UICancelOption enumeration)*
:   The progress window includes a Cancel button. When pressed, the method takes action based on this parameter. One of the following *Microsoft.VisualBasic. FileIO.UICancelOption* enumeration values.

| Value | Description |
|---|---|
| DoNothing | Aborts the deletion but returns no information indicating that the deletion was cancelled |
| ThrowException | Throws an exception |

If this parameter is missing, ThrowException is used by default.

## Description

The *DeleteFile* method deletes the indicated file.

## Usage at a Glance

- Visual Basic includes a `Kill` procedure that also deletes files.
- An exception is thrown if the path parameter is missing or invalid.
- An exception is thrown if the file does not exist or is in use.
- An exception is thrown if the user lacks sufficient file access permissions.

## Example

The following example sends a file to the Recycle Bin.

```
My.Computer.FileSystem.DeleteFile( _
    ("C:\workfile.txt", OnlyErrorDialogs, SendToRecycleBin)
```

## Related Framework Entries

- Microsoft.VisualBasic.FileIO.FileSystem.DeleteFile Method
- Microsoft.VisualBasic.MyServices.FileSystemProxy.DeleteFile Method
- System.IO.File.Delete Method

## See Also

CopyDirectory Method, CopyFile Method, CreateDirectory Method, DeleteDirectory Method, FileSystem Object, MoveDirectory Method, MoveFile Method, RenameDirectory Method, RenameFile Method

---

# Delimiters Property

## Location

TextFieldParser.Delimiters

## Syntax

```
Dim fileParser As FileIO.TextFieldParser
' ...later...
Dim result As String() = fileParser.Delimiters
```

or:

```
fileParser.Delimiters = setOfDelimiters
```

*setOfDelimiters (required; String array)*
> An array of the character or multicharacter values that identify the delimiters used to separate data fields in each input line of a delimited text file being parsed by a *TextFieldParser* object. End-of-line characters may not be used as field delimiters.

## Description

The *Delimiters* property sets or retrieves the field delimiters used in delimited text-file parsing. Although you can define more than one delimiter, most input files will use a single field delimiter, such as a comma or a tab character.

You can also set the delimiters with the *TextFieldParser* object's *SetDelimiters* method.

---

## Usage at a Glance

- The *Delimiters* property is only useful with delimited input files, not fixed-width files.

- Setting the *Delimiters* property does not alter the current value of the *TextField-Type* property.

- An exception is thrown if you attempt to use line-termination characters, zero-length strings, or Nothing as a field delimiter.

- You must close the *TextFieldParser* object when finished with it. Use the object's *Close* method or create the object instance with the Using keyword. See the *Text-FieldParser Object* entry in this chapter for an example.

## Example

The following example uses the *Delimiters* property to indicate the comma character as the field delimiter.

```
Dim scanInput As Microsoft.VisualBasic.FileIO.TextFieldParser
' ...later...
scanInput.TextFieldType = _
    Microsoft.VisualBasic.FileIO.FieldType.Delimited
scanInput.Delimiters = New String() {","}
```

## Related Framework Entries

- Microsoft.VisualBasic.FileIO.TextFieldParser.Delimiters Property

## See Also

FieldWidths Property, HasFieldsEnclosedInQuotes Property, ReadFields Method, SetDelimiters Method, SetFieldWidths Method, TextFieldParser Object, TextField-Type Property, TrimWhiteSpace Property

---

# Deployment Property

## Location

My.Application.Deployment

## Syntax

```
Dim result As System.Deployment.Application. _
    ApplicationDeployment = My.Application.Deployment
```

## Description

The *Deployment* property returns the application's ClickOnce deployment object. This object provides features that let you update the application's installation. It includes features to check for the presence of an update and features that let you download updates interactively or in the background.

## Public Members

The returned *ApplicationDeployment* object includes the following notable public members.

| Member | Description |
|---|---|
| CheckForDetailedUpdate | Method. Queries the network source for the deployment to see if an updated version exists. If so, the returned *System.Deployment.Application.UpdateCheckInfo* object includes information about the update, such as its version number and size. An asynchronous version of this method also exists. |
| CheckForUpdate | Method. Returns a Boolean that indicates whether an update is available (True) or not (False). |
| CurrentVersion | Property. Indicates the version number of the currently deployed instance. |
| DownloadFileGroup | Method. Downloads a specific subgroup of deployment files from the network source. An asynchronous version of this method also exists. |
| Update | Method. Immediately updates this deployment from its network source. An asynchronous version of this method also exists. |

## Usage at a Glance

- This property is read-only.

- An exception is thrown if the application is not deployed as a ClickOnce application. Always use the *My.Application.IsNetworkDeployed* property first to confirm that the application was installed using ClickOnce.

## Example

This sample code checks for an update.

```
Public Sub CheckSoftwareUpdate( )
    ' ----- Ask the user about updating the software.
    If (My.Application.IsNetworkDeployed = False) Then Exit Sub
    Dim updateInfo As System.Deployment.Application. _
        ApplicationDeployment = My.Application.Deployment
    Dim details As System.Deployment.Application.UpdateCheckInfo
    details = updateInfo.CheckForDetailedUpdate( )
    If (details.UpdateAvailable = True) Then
        If (MsgBox("Version " & details.AvailableVersion.ToString & _
            " is available for download. Update now?", _
            MsgBoxStyle.Question Or MsgBoxStyle.YesNo, "Update") _
            = MsgBoxResult.Yes) Then
            ' ----- Continue with the update.
            updateInfo.Update( )
        End If
    End If
End Sub
```

## Related Framework Entries

- Microsoft.VisualBasic.ApplicationServices.ConsoleApplicationBase.Deployment Property
- System.Deployment.Application.ApplicationDeployment

## See Also

Application Object, IsNetworkDeployed Property

# Description Property

## Location
My.Application.Info.Description

## Syntax
```
Dim result As String = My.Application.Info.Description
```

## Description
The *Description* property returns the application description as defined in the informational section of the assembly.

## Usage at a Glance
- This property is read-only.
- An exception occurs if the description attribute, *AssemblyDescriptionAttribute* (or `<AssemblyDescription>`), is undefined in the active assembly.

## Related Framework Entries
- Microsoft.VisualBasic.ApplicationServices.AssemblyInfo.Description Property
- System.Diagnostics.FileVersionInfo.FileDescription Property

## See Also
CompanyName Property, Copyright Property, Info Object (My.Application), ProductName Property, Title Property, Trademark Property

---

# Desktop Property

## Location
My.Computer.FileSystem.SpecialDirectories.Desktop

## Syntax
```
Dim result As String = My.Computer.FileSystem. _
    SpecialDirectories.Desktop
```

## Description
The *Desktop* property returns the full path name to the Desktop folder for the current user on the local workstation. Usually, this directory is found at *C:\Documents and Settings*\user\*Desktop*, but it may vary from system to system.

## Usage at a Glance
- This property is read-only.
- This folder contains items that appear on the user's Windows desktop.
- This path may not be defined in some cases. In such cases, use of this property generates an exception.
- The returned path will never have a backslash "\" character at the end.

**Related Framework Entries**

- Microsoft.VisualBasic.MyServices.SpecialDirectoriesProxy.Desktop Property
- Microsoft.VisualBasic.FileIO.SpecialDirectories.Desktop Property

**See Also**

AllUsersApplicationData Property, CurrentUserApplicationData Property, MyDocuments Property, MyMusic Property, MyPictures Property, ProgramFiles Property, Programs Property, SpecialDirectories Object, Temp Property

## DirectoryExists Method

**Location**

My.Computer.FileSystem.DirectoryExists

**Syntax**

```
Dim result As Boolean = _
    My.Computer.FileSystem.DirectoryExists(path)
```

*path (required; String)*
    The full path to a directory

**Description**

The *DirectoryExists* method indicates whether the supplied directory path exists (True) or not (False).

**Usage at a Glance**

This method returns False if the user lacks sufficient file system access privileges.

**Related Framework Entries**

- Microsoft.VisualBasic.MyServices.FileSystemProxy.DirectoryExists Method
- Microsoft.VisualBasic.FileIO.FileSystem.DirectoryExists Method
- System.IO.Directory.Exists Method

**See Also**

FileSystem Object, FileExists Method

## DirectoryPath Property

**Location**

My.Application.Info.DirectoryPath

**Syntax**

```
Dim result As String = My.Application.Info.DirectoryPath
```

**Description**

The *DirectoryPath* property returns the name of the directory containing the active application.

## Usage at a Glance

- This property is read-only.
- The returned path does not include a trailing backslash ("\").

## Related Framework Entries

- Microsoft.VisualBasic.ApplicationServices.AssemblyInfo.DirectoryPath Property
- System.Reflection.Assembly.Location Property

## See Also

AssemblyName Property, Info Object (My.Application), LoadedAssemblies Property

---

# DoEvents Method

## Location

My.Application.DoEvents

## Syntax

```
My.Application.DoEvents( )
```

The 'My' Reference

## Description

The *DoEvents* method temporarily relinquishes control from the current block of code so that other pending Windows messages can be processed. Using this method in a block of processing-intensive code can make your application feel more responsive. In some instances, it may be better to use multiple threads within your application to achieve this same goal.

Messages in the message queue for your application are normally processed one at a time by event handlers. If you take a long time to complete processing for a single message, all other messages in the queue will be blocked until the active event completes. Using the *DoEvents* method allows these other messages to be processed.

## Usage at a Glance

- This method is only valid in Windows Forms applications.
- When *DoEvents* is called from an event handler, it is possible that one of the messages being handled will also call the same event handler.

## Related Framework Entries

- System.Windows.Forms.Application.DoEvents Method

## See Also

Application Object

---

# DownloadFile Method

## Location

My.Computer.Network.DownloadFile

## Syntax

```
My.Computer.Network.DownloadFile(address, destinationFileName _
    [, username, password [, showUI, connectionTimeout, _
    overwrite [, onUserCancel]]])
```

or:

```
My.Computer.Network.DownloadFile(uri, destinationFileName _
    [, username, password [, showUI, connectionTimeout, _
    overwrite [, onUserCancel]]])
```

or:

```
My.Computer.Network.DownloadFile(uri, destinationFileName, _
    networkCredentials, showUI, connectionTimeout, overwrite _
    [, onUserCancel])
```

*address (required in syntax 1; String)*
The file to download, including its full URL path.

*uri (required in syntax 2 and 3; System.URI)*
The uniform resource identifier (URI) of the file to download.

*destinationFileName (required; String)*
The local destination path for the downloaded file.

*username (optional; String)*
The network user name for authentication purposes. If supplied, *password* must also be used.

*password (optional; String)*
The network password for authentication purposes. If supplied, *username* must also be used.

*showUI (optional; Boolean)*
Indicates whether a progress window should appear during the download. By default, no progress window appears.

*connectionTimeout (optional; Integer)*
The number of seconds to wait before failure. By default, the timeout is 100 seconds.

*overwrite (optional; Boolean)*
Indicates whether any existing file at the destination location should be overwritten. By default, existing files are not overwritten.

*onUserCancel (optional; UICancelOption enumeration)*
The progress window includes a Cancel button. When pressed, the method takes action based on this parameter. One of the following *Microsoft.VisualBasic. FileIO.UICancelOption* enumeration values.

| Value | Description |
|---|---|
| DoNothing | Aborts the download but returns no information indicating that the download was cancelled |
| ThrowException | Throws an exception |

If this parameter is missing, ThrowException is used by default.

*networkCredentials (required in syntax 3; ICredentials interface)*
The credentials to be supplied for authentication purposes, based on the *System. Net.ICredentials* interface.

## Description

The *DownloadFile* method downloads a file from a network location, saving it in a specified destination on the local computer.

## Usage at a Glance

- An exception is thrown if the source or destination path is invalid, or if the source web site denies the request.
- An exception is thrown if the user has invalid or insufficient security permissions to perform the download.
- An exception is thrown if a connection timeout occurs due to a lack of server response.

## Example

The following example downloads a file from a web site and saves it to a path on the local hard drive.

```
My.Computer.Network.DownloadFile _
    ("http://www.oreilly.com/PriceList.txt", "C:\PriceList.txt")
```

## Related Framework Entries

- Microsoft.VisualBasic.Devices.Network.DownloadFile Method

## See Also

Network Object, UploadFile Method

---

# Drives Property

## Location

My.Computer.FileSystem.Drives

## Syntax

```
Dim result As System.Collections.ObjectModel.ReadOnlyCollection( _
    Of System.IO.DriveInfo) = My.Computer.FileSystem.Drives
```

## Description

The *Drives* property returns a collection of *System.IO.DriveInfo* objects that represents the available logical disk drives currently configured on the local workstation.

## Public Members

Each *DriveInfo* object in the returned collection has many useful members that provide information about each logical drive. See the *GetDriveInfo* entry in this chapter for a summary of the members of this object.

## Usage at a Glance

- The returned collection is read-only.
- An error occurs if the user lacks sufficient privileges to retrieve the drive list.

## Related Framework Entries

- Microsoft.VisualBasic.MyServices.FileSystemProxy.Drives Propertry
- Microsoft.VisualBasic.FileIO.FileSystem.Drives Propertry
- System.IO.DriveInfo.GetDrives Method

## See Also

CurrentDirectory Property, FileSystem Object, FindInFiles Method, GetDirectories Method, GetDirectoryInfo Method, GetDriveInfo Method, GetFileInfo Method, GetFiles Method, GetTempFileName Method

# DynData Property

## Location

My.Computer.Registry.DynData

## Syntax

```
Dim result As Microsoft.Win32.RegistryKey = _
    My.Computer.Registry.DynData
```

## Description

The *DynData* property returns a *Microsoft.Win32.RegistryKey* object that refers to the HKEY_DYNDATA location in the Windows registry. This entry point is used primarily to store dynamic registry data.

## Usage at a Glance

- This property is read-only.
- You must have sufficient security permissions to read or write keys and values in the registry.

## Example

The following example displays all of the sub-elements of the HKEY_DYNDATA registry key element in a listbox control. The example assumes that you are using this code on a form with a defined ListBox1 control.

```
ListBox1.DataSource = My.Computer.Registry.DynData.GetSubKeyNames()
```

## Related Framework Entries

- Microsoft.VisualBasic.MyServices.RegistryProxy.DynData Property
- Microsoft.Win32.Registry.DynData Property

## See Also

ClassesRoot Property, CurrentConfig Property, CurrentUser Property, GetValue Method, LocalMachine Property, PerformanceData Property, Registry Object, SetValue Method, Users Property

## EndOfData Property

### Location
TextFieldParser.EndOfData

### Syntax
```
Dim fileParser As FileIO.TextFieldParser
' ...later...
Dim result As Boolean = fileParser.EndOfData
```

### Description
The *EndOfData* property indicates whether the parser has passed the final valid data record in the file (True) or not (False).

### Usage at a Glance
- This property only considers valid record entries. If there are blank lines or other non-data lines between the current position and the true end of the file, those are ignored.
- You must close the *TextFieldParser* object when finished with it. Use the object's *Close* method or create the object instance with the Using keyword. See the *TextFieldParser Object* entry in this chapter for an example.

### Example
The *EndOfData* property provides a convenient method to check for the end of the input data when parsing the entire contents of a file.
```
Dim fileParser As FileIO.TextFieldParser
' ...later...
Do While Not fileParser.EndOfData
   ' ----- Read and process one record of data here.
Loop
fileParser.Close
```

### Related Framework Entries
- Microsoft.VisualBasic.FileIO.TextFieldParser.EndOfData Property

### See Also
Close Method, LineNumber Property, PeekChars Method, ReadFields Method, ReadLine Method, ReadToEnd Method, TextFieldParser Object

---

## ErrorLine Property

### Location
TextFieldParser.ErrorLine

### Syntax
```
Dim fileParser As FileIO.TextFieldParser
' ...later...
Dim result As String = fileParser.ErrorLine
```

## Description

The *ErrorLine* property returns the contents of the most recent data input line that could not be parsed by the *TextFieldParser* object. Failed parsing is indicated by the *Microsoft.VisualBasic.FileIO.MalformedLineException* exception being thrown during a read operation. The *ErrorLineNumber* property returns the numeric line position of the errant line.

## Usage at a Glance

- This property is read-only.
- In the absence of malformed line errors, this property returns an empty string.
- You must close the *TextFieldParser* object when finished with it. Use the object's *Close* method or create the object instance with the Using keyword. See the *TextFieldParser Object* entry in this chapter for an example.

## Example

The following code imports a comma-delimited file, monitoring the input for errors.

```
Dim oneLine( ) As String
Dim inputFile As New FileIO.TextFieldParser("c:\temp\data.txt")

inputFile.SetDelimiters(",")
Try
    Do While Not inputFile.EndOfData
        oneLine = inputFile.ReadFields( )
        ' ----- Process data here...
    Loop
Catch ex As FileIO.MalformedLineException
    ' ----- Bad data.
    MsgBox("Bad data found at line " & inputFile.ErrorLineNumber & _
        ":" & vbCrLf & vbCrLf & inputFile.ErrorLine & vbCrLf & _
        vbCrLf & "Processing aborted.")
Finally
    inputFile.Close( )
End Try
```

## Related Framework Entries

- Microsoft.VisualBasic.FileIO.TextFieldParser.ErrorLine Property

## See Also

EndOfData Property, ErrorLineNumber Property, LineNumber Property, ReadFields Method, TextFieldParser Object

---

# ErrorLineNumber Property

## Location

TextFieldParser.ErrorLineNumber

## Syntax

```
Dim fileParser As FileIO.TextFieldParser
' ...later...
Dim result As Long = fileParser.ErrorLineNumber
```

---

## Description

The *ErrorLineNumber* property returns the line number of the most recent data input line that could not be parsed by the *TextFieldParser* object. Failed parsing is indicated by the *Microsoft.VisualBasic.FileIO.MalformedLineException* exception being thrown during a read operation. The *ErrorLine* property returns the text of the errant line.

## Usage at a Glance

- This property is read-only.
- The first line in the file is line number 1.
- Blank lines and comment lines are counted as valid lines when determining the line position.
- In the absence of malformed line errors, this property returns -1.
- You must close the *TextFieldParser* object when finished with it. Use the object's *Close* method or create the object instance with the Using keyword. See the *TextFieldParser Object* entry in this chapter for an example.

## Example

See the example in the *ErrorLine Property* entry.

## Related Framework Entries

- Microsoft.VisualBasic.FileIO.TextFieldParser.ErrorLineNumber Property

## See Also

EndOfData Property, ErrorLine Property, LineNumber Property, ReadFields Method, TextFieldParser Object

---

# FieldWidths Property

## Location

TextFieldParser.FieldWidths

## Syntax

```
Dim fileParser As FileIO.TextFieldParser
' ...later...
Dim result As Integer() = fileParser.FieldWidths
```

or:

```
fileParser.FieldWidths = setOfWidths
```

setOfWidths *(required; Integer array)*

An array of values, each of which indicates the character length of a positional field within a fixed-width text file being parsed by a *TextFieldParser* object. All field widths must be greater than zero, although the last array element may be less than or equal to zero to indicate a final variable-width field.

## Description

The *FieldWidths* property sets or retrieves the number of characters used for each field in fixed-width text-file parsing. The first field begins with the first character on each record line, and subsequent fields immediately follow the fields before. You can indicate that the last field is of variable length (that is, it includes all characters until the end of the line) by setting the last field width to -1.

You can also set the field widths with the *TextFieldParser* object's *SetFieldWidths* method.

### Usage at a Glance

- The *FieldWidths* property is only useful with fixed-width input files, not delimited files.
- Setting the *FieldWidths* property does not alter the current value of the *TextField-Type* property.
- An exception is thrown if you assign a zero or negative value to any field width other than the last one.
- You must close the *TextFieldParser* object when finished with it. Use the object's *Close* method or create the object instance with the Using keyword. See the *Text-FieldParser Object* entry in this chapter for an example.

### Example

The following example uses the *FieldWidths* property to indicate that each line in the input file contains three fields: a 3-character field, a 30-character field, and a 5-character field.

```
Dim scanInput As Microsoft.VisualBasic.FileIO.TextFieldParser
' ...later...
scanInput.TextFieldType = _
    Microsoft.VisualBasic.FileIO.FieldType.FixedWidth
scanInput.FieldWidths = New Integer() {3, 30, 5}
```

### Related Framework Entries

- Microsoft.VisualBasic.FileIO.TextFieldParser.FieldWidths Property

### See Also

Delimiters Property, ReadFields Method, SetDelimiters Method, SetFieldWidths Method, TextFieldParser Object, TextFieldType Property

---

## FileExists Method

### Location

My.Computer.FileSystem.FileExists

### Syntax

```
Dim result As Boolean = My.Computer.FileSystem.FileExists(path)
```
*path (required; String)*
    The full path to a file

### Description

The *FileExists* method indicates whether the supplied file path exists (True) or not (False).

## Usage at a Glance

This method returns False if the user lacks sufficient file system access privileges.

## Related Framework Entries

- Microsoft.VisualBasic.MyServices.FileSystemProxy.FileExists Method
- Microsoft.VisualBasic.FileIO.FileSystem.FileExists Method
- System.IO.File.Exists Method

## See Also

DirectoryExists Method, FileSystem Object

---

# FileSystem Object

## Location

My.Computer.FileSystem

## Description

Use the *FileSystem* object to examine and manipulate drives, directories, and files.

## Public Members

The following members of the *My.Computer.FileSystem* object have their own entries elsewhere in this chapter.

- CombinePath Method
- CopyDirectory Method
- CopyFile Method
- CreateDirectory Method
- CurrentDirectory Property
- DeleteDirectory Method
- DeleteFile Method
- DirectoryExists Method
- Drives Property
- FileExists Method
- FindInFiles Method
- GetDirectories Method
- GetDirectoryInfo Method
- GetDriveInfo Method
- GetFileInfo Method
- GetFiles Method
- GetName Method
- GetParentPath Method
- GetTempFileName Method
- MoveDirectory Method

- MoveFile Method
- OpenTextFieldParser Method
- OpenTextFileReader Method
- OpenTextFileWriter Method
- ReadAllBytes Method
- ReadAllText Method
- RenameDirectory Method
- RenameFile Method
- SpecialDirectories Object
- WriteAllBytes Method
- WriteAllText Method

**Related Framework Entries**
- Microsoft.VisualBasic.FileIO.FileSystem
- Microsoft.VisualBasic.MyServices.FileSystemProxy

**See Also**
Computer Object, SpecialDirectories Object

---

## FindInFiles Method

### Location
My.Computer.FileSystem.FindInFiles

### Syntax
```
Dim result As System.Collections.ObjectModel.ReadOnlyCollection( _
    Of String) = My.Computer.FileSystem.FindInFiles(path, _
    containsText, ignoreCase, searchType[, wildcard])
```

*path (required; String)*
The path to the directory that includes the files to search.

*containsText (required; String)*
The text to search for in each file.

*ignoreCase (required; Boolean)*
Indicates whether the search should be case-sensitive (False) or case-insensitive (True).

*searchType (optional; SearchOption enumeration)*
The type of search to perform. One of the following *Microsoft.VisualBasic.FileIO. SearchOption* enumeration values.

| Value | Description |
|---|---|
| SearchAllSubDirectories | Includes all files found directly under the specified path and also in all descendant subdirectories below the specified path |
| SearchTopLevelOnly | Includes only those files found immediately under the specified path; does not include files found in other descendant subdirectories |

*wildcard (optional; String)*

A pattern used to match file names. If missing, all names are matched. Use the asterisk character (*) to match zero or more characters or the question mark character (?) to match exactly one character.

## Description

The *FindInFiles* method returns a collection of strings, each one the name of a file within the specified directory that includes the specified search text. The set of files to search may be limited using the *wildcard* parameter. If no searched files include the specified search text, an empty collection is returned.

## Usage at a Glance

- The returned collection is read-only.
- An exception is thrown if the supplied path is missing or invalid or if an invalid wildcard expression appears.
- An exception is thrown if the user lacks sufficient file system privileges.

## Example

The following statement searches for files that contain the text "virus" (independent of case) in the current user's *MyDocuments* folder, ignoring any subdirectories.

```
Dim result As System.Collections.ObjectModel.ReadOnlyCollection( _
    Of String) = My.Computer.FileSystem.FindInFiles( _
    My.Computer.FileSystem.SpecialDirectories.MyDocuments, _
    "VIRUS", True, FileIO.SearchOption.SearchTopLevelOnly)
```

## Related Framework Entries

- Microsoft.VisualBasic.MyServices.FileSystemProxy.FindInFiles Method
- Microsoft.VisualBasic.FileIO.FileSystem.FindInFiles Method

## See Also

CurrentDirectory Property, Drives Property, FileSystem Object, GetDirectories Method, GetDirectoryInfo Method, GetDriveInfo Method, GetFileInfo Method, GetFiles Method, GetTempFileName Method

---

# Forms Object

## Location

My.Forms

## Description

The *My.Forms* object provides design-time and runtime access to all defined forms in a Windows Forms project. As forms are added to the project, this object is automatically updated to include the new form. For instance, if your project contains a form named "Form1," it is accessed through:

```
My.Forms.Form1
```

This returns a reference to the *System.Windows.Forms.Form* object for Form1, from which all of the relevant members can be accessed.

As a shortcut, the "My.Forms" prefix can be left off of references to forms. This allows your code to reference forms as was done in pre-.NET Visual Basic. The statement:

```
Form1.Show( )
```

is equivalent to:

```
My.Forms.Form1.Show( )
```

For code located within Form1, all references to itself should use Me instead of Form1.

```
Me.Show( )
```

If you use *My.Forms* to access a form that has not yet been instantiated, it is instantiated immediately. Setting this instance to Nothing will release the instance.

```
My.Forms.Form1 = Nothing
```

To test whether a form has yet been instantiated, test the *My.Forms* reference for Nothing.

```
If (My.Forms.Form1 Is Nothing) Then...
```

### Public Members

The *My.Forms* object has no members other than each specific form defined within the project.

### Usage at a Glance

- This object and its members are only valid in Windows Forms applications.
- Use the *My.Application.OpenForms* property to retrieve a collection of all forms currently open within the application.

### Example

This sample displays a specific form if it is not yet displayed.

```
If (My.Forms.ToolboxForm Is Nothing) Then _
    My.Forms.ToolboxForm.Show( )
```

### Related Framework Entries

- System.Windows.Forms.Form Class

### See Also

My Namespace, OpenForms Property, Resources Object, Settings Object, WebServices Object

---

## GetAudioStream Method

### Location

My.Computer.Clipboard.GetAudioStream

### Syntax

```
Dim result As System.IO.Stream = _
    My.Computer.Clipboard.GetAudioStream( )
```

## Description

The *GetAudioStream* method returns a stream object from the system clipboard that contains audio data.

## Usage at a Glance

- This method is only valid in non-server applications.
- Always use the *My.Computer.Clipboard.ContainsAudio* method to check for the presence of audio data before using this method.
- Security restrictions in place for the active user may limit access to the system clipboard.

## Example

The following example plays audio data from the system clipboard if such data is present.

```
Dim soundToPlay As System.IO.Stream
If (My.Computer.Clipboard.ContainsAudio( ) = True) Then
    soundToPlay = My.Computer.Clipboard.GetAudioStream
    My.Computer.Audio.Play(soundToPlay, AudioPlayMode.Background)
End If
```

## Related Framework Entries

- Microsoft.VisualBasic.MyServices.ClipboardProxy.GetAudioStream Method
- System.Windows.Forms.Clipboard.GetAudioStream Method

## See Also

Clipboard Object, ContainsAudio Method, GetData Method, GetDataObject Method, GetFileDropList Method, GetImage Method, GetText Method, SetAudio Method

---

# GetData Method

## Location

My.Computer.Clipboard.GetData

## Syntax

```
Dim result As Object = My.Computer.Clipboard.GetData(format)
```
format *(required; String)*
   The named format of the data to return from the clipboard

## Description

The *GetData* method returns data from the system clipboard in the specified custom named format.

## Usage at a Glance

- This method is only valid in non-server applications.
- Always use the *My.Computer.Clipboard.ContainsData* method to check for the presence of the specified named custom data before using this method.

- Security restrictions in place for the active user may limit access to the system clipboard.

### Example

The following example reads specialized data from the system clipboard and acts on it.

```
Dim secretData As Object
If (My.Computer.Clipboard.ContainsData("secretCode") = True) Then
    secretData = My.Computer.Clipboard.GetData("secretCode")
    MsgBox(DecodeSecret(secretData))
End If
```

### Related Framework Entries

- Microsoft.VisualBasic.MyServices.ClipboardProxy.GetData Method
- System.Windows.Forms.Clipboard.GetData Method

### See Also

Clipboard Object, ContainsData Method, GetAudioStream Method, GetDataObject Method, GetFileDropList Method, GetImage Method, GetText Method, SetData Method

---

## GetDataObject Method

### Location

My.Computer.Clipboard.GetDataObject

### Syntax

```
Dim result As System.Windows.Forms.IDataObject = _
    My.Computer.Clipboard.GetDataObject( )
```

### Description

The *GetDataObject* method returns an object that supports the interface *System. Windows.Forms.IDataObject* using data from the system clipboard. The *IDataObject* interface allows a single object to store the same data in multiple formats. For instance, a single data object could store the same data in plain text, Rich Text Format, and HTML.

### Usage at a Glance

- This method is only valid in non-server applications.
- Security restrictions in place for the active user may limit access to the system clipboard.

### Example

The following code displays the data formats current stored on the system clipboard.

```
Dim clipboardFormats As System.Windows.Forms.IDataObject
Dim formatNames( ) As String
clipboardFormats = My.Computer.Clipboard.GetDataObject( )
formatNames = clipboardFormats.GetFormats(True)
MsgBox(Join(formatNames, vbCrLf))
```

---

# GetDirectories Method

## Location

My.Computer.FileSystem.GetDirectories

## Syntax

```
Dim result As System.Collections.ObjectModel.ReadOnlyCollection( _
    Of String) = My.Computer.FileSystem.GetDirectories( _
    path[, searchType, wildcard])
```

*path (required; String)*
  The path to the directory that includes the subdirectories to return.

*searchType (optional; SearchOption enumeration)*
  The type of search to perform. One of the following *Microsoft.VisualBasic.FileIO. SearchOption* enumeration values.

| Value | Description |
|---|---|
| SearchAllSubDirectories | Includes all subdirectories found directly under the specified path and all descendant subdirectories below them |
| SearchTopLevelOnly | Includes only those subdirectories found immediately under the specified path; does not include descendants of those subdirectories |

If this parameter is missing, it defaults to SearchTopLevelOnly.

*wildcard (optional; String)*
  A pattern used to match directory names. If missing, all names are matched. Use the asterisk character (*) to match zero or more characters or the question mark character (?) to match exactly one character.

## Description

The *GetDirectories* method returns a collection of strings, each one the name of a subdirectory within the specified directory. If no directories are found or match the specified wildcard, an empty collection is returned.

## Usage at a Glance

- The returned collection is read-only.
- An exception is thrown if the supplied path is missing or invalid or if an invalid wildcard expression appears.

- An exception is thrown if the user lacks sufficient file system privileges.
- Each returned directory name includes the full path to that directory, not just the relative directory name.

## Example

The following example lists all subdirectories in the current directory.

```
Dim dirList As String = ""
Dim currentDir As System.Collections.ObjectModel. _
    ReadOnlyCollection(Of String) = _
    My.Computer.FileSystem.GetDirectories(".")

For Each oneSubDir As String In currentDir
    dirList &= "|" & oneSubDir
Next oneSubDir
MsgBox("The current directory contains the following " & _
    "sub-directories:" & Replace(dirList, "|", vbCrLf))
```

## Related Framework Entries

- Microsoft.VisualBasic.MyServices.FileSystemProxy.GetDirectories Method
- Microsoft.VisualBasic.FileIO.FileSystem.GetDirectories Method
- System.IO.DirectoryInfo.GetDirectories Method

## See Also

CurrentDirectory Property, Drives Property, FileSystem Object, FindInFiles Method, GetDirectoryInfo Method, GetDriveInfo Method, GetFileInfo Method, GetFiles Method, GetTempFileName Method

---

# GetDirectoryInfo Method

## Location

My.Computer.FileSystem.GetDirectoryInfo

## Syntax

```
Dim result As System.IO.DirectoryInfo = _
    My.Computer.FileSystem.GetDirectoryInfo(path)
```

*path (required; String)*
The path to the directory to be examined; an absolute or relative path

## Description

The *GetDirectoryInfo* method returns a *System.IO.DirectoryInfo* object for the indicated directory.

## Public Members

The returned *System.IO.DirectoryInfo* object includes the following notable public members.

| Member | Description |
|---|---|
| Create | Method. Creates the directory itself. Only useful when the *Exists* member returns False. |
| CreateSubdirectory | Method. Creates a subdirectory within the directory. |
| Delete | Method. Deletes the directory. |
| Exists | Property. Indicates whether the directory exists (True) or not (False). |
| FullName | Property. The full path text of the directory. |
| GetDirectories | Method. Returns a collection of subdirectories in the directory. |
| GetFiles | Method. Returns a collection of files in the directory. |
| MoveTo | Method. Moves the directory to a different location on the same drive. |
| Name | Property. The name of the directory without its full path. |
| Parent | Property. The parent folder of the directory. |
| Root | Property. The root directory that contains the directory, such as "C:\." |

## Usage at a Glance

- An exception is thrown if the path parameter is missing or invalid.
- An exception is thrown if the user lacks sufficient file-access privileges.
- If the indicated directory path does not exist, this function may complete successfully with no exception thrown. However, an exception will be thrown when accessing most members of the returned object. Use the *Exists* property to test for the directory if you are unsure of its existence, or use the *Create* method member to create the new indicated directory.

## Related Framework Entries

- Microsoft.VisualBasic.MyServices.FileSystemProxy.GetDirectoryInfo Method
- Microsoft.VisualBasic.FileIO.FileSystem.GetDirectoryInfo Method
- System.IO.DirectoryInfo Class

## See Also

CurrentDirectory Property, Drives Property, FileSystem Object, FindInFiles Method, GetDirectories Method, GetDriveInfo Method, GetFileInfo Method, GetFiles Method, GetTempFileName Method

---

# GetDriveInfo Method

## Location

My.Computer.FileSystem.GetDriveInfo

## Syntax

```
Dim result As System.IO.DriveInfo = _
    My.Computer.FileSystem.GetDriveInfo(drive)
```

*drive (required; String)*
> The letter of the drive to be examined. The supplied string is normally just the single-character drive letter. You can supply an absolute path as long as it begins with a drive letter; only the first letter of the string will be examined.

## Description

The *GetDriveInfo* method returns a *System.IO.DriveInfo* object for the indicated drive.

## Public Members

The returned *System.IO.DriveInfo* object includes the following notable public members.

| Member | Description |
| --- | --- |
| AvailableFreeSpace | Property. The available free space on the drive, in bytes, possibly limited by in-effect quotas. |
| DriveFormat | Property. The name of the format structure used on the drive, such as "NTFS" or "FAT32." |
| DriveType | Property. The type of drive, from the *System.IO.DriveType* enumeration. |
| IsReady | Property. Indicates whether the drive is ready for use (True) or not (False). This is useful for removable media drives, such as DVD drives. |
| Name | Property. The name of the drive, "C:" for example. |
| RootDirectory | Property. The root directory of the drive as a *System.IO.DirectoryInfo* object. |
| TotalFreeSpace | Property. The available free space on the drive in bytes. |
| TotalSize | Property. The total size of the drive in bytes, including both free and used portions of the drive. |
| VolumeLabel | Property. A short, friendly name for this drive. |

The *DriveType* property uses one of the following *System.IO.DriveType* enumeration values.

| Value | Description |
| --- | --- |
| CDRom | A CD-ROM device |
| Fixed | A fixed disk, such as an internal hard disk |
| Network | A nonlocal drive found on the network |
| NoRootDirectory | A drive with no root directory |
| Ram | A RAM disk |
| Removable | A drive with removable media |
| Unknown | Unknown device |

## Usage at a Glance

- An exception is thrown if the drive parameter is missing or invalid. You can supply an absolute path as the argument to the *GetDriveInfo* method, but the first letter of that path must be a drive letter.
- An exception is thrown if the user lacks sufficient file access privileges.

## Example

The following example displays the amount of free space on the C drive.

```
Dim cDrive As System.IO.DriveInfo
cDrive = My.Computer.FileSystem.GetDriveInfo("C:\")
MsgBox("Free space on the C drive: " & Format( _
    cDrive.TotalFreeSpace / (1024 * 1024), "0.00") & " MB")
```

---

# GetEnvironmentVariable Method

## Location

My.Application.GetEnvironmentVariable

## Syntax

```
Dim result As String = My.Application.GetEnvironmentVariable(name)
```

*name (required; String)*
The name of the environment variable value to return

## Description

The *GetEnvironmentVariable* method returns the value of the named Windows environment variable.

## Usage at a Glance

- An exception is thrown if an invalid or unknown name is used.
- An exception is thrown if the current user lacks sufficient security privileges to query environment variables.

## Example

The following example displays the value of the TriggerValue environment variable.

```
Try
    MsgBox("Application triggered at " & _
        My.Application.GetEnvironmentVariable("TriggerValue"))
Catch ex As System.ArgumentException
    MsgBox("Trigger value not configured.")
End Try
```

## Related Framework Entries

- System.Environment.GetEnvironmentVariable Method

## See Also

Application Object, CommandLineArgs Property

## GetFileDropList Method

### Location
My.Computer.Clipboard.GetFileDropList

### Syntax
```
Dim result As System.Collections.Specialized.StringCollection = _
    My.Computer.Clipboard.GetFileDropList()
```

### Description
The *GetFileDropList* method returns a collection of strings from the system clipboard, each containing a file path.

### Usage at a Glance
- This method is only valid in non-server applications.
- Always use the *My.Computer.Clipboard.ContainsFileDropList* method to check for the presence of the desired data format before using this method.
- Security restrictions in place for the active user may limit access to the system clipboard.

### Example
The following code displays the clipboard's file list.
```
Dim dropFiles As System.Collections.Specialized.StringCollection
If My.Computer.Clipboard.ContainsFileDropList() Then
    dropFiles = My.Computer.Clipboard.GetFileDropList()
    For Each oneFile As String In dropFiles
        ListBox1.Items.Add(oneFile)
    Next oneFile
End If
```

### Related Framework Entries
- Microsoft.VisualBasic.MyServices.ClipboardProxy.GetFileDropList Method
- System.Windows.Forms.Clipboard.GetFileDropList Method

### See Also
Clipboard Object, ContainsFileDropList Method, GetAudioStream Method, GetData Method, GetDataObject Method, GetImage Method, GetText Method, SetFile-DropList Method

---

## GetFileInfo Method

### Location
My.Computer.FileSystem.GetFileInfo

### Syntax
```
Dim result As System.IO.FileInfo = _
    My.Computer.FileSystem.GetFileInfo(path)
```

*path (required; String)*
    The path to the file to be examined

## Description

The *GetFileInfo* method returns a *System.IO.FileInfo* object for the indicated file.

## Public Members

The returned *System.IO.FileInfo* object includes the following notable public members.

| Member | Description |
|---|---|
| Attributes | Property. Gets or sets the attributes, using the *System.IO.FileAttributes* enumeration. |
| CopyTo | Method. Copies the file to a new location. |
| Create | Method. Creates a new file and opens it for writing. |
| Delete | Method. Deletes the file. |
| Directory | Property. The immediate directory of the file. |
| DirectoryName | Property. The full path of the directory containing the file. |
| Exists | Property. Indicates whether the file exists (True) or not (False). |
| FullName | Property. The full path to the file. |
| IsReadOnly | Property. Indicates whether the file is read only (True) or not (False). |
| Length | Property. The size of the file in bytes. |
| MoveTo | Method. Moves the file to a new location. |
| Name | Property. The name of the file without its full path. |
| Open | Method. Opens the file for reading or writing. |

## Usage at a Glance

- An exception is thrown if the path parameter is missing or invalid.
- An exception is thrown if the user lacks sufficient file-access privileges.
- If the indicated file does not exist, this function may complete successfully with no exception thrown. However, an exception will be thrown when accessing most members of the returned object. Use the *Exists* property to test for the file if unsure of its existence.

## Example

The following example reports a file's size.

```
Public Sub ShowFileSize(filePath As String)
    Dim theFile As System.IO.FileInfo
    theFile = My.Computer.FileSystem.GetFileInfo(filePath)
    If (theFile.Exists = True) Then
        MsgBox("'" & filePath & "' does not exist.")
    Else
        MsgBox("'" & filePath & "' size: " & _
            theFile.Length & "bytes")
    End If
End Sub
```

### Related Framework Entries

- Microsoft.VisualBasic.MyServices.FileSystemProxy.GetFileInfo Method
- Microsoft.VisualBasic.FileIO.FileSystem.GetFileInfo Method
- System.IO.FileInfo Class

### See Also

CurrentDirectory Property, Drives Property, FileSystem Object, FindInFiles Method, GetDirectories Method, GetDirectoryInfo Method, GetDriveInfo Method, GetFiles Method, GetTempFileName Method

---

## GetFiles Method

### Location

My.Computer.FileSystem.GetFiles

### Syntax

```
Dim result As System.Collections.ObjectModel.ReadOnlyCollection( _
    Of String) = My.Computer.FileSystem.GetFiles( _
    path[, searchType, wildcard])
```

*path (required; String)*
   The path to the directory that includes the files to return.

*searchType (optional; SearchOption enumeration)*
   The type of search to perform. One of the following *Microsoft.VisualBasic.FileIO. SearchOption* enumeration values.

| Value | Description |
|---|---|
| SearchAllSubDirectories | Includes all files found directly under the specified path and also in all descendant subdirectories below the specified path |
| SearchTopLevelOnly | Includes only those files found immediately under the specified path; does not include files found in other descendant subdirectories |

   If this parameter is missing, it defaults to SearchTopLevelOnly.

*wildcard (optional; String)*
   A pattern used to match file names. If missing, all names are matched. Use the asterisk character (*) to match zero or more characters or the question mark character (?) to match exactly one character.

### Description

The *GetFiles* method returns a collection of strings, each one the name of a file within the specified directory. If no files are found or match the specified wildcard, an empty collection is returned.

### Usage at a Glance

- The returned collection is read-only.
- An exception is thrown if the supplied path is missing or invalid or if an invalid wildcard expression appears.

---

- An exception is thrown if the user lacks sufficient file-system privileges.
- Each returned file name includes the full path to that file, not just the relative file name.

## Example

The following example lists all files in the current directory.

```
Dim fileList As String = ""
Dim currentDir As System.Collections.ObjectModel. _
    ReadOnlyCollection(Of String) = _
    My.Computer.FileSystem.GetFiles(".")

For Each oneFile As String In currentDir
    fileList &= "|" & oneFile
Next oneFile
MsgBox("The current directory contains the following " & _
    "files:" & Replace(fileList, "|", vbCrLf))
```

## Related Framework Entries

- Microsoft.VisualBasic.MyServices.FileSystemProxy.GetFiles Method
- Microsoft.VisualBasic.FileIO.FileSystem.GetFiles Method
- System.IO.Directory.GetFiles Method

## See Also

CurrentDirectory Property, Drives Property, FileSystem Object, FindInFiles Method, GetDirectories Method, GetDirectoryInfo Method, GetDriveInfo Method, GetFileInfo Method, GetTempFileName Method

---

# GetImage Method

## Location

My.Computer.Clipboard.GetImage

## Syntax

```
Dim result As System.Drawing.Image = _
    My.Computer.Clipboard.GetImage( )
```

## Description

The *GetImage* method returns an image from the system clipboard.

## Usage at a Glance

- This method is only valid in non-server applications.
- Always use the *My.Computer.Clipboard.ContainsImage* method to check for the presence of the desired data format before using this method.
- Security restrictions in place for the active user may limit access to the system clipboard.
- If the clipboard does not contain image data, Nothing is returned.

## Example

The following example displays an image from the system clipboard if it contains an image. This example assumes that your form includes a picture box control named PictureBox1.

```
If (My.Computer.Clipboard.ContainsImage( ) = True) Then
    PictureBox1.Image = My.Computer.Clipboard.GetImage( )
End If
```

## Related Framework Entries

- Microsoft.VisualBasic.MyServices.ClipboardProxy.GetImage Method
- System.Windows.Forms.Clipboard.GetImage Method

## See Also

Clipboard Object, ContainsImage Method, GetAudioStream Method, GetData Method, GetDataObject Method, GetFileDropList Method, GetImage Method, GetText Method, SetImage Method

---

## GetName Method

### Location

My.Computer.FileSystem.GetName

### Syntax

```
Dim result As String = My.Computer.FileSystem.GetFileName(path)
```

*path (required; String)*
    The path to be examined

### Description

The *GetName* method examines a valid filename path and returns only the filename portion, with all drive letters, folders, and directories removed.

### Usage at a Glance

The original path must be correctly formatted, but it does not need to refer to an actual file on the file system.

### Related Framework Entries

- Microsoft.VisualBasic.MyServices.FileSystemProxy.GetName Method
- Microsoft.VisualBasic.FileIO.FileSystem.GetName Method
- System.IO.Path.GetFileName Method

### See Also

CombinePath Method, FileSystem Object, GetParentPath Method

# GetParentPath Method

## Location
My.Computer.FileSystem.GetParentPath

## Syntax
```
Dim result As String = My.Computer.FileSystem.GetParentPath(path)
```
*path (required; String)*
    The path to be examined; an absolute or relative path

## Description
The *GetParentPath* method examines a valid path and returns the parent portion. The *path* supplied to the method does not have to exist, but it must be in a valid format. Whether you supply the full path to a file or a directory, *GetParentPath* simply removes the final portion.

You can supply a relative path, but if you supply only a single path component (such as ".."), an empty string will be returned.

## Usage at a Glance
- The source path supplied does not need to exist in the file system.
- An exception occurs if the source path is in an invalid format, or if the path is a "root" path that has no further parent.

## Example
```
workFolder = My.Computer.FileSystem.GetParentPath(workFile)
```

## Related Framework Entries
- Microsoft.VisualBasic.MyServices.FileSystemProxy.GetParentPath Method
- Microsoft.VisualBasic.FileIO.FileSystem.GetParentPath Method
- System.IO.Directory.GetParent Method
- System.IO.Path.GetDirectoryName Method

## See Also
CombinePath Method, FileSystem Object, GetName Method

# GetTempFileName Method

## Location
My.Computer.FileSystem.GetTempFileName

## Syntax
```
Dim result As String = My.Computer.FileSystem.GetTempFileName( )
```

## Description

The *GetTempFileName* method creates a temporary file name in the user's temporary files folder and returns the full path to that new file as a string. The new file name will be unique and will initially be empty. The file name always ends with a ".tmp" extension.

## Usage at a Glance

- An exception occurs if the active user lacks sufficient privileges to create the file.

## Related Framework Entries

- Microsoft.VisualBasic.MyServices.FileSystemProxy.GetTempFileName Method
- Microsoft.VisualBasic.FileIO.FileSystem.GetTempFileName Method
- System.IO.Path.GetTempFileName Method

## See Also

CurrentDirectory Property, Drives Property, FileSystem Object, FindInFiles Method, GetDirectories Method, GetDirectoryInfo Method, GetDriveInfo Method, GetFileInfo Method, GetFiles Method, Temp Property

# GetText Method

## Location

My.Computer.Clipboard.GetText

## Syntax

```
Dim result As String = My.Computer.Clipboard.GetText([format])
```

*format (optional; TextDataFormat enumeration)*
The specific format of the text to retrieve from the system clipboard. One of the following *System.Windows.Forms.TextDataFormat* enumeration values.

| Value | Description |
| --- | --- |
| *Not supplied* | Any type of text |
| CommaSeparatedValue | Comma-separated fields of data in one or more records |
| Html | HTML format |
| Rtf | Rich Text Format |
| UnicodeText | 16-bit Unicode character text |

If this parameter is not specified, CommaSeparatedValue is used by default.

## Description

The *GetText* method returns a String of text retrieved from the system clipboard in a specified text format. If the specified text data is not present on the clipboard, an empty string is returned.

### Usage at a Glance

- This method is only valid in non-server applications.
- Security restrictions in place for the active user may limit access to the system clipboard.

### Related Framework Entries

- Microsoft.VisualBasic.MyServices.ClipboardProxy.GetText Method
- System.Windows.Forms.Clipboard.GetText Method

### See Also

Clipboard Object, ContainsText Method, GetAudioStream Method, GetData Method, GetDataObject Method, GetFileDropList Method, GetImage Method, GetText Method, SetText Method

---

## GetValue Method

### Location

My.Computer.Registry.GetValue

### Syntax

```
Dim result As Object = My.Computer.Registry.GetValue(keyName, _
    valueName, defaultValue)
```

*keyName (required; String)*
  The hierarchy key under which to query the value for data.

*valueName (required; Object)*
  The name of the value to be queried within the key. To retrieve the default value (the "(Default)" entry) for a particular key, use Nothing or an empty string for this parameter.

*defaultValue (required; Object)*
  The default data to be returned if the value does not exist. To indicate no default value, use the Nothing keyword for this parameter.

### Description

The *GetValue* method returns the data for a value entry in the registry. All values are stored within "keys," the main hierarchy nodes within the registry.

### Usage at a Glance

- You must have sufficient security permissions to read or write keys and values in the registry.
- *keyName* must start with the name of a valid registry hive, such as HKEY_CURRENT_USER.
- This function returns data as type Object. If Option Strict is set to True, you will likely need to convert the data to another type before use. For example, when retrieving string results, use the CStr function to convert the result to a String.

## Example

The following code retrieves a string from the registry.

```
' ----- If the error limit is not recorded in the registry,
'       use a reasonable value like 5.
Dim errorLimit As String = CStr(My.Computer.Registry.GetValue( _
    "HKEY_CURRENT_USER\Software\MyCompany\MySoftware", _
    "ErrorLimit", "5"))
```

## Related Framework Entries

- Microsoft.VisualBasic.MyServices.RegistryProxy.GetValue Method
- Microsoft.Win32.RegistryKey.GetValue Method

## See Also

ClassesRoot Property, CurrentConfig Property, CurrentUser Property, DynData Property, LocalMachine Property, PerformanceData Property, Registry Object, SetValue Method, Users Property

---

# GmtTime Property

## Location

My.Computer.Clock.GmtTime

## Syntax

```
Dim result As Date = My.Computer.Clock.GmtTime
```

## Description

The *GmtTime* property returns the current date and time as represented in Universal Coordinated Time (UTC), which is equivalent to Greenwich Mean Time (GMT).

## Usage at a Glance

This property is read-only.

## Example

The following code displays the current UTC time in a message box.

```
MsgBox("If you were in London, your watch would read " & _
    Format(My.Computer.Clock.GmtTime, "HH:mm"))
```

## Related Framework Entries

- Microsoft.VisualBasic.Devices.Clock.GmtTime Property
- System.DateTime.UtcNow Property

## See Also

Clock Object, LocalTime Property, TickCount Property

# HasFieldsEnclosedInQuotes Property

## Location

TextFieldParser.HasFieldsEnclosedInQuotes

## Syntax

```
Dim fileParser As FileIO.TextFieldParser
' ...later...
Dim result As Boolean = fileParser.HasFieldsEnclosedInQuotes
```

or:

```
Dim fileParser As FileIO.TextFieldParser
' ...later...
fileParser.HasFieldsEnclosedInQuotes = hasQuotes
```

*hasQuotes (required; Boolean)*
  Indicates whether the delimited strings in the file represented by fileParser are surrounded by quotation marks (True) or not (False).

## Description

The *HasFieldsEnclosedInQuotes* property gets or sets a value that indicates whether the delimited fields parsed by a *TextFieldParser* object should accept quotation marks as field boundaries (True) or not (False). If you do not specifically set this field, it defaults to True.

If this property is set to True and a field is enclosed by quotes, any active delimiters (such as commas) found between the quotation marks are considered part of the field and are not used to delimit portions of that field. For instance, if comma is used as a delimiter, in the input line:

```
field1,field2,"field3,field4",field5
```

there are only four fields represented, since "field3,field4" is a single field containing a comma.

## Usage at a Glance

- The *HasFieldsEnclosedInQuotes* property is only useful with delimited input files, not fixed-width files.
- You must close the *TextFieldParser* object when finished with it. Use the object's *Close* method or create the object instance with the Using keyword. See the *TextFieldParser Object* entry in this chapter for an example.

## Related Framework Entries

- Microsoft.VisualBasic.FileIO.TextFieldParser.HasFieldsEnclosedInQuotes Property

## See Also

Delimiters Property, ReadFields Method, SetDelimiters Method, TextFieldParser Object, TextFieldType Property, TrimWhiteSpace Property

# Info Object (My.Application)

## Location
My.Application.Info

## Description
Use the *Info* object to access information about the current application.

## Public Members
The following members of the *My.Application.Info* object have their own entries elsewhere in this chapter.

- AssemblyName Property
- CompanyName Property
- Copyright Property
- Description Property
- DirectoryPath Property
- LoadedAssemblies Property
- ProductName Property
- StackTrace Property
- Title Property
- Trademark Property
- Version Property
- WorkingSet Property

## Related Framework Entries
- Microsoft.VisualBasic.ApplicationServices.AssemblyInfo Class
- System.Diagnostics.FileVersionInfo Class

## See Also
Application Object, Info Object (My.Computer)

# Info Object (My.Computer)

## Location
My.Computer.Info

## Description
Use the *Info* object to access information about the local computer.

## Public Members
The following members of the *My.Computer.Info* object have their own entries elsewhere in this chapter.

- AvailablePhysicalMemory Property
- AvailableVirtualMemory Property

- InstalledUICulture Property
- OSFullName Property
- OSPlatform Property
- OSVersion Property
- TotalPhysicalMemory Property
- TotalVirtualMemory Property

### Related Framework Entries
- Microsoft.VisualBasic.Devices.ComputerInfo Class

### See Also
Info Object (My.Application)

## InitializeWithWindowsUser Method

### Location
My.User.InitializeWithWindowsUser

### Syntax
```
My.User.InitializeWithWindowsUser( )
```

### Description
The *My.User* object generally refers to the user that owns the current execution thread. The *InitializeWithWindowsUser* method resets the *My.User* object to the user that started the application.

### Usage at a Glance
- While this method will work in ASP.NET applications, its use has no true impact on the *My.User* object.

### Related Framework Entries
- Microsoft.VisualBasic.ApplicationServices.User.InitializeWithWindowsUser Method
- Microsoft.VisualBasic.ApplicationServices.WebUser.InitializeWithWindowsUser Method

### See Also
CurrentPrincipal Property, IsAuthenticated Property, IsInRole Method, Name Property (My.User), User Object

## InstalledUICulture Property

### Location
My.Computer.Info.InstalledUICulture

### Syntax

```
Dim result As System.Globalization.CultureInfo = _
    My.Computer.Info.InstalledUICulture
```

### Description

The *InstalledUICulture* property returns a *System.Globalization.CultureInfo* object that describes the user interface culture of the operating system. It is especially useful when working with localized operating systems.

### Usage at a Glance

This property is read-only.

### Example

On a typical Windows system in the United States, this code:

```
MsgBox(My.Computer.Info.InstalledUICulture.DisplayName)
```

displays the following message:

```
English (United States)
```

### Related Framework Entries

- Microsoft.VisualBasic.Devices.ComputerInfo.InstalledUICulture Property
- System.Globalization.CultureInfo.InstalledUICulture Property

### See Also

ChangeUICulture Method, Info Object (My.Computer), UICulture Property

---

## IsAuthenticated Property

### Location

My.User.IsAuthenticated

### Syntax

```
Dim result As Boolean = My.User.IsAuthenticated
```

### Description

The *IsAuthenticated* property indicates whether the current user has been successfully authenticated (True) or not (False).

### Usage at a Glance

- This property is read-only.
- Some systems do not support authentication, such as Windows 95 and Windows 98. On these systems, this property always returns False.

### Related Framework Entries

- Microsoft.VisualBasic.ApplicationServices.User.IsAuthenticated Property
- Microsoft.VisualBasic.ApplicationServices.WebUser.IsAuthenticated Property
- System.Security.Principal.IIdentity.IsAuthenticated Property

## IsAvailable Property

### Location
My.Computer.Network.IsAvailable

### Syntax
```
Dim result As Boolean = My.Computer.Network.IsAvailable
```

### Description
The *IsAvailable* property indicates whether the network connected to the computer is available (True) or not (False).

### Usage at a Glance
- This property is read-only.
- This property will always return False when called by a user who does not have the *NetworkInformationPermission* permission.
- This property always returns False from ClickOnce-deployed applications.

### Related Framework Entries
- Microsoft.VisualBasic.Devices.Network.IsAvailable Property
- System.Net.NetworkInformation.NetworkInterface.GetIsNetworkAvailable Method

### See Also
Network Object

## IsInRole Method

### Location
My.User.IsInRole

### Syntax
```
Dim result As Boolean = My.User.IsInRole(role)
```
or
```
Dim result As Boolean = My.User.IsInRole(builtInRole)
```
*role (required in syntax 1; String)*
The role against which the user will be compared for inclusion.

*builtInRole (required in syntax 2; BuiltInRole enumeration)*
The predefined role against which the user will be compared for inclusion. One of the following *Microsoft.VisualBasic.ApplicationServices.BuiltInRole* enumeration values.

| Value | Description |
|---|---|
| AccountOperator | Users who manage local or domain user accounts |
| Administrator | Users who have full access to local or domain resources |
| BackupOperator | Users who back up local or domain files and require temporary yet extensive access |
| Guest | Users with minimal security access |
| PowerUser | Users with sufficient understanding of the local or domain environment to warrant enhanced security but not at the level of an administrator |
| PrintOperator | Users who control or manage the printers |
| Replicator | Users who control or manage file replication in a domain |
| SystemOperator | Users who have operational control over a local computer |
| User | Ordinary users with access to specific resources as assigned by an administrator |

### Description

The *IsInRole* method indicates whether the current user belongs to the indicated role (True) or not (False). The function accepts a predefined member of the *BuiltInRole* enumeration or a String with the name of a role.

### Usage at a Glance

If the current user is using a non-Windows authentication method and the *BuiltInRole* enumeration syntax of this method is used, the final part of the enumeration name is converted into a string, and that text is used as a lookup, as if the String syntax of this method had been called instead.

### Related Framework Entries

- Microsoft.VisualBasic.ApplicationServices.BuiltInRole Enumeration
- Microsoft.VisualBasic.ApplicationServices.User.IsInRole Method
- Microsoft.VisualBasic.ApplicationServices.WebUser.IsInRole Method
- System.Security.Principal.IPrincipal.IsInRole Method

### See Also

CurrentPrincipal Property, InitializeWithWindowsUser Method, IsAuthenticated Property, Name Property (My.User), User Object

---

## IsNetworkDeployed Property

### Location

My.Application.IsNetworkDeployed

### Syntax

```
Dim result As Boolean = My.Application.IsNetworkDeployed
```

### Description

The *IsNetworkDeployed* property indicates whether the application was deployed from a network using ClickOnce (True) or not (False).

## Usage at a Glance

- This property is read-only.

- This property is only valid in Windows Forms and console applications.

- Always use this property before using the *My.Application.Deployment* property. The *Deployment* property is only valid when the *IsNetworkDeployed* property is True.

## Example

The following example attempts to update the application, but only if it is a Click-Once installation deployed over a network.

```
If (My.Application.IsNetworkDeployed = True) Then _
    My.Application.Deployment.Update( )
```

## Related Framework Entries

- Microsoft.VisualBasic.ApplicationServices.ConsoleApplicationBase.,IsNetwork-Deployed Property

## See Also

Application Object, Deployment Property

# Keyboard Object

## Location

My.Computer.Keyboard

## Description

Use the *Keyboard* object to access the current keyboard-related state and to send keystroke sequences to applications.

## Public Members

The following members of the *My.Computer.Keyboard* object have their own entries elsewhere in this chapter.

- AltKeyDown Property
- CapsLock Property
- CtrlKeyDown Property
- NumLock Property
- ScrollLock Property
- SendKeys Method
- ShiftKeyDown Property

## Usage at a Glance

- This object and its members are only valid in non-server applications.

## Related Framework Entries

- Microsoft.VisualBasic.Devices.Keyboard Class

Computer Object, Mouse Object

---

## LineNumber Property

### Location
TextFieldParser.LineNumber

### Syntax
```
Dim fileParser As FileIO.TextFieldParser
' ...later...
Dim result As Long = fileParser.LineNumber
```

### Description
The *LineNumber* property returns the 1-based current line number (the line about to be read) within the file being parsed by a *TextFieldParser* object. If the end of the file has been reached, this property returns -1.

### Usage at a Glance
- This property is read-only.
- This property considers blank lines and comment lines. It is a line counter, not a record counter. This property may return a value other than -1 even when the object's *EndOfData* property returns True.
- You must close the *TextFieldParser* object when finished with it. Use the object's *Close* method or create the object instance with the Using keyword. See the *Text-FieldParser Object* entry in this chapter for an example.

### Example
The following example looks for "EOF" as an end-of-file marker.
```
Dim fileParser As FileIO.TextFieldParser
Dim oneLine( ) As String
Dim lastLine As Long
Dim markerFound As Boolean = False

fileParser = New FileIO.TextFieldParser(dataFile)
fileParser.SetDelimiters(",")
Do While (fileParser.LineNumber <> -1)
   lastLine = fileParser.LineNumber
   oneLine = fileParser.ReadFields( )
   If (UCase(oneLine(0)) = "EOF") Then
      MsgBox("Found EOF marker at line " & lastLine)
      markerFound = True
      Exit Do
   End If
Loop
fileParser.Close( )
If (markerFound = False) Then MsgBox("EOF marker not found.")
```

## Related Framework Entries

- Microsoft.VisualBasic.FileIO.TextFieldParser.LineNumber Property

## See Also

EndOfData Property, ErrorLineNumber Property, PeekChars Method, ReadFields Method, ReadLine Method, ReadToEnd Method, TextFieldParser Object

# LoadedAssemblies Property

## Location

My.Application.Info.LoadedAssemblies

## Syntax

```
Dim result As System.Collections.ObjectModel. _
    ReadOnlyCollection(Of System.Reflection.Assembly) = _
    My.Application.Info.LoadedAssemblies
```

## Description

The *LoadedAssemblies* property returns a collection of all assemblies currently loaded by the active application, with each element of type *System.Reflection.Assembly*.

## Usage at a Glance

- This property is read-only.
- An application may include multiple loaded assemblies, including the primary application assembly and associated libraries (DLLs).
- An exception is thrown if the application domain is not loaded.

## Example

The following example displays the names of all currently loaded assemblies in a message box.

```
Dim assemblyList As String = ""
Dim allAssemblies As System.Collections.ObjectModel. _
    ReadOnlyCollection(Of System.Reflection.Assembly) = _
    My.Application.Info.LoadedAssemblies
For Each oneAssembly As System.Reflection.Assembly _
        In allAssemblies
    assemblyList &= "|" & oneAssembly.FullName
Next oneAssembly
MsgBox("The following assemblies are currently loaded:" & _
    Replace(assemblyList, "|", vbCrLf))
```

## Related Framework Entries

- Microsoft.VisualBasic.ApplicationServices.AssemblyInfo.LoadedAssemblies Property
- System.AppDomain.GetAssemblies Method

## See Also

AssemblyName Property, DirectoryPath Property, Info Object (My.Application)

# LocalMachine Property

## Location

My.Computer.Registry.LocalMachine

## Syntax

```
Dim result As Microsoft.Win32.RegistryKey = _
    My.Computer.Registry.LocalMachine
```

## Description

The *LocalMachine* property returns a *Microsoft.Win32.RegistryKey* object that refers to the HKEY_LOCAL_MACHINE location in the Windows registry. This entry point is used primarily to store application and system settings that apply to all users on the local computer. It contains five major subkeys: Hardware, SAM, Security, Software, and System.

## Usage at a Glance

- This property is read-only.
- You must have sufficient security permissions to read or write keys and values in the registry.

## Example

The following example displays all of the sub-elements of the HKEY_LOCAL_MACHINE registry key element in a listbox control. The example assumes that you are using this code on a form with a defined ListBox1 control.

```
ListBox1.DataSource = _
    My.Computer.Registry.LocalMachine.GetSubKeyNames()
```

## Related Framework Entries

- Microsoft.VisualBasic.MyServices.RegistryProxy.LocalMachine Property
- Microsoft.Win32.Registry.LocalMachine Property

## See Also

ClassesRoot Property, CurrentConfig Property, CurrentUser Property, DynData Property, GetValue Method, PerformanceData Property, Registry Object, SetValue Method, Users Property

# LocalTime Property

## Location

My.Computer.Clock.LocalTime

## Syntax

```
Dim result As Date = My.Computer.Clock.LocalTime
```

## Description

The *LocalTime* property returns the current date and time as represented by the current time zone settings.

## Usage at a Glance

This property is read-only.

## Example

The following code displays the current local time in a message box.

```
MsgBox("Look at your watch; it's " & _
    Format(My.Computer.Clock.LocalTime, "h:mm tt"))
```

## Related Framework Entries

- Microsoft.VisualBasic.Devices.Clock.LocalTime Property
- System.DateTime.Now Property

## See Also

Clock Object, GmtTime Property, TickCount Property

# Log Object (My)

## Location

My.Log

## Description

The *Log* object provides features that let you add content to one of the system logs. The *My.Log* object is only available in ASP.NET applications. For client applications, use the *My.Application.Log* object instead. Except for this difference in where the *Log* object resides in the *My* hierarchy, the two objects are functionally equivalent. See the *Log Object (My.Application)* entry in this chapter for combined information about the *Log* object and its members.

# Log Object (My.Application)

## Location

My.Application.Log

## Description

The *Log* object provides features that let you add content to one of the system logs. The *My.Application.Log* object is only available in client applications. For ASP.NET applications, use the *My.Log* object instead. Except for this difference in where the *Log* object resides in the *My* hierarchy, the two objects are functionally equivalent.

## Public Members

The following members of the *My.Log* and *My.Application.Log* objects have their own entries elsewhere in this chapter.

- DefaultFileLogWriter Property
- TraceSource Property
- WriteEntry Method
- WriteException Method

## Usage at a Glance

- The *My.Application.Log* object and its members are only valid in client applications.
- The *My.Log* object and its members are only valid in ASP.NET applications.

## Related Framework Entries

- Microsoft.VisualBasic.Logging.Log Class

## See Also

Log Object (My)

---

# MinimumSplashScreenDisplayTime Property

## Location

My.Application.MinimumSplashScreenDisplayTime

## Syntax

```
Dim result As Integer = _
    My.Application.MinimumSplashScreenDisplayTime
```

or:

```
My.Application.MinimumSplashScreenDisplayTime = showTime
```

*showTime* *(required; Integer)*
The minimum number of milliseconds that the application's splash screen should be displayed.

## Description

The *MinimumSplashScreenDisplayTime* property gets or sets the number of milliseconds specified for display of the application's "splash screen," the screen that first appears when the application is run. At the earliest, the application's "main form" will not be displayed until this minimum time has elapsed.

## Usage at a Glance

This property is only valid in Windows Forms applications.

## Example

To set this property, you will need to override one of the application framework events, either *OnInitialize* or *OnCreateSplashScreen*. These are methods of the *WindowsFormsApplicationBase* class; you can override them in the *ApplicationEvents. vb* file. For instance, to set this value in the *OnCreateSplashScreen* method, use code similar to the following block.

```
Namespace My
    Partial Friend Class MyApplication
```

---

```
Protected Overrides Sub OnCreateSplashScreen()
    ' ----- Show the splash screen for 3 seconds.
    My.Application.MinimumSplashScreenDisplayTime = 3000
    MyBase.OnCreateSplashScreen()
  End Sub
End Class
End Namespace
```

### Related Framework Entries

- Microsoft.VisualBasic.ApplicationServices.WindowsFormsApplicationBase.MinimumSplashScreenDisplayTime Property

### See Also

Application Object, SplashScreen Property

## Mouse Object

### Location

My.Computer.Mouse

### Descripon

Use the *Mouse* object to determine the configuration and settings of the mouse attached to the local computer.

### Public Members

The following members of the *My.Computer.Mouse* object have their own entries elsewhere in this chapter.

- ButtonsSwapped Property
- WheelExists Property
- WheelScrollLines Property

### Usage at a Glance

This object and its members are only valid in non-server applications.

### Related Framework Entries

- Microsoft.VisualBasic.Devices.Mouse Class

### See Also

Computer Object, Keyboard Object

## MoveDirectory Method

### Location

My.Computer.FileSystem.MoveDirectory

## Syntax

```
My.Computer.FileSystem.MoveDirectory(source, _
    destination[, overwrite])
```

or:

```
My.Computer.FileSystem.MoveDirectory(source, _
    destination, showUI[, onUserCancel])
```

*source (required; String)*
The path of the directory to be moved.

*destination (required; String)*
The path of the parent directory to which the source directory will be moved.

*overwrite (optional; Boolean)*
Indicates whether an existing directory at the destination should be overwritten (True) or not (False). If this parameter is missing from the first syntax, it defaults to False.

*showUI (required in syntax 2; UIOption enumeration)*
Indicates whether error or progress dialog windows should appear during the move. One of the following *Microsoft.VisualBasic.FileIO.UIOption* enumeration values.

| Value | Description |
|---|---|
| OnlyErrorDialogs | Only shows error dialog boxes; does not display progress |
| AllDialogs | Shows progress and error dialogs |

If this parameter is missing, OnlyErrorDialogs is used by default.

*onUserCancel (optional; UICancelOption enumeration)*
The progress window includes a Cancel button. When pressed, the method takes action based on this parameter. One of the following *Microsoft.VisualBasic. FileIO.UICancelOption* enumeration values.

| Value | Description |
|---|---|
| DoNothing | Aborts the move but returns no information indicating that the move was cancelled |
| ThrowException | Throws an exception |

If this parameter is missing, ThrowException is used by default.

## Description

The *MoveDirectory* method moves the indicated directory and all files within it to a new parent directory.

## Usage at a Glance

- If the destination directory, though valid, does not exist, it will be created.
- An exception is thrown if the source or destination parameters are missing or invalid.
- An exception is thrown if the source directory does not exist or is in use (including any included files), or if a directory to be overwritten is in use.
- An exception is thrown if the user lacks sufficient file access permissions.
- An exception is thrown if the source and destination are the same or the source contains the destination.

## Example

The following example moves a directory to a new parent directory.

```
My.Computer.FileSystem.MoveDirectory( _
    ("C:\Project\Documents", "C:\Archive")
```

## Related Framework Entries

- Microsoft.VisualBasic.FileIO.FileSystem.MoveDirectory Method
- Microsoft.VisualBasic.MyServices.FileSystemProxy.MoveDirectory Method
- System.IO.Directory.Move Method

## See Also

CopyDirectory Method, CopyFile Method, CreateDirectory Method, DeleteDirectory Method, DeleteFile Method, FileSystem Object, MoveFile Method, RenameDirectory Method, RenameFile Method

---

# MoveFile Method

## Location

My.Computer.FileSystem.MoveFile

## Syntax

```
My.Computer.FileSystem.MoveFile(source, destination[, overwrite])
```

or:

```
My.Computer.FileSystem.MoveFile(source, destination, _
    showUI[, onUserCancel])
```

*source (required; String)*
The path of the file to be moved.

*destination (required; String)*
The path of the directory to which the file will be moved.

*overwrite (optional; Boolean)*
Indicates whether an existing file at the destination should be overwritten (True) or not (False). If this parameter is missing from the first syntax, it defaults to False.

*showUI (required in syntax 2; UIOption enumeration)*
Indicates whether error or progress dialog windows should appear during the move. One of the following *Microsoft.VisualBasic.FileIO.UIOption* enumeration values.

| Value | Description |
|---|---|
| OnlyErrorDialogs | Only shows error dialog boxes; does not display progress |
| AllDialogs | Shows progress and error dialogs |

If this parameter is missing, OnlyErrorDialogs is used by default.

---

*onUserCancel (optional; UICancelOption enumeration)*

The progress window includes a Cancel button. When pressed, the method takes action based on this parameter. One of the following *Microsoft.VisualBasic. FileIO.UICancelOption* enumeration values.

| Value | Description |
|---|---|
| DoNothing | Aborts the move but returns no information indicating that the move was cancelled |
| ThrowException | Throws an exception |

If this parameter is missing, ThrowException is used by default.

## Description

The *MoveFile* method moves the indicated file to a new directory.

## Usage at a Glance

- If the destination directory, though valid, does not exist, it will be created.
- An exception is thrown if the source or destination parameters are missing or invalid.
- An exception is thrown if the source file does not exist or is in use, or if a file to be overwritten is in use.
- An exception is thrown if the user lacks sufficient file access permissions.

## Example

The following example moves a file to a new directory, overwriting any existing file of the same name.

```
My.Computer.FileSystem.MoveFile( _
    ("C:\SourceDir\workfile.txt", "C:\DestDir", True)
```

## Related Framework Entries

- Microsoft.VisualBasic.FileIO.FileSystem.MoveFile Method
- Microsoft.VisualBasic.MyServices.FileSystemProxy.MoveFile Method
- System.IO.File.Move Method

## See Also

CopyDirectory Method, CopyFile Method, CreateDirectory Method, DeleteDirectory Method, DeleteFile Method, FileSystem Object, MoveDirectory Method, RenameDirectory Method, RenameFile Method

# My Namespace

## Location

My

## Description

The *My* Namespace feature provides access to many useful features of the .NET Framework Class Library (FCL). These features are arranged in a hierarchy according to functionality, and some of the features have simplified interfaces when compared to the original features in the FCL.

*My* acts as both a namespace of objects and as a Visual Basic-specific keyword. Some of its features are dynamic in nature (as with the project-specific members of the *My.Forms* object), quite unlike the behavior found in ordinary namespaces. But in practical use, it works just like a namespace, with its "dot" notation and its extensibility.

## Public Members

The following members of the *My* Namespace feature have their own entries elsewhere in this chapter.

- Application Object
- Computer Object
- Forms Object
- Log Object (My)
- Request Object
- Resources Object
- Response Object
- Settings Object
- User Object
- WebServices Object

## Usage at a Glance

Certain branches of the *My* namespace may be unavailable in your project. Some branches are not relevant to all project types, and Visual Basic disables access to those branches that are not relevant to the active project. The entries in this chapter indicate the types of projects for which they are unavailable.

## See Also

Application Object, Computer Object, Forms Object, Log Object (My), Request Object, Resources Object, Response Object, Settings Object, User Object, WebServices Object

---

# MyDocuments Property

## Location

My.Computer.FileSystem.SpecialDirectories.MyDocuments

## Syntax

```
Dim result As String = My.Computer.FileSystem. _
    SpecialDirectories.MyDocuments
```

## Description

The *MyDocuments* property returns the full path name to the "My Documents" folder for the current user on the local workstation. Usually, this directory is found at *C:\Documents and Settings*\user\*My Documents*, but it may vary from system to system.

The 'My' Reference

### Usage at a Glance

- This property is read-only.
- This folder contains user-specific files and directories.
- This path may not be defined in some cases. In such cases, use of this property generates an exception.
- The returned path will never have a backslash "\" character at the end.
- The path used for "My Documents" varies between the different Windows operating systems. Windows Vista excludes the "My" prefix from the user-specific folder name, although the *MyDocuments* property will retain its current name.

### Related Framework Entries

- Microsoft.VisualBasic.MyServices.SpecialDirectoriesProxy.MyDocuments Property
- Microsoft.VisualBasic.FileIO.SpecialDirectories.MyDocuments Property

### See Also

AllUsersApplicationData Property, CurrentUserApplicationData Property, Desktop Property, MyMusic Property, MyPictures Property, ProgramFiles Property, Programs Property, SpecialDirectories Object, Temp Property

---

## MyMusic Property

### Location

My.Computer.FileSystem.SpecialDirectories.MyMusic

### Syntax

```
Dim result As String = My.Computer.FileSystem. _
    SpecialDirectories.MyMusic
```

### Description

The *MyMusic* property returns the full path name to the "My Music" folder for the current user on the local workstation. Usually, this directory is found at *C:\Documents and Settings\user\My Documents\My Music*, but it may vary from system to system.

### Usage at a Glance

- This property is read-only.
- This folder contains music and multimedia files.
- This path may not be defined in some cases. In such cases, use of this property generates an exception.
- The returned path will never have a backslash "\" character at the end.
- The path used for "My Music" varies between the different Windows operating systems. Windows Vista excludes the "My" prefix from the user-specific folder name, although the *MyMusic* property will retain its current name.

- Microsoft.VisualBasic.MyServices.SpecialDirectoriesProxy.MyMusic Property
- Microsoft.VisualBasic.FileIO.SpecialDirectories.MyMusic Property

**See Also**

AllUsersApplicationData Property, CurrentUserApplicationData Property, Desktop Property, MyDocuments Property, MyPictures Property, ProgramFiles Property, Programs Property, SpecialDirectories Object, Temp Property

## MyPictures Property

### Location

My.Computer.FileSystem.SpecialDirectories.MyPictures

### Syntax

```
Dim result As String = My.Computer.FileSystem. _
    SpecialDirectories.MyPictures
```

### Description

The *MyPictures* property returns the full path name to the "My Pictures" folder for the current user on the local workstation. Usually, this directory is found at *C:\Documents and Settings\user\My Documents\My Pictures*, but it may vary from system to system.

### Usage at a Glance

- This property is read-only.
- This folder contains image and multimedia files.
- This path may not be defined in some cases. In such cases, use of this property generates an exception.
- The returned path will never have a backslash "\" character at the end.

### Related Framework Entries

- Microsoft.VisualBasic.MyServices.SpecialDirectoriesProxy.MyPictures Property
- Microsoft.VisualBasic.FileIO.SpecialDirectories.MyPictures Property

### See Also

AllUsersApplicationData Property, CurrentUserApplicationData Property, Desktop Property, MyDocuments Property, MyMusic Property, ProgramFiles Property, Programs Property, SpecialDirectories Object, Temp Property

## Name Property (My.Computer)

### Location

My.Computer.Name

## Syntax

```
Dim result As String = My.Computer.Name
```

## Description

The *Name* property returns the name of the local computer.

## Usage at a Glance

This property is read-only.

## Related Framework Entries

- Microsoft.VisualBasic.Devices.Computer.Name Property
- Microsoft.VisualBasic.Devices.ServerComputer.Name Property
- System.Environment.MachineName Property

## See Also

Computer Object, Name Property (My.User)

---

# Name Property (My.User)

## Location

My.User.Name

## Syntax

```
Dim result As String = My.User.Name
```

## Description

The *Name* property returns the name of the current user. For most Windows applications, this name will be in the format *domain\user*.

## Usage at a Glance

- This property is read-only.
- This property returns an empty string on systems that do not support authentication, such as Windows 95 and Windows 98.

## Example

The following example obtains the user name. This example checks if the application is using Windows or custom authentication, and it uses that information to parse the *My.User.Name* property.

```
Public Function GetCurrentUserName( ) As String
    If TypeOf My.User.CurrentPrincipal Is _
            System.Security.Principal.WindowsPrincipal Then
        ' ----- Windows username = "domain\user".
        Return Mid(My.User.Name, Instr(My.User.Name, "\") + 1)
    Else
        ' ----- Some other custom type of user.
        Return My.User.Name
    End If
End Function
```

### Related Framework Entries

- Microsoft.VisualBasic.ApplicationServices.User.Name Property
- Microsoft.VisualBasic.ApplicationServices.WebUser.Name Property
- System.Security.Principal.IIdentity.Name Property

### See Also

CurrentPrincipal Property, InitializeWithWindowsUser Method, IsAuthenticated Property, IsInRole Method, Name Property (My.Computer), User Object

## Network Object

### Location

My.Computer.Network

### Description

Use the *Network* object to access features and information related to the computer's network.

### Public Members

The following members of the *My.Computer.Network* object have their own entries elsewhere in this chapter.

- DownloadFile Method
- IsAvailable Property
- NetworkAvailabilityChanged Event (My.Computer.Network)
- Ping Method
- UploadFile Method

### Related Framework Entries

- Microsoft.VisualBasic.Devices.Network Class

### See Also

Computer Object

## NetworkAvailabilityChanged Event (My.Application)

### Location

My.Application.NetworkAvailabilityChanged

### Syntax

```
Public Sub Me_NetworkAvailabilityChanged(ByVal sender As Object, _
    ByVal e As NetworkAvailableEventArgs) _
    Handles Me.NetworkAvailabilityChanged
End Sub
```

*sender (required; Object)*
>The control or object that raised the event

*e (required; NetworkAvailableEventArgs)*
>An event parameter that contains information about the network, using the *Microsoft.VisualBasic.Devices.NetworkAvailableEventArgs* class.

### Description

The *NetworkAvailabilityChanged* event occurs whenever the network availability changes.

### Public Members

The *e* argument for this event, as an instance of the *NetworkAvailableEventArgs* class, includes the following notable public members.

| Member | Description |
| --- | --- |
| IsNetworkAvailable | Property. A Boolean that indicates whether the new state of the network is available (True) or not (False). |

### Usage at a Glance

- This event is only available in Windows Forms applications. A similar event, accessible to all application types, exists in the *My.Computer.Network* object. See the *NetworkAvailabilityChangedEvent (My.Computer.Network)* entry in this chapter for information on that event.

- This event handler can be found in the *ApplicationEvents.vb* source code file for your project. This file is normally hidden but can be viewed by toggling the *Show All Files* button in the Solution Explorer window in Visual Studio.

- This event does not occur on Windows 95 and Windows 98 systems.

### Related Framework Entries

- Microsoft.VisualBasic.ApplicationServices.WindowsFormsApplicationBase Class
- Microsoft.VisualBasic.Devices.NetworkAvailableEventArgs Class

### See Also

Application Object, NetworkAvailabilityChanged Event (My.Computer.Network)

---

## NetworkAvailabilityChanged Event (My.Computer.Network)

### Location

My.Computer.Network.NetworkAvailabilityChanged

### Syntax

```
Public Sub MyComputerNetwork_NetworkAvailabilityChanged( _
    ByVal sender As Object, _
    ByVal e As NetworkAvailableEventArgs)
End Sub
```

Elsewhere:

```
AddHandler My.Computer.Network.NetworkAvailabilityChanged, _
    AddressOf MyComputerNetwork_NetworkAvailabilityChanged
```

*sender (required; Object)*
The control or object that raised the event

*e (required; NetworkAvailableEventArgs)*
An event parameter that contains information about the network, using the
*Microsoft.VisualBasic.Devices.NetworkAvailableEventArgs* class.

## Description

The *NetworkAvailabilityChanged* event occurs whenever the network availability
changes.

## Public Members

The *e* argument for this event, as an instance of the *NetworkAvailableEventArgs* class,
includes the following notable public members.

| Member | Description |
| --- | --- |
| IsNetworkAvailable | Property. A Boolean that indicates whether the new state of the network is available (True) or not (False) |

## Usage at a Glance

- This event is available to any type of application. A similar event, only available in
  Windows Forms applications, exists in the *My.Application* object. See the
  *NetworkAvailabilityChangedEvent (My.Application)* entry in this chapter for infor-
  mation on that event.

- You cannot use the Handles keyword when defining the event procedure for this
  event. You must attach the event procedure to the event using the AddHandler
  statement.

- This event does not occur on Windows 95 and Windows 98 systems.

## Related Framework Entries

- Microsoft.VisualBasic.Devices.Network Class
- Microsoft.VisualBasic.Devices.NetworkAvailableEventArgs Class

## See Also

Network Object, NetworkAvailabilityChanged Event (My.Application)

---

# NumLock Property

## Location

My.Computer.Keyboard.NumLock

## Syntax

```
Dim result As Boolean = My.Computer.Keyboard.NumLock
```

## Description

The *NumLock* property indicates the current state of the Num Lock key, whether on (True) or off (False).

## Usage at a Glance

- This property is read-only.
- This property is only valid in non-server applications.

## Related Framework Entries

- Microsoft.VisualBasic.Devices.Keyboard.NumLock Property

## See Also

CapsLock Property, Keyboard Object, ScrollLock Property

---

# OpenForms Property

## Location

My.Application.OpenForms

## Syntax

```
Dim result As System.Windows.Forms.FormCollection = _
    My.Application.OpenForms
```

## Description

The *OpenForms* property returns a collection of the application's currently open forms.

## Usage at a Glance

- This property is read-only.
- This property is only valid in Windows Forms applications.
- An exception may be thrown if you try to access a form opened by another thread of your application. This property returns all forms currently open by all threads of the application. You may be limited in which open forms you can access from the current thread. For a given form, examine the *System.Windows.Forms.Control. InvokeRequired* property, which returns True if the form was created by another thread. If True, you can access that form by using its *System.Windows.Forms. Control.Invoke* method.

## Example

The following code saves the location of each form to the application's area of the registry.

```
Dim scanForm As System.Windows.Forms.Form
For Each scanForm In My.Application.OpenForms
    SaveSetting("MySoftware", "FormPositions", _
        TypeName(scanForm), scanForm.Left & "," & scanForm.Top)
Next scanForm
```

### Related Framework Entries

- Microsoft.VisualBasic.ApplicationServices.WindowsFormsApplicationBase. OpenForms Property
- System.Windows.Forms.Application.OpenForms Property

### See Also

Application Object, SplashScreen Property

---

## OpenSerialPort Method

### Location

My.Computer.Ports.OpenSerialPort

### Syntax

```
Dim result As System.IO.Ports.SerialPort = _
    My.Computer.Ports.OpenSerialPort(portName[, baudRate _
    [, parity [, dataBits [, stopBits]]]])
```

*portName (required; String)*
The name of the port to open. Typically, this will be a numbered "COM" serial port, as in "COM1."

*baudRate (optional; Integer)*
The desired baud rate of the port. The value you supply must be supported by the port you are trying to open. By default, a value of 9600 bits per second (bps) is used.

*parity (optional; Parity enumeration)*
The parity settings of the port. One of the following *System.IO.Ports.Parity* enumeration values.

| Value | Description |
|-------|-------------|
| Even | Sets the parity bit so that the count of bits set within each unit is always an even number of bits |
| Mark | Always sets the parity bit to 0 |
| None | Skips all parity checks |
| Odd | Sets the parity bit so that the count of bits set within each unit is always an odd number of bits |
| Space | Always sets the parity bit to 1 |

*dataBits (optional; Integer)*
Data-bit setting of the port. This value ranges from 5 to 8 and is set to 8 by default.

*stopBits (optional; StopBits enumeration)*
Stop-bit setting of the port, indicating the number of bits used to separate each unit of data. One of the following *System.IO.Ports.StopBits* enumeration values.

| Value | Description |
|-------|-------------|
| None | Uses no stop bits |
| One | Uses one stop bit |

| Value | Description |
|---|---|
| OnePointFive | Uses 1.5 stop bits |
| Two | Uses two stop bits |

## Description

The *OpenSerialPort* method opens one of the serial ports on the local computer and returns an instance of *System.IO.Ports.SerialPort* for that port.

## Usage at a Glance

- This method is not valid in ASP.NET applications.
- This serial port must be closed and disposed of when finished. Normally, this is done by using the *Close* method on the object returned from the *OpenSerialPort* method. You may also close it automatically by using the Using keyword. The example provided in this entry shows how to do this.
- An exception is thrown if any of the parameters passed are invalid or are not available through the specified port.

## Example

The following example opens the computer's COM1 serial port and sends a single line of text data. The serial port is closed implicitly through the use of the Using keyword. The *System.IO.Ports.SerialPort.WriteLine* method sends the data to the serial port.

```
Public Sub SendTextToCOM1(ByVal textToSend As String)
    ' ----- Open COM1 and send some text.
    Dim comPort As System.IO.Ports.SerialPort
    Using comPort = My.Computer.Ports.OpenSerialPort("COM1")
        comPort.WriteLine(textToSend)
    End Using
End Function
```

## Related Framework Entries

- Microsoft.VisualBasic.Devices.Ports.OpenSerialPort Method
- System.IO.Ports.SerialPort.Open Method

## See Also

Ports Object, SerialPortNames Property

# OpenTextFieldParser Method

## Location

My.Computer.FileSystem.OpenTextFieldParser

## Syntax

```
Dim result As FileIO.TextFieldParser = _
    My.Computer.FileSystem.OpenTextFieldParser(path[, delimiters])
```

or:

```
Dim result As FileIO.TextFieldParser = _
    My.Computer.FileSystem.OpenTextFieldParser(path[, fieldWidths])
```

*path (required; String)*
The path to the file to be read.

*delimiters (optional; String array)*
An array of the character or multicharacter values that identify the delimiters used to separate data fields in each input line of a delimited text file being parsed by a *TextFieldParser* object. End-of-line characters may not be used as field delimiters. If you only require a single delimiter, passing an ordinary string is acceptable.

*fieldWidths (optional; Integer array)*
An array of values, each of which indicates the character length of a positional field within a fixed-width text file being parsed by a *TextFieldParser* object. All field widths must be greater than zero, although the last array element may be less than or equal to zero to indicate a final variable-width field.

### Description

The *OpenTextFieldParser* method creates a *Microsoft.VisualBasic.FileIO.TextField-Parser* object, which represents each data row of the text input file, broken up into distinct fields. You can specify either fixed-position fields or fields delimited by a specific delimiter.

### Public Members

See the *TextFieldParser Object* entry in this chapter for additional information.

### Usage at a Glance

- The *delimiters* and *fieldWidths* parameters can also be set with the *TextField-Parser*'s *Delimiters* and *FieldWidths* properties or with the *SetDelimiters* and *SetFieldWidths* methods.

- An exception is thrown if the path parameter is missing or invalid, or if the file it refers to does not exist.

- An exception is thrown if the user lacks sufficient file access permissions.

- An exception is thrown if a row of the file's text data cannot be parsed according to the parameters supplied through this method. The exception thrown is *Microsoft.VisualBasic.FileIO.TextFieldParser.MalformedLineException*.

### Example

This code opens a tab-delimited file for scanning.

```
Dim oneLine( ) As String
Dim inputFile As FileIO.TextFieldParser = _
    My.Computer.FileSystem.OpenTextFieldParser( _
    "c:\temp\data.txt", vbTab)

Do While Not inputFile.EndOfData
    oneLine = inputFile.ReadFields( )
    ' ----- Process data here...
Loop
inputFile.Close( )
```

### Related Framework Entries

- Microsoft.VisualBasic.FileIO.FileSystem.OpenTextFieldParser Method
- Microsoft.VisualBasic.FileIO.TextFieldParser Class

- Microsoft.VisualBasic.MyServices.FileSystemProxy.OpenTextFieldParser Method

## See Also

FileSystem Object, OpenTextFileReader Method, OpenTextFileWriter Method, Read-AllBytes Method, ReadAllText Method, TextFieldParser Object, WriteAllBytes Method, WriteAllText Method

---

# OpenTextFileReader Method

## Location

My.Computer.FileSystem.OpenTextFileReader

## Syntax

```
Dim result As System.IO.StreamReader = _
    My.Computer.FileSystem.OpenTextFileReader(path[, encoding])
```

*path (required; String)*
   The path of the file to read.

*encoding (optional; Encoding)*
   The character encoding method to use, as a *System.Text.Encoding* object. If this parameter is missing, ASCII is used as the default encoding method.

## Description

The *OpenTextFileReader* opens a file for text reading and returns a stream of type *System.IO.StreamReader*.

## Public Members

The returned *StreamReader* object includes the following notable public members.

| Member | Description |
|---|---|
| Close | Method. Closes the file. |
| ReadLine | Method. Reads one line from the file and returns it as a string. |

## Usage at a Glance

- An exception is thrown if the path parameter is missing or invalid, or if the file it refers to does not exist.
- An exception is thrown if the user lacks sufficient file access permissions.

## Example

```
Dim oneLine As String
Dim inputFile As System.IO.StreamReader = _
    My.Computer.FileSystem.OpenTextFileReader("c:\temp\data.txt")
Do While inputFile.EndOfStream = False
    oneLine = inputFile.ReadLine( )
    ' ----- Process data here...
Loop
inputFile.Close( )
```

## Related Framework Entries

- Microsoft.VisualBasic.FileIO.FileSystem.OpenTextFileReader Method
- Microsoft.VisualBasic.MyServices.FileSystemProxy.OpenTextFileReader Method
- System.IO.StreamReader Class
- System.IO.TextReader Class

## See Also

FileSystem Object, OpenTextFieldParser Method, OpenTextFileWriter Method, ReadAllBytes Method, ReadAllText Method, WriteAllBytes Method, WriteAllText Method

---

# OpenTextFileWriter Method

## Location

My.Computer.FileSystem.OpenTextFileWriter

## Syntax

```
Dim result As System.IO.StreamWriter = _
    My.Computer.FileSystem.OpenTextFileWriter( _
    path, append[, encoding])
```

*path (required; String)*
The path of the file to written.

*append (required; Boolean)*
Indicates whether newly written text will be appended to the end of the file's existing content (True) or used to replace any existing content (False).

*encoding (optional; Encoding)*
The character-encoding method to use, as a *System.Text.Encoding* object. If this parameter is missing, ASCII is used as the default encoding method.

## Description

The *OpenTextFileWriter* opens or creates a file for text writing and returns a stream of type *System.IO.StreamWriter*.

## Public Members

The returned *StreamWriter* object includes the following notable public members.

| Member | Description |
|---|---|
| Close | Method. Completes all pending writes and closes the file. |
| Flush | Method. Forces any pending buffered writes to be sent to the file immediately. You can also set the related *AutoFlush* property to True to perform a *Flush* after every write. |
| Write | Method. Writes data to the stream. |
| WriteLine | Mathod. Writes data to the stream, followed by a line-termination character. |

## Usage at a Glance

- An exception is thrown if the path parameter is missing or invalid or if the file exists and is in use.
- An exception is thrown if the user lacks sufficient file-access permissions.

- If the file already exists and uses an encoding method other than the one specified by this method, the original encoding method of the file will prevail.

### Example

The following code creates or overwrites a file with some simple text data.

```
Dim counter As Integer
Dim outputFile As System.IO.StreamWriter = _
    My.Computer.FileSystem.OpenTextFileWriter( _
    "c:\temp\data.txt", False)  ' False = Overwrite
For counter = 1 To 10
    outputFile.WriteLine("This is line " & counter & ".")
Next counter
outputFile.Close( )
```

### Related Framework Entries

- Microsoft.VisualBasic.FileIO.FileSystem.OpenTextFileWriter Method
- Microsoft.VisualBasic.MyServices.FileSystemProxy.OpenTextFileWriter Method
- System.IO.StreamWriter Class
- System.IO.TextWriter Class

### See Also

FileSystem Object, OpenTextFieldParser Method, OpenTextFileReader Method,
ReadAllBytes Method, ReadAllText Method, WriteAllBytes Method, WriteAllText
Method

---

## OSFullName Property

### Location

My.Computer.Info.OSFullName

### Syntax

```
Dim result As String = My.Computer.Info.OSFullName
```

### Description

The *OSFullName* property returns the full name of the operating system.

### Usage at a Glance

- This property is read-only.
- An exception is thrown if the user does not have sufficient security privileges to
access system information.
- If Windows Management Instrumentation (WMI) is not installed on the local
computer, this property returns the same data as the *My.Computer.Info.OSPlat-
form* property.

### Example

The text returned by this property varies by operating system. For instance, the text
returned for Windows XP Professional is, as expected, "Microsoft Windows XP
Professional."

---

### Related Framework Entries

- Microsoft.VisualBasic.Devices.ComputerInfo.OSFullName Property

### See Also

Info Object (My.Computer), OSPlatform Property, OSVersion Property

---

## OSPlatform Property

### Location

My.Computer.Info.OSPlatform

### Syntax

```
Dim result As String = My.Computer.Info.OSPlatform
```

### Description

The *OSPlatform* property returns the basic platform name of the operating system.

### Usage at a Glance

- This property is read-only.
- An exception is thrown if the user does not have sufficient security privileges to access system information.
- If Windows Management Instrumentation (WMI) is installed on the local computer, the *My.Computer.Info.OSFullName* property will provide much more detailed information than this property.

### Example

The text returned by this property varies by operating system. For instance, the text returned for Windows XP Professional is "Win32NT."

### Related Framework Entries

- Microsoft.VisualBasic.Devices.ComputerInfo.OSPlatform Property
- System.Environment.OSVersion Property
- System.OperatingSystem.Platform Property

### See Also

Info Object (My.Computer), OSFullName Property, OSVersion Property

---

## OSVersion Property

### Location

My.Computer.Info.OSVersion

### Syntax

```
Dim result As String = My.Computer.Info.OSVersion
```

## Description

The *OSVersion* property returns the version of the operating system, a set of four numbers in the format "*major.minor.build.revision.*"

## Usage at a Glance

- This property is read-only.
- An exception is thrown if the user does not have sufficient security privileges to access system information.

## Example

The text returned by this property varies by operating system and installed features. For instance, the text returned for a sample Windows XP Professional system with Service Pack 2 and several hot fixes installed was "5.1.2600.131072."

## Related Framework Entries

- Microsoft.VisualBasic.Devices.ComputerInfo.OSFullName Property
- System.Environment.OSVersion Property
- System.OperatingSystem.Version Property

## See Also

Info Object (My.Computer), OSFullName Property, OSPlatform Property

---

# PeekChars Method

## Location

TextFieldParser.PeekChars

## Syntax

```
Dim fileParser As FileIO.TextFieldParser
' ...later...
Dim result As String = fileParser.PeekChars(peekLength)
```

*peekLength (required; Integer)*
The number of characters to read and return

## Description

The *PeekChars* method returns the specified number of characters from the current position in the input file, but it does not alter the current position. Blank lines are ignored when using this method.

## Usage at a Glance

- This method never returns characters beyond the end of the current line, no matter now many characters were requested.
- You must close the *TextFieldParser* object when finished with it. Use the object's *Close* method or create the object instance with the Using keyword. See the *TextFieldParser Object* entry in this chapter for an example.

## Example

This code opens a tab-delimited file for scanning but stops early if it detects an artificial end-of-file marker.

```
Dim oneLine( ) As String
Dim inputFile As FileIO.TextFieldParser = _
    My.Computer.FileSystem.OpenTextFieldParser( _
    "c:\temp\data.txt", vbTab)

Do While Not inputFile.EndOfData
    ' ----- Check for the EOF marker.
    If (inputFile.PeekChars(3) = "EOF") Then Exit Do

    ' ----- OK to process this line.
    oneLine = inputFile.ReadFields( )
    ' ----- Process data here...
Loop
inputFile.Close( )
```

## Related Framework Entries

- Microsoft.VisualBasic.FileIO.TextFieldParser.PeekChars Method

## See Also

EndOfData Property, LineNumber Property, ReadFields Method, ReadLine Method, ReadToEnd Method, TextFieldParser Object

---

# PerformanceData Property

## Location

My.Computer.Registry.PerformanceData

## Syntax

```
Dim result As Microsoft.Win32.RegistryKey = _
    My.Computer.Registry.PerformanceData
```

## Description

The *PerformanceData* property returns a *Microsoft.Win32.RegistryKey* object that refers to the HKEY_PERFORMANCE_DATA location in the Windows registry. This key refers to information that is not actually stored in the registry, but the registry is the access point for this dynamically generated data. The data includes performance counts and statistics, many of which are displayed through the *Performance* control panel applet.

## Usage at a Glance

- This property is read-only.
- You must have sufficient security permissions to read or write keys and values in the registry.

## Related Framework Entries

- Microsoft.VisualBasic.MyServices.RegistryProxy.PerformanceData Property
- Microsoft.Win32.Registry.PerformanceData Property

## See Also

ClassesRoot Property, CurrentConfig Property, CurrentUser Property, DynData Property, GetValue Method, LocalMachine Property, Registry Object, SetValue Method, Users Property

## Ping Method

### Location

My.Computer.Network.Ping

### Syntax

```
Dim result As Boolean = My.Computer.Network.Ping(host[, timeout])
```

or:

```
Dim result As Boolean = My.Computer.Network.Ping(uri[, timeout])
```

*host (required in syntax 1; String)*
The IP address, Internet domain, URL, or computer name of the system to ping.

*uri (required in second syntax; System.Uri)*
The uniform resource identifier of the system to ping.

*timeout (optional; Integer)*
The number of milliseconds to wait before skipping a ping request. By default, the timeout is 500 milliseconds.

### Description

The *Ping* method can be used to test for the presence of another system by making an ICMP protocol echo request over an IP network. This method returns True if the destination system was successfully Ping'd or False on a lack of success.

### Usage at a Glance

Even if the *Ping* method returns False, the destination system may still be running and on the network. Causes for failure include the ping protocol being turned off on the target system, the ping request being blocked by a firewall, or a failure of the packet to reach the target system due to other network issues.

### Related Framework Entries

- Microsoft.VisualBasic.Devices.Network.Ping Method
- System.Net.NetworkInformation.Ping Class

### See Also

Network Object

## Play Method

### Location

My.Computer.Audio.Play

## Syntax

```
My.Computer.Audio.Play(location[, playMode])
```

or:

```
My.Computer.Audio.Play(data, playMode)
```

or:

```
My.Computer.Audio.Play(stream, playMode)
```

*location (required; String)*
The path to the sound file.

*data (required in syntax 2; Byte array)*
The binary content of a sound file stored in a Byte array.

*stream (required in syntax 3; Stream)*
The binary content of a sound file accessed through a *System.IO.Stream* object.

*playMode (optional in syntax 1; AudioPlayMode enumeration)*
The method by which the sound should be played. One of the following *Microsoft.VisualBasic.AudioPlayMode* enumeration values.

| Value | Description |
|-------|-------------|
| Background | Starts playing the sound in the background one time. The program continues with the next source-code statement. |
| BackgroundLoop | Starts playing the sound in the background in a loop until stopped with the *My.Computer.Audio.Stop* method. The program continues with the next source-code statement. |
| WaitToComplete | Plays the sound but does not continue with the next source-code statement until the playing of the sound ends. |

If omitted, the default value is Background.

## Description

The *Play* method plays a sound (WAV) through the system speakers. The WAV sound content can be accessed as a file, a Byte array, or a *Stream*.

## Usage at a Glance

- This method is only valid in non-server applications.
- Using an invalid or empty data source will cause an exception, as will using an invalid play mode.
- Trying to play a file-based sound without sufficient privileges will cause an exception.

## Example

The following example plays a disk-based WAV file and waits for it to complete.

```
My.Computer.Audio.Play("C:\YouWin.wav", _
    AudioPlayMode.WaitToComplete)
```

## Related Framework Entries

- Microsoft.VisualBasic.Devices.Audio.Play Method
- System.Media.SoundPlayer Class

- System.Media.SoundPlayer.Play Method
- System.Media.SoundPlayer.PlayLooping Method
- System.Media.SoundPlayer.PlaySyncMethod

**See Also**

Audio Object, PlaySystemSound Method, Stop Method

---

## PlaySystemSound Method

### Location

My.Computer.Audio.PlaySystemSound

### Syntax

```
My.Computer.Audio.PlaySystemSound(systemSound)
```

*systemSound (required; SystemSound enumeration)*
The system sound to play. One of the following *System.Media.SystemSounds* enumeration values.

| Value | Description |
| --- | --- |
| Asterisk | The sound played with an "asterisk" message box |
| Beep | The default system "beep" sound |
| Exclamation | The sound played with an "exclamation" message box |
| Hand | The sound played with a "hand" message box |
| Question | The sound played with a "question" message box |

### Description

The *PlaySystemSound* method plays a system sound, one of the sounds linked to a specific system-initiated action. The sound is played in the background one time.

### Usage at a Glance

- This method is only valid in non-server applications.
- Specifying an invalid system sound will cause an exception.

### Example

The following example plays the system "Beep" sound.

```
My.Computer.Audio.PlaySystemSound( _
    System.Windows.Forms.SystemSounds.Beep)
```

### Related Framework Entries

- Microsoft.VisualBasic.Devices.Audio.PlaySystemSound Method
- System.Media.SystemSound Class
- System.Media.SystemSound.Play Method
- System.Media.SystemSounds Class

Audio Object, Play Method, Stop Method

## Ports Object

### Location
My.Computer.Ports

### Description
Use the *Ports* object to access features related to the computer's serial ports.

### Public Members
The following members of the *My.Computer.Ports* object have their own entries elsewhere in this chapter.

- OpenSerialPort Method
- SerialPortNames Property

### Usage at a Glance
- This object and its members are not valid in ASP.NET applications.

### Related Framework Entries
- Microsoft.VisualBasic.Devices.Ports Class
- System.IO.Ports.SerialPort Class

### See Also
Computer Object

## ProductName Property

### Location
My.Application.Info.ProductName

### Syntax
```
Dim result As String = My.Application.Info.ProductName
```

### Description
The *ProductName* property returns the product name as defined in the informational section of the assembly.

### Usage at a Glance
- This property is read-only.
- An exception occurs if the product name attribute, *AssemblyProductAttribute* (or `<AssemblyProduct>`), is undefined in the active assembly.

### Related Framework Entries

- Microsoft.VisualBasic.ApplicationServices.AssemblyInfo.ProductName Property
- System.Diagnostics.FileVersionInfo.ProductName Property

### See Also

CompanyName Property, Copyright Property, Description Property, Info Object (My. Application), Title Property, Trademark Property

## ProgramFiles Property

### Location

My.Computer.FileSystem.SpecialDirectories.ProgramFiles

### Syntax

```
Dim result As String = My.Computer.FileSystem. _
    SpecialDirectories.ProgramFiles
```

### Description

The *ProgramFiles* property returns the full path name to the "Program Files" folder for the local workstation. Usually, this directory is found at *C:\Program Files*, but it may vary from system to system.

### Usage at a Glance

- This property is read-only.
- This folder contains application files for installed programs.
- This path may not be defined in some cases. In such cases, use of this property generates an exception.
- The returned path will never have a backslash "\" character at the end.

### Related Framework Entries

- Microsoft.VisualBasic.MyServices.SpecialDirectoriesProxy.ProgramFiles Property
- Microsoft.VisualBasic.FileIO.SpecialDirectories.ProgramFiles Property

### See Also

AllUsersApplicationData Property, CurrentUserApplicationData Property, Desktop Property, MyDocuments Property, MyMusic Property, MyPictures Property, Programs Property, SpecialDirectories Object, Temp Property

## Programs Property

### Location

My.Computer.FileSystem.SpecialDirectories.Programs

### Syntax

```
Dim result As String = My.Computer.FileSystem. _
    SpecialDirectories.Programs
```

## Description

The *Programs* property returns the full path name to the start menu's "Programs" folder for the current user. Usually, this directory is found at *C:\Documents and Settings\user\Start Menu\Programs*, but it may vary from system to system.

## Usage at a Glance

- This property is read-only.
- This folder contains user shortcuts for installed programs.
- This path may not be defined in some cases. In such cases, use of this property generates an exception.
- The returned path will never have a backslash "\" character at the end.

## Related Framework Entries

- Microsoft.VisualBasic.MyServices.SpecialDirectoriesProxy.Programs Property
- Microsoft.VisualBasic.FileIO.SpecialDirectories.Programs Property

## See Also

AllUsersApplicationData Property, CurrentUserApplicationData Property, Desktop Property, MyDocuments Property, MyMusic Property, MyPictures Property, Program-Files Property, SpecialDirectories Object, Temp Property

# ReadAllBytes Method

## Location

My.Computer.FileSystem.ReadAllBytes

## Syntax

```
Dim result As Byte( ) = My.Computer.FileSystem.ReadAllBytes(path)
```
*path (required; String)*
The path of the file to read

## Description

The *ReadAllBytes* method returns the entire contents of a text file as a Byte array.

## Usage at a Glance

- An exception is thrown if the path parameter is missing or invalid, or if the file it refers to does not exist.
- An exception is thrown if the user lacks sufficient file access permissions.
- An exception is thrown if the file content is too large for available memory.

## Related Framework Entries

- Microsoft.VisualBasic.FileIO.FileSystem.ReadAllBytes Method
- Microsoft.VisualBasic.MyServices.FileSystemProxy.ReadAllBytes Method

FileSystem Object, OpenTextFieldParser Method, OpenTextFileReader Method, OpenTextFileWriter Method, ReadAllText Method, WriteAllBytes Method, WriteAll-Text Method

## ReadAllText Method

### Location
My.Computer.FileSystem.ReadAllText

### Syntax
```
Dim result As String = My.Computer.FileSystem.ReadAllText( _
    path[, encoding])
```
*path (required; String)*
The path of the file to read.

*encoding (optional; Encoding)*
The character-encoding method to use as a *System.Text.Encoding* object. If this parameter is missing, UTF-8 is used as the default encoding method.

### Description
The *ReadAllText* method returns the entire contents of a text file as a String. For information on code pages and encoding, see the *System.Text.Encoding* entry in the documentation supplied with the .NET Framework.

### Usage at a Glance
- An exception is thrown if the path parameter is missing or invalid or if the file it refers to does not exist.
- An exception is thrown if the user lacks sufficient file-access permissions.
- An exception is thrown if the file content is too large for available memory.

### Example
The following example reads in the contents of a file.
```
Dim errorText As String
errorText = My.Computer.FileSystem.ReadAllText("C:\error.log")
If (Len(Trim(errorText)) <> 0) Then _
    MsgBox("The following error was recorded:" & vbCrLf & _
    vbCrLf & errorText)
```

### Related Framework Entries
- Microsoft.VisualBasic.FileIO.FileSystem.ReadAllText Method
- Microsoft.VisualBasic.MyServices.FileSystemProxy.ReadAllText Method

### See Also
FileSystem Object, OpenTextFieldParser Method, OpenTextFileReader Method, OpenTextFileWriter Method, ReadAllBytes Method, WriteAllBytes Method, WriteAll-Text Method

# ReadFields Method

## Location
TextFieldParser.ReadFields

## Syntax
```
Dim fileParser As FileIO.TextFieldParser
' ...later...
Dim result As String( ) = fileParser.ReadFields( )
```

## Description
The *ReadFields* method is the main processing method of the *TextFieldParser* object. It reads all delimited or fixed-width fields in the current record of the input file and returns those fields as a string array. The fields returned from a delimited input file may be altered in content through the *HasFieldsEnclosedInQuotes* and *TrimWhiteSpace* properties. Blank lines and comment lines are always ignored.

After reading the record, the current file position advances to the start of the next record.

## Usage at a Glance
An exception is thrown if the parser is unable to extract the delimited or fixed-width fields currently configured through the *TextFieldParser* object. The *ErrorLine* and *ErrorLineNumber* properties will provide details on the errant record.

## Example
This code processes a tab-delimited file using the *ReadFields* method.
```
Dim oneLine( ) As String
Dim inputFile As FileIO.TextFieldParser = _
    My.Computer.FileSystem.OpenTextFieldParser( _
    "c:\temp\data.txt", vbTab)

Do While Not inputFile.EndOfData
    oneLine = inputFile.ReadFields( )
    ' ----- Process data here...
Loop
inputFile.Close( )
```

## Related Framework Entries
- Microsoft.VisualBasic.FileIO.TextFieldParser.ReadFields Method

## See Also
Close Method, CommentTokens Property, Delimiters Property, EndOfData Property, ErrorLine Property, ErrorLineNumber Property, FieldWidths Property, HasFieldsEnclosedInQuotes Property, LineNumber Property, PeekChars Method, ReadLine Method, ReadToEnd Method, SetDelimiters Method, SetFieldWidths Method, TextFieldParser Object, TextFieldType Property, TrimWhiteSpace Property

# ReadLine Method

## Location

TextFieldParser.ReadLine

## Syntax

```
Dim fileParser As FileIO.TextFieldParser
' ...later...
Dim result As String = fileParser.ReadLine( )
```

## Description

The *ReadLine* method reads and returns the current line from a file being parsed with the *TextFieldParser* object. The returned line is not parsed into distinct fields. If the file position is already at the end of the file, this method returns an empty string.

This method advances the current file position to the start of the next line.

## Usage at a Glance

You must close the *TextFieldParser* object when finished with it. Use the object's *Close* method or create the object instance with the Using keyword. See the *TextFieldParser Object* entry in this chapter for an example.

## Example

This code opens a tab-delimited file for scanning but performs a different type of processing on lines marked by a special preamble.

```
Dim oneLine As String
Dim fieldSet( ) As String
Dim inputFile As FileIO.TextFieldParser = _
    My.Computer.FileSystem.OpenTextFieldParser( _
    "c:\temp\data.txt", vbTab)

Do While Not inputFile.EndOfData
    ' ----- Check for the special processing flag.
    If (inputFile.PeekChars(5) = "SPEC:") Then
        ' ----- Do special processing of this line.
        oneLine = inputFile.ReadLine( )
        ' ----- Process data here...
    Else
        ' ----- OK to process this line normally.
        fieldSet = inputFile.ReadFields( )
        ' ----- Process data here...
    End If
Loop
inputFile.Close( )
```

## Related Framework Entries

- Microsoft.VisualBasic.FileIO.TextFieldParser.ReadLine Method

Close Method, CommentTokens Property, EndOfData Property, LineNumber Property, PeekChars Method, ReadFields Method, ReadToEnd Method, TextFieldParser Object

# ReadToEnd Method

## Location
TextFieldParser.ReadToEnd

## Syntax
```
Dim fileParser As FileIO.TextFieldParser
' ...later...
Dim result As String = fileParser.ReadToEnd( )
```

## Description
The *ReadToEnd* method reads and returns the remaining text in a file being parsed with the *TextFieldParser* object, starting from the current file position. The text returned is not parsed into distinct fields and may include blank lines and comment lines. If the file position is already at the end of file, this method returns an empty string.

This method advances the current file position to the end of the file and sets the parser's *LineNumber* property to -1.

## Usage at a Glance
You must close the *TextFieldParser* object when finished with it. Use the object's *Close* method or create the object instance with the Using keyword. See the *TextFieldParser Object* entry in this chapter for an example.

## Example
This code opens a tab-delimited file for scanning but looks for non-delimited data near the end of the file.
```
Dim oneLine( ) As String
Dim commentary As String
Dim inputFile As FileIO.TextFieldParser = _
    My.Computer.FileSystem.OpenTextFieldParser( _
    "c:\temp\data.txt", vbTab)

Do While Not inputFile.EndOfData
    ' ----- Check for the start of the commentary.
    If (inputFile.PeekChars(9) = "COMMENTS:") Then
        ' ----- Skip the first line.
        commentary = inputFile.ReadLine( )
        commentary = inputFile.ReadToEnd( )
    Else
        ' ----- OK to process this line.
        oneLine = inputFile.ReadFields( )
        ' ----- Process data here...
    End If
Loop
inputFile.Close( )
```

The 'My' Reference

### Related Framework Entries

- Microsoft.VisualBasic.FileIO.TextFieldParser.ReadToEnd Method

### See Also

Close Method, CommentTokens Property, EndOfData Property, LineNumber Property, PeekChars Method, ReadFields Method, ReadLine Method, TextFieldParser Object

## Registry Object

### Location

My.Computer.Registry

### Description

Use the *Registry* object to query or update keys and values in the Windows registry. The registry is a hierarchy of data values used by both Windows and other applications to manage user and system settings. You must have sufficient security privileges to use the members of this object.

### Public Members

The following members of the *My.Computer.Registry* object have their own entries elsewhere in this chapter.

- ClassesRoot Property
- CurrentConfig Property
- CurrentUser Property
- DynData Property
- GetValue Method
- LocalMachine Property
- PerformanceData Property
- SetValue Method
- Users Property

### Related Framework Entries

- Microsoft.VisualBasic.MyServices.RegistryProxy Class
- Microsoft.Win32.Registry Class

### See Also

Computer.Object

## RenameDirectory Method

### Location

My.Computer.FileSystem.RenameDirectory

## Syntax

```
My.Computer.FileSystem.RenameDirectory(path, newName)
```

*path (required; String)*
The path to the directory to be renamed.

*newName (required; String)*
The new name of the directory. Include the basic directory name only; do not include drive, parent directory, or path information.

## Description

The *RenameDirectory* method renames an existing directory, keeping it in the same parent directory.

## Usage at a Glance

- The renamed directory always remains in the original parent directory. To move a directory to a different location on the same drive and rename it at the same time, use the *MoveDirectory* method instead.

- Visual Basic includes a Rename statement that also renames directories.

- An exception is thrown if the *path* or *newName* parameters are missing or invalid or if the *newName* parameter contains any path-specific information.

- An exception is thrown if the directory does not exist or is in use (including any files contained within it) or if there is already a file or directory using the new name.

- An exception is thrown if the user lacks sufficient file-access permissions.

## Example

The following example renames a directory.

```
My.Computer.FileSystem.RenameDirectory("C:\vb_data", "vb_info")
```

## Related Framework Entries

- Microsoft.VisualBasic.FileIO.FileSystem.RenameDirectory Method
- Microsoft.VisualBasic.MyServices.FileSystemProxy.RenameDirectory Method
- System.IO.Directory.Move Method (if moving in same parent directory)

## See Also

CopyDirectory Method, CopyFile Method, CreateDirectory Method, DeleteDirectory Method, DeleteFile Method, FileSystem Object, MoveDirectory Method, MoveFile Method, RenameFile Method

# RenameFile Method

## Location

My.Computer.FileSystem.RenameFile

## Syntax

```
My.Computer.FileSystem.RenameFile(path, newName)
```

*path (required; String)*
    The path to the file to be renamed.

*newName (required; String)*
    The new name of the file. Include the basic filename and extension only; do not include drive, directory, or path information.

### Description

The *RenameFile* method renames an existing file, keeping it in the same directory.

### Usage at a Glance

- The renamed file always remains in the original directory. To move a file to a different directory and rename it at the same time, use the *MoveFile* method instead.

- Visual Basic includes a `Rename` statement that also renames files.

- An exception is thrown if the *path* or *newName* parameters are missing or invalid, or if the *newName* parameter contains any path-specific information.

- An exception is thrown if the file does not exist or is in use, or if there is already a file or directory using the new name.

- An exception is thrown if the user lacks sufficient file-access permissions.

### Example

The following example renames a file.

```
My.Computer.FileSystem.RenameFile("C:\workfile.txt", "playfile.txt")
```

### Related Framework Entries

- Microsoft.VisualBasic.FileIO.FileSystem.RenameFile Method
- Microsoft.VisualBasic.MyServices.FileSystemProxy.RenameFile Method
- System.IO.File.Rename Method

### See Also

CopyDirectory Method, CopyFile Method, CreateDirectory Method, DeleteDirectory Method, DeleteFile Method, FileSystem Object, MoveDirectory Method, MoveFile Method, RenameDirectory Method

## Request Object

### Location

My.Request

### Description

Use the *Request* object within ASP.NET applications to access the details of the active HTTP request.

### Usage at a Glance

- This object and its members are only valid in ASP.NET applications.

- The *Request* object parallels the functionality of the original *Request* object found in the pre-.NET Active Server Pages platform.

- System.Web.HttpRequest Object

**See Also**

Response Object

# Resources Object

## Location

My.Resources

## Description

Use the *My.Resources* object to access the global culture-specific resources for the active application. Resources are initially managed in Visual Studio using the new *Resources* panel of the project's *Properties* window. (Access this window by double-clicking on the "My Project" item in the *Solution Explorer* or by selecting *Properties* from Visual Studio's *Project* menu.) This form lets you add resources to a project, including named strings, images, icons, and other file-based resources. You can also add file-based resources to the project as standard items in the Solution Explorer.

All added resources are defined through the project's *Resources.resx* (or similar) resource file. To support the features required by *My.Resources*, Visual Studio also creates a separate *Resources.Designer.vb* file. This file includes standard Visual Basic source code that provides property-based retrieval of resources from the project's resource file.

As resources are added to a project, they are dynamically added as properties in the *My.Resources* object. For example, if you add a string resource named ConfirmDataDelete, it can be accessed in your code as:

```
My.Resources.ConfirmDataDelete
```

and it will be strongly typed as a String. For those resources added as file items to the project, the resource is referenced as:

```
My.Resources.resourceFile.resourceName
```

All resource properties available through *My.Resources* are read-only.

*My.Resources* uses the resources associated with the *My.Application.CurrentUICulture* culture, although you can override this default and use a different culture.

## Public Members

Each resource added to your project becomes a property in the *My.Resources* object. In addition to these, there are two members used to manage access to the resources.

| Member | Description |
|---|---|
| Culture | Property. Allows you to override the default culture used for resource retrieval. Assigned culture objects of type *System.Globalization.CultureInfo*. |
| ResourceManager | Property. Provides access to an object of type *System.Resources.ResourceManager* that provides more traditional .NET access to resources. |

## Usage at a Glance

Only application-wide resources are accessible through *My.Resources*; form-level resources (often used for culture-specific labels) are not available through this object.

## Related Framework Entries

- System.Resources.ResourceManager

## See Also

Forms Object, My Namespace, ChangeUICulture Method, Settings Object, UICulture Property, WebServices Object

# Response Object

## Location

My.Response

## Description

Use the *Response* object within ASP.NET applications to alter the content to be returned to the web-based user who initiated the HTTP request.

## Usage at a Glance

- This object and its members are only valid in ASP.NET applications.
- The *Response* object parallels the functionality of the original *Response* object found in the pre-.NET Active Server Pages platform.
- While you can use the *Response.Write* method to insert data into the outgoing HTTP content stream, it is recommended that you instead use the control-specific features available through ASP.NET.

## Related Framework Entries

- System.Web.HttpResponse

## See Also

Request Object

# Run Method

## Location

My.Application.Run

## Syntax

```
My.Application.Run(commandLine)
```

*commandLine (required; String array)*
    The command line used to start the application as an array of String values.

## Description

The *Run* method starts an instance of the current Windows Forms application using the Visual Basic Startup/Shutdown Application Framework for Windows Forms. This model supports startup and shutdown events, a splash screen, and the display and monitoring of a main application form, among other features.

## Usage at a Glance

- This method is only valid in Windows Forms applications that use the Windows Forms Application Framework introduced with Visual Basic 2005.
- Only use this method in the "Sub Main" procedure of an application.

## Related Framework Entries

- Microsoft.VisualBasic.ApplicationServices.WindowsFormsApplicationBase.Run Method

## See Also

Application Object, Shutdown Event, SplashScreen Property, Startup Event, Startup-NextInstance Event

---

# SaveMySettingsOnExit Property

## Location

My.Application.SaveMySettingsOnExit

## Syntax

```
Dim result As Boolean = My.Application.SaveMySettingsOnExit
```

or:

```
My.Application.SaveMySettingsOnExit = value
```

*value (required; Boolean)*
Indicates whether the settings should be saved on exit (`True`) or not (`False`)

## Description

The *SaveMySettingsOnExit* property indicates whether changes made to entries in the *My.Settings* object will be saved automatically when the application exits (`True`) or not (`False`). You can also modify this property while your application is running.

## Usage at a Glance

Although you can modify this setting when your application is running, its value will revert to its design-time setting the next time the application is run. To permanently change the value, modify the project's Application Properties and set the "Save My Settings on Shutdown" as desired.

## Related Framework Entries

- Microsoft.VisualBasic.ApplicationServices.WindowsFormsApplicationBase.SaveMySettingsOnExit Property
- System.Configuration.ApplicationSettingsBase.Save Method

## Screen Property

### Location
My.Computer.Screen

### Syntax
```
Dim result As System.Windows.Forms.Screen = My.Computer.Screen
```

### Description
The *Screen* property returns an object of type *System.Windows.Forms.Screen*, which contains various informational properties about the primary system display.

### Public Members
The *Screen* object returned from this property includes the following notable public members.

| Member | Description |
|---|---|
| AllScreens | Property. For systems with multiple attached displays, this property returns an array of all displays. |
| BitsPerPixel | Property. The number of color-related bits used for each pixel of the display. |
| Bounds | Property. Returns a *Drawing.Rectangle* object that identifies the bounds of the display. |
| DeviceName | Property. Returns the device name for the display. |
| Primary | Property. Indicates whether this is the primary display or not. |
| PrimaryScreen | Property. When using a *Screen* object for a secondary display, this property returns the object for the system's primary display. |
| WorkingArea | Property. Returns a *Drawing.Rectangle* object that identifies the working area of the display, which is the desktop area of the display minus any docked elements. |

### Usage at a Glance
- This property is read-only.
- This property is only valid in non-server applications.

### Example
This example displays the name of the screen device.
```
MsgBox("The primary screen's device name is: " & _
    My.Computer.Screen.DeviceName)
```

### Related Framework Entries
- Microsoft.VisualBasic.Devices.Computer.Screen Property
- System.Windows.Forms.Screen.PrimaryScreen Class

### See Also
Computer Object

## ScrollLock Property

### Location
My.Computer.Keyboard.ScrollLock

### Syntax
```
Dim result As Boolean = My.Computer.Keyboard.ScrollLock
```

### Description
The *ScrollLock* property indicates the current state of the Scroll Lock key, whether on (True) or off (False).

### Usage at a Glance
- This property is read-only.
- This property is only valid in non-server applications.

### Related Framework Entries
- Microsoft.VisualBasic.Devices.Keyboard.ScrollLock Property

### See Also
CapsLock Property, Keyboard Object, NumLock Property

The 'My' Reference

## SendKeys Method

### Location
My.Computer.Keyboard.SendKeys

### Syntax
```
My.Computer.Keyboard.SendKeys(keys[, wait])
```
*keys (required; String)*
A string of standard and special keys to send to the active window.

*wait (optional; Boolean)*
Indicates whether to wait for the sent keys to be processed (True) or not (False) before continuing with the next source-code statement. The default is True.

### Description
The *SendKeys* method simulates the typing of one or more keys in the active window.

To send plain text, simply include that text in the *keys* argument. For instance, using "abc" for the *keys* argument will send the characters a, b, and c, one at a time, to the active window. To have the Shift key held down with a key, precede that key with a plus sign (+). To use the Control key with another key, precede that key with the caret (^). To use the Alt key with another key, precede that key with the percent sign (%). To use one of these special keys with multiple other keys, enclose those other keys in parentheses. For instance, "+(abc)" sends a, b, and c with the Shift key held down.

You can repeat a key multiple times by using the syntax "{*key count*}" (that is, the character, then a space, then a numeric value, all within braces). For example, "{a 25}" will send the "a" key 25 times.

*SendKeys* supports several special keys, such as the Left Arrow key. Also, some standard keys must be enclosed in a set of braces to be recognized as a standard key. The following table lists all of these special keys and special-use standard keys.

| To include | Use this text |
| --- | --- |
| Backspace | {BACKSPACE} or {BS} or {BKSP} |
| Break | {BREAK} |
| Caps Lock | {CAPSLOCK} |
| Caret (^) | {^} |
| Clear | {CLEAR} |
| Close Brace (}) | {}} |
| Close Bracket (]) | {]} |
| Close Parenthesis (")") | {)} |
| Delete | {DELETE} or {DEL} |
| Down Arrow | {DOWN} |
| End | {END} |
| Enter | ~ |
| Escape | {ESCAPE} or {ESC} |
| F1 through F16 | {F1} through {F16} |
| Help | {HELP} |
| Home | {HOME} |
| Insert | {INSERT} or {INS} |
| Keypad Add | {ADD} |
| Keypad Divide | {DIVIDE} |
| Keypad Enter | {ENTER} |
| Keypad Multiply | {MULTIPLY} |
| Keypad Subtract | {SUBTRACT} |
| Left Arrow | {LEFT} |
| Num Lock | {NUMLOCK} |
| Open Brace ({) | {{} |
| Open Bracket ([) | {[} |
| Open Parenthesis (" (") | {(} |
| Page Down | {PGDN} |
| Page Up | {PGUP} |
| Percent Sign (%) | {%} |
| Plus (+) | {+} |
| Print Screen | {PRTSC} |
| Return | {RETURN} |
| Right Arrow | {RIGHT} |
| Scroll Lock | {SCROLLLOCK} |

| To include | Use this text |
|---|---|
| Tab | {TAB} |
| Tilde (~) | {~} |
| Up Arrow | {UP} |

## Usage at a Glance

- This method is only valid in non-server applications.
- This method sends keystrokes to the current active window, whether that window is part of your application or not. Also, some keystrokes you send may cause a different window to become active, depending on the functionality of that window.
- If you lack the necessary permissions to send the keystrokes to another application, an exception is raised.

## Example

The following example starts up Notepad, adds some text to its editing area, copies that text to the clipboard, and exits the program without saving changes.

```
Dim notepadID As Integer

' ----- Start and activate the Notepad application.
notepadID = Shell("notepad.exe", AppWinStyle.NormalFocus)
AppActivate(notepadID)
My.Application.DoEvents()

' ----- Add some text.
My.Computer.Keyboard.SendKeys("+visual +basic~", True)
My.Computer.Keyboard.SendKeys("{- 12}~", True)
My.Computer.Keyboard.SendKeys("+it's fun{!}", True)

' ----- Select all text with Control+A, then copy with Control+C.
My.Computer.Keyboard.SendKeys("^(a)", True)
My.Computer.Keyboard.SendKeys("^(c)", True)

' ----- Quit Notepad.
My.Computer.Keyboard.SendKeys("%{F4}", True)
My.Computer.Keyboard.SendKeys("n", True)

' ----- See if we copied the text correctly.
MsgBox(My.Computer.Clipboard.GetText())
```

## Related Framework Entries

- Microsoft.VisualBasic.Devices.Keyboard.SendKeys Method
- System.Windows.Forms.SendKeys.Send Method
- System.Windows.Forms.SendKeys.SendWait Methods

## See Also

Keyboard Object

## SerialPortNames Property

### Location
My.Computer.Ports.SerialPortNames

### Syntax
```
Dim result As System.Collections.Generic.ReadOnlyCollection( _
    Of String) = My.Computer.Ports.SerialPortNames
```

### Description
The *SerialPortNames* property returns a collection of serial port names available on the local computer.

### Usage at a Glance
- This property is read-only.
- This property is not valid in ASP.NET applications.

### Example
The following example displays all serial port names in a list box.
```
ListBox1.DataSource = My.Computer.Ports.SerialPortNames
```

### Related Framework Entries
- Microsoft.VisualBasic.Devices.Ports.SerialPortNames Property
- System.IO.Ports.SerialPort.GetPortNames Method

### See Also
OpenSerialPort Method, Ports Object

## SetAudio Method

### Location
My.Computer.Clipboard.SetAudio

### Syntax
```
My.Computer.Clipboard.SetAudio(audioBytes)
```
or:
```
My.Computer.Clipboard.SetAudio(audioStream)
```

*audioBytes (required in syntax 1; Byte array)*
> A Byte array of the audio data to be written to the system clipboard

*audioStream (required in syntax 2; Stream)*
> A *System.IO.Stream* object indicating the audio data content to be written to the system clipboard

## Description

The *SetAudio* method writes audio data to the system clipboard. Separate overloads allow you to write the data from a *Stream* or a Byte array.

## Usage at a Glance

- This method is only valid in non-server applications.
- Security restrictions in place for the active user may limit access to the system clipboard.

## Example

The following example reads data from an audio file and saves it to the clipboard.

```
Dim audioData As Byte( ) = _
    My.Computer.FileSystem.ReadAllBytes("c:\temp\SoundFile.wav")
My.Computer.Clipboard.SetAudio(audioData)
```

## Related Framework Entries

- Microsoft.VisualBasic.MyServices.ClipboardProxy.SetAudio Method
- System.Windows.Forms.Clipboard.SetAudio Method

## See Also

Clipboard Object, ContainsAudio Method, GetAudioStream Method, SetAudio Method, SetData Method, SetDataObject Method, SetFileDropList Method, SetImage Method, SetText Method

# SetData Method

## Location

My.Computer.Clipboard.SetData

## Syntax

```
My.Computer.Clipboard.SetData(format, data)
```

*format (required; String)*
    The named custom format of the data to be written to the system clipboard

*data (required; Object)*
    The data to be written to the system clipboard

## Description

The *SetData* method writes data in a named custom format to the system clipboard.

## Usage at a Glance

- This method is only valid in non-server applications.
- Security restrictions in place for the active user may limit access to the system clipboard.

## Example

This sample writes custom text data to the clipboard, but the data could also be in a non-text format.

```
My.Computer.Clipboard.SetData("Japanese-Romaji", _
    "Kore wa pen desu.")
```

### Related Framework Entries

- Microsoft.VisualBasic.MyServices.ClipboardProxy.SetData Method
- System.Windows.Forms.Clipboard.SetData Method

### See Also

Clipboard Object, ContainsData Method, GetData Method, SetAudio Method, SetData Method, SetDataObject Method, SetFileDropList Method, SetImage Method, SetText Method

---

# SetDataObject Method

### Location

My.Computer.Clipboard.SetDataObject

### Syntax

```
My.Computer.Clipboard.SetDataObject(data)
```

*data (required; DataObject)*
The *System.Windows.Forms.DataObject* object to be written to the system clipboard

### Description

The *SetDataObject* method writes an object of type *System.Widows.Forms.DataObject* to the system clipboard. The *DataObject* class allows a single object to store the same data in multiple formats. For instance, a single data object could store the same data in plain text, Rich Text Format, and HTML.

### Usage at a Glance

- This method is only valid in non-server applications.
- Security restrictions in place for the active user may limit access to the system clipboard.

### Example

The following code adds two types of data to the clipboard.

```
Dim pasteData As New System.Windows.Forms.DataObject
pasteData.SetText("This is a pen.")
pasteData.SetData("Japanese-Romaji", "Kore wa pen desu.")
My.Computer.Clipboard.SetDataObject(pasteData)
```

### Related Framework Entries

- Microsoft.VisualBasic.MyServices.ClipboardProxy.SetDataObject Method
- System.Windows.Forms.Clipboard.SetDataObject Method

---

- System.Windows.Forms.DataObject Class
- System.Windows.Forms.IDataObject Interface

### See Also

Clipboard Object, GetDataObject Method, SetAudio Method, SetData Method, SetDataObject Method, SetFileDropList Method, SetImage Method, SetText Method

## SetDelimiters Method

### Location

TextFieldParser.SetDelimiters

### Syntax

```
Dim fileParser As FileIO.TextFieldParser
' ...later...
fileParser.SetDelimiters(setOfDelimiters)
```

*setOfDelimiters* (required; String array)
> An array of the character or multicharacter values that identify the delimiters used to separate data fields in each input line of a delimited text file being parsed by a *TextFieldParser* object. End-of-line characters may not be used as field delimiters.

**The 'My' Reference**

### Description

The *SetDelimiters* method sets the field delimiters used in delimited text file parsing. This method also sets the *TextFieldParser* object's *TextFieldType* property to *Microsoft.VisualBasic.FileIO.FieldType.Delimited.* Although you can define more than one delimiter, most input files will use a single field delimiter, such as a comma or a tab character.

You can use the *TextFieldParser* object's *Delimiters* property to set the delimiters as well, but that property does not alter the *TextFieldType* property.

### Usage at a Glance

- The *SetDelimiters* method is only useful with delimited input files, not fixed-width files.

- An exception is thrown if you attempt to use line-termination characters, zero-length strings, or Nothing as field delimiters.

- If the file being parsed only uses a single delimiter, you can pass a standard string with that delimiter to the *SetDelimiters* method.

- You must close the *TextFieldParser* object when finished with it. Use the object's *Close* method or create the object instance with the Using keyword. See the *TextFieldParser Object* entry in this chapter for an example.

### Example

The following example uses the *SetDelimiters* method to indicate the comma character as the field delimiter.

```
Dim scanInput As Microsoft.VisualBasic.FileIO.TextFieldParser
' ...later...
scanInput.SetDelimiters(New String() {","})
```

- Microsoft.VisualBasic.FileIO.TextFieldParser.SetDelimiters Method

**See Also**

CommentTokens Property, Delimiters Property, FieldWidths Property, HasFields-
EnclosedInQuotes Property, ReadFields Method, SetFieldWidths Method,
TextFieldParser Object, TextFieldType Property, TrimWhiteSpace Property

# SetFieldWidths Method

**Location**

TextFieldParser.SetFieldWidths

**Syntax**

```
Dim fileParser As FileIO.TextFieldParser
' ...later...
fileParser.SetFieldWidths(setOfWidths)
```

*setOfWidths (required; Integer array)*

An array of the Integer values that each indicate the character length of a positional field within a fixed-width text file being parsed by a *TextFieldParser* object.
All field widths must be greater than zero, although the last array element may be
less than or equal to zero to indicate a final variable-width field.

**Description**

The *SetFieldWidths* method sets the number of characters used for each field in fixed-
width text file parsing. This method also sets the *TextFieldParser* object's *TextField-
Type* property to *Microsoft.VisualBasic.FileIO.FieldType.FixedWidth*. The first field
begins with the first character on each record line, and subsequent fields immediately
follow the fields before. You can indicate that the last field is of variable length (that is,
it includes all characters until the end of the line) by setting the last field width to -1.

You can use the *TextFieldParser* object's *FieldWidths* property to set the field widths as
well, but that property does not alter the *TextFieldType* property.

**Usage at a Glance**

- The *SetFieldWidths* method is only useful with fixed-width input files, not delimited files.

- An exception is thrown if you assign a zero or negative value to any field width
  other than the last one.

- If the file being parsed only uses a single fixed-width column, you can pass a standard integer with that width to the *SetFieldWidths* method.

- You must close the *TextFieldParser* object when finished with it. Use the object's
  *Close* method or create the object instance with the Using keyword. See the *Text-
  FieldParser Object* entry in this chapter for an example.

## Example

The following example uses the *SetFieldWidths* method to indicate that each line in the input file contains three fields: a 3-character field, a 30-character field, and a 5-character field.

```
Dim scanInput As Microsoft.VisualBasic.FileIO.TextFieldParser
' ...later...
scanInput.SetFieldWidths(New Integer( ) {3, 30, 5})
```

## Related Framework Entries

- Microsoft.VisualBasic.FileIO.TextFieldParser.SetFieldWidths Method

## See Also

CommentTokens Property, Delimiters Property, FieldWidths Property, ReadFields Method, SetDelimiters Method, TextFieldParser Object, TextFieldType Property

# SetFileDropList Method

## Location

My.Computer.Clipboard.SetFileDropList

## Syntax

```
My.Computer.Clipboard.SetFileDropList(filePaths)
```

*filePaths* (required; StringCollection)
  The set of file paths to be added to the clipboard, based on the collection *System. Collections.Specialized.StringCollection.*

## Description

The *SetFileDropList* method writes a collection of strings to the system clipboard, where each string contains a file path.

## Usage at a Glance

- This method is only valid in non-server applications.
- Security restrictions in place for the active user may limit access to the system clipboard.

## Example

The following code adds a list of files to the clipboard as a file drop list.

```
Dim pasteFiles As New _
    System.Collections.Specialized.StringCollection
pasteFiles.Add("c:\temp\file1.txt")
pasteFiles.Add("c:\temp\file2.txt")
My.Computer.Clipboard.SetFileDropList(pasteFiles)
```

## Related Framework Entries

- Microsoft.VisualBasic.MyServices.ClipboardProxy.SetFileDropList Method
- System.Windows.Forms.Clipboard.SetFileDropList Method

Clipboard Object, ContainsFileDropList MethodGetFileDropList Method, SetAudio Method, SetData Method, SetDataObject Method, SetFileDropList Method, SetImage Method, SetText Method

## SetImage Method

### Location
My.Computer.Clipboard.SetImage

### Syntax
```
My.Computer.Clipboard.SetImage(image)
```
*image (required; Image)*
> The *System.Drawing.Image* object to write to the system clipboard

### Description
The *SetImage* method writes an image to the system clipboard.

### Usage at a Glance
- This method is only valid in non-server applications.
- Security restrictions in place for the active user may limit access to the system clipboard.

### Related Framework Entries
- Microsoft.VisualBasic.MyServices.ClipboardProxy.SetImage Method
- System.Windows.Forms.Clipboard.SetImage Method

### See Also
Clipboard Object, ContainsImage Method, GetImage Method, SetAudio Method, SetData Method, SetDataObject Method, SetFileDropList Method, SetImage Method, SetText Method

## SetText Method

### Location
My.Computer.Clipboard.SetText

### Syntax
```
My.Computer.Clipboard.SetText(text[, format])
```
text *(required; String)*
> The text to be written to the system clipboard.

format *(optional; TextDataFormat enumeration)*
> The specific format of the text to write to the system clipboard. One of the following *System.Windows.Forms.TextDataFormat* enumeration values.

| Value | Description |
|---|---|
| *Not supplied* | Any type of text |
| CommaSeparatedValue | Comma-separated fields of data in one or more records |
| Html | HTML format |
| Rtf | Rich Text Format |
| UnicodeText | 16-bit Unicode character text |

If this parameter is not specified, UnicodeText is used by default.

## Description

The *SetText* method writes a string of text to the system clipboard in a specified text format. If no specific format is indicated, text is written as plain Unicode text.

## Usage at a Glance

- This method is only valid in non-server applications.
- Security restrictions in place for the active user may limit access to the system clipboard.
- An exception is thrown if invalid or missing string data is passed to the method.

## Example

The following code adds basic text to the clipboard.

```
My.Computer.Clipboard.SetText("This text is simple.")
```

## Related Framework Entries

- Microsoft.VisualBasic.MyServices.ClipboardProxy.SetText Method
- System.Windows.Forms.Clipboard.SetText Method

## See Also

Clipboard Object, ContainsText Method, GetText Method, SetAudio Method, SetData Method, SetDataObject Method, SetFileDropList Method, SetImage Method, SetText Method

The 'My' Reference

---

# Settings Object

## Location

My.Settings

## Description

Use the *My.Settings* object to manage application-specific and user-specific settings for an application. The 2002 and 2003 releases of Visual Basic included a generic configuration system for projects, but it had certain deficiencies, including the inability to manage strongly typed data. The new configuration system included with Visual Basic 2005 resolves many of the deficiencies present in those earlier releases.

Settings are initially managed in Visual Studio through the new *Settings* panel of the project's *Properties* window. (Access this window by double-clicking on the "My

Project" item in the Solution Explorer or by selecting *Properties* from Visual Studio's *Project* menu.) This form lets you add configuration settings to a project, including the name, data type, scope (application or user), and initial value of each setting.

The name of each setting automatically becomes a property of the *My.Settings* object. For example, if you add an `Integer` setting called `AlarmDuration` to the list of settings, it can be accessed in your code as:

```
My.Settings.AlarmDuration
```

and it will be strongly typed as an `Integer`. If it is a user-scoped value, the code can update its value through direct assignment.

```
My.Settings.AlarmDuration = 5
```

The settings are automatically saved when the programs exits, depending on the setting of the *My.Application.SaveMySettingsOnExit* property.

When developing an application in Visual Studio, the settings defined through the Project Properties window are stored in the *app.config* file for the project.

Once your application is deployed, the application-scoped settings and the user-scoped settings for each user are stored in different files. Each user's settings are usually stored in:

```
C:\DocumentsandSettings\LocalSettings\ApplicationData\companyName\
hashedAppDomain\version\user.config
```

where *companyName* is the assembly-defined company name for your project, *hashedAppDomain* is constructed from the application-related values, and *version* is the four-part, dot-delimited assembly version number. It's somewhat complex, but it is also uniquely identifiable.

The application-scoped settings (and the default versions of all user-scoped setting) are stored in the *Settings.settings* file, found in the same folder as the assembly file.

### Public Members

Each setting added to your project through the Project Properties window becomes a property in the *My.Settings* object. In addition to these, there are several members used to manage the settings.

| Member | Description |
|---|---|
| GetPreviousVersion | Method. Retrieves the value for a specific setting as stored in the settings file for a previous version of the assembly. |
| Reload | Method. Reloads all settings to the values they contained before this instance of the application was started. This is useful for discarding changes made during the current application session. |
| Reset | Method. Reloads all settings based on their default values. This discards any changes made since the application (or a specific version) was installed. |
| Save | Method. Immediately saves all modifications made to settings. |

### Usage at a Glance

- Settings that have an application-level scope are read-only and cannot be modified through *My.Settings*. Settings with user-level scope can be modified.
- The settings functionality is extensible, so that additional providers that manage the settings can be added.

## Related Framework Entries

- System.Configuration.ApplicationSettingsBase

## See Also

Forms Object, My Namespace, Resources Object, SaveMySettingsOnExit Property, WebServices Object

# SetValue Method

## Location

My.Computer.Registry.SetValue

## Syntax

```
My.Computer.Registry.SetValue(keyName, valueName, value _
    [, valueKind])
```

*keyName (required; String)*
The hierarchy key under which to write the data for a value.

*valueName (required; Object)*
The name of the value to be added or updated. To set the default value (the "(Default)" entry) for a particular key, use Nothing or an empty string for this parameter.

*value (required; Object)*
The data to be written to the new or existing value. This parameter cannot be set to Nothing.

*valueKind (optional; RegistryValueKind enumeration)*
The type of data to be written. One of the following *Microsoft.Win32.RegistryValueKind* enumeration values.

| Value | Description |
|---|---|
| Binary | Binary data. |
| DWord | A 32-bit "double word" numeric value. |
| ExpandString | A null-terminated path string with embedded environment variables. Surround such environment variables with matching percent signs (like "%PATH%"). All embedded environment variables are expanded to their current settings when this registry value is read later. |
| MultiString | An array of strings. Each string is followed by a null character, and the full value is terminated by two null characters. |
| QWord | A 64-bit "quad word" numeric value. |
| String | A null-terminated string. |
| Unknown | Lets the *SetValue* method determine the correct storage method automatically. |

## Description

The *SetValue* method writes or updates a new or existing data value within a registry key location.

## Usage at a Glance

- If the specified key or value does not exist, it is created. This includes any middle-level entries in the hierarchy leading to the key. For instance, if you specify "HKEY_ CURRENT_USER\Level1\Level2" and neither Level1 nor Level2 exist, they will both be created.

- *keyName* must start with the name of a valid registry hive, such as HKEY_CURRENT_ USER.

- To clear a registry value (but not delete it), send an empty version of its data type. For instance, to clear a string value, send an empty string (""). The *value* parameter cannot be set to Nothing.

- You must have sufficient security permissions to read or write keys and values in the registry.

- Avoid setting *valueKind* to Unknown when possible, as it reduces your application's control over its own stored data.

## Example

The following code updates a string in the registry.

```
' ----- Store the screen position for next time.
My.Computer.Registry.SetValue( _
    "HKEY_CURRENT_USER\Software\MyCompany\MySoftware", _
    "ScreenPosition", Me.Left & "," & Me.Top, _
    Microsoft.Win32.RegistryValueKind.String)
```

## Related Framework Entries

- Microsoft.VisualBasic.MyServices.RegistryProxy.SetValue Method
- Microsoft.Win32.RegistryKey.SetValue Method

## See Also

ClassesRoot Property, CurrentConfig Property, CurrentUser Property, DynData Property, GetValue Method, LocalMachine Property, PerformanceData Property, Registry Object, Users Property

---

# ShiftKeyDown Property

## Location

My.Computer.Keyboard.ShiftKeyDown

## Syntax

```
Dim result As Boolean = My.Computer.Keyboard.ShiftKeyDown
```

## Description

The *ShiftKeyDown* property indicates the current state of the Shift key, whether down (True) or up (False).

## Usage at a Glance

- This property is read-only.
- This property is only valid in non-server applications.
- For systems with two Shift keys, this setting indicates whether either Shift key is pressed. To examine the state of a specific Shift key during a control event, perform a bitwise comparison of the control's *ModifierKeys* property with the *Keys.LShiftKey* or *Keys.RShiftKey* enumeration value.

## Related Framework Entries

- Microsoft.VisualBasic.Devices.Keyboard.ShiftKeyDown Property
- System.Windows.Forms.Control.ModifierKeys Property
- System.Windows.Forms.Keys Enumeration

## See Also

AltKeyDown Property, CtrlKeyDown Property, Keyboard Object

# Shutdown Event

## Location

My.Application.Shutdown

## Syntax

```
Public Sub Me_Shutdown(ByVal sender As Object, _
    ByVal e As EventArgs) Handles Me.Shutdown
End Sub
```

*sender (required; Object)*
    The object that raised the event

*e (required; EventArgs)*
    An event parameter of type *System.EventArgs*, with no special members

## Description

The *Shutdown* event occurs when the application shuts down.

## Usage at a Glance

- This event is only available in Windows Forms applications.
- This event handler can be found in the *ApplicationEvents.vb* source code file for your project. This file is normally hidden, but it can be viewed by toggling the *Show All Files* button in the Solution Explorer window in Visual Studio.

## Example

The *Shutdown* event's code appears in the *ApplicationEvents.vb* file in a Windows Forms application.

```
Namespace My
    Class MyApplication
        Private Sub MyApplication_Shutdown(ByVal sender As Object, _
            ByVal e As System.EventArgs) Handles Me.Shutdown
```

```
        Console.WriteLine("See you later.")
      End Sub
   End Class
End Namespace
```

**Related Framework Entries**

- Microsoft.VisualBasic.ApplicationServices.WindowsFormsApplicationBase.Shutdown Event

**See Also**

Application Object, Startup Event, StartupNextInstance Event, UnhandledException Event

---

## SpecialDirectories Object

**Location**

My.Computer.FileSystem.SpecialDirectories

**Description**

Use the *SpecialDirectories* object to access many special windows folders, such as "Program Files" and "My Documents."

**Public Members**

The following members of the *My.Computer.FileSystem.SpecialDirectories* object have their own entries elsewhere in this chapter.

- AllUsersApplicationData Property
- CurrentUserApplicationData Property
- Desktop Property
- MyDocuments Property
- MyMusic Property
- MyPictures Property
- ProgramFiles Property
- Programs Property
- Temp Property

**Related Framework Entries**

- Microsoft.VisualBasic.MyServices.SpecialDirectoriesProxy Class
- Microsoft.VisualBasic.FileIO.SpecialDirectories Class

**See Also**

FileSystem Object

# SplashScreen Property

## Location
My.Application.SplashScreen

## Syntax
```
Dim result As System.Windows.Forms.Form = _
    My.Application.SplashScreen
```
or:
```
My.Application.SplashScreen = someForm
```
*someForm (required; Form)*
An instance of *System.Windows.Forms.Form* that represents the application's "splash" or informational startup form

## Description
The *SplashScreen* property returns the instance of the application's form used as a "splash screen," the informational form that first appears when starting up the application. To change the splash screen for your application, assign this property a different form instance.

## Usage at a Glance
- This property is only valid in Windows Forms applications.
- An exception is thrown if Nothing is assigned to this property.
- Changes made to this property persist only until the application exits. When the application is run again, the *SplashScreen* property will expose the settings defined at design time.

## Related Framework Entries
- Microsoft.VisualBasic.ApplicationServices.WindowsFormsApplicationBase. SplashScreen Property
- System.Windows.Forms.Form Class

## See Also
Application Object, MinimumSplashScreenDisplayTime Property, OpenForms Property

---

# StackTrace Property

## Location
My.Application.Info.StackTrace

## Syntax
```
Dim result As String = My.Application.Info.StackTrace
```

## Description

The *StackTrace* property returns the current stack trace information. The stack appears in order, from the closest procedure down to the original procedure, each on a separate text line.

## Usage at a Glance

- This property is read-only.
- Some fields may be absent from the returned trace if debugging symbols have been excluded from the project build.
- An exception is thrown if the stack trace is out of range or cannot be gathered from the current context.

## Example

Creating a new Windows Forms project and adding the following code to Form1's source code:

```
Public Class Form1
    Private Sub Form1_Click(ByVal sender As Object, _
        ByVal e As System.EventArgs) Handles Me.Click
        MsgBox(My.Application.Info.StackTrace)
    End Sub
End Class
```

produced these results when clicking on the form (slightly formatted to fit this page):

```
at System.Environment.GetStackTrace(Exception e,
   Boolean needFileInfo)
at System.Environment.get_StackTrace( )
at Microsoft.VisualBasic.ApplicationServices.AssemblyInfo.
   get_StackTrace( )
at WindowsApplication1.Form1.Form1_Click(Object sender,
   EventArgs e) in C:\temp\WindowsApplication1\Form1.vb:line 4
at System.Windows.Forms.Control.OnClick(EventArgs e)
at System.Windows.Forms.Control.WmMouseUp(Message& m,
   MouseButtons button, Int32 clicks)
at System.Windows.Forms.Control.WndProc(Message& m)
at System.Windows.Forms.ScrollableControl.WndProc(Message& m)
at System.Windows.Forms.ContainerControl.WndProc(Message& m)
at System.Windows.Forms.Form.WndProc(Message& m)
at System.Windows.Forms.Control.ControlNativeWindow.
   OnMessage(Message& m)
at System.Windows.Forms.Control.ControlNativeWindow.
   WndProc(Message& m)
at System.Windows.Forms.NativeWindow.DebuggableCallback(
   IntPtr hWnd, Int32 msg, IntPtr wparam, IntPtr lparam)
at System.Windows.Forms.UnsafeNativeMethods.
   DispatchMessageW(MSG& msg)
at System.Windows.Forms.Application.ComponentManager.
   System.Windows.Forms.UnsafeNativeMethods.
   IMsoComponentManager.FPushMessageLoop(Int32 dwComponentID,
   Int32 reason, Int32 pvLoopData)
at System.Windows.Forms.Application.ThreadContext.
   RunMessageLoopInner(Int32 reason, ApplicationContext context)
at System.Windows.Forms.Application.ThreadContext.
```

```
    RunMessageLoop(Int32 reason, ApplicationContext context)
  at System.Windows.Forms.Application.Run(
    ApplicationContext context)
  at Microsoft.VisualBasic.ApplicationServices.
    WindowsFormsApplicationBase.OnRun()
  at Microsoft.VisualBasic.ApplicationServices.
    WindowsFormsApplicationBase.DoApplicationModel()
  at Microsoft.VisualBasic.ApplicationServices.
    WindowsFormsApplicationBase.Run(String[] commandLine)
  at WindowsApplication1.My.MyApplication.Main(String[] Args)
    in 17d14f5c-a337-4978-8281-53493378c1071.vb:line 76
  at System.AppDomain.nExecuteAssembly(Assembly assembly,
    String[] args)
  at System.AppDomain.ExecuteAssembly(String assemblyFile,
    Evidence assemblySecurity, String[] args)
  at Microsoft.VisualStudio.HostingProcess.
    HostProc.RunUsersAssembly()
  at System.Threading.ThreadHelper.
    ThreadStart_Context(Object state)
  at System.Threading.ExecutionContext.Run(
    ExecutionContext executionContext,
    ContextCallback callback, Object state)
  at System.Threading.ThreadHelper.ThreadStart()
```

### Related Framework Entries

- Microsoft.VisualBasic.ApplicationServices.AssemblyInfo.StackTrace Property
- System.Environment.StackTrace Property

### See Also

Info Object (My.Application)

---

## Startup Event

### Location

My.Application.Startup

### Syntax

```
Public Sub Me_Startup(ByVal sender As Object, _
  ByVal e As StartupEventArgs) Handles Me.Startup
End Sub
```

sender *(required; Object)*
> The object that raised the event

e *(required; StartupEventArgs)*
> An event parameter that contains information about the command-line arguments, using the *Microsoft.VisualBasic.ApplicationServices.StartupEventArgs* class

### Description

The *Startup* event occurs when the application first starts. For single-instance applications, this event only occurs for the initial application startup.

## Public Members

The e argument to this event, as an instance of the *StartupEventArgs* class, includes the following notable public members.

| Member | Description |
|--------|-------------|
| Cancel | Property. Setting this Boolean value to True causes the application to exit without displaying its main form. |
| CommandLine | Property. A collection of the command-line arguments. The application path itself is not one of the collection members; the first member is the first true argument. |

## Usage at a Glance

- This event is only available in Windows Forms applications.
- This event handler can be found in the *ApplicationEvents.vb* source code file for your project. This file is normally hidden, but it can be viewed by toggling the *Show All Files* button in the Solution Explorer window in Visual Studio.

## Example

The *Startup* event's code appears in the *ApplicationEvents.vb* file in a Windows Forms application.

```
Namespace My
    Class MyApplication
        Private Sub MyApplication_Startup(ByVal sender As Object, _
            ByVal e As Microsoft.VisualBasic.ApplicationServices. _
            StartupEventArgs) Handles Me.Startup
            Console.WriteLine("Welcome.")
        End Sub
    End Class
End Namespace
```

## Related Framework Entries

- Microsoft.VisualBasic.ApplicationServices.StartupEventArgs Class
- Microsoft.VisualBasic.ApplicationServices.WindowsFormsApplicationBase. Startup Event

## See Also

Application Object, CommandLineArgs Property, Shutdown Event, StartupNextInstance Event, UnhandledException Event

---

## StartupNextInstance Event

### Location

My.Application.StartupNextInstance

### Syntax

```
Public Sub Me_StartupNextInstance(ByVal sender As Object, _
    ByVal e As StartupNextInstanceEventArgs) _
    Handles Me.StartupNextInstance
End Sub
```

sender *(required; Object)*
    The object that raised the event

e *(required; StartupEventArgs)*
    An event parameter that contains information about the command-line argu-
    ments, using the *Microsoft.VisualBasic.ApplicationServices.StartupEventArgs* class

## Description

The *StartupNextInstance* event occurs in single-instance applications when subsequent instances of the application begin. The initial use of the application fires the
*Startup* event, not the *StartupNextInstance* event. Non-single-instance applications
never call the *StartupNextInstance* event.

## Public Members

The e argument to this event, as an instance of the *StartupEventArgs* class, includes the
following notable public members.

| Member | Description |
| --- | --- |
| Cancel | Property. Setting this Boolean value to True causes the newly initiated instance of the application to exit without continuing. |
| CommandLine | Property. A collection of the command-line arguments used to start this specific instance of the application. The application path itself is not one of the collection members; the first member is the first true argument. Do not use the *My.Application.CommandLineArgs* property, as that only includes the arguments for the initial instance. |

## Usage at a Glance

- This event is only available in Windows Forms applications.

- This event handler can be found in the *ApplicationEvents.vb* source code file for
  your project. This file is normally hidden, but it can be viewed by toggling the
  *Show All Files* button in the Solution Explorer window in Visual Studio.

- Applications are multi-instance by default. To set an application as single-
  instance, alter the project's Application Properties, setting the "Make single
  instance application" field.

## Example

The *StartupNextInstance* event's code appears in the *ApplicationEvents.vb* file in a
Windows Forms application.

```
Namespace My
    Class MyApplication
        Private Sub MyApplication_StartupNextInstance( _
            ByVal sender As Object, ByVal e As _
            Microsoft.VisualBasic.ApplicationServices. _
            StartupNextInstanceEventArgs) _
            Handles Me.StartupNextInstance
            Console.WriteLine("I'm already running!")
        End Sub
    End Class
End Namespace
```

- Microsoft.VisualBasic.ApplicationServices.StartupEventArgs Class
- Microsoft.VisualBasic.ApplicationServices.WindowsFormsApplicationBase.StartupNextInstance Event

**See Also**

Application Object, CommandLineArgs Property, Shutdown Event, Startup Event, UnhandledException Event

---

## Stop Method

**Location**

My.Computer.Audio.Stop

**Syntax**

```
My.Computer.Audio.Stop( )
```

**Description**

The *Stop* method stops playing a WAV sound previously started in the background using the *My.Computer.Audio.Play* method.

**Usage at a Glance**

- This method is only valid in non-server applications.
- Only sounds initiated by the same application are stopped.

**Related Framework Entries**

- Microsoft.VisualBasic.Devices.Audio.Stop Method
- System.Media.SoundPlayer Class
- System.Media.SoundPlayer.Stop Method

**See Also**

Audio Object, Play Method, PlaySystemSound Method

---

## Temp Property

**Location**

My.Computer.FileSystem.SpecialDirectories.Temp

**Syntax**

```
Dim result As String = My.Computer.FileSystem. _
    SpecialDirectories.Temp
```

**Description**

The *Temp* property returns the full path name to the temporary files folder for the current user on the local workstation. Usually, this directory is found at *C:\Documents and Settings\user\Local Settings\Temp*," but it may vary from system to system.

---

## Usage at a Glance

- This property is read-only.
- This folder contains application-generated temporary files and directories.
- This path may not be defined in some cases. In such cases, use of this property generates an exception.
- The returned path will never have a backslash "\" character at the end.

## Related Framework Entries

- Microsoft.VisualBasic.MyServices.SpecialDirectoriesProxy.Temp Property
- Microsoft.VisualBasic.FileIO.SpecialDirectories.Temp Property

## See Also

AllUsersApplicationData Property, CurrentUserApplicationData Property, Desktop Property, MyDocuments Property, MyMusic Property, MyPictures Property, Program-Files Property, Programs Property, SpecialDirectories Object

# TextFieldParser Object

## Location

Microsoft.VisualBasic.FileIO.TextFieldParser

## Description

The *TextFieldParser* object simplifies the process of extracting data fields from delimited and fixed-width text data files. Existing data files are opened with the *My. Computer.FileSystem.OpenTextFieldParser* method, which returns an object of type *TextFieldParser*. You can also create a new instance of *TextFieldParser* directly, passing the file name as a constructor parameter. The object includes several useful members for extracting data from the data file.

You must close the *TextFieldParser* object when finished with it. This is normally done by calling the object's *Close* method. However, you can also use the Using statement to release all parser-related resources when the Using statement is complete.

```
Using fileParser As New FileIO.TextFieldParser(dataFile)
    ...code to parse the file goes here...
End Using
```

## Public Members

The following members of the *TextFieldParser* object have their own entries elsewhere in this chapter.

- Close Method
- CommentTokens Property
- Delimiters Property
- EndOfData Property
- ErrorLine Property
- ErrorLineNumber Property
- FieldWidths Property

- HasFieldsEnclosedInQuotes Property
- LineNumber Property
- PeekChars Method
- ReadFields Method
- ReadLine Method
- ReadToEnd Method
- SetDelimiters Method
- SetFieldWidths Method
- TextFieldType Property
- TrimWhiteSpace Property

**Related Framework Entries**
- Microsoft.VisualBasic.FileIO.TextFieldParser Class

**See Also**
My Namespace, OpenTextFieldParser Method

## TextFieldType Property

### Location
TextFieldParser.TextFieldType

### Syntax
```
Dim fileParser As FileIO.TextFieldParser
' ...later...
Dim result As Microsoft.VisualBasic.FileIO.FieldType = _
    fileParser.TextFieldType
```
or:
```
fileParser.TextFieldType = useFieldType
```
*useFieldType (required; FieldType enumeration)*
Indicates the parsing method to be used. One of the following *Microsoft.Visual-Basic.FileIO.FieldType* enumeration values.

| Value | Description |
|---|---|
| Delimited | Retrieves fields that are separated by a delimiter |
| FixedWidth | Retrieves fields at specific positions and character lengths |

### Description
The *TextFieldType* property indicates the method used to retrieve fields from each record in the input file. Set this property before processing the first record of the file.

### Usage at a Glance
- If this property is not set before reading the first record, the object assumes delimited input fields.

- You must close the *TextFieldParser* object when finished with it. Use the object's *Close* method or create the object instance with the Using keyword. See the *TextFieldParser Object* entry in this chapter for an example.

### Related Framework Entries
- Microsoft.VisualBasic.FileIO.FieldType Enumeration
- Microsoft.VisualBasic.FileIO.TextFieldParser.TextFieldType Property

### See Also
Delimiters Property, FieldWidths Property, ReadFields Method, SetDelimiters Method, SetFieldWidths Method, TextFieldParser Object

---

# TickCount Property

### Location
My.Computer.Clock.TickCount

### Syntax
```
Dim result As Integer = My.Computer.Clock.TickCount
```

### Description
The *TickCount* property returns the current millisecond count of the system timer, although with limited granularity.

### Usage at a Glance
- This property is read-only.
- The system timer has a limited resolution and is not accurate to more than 500 milliseconds.
- After about 24.9 days, the *TickCount* value reaches the maximum integer value (*System.Int32.MaxValue*). It then jumps to the minimum integer value, a negative number (*System.Int32.MinValue*), and continues incrementing in the positive direction.
- The system timer may stop incrementing when the system is in certain power-saving states, such as hibernation.

### Example
The following example returns the number of milliseconds that have elapsed since the last time the function was called.
```
Public Function SinceLastCall( ) As Integer
   ' ----- Return the number of milliseconds since the
   '       last call of this routine.
   Static lastTime As Integer = -1
   Dim thisTime As Integer

   ' ----- Get the current tick count and compare to last time.
   thisTime = My.Computer.Clock.TickCount
   If (lastTime = -1) Then lastTime = thisTime
```

```
If (thisTime < lastTime) Then
    ' ----- The integer value wrapped.
    SinceLastCall = (Integer.MaxValue - lastTime) + _
        (thisTime - Integer.MinValue)
Else
    ' ----- Simple advance of the timer.
    SinceLastCall = thisTime - lastTime
End If
lastTime = thisTime
End Function
```

### Related Framework Entries

- Microsoft.VisualBasic.Devices.Clock.TickCount Property
- System.Environment.TickCount Property

### See Also

Clock Object, GmtTime Property, LocalTime Property

---

## Title Property

### Location

My.Application.Info.Title

### Syntax

```
Dim result As String = My.Application.Info.Title
```

### Description

The *Title* property returns the application title as defined in the informational section of the assembly.

### Usage at a Glance

- This property is read-only.
- An exception occurs if the title attribute, *AssemblyTitleAttribute* (or <AssemblyTitle>), is undefined in the active assembly.

### Related Framework Entries

- Microsoft.VisualBasic.ApplicationServices.AssemblyInfo.Title Property
- System.Diagnostics.FileVersionInfo.FileDescription Property

### See Also

CompanyName Property, Copyright Property, Description Property, Info Object (My. Application), ProductName Property, Trademark Property

---

## TotalPhysicalMemory Property

### Location

My.Computer.Info.TotalPhysicalMemory

### Syntax

```
Dim result As ULong = My.Computer.Info.TotalPhysicalMemory
```

### Description

The *TotalPhysicalMemory* property returns the total amount of installed bytes of physical memory on the local computer.

### Usage at a Glance

- This property is read-only.
- This property only works on platforms that make the information available. This includes Windows XP, Windows 2000 Professional, Windows Server 2003, Windows 2000 Server, or any later versions of these systems.
- An exception is thrown if for any reason the application is unable to determine the current status of memory on the system.

### Related Framework Entries

- Microsoft.VisualBasic.Devices.ComputerInfo.TotalPhysicalMemory Property

### See Also

AvailablePhysicalMemory Property, AvailableVirtualMemory Property, Info Object (My.Computer), TotalVirtualMemory Property

---

## TotalVirtualMemory Property

### Location

My.Computer.Info.TotalVirtualMemory

### Syntax

```
Dim result As ULong = My.Computer.Info.TotalVirtualMemory
```

### Description

The *TotalVirtualMemory* property returns the total amount of configured bytes of virtual address space on the local computer.

### Usage at a Glance

- This property is read-only.
- This property only works on platforms that make the information available. This includes Windows XP, Windows 2000 Professional, Windows Server 2003, Windows 2000 Server, or any later versions of these systems.
- An exception is thrown if for any reason the application is unable to determine the current status of memory on the system.

### Related Framework Entries

- Microsoft.VisualBasic.Devices.ComputerInfo.TotalVirtualMemory Property

AvailablePhysicalMemory Property, AvailableVirtualMemory Property, Info Object (My.Computer), TotalPhysicalMemory Property

## TraceSource Property

### Location
My.Application.Log.TraceSource

My.Log.TraceSource

### Syntax
For client applications:

```
Dim result As System.Diagnostics.TraceSource = _
    My.Application.Log.TraceSource
```

For ASP.NET applications:

```
Dim result As System.Diagnostics.TraceSource = My.Log.TraceSource
```

### Description
The *TraceSource* property returns an object of type *System.Diagnostics.TraceSource* that identifies the current configuration of the relevant *Log* object.

### Usage at a Glance
- This property is read-only.
- Diagnostic content written using the various *Debug.Write* methods is not sent to the trace listeners.
- This property is only valid in client and ASP.NET applications. For client applications, use *My.Application.Log.TraceSource*. For ASP.NET applications, use *My. Log.TraceSource*.

### Example
The following code adds a text file output method to the collection of listeners. As a result, all *Debug.Write* and similar methods will not only send the output to the Output Window (the default listener) but also to the text file.

```
' ----- Uses "Imports System.IO" above.

' ----- Define a new listener object.
Dim fileTrace As New TextWriterTraceListener()

' ----- Since the listener is generic and doesn't have any
'           specific destination, the code needs to create the
'           destination and associate it with the listener. In
'           this case, the destination will be a file stream.
Dim traceStream As FileStream = New FileStream("c:\log.txt", _
    FileMode.Append, FileAccess.Write)
fileTrace.Writer = New StreamWriter(traceStream)
```

```
' ----- Now the listener is ready to be used.
My.Application.Log.TraceSource.Listeners.Add(fileTrace)

' ----- Add an entry to the log.
My.Application.Log.WriteEntry("Diagnostic status line 1.")

' ----- Test complete. Close all opened resources.
My.Application.Log.TraceSource.Listeners.Remove(fileTrace)
fileTrace.Close( )
traceStream.Close( )

' ----- This Debug statement goes only to the Output Window.
My.Application.Log.WriteEntry("Diagnostic status line 2.")
```

### Related Framework Entries

- Microsoft.VisualBasic.Logging.Log.TraceSource Property
- System.Diagnostics.TraceSource Class

### See Also

DefaultFileLogWriter Property, Log Object (My), Log Object (My.Application), WriteEntry Method, WriteException Method

---

## Trademark Property

### Location

My.Application.Info.Trademark

### Syntax

```
Dim result As String = My.Application.Info.Trademark
```

### Description

The *Trademark* property returns the legal trademark as defined in the informational section of the assembly.

### Usage at a Glance

- This property is read-only.
- An exception occurs if the trademark attribute, *AssemblyTrademarkAttribute* (or <AssemblyTrademark>), is undefined in the active assembly.

### Related Framework Entries

- Microsoft.VisualBasic.ApplicationServices.AssemblyInfo.Trademark Property
- System.Diagnostics.FileVersionInfo.LegalTrademark Property

### See Also

CompanyName Property, Copyright Property, Description Property, Info Object (My. Application), ProductName Property, Title Property

# TrimWhiteSpace Property

## Location

TextFieldParser.TrimWhiteSpace

## Syntax

```
Dim fileParser As FileIO.TextFieldParser
' ...later...
Dim result As Boolean = fileParser.TrimWhiteSpace
```

or:

```
fileParser.TrimWhiteSpace = whiteSpace
```

*whiteSpace (required; Boolean)*
Indicates whether whitespace around returned fields should be trimmed before those fields are returned (True) or not (False).

## Description

The *TrimWhiteSpace* property gets or sets a value that indicates whether leading and trailing whitespace characters surrounding delimited fields as parsed with the *TextFieldParser* object should be removed from each field before use (True) or not (False). If you do not specifically set this field, it defaults to True.

## Usage at a Glance

- The *TrimWhiteSpace* property is only useful with delimited input files, not fixed-width files.
- You must close the *TextFieldParser* object when finished with it. Use the object's *Close* method or create the object instance with the Using keyword. See the *TextFieldParser* Object entry in this chapter for an example.

## Related Framework Entries

- Microsoft.VisualBasic.FileIO.TextFieldParser.TrimWhiteSpace Property

## See Also

Delimiters Property, HasFieldsEnclosedInQuotes Property, ReadFields Method, SetDelimiters Method, TextFieldParser Object, TextFieldType Property

# UICulture Property

## Location

My.Application.UICulture

## Syntax

```
Dim result As System.Globalization.CultureInfo = _
    My.Application.UICulture
```

## Description

The *UICulture* property returns a *System.Globalization.CultureInfo* object that indicates the regional resource selections used by the active thread for user interface display.

## Usage at a Glance

This property impacts the application's interaction with the Resource Manager, and alters the behavior of the *My.Resources* object.

## Related Framework Entries

- System.Globalization.CultureInfo Class
- System.Threading.Thread.CurrentUICulture Property

## See Also

ChangeUICulture Method, Culture Property, InstalledUICulture Property, Resources Object

---

# UnhandledException Event

## Location

My.Application.UnhandledException

## Syntax

```
Public Sub Me_UnhandledException(ByVal sender As Object, _
    ByVal e As UnhandledExceptionEventArgs) _
    Handles Me.UnhandledException
End Sub
```

sender *(required; Object)*
    The control or object that raised the event

e *(required; StartupEventArgs)*
    An event parameter that contains information about the error or exception, using the *Microsoft.VisualBasic.ApplicationServices.UnhandledExceptionEventArgs* class

## Description

The *UnhandledException* event occurs when an exception occurs in your application that is not handled by any other exception handle. Normally, when an exception occurs, it is handled by the surrounding Try...Catch statement or by the On Error handler in effect for the procedure. If such handlers do not exist, the exception moves up the call stack, checking for active event handlers at each procedure in the stack. If there are no active event handlers in any of those procedures, the *UnhandledException* event is ultimately called.

## Public Members

The e argument to this event, as an instance of the *UnhandledExceptionEventArgs* class, includes the following notable public members.

| Member | Description |
| --- | --- |
| Exception | Property. A *System.Exception* instance that provides the details of the exception. |
| ExitApplication | Property. By default, this `Boolean` property is set to `True`, which causes the application to exit when the event exits. Setting this property to `False` keeps the application running. |

### Usage at a Glance

- This event is only available in Windows Forms applications.
- This event never fires when running an application built using the "Debug" compile target.
- This event does not fire when running an application from within the Visual Studio IDE.
- This event handler can be found in the *ApplicationEvents.vb* source code file for your project. This file is normally hidden, but it can be viewed by toggling the *Show All Files* button in the Solution Explorer window in Visual Studio.

### Example

The *UnhandledException* event's code appears in the *ApplicationEvents.vb* file in a Windows Forms application.

```
Namespace My
    Class MyApplication
        Private Sub MyApplication_UnhandledException( _
            ByVal sender As Object, ByVal e As _
            Microsoft.VisualBasic.ApplicationServices. _
            UnhandledExceptionEventArgs) _
            Handles Me.UnhandledException
            MsgBox("I can't handle it!")
            e.ExitApplication = True
        End Sub
    End Class
End Namespace
```

### Related Framework Entries

- Microsoft.VisualBasic.ApplicationServices.UnhandledExceptionEventArgs
- System.Exception Class

### See Also

Application Object, Shutdown Event, Startup Event, StartupNextInstance Event

---

## UploadFile Method

### Location

My.Computer.Network.UploadFile

### Syntax

```
My.Computer.Network.UploadFile(sourceFileName, address _
    [, username, password[, showUI, connectionTimeout _
    [, onUserCancel]]])
```

or:

```
My.Computer.Network.UploadFile(sourceFileName, uri _
    [, username, password[, showUI, connectionTimeout _
    [, onUserCancel]]])
```

or:

```
My.Computer.Network.UploadFile(sourceFileName, uri, _
    networkCredentials, showUI, connectionTimeout[, onUserCancel])
```

*sourceFileName (required; String)*
The local source path of the file to be uploaded.

*address (required in syntax 1; String)*
The destination web site address, including the full URL path.

*uri (required in syntax 2 and 3; System.Uri)*
The uniform resource identifier (URI) of the destination web site address.

*username (optional; String)*
The network user name for authentication purposes. If supplied, *password* must also be used.

*password (optional; String)*
The network password for authentication purposes. If supplied, *username* must also be used.

*showUI (optional; Boolean)*
Indicates whether a progress window should appear during the upload. By default, no progress window appears.

*connectionTimeout (optional; Integer)*
The number of seconds to wait before failure. By default, the timeout is 100 seconds.

*onUserCancel (optional; UICancelOption enumeration)*
The progress window includes a Cancel button. When pressed, the method takes action based on this parameter. One of the following *Microsoft.VisualBasic. FileIO.UICancelOption* enumeration values.

| Value | Description |
|---|---|
| DoNothing | Aborts the upload but returns no information indicating that the upload was cancelled |
| ThrowException | Throws an exception |

If this parameter is missing, ThrowException is used by default.

*networkCredentials (required in syntax 3; ICredentials interface)*
The credentials to be supplied for authentication purposes, based on the *System. Net.ICredentials* interface.

## Description

The *UploadFile* method sends a local file to a remote server via a web page that supports file uploading.

## Usage at a Glance

- An exception is thrown if the source or destination path is invalid, or if the destination web site denies the request.

- An exception is thrown if the user has invalid or insufficient security permissions to perform the download.
- An exception is thrown if a connection timeout occurs due to a lack of server response.

### Example

The following example uploads a local file to a web site.

```
My.Computer.Network.UploadFile _
    ("C:\PriceList.txt", "http://www.oreilly.com/upload.aspx", )
```

### Related Framework Entries

- Microsoft.VisualBasic.Devices.Network.UploadFile Method

### See Also

Network Object, DownloadFile Method

---

# User Object

### Location

My.User

### Description

Use the *My.User* object to access information about the active Windows user.

### Public Members

The following members of the *My.User* object have their own entries elsewhere in this chapter.

- CurrentPrincipal Property
- InitializeWithWindowsUser Method
- IsAuthenticated Property
- IsInRole Method
- Name Property (My.User)

### Usage at a Glance

This object's members provide varying functionality, depending on the type of application.

### Related Framework Entries

- Microsoft.VisualBasic.ApplicationServices.User Class
- Microsoft.VisualBasic.ApplicationServices.WebUser Class
- System.Web.HttpContext.User Class

### See Also

CurrentPrincipal Property, InitializeWithWindowsUser Method, IsAuthenticated Property, IsInRole Method, Name Property (My.User)

## Users Property

### Location
My.Computer.Registry.Users

### Syntax
```
Dim result As Microsoft.Win32.RegistryKey = _
    My.Computer.Registry.Users
```

### Description
The *Users* property returns a *Microsoft.Win32.RegistryKey* object that refers to the HKEY_USERS location in the Windows registry. This entry point is used primarily to store default settings for new Windows users.

### Usage at a Glance
- This property is read-only.
- To access the settings for the current Windows user, use the *My.Computer. Registry.CurrentUser* property instead.
- You must have sufficient security permissions to read or write keys and values in the registry.

### Example
The following example displays all of the sub-elements of the HKEY_USERS registry key element in a listbox control. The example assumes that you are using this code on a form with a defined ListBox1 control.
```
ListBox1.DataSource = My.Computer.Registry.Users.GetSubKeyNames()
```

### Related Framework Entries
- Microsoft.VisualBasic.MyServices.RegistryProxy.Users Property
- Microsoft.Win32.Registry.Users Property

### See Also
ClassesRoot Property, CurrentConfig Property, CurrentUser Property, DynData Property, GetValue Method, LocalMachine Property, PerformanceData Property, Registry Object, SetValue Method

The 'My' Reference

---

## Version Property

### Location
My.Application.Info.Version

### Syntax
```
Dim result As System.Version = My.Application.Info.Version
```

### Description

The *Version* property returns the version and revision numbers of the application as recorded in the assembly. The values are returned through an instance of the *System.Version* class.

### Public Members

The *System.Version* object returned by this property includes the following version-specific components, each of type `Integer`.

- Major
- Minor
- Build
- Revision

Version numbers are generally presented to the user in the format:

*Major.Minor.Build.Revision*

*Build* and *Revision* are optional, and when not defined, their properties will return -1. *Major* and *Minor* are required.

### Usage at a Glance

- This property is read-only.
- Use the *ToString* member of the returned object to generate a version number in a user-friendly display format.
- An exception occurs if the user does not have sufficient privileges to examine the version number of the assembly.
- Do not use this property from ClickOnce-deployed applications. Instead, use the *My.Application.Deployment.CurrentVersion* property.

### Example

The following example displays the version number of the application.

```
MsgBox("You are using version " & _
    My.Application.Info.Version.ToString)
```

### Related Framework Entries

- Microsoft.VisualBasic.ApplicationServices.AssemblyInfo.Version Property
- System.Deployment.Application.ApplicationDeployment.CurrentVersion Property
- System.Diagnostics.FileVersionInfo.FileVersion Property
- System.Diagnostics.FileVersionInfo.ProductVersion Property

### See Also

Info Object (My.Application)

---

# WebServices Object

### Location

My.WebServices

## Description

Use the *WebServices* object to access an instance of each XML Web service currently available to your application. The instances are created as needed, when you first reference an XML Web service through *My.WebServices*. This object lists those XML Web services that have been added as references to the application or those that are added at runtime. It is not available in ASP.NET applications.

XML Web services made available through a DLL associated with your running application are not added to *My.WebServices*. Access those services directly through the features provided by the DLL.

If you have a reference to an XML Web service named `TransferFunds`, access to that service is done by referencing that service as a property of *My.WebServices*:

```
My.WebServices.TransferFunds
```

When you are finished with an XML Web service and wish to dispose of it, set it to `Nothing`.

```
My.WebServices.TransferFunds = Nothing
```

You can test whether an instance of an XML Web service has already been created using the `Is` or `IsNot` operator:

```
If (My.WebServices.TransferFunds Is Nothing) Then...
```

## Public Members

The only public members of *My.WebServices* are the web services that have been referenced in your application.

## Usage at a Glance

This object and its members are not valid in ASP.NET applications.

## Related Framework Entries

• System.Web.Services Namespace

## See Also

Forms Object, My Namespace, Resources Object, Settings Object

---

# WheelExists Property

## Location

My.Computer.Mouse.WheelExists

## Syntax

```
Dim result As Boolean = My.Computer.Mouse.WheelExists
```

## Description

The *WheelExists* property indicates whether the mouse installed on the local computer includes a "mouse wheel" (`True`) or not (`False`).

## Usage at a Glance

• This property is read-only.

• This property is only valid in non-server applications.

- An exception is thrown if the computer does not have an installed mouse.
- Always use this property to detect the presence of a mouse wheel before using the *My.Computer.Mouse.WheelScrollLines* property.

**Related Framework Entries**
- Microsoft.VisualBasic.Devices.Mouse.WheelExists Property
- System.Windows.Forms.SystemInformation.MouseWheelPresent Property

**See Also**
ButtonsSwapped Property, Mouse Object, WheelScrollLines Property

---

## WheelScrollLines Property

### Location
My.Computer.Mouse.WheelScrollLines

### Syntax
```
Dim result As Integer = My.Computer.Mouse.WheelScrollLines
```

### Description
On systems that have a "mouse wheel" included on the installed mouse, the *WheelScrollLines* indicates how far the context should be scrolled when the wheel is rotated one position.

### Usage at a Glance
- This property is read-only.
- This property is only valid in non-server applications.
- An exception is thrown if the computer does not have an installed mouse.
- An exception is thrown if the installed mouse does not include a mouse wheel.
- Always use the *My.Computer.Mouse.WheelExists* property to detect the presence of a mouse wheel before using the *WheelScrollLines* property.

### Example
The following example displays the scroll amount for each mouse wheel rotation position.
```
If My.Computer.Mouse.WheelExists Then
    MsgBox("Mouse wheel scroll amount is " & _
        Abs(My.Computer.Mouse.WheelScrollLines) & ".")
Else
    MsgBox("No mouse scroll wheel present.")
End If
```

### Related Framework Entries
- Microsoft.VisualBasic.Devices.Mouse.WheelScrollLines Property
- System.Windows.Forms.SystemInformation.MouseWheelScrollLines Property

ButtonsSwapped Property, Mouse Object, WheelExists Property

---

## WorkingSet Property

### Location
My.Application.Info.WorkingSet

### Syntax
```
Dim result As Long = My.Application.Info.WorkingSet
```

### Description
The *WorkingSet* property identifies the number of bytes of physical memory mapped to this process context.

### Usage at a Glance
- This property is read-only.
- An exception is thrown if the user lacks sufficient privileges to query this value.
- This property always returns zero in Windows 98 and Windows Millenium Edition.

### Related Framework Entries
- Microsoft.VisualBasic.ApplicationServices.AssemblyInfo.WorkingSet Property
- System.Environment.WorkingSet Property

### See Also
Info Object (My.Application)

---

## WriteAllBytes Method

### Location
My.Computer.FileSystem.WriteAllBytes

### Syntax
```
My.Computer.FileSystem.WriteAllBytes(path, byteData, append)
```
*path (required; String)*
The path of the file to be written

*byteData (required; Byte array)*
The data to be written to the file

*append (required; Boolean)*
Indicates whether the data will be appended to the end of the file's existing content (True) or replaces any existing content (False)

## Description

The *WriteAllBytes* method writes the content of a Byte array to a specified file. If the file does not exist, it will be created, as long as the path specified with the file name is valid.

## Usage at a Glance

- An exception is thrown if the path parameter is missing or invalid, or if the file exists and is in use.
- An exception is thrown if the user lacks sufficient file-access permissions.

## Related Framework Entries

- Microsoft.VisualBasic.FileIO.FileSystem.WriteAllBytes Method
- Microsoft.VisualBasic.MyServices.FileSystemProxy.WriteAllBytes Method

## See Also

FileSystem Object, OpenTextFieldParser Method, OpenTextFileReader Method, OpenTextFileWriter Method, ReadAllBytes Method, ReadAllText Method, WriteAll-Text Method

---

# WriteAllText Method

## Location

My.Computer.FileSystem.WriteAllText

## Syntax

```
My.Computer.FileSystem.WriteAllText(path, textData, _
    append[, encoding])
```

*path (required; String)*
> The path of the file to be written.

*textData (required; String)*
> The text to be written to the file.

*append (required; Boolean)*
> Indicates whether the text will be appended to the end of the file's existing content (True) or replaces any existing content (False).

*encoding (optional; Encoding)*
> The character-encoding method to use as a *System.Text.Encoding* object. If this parameter is missing, UTF-8 is used as the default encoding method.

## Description

The *WriteAllText* method writes the content of a string to a specified file. If the file does not exist, it will be created, as long as the path specified with the file name is valid.

## Usage at a Glance

- An exception is thrown if the path parameter is missing or invalid or if the file exists and is in use.

---

- An exception is thrown if the user lacks sufficient file-access permissions.
- If the file already exists and uses an encoding method other than the one specified by this method, the original encoding method of the file will prevail.

## Example

The following example appends text to a file.

```
Public Sub RecordError(ByVal errorText As String)
    My.Computer.FileSystem.WriteAllText("C:\error.log", _
        errorText & vbCrLf, True)
End Sub
```

## Related Framework Entries

- Microsoft.VisualBasic.FileIO.FileSystem.WriteAllText Method
- Microsoft.VisualBasic.MyServices.FileSystemProxy.WriteAllText Method

## See Also

FileSystem Object, OpenTextFieldParser Method, OpenTextFileReader Method, OpenTextFileWriter Method, ReadAllBytes Method, ReadAllText Method, WriteAllBytes Method

# WriteEntry Method

## Location

My.Application.Log.WriteEntry

My.Log.WriteEntry

## Syntax

For client applications:

```
My.Application.Log.WriteEntry(message[, severity[, id]])
```

For ASP.NET applications:

```
My.Log.WriteEntry(message[, severity[, id]])
```

*message (required; String)*
> The message to log or an empty string if there is no message.

*severity (optional; TraceEventType enumeration)*
> The type of message to log. One of the following *System.Diagnostics.TraceEventType* enumeration values.

| Value | Description | Default ID |
|---|---|---|
| Critical | Application fatal error or crash event | 3 |
| Error | Recoverable error event | 2 |
| Information | Non-debugging informational message | 0 |
| None | Undefined event type | |
| Resume | Resumption of a logical operation | 7 |
| Start | Starting of a logical operation | 4 |

| Value | Description | Default ID |
|---|---|---|
| Stop | Stopping of a logical operation | 5 |
| Suspend | Suspension of a logical operation | 6 |
| Transfer | Transfer of control to another logical operation | 9 |
| Verbose | Debugging informational message | 8 |
| Warning | Noncritical event | 1 |

If severity is not supplied, Information is used by default.

*id (optional; Integer)*

The programmer-defined identifier for this entry. If *id* is not supplied, a predefined value associated with the *TraceEventType* enumeration is used. See the *Default ID* column in the table of *TraceEventType* enumeration values discussed above in the entry for the *severity* parameter.

### Description

The *WriteEntry* method writes a message to the application's configured event log listeners.

### Usage at a Glance

- This method is only valid in client and ASP.NET applications. For client applications, use *My.Application.Log.WriteEntry*. For ASP.NET applications, use *My. Log.WriteEntry*.
- For more information about using log listeners, see the *TraceSource Property* entry.
- An exception is thrown if you lack sufficient privileges to write to one of the configured log listeners.
- An exception is thrown if you specify an invalid *severity*.

### Example

The following example writes an informational message (the default) to the configured logs from a client application.

```
My.Application.Log.WriteEntry("Please read this; it's important.")
```

To write the same log message from an ASP.NET application, use this statement instead.

```
My.Log.WriteEntry("Please read this; it's important.")
```

### Related Framework Entries

- Microsoft.VisualBasic.Logging.Log.WriteEntry Method
- System.Diagnostics.TraceListener Class

### See Also

DefaultFileLogWriter Property, Log Object (My), Log Object (My.Application), TraceSource Property, WriteException Method

# WriteException Method

## Location

My.Application.Log.WriteException

My.Log.WriteException

## Syntax

For client applications:

```
My.Application.Log.WriteException(ex[, severity, _
    additionalInfo[, id]])
```

For ASP.NET applications:

```
My.Log.WriteException(ex[, severity, additionalInfo[, id]])
```

*ex (required; System.Exception)*
    The content of the exception to send to the log.

*severity (optional; TraceEventType enumeration)*
    The type of message to log. One of the following *System.Diagnostics.TraceEvent-Type* enumeration values.

| Value | Description | Default ID |
| --- | --- | --- |
| Critical | Application fatal error or crash event | 3 |
| Error | Recoverable error event | 2 |
| Information | Non-debugging informational message | 0 |
| None | Undefined event type | |
| Resume | Resumption of a logical operation | 7 |
| Start | Starting of a logical operation | 4 |
| Stop | Stopping of a logical operation | 5 |
| Suspend | Suspension of a logical operation | 6 |
| Transfer | Transfer of control to another logical operation | 9 |
| Verbose | Debugging informational message | 8 |
| Warning | Noncritical event | 1 |

If severity is not supplied, Information is used by default.

*additionalInfo (optional; String)*
    A message that is appended to the logged message.

*id (optional; Integer)*
    The programmer-defined identifier for this entry. If *id* is not supplied, a predefined value associated with the *TraceEventType* enumeration is used. See the *Default ID* column in the table of *TraceEventType* enumeration values discussed above in the entry for the *severity* parameter.

## Description

The *WriteException* method writes an exception entry to the application's configured event log listeners.

## Usage at a Glance

- This method is only valid in client and ASP.NET applications. For client applications, use *My.Application.Log.WriteException*. For ASP.NET applications, use *My.Log.WriteException*.
- For more information about using log listeners, see the *TraceSource Property* entry.
- An exception is thrown if you lack sufficient privileges to write to one of the configured log listeners.
- An exception is thrown if you specify an invalid *severity*.

## Example

The following example writes a exception warning message to the configured logs from a client application.

```
Try
    ' ----- Important but exception-prone code here.
Catch ex As System.Exception
    My.Application.Log.WriteException(ex, TraceEventType.Warning, _
        "Will try again in five minutes.")
End Try
```

To write the same log message from an ASP.NET application, use this statement instead.

```
Try
    ' ----- Important but exception-prone code here.
Catch ex As System.Exception
    My.Log.WriteException(ex, TraceEventType.Warning, _
        "Will try again in five minutes.")
End Try
```

## Related Framework Entries

- Microsoft.VisualBasic.Logging.Log.WriteException Method
- System.Diagnostics.TraceListener Class

## See Also

DefaultFileLogWriter Property, Log Object (My), Log Object (My.Application), Trace-Source Property, WriteEntry Method

# III

# Appendixes

Part III contains eight appendixes that supplement the core reference material provided in Parts I and II. These include:

- Appendix A, *Language Elements by Category*, which lists each entry from Chapter 12, grouped into several different categories. You can use this appendix to locate a particular language element by usage and, having obtained its name, look it up in Chapter 12.

- Appendix B, *Namespace Hierarchy*, which lists the *My* namespace entries from Chapter 13 in their original hierarchical arrangement. Also included is a hierarchical listing of many of the namespaces included in the .NET Framework Class Library.

- Appendix C, *Constants and Enumerations*, which lists VB intrinsic constants, as well as .NET enumerations that are specific to VB.

- Appendix D, *What's New and Different in Visual Basic .NET 2002*, which surveys the extensive changes the language experienced with the original release of Visual Basic for the .NET platform.

- Appendix E, *What's New and Different in Visual Basic .NET 2003*, which extends Appendix D by documenting changes introduced with Visual Basic .NET 2003 and Version 1.1 of the .NET Framework.

- Appendix F, *What's New and Different in Visual Basic 2005*, which further extends Appendixes D and E by documenting changes introduced with Visual Basic 2005 and Version 2.0 of the .NET Framework.

- Appendix G, *VB6 Language Elements No Longer Supported*, which lists the elements that have dropped out of the Visual Basic language as a result of its transition to the .NET Framework.

- Appendix H, *The Visual Basic Command-Line Compiler*, which documents the operation and options of the Visual Basic command-line compiler.

# A

# Language Elements by Category

This appendix lists by category all the directives, statements, functions, proce-dures, and classes available within the Visual Basic language. Also included are those Foundation Class Library members that are documented in Chapter 12. The categories are:

Array Handling
Clipboard
Collection Objects
Common Dialogs
Conditional Compilation
Conversion: Data Type Conversion and Other Conversion
Date and Time
Debugging
Declaration
Error Handling
File System
Financial
Information
Input/Output
Integrated Development Environment
Interaction
Mathematics
Program Structure and Flow
Programming: Object Programming and Miscellaneous Programming
Registry
String Manipulation

Some individual entries appear in more than one category. Also, this appendix does not list any members of the *My* Namespace feature. See Appendix B for a hierarchical listing of the *My* Namespace feature members.

# Array Handling

| Element | Description |
| --- | --- |
| Array Class | Represents an array |
| Array.BinarySearch Method | Searches for a value in a sorted one-dimensional array |
| Array.Copy Method | Copies all or part of an array |
| Array.IndexOf Method | Searches for the first occurrence of a value in an unsorted one-dimensional array |
| Array.LastIndexOf Method | Searches for the last occurrence of a value in an unsorted one-dimensional array |
| Array.Reverse Method | Reverses the order of elements in an array dimension |
| Array.Sort Method | Sorts the elements of an array dimension |
| Erase Statement | Resets an array to its uninitialized state |
| IsArray Function | Indicates whether a variable is an array |
| Join Function | Concatenates an array of values into a delimited string |
| LBound Function | Returns the lower boundary of an array |
| ReDim Statement | Adjusts the bounds of an array dimension |
| UBound Function | Returns the upper boundary of an array |
| VBFixedArray Attribute | Defines a fixed-length array |

# Clipboard

| Element | Description |
| --- | --- |
| Clipboard Class | Encapsulates functionality related to the system clipboard |
| Clipboard.GetDataObject Method | Places data on the clipboard |
| Clipboard.SetDataObject Method | Retrieves an *IDataObject* object representing data on the clipboard |
| IDataObject Interface | Defines an interface for clipboard format management |
| IDataObject.GetData Method | Retrieves data from the clipboard in a given format |
| IDataObject.GetDataPresent Method | Indicates whether the clipboard holds data of a particular format |
| IDataObject.GetFormats Method | Retrieves a list of all the formats with which the clipboard data is associated or to which it can be converted |

# Collection Objects

| Element | Description |
| --- | --- |
| Collection Class | Implements a Collection object that manages a set of related objects. |
| Collection.Add Method | Adds a member to a Collection object. |
| Collection.Count Property | Indicates the number of items stored to a Collection object. |
| Collection.Item Property | Retrieves a member from a Collection object based on its key value or ordinal position . |
| Collection.Remove Method | Removes the member associated with a given key or ordinal position from a Collection object. |
| Hashtable Class | Encapsulates a hashtable collection. |

| Element | Description |
|---|---|
| Hashtable.Add Method | Adds a key-value pair to a *Hashtable* object. |
| Hashtable.ContainsKey Method | Indicates whether a given key exists among the hashtable's items. |
| Hashtable.ContainsValue Method | Indicates whether a given value exists among the hashtable's items. |
| Hashtable.CopyTo Method | Copies hashtable values into an array of *DictionaryEntry* structures. |
| Hashtable.Item Property | Retrieves the value of a *Hashtable* item given its key. |
| Hashtable.Keys Property | Returns an *ICollection* object that contains the keys in the hashtable. |
| Hashtable.Remove Method | Removes a key/value pair from a *Hashtable* object. |
| Hashtable.Values Property | Returns an *ICollection* object that contains the values in the hashtable. |
| Of Keyword | *New in 2005.* Enables generics on a type or member definition. |
| Queue Class | Encapsulates a queue-style collection. |
| Queue.Contains Method | Indicates whether a *Queue* contains a particular item. |
| Queue.CopyTo Method | Copies the *Queue* items to an array. |
| Queue.Dequeue Method | Removes an item from a *Queue* object. |
| Queue.Enqueue Method | Places an item at the end of a *Queue*. |
| Queue.Peek Method | Returns the first item in a *Queue*. |
| Queue.ToArray Method | Copies the *Queue* items to an array. |
| Stack Class | Encapsulated a stack-style collection. |
| Stack.Contains Method | Indicates whether a *Stack* contains a particular item. |
| Stack.CopyTo Method | Copies the items in a *Stack* to an array. |
| Stack.Peek Method | Returns the item at the top of a *Stack*. |
| Stack.Pop Method | Removes the topmost item from a *Stack*. |
| Stack.Push Method | Places an item at the top of a *Stack*. |
| Stack.ToArray Method | Copies the items on a *Stack* to an array. |

# Common Dialogs

| Element | Description |
|---|---|
| ColorDialog Class | Allows programmatic control of the Windows Common Color dialog box |
| FontDialog Class | Allows programmatic control of the Windows Common Font dialog box |
| OpenFileDialog Class | Allows programmatic control of the Windows File Open dialog box |
| SaveFileDialog Class | Allows programmatic control of the Windows Save As dialog box |

# Conditional Compilation

| Element | Description |
|---|---|
| #Const Directive | Declares a conditional compiler constant |
| #If...Then...#Else Directive | Defines a block of code that will only be compiled into the program if the expression evaluates to True |

# Conversion

## Data Type Conversion

| Element | Description |
| --- | --- |
| CBool Function | Converts an expression to a `Boolean` data type. |
| CByte Function | Converts an expression to a `Byte` data type. |
| CChar Function | Converts a string expression to a `Char` data type. |
| CDate Function | Converts an expression to a `Date` data type. |
| CDbl Function | Converts an expression to a `Double` data type. |
| CDec Function | Converts an expression to a `Decimal` data type. |
| CInt Function | Converts an expression to an `Integer` data type. |
| CLng Function | Converts an expression to a `Long` data type. |
| CObj Function | Converts an expression to an `Object` data type. |
| CSByte Function | *New in 2005.* Converts an expression to an `SByte` data type. |
| CShort Function | Converts an expression to a `Short` data type. |
| CSng Function | Converts an expression to a `Single` data type. |
| CStr Function | Converts an expression to a `String` data type. |
| CType Function | Converts an expression to any valid data type, structure, object type, or interface. |
| CUInt Function | *New in 2005.* Converts an expression to a `UInteger` data type. |
| CULng Function | *New in 2005.* Converts an expression to a `ULong` data type. |
| CUShort Function | *New in 2005.* Converts an expression to a `UShort` data type. |
| DateValue Function | Converts the string representation of a date to a `Date` data type. |
| DirectCast Function | Converts a variable to its runtime type. |
| GetType Operator | Returns the type of a given object. |
| Option Strict Statement | Determines whether narrowing operations are allowed. |
| Str Function | Converts a numeric value to a string. |
| TimeValue Function | Converts a string representation of time to a `Date` data type. |
| TryCast Function | *New in 2005.* Converts a variable to a specified type, if possible. |
| Val Function | Converts a numeric string to a number . |

## Other Conversion

| Element | Description |
| --- | --- |
| ErrorToString Function | Returns the descriptive error message corresponding to a particular error code |
| Fix Function | Returns the integer portion of a number |
| Hex Function | Converts a number to a string representing its hexadecimal equivalent |
| Int Function | Returns the integer portion of a number |
| Oct Function | Converts a number to a string representing its octal equivalent |
| QBColor Function | Converts a QBasic color code to an RGB color value |
| RGB Function | Returns a system color code that can be assigned to object color properties |

# Date and Time

| Element | Description |
|---------|-------------|
| DateAdd Function | Returns the result of adding or subtracting a date or time |
| DateDiff Function | Returns the difference between two dates |
| DatePart Function | Returns the part (month, day, year) of the date requested |
| DateSerial Function | Returns a date from month, day, and year components |
| DateString Property | Retrieves or sets the current system date |
| DateValue Function | Converts the string representation of a date to a `Date` data type |
| Day Function | Returns a number representing the day of the month |
| GetTimer Function | Returns the number of seconds since midnight |
| Hour Function | Extracts the hour element from a time |
| Minute Function | Extracts the minutes element from a time |
| Month Function | Extracts the month element from a date |
| MonthName Function | Returns the name of the month for a given date |
| Now Property | Returns the current system date and time |
| Second Function | Extracts the seconds element from a time |
| TimeOfDay Property | Sets or retrieves the current system time |
| Timer Property | Returns the number of seconds that have elapsed since midnight |
| TimeSerial Function | Returns a time from its hour, minute, and second components |
| TimeString Property | Sets or returns the current system time |
| TimeValue Function | Converts a string representation of time to a `Date` data type |
| Today Property | Sets or retrieves the current system date |
| Weekday Function | Determines the day of the week for a given date |
| WeekdayName Function | Returns the weekday name for a given weekday number |
| Year Function | Returns the year element from a date |

# Debugging

| Element | Description |
|---------|-------------|
| Debug.Assert Method | Outputs a message if an expression is `False` |
| Debug.AutoFlush Property | Determines whether each write operation should be followed by a call to the *Flush* method |
| Debug.Close Method | Flushes the output buffer and closes any listeners except the Output window |
| Debug.Flush Method | Flushes the output buffer |
| Debug.Indent Method | Increases the value of the *IndentLevel* property by 1 |
| Debug.IndentLevel Property | Determines the indent level for *Debug* object output |
| Debug.IndentSize Property | Defines the current indent size in number of spaces |
| Debug.Listeners Property | Returns a collection of all *TraceListener* objects that are monitoring the *Debug* object's output |
| Debug.Unindent Method | Decreases the value of the *IndentLevel* property by 1 |
| Debug.Write Method | Sends output to the Output window and other listeners |
| Debug.WriteIf Method | Sends output to the Output window and other listeners if an expression is `True` |

| Element | Description |
|---|---|
| Debug.WriteLine Method | Writes output along with a newline character to the Output window |
| Debug.WriteLineIf Method | Writes output along with a newline character to the Output window if an expression is `True` |

# Declaration

| Element | Description |
|---|---|
| Const Statement | Declares a constant. |
| Class...End Class Statement | Defines a class and its members |
| Custom Event Statement | *New in 2005*. Declares a custom event with specialized declaration handlers. |
| Declare Statement | Defines a prototype for a call to an external DLL library procedure. |
| Dim Statement | Declares a variable. |
| Enum Statement | Defines a series of constants as an enumerated type. |
| Flags Attribute | Indicates that an enumeration should be treated as a set of flags. |
| Function Statement | Defines a function. |
| Friend Keyword | Makes a procedure in a class callable from outside the class but within the project in which the class is defined. |
| New Keyword | Creates a new instance of an object. |
| Nothing Keyword | The value of an undefined object. |
| Of Keyword | *New in 2005*. Enables generics on a type or member definition. |
| Operator Statement | *New in 2005*. Defines an overloaded operator. |
| Option Explicit Statement | Requires declaration of all variables. |
| Partial Keyword | *New in 2005*. Allows a type to be divided among multiple source code files. |
| Private Statement | Declares a local variable. |
| Property Statement | Defines a property. |
| Protected Keyword | Declares a protected class member. |
| Public Keyword | Declares a public or global variable. |
| Shared Keyword | Defines a shared member of a type that does not depend on an instance. |
| Static Statement | Declares a static variable. |
| Structure...End Structure Statement | Declares a structure or user-defined type. |
| Sub Statement | Declares a subroutine. |

# Error Handling

| Element | Description |
|---|---|
| Erl Property | Indicates the line number at which an error occurred |
| Err Object | Encapsulates an error |
| Err.Clear Method | Clears the `Err` object |
| Err.Description Property | Provides a textual description of an error |
| Err.GetException Method | Returns the *Exception* object associated with the current error |
| Err.HelpContext Property | Returns or sets the help file ID for the current error |

| Element | Description |
|---|---|
| Err.HelpFile Property | Returns or sets the name and path of the help file containing information about the current error |
| Err.LastDLLError Property | Returns the error number from an error raised by a system API DLL |
| Err.Number Property | Returns or sets the current error code |
| Err.Raise Method | Generates a user-defined error |
| Err.Source Property | Returns or sets the source of an error |
| Error Statement | Raises an error |
| ErrorToString Function | Returns the descriptive error message corresponding to a particular error code |
| Exception Class | Base class for all exceptions |
| IsError Function | Determines whether an object is an exception type |
| On Error Statement | Enables or disables an error handler |
| Resume Statement | Transfers control from an error handler |
| Throw Statement | Throws an exception |
| Try...Catch...Finally Statement | Handles particular errors that may occur in a block of code through structured exception handling |

# File System

| Element | Description |
|---|---|
| ChDir Procedure | Changes the current directory |
| ChDrive Procedure | Changes the current drive |
| CurDir Function | Returns the current directory of a drive |
| Dir Function | Returns the name of a file or directory matching a file specification and having particular file attributes |
| Directory Class | Encapsulates various features related to file system directory information |
| Directory.CreateDirectory Method | Creates a new directory |
| Directory.Delete Method | Deletes a directory |
| Directory.Exists Method | Indicates whether a particular directory exists |
| Directory.GetCreationTime Method | Retrieves the date and time the directory was created |
| Directory.GetDirectories Method | Retrieves the names of the subdirectories of a given directory |
| Directory.GetDirectoryRoot Method | Retrieves the name of the root directory of a given directory |
| Directory.GetFiles Method | Retrieves the names of the files in a given directory |
| Directory.GetFileSystemEntries Method | Retrieves the names of file system objects (files and directories) in a given directory |
| Directory.GetLogicalDrives Method | Retrieves the set of logical drives available on the local system |
| Directory.GetParent Method | Retrieves a *DirectoryInfo* object representing the parent of a specified directory |
| Directory.Move Method | Moves a directory and its contents, including nested subdirectories, to a new location |
| File Class | Encapsulates various features related to file system file information |
| File.Exists Method | Indicates whether a specified file exists |
| FileCopy Procedure | Copies a file |
| FileDateTime Function | Returns the date and time of file creation or last access |

| Element | Description |
|---|---|
| GetAttr Function | Returns the attributes of a given file or directory |
| Kill Procedure | Deletes one or more files |
| MkDir Procedure | Creates a new directory |
| Rename Procedure | Renames a file or directory |
| RmDir Procedure | Removes a directory |
| SetAttr Procedure | Sets a file or directory's attributes |

# Financial

| Element | Description |
|---|---|
| DDB Function | Returns double-declining balance depreciation of an asset for a specific period |
| FV Function | Calculates the future value of an annuity |
| IPmt Function | Computes the interest payment for a given period of an annuity |
| IRR Function | Calculates the internal rate of return for a series of periodic cash flows |
| MIRR Function | Calculates the modified internal rate of return |
| NPer Function | Determines the number of payment periods for an annuity, based on fixed periodic payments and a fixed interest rate |
| NPV Function | Calculates the net present value of an investment |
| Pmt Function | Calculates the payment for an annuity |
| PPmt Function | Computes the payment of principal for a given period of an annuity |
| PV Function | Calculates the present value of an annuity |
| Rate Function | Returns the interest rate per period for an annuity |
| SLN Method | Computes the straight-line depreciation of an asset |
| SYD Function | Computes the sum-of-years' digits depreciation of an asset for a specified period |

# Information

| Element | Description |
|---|---|
| Application Class | Includes features and informational properties related to the application |
| Application.CompanyName Property | Returns the name of the company that created the application |
| Application.ExecutablePath Property | Returns the executable path to the application |
| Application.ProductName Property | Returns the application's product name |
| Application.ProductVersion Property | Returns the application's version number |
| AssemblyVersion Attribute | Defines the version information for an assembly |
| Erl Function | Indicates the line number at which an error occurred |
| Global Keyword | *New in 2005*. Removes ambiguity from similarly named types and namespaces |
| IsArray Function | Indicates whether a variable is an array |
| IsDate Function | Indicates whether an argument is, or can be converted to, a date |
| IsDBNull Function | Determines whether an expression evaluates to *DbNull* |
| IsError Function | Determines whether an object is an exception type |
| IsNothing Function | Determines if an object reference evaluates to Nothing |

| Element | Description |
|---|---|
| IsNumeric Function | Determines if an expression is, or can be converted to, a number |
| IsReference Function | Determines if an expression is a reference type rather than a value type |
| Nothing Keyword | The value of an undefined object |
| RGB Function | Returns a system color code that can be assigned to object color properties |
| Rem Statement | Indicates a remark or comment placed within the code |
| ScriptEngine Property | Returns the name of the programming language |
| ScriptEngineBuildVersion Property | Returns the build number of the programming language |
| ScriptEngineMajorVersion Property | Returns the major version of the programming language |
| ScriptEngineMinorVersion Property | Returns the minor version of the programming language |
| SystemTypeName Function | Returns the name of the .NET data type corresponding to a VB data type |
| TypeName Function | Returns the data type name of a variable |
| TypeOf Operator | Compares an object to a defined type |
| VarType Function | Returns a constant indicating the data type of a variable |
| VbTypeName Function | Returns the name of a VB data type that corresponds to a .NET data type |

# Input/Output

| Element | Description |
|---|---|
| EOF Function | Returns a flag denoting the end of a file |
| FileAttr Function | Returns the file-access mode for a file opened using the `FileOpen` procedure |
| FileClose Procedure | Closes one or more open files |
| FileGet, FileGetObject Procedures | Reads from a file to a variable |
| FileLen Function | Returns the size of an open file |
| FileOpen Procedure | Opens a file |
| FilePut, FilePutObject Procedures | Writes from a variable to a file |
| FileWidth Procedure | Sets the line width of a file opened using the `FileOpen` procedure |
| FreeFile Function | Returns the number of the next available file |
| Input Procedure | Reads delimited data from a sequential file |
| InputString Function | Reads a designated number of characters from a file |
| LineInput Function | Returns a string containing a line read from a file |
| Loc Function | Returns the current position of the read/write pointer in a file |
| Lock Procedure | Locks a file, section of a file, or record in a file to prevent access by another process |
| LOF Function | Returns the size of an open file in bytes |
| Print, PrintLine Functions | Writes formatted data to a sequential file |
| Reset Procedure | Closes all open files |
| Seek Function | Returns the position of the file pointer |
| Seek Procedure | Sets the position of the file pointer |
| SPC Function | Inserts spaces between expressions in output |
| TAB Function | Moves the text-insertion point to a given column or to the start of the next print zone |
| Unlock Procedure | Removes a file or file section lock previously set with the `Lock` procedure |
| Write, WriteLine Procedures | Writes data to a file |

# Integrated Development Environment

| Element | Description |
| --- | --- |
| #Region...#End Region Directive | Defines collapsible sections of code in VB source code files |
| Debug Class | Provides debugging services for the Output window and other listeners |

# Interaction

| Element | Description |
| --- | --- |
| AppActivate Procedure | Gives the focus to a window based on its title or task ID |
| Beep Procedure | Sounds a note using the computer speaker |
| Choose Function | Returns a value from a list based on its index |
| Command Function | Returns the argument portion of the command line |
| Environ Function | Retrieves the value of an environment variable |
| IIf Function | Returns one of two values based on the evaluation of a Boolean expression |
| InputBox Function | Returns user input from a simple dialog box |
| MsgBox Function | Displays a message box with buttons, an icon, and a message, and it returns the response selected by the user |
| Shell Function | Launches an external application |
| Switch Function | Returns the first value or expression in a list that is `True` |
| Send, SendWait Methods | Sends keystrokes to the active window |

# Mathematics

| Element | Description |
| --- | --- |
| Abs Function | Returns the absolute value of a number |
| Acos Function | Returns the arccosine in radians |
| Asin Function | Returns the angle in radians of a sine |
| Atan Function | Returns the arctangent in radians of a tangent |
| Atan2 Function | Returns the angle in the Cartesian plane formed by the x-axis and a vector starting from the origin (0, 0) and terminating at a point (x, y) |
| Ceiling Function | Returns the smallest integer that is greater than or equal to a number |
| Cos Function | Returns the cosine of an angle |
| Cosh Function | Returns the hyperbolic cosine of an angle |
| E Field | Returns the approximate value of the irrational number $e$ |
| Exp Function | Returns the base of a natural logarithm raised to a power |
| Fix Function | Returns the integer portion of a number |
| Floor Function | Returns the largest integer less than or equal to a number |
| IEEERemainder Function | Returns the remainder resulting from division |
| Int Function | Returns the integer portion of a number |

| Element | Description |
| --- | --- |
| Log Function | Returns the natural (base *e*) logarithm of a given number |
| Log10 Function | Returns the common (base 10) logarithm of a given number |
| Max Function | Returns the larger of two numbers |
| Min Function | Returns the smaller of two numbers |
| Mod Operator | Returns the modulus (the remainder after division) |
| Partition Function | Returns a string indicating the range in which a number appears |
| PI Field | Returns the approximate value of $\pi$ |
| Pow Function | Returns the result of a number raised to a specified power |
| Randomize Procedure | Initializes the random-number generator |
| Rnd Function | Returns a random number |
| Round Function | Rounds a number to a specified number of decimal places |
| Sign Function | Determines the sign of a number |
| Sin Function | Returns the sine of an angle |
| Sinh Function | Returns the hyperbolic sine of an angle |
| Sqrt Function | Calculates the square root of a number |
| Tan Function | Returns the ratio of two sides of a right triangle |
| Tanh Function | Returns the hyperbolic tangent of an angle |

# Program Structure and Flow

| Element | Description |
| --- | --- |
| Call Statement | Calls an intrinsic or user-defined procedure or function, a method, or a routine in a dynamic link library. |
| CallByName Function | Dynamically executes a class method or property. |
| Continue Statement | *New in 2005.* Continues with the next cycle of the current loop block. |
| Do...Loop Statement | Repeatedly executes a block of code while or until a condition is true. |
| Exit Statement | Prematurely exits a code block. |
| End Statement | Marks the end of a block of code or an entire program. |
| For...Next Statement | Iterates through a section of code a given number of times. |
| For Each...Next Statement | Iterates through a collection or array of objects or values, returning a reference to each of the members. |
| GoTo Statement | Passes program flow to a portion of code marked by a label. |
| If...Then...Else Statement | Defines conditional blocks of code. |
| Operator Statement | *New in 2005.* Defines an overloaded operator. |
| Return Statement | Exits a function or procedure and returns a value from a function. |
| Select Case Statement | Executes one out of a series of code blocks based on the value of an expression. |
| Stop Statement | Suspends program execution. |
| Using...End Using Statement | *New in 2005.* Automatically releases allocated resources used within a code block. |
| While...End While Statement | Executes a block of code until a condition becomes `False`. |
| With...End With Statement | Enables simplified object referencing. |

# Programming

## Object Programming

| Element | Description |
|---|---|
| AddHandler Statement | Dynamically binds an event handler to an event. |
| AddressOf Operator | Creates a procedure delegate instance that references a particular procedure. |
| AttributeUsage Attribute | Defines which elements support a particular custom attribute. |
| Class...End Class Statement | Defines a class and its members. |
| COMClass Attribute | Allows a .NET component to be exposed as a COM object. |
| CreateObject Function | Creates a new instance of a COM (ActiveX) object. |
| Custom Event Statement | *New in 2005.* Declares a custom event with specialized declaration handlers. |
| DefaultMember Attribute | Indicates which member of a type is considered the "default" member. |
| Delegate Statement | Declares a delegate. |
| Event Statement | Declares an event. |
| Get Statement | Defines a `Property Get` procedure that returns a property value to the caller. |
| GetObject Function | Returns a reference to a COM (ActiveX) object. |
| Handles Keyword | Indicates that the procedure serves as a handler for an event. |
| Implements Keyword | Indicates that a class member implements a property, function, procedure, or event of an abstract base class. |
| Implements Statement | Specifies one or more interfaces that are implemented by a class. |
| Imports Statement | Imports a namespace from a project or an assembly, making its types and their members accessible to the current project. |
| Inherits Statement | Indicates that a class is derived from a base class. |
| Interface...End Interface Statement | Defines an interface and its members. |
| Is Operator | Compares two object references for equality. |
| IsNot Operator | *New in 2005.* Compares two object references for inequality. |
| MarshalAs Attribute | Defines the conversion method between a COM data element and its .NET counterpart. |
| Me Keyword | Represents the current class instance. |
| Module...End Module Statement | Defines a code module and its members. |
| MyBase Keyword | Represents the base class from which an inherited class is derived. |
| MyClass Keyword | Represents the current class instance. |
| Namespace Statement | Declares the name of a namespace. |
| Operator Statement | *New in 2005.* Defines an overloaded operator. |
| Partial Keyword | *New in 2005.* Allows a type to be divided among multiple source code files. |
| Property Statement | Defines a property. |
| RaiseEvent Statement | Raises a custom event. |
| RemoveHandler Statement | Disassociates an event from an event handler defined using the `AddHandler` statement. |
| Set Statement | Defines a `Property Set` procedure that assigns a property value. |

| Element | Description |
| --- | --- |
| Shadows Keyword | Indicates that a derived class hides an identically named member in a base class. |
| Shared Keyword | Defines a shared member of a type that does not depend on an instance. |
| WithEvents Keyword | Receives notification of events raised by an object. |

## Miscellaneous Programming

| Element | Description |
| --- | --- |
| AddressOf Operator | Creates a procedure delegate instance that references a particular procedure |
| Application.DoEvents Method | Allows the operating system to process events and messages waiting in the message queue |
| CLSCompliant Attribute | Indicates that an element is compliant with the minimal Common Language Specification |
| Declare Statement | Defines a prototype for a call to an external DLL library procedure |
| Environ Function | Retrieves the value of an environment variable |
| Guid Attribute | Assigns a GUID to a program element |
| Len Function | Counts the number of characters in a string |
| MTAThread Attribute | Indicates that the multithreaded apartment model is to be used for a class or application |
| Obsolete Attribute | Indicates that a program element is obsolete or deprecated |
| Out Attribute | Indicates that a parameter is an "out" parameter for data returned from a procedure |
| ParamArray Attribute | Indicates that a parameter is a "parameter array" element |
| STAThread Attribute | Indicates that the single-threaded apartment model is to be used for a class or application |
| SyncLock Statement | Prevents multiple threads of execution in the same process from accessing shared data or resources at the same time |
| ThreadStatic Attribute | Indicates that each thread maintains its own image of a static value |

## Registry

| Element | Description |
| --- | --- |
| DeleteSetting Procedure | Removes a complete application key, one of its subkeys, or a single value entry from the system registry |
| GetAllSettings Function | Returns all values from an application key in the system registry |
| GetSetting Function | Returns a specific value from an application key in the system registry |
| SaveSetting Procedure | Creates or saves a value in the system registry |

## String Manipulation

| Element | Description |
| --- | --- |
| Asc, AscW Functions | Returns the character code of the first character of a string |
| Chr, ChrW Functions | Returns a string containing a character based on its numeric code |
| Filter Function | Returns an array of strings matching (or not matching) a specified value |

| Element | Description |
|---|---|
| Format Function | Returns a string formatted to a given specification |
| FormatCurrency, FormatNumber, FormatPercent Functions | Returns a numeric value formatted as indicated by the name of the specific function |
| FormatDateTime Function | Returns a string formatted using the date/time setting for the current locale |
| GetChar Function | Returns a Char containing the character at a particular position in a string |
| InStr Function | Finds the starting position of a substring within a string |
| InStrRev Function | Returns the first occurrence of a string within another string by searching from the end of the string |
| Join Function | Concatenates an array of values into a delimited string |
| LCase Function | Converts a character or string to lowercase |
| Left Function | Returns a string containing a specific number of characters from the beginning of a string |
| Len Function | Counts the number of characters in a string |
| Like Operator | Compares two strings |
| LSet Function | Left-aligns a string |
| LTrim Function | Removes characters from the beginning of a string |
| Mid Function | Extracts a substring from a larger string |
| Mid Statement | Replaces a substring in a larger string |
| Option Compare Statement | Sets the default method for comparing string data |
| Replace Function | Replaces one or more occurrences of a substring within a larger string |
| Right Function | Returns a string containing a specific number of characters from the end of a string |
| RSet Function | Right-aligns a string |
| RTrim Function | Removes characters from the end of a string |
| Str Function | Converts a numeric value to a string |
| SPC Function | Inserts spaces between expressions in output |
| Space Function | Fills a string with a given number of spaces |
| Split Function | Returns an array of strings from a single delimited string |
| StrComp Function | Returns the result of comparing two strings |
| StrConv Function | Returns the result of converting a string in a number of possible ways |
| StrDup Function | Returns a string consisting of the first character of another string duplicated a given number of times |
| StrReverse Function | Reverses the characters of a string |
| Trim Function | Removes characters from the beginning and end of a string |
| UCase Function | Converts a string to uppercase |
| Val Function | Converts a numeric string to a number |
| VBFixedString Attribute | Defines a fixed-length string |

# B

## Namespace Hierarchy

The .NET Framework Class Library (FCL) is organized as a hierarchy, yet you rarely get to see it in that format—but you will in this appendix. Here you will find two hierarchical listings, one that shows each major element in the *My* Namespace feature, and one that shows all major namespaces within the master *System* namespace. The *My* Namespace hierarchy listing includes all nodes and elements listed in Chapter 13, but in hierarchy order instead of merged alphabetical order.

## 'My' Namespace Hierarchy

```
My Namespace
    Application Object
        ApplicationContext Property
        ChangeCulture Method
        ChangeUICulture Method
        CommandLineArgs Property
        Culture Property
        Deployment Property
        DoEvents Method
        GetEnvironmentVariable Method
        Info Object
            AssemblyName Property
            CompanyName Property
            Copyright Property
            Description Property
            DirectoryPath Property
            LoadedAssemblies Property
            ProductName Property
            StackTrace Property
            Title Property
            Trademark Property
            Version Property
            WorkingSet Property
```

```
        IsNetworkDeployed Property
        Log Object
            TraceSource Property
            WriteEntry Method
            WriteException Method
        NetworkAvailabilityChanged Event
        OpenForms Property
        Run Method
        SaveMySettingsOnExit Property
        Shutdown Event
        SplashScreen Property
        Startup Event
        StartupNextInstance Event
        UICulture Property
        UnhandledException Event
    Computer Object
        Audio Object
            Play Method
            PlaySystemSound Method
            Stop Method
        Clipboard Object
            Clear Method
            ContainsAudio Method
            ContainsData Method
            ContainsFileDropList Method
            ContainsImage Method
            ContainsText Method
            GetAudioStream Method
            GetData Method
            GetDataObject Method
            GetFileDropList Method
            GetImage Method
            GetText Method
            SetAudio Method
            SetData Method
            SetDataObject Method
            SetFileDropList Method
            SetImage Method
            SetText Method
        Clock Object
            GmtTime Property
            LocalTime Property
            TickCount Property
        FileSystem Object
            CombinePath Method
            CopyDirectory Method
            CopyFile Method
            CreateDirectory Method
            CurrentDirectory Property
            DeleteDirectory Method
            DeleteFile Method
            DirectoryExists Method
            Drives Property
            FileExists Method
            FindInFiles Method
```

Namespace
Hierarchy

```
                UploadFile Method
            Ports Object
                OpenSerialPort Method
                SerialPortNames Property
            Registry Object
                ClassesRoot Property
                CurrentConfig Property
                CurrentUser Property
                DynData Property
                GetValue Method
                LocalMachine Property
                PerformanceData Property
                SetValue Method
                Users Property
            Screen Property
        Forms Object
        Log Object
            TraceSource Property
            WriteEntry Method
            WriteException Method
        Request Object
        Resources Object
        Response Object
        Settings Object
        User Object
            CurrentPrincipal Property
            InitializeWithWindowsUser Method
            IsAuthenticated Property
            IsInRole Method
            Name Property
        WebServices Object
    TextFieldParser Object
        Close Method
        CommentTokens Property
        Delimiters Property
        EndOfData Property
        ErrorLine Property
        ErrorLineNumber Property
        FieldWidths Property
        HasFieldsEnclosedInQuotes Property
        LineNumber Property
        PeekChars Method
        ReadFields Method
        ReadLine Method
        ReadToEnd Method
        SetDelimiters Method
        SetFieldWidths Method
        TextFieldType Property
        TrimWhiteSpace Property
```

# System Namespace Hierarchy

```
System
    CodeDom
```

```
        Compiler
Collections
        Generic
        ObjectModel
        Specialized
ComponentModel
        Design
                Data
                Serialization
Configuration
        Assemblies
        Install
        Internal
        Provider
Data
        Common
        Design
        Odbc
        OleDb
        OracleClient
        Sql
        SqlClient
        SqlServerCe
        SqlTypes
Deployment
        Application
        Internal
DeploymentFramework
        FileTypes
Diagnostics
        CodeAnalysis
        Design
        SymbolStore
DirectoryServices
        ActiveDirectory
        Protocols
Drawing
        Design
        Drawing2D
        Imaging
        Printing
        Text
EnterpriseServices
        CompensatingResourceManager
        Internal
Globalization
IO
        Compression
        IsolatedStorage
        Ports
Management
        Instrumentation
Media
Messaging
        Design
```

```
Net
    Cache
    Configuration
    Mail
    Mime
    NetworkInformation
    Security
    Sockets
Reflection
    Emit
Resources
    Tools
Runtime
    CompilerServices
    ConstrainedExecution
    Hosting
    InteropServices
    ComTypes
        CustomMarshalers
        Expando
    Remoting
        Activation
        Channels
            Http
            Ipc
            Tcp
        Contexts
        Lifetime
        Messaging
        Metadata
            W3cXsd2001
        MetadataServices
        Proxies
        Services
    Serialization
        Formatters
            Binary
            Soap
    Versioning
Security
    AccessControl
    Authentication
    Cryptography
        Pkcs
        X509Certificates
        Xml
    Permissions
    Policy
    Principal
ServiceProcess
    Design
Text
    RegularExpressions
Threading
```

```
Timers
Transactions
    Configuration
Web
    Caching
    Compilation
    Configuration
        Internal
    Handlers
    Hosting
    Mail
    Management
    Mobile
    Profile
    RegularExpressions
    Security
    Services
        Configuration
        Description
        Discovery
        Protocols
    SessionState
    UI
        Adapters
        Design
            MobileControls
                Converters
            WebControls
                WebParts
        HtmlControls
        MobileControls
            Adapters
                XhtmlAdapters
        WebControls
            Adapters
            WebParts
    Util
Windows
    Forms
        ComponentModel
            Com2Interop
        Design
            Behavior
        Layout
        PropertyGridInternal
        VisualStyles
Xml
    Schema
    Serialization
        Advanced
        Configuration
    XPath
    Xsl
        Runtime
```

# C

# Constants and Enumerations

This appendix consists of a reference for Visual Basic's built-in constants and enumerations.

Visual Basic defines several enumerations in the *Microsoft.VisualBasic* namespace. For instance, the *CompareMethod* enumeration is defined as:

```
Enum CompareMethod
    Binary = 0
    Text = 1
End Enum
```

Thus, you can use the following expressions in VB code:

```
CompareMethod.Binary
CompareMethod.Text
```

Visual Basic also defines two equivalent built-in constants in the *Constants* class of the *Microsoft.VisualBasic* namespace that serve the same purpose:

```
vbBinaryCompare
vbTextCompare
```

While this is convenient, VB does not define built-in constants corresponding to every member of every enumeration. For instance, there are no built-in constants that correspond to the *OpenMode* enumeration members, used with the *FileOpen* procedure:

```
Enum OpenMode
    Input = 1
    Output = 2
    Random = 4
    Append = 8
    Binary = 32
End Enum
```

# Visual Basic Intrinsic Constants

Table C-1 contains an alphabetical listing of VB's built-in symbolic constants. They are actually implemented as fields of the *Constants* class in the *Microsoft. VisualBasic* namespace.

*Table C-1. Visual Basic constants*

| Constant | Value |
| --- | --- |
| vbAbort | 3 |
| vbAbortRetryIgnore | &H00000002 |
| vbApplicationModal | &H00000000 |
| vbArchive | 32 |
| vbArray | 8192 |
| vbBack | Chr(8) |
| vbBinaryCompare | 0 |
| vbBoolean | 11 |
| vbByte | 17 |
| vbCancel | 2 |
| vbCr | Chr(13) |
| vbCritical | &H00000010 |
| vbCrLf | Chr(13) & Chr(10) |
| vbCurrency | 6 |
| vbDate | 7 |
| vbDecimal | 14 |
| vbDefaultButton1 | &H00000000 |
| vbDefaultButton2 | &H00000100 |
| vbDefaultButton3 | &H00000200 |
| vbDirectory | 16 |
| vbDouble | 5 |
| vbEmpty | 0 |
| vbExclamation | &H00000030 |
| vbFalse | 0 |
| vbFirstFourDays | 2 |
| vbFirstFullWeek | 3 |
| vbFirstJan1 | 1 |
| vbFormFeed | Chr(12) |
| vbFriday | 6 |
| vbGeneralDate | 0 |
| vbGet | 2 |
| vbHidden | 2 |
| vbHide | 0 |
| vbHiragana | 32 |
| vbIgnore | 5 |
| vbInformation | &H00000040 |
| vbInteger | 3 |
| vbKatakana | 16 |
| vbLet | 4 |

*Table C-1. Visual Basic constants  (continued)*

| Constant | Value |
| --- | --- |
| vbLf | Chr(10) |
| vbLinguisticCasing | 1024 |
| vbLong | 20 |
| vbLongDate | 1 |
| vbLongTime | 3 |
| vbLowerCase | 2 |
| vbMaximizedFocus | 3 |
| vbMethod | 1 |
| vbMinimizedFocus | 2 |
| vbMinimizedNoFocus | 6 |
| vbMonday | 2 |
| vbMsgBoxHelp | &H00004000 |
| vbMsgBoxRight | &H00080000 |
| vbMsgBoxRtlReading | &H00100000 |
| vbMsgBoxSetForeground | &H00010000 |
| vbNarrow | 8 |
| vbNewLine | Chr(13) & Chr(10) |
| vbNo | 7 |
| vbNormal | 0 |
| vbNormalFocus | 1 |
| vbNormalNoFocus | 4 |
| vbNull | 1 |
| vbNullChar | Chr(0) |
| vbNullString | |
| vbObject | 9 |
| vbObjectError | &H80040000 |
| vbOK | 1 |
| vbOKCancel | &H00000001 |
| vbOKOnly | &H00000000 |
| vbProperCase | 3 |
| vbQuestion | &H00000020 |
| vbReadOnly | 1 |
| vbRetry | 4 |
| vbRetryCancel | &H00000005 |
| vbSaturday | 7 |
| vbSet | 8 |
| vbShortDate | 2 |
| vbShortTime | 4 |
| vbSimplifiedChinese | 256 |
| vbSingle | 4 |
| vbString | 8 |
| vbSunday | 1 |
| vbSystem | 4 |
| vbSystemModal | &H00001000 |
| vbTab | Chr(9) |

*Table C-1. Visual Basic constants  (continued)*

| Constant | Value |
|---|---|
| vbTextCompare | 1 |
| vbThursday | 5 |
| vbTraditionalChinese | 512 |
| vbTrue | 1 |
| vbTuesday | 3 |
| vbUpperCase | 1 |
| vbUseDefault | &HFFFFFFFE |
| vbUserDefinedType | 36 |
| vbUseSystem | 0 |
| vbUseSystemDayOfWeek | 0 |
| vbVariant | 12 |
| vbVerticalTab | Chr(11) |
| vbVolume | 8 |
| vbWednesday | 4 |
| vbWide | 4 |
| vbYes | 6 |
| vbYesNo | &H00000004 |
| vbYesNoCancel | &H00000003 |

# ControlChars Class

The *Microsoft.VisualBasic* namespace includes a *ControlChars* class with shared fields that can be used for device control and outputting special characters. Most of the shared fields also have equivalent Visual Basic intrinsic constants.

| Field | Value | Intrinsic constant |
|---|---|---|
| Back | Chr(8) | vbBack |
| Cr | Chr(13) | vbCr |
| CrLf | Chr(13) & Chr(10) | vbCrLf |
| FormFeed | Chr(12) | vbFormFeed |
| Lf | Chr(10) | vbLf |
| NewLine | Chr(13) & Chr(10) | vbNewLine |
| NullChar | Chr(0) | vbNullChar |
| Quote | Chr(34) | |
| Tab | Chr(9) | vbTab |
| VerticalTab | Chr(11) | vbVerticalTab |

These constants must be qualified with their class name, as in:

```
If (dataString = ControlChars.CrLf) Then
```

# Visual Basic Enumerations

The following is a list of the major VB-defined enumerations. Many of the enumeration values have equivalent VB constants, which appear in the comments to the right of each value. In general, you will need to qualify enumeration members with the enumeration name when using them in your code.

## AppWinStyle Enumeration

```
Enum AppWinStyle
    Hide = 0                      ' vbHide
    NormalFocus = 1               ' vbNormalFocus
    MinimizedFocus = 2            ' vbMinimizedFocus
    MaximizedFocus = 3            ' vbMaximizedFocus
    NormalNoFocus = 4             ' vbNormalNoFocus
    MinimizedNoFocus = 6          ' vbMinimizedNoFocus
End Enum
```

## AudioPlayMode Enumeration

This enumeration is *new with Visual Basic 2005.*

```
Enum AudioPlayMode
    WaitToComplete = 0
    Background = 1
    BackgroundLoop = 2
End Enum
```

## BuiltInRole Enumeration

This enumeration is *new with Visual Basic 2005.*

```
Enum BuiltInRole
    Administrator = 544
    User = 545
    Guest = 546
    PowerUser = 547
    AccountOperator = 548
    SystemOperator = 549
    PrintOperator = 550
    BackupOperator = 551
    Replicator = 552
End Enum
```

## CallType Enumeration

```
Enum CallType
    Method = 1                    ' vbMethod
    Get = 2                       ' vbGet
    Let = 4                       ' vbLet
    Set = 8                       ' vbSet
End Enum
```

## CompareMethod Enumeration

```
Enum CompareMethod
    Binary = 0                    ' vbBinaryCompare
    Text = 1                      ' vbTextCompare
End Enum
```

## DateFormat Enumeration

```
Enum DateFormat
    GeneralDate = 0          ' vbGeneralDate
    LongDate = 1             ' vbLongDate
    ShortDate = 2            ' vbShortDate
    LongTime = 3             ' vbLongTime
    ShortTime = 4            ' vbShortTime
End Enum
```

## DateInterval Enumeration

```
Enum DateInterval
    Year = 0
    Quarter = 1
    Month = 2
    DayOfYear = 3
    Day = 4
    WeekOfYear = 5
    Weekday = 6
    Hour = 7
    Minute = 8
    Second = 9
End Enum
```

## DeleteDirectoryOption Enumeration

This enumeration is *new with Visual Basic 2005*.

```
Enum DeleteDirectoryOption
    ThrowIfDirectoryNonEmpty = 0
    DeleteAllContents = 1
End Enum
```

## DueDate Enumeration

```
Enum DueDate
    EndOfPeriod = 0
    BegOfPeriod = 1
End Enum
```

## FieldType Enumeration

This enumeration is *new with Visual Basic 2005*.

```
Enum FieldType
    Delimited = 0
    FixedWidth = 1
End Enum
```

## FileAttribute Enumeration

```
Enum FileAttribute
    Normal = 0               ' vbNormal
    ReadOnly = 1             ' vbReadOnly
```

```
      Hidden = 2              ' vbHidden
      System = 4              ' vbSystem
      Volume = 8              ' vbVolume
      Directory = 16          ' vbDirectory
      Archive = 32            ' vbArchive
    End Enum
```

## FirstDayOfWeek Enumeration

```
    Enum FirstDayOfWeek
      System = 0              ' vbUseSystemDayOfWeek
      Sunday = 1              ' vbSunday
      Monday = 2              ' vbMonday
      Tuesday = 3             ' vbTuesday
      Wednesday = 4           ' vbWednesday
      Thursday = 5            ' vbThursday
      Friday = 6              ' vbFriday
      Saturday = 7            ' vbSaturday
    End Enum
```

## FirstWeekOfYear Enumeration

```
    Enum FirstWeekOfYear
      System = 0             ' vbUseSystem
      Jan1 = 1               ' vbFirstJan1
      FirstFourDays = 2      ' vbFirstFourDays
      FirstFullWeek = 3      ' vbFirstFullWeek
    End Enum
```

## MsgBoxResult Enumeration

```
    Enum MsgBoxResult
      OK = 1                 ' vbOK
      Cancel = 2             ' vbCancel
      Abort = 3              ' vbAbort
      Retry = 4              ' vbRetry
      Ignore = 5             ' vbIgnore
      Yes = 6                ' vbYes
      No = 7                 ' vbNo
    End Enum
```

## MsgBoxStyle Enumeration

```
    Enum MsgBoxStyle
      DefaultButton1 = &H00000000      ' vbDefaultButton1
      ApplicationModal = &H00000000    ' vbApplicationModal
      OKOnly = &H00000000              ' vbOKOnly
      OKCancel = &H00000001            ' vbOKCancel
      AbortRetryIgnore = &H00000002    ' vbAbortRetryIgnore
      YesNoCancel = &H00000003         ' vbYesNoCancel
      YesNo = &H00000004               ' vbYesNo
      RetryCancel = &H00000005         ' vbRetryCancel
      Critical = &H00000010            ' vbCritical
      Question = &H00000020            ' vbQuestion
```

```
    Exclamation = &H00000030          ' vbExclamation
    Information = &H00000040          ' vbInformation
    DefaultButton2 = &H00000100       ' vbDefaultButton2
    DefaultButton3 = &H00000200       ' vbDefaultButton3
    SystemModal = &H00001000          ' vbSystemModal
    MsgBoxHelp = &H00004000           ' vbMsgBoxHelp
    MsgBoxSetForeground = &H00010000  ' vbMsgBoxSetForeground
    MsgBoxRight = &H00080000          ' vbMsgBoxRight
    MsgBoxRtlReading = &H00100000     ' vbMsgBoxRtlReading
End Enum
```

## OpenAccess Enumeration

```
Enum OpenAccess
    Default = &HFFFFFFFF
    Read = 1
    Write = 2
    ReadWrite = 3
End Enum
```

## OpenMode Enumeration

```
Enum OpenMode
    Input = 1
    Output = 2
    Random = 4
    Append = 8
    Binary = 32
End Enum
```

## OpenShare Enumeration

```
Enum OpenShare
    Default = &HFFFFFFFF
    LockReadWrite = 0
    LockWrite = 1
    LockRead = 2
    Shared = 3
End Enum
```

## RecycleOption Enumeration

This enumeration is *new with Visual Basic 2005*.

```
Enum RecycleOption
    DeletePermanently = 0
    SendToRecycleBin = 1
End Enum
```

## SearchOption Enumeration

This enumeration is *new with Visual Basic 2005*.

```
Enum SearchOption
    SearchTopLevelOnly = 0
```

```
            SearchAllSubDirectories = 1
        End Enum
```

## TriState Enumeration

```
    Enum TriState
        UseDefault = &HFFFFFFFE          ' vbUseDefault
        False = 0                        ' vbFalse
        True = 1                         ' vbTrue
    End Enum
```

## UICancelOption Enumeration

This enumeration is *new with Visual Basic 2005.*

```
    Enum UICancelOption
        DoNothing = 0
        ThrowException = 1
    End Enum
```

## UIOption Enumeration

This enumeration is *new with Visual Basic 2005.*

```
    Enum UIOption
        OnlyErrorDialogs = 0
        AllDialogs = 1
    End Enum
```

## VariantType Enumeration

```
    Enum VariantType
        Empty = 0                        ' vbEmpty
        Null = 1                         ' vbNull
        Short = 2
        Integer = 3                      ' vbInteger
        Single = 4                       ' vbSingle
        Double = 5                       ' vbDouble
        Currency = 6                     ' vbCurrency
        Date = 7                         ' vbDate
        String = 8                       ' vbString
        Object = 9                       ' vbObject
        Error = 10
        Boolean = 11                     ' vbBoolean
        Variant = 12                     ' vbVariant
        DataObject = 13
        Decimal = 14                     ' vbDecimal
        Byte = 17                        ' vbByte
        Char = 18
        Long = 20                        ' vbLong
        UserDefinedType = 36             ' vbUserDefinedType
        Array = 8192                     ' vbArray
    End Enum
```

# VbStrConv Enumeration

```
Enum VbStrConv
    None = 0
    UpperCase = 1                        ' vbUpperCase
    LowerCase = 2                        ' vbLowerCase
    ProperCase = 3                       ' vbProperCase
    Wide = 4                             ' vbWide
    Narrow = 8                           ' vbNarrow
    Katakana = 16                        ' vbKatakana
    Hiragana = 32                        ' vbHiragana
    SimplifiedChinese = 256              ' vbSimplifiedChinese
    TraditionalChinese = 512             ' vbTraditionalChinese
    LinguisticCasing = 1024              ' vbLinguisticCasing
End Enum
```

# D

# What's New and Different
# in Visual Basic .NET 2002

This appendix is for readers who are familiar with pre-.NET versions of Visual Basic, specifically Version 6. The text describes the basic changes to the Visual Basic language, both in terms of syntax and usage. General functional changes appear as well, including topics such as error handling and objected-oriented programming support.

This appendix assumes that you are familiar with VB 6, so it does not go into the details of how VB 6 handles a given language feature, unless the contrast is specifically helpful. Readers familiar only with versions of Visual Basic before Version 6 will also benefit from this chapter, although only changes made since Version 6 appear here.

## Language Changes in VB.NET 2002

This section outlines the changes made to the Visual Basic language from Version 6 to Visual Basic .NET 2002. These language changes were made to bring VB under the umbrella of the .NET Framework and to provide VB access to the Common Language Runtime shared by all languages in the Visual Studio .NET family of languages.

### Data Types

There have been fundamental changes to data types in the transition to VB.NET. The most important change is that all .NET-compliant languages (including VB, C#, and Managed C++) now implement a subset of a *common set* of data types, defined in the .NET Framework's Base Class Library (BCL); specific languages, including VB.NET 2002, do not implement all available BCL data types. Each data type in the BCL is implemented either as a class or as a structure and, as such, has members. The VB.NET data types are wrappers for the corresponding BCL data types. Because of this, any feature of the .NET Framework that uses a specific BCL data type will work seamlessly with the equivalent VB.NET data type. For more discussion on data types, see Chapter 4.

## Strings

In VB 6, strings were implemented as BSTRs ("B-Strings"). A BSTR is a pointer to a character array that is preceded by a 4-byte Long specifying the length of the array. In VB.NET, strings are implemented as objects of the *System.String* class.

One consequence of this reimplementation of strings is that VB.NET does not support fixed-length strings, as did VB 6. Thus, the following code is illegal:

```
Dim sName As String * 30
```

Strings in .NET are immutable. Once you assign a value to a string, neither its length nor its content changes. If you change a string, the .NET Common Language Runtime actually gives you a reference to a new *String* object. (For more on this, see Chapter 4.)

## Integer/Long data-type changes

Visual Basic .NET 2002 defines the following signed-integer data types:

Short
> A 16-bit integer data type, based on the *System.Int16* data type.

Integer
> A 32-bit integer data type, based on the *System.Int32* data type.

Long
> A 64-bit integer data type, based on the *System.Int64* data type.

This means that in the transition from VB 6 to VB.NET:

- The VB 6 Integer data type became the VB.NET Short data type.
- The VB 6 Long data type became the VB.NET Integer data type.
- The VB.NET Long data type has no direct equivalent in VB 6.

## Variant data type

VB.NET does not support the Variant data type. The Object data type is VB. NET's *universal data type*; it can hold data of any other data type. Although its use is somewhat different from the Variant data type, both data types provide a general way to refer to a variety of data.

There are several penalties associated with using a universal data type, including poor performance and poor program readability. While VB.NET still provides this opportunity through the Object data type, its use is not recommended simply to avoid the clear categorization of your data values.

The VarType function, which was used in VB 6 to determine the type of data stored in a Variant variable (that is, it returned the Variant's data *subtype*), now reports the true data type of the Object instance instead. VB.NET still supports the TypeName function, which is used to return the name of the true data type of an Object variable.

### Other data-type changes

Here are some additional changes in data types:

- The Def*type* statements (DefBool, DefByte, etc.), which were used to define the default data type for variables with names that began with particular letters of the alphabet, are not supported in VB.NET.

- The Currency data type is not supported in VB.NET. However, VB.NET's Decimal data type can handle more digits on both sides of the decimal point than did the Currency data type, and it is a superior replacement. The VB. NET Decimal data type is a true data type; VB 6's Currency data type was a Variant subtype, and a variable could be cast as a Decimal in VB 6 only by calling the CDec conversion function.

- In VB 6, dates and times were stored in a Double format using four bytes. In VB.NET, the Date data type is an 8-byte integral data type with a range of values that is from January 1, 1 to December 31, 9999 in the Gregorian calendar.

## Variables and Their Declaration

Visual Basic .NET 2002 introduced several changes related to variable use.

### Variable declaration

The syntax used to declare variables changed with VB.NET, making it more flexible. In VB.NET, when multiple variables are declared on the same line, if a variable is not declared with a type explicitly, then its type is that of the next variable with an explicit type declaration. Thus, in the line:

```
Dim first As Long, second, third, fourth As Integer
```

the variables second, third, and fourth are of type Integer. Using this same statement in VB 6 would have defined second and third as type Variant, and only the variable fourth would have been an Integer.

When declaring external procedures using the Declare statement, VB.NET does not support the As Any type declaration clause. All parameters must have a specific type declaration.

### Variable initialization

VB.NET permits the initialization of variables on the same line as their declaration. The statement:

```
Dim x As Integer = 5
```

declares an Integer variable x and initializes its value to 5. More than one variable declaration and assignment may appear on a single line:

```
Dim x As Integer = 6, y As Integer = 9
```

### Variable scope changes

In VB 6, a variable that is declared *anywhere* in a procedure has *procedure scope*; the variable is visible to all code in the procedure. In VB.NET, if a variable is

defined inside a *code block* (a set of statements that is terminated by an End...,
Loop, Next, or similar block closing keyword), then the variable has *block-level
scope*; it is visible only within that block. For example, consider the following
VB.NET code:

```
Public Sub Test(sourceValue As Integer)
    If (sourceValue <> 0) Then
        Dim inverseResult As Integer
        inverseResult = 1 / sourceValue
    End If
    ' ----- The next line is invalid.
    MsgBox(CStr(inverseResult))
End Sub
```

In this code, the variable inverseResult is not recognized outside the block in
which it is defined, so the final statement will produce a compile-time error.

The *lifetime* of a local variable is always that of the entire procedure, even if the
variable's scope is block-level. This implies that if a block is entered more than
once, a block-level variable will retain its value from the previous time through the
code block.

### Arrays and array declarations

VB 6 permitted you to define the lower bound of a specific array, as well as the
default lower bound of arrays with a lower bound that was not explicitly specified. In VB.NET, the lower bound of every array dimension is zero and cannot be
changed. The following examples show how to declare a one-dimensional array,
with or without an explicit size and initialization:

```
' Implicit constructor: No initial size and no initialization
Dim days() As Integer

' Explicit constructor: No initial size and no initialization
Dim days() As Integer = New Integer() {}

' Implicit constructor: Initial size but no initialization
Dim days(6) As Integer

' Explicit constructor: Initial size but no initialization
Dim days() As Integer = New Integer(6) {}

' Implicit constructor: Initial size implied by initialization
Dim days() As Integer = {1, 2, 3, 4, 5, 6, 7}

' Explicit constructor: Initial size and initialization
Dim days() As Integer = New Integer(6) {1, 2, 3, 4, 5, 6, 7}
```

In the declaration:

```
Dim arrayName(upperBound) As arrayType
```

the number *upperBound* is the upper bound of the array. Thus, the array has size
*upperBound* + 1, with elements 0 through *upperBound*.

Multidimensional arrays are declared similarly. The following example declares and initializes a two-dimensional array:

```
Dim someData(,) As Integer = {{1, 2, 3}, {4, 5, 6}}
```

The following code displays the contents of that array:

```
Debug.Write(someData(0, 0))
Debug.Write(someData(0, 1))
Debug.WriteLine(someData(0, 2))
Debug.Write(someData(1, 0))
Debug.Write(someData(1, 1))
Debug.WriteLine(someData(1, 2))

' ----- The output is:
123
456
```

In VB.NET, all arrays are dynamic; there is no such thing as a fixed-size array. The declared size should be thought of simply as the initial size of the array, which is subject to change using the ReDim statement. The number of dimensions of an array cannot be changed.

The ReDim statement in VB.NET cannot be used for array declaration but only for array resizing, which differs from the functionality in VB 6. All arrays must be declared initially using the Dim (or equivalent) statement.

### Structure/user-defined type declarations

In VB 6, a structure or user-defined type is declared using the Type...End Type syntax. In VB.NET, the Type statement isn't supported. Structures are declared using the Structure...End Structure construct. Each member of this structure must be assigned an access modifier, which can be Public, Protected, Friend, Protected Friend, or Private. (The Dim keyword is equivalent to Public in this context.)

For instance, the VB 6 user-defined type:

```
Type RECT
    Left As Long
    Top As Long
    Right As Long
    Bottom As Long
End Type
```

has the following equivalent VB.NET declaration:

```
Structure RECT
    Public Left As Integer
    Public Top As Integer
    Public Right As Integer
    Public Bottom As Integer
End Structure
```

VB.NET Structure types are far more reaching than their VB 6 user-defined type counterparts. Structures in .NET have many properties in common with classes, such as the presence of members (like properties and methods). Structures are discussed in detail in Chapter 4.

## Logical and Bitwise Operators

Eqv and Imp, two infrequently used VB 6 logical and bitwise operators, have been removed from VB.NET.

In VB 6, Eqv is the equivalence operator. As a logical operator, it returns True if both operands are either True or False, but it returns False if one is True while the other is False. As a bitwise operator, it returns 1 for a given bit if both source bits are the same (that is, if both are 1 or both are 0), but it returns 0 if they are different. In VB.NET, Eqv can be replaced with the Equal To (=) comparison operator for logical operations. If you require the true bitwise result of the equivalence operation, use the following code.

```
Public Function BitwiseEqv(ByVal x1 As Byte, ByVal x2 As Byte) As Byte
    ' ----- Functional equivalent to the VB 6 'Eqv' keyword.
    Dim bit1 As Byte
    Dim bit2 As Byte
    Dim result As Byte = 0
    Dim counter as Integer

    ' ----- Scan each of the eight bits.
    For counter = 0 To 7
        ' ----- Compare this specific bit.
        bit1 = x1 And 2 ^ counter
        bit2 = x2 And 2 ^ counter
        If (bit1 = bit2) Then result += 2 ^ counter
    Next counter
    Return result
End Function
```

In VB 6, Imp is the implication operator. As a logical operator, it returns True in all cases except when the first operand is True and the second is False. As a bitwise operator, it returns 1 in a bit position in all cases, except when that positional bit in the first operand is 1 and the same bit in the second operand is 0. In VB.NET, Imp can be replaced with a combination of the Not and Or operators for logical operations. For example, the statement:

```
result = (Not flag1) Or flag2
```

is equivalent to the VB 6 statement:

```
result = flag1 Imp flag2
```

For bitwise operations, a bit-by-bit comparison is again necessary. The following code implements the missing functionality.

```
Public Function BitwiseImp(ByVal x1 As Byte, _
        ByVal x2 As Byte) As Byte
    ' ----- Functional equivalent to the VB 6 'Imp' keyword.
    Dim bit1 As Byte
    Dim bit2 As Byte
    Dim result As Byte = 0
    Dim counter As Integer

    ' ----- Scan each of the eight bits.
    For counter = 0 to 7
```

```
      bit1 = Not(x1) And 2 ^ counter
      bit2 = x2 And 2 ^ counter
      If (bit1 Or bit2) Then result += 2 ^ counter
   Next counter
   Return result
End Function
```

Many programming languages support *short-circuiting*, which allows the language to abort evaluation of a complex conditional expression early when it is already clear what the final logical result will be. As expressions are evaluated from left to right, once the eventual truth or falsity of the whole condition is known, the remaining expressions are skipped. For instance, if a condition includes two expressions joined with an "And" logical operator, short-circuiting ceases evaluation if the first expression evaluates to False, since the value of the second expression will not impact the final result.

Visual Basic 6 did not support short-circuiting, but VB.NET now supports it through the AndAlso and OrElse logical operators. If these operators are used (instead of the non-short-circuiting And and Or logical operators), the condition may exit early if warranted. For example, consider the statement:

```
   If (X AndAlso Y) Then
```

If X is False, then Y is not evaluated, because the entire statement is False regardless of the truth value of Y.

VB.NET introduced new operators to support short-circuiting rather than simply modifying the behavior of And and Or, largely for reasons of compatibility. In most cases, short-circuiting has no effect on a program's execution other than an improvement in performance and an increase in robustness (expressions that are not evaluated cannot raise errors or consume CPU cycles). However, care must be taken when the second expression includes function calls. For example:

```
   If Increment(x) AndAlso Increment(y) Then
      ' ----- Do something.
   End If
   ...

   Private Function Increment(ByRef n As Integer) As Boolean
      If (n < 10) Then
         n += 1
         Return True
      Else
         Return False
      End If
   End Function
```

The original condition is somewhat ambiguous, since y will be incremented only sometimes. In such cases, it may be preferable to avoid short-circuiting with AndAlso in favor of the And operator.

## Changes Related to Procedures

VB.NET includes several changes in the way that procedures are defined and called, with clearer and more consistent results.

---

## Calling a procedure

In VB 6, parentheses are required around arguments when making function calls, but when calling subroutines, argument parentheses are only used with the Call keyword. In VB.NET, parentheses are always required around a *non-empty* argument list for any procedure call—function or subroutine. (In subroutine calls, the Call statement is still optional.) When calling a procedure with no arguments, empty parentheses are optional.

## Default method of passing arguments

In VB 6, if the parameters to a function or subroutine are not explicitly prefaced with the ByVal or ByRef keywords, arguments are passed to that routine *by reference*, and modifications made to the argument in the function or subroutine are reflected in the variable's value once control returns to the calling routine. In VB.NET, if the ByRef or ByVal keyword is not used with a parameter, the argument is passed to the routine *by value*, and modifications made to the argument in the function or subroutine are discarded once control returns to the calling routine.

## Optional arguments

In VB 6, a procedure parameter can be declared as Optional without specifying a default value. For optional Variant parameters, the IsMissing function determines whether the parameter is present. In VB.NET, an optional parameter must declare a default value, which is passed to the routine if the calling code does not supply an argument. The IsMissing function is not supported. The following example shows an optional parameter declaration in VB.NET:

```
Public Sub Calculate(Optional ByVal silent As Boolean = False)
```

## GoSub and Return statements

In VB 6, the GoSub and Return statements provide support for a subroutine-like block of code within a larger procedure. VB.NET no longer supports this construct. The GoSub statement has been removed from the language, and the Return statement is now used to exit a procedure immediately, with the option of setting the return value, as demonstrated in the following VB.NET code:

```
Public Function SafeDivide(numerator As Decimal, _
    denominator As Decimal) As Decimal
' ----- Division with a check for divide-by-zero.
If (denominator = 0) Then
    Return 0
Else
    Return numerator / denominator
End If
End Function
```

## Passing Property parameters in procedures

In VB 6, properties passed as arguments to procedures were always passed by value, even if the procedure defined the argument as ByRef.

```
Public Sub ShrinkToHalf(ByRef lSize As Long)
    lSize = CLng(lSize / 2)
End Sub

' ----- In some other routine...
Call ShrinkToHalf(Text1.Height)
```

In VB 6, `Text1.Height` remains unaltered by the `ShrinkToHalf` routine. In VB.NET, properties passed to `ByRef` parameters will be updated to reflect any changes made within the procedure.

### ParamArray parameters

In VB 6, a parameter marked with the `ParamArray` keyword only accepts arguments through the `Variant` data type, and the arguments are passed `ByRef`. In VB.NET, `ParamArray` parameters are always passed `ByVal`, and the parameters in the array may be of any data type.

## Miscellaneous Language Changes

VB.NET includes several miscellaneous language changes that don't fit into other broad categories.

### Line numbers

Visual Basic .NET requires that every line number be followed immediately by a colon (:). A statement can optionally follow the colon. In VB 6, nonnumeric line labels had to include a colon, but numeric line numbers did not.

### On GoSub and On GoTo statements

The `On...GoSub` and `On...GoTo` value-based branching constructs are no longer supported. However, VB.NET still supports the `On Error GoTo` statement.

### While statement

VB 6 included a `While...Wend` conditional loop construct. Although VB.NET retains this statement, it replaces the `Wend` keyword with the `End While` keyword pair.

# Changes to Programming Elements

VB.NET has removed support for several programming elements because the underlying .NET Framework Class Library and the Common Language Runtime (CLR) contain equivalent functionality. Other syntax and usage changes have been made as well.

## Constants

Many predefined constants available in VB 6, such as the familiar `vbCrLf` constant, are now part of VB.NET's *Microsoft.VisualBasic.Constants* class. They can be used in VB.NET just as they were used in VB 6. However, some constants, such as the color constants vbRed and vbBlue, are no longer directly supported. The color constants are part of the *System.Drawing* namespace's *Color* structure and are accessed as follows:

```
Me.BackColor = System.Drawing.Color.BlanchedAlmond
```

When using most constants, other than those in the *Microsoft.VisualBasic. Constants* class, you will need to include some or all of their namespace and class name prefix. For example, the vbYes constant in VB 6 continues to exist in VB.NET as a member of the MsgBoxResult enumeration. It can be used as follows:

```
If (MsgBoxResult.Yes = MsgBox("OK to proceed?", ...
```

For a list of built-in constants and enumerations, see Appendix C.

## String Functions

The String function has been removed from VB.NET. Its functionality now appears as part of the String data-type constructor.

```
Dim giveThemAnA As New String("A"c, 5)
```

which defines a string containing five As. The c modifier in "A"c indicates a character literal (data type Char) as opposed to a standard one-character string (data type String).

## Emptiness

In VB 6, the Empty keyword indicated an uninitialized variable, and the Null keyword was used when a variable contained no valid data. VB.NET does not support either keyword but uses the Nothing keyword in both of these cases. The Null keyword continues to be a reserved word in VB.NET, but it has no functionality.

The IsEmpty function is no longer supported in VB.NET; use the IsNothing function instead.

## Graphical Functionality

The *System.Drawing* namespace contains classes that implement graphical methods. Its *Graphics* class contains methods such as *DrawEllipse* and *DrawLine*. As a result, the VB 6 Circle and Line methods, associated with Forms and other drawing surfaces, have been removed.

VB 6's PSet and Scale methods are no longer supported, and they have no direct equivalents in the *System.Drawing* namespace.

## Mathematical Functionality

Mathematical functions are implemented as members of .NET's *System.Math* class. All VB 6 math functions, such as the trigonometric functions, have been dropped from the VB.NET language itself, replaced with members of *System. Math*. Typical using is:

```
result = Math.Cos(1)
```

The Round function has been replaced by the *Round* method of the *System.Math* class.

## Diagnostics

The *System.Diagnostics* namespace provides classes related to programming diagnostics. Most notably, the VB 6 Debug object is gone, but its functionality is implemented in the *System.Diagnostics.Debug* class, which has methods such as *Write*, *WriteLine* (replacing *Print*), *WriteIf*, and *WriteLineIf*.

### Miscellaneous

Here are a few additional changes to consider.

- The VB 6 DoEvents statement has been replaced by the *DoEvents* method of the *System.Windows.Forms.Application* class.

- The VB 6 IsNull and IsObject functions have been replaced by the IsDBNull and IsReference methods respectively, both part of the *Information* class in the *Microsoft.VisualBasic* namespace.

- Several VB 6 functions have two versions: a string version (such as Trim$) and a variant version (Trim). In VB.NET, these functions are replaced by a single overloaded function. The Trim function can now be called directly using either a String or Object argument.

## Obsolete Programming Elements

Several features of Visual Basic 6 are no longer supported by Visual Basic .NET or have been replaced by equivalent functionality elsewhere in the .NET Framework. See Appendix G for a listing of these unsupported or redirected elements.

## Structured Exception Handling

VB.NET has added a significant new technique for error handling. Along with the traditional unstructured error handling through On Error GoTo statements, VB.NET adds *structured exception handling*, using the Try...Catch...Finally syntax supported in other languages, such as C++. This new syntax is discussed in detail in Chapter 11.

## Changes in Object Orientation

Visual Basic has implemented some features of object-oriented programming (OOP) since Version 4. However, the OOP changes made between VB 6 and VB.NET are very significant. Some people did not consider VB 6 (or earlier versions) to be a true object-oriented programming language. VB.NET 2002 includes support for most major OOP concepts, and the general changes introduced with VB.NET appear in this section. Chapter 3 includes a general overview of OOP concepts and introduces VB.NET's specific OOP implementation.

# Inheritance

VB.NET supports object-oriented *inheritance* (but not multiple inheritance). This means that a class can derive from another (base) class, thereby inheriting all of the properties, methods, events, and other types of the base class. Since .NET forms are classes, inheritance applies to them as well. This allows new forms to be created based on existing control-laden forms.

# Overloading

VB.NET supports a language feature known as *function overloading*. Within a class, a single method can include multiple argument signature variations. That is, the number and data type of each method argument can vary between the different versions, despite the method having the same name in each version. The following declarations are valid in the same class.

```
Public Overloads Sub OpenFile( )
    ' ----- Prompt user for file to open, and open it.
End Sub

Public Overloads Sub OpenFile(ByVal fileToOpen As String)
    ' ----- Open the specified file.
End Sub
```

# Object Creation

VB 6 supports a form of object creation called *implicit object creation*. If an object variable is declared using the New keyword, as in:

```
Dim obj As New SomeClass
```

then the object is created the first time it is used in code. More specifically, the object variable is initially given the value Nothing, and then every time the variable is encountered during code execution, VB checks to see if the variable is Nothing. If so, the object is created at that time. (This behavior was changed somewhat in a Visual Studio 6.0 service pack.)

VB.NET does not support implicit object creation. If an object variable contains Nothing when it is encountered, it is left unchanged, and no object is created.

VB.NET supports object creation in the declaration statement, as with:

```
Dim someInstance As SomeClass = New SomeClass
```

or the shorter equivalent:

```
Dim someInstance As New SomeClass
```

If the object's class constructor takes parameters, they can be included, as with:

```
Dim someInstance As SomeClass = New SomeClass(arg1, arg2, ...)
```

or the shorter equivalent:

```
Dim someInstance As New SomeClass(arg1, arg2, ...)
```

# Properties

There have been a few changes in how VB handles properties, particularly default properties and property declarations.

## Default properties

VB 6 supports default properties. For instance, if txtQuote is a TextBox control, then:

```
txtQuote = "To be or not to be"
```

assigns the string "To be or not to be" to the default Text property of txtQuote.

However, this can sometimes lead to ambiguity. For example, if TextBox1 and TextBox2 are TextBox controls on a form, what does the following statement do?

```
TextBox1 = TextBox2
```

In VB 6, this assigns the default property of TextBox2 (the Text property) to the same property in TextBox1, although it looks like the object itself is being assigned. Object assignment in VB 6 uses the Set keyword, as in the following syntax:

```
Set TextBox1 = TextBox2
```

But in VB.NET, the Set keyword is no longer used for object assignment. Therefore, to avoid any ambiguity, default properties in VB.NET are not supported *unless* the property takes one or more parameters. In VB.NET, the line:

```
TextBox1 = TextBox2
```

is an object assignment statement. To copy the contents of the Text property, the following syntax is required:

```
TextBox1.Text = TextBox2.Text
```

For object variable *comparison*, VB.NET uses the Is operator rather than the Equal To (=) comparison operator, as in:

```
If (TextBox1 Is TextBox2) Then
```

or:

```
If Not (TextBox1 Is TextBox2) Then
```

## Property declarations

In VB 6, properties are defined using Property Let, Property Set, and Property Get procedures. VB.NET uses a modified Property statement syntax.

```
Property Salary( ) As Decimal
    Get
        Salary = employeeSalary
    End Get
    Set(ByVal value As Decimal)
        employeeSalary = value
    End Set
End Property
```

The former differentiation between Property Let and Property Set no longer exists in VB.NET due to default property changes; only Property Set is retained.

VB.NET does not support ByRef property parameters. All property parameters are passed ByVal.

# E

# What's New and Different
# in Visual Basic .NET 2003

If Visual Basic .NET 2002 represented a monumental leap in the path of the Visual Basic language, the 2003 release of Visual Basic .NET was, in many ways, the extra step you take to balance yourself after making the first big leap. VB.NET 2003 was a minor upgrade to the language, as acknowledged by its internal version number, 7.1. Its release paralleled the upgrade to the .NET Framework, also short-stepping to just Version 1.1.

This is not to say that there were no benefits to the programmer in this release. There were clearly improvements in terms of both performance and usability, especially through changes made to the Visual Studio environment. However, changes to the Visual Basic language itself were limited.

## Language Changes in VB.NET 2003

Visual Basic .NET 2003 included two changes of note in its implementation of the Visual Basic language.

### Bit Shift Operators

The collection of bitwise operators increased in 2003 with the addition of the bit shift operators, << (Shift Left) and >> (Shift Right). Also added were their assignment operator equivalents, <<= and >>=. These operators are discussed in Chapter 5.

### Declaration in For Loops

Visual Basic .NET 2002 introduced block-level declaration to the language, allowing you to use Dim statements within an If statement, a loop, or other block constructs and have that variable apply in scope only to that block. The other benefit of such usage was that a local variable could be defined at the moment of its first use in a procedure. However, this was not true for loop variables used to control For statements.

In the 2003 release, For statements can now include a declaration for the looping variable directly in the For statement. The new syntax adds an As clause to the loop variable name. The following VB.NET 2002 code:

```
Dim counter As Integer
For counter = 1 To 10
    MsgBox(counter)
Next counter
```

can now be written in VB.NET 2003 as:

```
For counter As Integer = 1 To 10
    MsgBox(counter)
Next counter
```

As with block variables, these For loop variables have valid scope only within the block (the For statement block, in this case). Also, if you want to add a second loop at the same block level to your code using the same variable name, you must include the As clause to that second loop, as its definition does not carry from one loop to the next.

This new syntax can also be used with For Each statements.

```
For Each player As TeamMember In baseballTeam
    MsgBox(player.Name)
Next player
```

# F

# What's New and Different in Visual Basic 2005

The 2005 release of Visual Basic includes major enhancements over the previous 2003 edition. Its internal version number is 8.0, and it matches a related major update of the .NET Framework, now at Version 2.0. Microsoft also removed the ".NET" term from the name of each product in the Visual Studio family. Visual Basic .NET is now known officially as Visual Basic.

This release includes many usability enhancements, many of which are realized only when using the Visual Studio 2005 product. For instance, Visual Basic now includes *Edit and Continue*, a feature available in all pre-.NET versions of Visual Basic, which allows source code to be modified in an actively running program. The changes are immediately reflected in the running code. A parallel change, *design-time expression evaluation*, processes individual source-code statements without the need to fully build an application (although Visual Studio actually builds a mini-application in the background to evaluate the expression).

The Visual Studio environment also includes *enhanced error reporting*, including recommendations on changing errant VB code. *Code snippets*, *auto-completion* features, and enhanced project and item *templates* also support faster code development.

While these and other Visual Studio-level enhancements make Visual Basic a more productive language, this appendix focuses on the language enhancements included in the 2005 release.

Visual Basic 2005 includes several new keywords that may have been used as variable or member names in your pre-2005 Visual Basic code. This release includes a command-line utility, *vb7to8.exe*, which checks existing Visual Basic code for keyword conflicts.

# Enhancements of Existing Functionality

Some of the changes included in Visual Basic 2005 modify or enhance existing Visual Basic features.

## Custom Event Statement

Events in Visual Basic are linked to event handlers either through the AddHandler statement or with the Handles clause on a member declaration. The process of adding and removing handlers is fully managed by the framework, as is the process of calling handlers when events occur.

Visual Basic 2005 adds a new *custom events* feature that allows your code to partner with the .NET Framework in the management of adding and removing handler, and in calling event handlers.

The general syntax of a custom event handler is as follows:

```
accessModifier Custom Event eventName As EventHandler
    AddHandler(ByVal value As EventHandler)
        ' ----- Special code when adding handlers.
    End AddHandler

    RemoveHandler(ByVal value As EventHandler)
        ' ----- Special code when removing handlers.
    End RemoveHandler

    RaiseEvent(ByVal sender As Object, ByVal e As System.EventArgs)
        ' ----- Special code when raising the event.
    End RaiseEvent
End Event
```

Your own custom code can be included in any of the three event procedures. Custom events are discussed in Chapter 8.

## Data-Type Additions

Visual Basic 2005 includes four new data types: SByte (signed byte), UShort (unsigned short), UInteger (unsigned integer), and ULong (unsigned long). Actually, these four data types existed in the .NET Framework from the initial release of .NET and could even be used from Visual Basic code. However, Visual Basic wrappers were not included for these data types as they were for all of the other core data types. These four new data types complete Visual Basic's implementation of the Base Class Library's basic data types.

These four data types are not compliant with the minimal *Common Language Specification*. Components and applications using that standard may not be compatible with applications that use SByte, UShort, UInteger, or ULong.

Additional information about these data types is available in Chapter 4.

# Global Keyword

If your application includes a namespace named something like *MyCompany. System*, and you use the `Imports MyCompany` statement in your code file, any reference to "System" becomes ambiguous. To resolve possible conflicts such as these, Visual Basic 2005 includes a new `Global` keyword.

When potential conflicts exist, the `Global` keyword can be used to provide a true top-level reference to the desired namespace-based type. To access the .NET-supplied *System* namespace, reference `Global.System`, which removes any ambiguity conflicts with *MyCompany.System*.

# IsNot Operator

Visual Basic has always included an `Is` operator, used to establish the equivalence of an object with another object or type. This operator is most often used in `If` statements.

```
If (someInstance Is SomeClass) Then
```

The operator is also used to test for an uninitialized object.

```
If (someInstance Is Nothing) Then
```

However, to reverse the statement to test for something that the object "is not," the `Not` operator had to be used separately.

```
If Not (someInstance Is SomeClass) Then
```

Visual Basic 2005 adds a new `IsNot` operator.

```
If (someInstance IsNot SomeClass) Then
```

The `IsNot` operator is functionally equivalent to the combined `Is` and `Not` operators, but it was added to increase readability of the source code.

# Lower Bound in Array Declarations

Pre-.NET versions of Visual Basic allowed both a lower bound and an upper bound in the sizing of an array dimension.

```
Dim dataArray(0 To 5) As Integer
```

Visual Basic .NET 2002 removed the lower bound declaration and the `To` keyword, since all arrays had a lower bound of zero.

```
Dim dataArray(5) As Integer
```

The 2005 update to Visual Basic restores the lower bound element and the `To` keyword; they can now be included, although they are optional. When included, the lower bound must still always be zero.

# Partial Types

In most Visual Basic code, each source-code file includes a single class or other similar type. The language also permitted any number of classes or types to appear in a single source code file, but a class could not be split between multiple source-code files. This has changed with the 2005 release.

Visual Basic now permits classes and structures to be split across multiple source-code files in the same project. This change permits Microsoft to move the Windows Forms-specific initialization code, previously contained in a #Region block, into its own source code file.

To use this feature, begin a class or structure definition with the new Partial keyword.

```
Partial Friend Class Employee
    ...
End Class
```

At least one of the class portions must include the Partial keyword. See the "Partial Keyword" entry in Chapter 12 for additional usage information.

## Property Accessor Enhancements

In Visual Basic .NET 2002 and 2003, the Get and Set portions of a Property member always had the same level of access, such as Public or Private. The 2005 update to the language allows each of the two portions to have different levels of accessibility.

The syntax is generally unchanged, with a primary access modifier included with the Property statement itself. But an additional access modifier can be added to the start of the Get or Set statement.

```
Public Property Name( ) As String
    Get
        Return fullName
    End Get
    Friend Set(ByVal value As String)
        fullName = value
    End Set
End Property
```

The additional access modifier must always be more restrictive than the general modifier used for the Property statement itself.

## TryCast Function

Visual Basic permits general conversions of one class or data type to another using either the CType function or the DirectCast function. These functions both generate exceptions if the conversion cannot be performed successfully.

While an exception is a clear indication of a failed conversion, it is not the most elegant or straightforward, as you must set up explicit error handlers for such conditions. Therefore, Visual Basic 2005 includes a new TryCast function. It works just like a CType or DirectCast function, but it returns Nothing on failed conversions instead of generating an exception.

```
newObject = TryCast(origObject, NewType)
```

# The 'My' Namespace

One of the biggest features included with Visual Basic 2005 is the new *My* Namespace feature. This feature adds a new namespace named *My* at the top of the namespace hierarchy, parallel with the *System* namespace. This namespace contains a conveniently arranged subset of the features available in the Framework Class Library, designed to be as easy as possible to use. The *My* namespace is a hierarchy and contains different branches covering major subsets of functionality. For instance, the *My.Computer.Network* portion of the hierarchy provides access to properties and methods that relate to the local computer's network.

Most of the *My* namespace is static, with specific features permanently located at known locations. However, parts of the hierarchy are dynamic, with different items included depending on the configuration of the system and the application. One of these dynamic sections, *My.Forms*, makes available all of the forms in the current application. This collection changes dynamically as forms are added to the application, either at design time or at runtime.

One use of the *My.Forms* dynamic collection is the ability to reference a form directly and display it on-screen without first creating an instance of the form. The general syntax to display a form in this manner is:

```
My.Forms.Form1.Show( )
```

The same statement also appears in a simplified form:

```
Form1.Show( )
```

which is quite similar to the syntax used in VB 6. These *default instances* simplify the accessibility of forms.

Another new 2005 feature works hand in hand with some of the *My* Namespace feature elements. Portions of the namespace expose application-wide events, events that impact the entire application and not simply one control or class. To support these events, Visual Basic includes a new "application framework," a set of features that simplify the management of an application's lifetime, from startup to shutdown.

All of the *My* Namespace features are documented in Chapter 13. A hierarchical listing of the elements included in the *My* Namespace hierarchy appears in Appendix B.

# Other New Features

Some features included in Visual Basic 2005 are completely new, unrelated to any existing 2003 version features.

## ClickOnce Installation

Visual Studio has included features to develop Windows Installer-based setup projects since the initial .NET release. The 2005 releases of the .NET Framework and Visual Studio add a new installation type called *ClickOnce* that provides an alternative to the standard installation process. While not officially part of Visual Basic, this new feature impacts Visual Basic as if it were a language enhancement.

Normally, the installation of complex applications requires the person performing the installation to be at least a local administrator on the workstation. However, there may be instances where this is neither convenient nor possible. ClickOnce applications can be installed by any user without the assistance of a local administrator, although there may be limits on the system resources available to the application. ClickOnce applications can also be configured to support automatic updates of installed components from a web site or server.

## Continue Statement

Visual Basic includes various loops, including For, For Each, and Do...Loop constructs. It has always been possible to exit a loop immediately using a related Exit statement, such as Exit For. But there was no feature that would let you immediately skip to the next pass through the loop. Such an action required complex conditional constructs, or at least a GoTo statement.

```
For counter = 1 To 10
    ' ----- Do some processing here, then
    If (someCondition) Then GoTo NextIteration
    ' ----- More code here.

NextIteration:
    ' ----- This label exists simply to skip to the next loop counter.
Next counter
```

Visual Basic 2005 includes a new Continue statement that returns to the top of the loop with the next iteration in place, as if the current pass through the loop had been completed successfully.

```
For counter = 1 To 10
    ' ----- Do some processing here, then
    If (someCondition) Then Continue For
    ' ----- More code here.
Next counter
```

## Generics

The collection classes included in the .NET Framework (through *System.Collections*) and the Visual Basic Collection class (through *Microsoft.VisualBasic.Collection*) are great for managing a lot of objects, but each collection stores the objects in a weakly typed manner. You can put any type of object into the collection; each object you add to a collection instance can be of a unique type.

Visual Basic 2005 adds a new feature called *generics* that allows you to create a strongly typed collection. A collection, once bound to a specific class through the generics declaration, can only be used to store that specific class or its descendants; any other use will generate an exception. Several new generics-specific collection classes appear in the *System.Collections.Generic* namespace.

A collection is bound to a type using the new Of keyword.

```
Dim oneClassOnly As System.Collections.Generic.List(Of Employee)
```

You can also use generics in the design of your own custom classes. Chapter 10 discusses the use and syntax of generics.

## Operator Overloading

Visual Basic has supported method overloading in classes since the initial .NET release of the language. Other languages, such as C#, also supported *operator overloading*, where standard language operators, such as the + addition operator, could be given custom meanings when used with specific classes. Visual Basic now includes this feature in its 2005 release.

Consider a class that manages video media. The code to join together two portions of video would likely be quite complex, but the *syntax* to join the videos could be straightforward.

```
Dim clip1, clip2, clip3 As VideoClip
...
clip3 = clip1 + clip2
```

The VideoClip class would include an overloaded operator definition that provides the logic to perform the custom addition.

```
Friend Class VideoClip
    Public Shared Operator +(ByVal firstClip As VideoClip, _
        ByVal secondClip As VideoClip) As VideoClip
        ' ----- Append one clip to another.
        Dim largerClip As New VideoClip
        ' ...more code here...
        Return largerClip
    End Operator
End Class
```

Your class can also define custom conversions from one class or data type to another by overloading the CType conversion function. Operator overloading is discussed in the "Operator Overloading" section of Chapter 5.

## Using Statement

Some classes acquire resources that must be manually released when an instance of the class is no longer needed. This is done by calling the class's *Dispose* method. Visual Basic 2005 includes the new Using statement to simplify the process of resource acquisition and release.

The Using statement is a block construct that includes code at the start that acquires the resource to use. For instance, "pens" used to draw on the display screen or other drawing surface, defined in the *System.Drawing.Pen* class, must be disposed of when no longer needed. This is normally done with a separate call to the class's *Dispose* method. But it can also be accomplished in a single Using statement.

```
Using redPen As System.Drawing.Pen = _
    New System.Drawing.Pen(Brushes.Red)
    ' ----- Add drawing code here.
End Using
```

The redPen instance is guaranteed to be disposed of properly, even if you jump out of the Using block abnormally. In this way, Using acts somewhat like the Finally block in a Try...Catch statement.

For more information on implementing the Using statement in your code, see its entry in Chapter 12.

## XML Comments

Visual Basic 2005 includes a new *XML Comments* feature that lets you decorate your class members with special XML-formatted comments. Visual Studio recognizes and uses these comments to enhance the development environment. To use XML comments, place the insertion point on a blank line in your code, just above a method definition, then type three single-quote marks. Immediately, even before pressing the Enter key, the following template (or one similar to it) appears.

```
''' <summary>
'''
''' </summary>
''' <param name="sender"></param>
''' <param name="e"></param>
''' <remarks></remarks>
```

Once these parts are filled in with the appropriate content, Visual Studio uses the information to display more verbose IntelliSense details concerning the related method. It also exports the XML content to a documentation file during the compile of the assembly.

# G

# VB 6 Language Elements No Longer Supported

This appendix provides an alphabetical list of language elements that are present in VB 6 but are not supported by Visual Basic .NET 2002, or in subsequent versions of the language. Several math-related functions, formerly part of the Visual Basic language but now located in the *System.Math* namespace, are not included in this appendix.

*Table G-1. VB 6 elements no longer supported*

| Element | Description |
|---------|-------------|
| Array Function | Returns a variant array with elements that contain the values passed as arguments to the function |
| Any Keyword | Used in `Declare` statements to indicate generic parameter data types; all parameters must now have a declared data type |
| AscB Function | Returns an integer representing the character code of the first byte of a string |
| Atn Function | Returns the arctangent of a number; replaced by the *Atan* method in the *System.Math* class |
| Calendar Property | Determines whether a project should use the Gregorian or Hijri calendar; replaced by classes in the *System.Globalization* namespace |
| CCur Function | Converts an expression into a `Currency` data type |
| ChrB Function | Returns the character corresponding to an 8-bit character code |
| Circle Method | Draws circles on a form, *PictureBox* control, or other drawing surface; replaced by features in the *System.Drawing* namespace |
| Close Statement | Closes a file opened with the Open statement |
| Currency Data Type | Data type for accurate financial calculations; replaced by the `Decimal` data type |
| CVar Function | Converts an expression into a `Variant` data type |
| CVDate Function | Returns a `Date` variant |
| CVErr Function | Returns an error from a procedure |
| Date, Date$ Functions | Returns the current system date; replaced by the *DateTime.Today* property |
| Date Statement | Sets the current system date; replaced by the *DateTime.Today* property |

| Element | Description |
| --- | --- |
| Debug.Assert Statement | Conditionally suspends execution based on a Boolean test; consider replacement with the *Debug.Assert* method in the *System.Diagnostics* namespace |
| Debug.Print Statement | Sends output to the Immediate window; consider replacement with the *Debug.Write-Line* method and similar methods in the *System.Diagnostics* namespace |
| DefBool Statement | Defines all otherwise undeclared variables beginning with particular alphabetical characters as Boolean |
| DefByte Statement | Defines all otherwise undeclared variables beginning with particular alphabetical characters as Byte |
| DefCur Statement | Defines all otherwise undeclared variables beginning with particular alphabetical characters as Currency |
| DefDate Statement | Defines all otherwise undeclared variables beginning with particular alphabetical characters as Date |
| Defdbl Statement | Defines all otherwise undeclared variables beginning with particular alphabetical characters as Double |
| Defdec Statement | Defines all otherwise undeclared variables beginning with particular alphabetical characters as Decimal |
| Defint Statement | Defines all otherwise undeclared variables beginning with particular alphabetical characters as Integer |
| DefLng Statement | Defines all otherwise undeclared variables beginning with particular alphabetical characters as Long |
| Defobj Statement | Defines all otherwise undeclared variables beginning with particular alphabetical characters as Object |
| Defsng Statement | Defines all otherwise undeclared variables beginning with particular alphabetical characters as Single |
| Defstr Statement | Defines all otherwise undeclared variables beginning with particular alphabetical characters as String |
| DefVar Statement | Defines all otherwise undeclared variables beginning with particular alphabetical characters as Variant |
| DoEvents Statement | Releases control to the application's message queue; replaced with the *DoEvents* method in the *Windows.Forms* namespace, or in *Visual Basic 2005* with the *My.Application.DoEvents* method |
| Empty Keyword | Indicates an empty or uninitialized data value; replaced by the Nothing keyword |
| Eqv Operator | Represents a logical equivalence operator; use the Equal To (=) comparison operator instead |
| Error Function | Returns a standard description of a particular error code |
| Get Statement | Retrieves data from a disk file into a program variable; replaced by the *FileGet* function |
| GoSub...Return Statement | Passes execution to, and returns from, a block subroutine within a procedure |
| Imestatus Function | Returns the state of the Input Method Editor, used for localized or specialized data input |
| Imp Operator | Represents a logical implication operator; use the expression "(Not A) Or B" instead |
| Initialize Event | Fires when an object is first used; use class constructors instead |
| InputB, InputB$ Functions | Reads a designated number of characters from a file opened in input or binary mode |
| Instancing Property | Defines how instances of a class are created; specify instancing in the class constructor instead |
| InStrB Function | Returns the position of a particular byte in a binary string |
| IsEmpty Function | Determines if a variable has been initialized; replaced by the IsNothing function |

*Table G-1. VB 6 elements no longer supported (continued)*

| Element | Description |
|---|---|
| IsMissing Function | Determines whether an argument has been passed to a procedure |
| Isnull Function | Indicates whether an expression contains Null data; replaced by the `IsDbNull` function |
| IsObject Function | Indicates whether a variable contains a reference to an object; replaced by the `IsReference` function |
| LeftB, LeftB$ Functions | Returns the leftmost specified number of bytes of binary data |
| LenB Function | Returns the actual size of a user-defined type in memory |
| Let Statement | Assigns the value of an expression to a variable; simply assign values without the `Let` keyword |
| Line Input # Statement | Retrieves a single line from an input file into a variable; replaced by the `LineInput` function |
| Line Method | Draws lines or boxes on a form, *PictureBox* control, or other drawing surface; replaced by features in the *System.Drawing* namespace |
| Load Statement | Loads a form or control into memory for use |
| LoadResData Function | Extracts a string containing a resource included in a resource project; in *Visual Basic 2005*, use the *My.Resources* object |
| LoadResPicture Function | Assigns a graphic from a resource file to the Picture property of an object; in *Visual Basic 2005*, use the *My.Resources* object |
| LoadResString Function | Retrieves a string from a resource file; in *Visual Basic 2005*, use the *My.Resources* object |
| MidB, MidB$ Functions | Returns a specified number of bytes from a larger binary string |
| MidB Statement | Replaces a specified number of bytes in a binary string |
| MTSTransactionMode Property | Indicates whether a component is an MTS object and, if so, determines its level of transaction support |
| Name Statement | Renames a disk file or directory; replaced by the *Rename* function |
| Null Keyword | Indicates a Null data value; use the *DBNull* class in the *System* namespace |
| ObjPtr Function | Returns a pointer to an object |
| On...GoSub Statement | Causes program execution to jump to a block subroutine based on the value of a control variable |
| On...Goto Statement | Causes program execution to jump to a label based on the value of a control variable |
| Open Statement | Opens a file; replaced by the `FileOpen` function |
| Option Base Statement | Defines the default lower bound for arrays dimensioned within a module; all arrays now have a lower bound of 0 |
| Option Private Module Statement | Restricts the scope and visibility of a module to the module's project; use access modifiers in each `Module` statement |
| Persistable Property | Determines whether a class in an ActiveX DLL project can be saved to disk |
| Property Statement | Declares procedures for read and write support of class property values; replaced with an updated `Property` statement syntax |
| PSet Method | Draws a colored point on a form, *PictureBox* control, or other drawing surface; replaced by features in the *System.Drawing* namespace |
| Put Statement | Writes data from a program variable to a disk file; replaced by the `FilePut` function |
| RightB, RightB$ Functions | Returns the rightmost bytes from a binary string |
| Scale Method | Defines a custom coordinate system on a form, *PictureBox* control, or other drawing surface; replaced by features in the *System.Drawing* namespace |
| Set Statement | Assigns an object reference to a variable; simply assign objects without the `Set` keyword |

*Table G-1. VB 6 elements no longer supported (continued)*

| Element | Description |
|---|---|
| Sgn Function | Determines the sign of a number; replaced by the *Sign* method in the *System.Math* class |
| Sqr Function | Calculates the square root of a number; replaced by the *Sqrt* method in the *System. Math* class |
| String Function | Creates a string composed of a single character repeated a given number of times; replaced by special constructors on the String data type |
| StrPtr Function | Returns a pointer to a BSTR (Visual Basic string) |
| Terminate Event | Fires when an object is destroyed; use the *Dispose* and *Finalize* methods of a class instead |
| Time Function | Returns the current system time; replaced by the *DateTime.TimeOfDay* property |
| Time Statement | Sets the current system time; replaced by the *DateTime.TimeOfDay* property |
| Type Statement | Defines a user-defined type; replaced by the Structure statement (or even the Class statement) |
| Unload Statement | Removes a form or a dynamically created member of a control array from memory |
| Variant Data Type | Generic data type; use the Object or other relevant data type instead |
| VarPtr Function | Returns a pointer to a variable |
| Wend Keyword | Terminates a While loop block; replaced by the End While keyword pair |
| Width# Statement | Specifies a virtual file width when working with files opened with the Open statement |

# H

# The Visual Basic Command-Line Compiler

Although the Visual Studio Integrated Development Environment (IDE) is an efficient tool for developing your VB applications, you can actually do all of your development in Notepad (a.k.a. "Visual Notepad") and compile the source code from the Windows command prompt. This appendix details the operation of the Visual Basic compiler, *vbc.exe*.

## Compiler Basics

The compiler uses command-line switches to control its operation. A command-line switch is designated by a slash or hyphen, followed by a keyword. If the keyword takes an argument, it is separated from the keyword by a colon (:). For example:

```
vbc sample1.vb /target:library
```

indicates that the compiler should generate a library (a DLL file) as the output target file type. In this case, target is the switch keyword and library is the argument. If multiple arguments are required, they are usually separated from one another by commas (unless otherwise noted). For example:

```
vbc sample1.vb /r:system.design.dll,system.messaging.dll
```

references the metadata in the *system.design.dll* and *system.messaging.dll* assemblies.

The minimal syntax required to compile a file named *sample1.vb* is:

```
vbc sample1.vb
```

This generates a console-mode application named *sample1.exe*. You can specify the type of component or application you wish to generate by using the /target (or /t) switch. To generate a Windows executable, you enter something like the following at the command line:

```
vbc sample1.vb /t:winexe /r:system.windows.forms.dll
```

The /r switch adds a reference to the assembly that contains the *System.Windows. Forms* namespace. You must explicitly add references to any assemblies your application requires, other than *mscorlib.dll* and *microsoft.visualbasic.dll*.

To compile multiple files, just list them on the command line using a space to separate them. For example:

```
vbc sample1.vb sample2.vb /t:winexe /r:system.windows.forms.dll
```

Since *sample1.vb* is the first file listed, and since a specific output filename is not indicated, the compiler will generate a Windows executable named *sample1.exe*.

# Command-Line Switches

The VB compiler supports the following command-line switches.

## Output Filename and File Type

| Switch | Description |
| --- | --- |
| /out:*<file>* | Defines the output filename. If not present, the output file will have the same root filename as the first input file. *<file>* need not include a file extension. |
| /target:*<type>* <br> or: <br> /t:*<type>* | Defines the type of file to be generated by the compiler. *<type>* can be any of the following keywords: exe (to create a console application), winexe (to create a Windows application), library (to create a library assembly in a DLL), or module (to create a ".netmodule" file that can be added to an assembly). If the switch is not present, *<type>* defaults to exe. |

## Input Files

| Switch | Description |
| --- | --- |
| /addmodule:*<file>* | Includes the ".netmodule" file named *<file>* in the output file. May include multiple comma-separated files. |
| /libpath:*<path>* | Specifies the directory or directories to search for metadata references (which are specified by the /reference switch) that are not found in either the current directory or the CLR's system directory. *<path>* is a list of directories, with multiple directories separated by semicolons. You can also use /*libpath* multiple times to add additional paths. By default, the global assembly cache is automatically searched for references. |
| /recurse:*<[dir\]wildcard>* | Compiles all files in the current directory and its subdirectories according to the wildcard specifications. For example: <br><br> ```vbc /recurse:*.vb /t:library``` <br> ```      /out:mylibrary.lib``` <br><br> If you use the /recurse switch, you do not have to name a specific file to compile; however, if you do, it should not match the specification provided as an argument to the /recurse switch. To start from a directory other than the current directory, prepend the wildcard with the directory path. |
| /reference:*<file>* <br> or: <br> /r:*<file>* | References metadata from the assemblies contained in *<file>*. May include multiple comma-separated files. Each filename in *<file>* must include a file extension. |

| Switch | Description |
|---|---|
| /sdkpath:*<path>* | *New in 2005.* Indicates the location of the main .NET library files *mscorlib.dll* and *microsoft.visualbasic.dll*. *<path>* indicates the folder. This switch is often used with the /netcf switch. |

# Resources

| Switch | Description |
|---|---|
| /linkresource:*<resinfo>*<br>or:<br>/linkres:*<resinfo>* | Links to a managed resource file without embedding it in the output file. *<resinfo>* has the form:<br>    *<file>*[,*<name>*[,public\|private]]<br>where *<file>* is the filename of the resource, *<name>* is the logical name used to load the resource, and the public and private keywords determine whether the resource is public or private in the assembly manifest. By default, resources are public. |
| /resource:*<resinfo>*<br>or:<br>/res:*<resinfo>* | Embeds the managed resource or resources named *<resinfo>* in the output file. *<resinfo>* takes the form:<br>    *<file>*[,*<name>*[,public\|private]]<br>where *<file>* is the filename of the resource, *<name>* is the logical name used to load the resource, and the public and private keywords determine whether the resource is public or private in the assembly manifest. By default, resources are public. The /resource switch cannot be used with the /target:module switch. |
| /win32icon:*<file>* | Indicates the path to the Win32 icon (.*ico*) file for the output file. |
| /win32resource:*<file>* | Indicates the path to a Win32 resource (.*res*) file to insert into the output file. |

# Code Generation

| Switch | Description |
|---|---|
| /netcf | *New in 2005.* Tells the compiler to target the .NET Compact Framework. This switch is often used with the /sdkpath switch. |
| /optimize[+\|-] | Enables (+) or disables ( ) the compiler's code optimizers. Optimizing generates smaller binary files that offer improved efficiency and performance but are more difficult to debug. Its default value is on (+). /optimize is equivalent to /optimize+. |
| /platform:*<type>* | *New in 2005.* Indicates the target processor platform. The <type> argument is one of the following: anycpu (any CPU), x86 (Intel 32-bit compatible processor), x64 (AMD 64-bit processor), or Itanium (Intel 64-bit processor). The default is to target any CPU. |
| /removeintchecks[+\|-] | Enables (-) or disables (+) integer overflow checks. (Yes, the options do seem reversed.) The default is to enable these checks (-), which improves safety but reduces performance. /removeintchecks is equivalent to /removeintchecks+. |

# Debugging

| Switch | Description |
|---|---|
| /debug[+\|-] | Instructs the compiler to include (+) or exclude (-) debugging information in the compiled output file. The default value is /debug-, which suppresses the generation of debug information. /debug+ and /debug are equivalent. |

| Switch | Description |
|---|---|
| /debug:full<br>or:<br>/debug:pdbonly | Defines the form of debugging information output by the compiler. The full option generates full debugging information and allows a debugger to be attached to the running program; this is the default value if debugging is enabled. The pdbonly option generates a debug symbol (*.pdb*) file only. It supports source-code debugging when the program is started in the debugger but displays assembler only when the running program is attached to the debugger. |

## Errors and Warnings

| Switch | Description |
|---|---|
| /bugreport:<*file*> | Generates a file named <*file*> that contains information needed to report a compiler bug. May be used with the /errorreport switch. |
| /errorreport:<*type*> | *New in 2005.* Indicates how internal errors in the compiler should be reported to Microsoft. The values for <type> include: prompt (ask whether to send the error to Microsoft or not, pending security settings), send (if security settings allow, send the error report to Microsoft automatically), and none (output errors to a text file, but do not report them to Microsoft). If this switch is not used, none is the default. May be used with the /bugreport switch. |
| /nowarn[:<*warnList*>] | Disables compiler-generated warnings about nonfatal code errors. *New variation in 2005*: You can include a comma-separated list of warning codes, <*warnlist*>, to suppress specific compiler warnings. |
| /unify | *New in 2005.* Suppresses warnings concerning mismatched assembly version numbers. |
| /warnaserror[+|-] | Instructs the compiler to abort (+) or continue (-) when encountering normally nonfatal code errors. That is, when this option is enabled, the compiler treats warnings as errors, preventing the code from compiling. Its default value is off (-). /warnaserror is equivalent to /warnaserror+. |

## Language

| Switch | Description |
|---|---|
| /define:<*symbol*><br>or:<br>/d:<*symbol*> | Declares global conditional compiler constants. <*symbol*> has the form *name=value*, with multiple name-value pairs separated by commas. See the *Conditional Compilation Constants* section later in this appendix for information on predefined constants. |
| /imports:<*namespace*> | Globally imports namespaces, eliminating the need to define them with individual Imports statements. <*namespace*> is a comma-delimited list of namespaces. |
| /optioncompare:<*type*> | Indicates the method used for string comparison. The values for <*type*> include: binary (case-sensitive comparisons) and text (case-insensitive comparisons). The default value is binary. This switch sets the default application-wide setting; it does not override any explicit Option Compare statements found in individual source-code files. |
| /optionexplicit[+|-] | Indicates that variables must be explicitly defined (+) or not (-) before they are used. The default setting is on (+). This switch sets the default application-wide setting; it does not override any explicit Option Explicit statements found in individual source-code files. /optionexplicit is the same as /optionexplicit+. |

| Switch | Description |
| --- | --- |
| /optionstrict[+\|-] | Indicates that implicit narrowing conversions should be allowed (-) or rejected (+) by the compiler. The default setting is off (-). This switch sets the default application-wide setting; it does not override any explicit Option Strict statements found in individual source-code files. /optionstrict is the same as /optionstrict. |
| /rootnamespace:<namespace> | Defines a root namespace for all type declarations. This means that an Imports statement need not be used to import the root namespace, and that the relative path of a type (starting from the root namespace) can be used in place of its fully qualified name. Any Imports statements, however, must contain the fully qualified namespace name. |

## Miscellaneous

| Switch | Description |
| --- | --- |
| /help<br><br>or:<br><br>/? | Displays information on compiler option usage. |
| /nologo | Suppresses the display of the compiler's copyright banner. |
| /quiet | Turns on quiet output mode; the compiler displays less information about errors than it does ordinarily. Specifically, it withholds the display of errant source code from error messages. |
| /verbose[+\|-] | Causes the compiler to emit verbose (+) or standard (-) status and error messages. The default setting is off (-). /verbose is the same as /verbose+. |

## Advanced

| Switch | Description |
| --- | --- |
| /baseaddress:<number> | Specifies the default base address at which a DLL library should be loaded. Runtime performance increases when all loaded DLLs for an application have a unique base address. <number> is a hexadecimal address. |
| /codepage:<id> | *New in 2005.* Indicates the code page that the compiler should use when generating the output file. <id> is the numeric identifier of the code page to use. |
| /delaysign[+\|-] | Indicates whether the generated assembly will be fully signed (-) or partially signed (+). Partially signed assemblies use only the public portion of the strong name key. The default setting is fully signed (-). The /delaysign option must be used with either the /keycontainer or /keyfile switch. |
| /doc[+\|-] | *New in 2005.* Indicates whether the compiler should generate an XML documentation file (+) or not (-). The default is to not generate the file (-). If generated, the XML file shares the same base name as the compiled output file but with a ".xml" extension. |
| /doc:<file> | *New in 2005.* Indicates that the compiler should generate an XML documentation file. <file> is the name of the file to generate. |
| /filealign:<number> | *New in 2005.* Specifies the boundary size used to align sections of the compiled output in bytes. <number> must be one of the following values: 512, 1024, 2048, 4096, or 8192. |
| /keycontainer:<container> | Specifies a strong-name key container with the assembly's key pair. The name of the container is indicated by <container>. May be used with the /delaysign switch. |

| Switch | Description |
|---|---|
| /keyfile:*<file>* | Specifies the file containing a key or key pair that will be used to give an assembly a strong name. The file name is indicated by *<file>*. May be used with the /delaysign switch. |
| /main:*<class>*<br>or:<br>/m:*<class>* | Specifies the class or module that contains *Sub Main*, the entry point for applications and components. This switch is particularly useful if more than one class or module in a project has a subroutine named *Main*. *<class>* can be a module name (optionally prefixed with a namespace) or a Windows Form class. |
| /noconfig | *New in 2005.* The *vbc.rsp* file, a response file found in the same directory as *vbc. exe*, contains default configuration settings for use by the compiler. This switch instructs the compiler to ignore the *vbc.rsp* file. See the *Using a Response File* section below for information on response files and their contents. |
| /nostdlib | *New in 2005.* By default, the compiler references the *Mscorlib.dll*, *System.dll*, and *Microsoft.VisualBasic.dll* assembly files when compiling source code. This switch instructs the compiler to ignore these assembly files. |
| /utf8output[+|-] | Emits compiler output in UTF8 character encoding (+) or with default encoding (-). UTF8 encoding is useful when local settings prevent compiler output from being displayed correctly on the console. The default value is off (-). /utf8output is the same as /utf8output+. |

# Using a Response File

The Visual Basic compiler allows you to specify command-line options and settings from a text file of settings called a *response file*. The syntax for using a response file is:

```
vbc @<file>
```

where *<file>* is the full or relative path of the response file. The response file contains source filenames and compiler switches; it is interpreted as if the filenames and compiler switches were entered directly on the command line.

The syntax of a response file is simple. Multiple filenames or switches can be included on a single line, or you can put each filename and switch on a line of its own. However, a single filename or switch cannot span multiple lines. The # symbol indicates a comment that continues until the end of the line.

Consider the following response file named *mylib.rsp*:

```
# Build the library
/target:library
/out:mylibrary
/debug+
/debug:full
libfunc1.vb
libproc1.vb
libstrings.vb
```

The compiler acts on this file by entering the following at the command prompt:

```
vbc @mylib.rsp
```

Even when using a response file, you can continue to use switches and filenames on the command line, and multiple response files can be used. The compiler processes all command-line arguments in the order in which they appear. This means that settings in a response file can be overridden by specifying command-line options after the response file name, or that command-line settings can be overridden by following them with a response filename. For example, the command line:

```
vbc libnumeric.vb @mylib.rsp /debug-
```

compiles a file named *libnumeric.vb*, in addition to the three files already named in *mylib.rsp*. It also reverses a setting from *mylib.rsp* by preventing debugging information from being included in the output file.

*New in 2005.* Beginning with the 2005 release of Visual Basic, the compiler automatically includes a response file named *vbc.rsp* each time it runs. This file is located in the same directory as the *vbc.exe* compiler itself. It includes all of the default files and switches that should be included in every compile, such as references to each of the core assemblies shipped with the .NET Framework. Modify this file if you wish to add files or switches to every compile event. You can also tell the compiler to exclude the *vbc.rsp* file by adding the /noconfig switch to the *vbc.exe* command.

## Conditional Compilation Constants

Visual Basic includes support for conditional compilation in your source code through the #Const and #If directives. While you can add your own constants, there are several predefined constants available for use in conditionally compiling your code.

| Constant | Description |
| --- | --- |
| CONFIG | *New in 2005.* This string indicates the current solution configuration in effect for the project from within the Visual Studio IDE. Typically, this constant is set to "Debug" or "Release." This constant is not set by default when using the command-line compiler. |
| DEBUG | A Boolean value that indicates whether debugging should be enabled (True) or disabled (False) in the compiled output. Code in the *System.Diagnostics.Debug* class responds to this constant. You can also use it to limit your own code. This constant is not set by default when using the command-line compiler. |
| TARGET | *New in 2005.* This string indicates the output target type as defined through the /target command-line switch. One of the following values: "exe" (console application), "winexe" (Windows application), "library" (DLL), or "module" (a ".netmodule" for later use in an assembly). |
| TRACE | A Boolean value that indicates whether tracing should be enabled (True) or disabled (False) in the compiled output. Code in the *System.Diagnostics.Trace* class responds to this constant. You can also use it to limit your own code. This constant is not set by default when using the command-line compiler. |
| VBC_VER | *New in 2005.* A numeric value that indicates the version number of Visual Basic being used to compile the application. Always in *major.minor* format. The Visual Basic 2005 compiler sets this constant to 8.0. |

| Constant | Description |
|---|---|
| _MYAPPLICA-TIONTYPE | *New in 2005.* Indicates the type of Windows-based (not Web-based) application for the active project. Set automatically based on the _MYTYPE compiler constant value. One of the following values.<br>• "Console" when _MYTYPE is set to "Console" or "WindowsFormsWithCustomSubMain"<br>• "Windows" when _MYTYPE is set to "Windows" or "" (empty string)<br>• "WindowsForms" when _MYTYPE is set to "WindowsForms"<br>For other _MYTYPE values, this constant is undefined. The *My.Application* namespace branch is unavailable when this constant is not one of the values listed above. When *My.Application* is available, its functionality varies based on this constant. |
| _MYCOMPUTER-TYPE | *New in 2005.* Indicates whether the active application is a Windows-based or Web-based application. Set automatically based on the _MYTYPE compiler constant value. One of the following values.<br>• "Web" for Web-based applications when _MYTYPE is set to "Web" or "WebControl"<br>• "Windows" for Windows-based applications when _MYTYPE is set to "Console," "Windows," "" (empty string), "WindowsForms," or "WindowsFormsWithCustomSubMain"<br>For other _MYTYPE values, this constant is undefined. The *My.Computer* namespace branch is unavailable when this constant is not one of the values listed above. When *My.Computer* is available, its functionality varies based on this constant. |
| _MYFORMS | *New in 2005.* Indicates whether the *My.Forms* namespace branch is available in the application. Set automatically based on the _MYTYPE compiler constant value. One of the following Boolean values.<br>• True when _MYTYPE is set to "WindowsForms" or "WindowsFormsWithCustomSubMain"<br>• False when _MYTYPE is set to "Web" or "WebControl"<br>For other _MYTYPE values, this constant is undefined. The *My.Forms* namespace branch is only available when this constant is set to True. |
| _MYTYPE | *New in 2005.* Indicates the general project type of the current application. This setting and others that begin with "_MY" are used in conjunction with the *My* namespace feature. Although this value is set automatically, if you choose to override it, you will alter the availability of different portions of the *My* namespace hierarchy. One of the following values.<br>• "Console" for console applications and windows services.<br>• "Custom" for a custom solution that disables most *My* namespace features. This value is never set automatically.<br>• "Web" for an ASP.NET-based standard application.<br>• "WebControl" for an ASP.NET-based web control application.<br>• "Windows" for a Windows Forms class library or control library. A _MYTYPE value of "" (empty string) has the same application impact as a setting of "Windows."<br>• "WindowsForms" for a Windows Forms application.<br>• "WindowsFormsWithCustomSubMain" for a Windows Forms application that has been altered to use a custom Sub Main entry point.<br>The *My.Log*, *My.Request*, and *My.Response* namespace branches are available only when this constant is set to "Web." |
| _MYUSERTYPE | *New in 2005.* Indicates the functionality of the *My.User* namespace branch. Set automatically based on the _MYTYPE compiler constant value. Always set to the same value as the _MYCOMPUTERTYPE constant.<br>• "Web" for Web-based applications when _MYTYPE is set to "Web" or "WebControl"<br>• "Windows" for Windows-based applications when _MYTYPE is set to "Console," "Windows," "" (empty string), "WindowsForms," or "WindowsFormsWithCustomSubMain"<br>For other _MYTYPE values, this constant is undefined. The *My.User* namespace branch is unavailable when this constant is not one of the values listed above. When *My.User* is available, its functionality varies based on this constant. |

| Constant | Description |
|---|---|
| _MYWEBSER-VICES | *New in 2005.* Indicates whether the *My.WebServices* namespace branch is available in the application. Set automatically based on the _MYTYPE compiler constant value. One of the following Boolean values.<br><br>• True when _MYTYPE is set to "WebControl," "Windows," "" (empty string), "Windows-Forms," or "WindowsFormsWithCustomSubMain"<br>• False when _MYTYPE is set to "Web"<br><br>For other _MYTYPE values, this constant is undefined. The *My.WebServices* namespace branch is only available when this constant is set to True. |

# Index

## Symbols

+ (addition) operator), 73
\ (division) operator, 74
^ (exponentiation) operator, 75
* (multiplication) operator, 74
<< (Shift Left) operator, 78
>> (Shift Right) operator, 79
- (subtraction) operator, 74
+ (unary) operator, 73

## A

Abs function, 162
abstraction, 25
Acos function, 163
AddHandler statement, 119, 163
addition (+) operator, 73
address variables, 62
AddressOf operator, 83, 164
AllUsersApplicationData property, 497
AltKeyDown property, 498
And operator, 76
AndAlso operator, 76
API (Application Programming
        Interface), x
AppActivate procedure, 164
Application class, 166
application deployment, 23
Application object, 499

Application.CompanyName
        property, 167
ApplicationContext property, 500
Application.DoEvents method, 167
Application.ExecutablePath
        property, 169
Application.ProductName
        property, 169
Application.ProductVersion
        property, 170
Application.Run method, 170
applications
        class libraries, 89
        console applications, 88
        entry points, 90–92
        types, 88–89
        Windows, 88
        Windows services, 89
AppWinStyle enumeration, 684
arguments
        attributes, 123
        events, 95
        introduction, 68
        optional, 71
        passing, 69
arithmetic operators, 73–75
Array class, 103–104, 171
array handling elements, 660
Array.BinarySearch method, 172

We'd like to hear your suggestions for improving our indexes. Send email to *index@oreilly.com*.

# F

FCL (Framework Class Library)
  namespace hierarchy
    my namespace, 673–676
    System namespace, 676–679
fields
  E, 261
  members, 31
  PI, 396
FieldType enumeration, 685
FieldWidths property, 541
File class, 281
FileAttr function, 282
FileAttribute enumeration, 685
FileClose procedure, 283
FileCopy procedure, 283
FileDateTime function, 284
File.Exists method, 281
FileExists method, 542
FileGet procedure, 285
FileGetObject procedure, 285
FileLen function, 286
FileOpen procedure, 287–289
FilePut procedure, 289
FilePutObject procedure, 289
filesystem elements, 665
FileSystem object, 543
FileWidth procedure, 291
Filter functions, 291
financial elements, 666
FindInFiles method, 544
FirstDayOfWeek enumeration, 686
FirstWeekOfYear enumeration, 686
Fix function, 292
Flags attribute, 293
Floor function, 293
FontDialog class, 294
For Each...Next statement, 297
Format function, 298–302
FormatCurrency function, 302
FormatDateTime function, 303
FormatNumber function, 302
FormatPercent function, 302
Forms object, 545
For...Next statement, 295–297
Framework Class Library, 11–13, 22
FreeFile function, 304
Friend keyword, 305
Function statement, 306–308
functions
  Abs, 162
  Acos, 163

Asc, 178
AscW, 178
Asin, 180
Atan, 180
Atan2, 181
CallByName, 184
CBool, 185
CByte, 186
CChar, 186
CDate, 187
CDbl, 187
CDec, 188
Ceiling, 189
Choose, 191
Chr, 192
ChrW, 192
CInt, 193
CLng, 196
CObj, 198
Command, 206
Cos, 210
Cosh, 210
CreateObject, 211
CSByte, 212
CShort, 213
CSng, 214
CStr, 214
CType, 215
CUInt, 217
CULng, 218
CurDir, 219
CUShort, 218
custom procedures, 97
DateAdd, 222
DateDiff, 223
DatePart, 225
DateSerial, 226
DateValue, 228
Day, 228
DDB, 229
Dir, 248
DirectCast, 249
Environ, 266
EOF, 267
ErrorToString, 276
Exp, 280
FileAttr, 282
FileDateTime, 284
FileLen, 286
Filter, 291
Fix, 292
Floor, 293

## G

garbage collection, 18, 36–37
generics
    constraints, 136–137
        multiple, 137
    introduction, 134
    methods, 139
    nested types, 139–140
    overloading methods, 140
    type parameters, 135–136
        members, 138–139
        multiple type parameters, 136
    types, overloading, 140
    VB 2005, 711
GetAllSettings function, 310
GetAttr function, 311
GetAudioStream method, 546
GetChar function, 312
GetData method, 547
GetDataObject method, 548
GetDirectories method, 549
GetDirectoryInfo method, 550
GetDriveInfo method, 551
GetEnvironmentVariable method, 553
GetFileDropList method, 554
GetFileInfo method, 554
GetFiles method, 556
GetImage method, 557
GetName method, 558
GetObject function, 312
GetParentPath method, 559
GetSetting function, 313
GetTempFileName method, 559
GetText method, 560
GetType operator, 83, 314
GetValue method, 561
Global keyword, 315, 708
GmtTime property, 562
GoTo statement, 316
Guid attribute, 317

## H

Handles keyword, 317
HasFieldsEnclosedInQuotes
        property, 563
Hashtable class, 319
Hashtable.Add method, 320
Hashtable.ContainsKey method, 320
Hashtable.ContainsValue method, 321
Hashtable.CopyTo method, 321
Hashtable.Item property, 322
Hashtable.Keys property, 323
Hashtable.Remove method, 323
Hashtable.Values property, 324
Hex function, 324
Hour function, 325

## I

IEEERemainder function, 325
#If...Then...#Else directive, 160
If...Then...Else statement, 326
IIf function, 327
IL (Intermediate Language) code, 18
Imp operator, 78
Implements keyword, 328
Implements statement, 329
Imports statement, 331
Info object (My.Application), 564
Info object (My.Computer), 564
information elements, 666
inheritance, 27, 40–42
Inherits statement, 332
InitializeWithWindowsUser
        method, 565
inline error handling, 144
Input procedure, 333–334
InputBox function, 335
input/output elements, 667
InputString function, 336
InstalledUICulture property, 565
instance members, shared members
        and, 35–36
InStr function, 337
InStrRev function, 338
Int function, 339
Integer data type, 53
integer division (\) operator, 74
integrated development environment
        elements, 668
interaction elements, 668
Interface...End Interface
        statement, 339–341
interfaces, 27, 38–39
IPmt function, 341
IRR function, 343
Is operator, 82, 344
IsArray function, 345
IsAuthenticated property, 566
IsAvailable property, 567
IsDate function, 345
IsDBNull function, 346

## About the Authors

**Tim Patrick** is the senior software architect at TiMaki Services, where he develops custom client/server and multi-tier software solutions targeting Microsoft Windows client workstations and Internet/Intranet/Extranet users. Tim has more than 20 years of experience in software development and software architecture. He is a Microsoft Certified Solution Developer (MCSD). He wrote *The Visual Basic Style Guide* and its successor, *The Visual Basic .NET Style Guide*. He has also published many magazine articles on topics related to Visual Basic development.

**Steven Roman, Ph.D.**, is a professor emeritus of mathematics at California State University, Fullerton. His previous books with O'Reilly include *Access Database Design and Programming*, *Writing Excel Macros with VBA*, and *Win32 API Programming with Visual Basic*.

**Ron Petrusha** is the author or co-author of many books, including *VBScript in a Nutshell*. He began working with computers in the mid 1970s, programming in SPSS and FORTRAN on the IBM 370 family. Since then, he has been a computer book buyer, an editor of a number of books on Windows and Unix, and a consultant on projects written in dBASE, Clipper, and Visual Basic.

**Paul Lomax** is the author of O'Reilly's *VB & VBA in a Nutshell* and a co-author of *VBScript in a Nutshell*, and is an experienced VB programmer with a passion for sharing his knowledge—and his collection of programming tips and techniques gathered from real-world experience.

## Colophon

The animal on the cover of *Visual Basic 2005 in a Nutshell*, Third Edition is a catfish. Catfish can be found all over the world, most often in freshwater environments. Catfish are identified by their whiskers, called "barbels," as well by as their scaleless skin; fleshy, rayless posterior fins; and sharp, defensive spines in the dorsal and shoulder fins. Catfish have complex bones and sensitive hearing. They are omnivorous feeders and skilled scavengers. A marine catfish can taste with any part of its body.

Though most madtom species of catfish are no more than 5 inches in length, some Danube catfish (called wels or sheatfish) reach lengths of up to 13 feet and weights of 400 pounds. Wels catfish (found mostly in the U.K.) are dark, flat, and black in color with white bellies. They breed in the springtime in shallow areas near rivers and lakes. The females hatch eggs in their mouths and leave them on plants for the males to guard. Two to three weeks later, the eggs hatch into tadpole-like fish, which grow quickly in size. The largest recorded wels catfish was 16 feet long and weighed 675 pounds.

The cover image is a 19th-century engraving from the Dover Pictorial Archive. The cover font is Adobe ITC Garamond. The text font is Linotype Birka; the heading font is Adobe Myriad Condensed; and the code font is LucasFont's TheSans Mono Condensed.